Art, Culture, and Cuisine

Art, Culture,

ANCIENT AND

PHYLLIS PRAY BOBER

THE UNIVERSITY OF CHICAGO PRESS

Chicago and London

and Cuisine

MEDIEVAL GASTRONOMY

Phyllis Pray Bober is professor emerita of History of Art and of Classical and Near Eastern Archaeology at Bryn Mawr College.

Book design: Adrianne Onderdonk Dudden

The University of Chicago Press, Chicago 60637
The University of Chicago Press, Ltd., London
© 1999 by Phyllis Pray Bober
All rights reserved. Published 1999
08 07 06 05 04 03 02 01 00   5 4 3 2

ISBN (cloth): 0-226-06253-8

Library of Congress Cataloging-in-Publication Data

Bober, Phyllis Pray.
    Art, culture, and cuisine : ancient and medieval gastronomy /
Phyllis Pray Bober.
        p.   cm.
    Includes bibliographical references and index.
    ISBN 0-226-06253-8 (alk. paper)
    1. Gastronomy.   2. Food—History.   3. Cookery.   I. Title.
TX637.B58   1999
641'.01'3—dc21   98-36867
                                                          CIP

Contents

Illustrations

3   MESOPOTAMIA

4   ANCIENT GREECE

5   HELLENISTIC GREECE

6   ROME

7 EARLY MIDDLE AGES

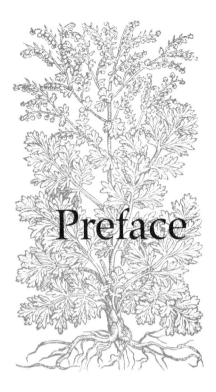

Preface

THIS BOOK HAS EVOLVED over many years. Because its text was completed in 1994, individual discussions may not reflect every fresh development in the burgeoning field of food history, although I have tried to bring all bibliographies up to date. There may be readers who, like many reviewers of nonfiction these days, will complain about an abundance of notes. This is not merely due to some academic habit of mind. A volume like mine addresses both a general public that loves to read anything having to do with cookery and also food professionals as well as a growing body of scholars devoted to interdisciplinary research and teaching in the field. Especially for the latter it is imperative to provide documentation for any given statement so that it may be verified and its evidence weighed. Also, numerous side issues that might obstruct the narrative for all but the most studious audience can be followed in the notes at will. Notes are never distractions, but are necessities for the serious reader.

My contribution to culinary history directly results from a course called "Culture and Cuisine" that I taught at Bryn Mawr College from 1987 through 1990 (also for undergraduates from Haverford and Swarthmore, thanks to our Three-College System). But, in far time, its origin goes back to the end of the 1960s at University College of New York University when Dean Frederick Ulfers, seeking to aid freshmen and sophomores closed out of registration in some of the most popular course offerings, enlisted faculty to teach "mini-

seminars" open only to these underclassmen and -women and in topics outside the normal curriculum. For the first time I had nine eager hands and a
decanal budget to teach "The Culinary Arts of Ancient Rome." And a huge
basement kitchen in an old house in the South Bronx that proved able to
contain our weekly shopping/cooking enterprise once we left the classroom
as well as, on one occasion, two curious little boys—my sons—and an entire
television crew with interviewer from *CBS Evening News*.

Until that time my love of both cookery and history had been limited to
cooking, say, a chicken by any usual method, then concocting a sauce from the
Latin cookbook attributed to Apicius. To that precious document I had been
introduced by friends in England, Barbara Flower and Elizabeth Rosenbaum
(later Alföldi), as they worked out their English translation together with
notes clarifying procedure and quantities for some selected recipes (an edition published in 1958). This had stimulated an instructional ploy for the
classroom: students in my courses in ancient art could more readily grasp the
change in style when Roman Republican sculptors gradually shed the "Italic"
tradition in portraiture to absorb the lessons of Greek masters if I brought out
an analogy with what happened in Latin kitchens at the same time.

Following the Roman seminar, a group of N.Y.U. scholars (who were able
to shape some of their courses if they could find a willing faculty member) persuaded me to lead a group exploring not only ancient Roman foodways but
those of ancient China and of five precolonial cultures among Amerindians.
Again Dean Ulfers provided a generous budget with which to purchase ingredients for the cooking sessions at my home, thus permitting indulgences
(never affordable before—or since!) such as oriental dried scallops and other
specialties whose cost puts that of caviar to shame.

My first and undergirding acknowledgments go to Fred Ulfers and to all
those N.Y.U. undergraduates who helped turn my engagement with the history of food and cookery from theory to practice, from avocation to, ultimately, a third, retirement career. My gratitude is belatedly expressed but
fundamental. From the first group I also learned how important it could be,
through study of the past and other cultures, to open people's minds—and
stomachs—to a wider range of foodstuffs and cooking procedures than characterize the American norm. Of the nine, all residents of one of the most cosmopolitan cities in the world and from affluent families, only one had ever
eaten lamb before we prepared it, none had eaten duck! I am happy that
one of them—a Latin major who could scarcely contain himself when Cato's

ritual bread, *libum,* came out of the oven: "The bread that won Carthage!"— has become a restaurant-owner.

My next public venture in gastronomic history came after a seven-year spell as Dean of the Graduate School of Arts and Sciences at Bryn Mawr College, when problems of graduate education absorbed most of my energies. In 1980 and 1981 I participated in the Bryn Mawr Forum, a program designed to serve the extramural community, by offering a lecture series on food history. First, eight weekly lectures considering focal periods (including Northern Sung China), each centered on a famous historical banquet; the following year, five more devoted to sacral elements of food. Both series ended with a recreated feast produced in a campus kitchen with the aid of what turned out to be a supremely skilled crew carefully selected from subscribers to the lectures. Thanks go to them and to our then head of food services, Gail Finan, for aid in expanding my repertoire, with a special nod to Alexa Aldridge, who managed to lard our 102-pound boar for the Roman bash, breaking one of my larding needles on his resistant flesh in the process. For the vicissitudes of preparing that boar, interested readers are referred to the Bryn Mawr *Alumnae Bulletin* for Spring 1990 or to the Guild of British Food Writers' *News,* no. 8 (Autumn–Winter 1992).

Such marriage of culinary research and direct practical experience explains why this text is followed by an appendix with suggestions for recreating a dinner in the style of each major period discussed. Heartfelt thanks go to my first editor, Karen Wilson, who, before she retired from Chicago University Press, not only solicited my book but encouraged inclusion of these recipes. Although I am neither a chef nor a cookbook writer (not to say that I may not indulge the latter bent in future), I have tried to be both authentic— as authentic as possible with modern ingredients—and nonprescriptive. Every good cook must get her or his own "feel" for the recipe, just as any cook of the past would have varied accepted procedure. Simply be careful not to add something anachronistic and remember that a food processor or blender does not achieve the same results as a mortar and pestle.

I must express appreciation to Oldways Preservation and Exchange Trust—Dun Gifford, Sara Baer-Sinnott, and, at the time, Greg Drescher— whose concern for sustainable agriculture, traditional foodways and healthful nutrition confirm my own beliefs in the significance of folk mores in cookery and preservation as remedies for modern problems of food supply and energy conservation. Their international conferences have given me the opportunity to test some of my theories about the expressive linkage between the culinary arts and the other arts called "fine." At the same time, these gatherings introduced me to so many food professionals who have become friends, many of them contributors to my understanding of particular ingredients and certain processes. Let me acknowledge collective thanks to Lidia Bastianich, Catherine Brandel, Claire Clifton (oh! the botanical lore), Naomi Duguid, Mary Ann Esposito, Jessica Harris (Bryn Mawrter, she), Suzanne Hamlin, Nancy Harmon Jenkins, Barbara Kafka, Aglaia Kremezi, Leslie Land, Jean Nathan, Claudia Roden, Mary Taylor Simeti (a veritable seminar on jujubes and cardoons), Colin Spencer, "Hoppin' John" Martin Taylor, Faith Willinger, Paula Wolfert, and Clifford Wright.

Participation in annual meetings of the Oxford Symposium on Food and Cookery has proved another source of generic support and learning in my new career, as has the inspiration of fellow dames among the Dames d'Escoffier, whom I was invited to join in 1995. I have learned so much from prolific Pennsylvania historians Dame Elisabeth Rozin and William Woys Weaver. And special recognition must go to my friend Chef Fritz Blank, microbiologist turned culinary star and owner of one of Philadelphia's premier restaurants, Deux Cheminées, for his interest in my work and his unflagging passion for the search after deeper meanings in the alimentary realm.

My indebtedness to colleagues is boundless. Nancy Dorian obligingly shared many of her insights into Celtic life and language; Dick Ellis was kind enough to help with many questions concerning ancient Egypt and Mesopotamia and to read those chapters, saving me from numerous errors; Steve Levine generously offered wise criticisms on my introduction; although not at Bryn Mawr, Martha McCrory served and continues to serve as a sort of discriminating clipping service, ferreting out journal tidbits and bibliography that would otherwise escape my notice. T. A. Carter generously shared her data on faunal remains from a Mesopotamian dig. Julius Held continues to extend a long-term loan of a rare German anthology of gastronomic writings. Bryn Mawr's Interlibrary Loan Librarian, Charles Burke, and Reference Librarian, Andrew Patterson, each deserve grateful recognition for aid and comfort beyond the call of duty. Those scholars who administer foreign libraries are owed my appreciative thanks, with special acknowledgment to Massimo Ceresa at the Vatican whose never-ending good will supports my ventures in culinary history now added to my more usual research on Roman humanism; also to Michelle Brown, Manuscript Librarian at the British Library, who is ever ready to share her unmatched knowledge of things medieval, including cuisine. A special bow to Ellie Robbins for her interest in my work as well as for her splendid zodiacal prints used to decorate my Petronian hors d'oeuvres when I produce a Roman dinner.

In terms of the book itself—the physical presence of its first installment— credit for its "readability" (if such there be) and attractiveness must go to my sympathetic editor, Susan Bielstein (who rescued me from a text more Ciceronian than any reader will now encounter), and to the gifted designer Adrianne Onderdonk Dudden (who is accustomed to work with volumes of greater insistence upon aesthetic integration of argument with the quality of illustrative material than is required here). I am inexpressibly grateful to them both.

Also, I must not neglect thanks to computer-wise rescuers who saved this technopeasant from calamities that would have discouraged further work on the book: Ria Ellis (whose expertise in the realm matches her authority in Assyriology), Alan Candor Esq. (retriever *par excellence*), and Sara Tuttle (student "angel" in the HELP service at Bryn Mawr's Computer Center).

There are others to whom I am indebted for much-valued assistance in my enterprise, but whose contributions will be explicitly acknowledged in a further volume. That final installment proves less difficult to write in certain ways—thanks to my own specialization in the Italian Renaissance as well as to the propensity of artists and new movements toward cultural change to seize upon the culinary as one of the modes to express or encode their aims. On the other hand, food history becomes necessarily a less unitary narrative, and will embrace diverse trends and allegiances from the Renaissance to post-Surrealism, ending as I project it now with John Cage's wonderful intaglio prints viewed in context with the macrobiotic breakfasts that are their substance.

A final word of gratitude to my sons Jonathan and David and to my "significant other," Ted Barnett, for their forbearance while this book of long gestation has meant dinners—even festive ones—eaten in the midst of a household's semiotic equivalent of contemporary chaos theory; papers and books, computer and printer, pushed aside at one end of a table in my workroom (the dining-room table being permanently encumbered with various other enterprises) and towering over our conviviality. At least, by common consent, the meals were delicious!

Introduction

FOR ALL LIVING CREATURES, including plants, drives to feed and to reproduce are inborn imperatives for survival not only of the self, but of the species. Food and sex regulate all else in life.[1] Seen as the most socializing proclivities of human beings, at the same time they most privately define our individual selves. Even tiny children learn self-realization, not to mention power, through expressing their likes and dislikes in the gustatory realm. (It takes a little longer to develop predilections in the other!)

The universality of such dominant propensities as food and sex make them prime subjects for investigating society and culture in every geographical area or historical era.[2] Together, they served a definition offered by a Chinese sage in the fourth century B.C.: Kao Tzu alleged that the appetite for food and sex is Nature.[3] The privacy of sex, however, makes it less useful than food as a metaphor for cultural history. It is food, transcending mere alimentary function and raised through cookery to social expression, exalted through cuisine to public display of status and power, that is the subject of this book. The lens used to examine cooking is determined by archaeology and the history of art in order to bring into the realm of the humanities that which is generally treated as a craft—its literature assigned in libraries to the category of technology.

A famous aphorism of the eighteenth-century gastronomer Jean Anthèlme Brillat-Savarin goes, "Tell me what you eat; I will tell you what you are."[4] Taken literally, this dictum is said to have led the famous actor Edmund Kean (1787–1833) to dine according to the character he was to play: if a lover, he ate mutton; if a murderer, beef; and if a tyrant, pork. (This all sounds fine for some of his favorite roles such as Othello or Richard III, but what did he have for dinner before performing his famed Shylock?)

Today biochemical research tells us that we are, indeed, what we eat, but on the basis of quite different concepts.[5] In Brillat-Savarin's context, however, it is likewise true that you are what you do *not* eat. Food taboos and food avoidance have always been supremely effective boundary mechanisms delimiting cultural groupings both large and small.[6] And culinary chauvinism, in a contrary and positively defining sense, gives us some of the most vivid writing from masters of the pen: Mark Twain (traveling in citadels of European gastronomy), homesick for the All-American foods he catalogued in *A Tramp Abroad*, summoning up his vision of a thick, rare Porterhouse steak, with native butter melting over it;[7] or, again, Robert Tristram Coffin enshrining the cookery of his Maine seacoast in paeans to products of Indian imagination united with Yankee ingenuity like "Kennebec Turkey" (smoked "red" herring), an Abenaki clambake, or his mother's smothered eels.[8] Devotees of other ethnicities and regions will think of their own examples, or of Roland Barthes' essay on the *boisson-totem* that wine represents for the French nation (not to mention their patriotic pride in 360 different kinds of cheese to go with the "wondrous substance" they consider a "blessing of their very own").[9]

Since the development in France of the *Annales* school to which Barthes belonged—historians who follow the lead of the anthropologist Claude Lévi-Strauss[10] in applying structural and semiotic methods of analysis as well as statistics to recover the lives and occupations of ordinary folk of the past—the "new historicism" has brought forth a vast literature on food and cookery as signs and symbols that encode social, psychological, economic and religious realities of past or present.

So Barthes defined *nourriture:* "What is food? Not solely an assemblage of products subject to statistical or nutritional analysis. It is at one and the same time a system of communication, a body of imagery, a protocol of customs, of situations, of behaviors. How does one study the alimentary reality, expanded to the image and to the sign?"[11] His own answers applied a trenchant Gallic wit in essays on contemporary food habits, French and American. Attempting to investigate an entire cultural system through food as expressive medium, the self-described functional structuralist, Mary Douglas, with fellow researchers, minutely analyzed British working-class "food events" of various

kinds to discover ordered patterns of the week, the day, the meal in syntag-
matic relationships.[12]

Another line of theoretical interpretation, also represented in Lévi-
Strauss's introduction to the science of mythology, descends from Norbert
Elias. This German sociologist put forward in the 1930s a truly hermeneutic
analysis of manners which regulate human interaction, including their role in
hospitality and dining as part of the civilizing process.[13] His work on strategies of conduct focused logically upon court society, which has been expanded
in recent years by C. Stephen Jaeger for the Middle Ages.[14] For the shaping
of more recent sensibilities in the same broad picture of court society, Marvin
Becker's study must be cited.[15] Here the Renaissance aesthetics of comport-
ment and government take one quite far from courtly life and the banquet
table, but a concentrated assessment of dining courtesies and rituals has been
published by Margaret Visser.[16]

In addition to studies devoted to theory, food history with all of its associated disciplines, from folklore and medicine to agriculture and the economics of commodity trade, enjoys many practitioners these days. My bibliography
will attest to the burgeoning richness of the field. A good number of studies
of culinary history from its origins already exist, at least one of which, Reay
Tannahill's *Food in History,* deals not only with the story of the West, but with
China and the Arab world as well. (I do not include these civilizations since I
am unable to read their primary sources in the original.) It would thus seem
that another general survey from prehistoric to contemporary times is far
from a scholarly necessity. However, to my knowledge no one has pursued
the particular theme I wish to set forth: the essential community of expression
in any given era between the culinary arts and other arts more regularly
termed "fine."

As an archaeologist I have learned to interpret minutiae of human relics
as evidence of lives once lived. As a historian of art, I am well accustomed to
interpreting artifacts as indices of culture. The unity of culture across all media of expression means that direct engagement with the art object, seeking
out its formal values, makes it possible to reconstruct its full context, societal
and intellectual. In the present case, seeking as well the environment of mind
and heart in those who practiced cookery or consumed it, my analysis of the
art of a period must necessarily be reduced in a miniaturized history of art
aimed at making a contemporary "gustatory code" revelatory. Culinary art is
the fundamental datum in this transmedial exploration. But setting the stage
through works of art serves my method of reading its message.

I fully subscribe to Alfred North Whitehead's dictum:

> In each age of the world distinguished by high activity there will be found . . .
> some profound . . . outlook, implicitly accepted . . . almost too obvious to need
> expression, and almost too general to be capable of expression. In each pe-
> riod there is a general form of the forms of thought; and, like the air we
> breathe, each form is so translucent, and so pervading, and so seemingly nec-
> essary, that only by extreme effort can we become aware of it.[17]

Artists are the ones who enlighten us.

It is these underlying assumptions in periods of "high activity" that I hope
to expose through the medium of cuisine and visual arts. I will attempt to peel
back as many layers of meaning as possible, using various methods appropriate to different epochs in my diachronic approach. Although some still-lifes
may be reproduced among my illustrations, analogies that bind forms of food
presentation and such pictorial motifs are too superficial to contribute to my
argument. An example here of the metaphoric value of certain depictions of
food would not be amiss, however.

We will encounter examples in seventeenth-century Dutch painting of
moral messages communicated through still-life, but others even more complex are encoded by certain sixteenth-century Flemish artists. Pieter Aertsen's
The Meat Stall of 1551 (fig. 1), is a splendid example of indirection. Overwhelmed by butchered animals, meats, and fish heaped into the foreground,
few observers will recognize the painting's moralizing discourse, even if familiar with concealed symbolism so frequently hiding beneath the everyday
naturalism of Netherlandish art.

Trained eyes are able to understand a message which "sets a contrast between corporeal food . . . [and] the idea of [its] temporal efficacy as against
the lasting effect of the spiritual food of Christ."[18] A signboard high on the
right, ostensibly advertising farmland for sale, calls attention to what lies "behind here": a scene of worldly consumption, of food, of drink, possibly a pre-
lude to sex. But, further back and to the center, a window opens on a scene
that requires no other sign than so many foreground objects and viands di-
recting the viewer to it. Experienced merely as a vignette, here—it may seem
perversely—is the main subject of the painting, the Flight into Egypt! The
Virgin pauses to offer bread to a little boy as an exemplum of charity and food
of the spirit; a file of worshippers moves across the landscape, seemingly in
progress toward a church-tower glimpsed through another window at far left.

Kenneth Craig makes a good case for an Antwerp church, and interprets the hanging pretzels, a little hanging bell (the *Sanctus* rung in the Mass at the moment of transubstantiation?), and other elements as symbols of the Eucharist. For Christological signs are everywhere in this still-life of animal "sacrifice." The dominating ox head replicates the ritual bucranium of antiquity, while carefully disposed fish, Christ's logo since Early Christian days, shape a cross echoed by other objects scattered throughout the painting.

There is more to Aertsen's occult message, but this is sufficient to anticipate one of the roles still-lifes of edibles play in later pages that deal with the Christian denigration of the senses and fear of the deadly sin of gluttony in conflict with joy in the good earth and in God's bounty. This particular work of art, like others by Aertsen and fellow painters of the sixteenth

1. Pieter Aertsen, The Meat Stall, *1551. Uppsala University, Sweden*

century, however, will prove much more valuable than any allegorizing intentions sketched at this point. We will discover the sociopolitical and psychological context for such willful dismantling of artistic traditions, for deliberate evasion of normative expectations, in the creations of certain artists — including chefs and maitres-d'hôtel — all over Europe during a period called "Mannerist."

It is in this more profound realm of analogy that we will explore foodstuffs, recipes, menus, and dining environments in concert with the arts and other cultural manifestations. Long ago my eloquent friend and colleague Blanche L. Brown started me thinking about revealing contrasts between two cuisines acknowledged to be preeminent, French and Chinese. She observed how like the painting of Poussin is the sense of structure, of classical order, in the presentation of a formal French meal. A Chinese menu, on the other hand, unfolds melodically with an ebb and flow like landscape painting on a horizontal scroll.

How perfect the comparison! though both cultures emphasize sophisticated aesthetics in the art of eating, stressing the finest ingredients and infinite care in their preparation. Both consider the art of cookery and refinement of taste to be among the highest values in life. French philosophers and literati from Ronsard to Dumas and Flaubert have occupied themselves with matters of cuisine, yet its themes are central to Chinese thinkers and poets as well. I do not know of anything in French literature to compare with sexual and gourmand sensualities interwoven as they are in the great Tang novel *The Golden Lotus.* Even Rabelais' *Gargantua,* book 4, cannot compare, since it exploits, above all, excess.

The deliberate geometry of a Poussin illustrates French rationalism. His *Self-portrait* (fig. 2) embodies a suitable contemporary of Descartes in which even the disposition of light obeys all rules of coordinate display. A sharp demarcation of illumination from shadow bisects a visage whose gaze, engaging us, is directed out of the picture. The resulting line down forehead and nose to chin — in a visual trick some paintings by Picasso have taught us to recognize — creates a profile in that full-front face, returning its form to the painting's grid of verticals and horizontals calculated to respond to boundaries of frame even as they are anchored firmly in parallel planes of depth. Is this not comparable in its French *clarté* to a classic Parisian — even provincial — menu built upon a fixed sequence of removes, each neatly discriminated from the following course in *grande cuisine* by a palate-cleansing sorbet? Then, each dish should ideally retain the integrity of its chief ingredient, complemented by

2. *Nicolas Poussin,*
Self-portrait, *1641.*
Paris, Louvre

others subtly harmonized among themselves as enhancement of the dominant savor. For discriminating diners, the pleasure of identifying them is part of the joy in eating, particularly when joined to a structured system of accompanying wine,

Unlike the French, the Chinese do not proselytize in matters gastronomic, well aware that the aesthetics of their best cuisine would prove inaccessible to those not immersed in their culture. The control of variant textures being essential to appreciation of a dish, cookery exploits all sorts of odd components they are certain a Westerner would reject: fish heads, duck feet, and such unlikely delicacies as jellyfish, sea-swallows' nests, tree fungus, and fish maw. The latter belong to a group of texture foods prized because they are practically tasteless and demand culinary artifice to lend them flavor. Between

3. Xia Gui, Scenic Spots along the River. *Southern Sung, 1127–79. Detail from a handscroll. Shanghai Museum*

crunchy and tender, elastic and gelatinous, lies a spectrum of textural sensation to be differentiated by the sophisticated palate, much as the connoisseur's eye is trained to value the most minute variations in the vitality of a brush stroke in calligraphy and in painting.

Westerners do esteem the art of Chinese landscape painting, such as this example from its high point in Southern Sung of the twelfth and thirteenth centuries (fig. 3). But how many are able fully to comprehend its subtleties: the way in which the hand scroll becomes a time growth, unrolling melodically, its voids as eloquent as its spaces, its ink as modulated in contrast and harmony as notes of music?[19] Just so a classic Chinese banquet unfolds in musical refinement, the ebb and flow of its courses rhythmically punctuated by aromatic soups serving as transitions one to another (quite unlike French palate-cleansing ices). Presentations — and a multitude of them! — blend to climaxes and recede to muted sonorities (sounds are also important, conveyed by crunchiness and by exotic quests — in the past we hope — for things that might squeak or cry out when eaten). If the menu is symphonic, the unit is of the nature of chamber music. Individual dishes exemplify the same musical development into a final harmonious, inextricable blend which may even counterfeit a given flavor. It is enough to make one construct a poetic confrontation between French and Chinese gastronomy, for all their shared commitment to gourmet tradition: the wave theory which once underlay oriental explanations of the cosmos, compared to atomic theory which has absorbed the West since formulation by the Greek philosopher Democritos.

As a further and more compelling example of aesthetic unity between the visual and the culinary arts, I submit an observation which has found favor among various food professionals before whom I have tested my theory. This involves Islamic culture, one which holds basically in the arts to a ban against representation of the human form. In my chapter on ancient Mesopotamian culinary arts the reader will find reference to an abiding prejudice in the Near East toward decorative patterning and a reliance upon the accumulation of myriad small units for both structural and coloristic effect. Beginning in A.D. 622 with lightning-swift conquests in the Middle East, then beyond across the maghreb (North Africa) and into Spain—to be stopped from gaining most of Europe only by Charles Martel at Tours in 732—Arabs brought half the Western world under the sway of Islam within two generations.

The Koran, sacred book of Islam, is curiously ordered by length of each passage as dictated to and written by Mohammed, rather than by content or chronology. It is taught to children and converts by rote and by repetition, in the same way prayers are effective through an almost mesmerizing iteration of single phrases as boundless as the forest of columns in a large hall of worship like the Great Mosque at Cordova. A perspective of supports and arches in every direction enhances the air or "aroma" of transcendence, of mystery, achieving its effects in the very opposite way that a Christian house of worship stimulates the spirituality of its communicants. Islam is a religion of individual communion with a Supreme Being through prayer, invisibly oriented, like the *mihrab* containing the Koran, to holy Mecca in the far beyond; Christianity has been developed as a congregational religion, the interior space of its churches focused, usually by an unrelenting, metronomic rhythm eastward of supports, toward a relatively small-scale *mensa*, or table, where an officiant mediates prayers and sanctifies symbolic consumption of the blood and substance of the Lord in the communal mystery of the Mass.

The sense of limitless and numberless units that expands architectural space at Cordova and elsewhere also pervades Islamic decoration. Muslim architects and craftsmen have reigned supreme in creating structures ornamented by encrustations of tile, and wood-, plaster-, and leather-work that stun by color and intricacy of design and workmanship. To my mind, the cellular agglomeration of the ceiling of a hall in the Alhambra at Granada or scintillating networks of tile express, like Islamic calligraphy — indeed, like all Islamic art — the aesthetic principles of Muslim cuisine. A superabundance of multiple units mounded on platters or in North African *tajines* — heady with the aroma of attars and spices traditional to Persian and Arabic gastronomy since antiquity, richly decorated in colorful patterns of dates, pomegranate seeds, or what have you — cumulatively resonates with all other Islamic arts in more ways than can be considered here.

It is such reciprocities between different modes of sociocultural expression that will be addressed in this book and in a future volume comprising the Renaissance to Modern periods. In some cases — preeminently the Egyptian — we will have no recipes to interpret, and I will be forced to build my argument about cooking style solely from archaeological data and works of art. In others, cookery will assume a speaking role in intellectual and artistic movements that defined themselves in part by their foodways — most notably futurism and surrealism in a modern time frame, but also tentatives in this regard by Renaissance humanists.

For every historical epoch, food serves as a template for examining numerous aspects of human experience — sacral and secular, personal and political, mythic and scientific. Because this is so, it is difficult to set out the full range of evidence I will use in each particular era. For certain periods methods derived from anthropology and sociology will prove of value; in others geography and economics will contribute, while medicine and theology will play a sustaining role. Beginning with the Middle Ages, music and theatral performance come into prominence, since their secular manifestations were born in banqueting and festivals.

Recipes and cookbooks are essential documents for culinary history, of course, joined by gardening treatises and works on natural history and botany. Paradoxically, one is on more contentious ground using such sources from the sixteenth century on, simply because of the vast amount of material compared with scattered fragments from antiquity or the handful of cookery manuscripts (except among the Arabs) before the invention of printing. One would have to be a bibliographic detective to be certain of the *stemma* of popular recipes, that is, to ascertain which cook invented a particular one and then construct a family tree of derivatives, both plagiarized and modified.[20]

In the matter of recipes, I had not intended to include a modernized version of any of my "documents." The idea spoke to me of technique instead of ideas, comparable to presenting works of art in terms of sizing a canvas, grinding colors, and considering which binder to use. However, I have been persuaded to place in an appendix a menu and constituent recipes for each of my focus periods, selected for topical interest and metaphoric or encoding value. In their very nature these represent, as does a major portion of this study, foodways of a societal elite, often on spectacular occasions. Although the folk arts of ancient Rome contribute in a positive sense, in only a few other chapters will the reader find more than brief reference to eating habits of the least members of society unless these offer a counterpoint to the main drama of culinary *art* rather than necessity. Throughout history until modern times in developed countries peasants and the urban poor have sustained life, alas, on the same basically carbohydrate diet, pulmentarian as it is proletarian.

In this context, on the other hand, I must emphasize my personal motives for having spent much of the past decades since the late 1960s in teaching various aspects of "culture and cuisine" as well as in undertaking the present book (so different from works in my proper métier). While it is true that I love to cook and am known as an adventurous trencherwoman, my passionate interest in culinary history derives from my concerns for hunger and malnutrition in the world. Equally, waste of the earth's resources — above all, food and energy — by us "haves" engages my attention. I believe that environmental degradation, loss of biological diversity and problems of feeding the world's expanding population may all be addressed in the long run by wider dissemination of the story of humankind's imagination and creativity in uniting the body's nutritional demands with the spirit's joys of the table.

Such concerns come readily to one raised as I was by a father who was a tireless gastronome, making distant forays to seek out items such as eggs, cheese, apples, and maple syrup that would meet his standards, and a mother renowned as a superb and at the same time nutrition-minded cook. She was of that World War I–generation of homemakers who gained from newly important postwar advances in dietetics and household management their devotion to "scientific" regimens for their families. Her food pyramid would rival today's government pronouncements; I still follow her insistence on a green and a "yellow" vegetable each day, plus one raw green one, and her methods of preserving all the "enzymes" by cooking them "without water." What is more, she was a French-Canadian by birth and a demon for making use of every scrap of food in some creative and delicious invention. Her boast was that she did not really need a garbage pail: coffee grounds and egg shells did something beneficial for plants, as I recall, while potato skins cleaned silver or

4. *Juan Sanchez Cotan,* Still-life, or Bodegón with Cardoon, *ca. 1603–5. Granada, Museo de Bellas Artes*

made heavenly crisp treats and citrus or watermelon rinds became prized marmalades and pickles. If I ever write a cookbook, it will be one for creative uses of leftovers.

Study of the history of art and archaeology has always powerfully counteracted ethnocentricity by bringing one to appreciate the wellsprings of other cultures. In like manner, in this age of multiculturalism, study of food history brings understanding, even beguilement, by the Other. Food is a system of communication beyond compare. In appreciation of a multitude of different systems of the remote or immediate past, we come to learn ways of utilizing every scrap of the plants and animals we consume — tickling our ingenuity with fresh ideas for our daily fare. Every one of us also needs mentors in a quest to use less energy on food preservation in freezer and refrigerator. For thousands of years people ate healthily and well without either, and only today are some few recovering techniques of salting, drying, pickling, smoking, and the like, long left to commercial providers.

On a broader, clearly political, level I hope that models from diverse cultures will encourage thoughtful participation in conservation practices of a different nature. Could tropical rain forests in South America be preserved if natives are helped to raise and to market a sustainable population of iguana for consumers who wish to enjoy a delicacy relished in Mexico? After all, Amazonian lands are being stripped, their soil ultimately exhausted by raising cattle which give back only about 4 percent of the energy they consume (as compared with about 20 percent in the case of pigs, a preferred aliment throughout antiquity). Are there more interesting vegetables which have fallen out of favor with growers that might enhance both taste and nutrition? For example, cardoons, a favorite in ancient times as well as for our own colonial ancestors, seen in a painting by the seventeenth-century Spanish painter, Sanchez Cotan (fig. 4), are now difficult to find outside of expensive urban specialty stores and a few Italian markets.

Enough, you see some of my hidden purposes. Be adventuresome and glean promising inspiration from food habits of earlier times and cultures! Good eating! — and, I hope, reading.

1 Prehistory

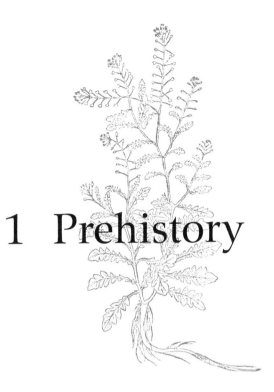

BECAUSE OUR INVESTIGATION of food history is concerned with questions of taste and aesthetics, with cookery seen in concert with "fine" arts as expressing the societal and cultural values of those who both produced and consumed it, it is next to impossible — even for an archaeologist — to deal with prehistoric "cuisine."

The concept, cuisine, itself demands a consciousness of self and of what one is eating that transcends simple diurnal filling of a clamoring belly or primitive testings of what might prove palatable and at the same time non-toxic. Before history, which means before human beings could record their present or their past, we can only depend upon researchers whose interpretations of constantly evolving scientific data are frequently used to serve current realities of politicized discourse. Theories about the diet of the first hominids; about which food strategy, hunting or "seeding," led isolated subsisters to come together to form the first rudimentary social groups that might seek larger game or shape the beginnings of agriculture; about the harnessing of fire beyond the myth of Prometheus; all these and more are today embroiled in the rhetoric of feminism and its backlash, in religious fundamentalism versus secular humanism, and in just plain academic rivalry.

Recent decades have brought an explosion of technological means to explore the diet and nutrition of ancient peoples. New methods in archaeology recover evidence of plant material and seeds for a revolutionary science of paleobotany. When I participated in field work years ago, a burned layer was noted in our diary, any tangible remains such as bones were carefully labeled and taken off to a specialist to be identified. Flotation techniques used by to-day's archaeologists preserve the least remnant of carbonized matter to speak of original substance as well as date. Thermoluminescence, DNA investigations, analysis of strontium in human bones, and a host of other tools of the nuclear age contribute new data to archaeologists seeking to answer questions that now focus as closely on the daily experience of ancient peoples — even the most common — as upon their artifacts and material culture.

The study of coprolites, that is, fossilized excrement, and chemical and microscopic analysis of the stomach contents of "bog people" — fortuitously preserved unfortunates drowned (or frozen) by accident or design in anaerobic contexts — ensure that specific items were truly ingested and not merely present in the environment. Cores taken from river and lake beds are analyzed to yield sequences of pollen counts which document plant species as well as evidence of wet or drought growing seasons. Fluoroluminescence, flotation sciences of paleoethnobotany, phytoarchaeology or bioarchaeology, all the techniques of modern science, yield more data than they bring about consensus on fundamental issues in the development of human culture — and, by extension, cuisine. For this reason, I intend to concentrate on the so-called Neolithic revolution, to forego consideration of competing theories as to the meaning of Old Stone Age cave paintings: whether they represent hunting magic or metaphoric and sexual summons to human fertility like even earlier sculptures which go by the name of Paleolithic "Venus" figures. Humans of the Pleistocene produced fire for cooking surely, but food preferences and its specific treatment we cannot know. We can only marvel at ecologies all around the globe that met the basic nutritional needs of their inhabitants, although with very diverse flora and fauna.

Once they had learned to exploit every available resource, it seems that omnivorous early peoples attained appropriately balanced diets without alimentary science to aid their ingenuity. Perhaps distinct "cravings" of the type that lead certain animals to seek out a purgative plant after ingesting something harmful led our ancestors to try what at first appeared unappetizing or dangerous things to eat. Consider the first eater of shellfish or lobster(!); the first Maya Indian to try to make something from the black smut that made its fungal appearance on his corn, today's delicacy, huitlacoche; snowbound Eskimos or Lapps who get requisite vitamins from ingesting the contents of the stomachs of caribou or reindeer; natives of South America who experimented with techniques to rid manioc (ultimately to become Africa's cassava) of its toxic chemicals in order to make it their staple starch; or, again, horsemen of the Asian steppes who learned to milk their mares and thereby not only gained vitamin C and other nutrients, but developed a means of fermenting it into an intoxicating drink.

In the past, many conclusions about Old Stone Age peoples were put forward on the basis of comparison with present-day hunters and gatherers like the Bushmen of southern Africa or primitive cultures in remote jungles of the Philippines. Today it is recognized that such methodology is misleading. After all, however technologically deprived these "primitives" may be, their social structures and cultural mores have evolved over thousands of years. Their patterns of culture are extremely variable and adapted to their environment. Also, generally they live in marginal geographical contexts not well endowed with an abundance and diversity of resources, factors that apparently fostered the origins of complex societies and what we term civilization.

Modern interdisciplinary research has invalidated a host of theories once held to explain the beginnings of village life with its domestication of animals and invention of agriculture. For one thing, it is now clear that prehistoric foragers—women gathering nuts, fruits, roots, and seeds as well as insects, snails, and, opportunistically, small animals and honey (fig. 5); and men fishing and hunting birds and larger prey—in many cases led semisettled rather than nomadic lives. Huts made of mammoth tusks, excavated from the permafrost of Siberia, and food storage pits discovered elsewhere date back ten and fifteen thousand years before the genesis of Neolithic cultures and agriculture, which took place about 10,000 B.C. Then, too, it is becoming increasingly clear that far-reaching trading networks were gradually built up over millennia.

Revisions in dating European phenomena have laid to rest for most prehistorians the idea that agriculture and husbandry in the West depended upon the diffusion of discoveries from the Near East. All over the world the independent development of techniques to cultivate wild plants and to domesticate wild creatures overthrew strictures upon population growth and led to advances in material culture by hunters and gatherers who needed to be mobile and to travel light.

However, with climates warmer and well-watered after the retreat of the last glaciation, it stands to reason that regions with a great variety of native

5. Gathering Honey. *Drawing after a prehistoric painting at a rock shelter. La Coimbra, Spain*

food resources would lead the rest in achieving more complex social organization and economies freed from mere subsistence. In Southeast Asia, in the Indus Valley of the subcontinent, on the "Hilly Flanks" of the Zagros Mountains, in the Jordan Valley north of what is today the Dead Sea, in uplands overlooking the Nile Valley, a beneficent instead of a vicious circle of factors brought humankind new ways of life stressing community, control of a food supply, plus diversification of talent leading to hierarchical distributions of power. Some individuals might gain status by making the best tools for barter and trade, others seemed more gifted in communication with unseen beings who must control the vagaries of nature, while still others distinguished themselves by prowess in fighting off threats to their settlements from mundane enemies. Did special kudos accrue to outstandingly accomplished cooks who could teach others how to make food more tasty, even though simply boiled or grilled? We may imagine that it was so, but have no means to prove it.

In any case, more reliable supply and better nutrition enhanced the brain's capacity to think up ever improved patterns of farming, of husbandry, of trade, and of craft production. It must surely have stimulated as well ingenuity and imagination that encouraged fresh culinary experiments in combining various ingredients and in enhancing their taste by what we term seasonings. Mammalian bodily demands for salt would long since have compelled the human animal to seek out sources of sodium compounds where these lie near the surface (salt licks and springs like Wadi Natroun in the western desert of Egypt) or at the sea. But needs for both salt and potassium can be met in part by the ash of cooking fires that inevitably clung to food cooked over open fires. Given documented trade in the long-range transportation of obsidian for New Stone Age perfecting of sharp-edged tools,[1] we may be able to extrapolate to commerce in commodities such as salt, a presage of its historical claims to economic preeminence. Neolithic invention would add this precious substance to such methods of food preservation as drying or smoking.

What then of other savors? By the Mesolithic period, if not before, the sweet delights of honey had been stolen from nests of wild bees. Was it during the New Stone Age that humans learned how to control production by those industrious insects so that one need not compete with bears and other equally avid creatures? This would explain the well-developed hives and apiculture of the Egyptian Old Kingdom.[2] How early did anyone discover that honey kept long enough will ferment? This boon of nature must have been discovered of grains and fruit juices as soon as people began to store them.

In the earliest civilizations of the Near East and Mediterranean, fundamental reliance on those "allies" in flavor—as they have punningly been called—the Alliaceae, or onion family, which includes garlic, reflects the prehistoric use of wild forebears that would not leave traces among the carbonized remains of seeds, husks, and fruit pits. But those seeds, which can withstand being consumed by fire, do substitute as evidence indicating the use of foraged herbs and spices as seasoning by ancient cooks. They are recovered from Neolithic sites, in quantities similar to the mustardseed and caraway found in Swiss Lake dwellings dated to around 8000 B.C.[3]

AN IMPORTANT NEOLITHIC TOWN

I have chosen a site in Anatolia to consider because it is one that I have visited with an already developed interest in local food resources and culinary possibilities. Çatal Hüyük, in the Konya Plain of modern Turkey, was excavated by James Mellaart in the 1960s.[4] Although not provided with Jericho's stunning eighth-millennium ramparts and funerary "portraits" modeled over skulls in clay, this is a site of extraordinary size and veritably urban evolvement, reaching back to circa 6500 B.C. In the words of its excavator, Çatal "deserves the name of city: it was a community with an extensive economic development, specialized crafts, a rich religious life, a surprising attainment in art and an impressive social organization."[5] More to the point for our purposes, it is a site where it is still possible to experience much of its ancient ecological context.

Situated on the alluvial plain where streams formed in the Taurus Mountains to the south fan out to water vast grasslands that once nourished a rich variety of animals, Çatal Hüyük in its day profited as well from forest stands of beneficial trees: oak, juniper, wild pistachio, almond, and apple. The bed of its (now diverted) Çarsamba River summons up the agricultural potential of this area, while twin cones of a volcano, Hasan Dağ, looming about 80 miles away to the east, speak of another probable source of the town's prosperity. From here and other volcanoes of Anatolia archaeologists have traced glasslike obsidian that served to make superior stone tools found at Çatal and was traded as far away as Syria, Palestine, Jordan, and Cyprus. In addition there is evidence that Çatal in its prime was a cult center for the surrounding region, since over forty structures among some hundred and fifty, at various levels, in the single small area dug, were designated shrines by their excavator. All were richly installed and decorated with reliefs and paintings of manifest religious significance (figs. 6, 9): jutting reworked skulls of auroch bulls and their horn cores often used in construction; jaws of boars imbedded in a wall to be covered in a subsequent stage with abstractly rendered female breasts; in relief, a spreadeagled goddess giving birth to a bull; leopards renewed again and again in replastering their confronted bodies; hunting scenes (the men girded with leopard skins); and the like.

Twelve separate levels of occupation were identified by Mellaart, with very limited excavation of the lower ones (VIII through X) in the single quarter explored. Several had been destroyed by fire—helpful in identifying carbonized plant material—although there seems to have been no evidence of invasion or a basic change of population. Before his level VIA (dated 5850–5600 B.C. according to carbon-14 evidence) Çatal was aceramic; the inhabitants did not use kiln pottery but had vessels of stone, painstakingly carved in wood, or basketry that could be lined with clay to be impermeable. Boiling or stewing was apparently accomplished in the manner used by Amerindians before the colonists brought metal pots: by adding stones heated in the cooking fire.

6.   *"Ritual Center" with reliefs including a large bull on the lateral wall and projecting breasts that enclose vultures' beaks. Çatal Hüyük, Turkey. Sixth millennium B.C. After Mellaart*

Dwellings at Çatal are built of molded mud brick, densely abutting one another about open courts, so that the entire town must have turned blank walls toward the outside world (fig. 7). Many observers have been reminded of the pueblos of America's Southwest, a resemblance enhanced by the fact that each house was accessible only from its flat roof (good for drying grains, seeds, and fruits), attained by a removable ladder while a fixed one led down into the residence, through an opening which doubled as a vent for smoke from below. In most dwellings, beneath this dual entrance/vent, an oval flat-topped oven was partly set into the (usually) southern wall (fig. 8) with a deep recess close by that evidently served for storage. Often these were supplemented by grain bins filled from the top and drawn off from below.

The hearth was toward the center of this living space, which was otherwise provided with built-in platforms for sitting and sleeping. The dead

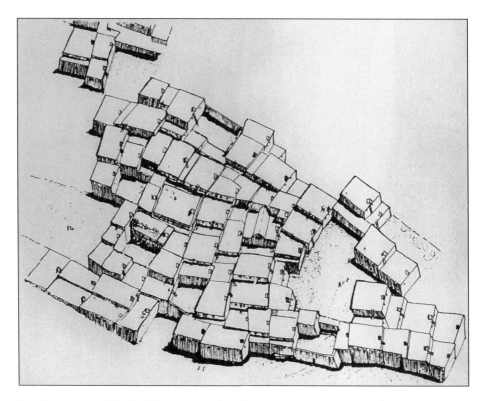

7. *Reconstruction of the Neolithic town of level VI. Çatal Hüyük. Drawing after Mellaart*

were apparently not regarded by these and other Neolithic people with the dread that affected later classical civilizations, for beneath these "divans" (as Mellaart termed them) burials were discovered. If gruesome thoughts of decaying flesh come to mind, be reassured. Mellaart interprets representations and other sacral evidence in a finding that bodies were first exposed in rites of excarnation (again bringing to mind certain Amerindians), to be picked clean by griffon vultures (fig. 9).[6] Thus, only the skeletons would be interred, keeping one's forebears as part of the community. As if to restore their power, red ocher (taken to be a substitute for blood) was included with Çatal's burials, a Paleolithic survival matched in other finds at this site: the same pigment outlining handprints on some walls and numbers of "mother goddess" figures in stone and clay whose superabundant flesh equals that of Old Stone Age examples.

What did the Neolithic "housewife"—as we intuit from historical practice when women or slaves minister in the kitchen while men act as professionals

8. *View down a ladder into one of the Neolithic houses, showing the rudimentary oven built up against the entrance wall, the hearth, and sleeping platforms. Çatal Hüyük. Drawing after Mellaart*

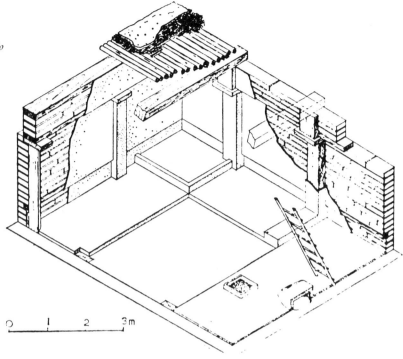

O 1 2 3 m

9. *"Shrine" with scenes that must relate to the exposure of corpses to vultures before burial of the cleaned bones. Çatal Hüyük. Drawing after Mellaart*

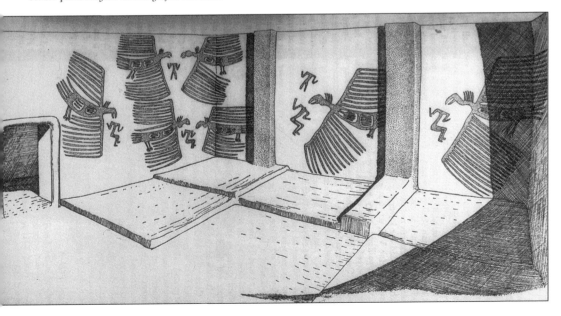

preparing formal and ritual meals—cook in these dwellings where one was forced to bend double to crawl through a low door into another room, if there was one? This we can answer more fully than in many a prehistoric site, but the details escape us. All about the mounds of its multileveled occupation, the flat plain is littered with what seem at first glance to be carcasses of small, worm-like creatures that turn out to be the dried husks of wild vetches. The distinguished Scandinavian paleobotanist Hans Helbaek identified two forms of vetch cultivated here in Neolithic times and surmised that they were useful as fodder for Çatal's domesticated animals, primarily goats and sheep,[7] although there is ample precedent for their being utilized equally, world-wide, for human sustenance. The species of ungulates Helbaek names were everywhere the first to be brought under human control and breeding; being by nature gregarious, living in large herds, socialized so to speak and ready to follow a leader;[8] the goats and sheep, even varieties of gazelle, like reindeer in far northern reaches of the globe, were domesticated in an initial phase of husbandry by at least the ninth millennium B.C. Cattle and pigs came under our sway a bit later. Interestingly, while cattle are massively represented at Çatal—whether fully domesticated or not at every level remains unclear— there were few pig remains, this despite their presence in large numbers at an associated Anatolian site, Hacilar.

No fewer than fourteen different food plants seem to have been cultivated by the residents of Çatal, aided by the alluvial soil and at least seasonal irrigation from their river. Helbaek's lists are from Level VIA, and it is significant that the grains indicate secondary agriculture after primary development elsewhere.[9] Wild progenitors do not exist in the area where the environment is not nor ever was suitable for any but the two-row hulled barley found here in small specimens. Instead, Çatal has six-row naked barley, an evolved hybrid form. Another import is its emmer wheat (tetraploid, naked and more easily threshed than hulled varieties). Most surprising of all was the presence of bread wheat (*Triticum aestivum*, hexaploid) at levels VI, V, and IV, because this is a hybrid that has no wild form.[10] Einkorn also appears at Çatal. Most of the houses had saddle querns for grinding these grains, but like flint sickles found at Jericho, these would not indicate cultivation without the evidence of the grains, since both implements could be used in a foraging stage as well.

Çatal dwellers surely boiled porridge even at preceramic stages, by the method already noted of heating stones in the fire and putting them into one of the wooden vessels discovered at the site. Flat breads would have been cooked on a stone at the hearth, others in ovens. Had wild yeasts now given them the experience at Level VI of some leavening? Did they know the secret of sourdough yet? A provocative possibility is raised by Helbaek's notes that acorns were found in three houses, in one case several at a fireplace as if ready for roasting. Acorn caps, as Mellaart writes,[11] are still used in the region today to start the process of making yogurt and the wonderfully refreshing fermented goats' milk called *ayran* in Turkish. Since sheep and goats were at hand at Çatal, one can perhaps believe that a similar product helped that bread wheat to rise. At level V–IV one house held a much larger oven than any other, which Mellaart interpreted as a bakery.

Two oil-bearing seeds were represented in Çatal's plant material: shepherd's purse *(Capsella bursa pastoris)* and another crucifer, *Erysimum sisymbrioides,* which might produce a good potherb with a garlicky savor. Another find that holds particular culinary interest and which still grows in irrigation canals of the area today in season is *Scirpus,* a rush with an edible tuber related to a water chestnut. With common field peas, a few representatives of the purple pea *(Pisum elatius),* and lentils — these pulses so beneficial to farmers because their nitrogen fixing capabilities improve the soil — all of us can begin to think of ways to cook up something delicious with all that game out on the plain. Our imaginary dish can be enhanced as well by wild fruits such as little tart apples and by gatherings from the bounty of almonds, pistachios, and juniper. Cultivation of fruit trees takes longer in the scheme of agricultural evolution, especially for species like the olive, grape, figs, date, and pomegranate, which require grafting rather than simple vegetative propagation.[12]

Helbaek made a further suggestion that would make Neolithic dining at Çatal Hüyük an engaging experience for most of us. His identification of hackberries at all levels made him think of wine from their juice. Mellaart had no hesitation in pronouncing that both wine and beer were evidently known.[13]

There are other substantial towns from this period of about 6000 B.C., but the extraordinary richness of agricultural finds as well as art at Çatal is sufficient to launch an exploration pointing toward the first great urban and historical cultures of Egypt and Mesopotamia. At Çatal Hüyük culture and cuisine have surpassed a subsistence economy, a complex and specialized society has been established, religious ritual is well developed, trade is organized, and already at Level VI we are able to see the end of the New Stone Age. There are a few finds of native copper implements. Crafts are plied skillfully — not merely fine ceramics in level VI, but weaving and those impressive wooden pots. I feel that we must believe that there were already creative cooks who could make something delicious from the contents of the storage bins and alcoves uncovered by archaeology and the flora identified by paleobotany. Let us look forward to more surprising finds in the future from a new enterprise undertaken at Çatal Hüyük by the British.

2 Ancient Egypt

WE TURN FROM following the Neolithic growth of differentiated societies to cultures far more structured in their organization, more reliant on specialized work and knowledge on the part of individuals, and now dependent on accurate record-keeping, that is, on writing. In a word, the urban revolution marks the next stage of human development. Tiny agricultural villages coalesce into, not merely larger, but complex, even hierarchical, social systems. Leading citizens gain power magnified to an extraordinary degree, whether acting as chief interrogator of the gods, chief negotiator in trade with other communities, or both—or, again, as wise mentor in the lore of farming and human development. With power comes a new kind of diversity of diet in keeping with one's status in society.

Social status must inevitably demand privileged modes of displaying it. Feasts that must once have originated in ritual contexts uniting primitive communities in thanks for bountiful harvests or fruitful hunts are transformed into displays of personal affluence and secular power. Wherever the urban revolution took place—almost simultaneously in beneficent areas of the Near East: Egypt and Mesopotamia—festal boards are spread by individuals to celebrate victory (fig. 10) or delectation in this life, anticipated in the next (fig. 11). Sensuous beguilements abound: the perfume of incense, the delicate strains of a harp, divine gifts of the vine that liberate creative visions, and poetry—all this newfound bounty of gregarious Culture with a capital C.

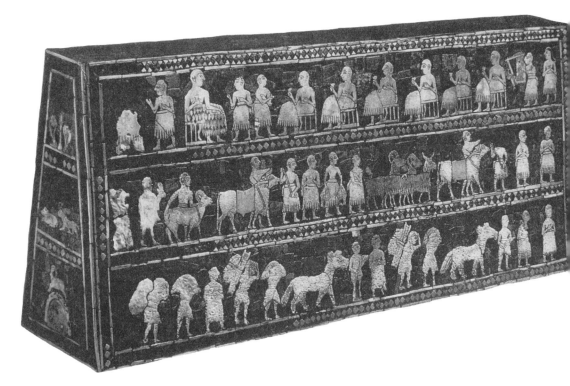

10. Banquet Celebrating a Victory. *Sumerian "standard" from the early third millennium* B.C., *found at Ur. Shell and lapis lazuli mosaic inlaid. London, British Museum*

Considering the vitality of the new urban culture, it is simplest to discuss Egypt first, as a more unitary civilization, protected on both sides by desert once the Nile, with its confining cliffs, had been tamed, and politically unified for some seven hundred miles of the river's course. Mesopotamia as a subject brings successive conquests, racial and linguistic transformations, in short, constant disruption. In Egypt we can speak of three thousand years of little fundamental change, a basic population and way of life that managed to captivate, even in decline, waves of foreign rulers: Hyksos, Assyrians, Persians, Greeks, and Romans. This is not to mention the Arab conquest of the seventh century A.D. that today challenges history with extraordinary tensions between tradition and revolution, Islamic fundamentalists against their brethren and, especially, Christian Copts. They are, one and all, heirs to the particular climate, fauna, and flora of their country, displaying a unique continuity in

11. Banquet. *Detail from the Tomb of Nebamun, Thebes, Valley of the Kings. New Kingdom, ca. 1400 B.C. London, British Museum*

gastronomic matters from pre-Dynastic times to our own. Modern visitors will delight in the grilled fowl, wild or domestic, once favored by Egyptian nobles on their country estates. They will dine on Nile and Mediterranean fish prepared with little change from antiquity; praise seasoning with the zesty onions and garlic nostalgically recalled by Israelites in their escape from bondage (Numbers 11:5); and find the national vegetable in a leafy plant that may have been gathered and enjoyed by prehistoric ancestors: *melukhiya.*[1]

Paradoxically, we know everything there is to know about the foodstuffs of ancient Egypt, the processes that made them ready for the kitchen, but almost nothing about cookery and gastronomy. I intend to set forth my own theory of how things were prepared and how they tasted, but this is pure hypothesis based on many characteristics of Egyptian language and art extrapolated to the realm of cuisine. Although the evidence comes from various periods in Egypt's long history, an inherent conservatism of its culture — that tendency to "keep the laws [and customs] of their forefathers" emphasized by the Greek historian, Herodotos,[2] who visited in the early fifth century B.C. — assures certain general conclusions. Our awe will come legitimately from admiration for the Egyptians' artful, sustainable exploitation of natural resources as well as research into their medicinal uses, rather than from mystical claims of our New Age contemporaries, beguiled by the cult of pyramids and much else shaped by a civilization remote in time (or in space, if one mindlessly follows the science-fiction pronouncements of writers who attribute its greatest monuments to interplanetary aliens). Even Greek geographers like Strabo[3] sought to explain the primacy of Egyptians in the realm of geometry (though he only refers to plane rather than the solid kind): because the Nile annually wiped out boundary lines of property, Egyptians early on had to invent a way of measuring land.

Enduring Egyptian ways of life and belief have always aroused wonder. A conservative like Plato, reacting to rapid change in fourth-century Athens, envied Nilotic stability over millennia. As recently as the Renaissance,[4] scholars have attributed the lore of Plato and of Moses to their apprenticeship under Egyptian priests. Freud went much further in exalting Moses as a high-born Egyptian rescuing the monotheism of Akhenaton by implanting it among alien residents, the Jews.[5] Today in the countryside, one is struck by villages of simple houses made from sun-dried brick and reeds, by farmers herding, plowing, irrigating and harvesting with age-old techniques familiar from tomb reliefs of the Old Kingdom (except that ankle-length caftans have replaced loincloths). In sharp contrast to modern city life, it is common to see women and children crouched before a threshold, readying the evening meal at a brazier or a *tandur* that looks like one three thousand years old (fig. 12).[6]

THE FORMAL CONVENTIONS OF EGYPTIAN ART

A justly famous work of Early Dynastic art, the ritual slate palette of King Narmer (fig. 13), represents in various paraphrases of symbolic form the unification of Egypt about 3000 B.C. Long since, a pictorial system of writing has been invented: signs for *n'r-mr*, the ruler's name, appear with a palace-façade hieroglyph atop each face, flanked by bull-horned Hathor heads. On one side two heraldic beasts, restrained by keepers, intertwine their elongated necks about a central well for ceremonially mixing kohl as eyeliner. Their inextricability seems to underscore the union of Upper (southern) and Lower

12.   *Tandur oven. Middle Kingdom.* "Flat breads" would be baked as they are today, slapped on the inside heated surface, giving them a curving shape. *Cairo Museum*

13.   Palette of Narmer. *Early dynastic period, ca. 3000 B.C. The obverse and reverse represent the unification of Upper and Lower Egypt. Slate. Cairo Museum*

(northern) Egypt, which all the other images commemorate. Already clearly ordered in registers, the actors on both obverse and reverse of the palette iterate the conquest over the North as well as the Delta. A majestic Narmer raises his mace to strike a fallen foe in a gesture outside of specific time or space that will be echoed again and again by later pharaohs throughout Egyptian history; it says "here is the conquering, invincible leader." In this case he wears the crown of Upper Egypt, while on the obverse, he marches with the crown of Lower Egypt toward the headless bodies of defeated enemies, accompanied by bearers of kingship symbols. Principles of artistic representation that will endure in the face of political and cultural change are proclaimed at the very beginning of Dynastic Egypt.

These principles include the refusal to suggest ephemeral aspects of phenomena observed in three-dimensional space. For the carver of Narmer's palette, the decapitated bodies are enumerated, as it were; most figures stand upon groundlines that isolate them on the plane rather than in depth, and in each register they display a hierarchy of proportions to distinguish the main protagonist from the accessory actor(s) on a scale of social and narratological value. An established code governs the rendering of each person and animal so as to maintain the integrity of the surface on which they appear and a literal inventory of their lineaments: animals in full, descriptive profile (exceptions, as we shall see, are birds in flight and the horns or ears of beasts like the bull surrogate for Narmer, where a strict side view would be ambiguous), humans in a fractional representation that dwells upon the most significant contour of each element. Thus, a front view of an eye in the profile face, of broad shoulders above profile hips and legs, and two left or right feet, because the most meaningful outline of a foot includes the big toe! Overlapping is avoided as much as possible, so that a group is strung out in a long frieze, and the "inward" arm is normally the most animated. Yet there is no impediment to depicting lively action, particularly in Old Kingdom workers who carry out the chores of daily life and bring offerings of every kind of thing to eat or drink to set before the deceased in his or her tomb (figs. 14, 21–23).

If each separate feature serving to make up the whole of a person — or in such an additive way to construct a scene — has the value of a word, that word is the most intensely vivid possible. Everything about Egyptians, their poetry above all, speaks of a people who treasured nature and sensuous enjoyment of the world around them. Herodotos had it exactly wrong when he claimed they were obsessed with an afterlife and prepared their tombs at the expense of pleasure in living. The fact that the Egyptians preserved the body itself by

14. *Food Offerings. Fifth Dynasty, ca. 2450 B.C. Saqqara, Tomb of Ptahhetep*

mummifying it and relied also on sculptural likenesses for its double, or *ka,* to inhabit after death, like all their funerary art, reflects delight in every manifestation of Nature and a reluctance to relinquish it in fear of the unknowable they hope to control. From the earliest dynasties to the most relaxed artistic expression of the New Kingdom (or Empire, 1552–1070 B.C., Dynasties XVIII–XX), we cannot help but be astonished at a keen observation and love of life that shines forth in renderings of the very least bit of the natural world — celebrating the fecundity of our earth in its flora and fauna with exquisite detail, as sensitive to animal psychology as to the animating human spirit that radiates from the magnificent but rather rigidly formulaic portrait statuary (fig. 15). Humor also strikes the person who can read the comments and songs set down in hieroglyphics beside actors in painted or carved scenes of farmhands and artisans at work, or, in the New Kingdom, guests and servants at banquet.[7] In the latter, a theme that will echo down the centuries appears: "Eat, drink, and be merry, for tomorrow we die."[8]

When we unite such passionate engagement with life — not forgetting its optimistic rituals or magic for sustaining its delights after death — with characteristics of every culture's most "speaking" aspect, its language, the first clues to Egyptian gastronomy begin to appear. I stress gastronomy because, as in most ancient or "undeveloped" societies, a hierarchy of social status determined one's diet. We know that certain priests were forbidden to eat either fish or pork.[9] We know that slave or peasant workers existed on a diet of barley or emmer wheat bread, certain pulses seasoned with onions, leeks, garlic, and wild herbs, plus beer, and whatever could be scrounged or pilfered to supplement limited fare — unless one were fortunate enough to participate in some great feast-day distribution that might include meat.

Egyptian writing has a dual system, pictographic on the one hand, and phonetic on the other. The possibility of confusing one meaning of a word with another can be obviated by determinatives set beside them. Like concrete details of nature's bounty for the artist, determinative pictographs stun by their consolidated tradition of sympathetic observation. The verb "to be angry" receives a baboon as the symbol of irritability. "To tremble" is distinguished by a marsh bird familiar to everyone for the shivering flutter of its wings.[10]

My question must be: would a people so attuned to the individual and specific, so conscious of the need to itemize each aspect of the human body in keeping with a schema of proportional values,[11] subscribe to a culinary code at variance with an attitude proclaimed by their art and language? Rooted in a cult of the dead, as provision for their sustenance in the Beyond, representations of agriculture and food offerings, lists of dedications in tombs and for temple rituals and the like give each item of food the discrete attention an inventory deserves. It is my contention that this paratactic habit of mind, joined with the particular quality of Egyptian feeling for Nature, could not help but affect what their cooks made of such bounteous provisions, that is, the aesthetics of their best cuisine.

I believe that the Egyptian culinary repertoire did not include many dishes that the French would call *composées*, no elaborate stews or creations demanding dozens of ingredients and seasonings, no complex sauces. I would also argue that, unlike the calculated, musical flow of savor and texture that characterizes Chinese cookery, of taste and aroma blending one into the other, the Egyptian menu would, more akin to the French, discriminate, perhaps contrast, one dish or ingredient with another — discrete, pure, and deceptively

15. Chephren. *Old Kingdom, ca. 2500 B.C. Diorite funerary statue in the Cairo Museum*

simple. "Simple" refers only to technique, given the character of kitchens we know from excavation or depiction, not to any lack of seasoning for a people so sensuously beguiled by every organ, including the nose. In the New Kingdom, representations of banquets (see, e.g., fig. 16) show them with cones of incense on their heads designed to melt during the meal (they are not shown eating, though food may be piled up before them, only engaged in pre- or post-prandial enjoyment of wine).

My argument would be weak against countervailing protests that, of

16.   Banquet. *New Kingdom, ca. 1400 B.C. Detail of a fresco from Thebes, Valley of the Kings. Note the cones of incense on the heads; foods include grapes, figs, and several types of bread, while both wine and beer stand beneath the table.*

17.   Daughter of Akhenaton *gnawing on a roasted duck. Sculptor's trial sketch from Tell el-Amarna in the Cairo Museum*

course, feeding the deceased or a divinity through word, picture, or modeled object functionally demands utmost clarity and itemization. However, archaeology supports me in many important ways. In an interlude in the New Kingdom (1352–1334 B.C.) when Akhenaton established his religious reforms and a new capital city at Amarna, artists basked in relaxation of those set rules of representation we have just considered. One trial image on a fragment of limestone sketches a young offspring of Akhenaton gnawing at a whole duck (fig. 17); before her stands a table bearing individual items to accompany it.[12] Centuries earlier, an actual funerary meal excavated from the rich harvest of Old Kingdom mastabas at Saqqara[13] presents an absolute contrast to a similar banquet laid out in an early Han tomb in China (fig. 18). The pottery platters and stone plates and bowls contained a porridge of ground barley; grilled quail (entire, with head tucked underneath the wing); two cooked kidneys; a cooked fish (headless); beef ribs; small triangular loaves of bread of a shape well represented in the Dokki Agricultural Museum and elsewhere, made of emmer wheat; some circular cakes; stewed fruit, probably figs; fresh *nabq* (Christ's thorn) berries[14] that are still a favorite today; and what is described as a stewed pigeon. For the last there is no indication of other ingredients or whether anything more than simmering with liquid had been involved. I would expect only an herb and possibly a little animal fat added to the fowl. Of course, this complete meal for a lady of the nobility also had some jars for wine as well as what analysis proved to be a form of cheese.[15]

One other detail interests me very much. All the dishes were set out to the east of the coffin. In a culture oriented to eternal verities of points of the compass, does this reflect the normal orientation of kitchens as we know them from the New Empire? They are almost invariably to be found at the east of the villas of Akhenaton's capital city of Tell el-Amarna and elsewhere, since breezes seldom blew from that direction and the smells of cookery would be confined to servant's quarters.[16]

It is instructive to compare the actual funerary meal considered above with a wall inscription of royal offerings in the Fifth Dynasty pyramid of King Unas, also at Saqqara. Milk, three kinds of beer, and five of wine (we will treat these anon) are listed, as are five kinds of oil. Ten "loaves" are distinguished from four breads, while fruit cakes are equally discriminated from ten deemed simply "cakes." Meats are cited by cut—cattle being understood: joints, roast, spleen, limb, breast, and tail. Fowl are represented by the favorite, goose, and by pigeons; chickens were latecomers to Egypt as use spread from their center of domestication in Southeast Asia.[17]

18. TOP: *Old Kingdom remains of a funerary meal left for the deceased in a mastaba, at Saqqara. From the excavation of W. B. Emery (1962);* BOTTOM: *Western Han China, mid-second century B.C. funerary meal for the deceased Marquess of Tai. Tomb near Ch'ang-sha, Hunan province*

THE STAFF OF LIFE: BREAD
AND ITS DERIVATIVE, BEER

As was the case for all ancient agriculturalists, Egyptians were sustained by a diet in which energy and nutrition were basically provided by grains. Chief among these—in a fertile Nilotic land that in later times became the "breadbasket" for wheat that kept a restive Roman proletariat content—was barley. Seemingly the earliest in cultivation and always less expensive than any variety of wheat, barley was the staple food among the lower classes in pharaonic Egypt as well as the common source for drink.[18] Among the wheats, emmer *(Triticum дicoccum)* was the usual variety until Ptolemaic times, utilized as porridge groats or pounded in a mortar to get rid of the hull and then ground on a hand quern into flour (fig. 19); rush or reed sieves were used to produce the finer grades destined for the elite. Whatever one's station in life, bread in a multitude of forms served not only as the staff of life (and death, as funerary offerings attest) but also as a favored offering for the temples of the gods. And what a variety of breads in every shape, flavor, and form! from flat, unleavened cakes of barley or emmer baked in ashes or slapped onto a hot stone or the sides of a *tandur* oven to the most carefully shaped wheaten loaves, sometimes baked in molds to a numinous pyramid, or in the form of some creature. The primacy of bread is reflected in countless examples of its use as wages to laborers; its diversity by the number of words for it in the Egyptian language, beginning with about a dozen different types in the Old Kingdom (ca. 2600–2180) and increasing to about forty breads and cakes in one New Kingdom listing.[19]

Figure 20 illustrates a few of the most prevalent shapes, including a fried variety that much resembles the Pennsylvania Dutch funnel cake. Leaven came from leftover dough that had soured, from the foam of fermenting beer, or from the action of fruit sugars that turned ordinary fare into special cakes. Different kinds of palm trees supplied either dates, so rich in protein and carbohydrates as well as sugars, or doum fruits, the flesh of which could be added to sweeten dough while the inner nut was often carved like ivory.[20] Honey served a major role in addition to fruit purées for sweetening cakes and pastries.

Egyptians of every class suffered from their fondness for bread and their rather primitive technology for grinding and sifting grain. On the saddle querns in use until rotary mills became widespread in the Roman period not only the stones themselves gave up grit into the flour, but it was customary to

19.   Woman grinder at a Quern. *Old Kingdom, ca. 2500 B.C. Berlin, Ägyptisches Museum*

20.   A Royal Bakery. *Drawing after the tomb of Rameses III, Thebes. Note variant bread and cake shapes, including tall molded pyramids, an animal effigy, and pin-wheels resembling funnel cakes.*

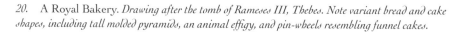

aid the grinding process by adding a small amount of sand as well. In Egyptian burials, gross attrition of teeth and resultant abscesses mark the dental health of even relatively young people.[21]

Bread also was used to make the universal beverage, beer *(hnqt),* in all its forms. Thus, in a pattern to be familiar down through history unto medieval monasteries, bakery and brewery shared quarters on an Egyptian's estate (fig. 21).[22] Part of the grain, generally barley unless "fine beer" was to be the end product, was set aside to be malted (soaked in water until it germinated),

21.   Production of Bread and Beer. *New Kingdom, ca. 1400 B.C. Painting in the tomb of Ken Amun, Thebes*

then sieved to eliminate husks, and finally lightly baked in the form of a rough loaf. This "beer-bread," after exposure to air-borne yeasts, was next broken up and set to ferment in water in a large vessel with added wheat, herbs, spices, or other seasonings such as dates or seeds of poppy and carob. The nomenclature shows that there were numerous kinds of beer (as well as imports), of which at least one is said to be essentially the same as today's *bouza* of Upper Egypt and Nubia. Different colors are cited, too, and an ancient myth about the origin of beer reflects one that gleamed distinctly red.

The story concerns the Sun god, Ra, and the goddess Hathor/Sekhmet whom he sent down to earth to punish a disrespectful mankind. Carried away by vengefulness, her fierce rage would have utterly destroyed human beings, if Ra had not relented and sent down red beer to cover fields, where it shone like a great mirror. Beguiled by her own reflection, the goddess drank from this pool that resembled blood, grew inebriated, and fell asleep, her dreadful mission forgotten.[23]

EGYPTIAN VITICULTURE

If beer so impressed Herodotos as the Egyptian national drink (and as wages, together with bread, in an exchange economy) that he could state that the Egyptians did not have vineyards, we are in a better position to assess the beverage of choice among the ruling classes. Vintaging scenes are favorites in the tombs, especially during the prosperous times of the New Kingdom when gracious living was extended to a broader segment of nobles and bureaucratic officials (figs. 22 and 23). Perhaps the Greek historian thought the wine he noted at certain festivals had been imported from elsewhere, and he paid no heed to wines made from dates, figs, pomegranates, and whatever to him seemed unlikely fruit. But how did he miss the vineyards that archaeology documents from the very first dynasties?[24]

It is from the New Kingdom that we find the most plentiful documentation of the Egyptian love of wine and of their refined knowledge of it.[25] Professor Leonard Lesko is our present leading oenophile and expert on ancient Egyptian vintages, having developed an after-dinner talk into his informative tract, *King Tut's Wine Cellar.*[26] From Tutankhamon's tomb, unopened wine jars with their labels confirm evidence from broken shards of such neck labels at other sites that estate, vineyard, wine-maker, and date were important to consumers. Lesko appears certain that their fine wines were appreciated neat, not mixed with water in the later classical manner. He states: "it seems that the

22.   Vintage. *New Kingdom, ca. 1400 B.C. Frescoes from the tomb of Nakht, Thebes, Valley of the Kings.*
See the men treading grapes in a vat.

23.   *Detail of a vintage relief showing men pressing grapes in a bag twisted by poles. Old Kingdom, ca.*
2000 B.C. Mastaba of Mereruka, Saqqara

24.   The Sculptor Ipy and His Family. *Nineteenth Dynasty, ca. 1200 B.C. Reproduction of a tomb painting from Thebes*

Egyptian wines would have been much more to our modern taste than the resinated, oil-covered, burned, and diluted concoctions served by Greeks and Romans."[27]

The oldest dated jar from Tutankhamon's tomb may have contained a vintage thirty-five years old at the time of the young king's burial, but Professor Lesko allows for the possibility that this amphora might have been reused (a practice for which there is much evidence) without erasing the old label or adding a new. Even in jars lined with gypsum, the porosity of clay makes it difficult to accept the possibility of vintages of such a venerable age, although aging was certainly one criterion for quality in wine. Other criteria are found in the frequent addition of adjectives to data on labels; it is notable that relatively few were deemed "sweet." One would dearly love to know what "The Green Eye of Horus" tasted like; this was one poetically named wine from the Western Oases that, with the Fayoum and Delta, comprised the best vine-growing areas.[28]

New Kingdom banqueting scenes (figs. 11, 25) concentrate on the joyous consumption of wine instead of depicting the dinner itself. Men and women usually do not sit together, but in separate groups, as servants tend the tall

25. Banquet. *New Kingdom, ca. 1400 B.C. Tomb of Rekhmire, Thebes, Valley of the Kings. This fresco shows the men and women separated. Especially noteworthy in the second frieze from the top is the maidservant who pours wine, turning into space in a break with normal Egyptian pictorial conventions.*

26. *Alabster lotus chalice, ca. 1375 B.C., from the tomb of Tutankhamon. Cairo Museum*

wine amphoras wreathed in flower garlands. Handmaidens, often clad in the transparently sheer garments that replaced the stiff linens of the Old and Middle Kingdoms, pass among the assembly to keep drinking vessels filled. Musicians play music that must be soothing — to judge by the ever-present harpist and a few tootling reed pipes and strings — to enhance the scent of lotus flowers everyone holds or presses for a neighbor's scenting and the melting incense cones on every head.[29] The relaxation is so palpable that the artist who painted the Theban tomb of Rekhmire — against all inherited artistic convention — even allowed himself the freedom of turning the figure of a lithe young serving girl into three-dimensional *space* as she offers to pour with the beguiling invitation spelled out by accompanying hieroglyphs: "For your soul *[ka]*. Make happy festival!" (fig. 25).

A further index of oenophilic pleasure among Egyptians of the upper classes is to be found in the elegance of drinking vessels found in tombs of the Empire period. Anyone who visited the exhibition of King Tut's Treasures when it toured the States will remember his alabaster chalice (fig. 26). This one may have been for ritual use, but wine goblets of alabaster, gold, and faience, or molded glass, are common archaeological finds of the Eighteenth and Twentieth Dynasties.[30]

THE CULINARY REPERTOIRE

An extraordinary range of ingredients was available to the privileged classes of Egyptian society, thanks to the bounty of their "Two Lands" and to the ingenuity which, from pre-dynastic times, marked their exploitation of natural resources. Animal husbandry accomplished marvels of herded wild oryx, ibex, and antelopes from the craggy desert boundaries of their lush valley. In exquisitely detailed low reliefs of the Old Kingdom we find depicted such experiments in adding game animals to others long domesticated, like the long-horned cattle favored in breeding.[31] Nor were ruminants the sole triumphs of domestication. Wild game birds were netted in the marshes to be raised and fattened with domestic fowl; even tall cranes appear in reliefs from the Fifth and Sixth Dynasties. And Egypt was in pharaonic times, as it still is, on a Near Eastern migratory flyway that seasonally brought all sorts of birds to the braziers of noble and peasant alike. Split and grilled, roasted whole on a spit, covered with clay and cooked under ashes, or — thinking of that Saqqara pigeon stew — simmered in liquid, avian fauna from quail and dove to rare, imported ostrich provided one of the most significant sources of animal protein. Until the Empire, poultry yards did not contain chickens, as was already explained. Eggs came primarily from ducks and geese, both fowl especially prominent in offering lists and representations.[32] Herodotos puzzled over Egyptian partiality to goose, an important item in the diet of priests though it was sacred to the Nile god; geese were kept in large flocks at some temple precincts and were frequent sacrificial victims. Other sacred birds were never eaten, of course: hawks, vultures, and the Nilotic ibis (extinct in Egypt since the late nineteenth century).

Speaking of geese brings to mind the value of animal fats in a culture that did not develop the capacity in bovines to give milk prodigally and continually. References to butter are few, and it had to be clarified to a product like ghee in order to last in a hot climate. But fats of every sort of animal, wild or domestic, as well as rich oils from seeds and nuts, supplied Egyptians with the means to fry foods and to enrich their cakes and pastries.[33] Aside from oils for ritual use and those employed chiefly in perfumes or medicine, culinary oils include two that may surprise us—from radish and lettuce seeds. Sesame oil is assumed, although records of it are not certain until the Greek period, given a host of terms for oils in the sources. By Greco-Roman times there is ample documentation for both sesame oil and paste *(halvah)*.[34]

Returning to animal protein, we should consider the staggering number of fish species that inhabited the Nile and its marshlands (fig. 27), because they were accessible to all—and crocodiles, as well.[35] Nowadays, when alligator is consumed with relish by bayou-dweller and urbanite alike, one wonders whether sacred animals such as the crocodile were ever considered food by meat-starved ancestors of the *fellahin*.[36] Curious is the lack of fish in Old Kingdom funerary offering lists, while a rich repertoire of representations appears in tomb reliefs of the period. This may result from the fact that fish were avoided by priests (and the ruler as high priest of state cults), which we know from later testimony of the Greeks. It may also speak to a snobbish abstention from a food too common among peasant classes. In any case, there were certain fish caught up in religious taboos both local and general. Among the latter, the oxyrhynchus was enmeshed from the end of the Old Kingdom in the spread of the worship of Osiris, the god of the underworld and resurrection; it had joined certain companions in devouring the genitals of the God after his murderous brother, Seth, butchered his body, scattering the pieces in the river (none of this preventing Isis, the faithful wife of Osiris, from gathering up the *membra disjecta* and conceiving the child, Horus).[37]

Given the Egyptian climate, a means of preserving fish had to be devel-

27. Netting Fish in the Nile. *Old Kingdom. Relief from the tomb of Akhethotep, Saqqara. Among the species depicted in this detail, an oxyrhynchus is to be noted at the lower right and, just above it, to the left, is a large tilapia. Paris, Louvre*

oped very early. Split and gutted, they were salted, pickled, or hung in the sun to dry, becoming an important export product. Delicate fish pickle from Egypt is praised by Roman aficionados. Representations of fish processing indicate that any roe was carefully removed, but there is no agreement on when or how this led to the salted, pressed cakes of mullet roe, dried hard, that the French call *boutargue* and which is relished by modern Egyptians as *batarekh*.[38] At the high end of the social scale, wealthy landowners could practice aquaculture in the fishponds of their gardens (fig. 28).

The trees encircling this Nineteenth-Dynasty piscina introduce the importance of fresh fruits in Egyptian nutrition and as a source of sweetening for beverages and cakes. Herodotos (II, 77) remarked upon the health of the Egyptians, attributing it less to their devoting three days each month to purging their systems with emetics and enemas than to the constancy of the climate. We might prefer to credit it to their "Mediterranean" diet featuring whole grain breads, moderate consumption of red meat — or none, depending on one's station in life — limited fats, and, above all, the quality and variety of their fruits and vegetables. Our illustration of a fragmentary painting from a Theban tomb of the Empire, wonderfully designed to clarify each element without the vagaries of spatial extension, distinguishes a striking variety of fruit trees: date-palm, fig, sycamore fig, doum palm, persea, pomegranate (a Levantine newcomer from the days of the Hyksos invaders who ruled Egypt from about 1780 to 1570 B.C., bringing the Iron Age to Egypt together with horses and chariots), and, I believe, carob.[39] The fruit of the last-named tree, *Ceratonia siliqua*, is familiar to frequenters of health food stores as a substitute for chocolate. Controversy surrounds its proper Egyptian name and whether it grew widely in the ancient land where it is today mostly restricted to a limited area on the northern coast. If it was an exotic for Egyptian gardens, this pod-bearing relative of the locust is nonetheless represented in archaeological contexts, and food historians may be forgiven for thinking that the high sugar content of the bean assured its use in ancient sweets.[40]

In the vegetable kingdom, members of the Allium family and of Cucurbitaceae dominated — among the former, onions, leeks, garlic; among the latter, various gourds, melons, and cucumbers.[41] One cannot help being struck,

28. Garden Pool of an Estate. *New Kingdom fresco from the Eighteenth-dynasty Tomb of Nebamun. The pool is surrounded by date palms, fig, sycamore fig, persea, and pmegranate trees; perhaps a carob tree at lower left. London, British Museum*

when looking at an offering tables of either the Old Kingdom or the Empire (figs. 14, 24), by the perfected menu in a hot climate for a people whose thought processes appear to have worked in terms of balanced antitheses—a harmony of opposites similar to Chinese principles of *yin* and *yang*. There are the various breads, the beer and wine, with choice cuts of meat for roasting or grilling contrasted to heaps of such cool, juice-laden vegetables and fruits. "Cool" need not be taken as subjective gastronomical inference either; as in the desert, the temperature differential between daytime heat and nighttime cold is sufficient to chill by evaporation produce or drink left outside—even to make ice.

Among food plants, there are three which, like the date-palm, merit special attention because of their symbolic eloquence: papyrus, sedge, and lettuce. From earliest pre-dynastic times wild Nile vegetation of the family Cyperaceae were exploited in Egypt for alimentary and other purposes. Vegetal forms in Egyptian architecture—translated into the petrified language of limestone—give vivid testimony to papyrus and reeds as building materials for prehistoric huts and protective palisades. But archaeological finds equally attest to the use of papyrus and sedge as foods, providing additional motivation for their later use as hieroglyphic symbols for Lower (northern) and Upper Egypt, respectively. The papyrus *(Cyperus papyrus)*, the fibrous upper stalk of which served to make writing material and give us our word "paper," could, like sugar cane, be chewed raw for its juices, while the lower stalk and roots could also be boiled or roasted.[42] As for *Cyperus esculentus*, the sedge that stands for the Upper Nile region and is also known as chufa, or nut-grass, American children growing up along the banks of the Delaware River all the way south to the lowlands of the Carolinas know how crunchily sweet are its tubers. Little wonder the earliest cultures found culinary use for it. Perhaps they also grated these "nuts" to make a refreshing drink, much as the Spanish do today; still, the Egyptians could not know what they were missing for lack of knowledge that its seeds could be used to brew a coffee-like drink as in Hungary!

"Lettuce," to a modern cook may bring to mind headed varieties—possibly even that tasteless iceberg type developed by U.S. agribusiness to travel long distances under refrigeration—but ancient species were tall and stalky. If you are given to entertaining in the mode of antiquity, you must use a cos lettuce, romaine for example, as the closest substitute. But even that will not show the milky juice that gives the plant its name, a sap that appears dripping from the stem when it is cut from the roots and that inspired its symbolic value for the ancients. Paradoxically, this exudation receives entirely opposite interpretation at different points in history, among different religious contexts. Because of the sap's supposed resemblance to male semen, some cultures have claimed lettuce as an aphrodisiac, while humoral theory developed by the Greeks emphasized the cold, wet nature of lettuce. Thus, as Marcel Detienne has shown us, it could stand for impotence and death. Clearly, for Egyptians, its referential value was the former; it is the offering of choice to the god of fertility and procreation, Min (fig. 29), and appears often among the tomb offerings of both the Old Kingdom and the New.[43]

Few Egyptians today forego their breakfast *ful*,[44] a dish of long-simmered brown beans garnished by the eater to choice with oil, lemon, garlic, minced parsley, cumin, or pepper. This is one more example of a long-enduring Egyptian tradition, for legumes were a staple food of the ancients, leading one to suspect that the era of the pharaohs may likewise have seen broad (fava) beans and chickpeas used to make the delicious fried cakes or balls we know as *falafel* (*ta'amya* throughout the Near East). We encountered such pulses (that is, legumes) in the Neolithic period, as well as lentils, lupines, and vetches, but these important sources of vegetable protein were especially favored among the Egyptians together with varieties peculiar to their agriculture. The "Egyptian bean" *par excellence,* as it was defined by the Greeks and Romans, appears to have been early confused with seeds of the aquatic pink lotus *(Nelumbium speciosum)* extracted from its bulbous head. At least that is what is carefully described by Theophrastos (IV, viii, 7–8). On the other hand, one authority has insisted that the most widely grown and consumed bean of pharaonic times was not a bean at all, but a *dolichus,* kin to our black-eyed pea.[45]

Given the conflicting linguistic evidence concerning identification of the most popular bean in the Egyptian dietary repertoire, it is difficult to tell which legume (or all of them?) was forbidden to be eaten by priests and rulers. This avoidance is a matter of interest, because the proscription came to be observed later among Greek and Roman followers of the philosopher Pythagoras. In his day — the Archaic age of the sixth century B.C. — Pythagoras studied the lore of priests in Egypt and was presumably influenced in this respect by their traditions. Why were beans considered to be unclean by the most elevated Egyptians when they were so basic to the daily fare of the lower classes and are found in tomb offerings of their betters? Any housewife who has sprouted them can readily suggest an answer: bean sprouts appear so miraculously when a dried legume has been moistened and kept in a dark

29. Offering of Senruset I to the God Min. *Middle Kingdom, ca. 1880 B.C. Relief in the Chapel of Senruset at Karnak. Note three lettuce plants behind Min.*

place, it suggests renascent life or soul resident within. The phenomenon must have been compelling, not only for Egyptian priests, but especially so for Pythagoras, with his development of the theory of transmigration of souls. The taboo surely has nothing to do with beans causing flatulence, as some have suggested.

We cannot leave ancient Egyptian cuisine without exploring a bit further details of taste and seasoning, of relishes and condiments. A culture that filled the entire wall of a temple precinct with inscribed recipes for ointments and perfumes, that experimented with chemical properties of substances in order to mummify its dead and to develop medicines to treat the living, can be expected to have spared no expense to import products from afar. The only question is whether spices and herbs used medicinally or in religious rites gave pleasure to the Egyptian palate as well; perhaps the cinnamon from far-off India which Ramesses III (1182–1151 B.C.) presented to the gods on several occasions did not enter the culinary chain of ordinary mortals. Herodotos (III, 110–111) later indulges in legends painting it as an incredibly exotic ingredient, and in Roman days it was reserved as an aromatic to cover the scent of burning flesh at cremations. Yet the land of the Nile had its own native spices: cumin, anise, coriander, fenugreek among them, as well as black mustard seed from at least the New Kingdom, making up for the lack of pepper before Roman days. Cedar, juniper, caper shrub, possibly even the clove tree enlarge the possibilities, while herbs like fennel and dill yielded both leaf and seed. Other herbs include mint, marjoram, thyme, sage and safflower.[46]

Egypt had many sources for salt, so necessary for curing and preserving meat and fish as well as for seasoning. Pans for evaporating sea water have been excavated in the Delta, though there is some evidence, however late, that priests abstained from sea salt, at least on ritual occasions, because of its association with the evil god Seth. Red salt came from a lake near Memphis, while a purple variety imported from Libya and Ethiopia provided yet another type. Western oases yielded not merely salt but another form of sodium, natron, that was very important in the mummification process; Wadi Natroun takes its name from this carbonate compound.[47]

A further question of savor eludes us: did Egyptians relish the contrast of sweet/sour combinations we know in other ancient cultures? To their honey and fruit pulps did they add vinegar, as we know they did during the Roman era? As one would expect, vinegar is not mentioned among offering lists of delicacies, and, in the technical analysis of excavated containers, cannot be distinguished from residues of wine and other substances that produce it through nature's processes. There is no question that vinegar occurred, whether it was exploited or not.

All things considered, it is possible to have confidence in an appetizing quality that enhanced a cuisine for which we have as yet no single recipe before Greco-Roman times. Always adding, of course, the caveat that we are not speaking of the ordinary mass of humble Egyptian workers.

3 Mesopotamia

HOW COMPARABLE, yet how profoundly different, appears the other great early civilization of the Near East set beside Egypt: Mesopotamia — often known as Babylonia, after its most famed and biblically infamous urban paradigm. The complex civilization of Mesopotamia is conjugated by competing states, radically transformed by incursions from elsewhere, and characterized by the very opposite of ethnic homogeneity. Even so, underlying continuity of religious and societal norms can be discerned, making it possible to put forward certain generic statements about food and foodways in the Tigris-Euphrates plain. Unlike the Nile inundation, predictable in its rise and benign in its annual deposit of fertile topsoil, floods in the land between the two rivers came less reliably and with decided violence. The story of a devastating flood that almost wiped out all life in that world is part of the belief system of all peoples in Mesopotamia, from the Sumerians who dominated the lower confluence of the rivers about 3500 B.C. to the Hebrews who set down the experience of Noah.[1]

Perhaps the necessity for elaborate systems of canals to control and distribute the waters led, at least at first, to a social and political organization quite different from Egypt's ideal of centralized power. Instead we find, from a period comparable to that of Narmer, individual city-states, each under the protection of a patron divinity, managed by a human steward/ruler in a sort of state socialism that saw to the rites of the deity, the efficient practice of agriculture and trade, and to the just allocation of resources among its population. In any case, southern Mesopotamian agriculture had to learn to deal with the silting up of irrigation channels and subsidence of the lower reaches of the rivers—a process that has continued over the millennia so that archaeological sites once close to the Persian Gulf are now more than a hundred miles inland—and with salinization of the irrigated soil. Some paleoethnobotanists believe that Mesopotamian farmers learned very early to counteract both adverse conditions, exploiting the marshes of the lower valley, home to Iraq's Marsh Arabs today, to foster date palms, which do enjoy brackish water, and were already empirically aware of the capability of leguminous plants to combat salinity as well as to fix nitrogen from the atmosphere to nourish the earth in which they grow.[2]

From the urban revolution of the fourth millennium B.C., trade relationships, both in terms of local commerce and longer distance trade routes, brought the products with which Mesopotamia was poorly endowed. This contrasts sharply with self-sufficient Egypt before the expansiveness of its New Kingdom empire opened its unitary culture to fresh influences and luxury items of consumption. Southern Mesopotamia had to import so much: stone, hardwoods, wheat, and wine from its western highlands, fruits such as apples and pears from temperate climates to the north, as well as certain nuts, and exotic imports that underline very early connections between this part of the Near East and comparable civilizations of the Indus Valley.

ART OF MESOPOTAMIA

Thorkild Jakobsen wrote more than fifty years ago of the difference in "mood" between the two great civilizations of the ancient Near East. "Were the Egyptian to come back today, he would undoubtedly take heart from the endurance of his pyramids, for he accorded to man and to man's tangible achievements more basic significance than most civilizations have been willing to do. Were the Mesopotamian to return, he could hardly feel deeply disturbed that *his* works have crumbled, for he always knew, and knew deeply, that as for 'mere man—his days are numbered, whatever he may do, he is but wind.'"[3] Indeed, an even more powerful metaphor for Mesopotamian cultures brought forth the words of Genesis 3:19: "for dust thou art, and unto dust shalt thou return," one that echoes in the mind at contemplation of the art and architecture in the region. We will see its relevance to foodways as well. Characteristically, since, unlike Egypt, topography did not bless the area between the Tigris and Euphrates with vast outcroppings of good stone for buildings or sculpture, the unit of construction was mud brick, dried in the sun; in sculpture, throughout the ascendencies of various peoples in the area, one senses the vision of a creator in clay, even when a work is crafted from imported stone. And the system of writing used by the Sumerians for their non-Semitic language, passed on to subsequent cultures, was also based on an accumulation of small indentations made by a stylus in a clay "brick," developing from pictographic shorthand to syllabic notation. Masses of such cuneiform tablets still await a first reading by scholars and some of them provide our first true "shopping lists" and recipes. Another characteristic devotion to the exploitation of clay resides in a ubiquitous use of cylinder seals carved with official emblems or personal "signatures" that could make a sort of frieze when rolled across the receptive surface of a damp, unbaked tablet.[4]

Compare with the Egyptian funerary statue (fig. 15), waiting to be animated by its *ka*, a lively Sumerian figure of the Early Dynastic period (3000–2340 B.C.) (fig. 30). It was made, like so much early Mesopotamian sculpture, as a votive suppliant to confront a deity in his or her temple, a stand-in for the worshipper who commissioned and dedicated it, most probably a priest or a ruler who, as the steward, administered a city possessed by the god. Aside from differences in scale, everything about the Egyptian shouts "carved," "lithic," and its cubic or stereometric quality derives from the process of carving back on each of four sides of a block the projected outline drawn on its surface; in the final image one often feels the original corners of that block in abrupt angles at which planes encounter one another. In contrast, every form of the Sumerian figure speaks rotundity, modeling, as in the process by which a child might fashion a figure of mud or Play-Doh, though, of course, the actual process involved carving a small piece of alabaster.[5] Another characteristic will be constant in the art of Mesopotamia whether Sumerian, Akkadian of the succeeding dynasties (2340–2180 B.C.), Babylonian of the hegemony of Hammurabi (1792–1750 B.C.), or from the Assyrians who began to conquer the entire Near East at the end of the second millennium, or anything in between. This is an extraordinary refinement and multiplicity of patterned designs, of elements stylized to replace those of nature in rendering details such as hair, beard, fleece, musculature, or flora.

In architecture, the cone and the cylinder, truly rolled from clay to be then

30. Standing figure, ca. 2400 B.C., from the Ishtar Temple at Assur. Berlin, Pergamon Museum

glazed and baked, emphasize even more compellingly the Mesopotamian reliance on the singular, small unit that, in the aggregate, makes up the total form, just as bricks serve the entire structure. At Uruk, the Biblical Erech, from the prehistoric (Protoliterate) period 3500 to 3000 B.C., archaeologists have uncovered one of the earliest sanctuaries of a Sumerian divinity. It is raised high on an artificial mound, a *ziggurat* by name—for us, prototype of the Biblical Tower of Babel; for Sumerians and their successors right down to the Assyrians, a symbolic mountain where one might experience the epiphany of a deity (and once, it seemed, a nostalgic remembrance of the mountains from which they might have come down to settle in the lower reaches of the Tigris-Euphrates plain). Aside from the symbolic religious value, another pragmatic purpose should be noted: inundation in Mesopotamia being so violent and unpredictable, sun-dried brick had in any case to be protected by at least a platform from swirling waters that might eat away its substance. At Uruk (fig. 31) were found early experiments at protecting and enlivening expanses of wall with colorful geometric designs in mosaic, shaped by cones of clay imbedded in the fabric with their bases protruding. Although there is but episodic development of this brilliant solution to pattern and color on architectural surfaces, it seems to anticipate the glazed relief bricks of the Ishtar Gate at Babylon through which the Israelites were led to captivity under Nebuchadnezzar (fig. 32).

The ingenuity of people building with small modular units like sun-dried bricks, and faced with a dearth of trees that might supply strong beams for roofing, led to the early development of the architectural principles of the arch (ultimately to be exploited by the Romans over wide spaces, once they invented concrete as a binding material), inimical to Egyptians with either ephemeral or dense stone material for public construction. Enclosed spaces in Mesopotamia tend, however, to be longer than wide as a result of barrel vaults which require thick walls to buttress the thrust of a continuous series of arches that, in an Arabic phrase, "never sleep." That principle ran counter to the Egyptian sense of perenduring stasis; they used arch and vaults solely in pragmatic solutions to problems of underground conduits or storage facilities.[6]

When it comes to representation of the daily lives of dwellers in Mesopotamian regions, artists of various successive cultures provide nothing analogous to the extensive description of typical occupations and diversions that we owe to Egyptian sculptors or painters who depicted earthly pleasures in tombs of the deceased. For the most part it is communal life and the exercise of power, divine and human, that serve as narrative material for Sumerians, for their Semitic successors, the Akkadians, or for empire-builders of the Bronze Age, like the Mitanni, the Hittites in Anatolia, or the Assyrians who conquered all the Near East, including Egypt, in the period from 1000 to

31. Sumerian Uruk. Ziggurat, and so-called White Temple. Detail of cone mosaics revetting architectural elements

612 B.C. One predilection, however, seems present from the beginning, to culminate in Assyrian journalistic reports of their preeminence in the arts of war and divinely aided administration of their conquests. This is an urge to document specific events, to represent *history* rather than generic verities of power or quotidian events as did the Egyptians.

In the hands of Assyrian builders of vast palace-cities, with ample supplies of good stone in northeastern Mesopotamia, wall revetments were expanded to extol in relief the occupations and notable deeds of a ruler. They introduce us to dimensions of war and of the hunt, each in its most fearsome aspects, that include topography, strategic planning, and every relevant activity. More important than the intimidating subjects of reliefs with which Assyrians lined the halls where emissaries from allies and tribute nations cooled their heels awaiting audience was this documentary intent. We will see shortly how this affects the Assyrian heirs of Mesopotamian civilization in respect to

32. Babylon, sixteenth century B.C. Neo-Babylonian Gate revetted with glazed bricks, as reconstructed in the Berlin Museum

food preparation in the field, so to speak, and dining on one particular cele-
bratory occasion (figs. 33, 42).

BEER AND BREAD/BREAD AND BEER
IN MESOPOTAMIA

Like the question "which came first, the chicken or the egg?" a similar query
may be applied to bread and beer. We have seen the symbiotic relationship between these mainstays of human well-being, physical and psychological, in
considering Egyptian production of both. In our chapter on prehistory we
traced the gradual taming of wild grasses that gave humans the possibility of
cereal cultivation and settled village life. With Mesopotamia it becomes necessary to admit a theory that it is beer which represents the first-born invention of culture versus nature (to use oppositions of Claude Lévi-Strauss's
"culinary triangle"). Initiated by Robert Braidwood and taken up most notably by the activism of Solomon Katz, Mary Voigt, and other enthusiasts at
the University of Pennsylvania,[7] is the beguiling idea that beer represents the
ur-source of all civilization; that grain, collected by hunters and gatherers,
then stored, spontaneously fermented under moistened conditions into something that could bring joy to the soul, persuaded people to settle down in com-
paniable villages, and gave a jump-start to society in the most ample sense of

*33.   Field Kitchen, in bird's-eye view, with cooks preparing food and stirring a huge cauldron. Ninth
century B.C. Assyrian limestone relief from the Northwest Palace of Assurnazirpal, Nimrud. London,
British Museum*

34. Hammurabi before the Sun-god. *Babylonian diorite stele, ca. 1760 B.C., with the Law code of Hammurabi. Paris, Louvre*

the word. All this *before* utilizing that grain to produce flour and the bread which ultimately transformed the process in ways we have seen. The grain was barley, the dominant cereal crop in lower Mesopotamia to an even more exclusive degree than in Egypt, since areas suitable for growing wheat lay in a more western region of the Fertile Crescent, or in the northern highlands.[8]

With the aid of a modern brewery owner, the Pennsylvania aficionados in 1990 recreated an ancient Sumerian beer, by interpreting a recipe embedded in a hymn to the goddess of beer, Ninkasi; the name of their brew—what else?—*Ninkasi.* The cuneiform tablet with the hymn dates from the Babylonian dynasty that included, Hammurabi, (1792–1750 B.C.), sponsor of the famous law code (fig. 34).[9] In this extraordinary document, preserved because a stele proclaiming it was later carried off as booty by raiding Elamites to be discovered by French excavators in Persia, regulations indicate that women were apparently what passed for barkeeps in those days, unless the taverns in question were at the same time brothels. Yet, the Ninkasi hymn would support a hypothesis that brewing and serving beer were feminine occupations, by this period intimately linked with the making of bread, as we have seen. Ninkasi mixes her barley cake, *bappir*, with sweet aromatics and honey to facilitate fermentation.[10] Professor Katz suggests that the sweet aromatics included skirret, that is, its licorice-tasting root. It is likely that the "honey" was normally a date syrup, since this was the ordinary sweetener of lower Mesopotamia where apiculture was not as widespread as in Egypt and jars of bee honey frequently appear among invoices of imports. Many representations of beer-drinking show that it was common to drink unfiltered beer through a drinking tube to avoid any residue from barley husks or the wild yeasts that aided fermentation (see fig. 35); a special silver, gold and lapis lazuli drinking straw of the kind was among the early Sumerian finds at Ur.[11]

As for wine, ever an upper class indulgence, viticulture was well established commercially in upper Mesopotamia and the Levant by the second millennium B.C. Mari seems to have been a redistribution point for imports from further west and north, from Carchemish for example; the taxes levied do not refer to vintages, but merely different grades of wine: "ordinary," "ordinary red," and the like.[12] In Biblical passages, the wines of Syria from Helbon (Ezekiel 27:18) and of Lebanon (Hosea 14:7) receive special notice, the latter used as metaphors for heady aroma. In Babylonia we have evidence of local wines, but temple vineyards and private plots seem not to have provided any threat to the dominance of date wine and beer as the favored drinks.

Whatever the liquor, intemperance appears to have been cultivated to a high degree. One reads nothing comparable to the mildly disapproving views on drunkenness that turn up in Egyptian comments, texts, and a few representations (or for that matter in the Biblical reproach the Lord visits on Noah). On the contrary, even the most elevated divinities and heroes are depicted in various stages of inebriation, from stupor or exalted vision to the most disgusting loss of bodily control. The unsophisticated Enkidu, one of two heroes of the epic, *Gilgamesh*, after his first encounter with a fermented beverage, stands for the transformative effect of liquor: "carefree became his mood (and) cheerful, / His heart exulted / And his face glowed."[13]

Not from Mesopotamia, but from the north Syrian coast comes an extraordinary image of a father of the gods. The chief divinity of the Canaanites, El, reveals the most gross results of overindulgence in an epic discovered at Ugarit (Ras Shamra): ". . . El drank wine to satiety, Must to drunkenness . . .

35. Banquet. *Third millennium B.C. Impression from a Sumerian cylinder seal showing the use of long curved tubes. Find from the Royal Graves at Ur. (After Leonard Woolley,* Excavations at Ur, *vol. 2, no. 10825)*

[he is helped to his house where a 'creeper' with two horns and a tail accosts him, a demon equivalent to a 'pink elephant']. He floundered in his excrement and urine. El collapsed, El like those who descend to Earth."[14]

CULINARY ARTS IN MESOPOTAMIA

Happily, for the first time we have actual recipes from various periods preserved among literally millions of cuneiform tablets. Written on several sides of sometimes damaged lumps of clay, these precious documents, like all cookery instructions from the distant past, give no quantities. They were clearly made as part of repertory standards for professional cooks. Many of the ingredients—particularly the meaning of Sumerian words—have yet to be agreed upon by philologists. But procedural sequence is generally clear and manifests decided sophistication in the arts of cuisine. Our knowledge of food preparation is enhanced also by other texts, notably kitchen inventories of palaces and reports by stewards of their supervision of storerooms and preparations for formal banquets.

The raw materials for Mesopotamian cuisine are substantially the same as those of Egypt (at least of the New Kingdom at the time of its imperial expansion into the Levant), with several significant differences. We find for basic nutrition the same reliance on grain (plus, of course, beer), with even more ingenuity attested in a multitude of variations from groats and porridge to breads differentiated by additives, by shape, and by purpose. The flour may be barley, millet, emmer wheat, or even chickpea; fats and sweeteners may be added, as well as fruits or nuts; shape may be flat, slapped on a hot surface or *tannur*,[15] or leavened by fermentation brought on by the action of wild yeasts on glucose or fructose, of sour dough, or of beer foam; and the use of molded shapes seems more widespread than in Egypt. Every sort of representation from animals to fecund nudes may be imprinted or molded on or in bread; by the second millennium B.C. a growing practice seems to replace actual sacrifice by such surrogate models among dwellers in Mesopotamia or among Hittite invaders from Anatolia (figs. 36, 37). In the kingdom of Mari, on the Middle Euphrates, palace storerooms yielded scores of molds.[16]

When it comes to sacrifices and to the consumption of meat by those fortunate enough to be entitled to it, it is possible to name the same basic sources of animal protein for gods or humans. But the relative proportions have changed. Cattle, including a different strain akin to the Indian zebu in early Sumerian representations, may be fattened for the gods and special uses, but the bull is more widely a symbol of divinity than even the Apis cult of Egypt would allow (a bull's horns distinguish the headdress of gods and their representatives, while Assyrian palaces are guarded by forbidding, huge winged bulls with human heads [fig. 38]). As such, they are all the less a staple of meat preparation. Exploited to a much greater degree than in Egypt are goats, sheep, and swine — and the sheep are developed especially for the Mesopotamian breed still coveted today, with a fat-swollen tail so enormously developed that it must sometimes be carried on a little cart drawn behind![17]

Pork and swine fat, lard, appears with regularity and forces one to ask why, in a Near East where tradition recommends eating this animal, favored by early people for rich flesh fostered by prehistoric stands of pistachio and other nut-bearing trees, and domesticated after the climate changed to a most satisfying household creature — needing no pen and helping to consume food

36.   *Terra cotta baking molds excavated in Room 77 of the Old Babylonian Palace at Mari, ca. 1780 B.C. Note the group in shape of a fish, upper right.*

37.   *Molds from Mari, showing cattle.*

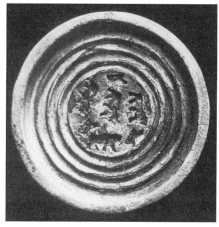

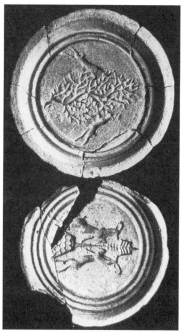

38.   ABOVE LEFT: *Assyrian Winged Bull, Divine Guardian* (lamassu), *Northwest Palace of Assurnazirpal II at Nimrud. Five legs make it read properly in frontal or in profile view. British Museum*

39.   ABOVE RIGHT: *Sumerian decoration of the soundbox of a lyre from the Royal Tombs of Ur, ca. 2600 B.C. Philadelphia, Museum of the University of Pennsylvania. Below a dominating hero, food and drink are readied for a banquet of animals. The meats apparently will be lamb and pork.*

discards in a village—why, I repeat, does one find in this very region the most intractable repugnance at eating pork on the part of Jewish and Muslim adherents of religious law?

Many scholars have tried to answer this question. Each one of their answers probably contains an element of "truth," while other details may yet wait to be elucidated.[18] One factor in a context of such ethnic mix must be that pork avoidance serves as a boundary mechanism, a culture marker of self-identification. But why pork? Another factor may have been conflict between early pastoralists like the Jews and agriculturalists, reflecting, as Simoons argues, the fact that pigs are not satisfactory herding animals. But the most compelling reason, put forward by Mary Douglas and Jean Soler, rests on the fact that swine and other "unclean" creatures simply violate one or more characteristics of their classification. Since it was considered ungodly to eat of animals who were themselves killers—eliminating raptor birds and all carnivores—licit sacrifice or food had to meet criteria of its specific category. Herbivores were defined by cloven hooves and the chewing of cud, while what lived in water must needs have scales and fins. Anomalies within their respective categories, pig and camel might have cloven hooves, but neither chewed its cud. Nor did the forbidden hare and rock badger manifest both legitimate characteristics. The justness of this explanation is underscored by the way in which medieval people interpreted the Bible in a different but comparable system. On days when it was forbidden to eat meat or animal products, dolphin, porpoise, and seals might be served, or even river otters, since these did not seem to fit their mammalian category, and could be classified with fish.

Though there is no evidence for their domestication, game animals such as deer, gazelles, antelope, and oryxes, were relished by the elite; Mesopotamia, too, abounded in all kinds of wild birds. Both the rivers and the sea yielded up to ancient nets enormous numbers of fish, their names translating often into affinitive characteristics: "fox fish," "pig fish," "lamb fish," "nun fish," "swallow fish," and the like. From early Sumerian times dams created fishponds to serve towns and temples with a ready supply, for, unlike Egypt, there was no proscription for any segment of the population: even the gods received fish among their offerings.[19] Among delicacies—one thinks of the same treats enjoyed by children in Africa and by everyone in Saudi Arabia nowadays—locusts stand out to a modern reader thinking of four species of them permitted in dietary rules set forth in Leviticus 11:21–22.

Foundation vegetables in Mesopotamian cuisine are the same flavorful trio beloved by Egyptians: garlic, onion, and leek.[20] Legumes also were grown in the Near East from neolithic times: lentils, lupins, chickpeas, vetches, peas, and broad beans. Greens such as lettuces, cabbage, garden cress, and cucumbers or other cucurbits stand out as well in lists of foodstuffs for Sumerian/Akkadian "dictionaries," or in the provision lists recovered from royal palaces like that at Mari or later Assyrian administrative centers.[21] From the Northwest Palace at Nimrud in the period of Assurnasirpal II in the ninth century B.C. comes an astounding list of provisions laid in for the dedication of a new palace-city at Kalhu.[22] For the festivities the ruler invited the gods and 69,574 people to be housed, wined, and feasted for ten days! These guests seem to have included not merely officials of various kinds, but thousands of workmen who had constructed the new center.

In the vocabularies of Mesopotamia, eighteen or twenty different kinds of cheeses appear, and Jean Bottéro has found over one hundred different soups and stews catalogued, all of them distinguished by the number and variety of the spices which season them. Aniseed, cumin, coriander, mint, juniper berries, cardamom, and fenugreek have been identified among the aromatics used; some names are subject to controversy among scholars, but mustard is accepted, and for the first time we seem to meet asafoetida, an umbelliferous plant still in use today in Arabic cookery as well as in India (where it is called *hing*); we will meet it again in the cuisine of ancient Rome.[23] Black cumin (*Nigella sativa*), which we are accustomed to seeing today sprinkled like comfits on Egyptian and Near Eastern breads and cakes, is well documented linguistically. Saffron from the crocus is conspicuous in catalogues, an ingredient to add both redolence and color. Although not identified in any listings, recent excavations at Terqa yielded some cloves; in a late-second-millennium context they are surprisingly far from their home in Indonesia.[24] Two seasonings called *samidu* and *suḫutinnû* have not been identified, though Bottéro believes they should join the favorite trinity of onion, garlic, and leek as members of the same family. For *zurummu* even he has no suggestion.[25]

Spices are used in concert, often four in a single recipe, supplemented by such flavorings as pomegranate juice, bitter almonds, mulberries, or date syrup, and various herbs, including rue. In the Greek geographer Strabo's day, the first century B.C., he marveled at the versatility of the date palm of Mesopotamia which still met "all their needs" for bread, wine, vinegar, honey [i.e., syrup] and meal (*alphita*), plus all kinds of woven articles, and the use of the stones of the fruit as charcoal, or, soaked in water, as food for cattle.[26] In modern times there have been periods of shortage when date stones were just so used, after soaking and grinding, to extend flour for humans.

The range of fruits and nuts is greater than in Old and Middle Kingdom Egypt: dates, pomegranates, grapes, apples, quince, medlars, plums, figs, sycamore figs, pears, and perhaps even the apricot, which some have considered a native of Armenia.[27] According to Henry W. F. Saggs, cherries were available from the Kurdish mountains, but this seems to have been a late discovery in the period of the Assyrian conqueror Sargon.[28] Pistachio and pine nuts are frequently named among lists of stores.

Fats and oils are exceedingly important in Mesopotamian cuisine and one gets the impression of greater concern for unctuous taste than Egyptian documentation affords. Both cultures were obliged to heat the impurities out of butter, making ghee to enhance its keeping qualities in hot climates. Both valued oil-producing plants such as flax (for linseed oil), castor bean, safflower, and the like. However, two oils of little culinary importance in Pharaonic Egypt are documented in Mesopotamia, one of them, sesame oil, being cultivated by at least the second millennium B.C.[29] An Egyptian popular tale of the Twelfth Dynasty tells the story of Sinhue [also spelled Sanahet] who, leaving Egypt to escape the palace intrigue that surrounded the death of Amenhemhet I, ultimately married the daughter of a foreign king to become himself a powerful ruler over a region of Syria. At the end of the story, when nostalgia and the pharaoh Senusret I bring him home to the Nile, he delights in his shaved, anointed body and exclaims, "Let them keep their 'tree-oil,' those who grease themselves with it."[30] The name for sesame meaning 'seed of the oil-tree,' is this evidence that its oil was used as early as the twentieth century B.C.? Olive oil was produced in the more northerly and western regions of Mesopotamia.

The Tale of Sinhue contains a letter the hero writes from Syria recounting the pleasures of his exalted position and summarizing his rich sustenance—abundant honey and oil, barley and emmer wheat, bread and wine, not only cattle but game, wild fowl, and every sort of fruit, plus milk dishes of all kinds (fig. 40).[31] Of course, Egyptians used milk and milk products, yet one has an impression that throughout Mesopotamia there was more culinary reliance in recipes upon milk, milk mixed with oil, and clabber or yogurt than in the Valley of the Nile. In any case, the cauldron is more prominent as a cooking vessel and compound dishes with many ingredients appear to have been stewed, as are those in the Yale recipe tablets.

Let us look at Bottéro's decipherment of those Babylonian tablets written about 1700 B.C. that enables him to characterize Mesopotamian cuisine as a sophisticated one, complex in both savor and modes of preparation. He gives a sampling of recipes from three tablets, one of which (in problematic

40.   Milking. *Detail of a Sumerian relief showing the Mesopotamian technique of milking from behind. Tell El-Obaid, 2900–2650 B.C. Baghdad Museum*

condition) concentrates on the cooking of various birds, while another presents twenty-one recipes for meat stews, plus four more in which vegetables figure as well. Although he warns that it is unlikely that one can duplicate them in modern times, since there is no way of knowing the "tricks of the trade" known to ancient chefs, and there are questions about some of the ingredients, a food historian did prepare a banquet from them.[32]

One recipe for a stew of kid was fairly widely disseminated in news reports. Before being put in the pot with the rest of the meat, the head, legs, and tail should be singed at the fire. Bring the water to a boil, adding fat, then garlic, onion, leek, *samidu,* some fresh cheese(?), and blood, all pounded together, and lastly an equal amount of plain *šuḫutinnû.* Another stew of some sort of little birds illustrates reliance on a sequence of cooking methods and pots: first you take the head and feet from the birds and open them to remove gizzards and pluck; split and peel gizzards and rinse and flatten(?) the birds. "Prepare a cauldron and put in birds, gizzards and pluck and place on the fire" [here I depart from Bottéro and imagine that this first application of heat, probably within a greased pot, is to lightly brown these ingredients]. The second stage involves a different pot set on the fire with fresh water and "beaten" milk [butter or cheese?], while the cauldron is drained, any inedible parts cut off the ingredients, and the rest salted, returned to the fire in the new milk pot, together with some fat and some cleaned rue. When the stew comes to a boil, a mince of onion, leek, garlic, and *samidu* is added with a little more water; here the text warns, "don't overdo the onion." While the stew cooks, the next step is to prepare a dough made of crushed grain, rinsed in water, softened in milk, and kneaded with sufficient milk and oil to make a soft dough, incorporating *samidu*, leeks, garlic, and a "salty condiment" that must be *siqqu*, a fermented table or cooking sauce made from fish or crustaceans that is the ancestor of one we will meet in Greece and Rome.[33] This dough is briefly exposed to the heat, then cut in two pieces. Here the tablet is so damaged that it is not clear what happens to one of these pieces; apparently it simply makes an unleavened flat bread. The other piece is set into a pot with milk, apparently so that it will rise and puff up a bit. To present the dish on a platter large enough to hold all the birds (whose number is never specified) this second dough is spread out, care being taken to see that it overhangs the rim only slightly. It is cooked on top of a clay *tandur* like that we met in Egypt (fig. 12), here called *tinuru.* Once cooked, it is seasoned with a sprinkling of more members of the onion family, the birds are arranged on it garnished with their innards; the sauce is added, and, covered, it is sent to the table.[34] (Compare the recipe in the appendix for "Pigeon Surprise.")

Such recipes are a far cry from simple spit-broiling or grilling methods that existed side by side with more elaborate fare. Presumably cooks of royal or noble households would have had no need for advice on simple procedures. Other stews of birds — pigeons for example — include pieces of meat as well, often the favorite lamb or mutton. Meats in the Yale tablets are always braised with fat added to the water, often with milk or fresh cheese, and always with many spices; in one case the meat is marinated in its own blood to make a "red stew." One stew even bears a name, *zukanda,* in the language of its foreign Elamite origin in southwestern Iran.[35] Turnips are the main ingredient in a vegetable stew, but there, too, meat was added. Here Bottéro argues that the word applied to this extra, *izzaz,* should be taken to mean "should be present" in the dish, rather than its alternative, "should be cut up in pieces." The major point of his argument is that the concoction is to be presented to a carver *(écuyer tranchant)*; without knowing cuneiform, I would prefer to think that the word for that "carving" simply refers to a steward dividing the portions for service. My reasoning about a fundamental aesthetic of Mesopotamian gastronomy explains why I devoted so much space to the art and architecture of Mesopotamia at the beginning of this section.

In keeping with my central premise concerning the unity of expression in the culinary as in the visual arts of a given period, I believe that Sumerian, Akkadian, Babylonian, or Assyrian cookery, whatever the regional variation, must have celebrated abundance by a piling up of many small units, a balanced construction of diverse, even conflicting, tastes and textures. Exception must be made for rulers and an elite who, as in every historical epoch, could indulge as well in the status-building display of large roasts of meat and demonstrations of power and hunting skills. Otherwise, the rich, fatty, and spice-perfumed dishes recorded in the vocabularies and recipes that have been decoded thus far bear out my hypothesis. So also does the proliferation of redolent stews in Arabic cookery from its earliest medieval cookbooks to today's Middle Eastern and North African cuisines. Think of a Tunisian or Moroccan *tajine* heaped upon a great platter, delectable bits of color and perfume ready for questing fingers, and I believe that you should summon up in the mind's eye an image of sun-dried bricks and those decorated clay cones embedded in patterns on the supports at Uruk, or, again, the mesmerizing rhythms of repeated units in the intricacies of Islamic ornament as we considered them in the introduction.

If mine is romantic nostalgia for reading cultural survivals into history — rather, retro-reading formal characteristics into the past — there is yet one further element of dining in old Mesopotamia that can be shown to perendure throughout antiquity from the time of its first appearance. The custom of reclining while eating at formal banquets and symposia among Greeks and Romans has its origin, it seems, in the Near East. It becomes the chief symbol of rewards in the afterlife — witness representations of the funerary banquet (fig. 41) — as it is for communication with the divine in this world through ritual meals at sanctuaries.[36]

By the eighth century B.C. the Hebrew prophet Amos (6:3–6) castigates Israel for her wantonness: "Ye . . . that lie upon beds of ivory, and stretch themselves upon their couches, and eat the lambs . . . and the calves . . . That

41. Funerary Meal of a Hero. *Hellenistic Greek votive relief.* Paris, Louvre

42. The King and His Wife Dining in a Garden. *Seventh century B.C. Assyrian limestone relief from the Palace of Assurbanipal, Nineveh. Note the variety of trees, which reflects the botanical collections of Assyrian monarchs and their arboreta; note also the head of the defeated enemy hanging at left.*

drink wine in bowls" (encompassing also the music and anointing with oil, all elements of corruption from the mainstream culture).[37] The earliest representation seems to be a famous Assyrian relief from the Palace of Assurbanipal at Nineveh (fig. 42) showing the king and his queen at dinner in the royal garden, filled with exotic plants. They are fanned by attendants as other servitors bring forth platters of delicacies and Assurbanipal raises his wine bowl to his lips. I understand that there are Assyriologists who believe that the king reclines because he is indisposed, but we meet here the iconography that is to have such a long life in the future. And clearly this tender scene *is* a celebration; the reason, a victory over Elamites at Tulliz, is not hard to detect: the head of the enemy ruler, Teumann, hangs on a tree at far left!

The Assurbanipal dining relief dates from the seventh century B.C., a time referred to in Greek archaeology as the Orientalizing period, because, throughout the Mediterranean world, peoples are inspired by Egyptian and Near Eastern prototypes. Etruscans in Italy, Phoenicians at outposts in North Africa, and Greeks on the mainland, in Asia Minor, or in distant colonies all revel in the fashion for "oriental" motives of art. By the latter part of the century the Greeks begin to emulate, ultimately to surpass, monumental public sculpture like that of the Egyptians and Assyrians. It is to Hellenic culinary history and inheritances that we now turn.

4 The Hellenic Experience

WHEN GREECE BECOMES our focus, the situation we encounter in developing a culinary history differs radically from that of Egypt and the Near East. In a sense, the Hellenes stand out as the world's first romantics, apparently the earliest people to seriously explore their own roots and history, whether as mythographers or as archaeologists.[1] We are no longer forced to rely upon funerary meals and items painstakingly culled from pictorial representations or lists of food products. The Greek obsession with analysis, ever seeking rational order in every aspect of nature and of human functioning within it, creates rich primary documentation to guide us. This includes a literary and philosophical concern for humankind's sustenance, looking back to a primitive tribal existence as well as examining contemporary practice, first in classical *poleis* (city-states), later among widely dispersed and pluralistic societies of the Hellenistic age following the conquests of Alexander the Great.

Equally important is the development of a true gastronomic tradition which could flourish above all in agriculturally well-endowed colonies of the western Greek world in Sicily and South Italy as well as, during Ptolomaic and Roman times, in the metropolis of Alexandria. From the latter center we have the single most valuable literary source from all antiquity: the

Deipnosophists (variously translatable as "The Gastronomers," "Sophists at Dinner") by Athenaeus, a Greco-Roman of Egypt active about A.D. 200. In a text that fills seven volumes in Gulick's Loeb Library edition, the author excerpts a vast antecedent literature through the device of showing off the lore and wit of a group of symposiasts discussing — with liberal allusions or quotations — wide-ranging topics connected with the preparation and ingestion of food. What a tantalizing array of specialized writings from Hellenic chefs and gourmet experts stands out among citations from philosophers, poets and playwrights!

It is enough to make anyone weep anew over destruction of the great Library, the Mouseion, of Alexandria to hear of lost works by Dorion *On Fish*, Chrysippos of Tyana (the "wise cake-doctor") *On Breadmaking*, Iatrokles *On Pastry*, and the like. However, from one of the most famous and influential writers we do have substantial fragments, notably those dealing with fish of all kinds. Archestratos of Gela, whose *bonne gueule* responds to refinements of high living in Sicilian circles of fourth-century tyrants of Syracuse, dwells in epic hexameter upon *Gastrology*.[2] A free translation of one entry by John Dillon, preserving poetic format, gives an idea of this lost treatise:

> The *amia** serve in the autumn, when the Pleiads are setting,
> prepared any fashion you wish. No song and dance need I make here.
> This fish you could not ruin, even were you to wish to.
> But my dear Moschus, if you must know also how best to prepare it,
> I tell you, wrap it in fig-leaves, adding just a pinch of marjoram —
> no cheese or nonsense like that! Just place it in the leaves,
> fasten them round it securely, and stick all in the hot embers.
> Now really the best *amia* you will get from the lovely Byzantium;
> any caught even near there will not be too bad; but the farther
> you get from the Hellespont, the worse those fish will become,
> and once you get them from well out in the briny Aegean
> they're not the same thing at all, and all my praise must be cancelled.
>
> [*Amia are smaller relatives of the tuna, identified by authorities on ancient fish as a bonito.][3]

From such remains of Archestratos and other bits and pieces of classic advisories, we learn that much culinary theory dwelt less upon recipes *per se* than it emphasized the best locales to find the "top of the line" in any category —

the experience of discriminating cooks and palates. Yet, for the first time, we gain clues to the *taste* of dishes from notes of cooking method and alternative ingredients. The possibilities of evaluating the flavor of a given preparation from authors of this type of gastronomic poetry are also immensely enhanced by passages from writers of comedy. Beginning with Aristophanes and culminating in the New Comedy that shapes Roman Plautus in the third century B.C., cooks are comic characters *par excellence* on the Greek stage.[4]

Although it is easy to poke fun at the cheekiness and foibles of cooks — especially those out for hire in the marketplace for special occasions — the literature also reflects serious consideration of the craft (*technē*, the only word for "art" in ancient Greek) of a master chef. One New Comedy cook explains the scientific principles genuine members of his profession must have at their command, including knowledge of astrological cosmology, architecture, geometry, natural history, military strategy, and, of course, medicine.[5]

In classical times the *mageiros* might reap as great renown as an Escoffier or Bocuse. His name derived from his original and most exalted function as sacrificial butcher, defining his skill in treating meat or fish and dishes in which these were the major components. There were no female *mageiroi*, but women could be special artisans (demiurges) when it came to preparing desserts and cakes.[6] Among the citizens of Sybaris — those South Italian, proverbial "highlivers" — caterers and cooks had patent privilege for a year in which no one else might copy the invention of a particularly choice dish (Athenaeus XII, 521 c–d)).

Gastronomic poetry may also contribute some feeling of the relish with which a particular dish had been enjoyed. Outstanding in the category is *The Banquet* by a dithyrambic poet named Philoxenos of Cythera (435–380 B.C.).[7] As a poet of dithyrambs dedicated to Apollo, Philoxenos lends us more gustatory (if less ingenious) value in his *Deipnon* than one Matron of Pitane who wrote on the same topic in parody of the *Iliad* and *Odyssey*.[8] But the rapture of a true epicure shines through Philoxenos' verse as he follows the banquet's profusion of dishes, beginning with the seafood of which he was said to be excessively fond. Anecdotes (Athenaeus VIII, 341) highlight his devotion to epulary delights. He would have loved to be blessed with a throat like a giraffe's, since he wished for one elongated like that of a crane to permit him to relish more than one food at a time, and to have the longest possible time in swallowing them. When he bought an octopus three feet long in Syracuse, he prepared and ate the entire thing at one go — all but the head. A dire case of indigestion ensued, and the doctor who was summoned judged him to be at

43. Black-figured vase showing men preparing the spit with offal, sixth century B.C.

death's door. Warning his patient of the diagnosis, he suggested that Philoxenos quickly make a will and put his affairs in order. "Oh," said the poet, outlining his bequests "everything is in order, but now when Charon summons me, to be certain I have myself all together on my way below, give me back the rest of that polypod!"

Philoxenos' *Banquet* is permeated with a sense of pleasure and delectation, of wonder at the size of offerings like a gray mullet as large as one of the tables; a "monstrous" slice of tuna from the meatiest part of its belly; a huge cauldron of eels; wheaten "puff-cakes" *(purnōn steganai phustai)* as large as their

pot (one imagines a giant sort of popover). It is appreciative of artful invention nonetheless, and his adjectives regale us, too, with such refinements as
the split head of a milk-fed kid slaughtered by strangling (to retain its blood);
flower-petaled cakes; "sweetest morsel" of underdone innards from both kids
and lambs (sausages? or the *kokoretsi* of modern Greece [fig. 43], now generally of lamb's pluck alone); bread "light and nicely folded" (probably made
with the fine bread flour characteristic of Attic imports from wheatlands of
the Black Sea area that was used to make starch, *amulos*)[9]; with yellow honey
and curds as well as "tender" cheese.

His appreciation for delicacies of dessert at "second table" is expressed
with even greater poetic fervor. A marrow pudding, "delight of mortals,"
hides in "robes as gossamer as a spiderweb," white with *amulon* and goat's milk
from the "backward flowing fountains of Aristaeus" (the udders named for a
patron divinity of farmers).[10] An "all-together" and other confections he can
only portray by portmanteau words compounded from as many as nine or
ten others—a challenge to Aristophanes' famous composite dish of fifty-nine
syllables that closes his *Ecclesiazusae*.[11] But Philoxenos' sweetmeats and cakes
are concocted from congenial elements and rendered by taste-provoking
adjectives. Then chickpeas are "saffron-mingled *[knakosum-migeis]*,[12] luxuri-
ant in their tender bloom"; almonds are so fresh that their skins are still soft
(malakophloïdōn); and the walnuts are as sweet as those munched by children.

EARLY GREECE

Masters of the culinary arts from the fifth century B.C. through Greco-Roman
times represent a sophisticated end product of a tradition that may be dimly
traced back into the Minoan-Mycenaean Bronze Age of about 1500–1200
B.C. And in stories being shaped in those by-gone days we hear an atavistic
echo from an even more remote past that might once have included cannibalism as a supplement to hunting and gathering. How else can we explain mythological episodes in the lineage of the lords of Mycenae: to serve
the gods, Tantalus stewing up his son Pelops, founder of this ruling house
in the Peloponnesus after the Olympians restore him to life (all but one
shoulder inadvertently eaten by Demeter, which had to be refashioned in
ivory); and Atreus, son of Pelops, punishing his own brother with a meal of
Thyestes' three sons, horrid cuisine of sacrifice revealed only after their father had consumed them? Nor are gods immune: witness the Dionysos child
butchered and cooked by the Titans in Orphic mythology. Greeks of later

historical periods ritualized these and similar tales in blood sacrifice and in their tragedies, while shuddering at the barbarity of Scythians drinking the blood of their first fallen foe. Thus Pindar suppresses in his odes such gory details as Tydeus, of *Seven Against Thebes* fame, eating the brains of his enemy Melanippus, and superhero Achilles being raised on the entrails and marrow of *living* beasts of prey.[13]

The Greek view of what to them was the Homeric age of heroes — purportedly the date of the expedition against Troy, about 1200 B.C., but related by Homer almost four hundred years later — stands in marked opposition to what we know today of human diets in those times and in even earlier prehistory, thanks to increasingly refined archaeological techniques and the decipherment of Mycenaean documents in Linear B. Today the evidence must be interpreted with reference to findings from Mesolithic habitation by cave-dwellers at Franchthi[14] — that is, the native exploitation of wild resources of mainland Greece before it was influenced by early agricultural developments in the eastern Mediterranean. It must also be viewed with a knowledge of the post-Mycenaean transformation caused by the collapse of that vivid Bronze Age culture, a "peasantization" of purely local life in the disruptions and migrations during centuries that used to be known as the "Dark Ages" of Greece.

One of Athenaeus' authorities remarks (with lewd asides omitted here): "when does any Achaean eat fish in Homer? and he never shows anyone boiling meat only roasting it" (I, 25c). The writer, a fourth-century comic poet named Eubulus, must have had in mind the feast prepared by Achilles and Patroclus in *Iliad* IX, 202ff.[15] There, indeed, haunches of sheep and goat as well as fat chine of hog are cut up, spitted and grilled over the glowing coals; but one of Athenaeus' companions corrects Eubulus' erroneous text, citing passages to prove the heroic consumption of fish and Homeric references to boiled meats. Indeed, the bounty of the Aegean and Mediterranean has always been exploited by the inhabitants of their shores, and seafood, both fresh and dried, was the preferred sustenance of historic Greek gourmets. If we add another modern observation to the argument, over and above reaction to the machismo expressed, it is that actual practice, as in many early cultures, is likely to have been a combination of both methods: simmering first, then spit-roasting the tenderized result.[16] The process is well represented in a sacrifice depicted on a Campanian black-figured vase of the late archaic period (fig. 44). Incidentally, this is one reason why structuralist interpretations such

44.   Sacrifice *(sequential scenes)*. *Black-figured hydria from South Italy (Campana group). Sixth century* B.C. *Private collection*

as Lévi-Strauss's "culinary triangle" do not reflect historical reality in setting up a forced binary opposition between boiled versus roasted.

Today's scholars are able to supplement Athenaeus' philological method with other research tools in seeking to recover either the food and drink of the besiegers of Troy or typical nutriment for later Greeks of Homer's day. Archaeological technology continues to develop new means to bring back to tangible life microscopic charred vegetable scraps or seeds and the residues that linger in the depths of containers; dendrochronology, now providing more than a three-thousand-year graph of tree-ring coordinates, joins climatology in recreating weather and growing conditions in the remote past; while wonders of biochemical research yield evidence from bones and teeth of dietary intake, even genetic heritage.[17]

In the Homeric passage cited above, Patroclus also seasons the meat with "holy" salt, evoking practical and symbolic values from time immemorial in a substance at once preservative and taste-enhancing.[18] Godlike Achilles carves while his friend passes a basket of bread that reminds the reader of how truly farinaceous was the diet of all ancient people. The word used for bread, *sitos*, denoted food generally, and later Greeks of an ordinary station in life would think of their customary barley porridge, called *maza*, which could also be baked as an unleavened cake (translated into Latin by the Romans as *polenta*).

The palatial culture of the Bronze Age, which Homer (and/or his alter egos) were attempting to recreate from bardic songs that shaped collective memory during long centuries after the collapse of Mycenaean hegemony, was alien in so many respects to his own era when the epic tradition crystallized. Centered about fortified palaces such as Tiryns, Mycenae (fig. 45), or Pylos, and even ruling over King Minos' Cretan complex at Knossos in its latest phases, the life of lords like Menelaos, Agamemnon, and Nestor was not unlike that of feudal barons in their castles. "Robber barons" might be an even more apposite name for them in regard to linked commercial acumen and military prowess. It is possible to look upon the Trojan expedition as a siege to win a strategic outpost to expand trading routes into the Black Sea, and earlier Achaeans of Middle Helladic shaft graves at Mycenae may have served as mercenaries in Egypt.

In any case, they surely loved warfare and the hunt, the last particularly if it involved dangerous wild boars and the lions that endured in Greece into the fifth century B.C. (figs. 46 and 47).[19] Game of all kinds must have starred among their viands, though we know that herding prospered where there was sufficient plain to provide grazing land as well as soil for cultivating

45. *The Lion Gate at Mycenae, the Palace of Agamemnon, ca. 1250 B.C.*

grain. Gradually they bred fierce descendants of *Bos primigenius* to become the farmer's friend and helpmeet. But cattle were not, and never were to be in future Greek husbandry, a major source of protein (unless they were the victims of ritual sacrifice) nor of milk and cheese. I take it that when Athena (disguised as Mentes) comes to visit Telemachos (*Odyssey*, I, 105–13) and finds Penelope's suitors not merely banqueting on all kinds of meats, but seated on hides of oxen they had slaughtered, this should be seen as a detail to enhance dramatically the degree to which they are decimating the patrimony of Odysseus' son. In a day when ox-hides were stretched on frames to make beds, drawn tautly to form shields, and sought for many other uses, they were as commercially valuable as the motive power of the live beast; in later times regulations permit officiating priests to retain and sell hides of sacrificial victims. Only a few regions in Greece were suitable for raising cattle in any number: Thessaly, for example, or Boeotia and Euboea whose very names canonize their role in supplying victims for later classical hecatombs.

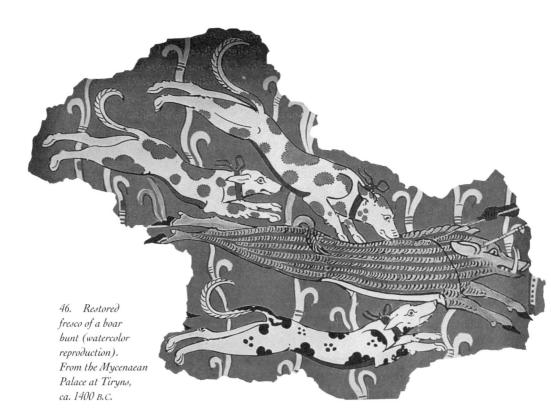

46. Restored
fresco of a boar
hunt (watercolor
reproduction).
From the Mycenaean
Palace at Tiryns,
ca. 1400 B.C.

47.   Trapping Wild
Bulls *(detail). Gold
repoussé cup found in a
Mycenaean tomb at
Vaphio. Athens, National
Museum*

Baronial meats of the domestic variety were from goats, sheep, and pigs, the last perhaps dominant before Neolithic and Early Bronze Age forests were cut down.[20] Homer acknowledges this in making his old swineherd welcome the stranger/Odysseus home, serving up, not the fatted calf, but porkers. With transhumance—moving sheep and goats to mountain pasturage during seasons when the land could yield crops for human sustenance—the Mycenaean *(w)anax,* or king, was able to rule over a redistributive economy, limited but able to support the specialization of labor at home and trading enterprises abroad. Remnants of the pre-Achaean population, called "Pelasgians" by the Hellenes, made up an underclass of farmers and herdsmen filling the storerooms of the palace with grain: emmer and einkorn, the husked wheats that must be roasted and pounded in order to free the glume (fig. 48), giving way to naked wheats and barley *(alphita),* which Homer justly terms "the marrow of men," as he envisages Athena provisioning Telemachus' boat (*Odyssey,* II, 290) with barley meal in sacks of skin and amphoras of wine—of which more anon.

48. Woman Making Bread *(with central scene of pounding grain in a tall mortar). Boeotian black-figured lecythos, mid-sixth century* B.C. *Private collection*

Women worked in the storehouse weaving textiles of wool and flax (some of which may still be wild, to judge from inventory tablets at Pylos).[21] These cloths and ceramics were traded throughout the Mediterranean and Aegean world, the pottery at least surviving to document lucrative trade with, for example, Syria and South Italy. It was bureaucratic management of storage and rations, if not commerce, that brings us the precious data on Linear B tablets that identify Mycenaean plants and products. The measures are Near Eastern, based on a sexagesimal system, using Semitic minas and talents.[22]

The range of spices and aromatics is impressive in Linear B archives, as are multiple attributes for differentiating oils by provenance and age—vintages, as it were—and flavors (from seeds and extracts of roses, sage, mint, and various herbs).[23] The oils themselves came from sesame (*sesama*, using its Semitic name, as Chadwick points out), flax and safflower in addition to the olive, which may give evidence of both wild and cultivated (grafted) trees.[24] Perhaps the poppies that figure in the lists served as another source for oil just as the seed had been exploited from Neolithic times in other parts of Europe.[25] But the olive clearly dominated production from at least the middle of the third millennium.

Among seeds and herbs, coriander is most frequently named, anticipating the favor it will find in the classical age. Fennel already has its classical Greek name, or the closest thing to it: *marath(w)on*, also transcribed as *maratuwo*, reminding us that it once flourished, eponymously, on the Attic plain where Miltiades repulsed the Persians in 490 B.C. and Pheidippides' run with the news created an enduring memorial race. *Marathon* resonates equally with the mythic origins of humankind's discovery of cookery in taming fire, since Prometheus brought this incalculable boon, stolen from the gods, smoldering like punk in a hollow stalk of giant fennel. Other favorites of subsequent generations such as aniseed have been documented through excavation rather than by inventory or ration lists, but the tablets give us cardamom, cumin (again, in its Semitic nomenclature), peppergrass, garden cress, calamint, pennyroyal, celery, gingergrass (?), and saffron.[26]

One plant of outstanding appeal to historic gastronomes, both Greek and Roman, may or may not have been appreciated by Mycenaean overlords. This is *silphion*, Latin and English silphium, which was to become the chief export of the Greek colony of Cyrene in Libya (fig. 49) but extinct since the first century A.D. (a signal warning to ourselves), although its proximate cousin survives as Indian *hing* or Arabic "devil's dung" (asafoetida).[27] Silphium grew as

49. *Coin of Cyrene representing the silphium plant. Sixth century* B.C.

a wild plant, inordinately attractive to grazing animals, frustrating to bring under cultivation, and perhaps popularized in culinary use as much for its supposed contraceptive effect as for its garlicky savor minus garlic's raunchy afterglow.[28] Sir Arthur Evans believed that he had found a sign for silphium in Cretan Linear A, but Minoan-Mycenaean importation is generally undocumented.[29] A Laconian (Spartan) cup of the sixth century B.C. showing bales of it (or, possibly, wool?) being loaded aboard a ship (fig. 50) may be the earliest witness to its exportation from Cyrene.

Linguistic evidence from classical Greek expands a catalogue of foodstuffs. Words ending in -*issos* or -*nthos* preserve terminations going back to pre-Greek Minoan words.[30] As one would expect from the ecstatic worship of nature by this culture which so strongly influenced the Mycenaean, many of the words are names of flowers: narcissus (Gk. *narkissos*) and hyacinth stand out among them, leading to speculation as to whether Achaeans were already devoted to eating bulbs as delicacies that would entice their descendants of the classical age — or of today (water hyacinth bulbs, *volvi,* pickled by modern

*50. Laconian cup possibly
representing silphium being
loaded aboard a ship at the
Spartan colony of Cyrenaica.
Sixth century B.C. Paris,
Bibliothèque Nationale*

Greeks and the same used in Italian regions of Magna Graecia, Apulian *lam-pascioni*). Hesiod, at the beginning of the seventh century B.C., speaks of asphodel bulbs as items of sustenance for his countrymen.[31]

Whether Laertes' and Alcinous' orchards described by Homer in the *Odyssey* best represent Mycenaean tree culture or that of his own day, their products are all well documented for the Bronze Age. Odysseus identifies himself to his father by citing the trees Laertes gave him in childhood (XXIV, 340f.): thirteen pear, ten apples, forty figs, plus fifty rows of vines. Alcinoos' palace and four-acre orchard adds pomegranates to the other fruits, while wild plums were native to Greece and to Asia Minor. The stunning proportion of fig trees highlights a significance these held for Greeks of all periods. Figs, together with acorns, were held to be the first nurture of humans, the one sacred to Zeus, the other to Demeter. The name of the wild fig, *olunthos*, again designates an indigenous pre-Greek origin. Fresh and dried, figs were already an important source of sustenance, as we know from ration lists for Mycenaean slaves—anticipating the later Roman reliance on them as energy food for those in bondage.

Other tree crops besides the olive are more problematic. An archival *ki-tano* may represent the "turpentine" tree, terebinth, in the same family as the pistachio we found as a favored element of diet in the prehistoric Near East. Almonds and dates (the last perhaps the "Phoenician" item recorded at Knossos) were probably imported.[32] At both Knossos and Pylos a condiment is named which is *Cyperus* in modern terminology. For Emily Vermeule, this is galingale (which seems unlikely); for Chadwick, a fragrant rush useful in perfume-making, *C. rotundus*.[33]

A good number of signs in Linear B archives have not yet been deciphered. Some must represent staples we know to have formed the basic vegetables of Mycenaean diet. In addition to onion, leek, and wild garlic, just as in the Near East, legumes were daily fare: peas, fava (broad) beans, lentils, and vetches, even though they do not figure in status food of meat and bread stressed for the aristocrats of the epics.[34] For ordinary souls of the Mycenaean age, typical "best company dinner" can be well represented by the story of Philemon and Baucis (although it is a myth told by the Roman Ovid) and their simple hospitality when visited by the father and messenger of the gods in disguise. A stew of pot herbs and bacon is served, accompanied by olives, cornel berries preserved in vinegar, radishes (wild ones were among Late Bronze Age stores excavated in Cyprus),[35] cheese, and eggs cooked in the ashes. Wine, "not the oldest," never ceased to flow from a pitcher, thanks to the miraculous power of their guests. For dessert there were apples and wild honey.

The eggs just mentioned in a late version of the tale of that primordial Phrygian couple introduce another problem. We have already learned that the chicken was a relative latecomer to the Near East from southeast Asia. If indeed it reached Egypt about 2500 B.C., the fowl seems to have been carried westward and northward sporadically through the first millennium B.C., often more important for purposes of divination or entertainment than as a food resource.[36] The sacred character that accrued to a cock which greeted the arrival of the sun each day is self-evident, and all sorts of predictive messages and omens might be read in patterns pecked by hens among scattered grains. Then there is the numinous egg. The Mycenaeans may not have exploited the chicken, but they surely did raise geese, and treasured their eggs as funerary gifts. Homer even makes reference to a goose bred within the household rather than in the feedyard (*Odyssey*, XV, 174), which may only mirror his own day.[37]

Apiculture must have developed early, spreading from Egypt via Crete.[38] Honey in the documents, which stress its ritual use as offerings to divinities, need not have come from domesticated hives, of course; however, from Pylos comes a tablet regarding land tenure citing the title "bee-keeper," and there is other evidence for officials in charge of the supply.[39] Honey's role as a sweetener included the enhancement of wine. At Pylos a wine storeroom yielded seals with the ideogram for wine joined with the one for honey. "Honeyed wine" introduces Homeric Pramnian wine, dark as the sea is always characterized, thick, and mixed with goat cheese and barley meal as a serious potion.[40]

Vitis vinifera, the sole genus of grapevine known before the discovery of America, is distinguished from its wild progenitors with difficulty, complicated by spontaneous crossings between wild vines and cultivated species. Morphological traits of cultivated versus wild pips show transition to the latter in the Aegean area in the course of the third millennium (Early and Middle Helladic periods).[41] Whatever its source, *(w)oinos*—wine—was surely the preferred drink among the lords of Mycenaean strongholds, although Sir Arthur Evans held that beer was the main Minoan drink.[42] A most startling discovery among the Linear B tablets at Mycenae, once the script was deciphered in 1952, was the appearance of the name of Dionysos *(Di(w)onu-sos)* on two fragments. It had always been assumed that the fertility divinity who became the god of wine was a latecomer to the Olympian pantheon, perhaps from Phrygia. The reverse of one tablet fragment may be a compound of the word for wine, but without further proof of the divinity of this "Dionysos," Chadwick feels "caution demands that we reserve judgement here."[43]

Ration lists generally do not show wine, indicating that it was a luxury not extended to lower orders or to slaves.[44] It was stored in huge terracotta vessels *(pithoi)* and other large jars, and some attempt was made to seal these with a soft clay filling and vine leaves, held in place by cords and covered with a potsherd.[45] Apparently with the intention to ensure against continued fermentation through porous baked clay, the inner face of storage vessels was often if not regularly smeared with resin—origin of the *retsina* that is still a favored white wine among Greeks and lovers of Greek popular cookery.[46]

Did the Achaeans dilute their wine with water as did later Greeks of historical epochs? Modern oenophiles may shudder at the idea of mixing in barley meal and goat cheese, but that at least makes for a nutritious and hearty potion—symbolic as well, one suspects, of basic food groups in demonstrating hospitality. I do not visualize hardened Mycenaean kings and nobles watering down the contents of their goblets or rhytons as a general rule. The relative scarcity of mixing bowls (kraters) among archaeological finds bears this out, especially when compared with almost three thousand drinking vessels discovered in storerooms at Pylos. The excavator, Carl Blegen, had a plausible interpretation of that staggering number: drinking sessions began, as we know, with a libation to a god or gods; such a supply must allow for smashing the goblet after that first incantation (Gentlemen, I give you the King!).[47]

To accompany a varied diet of seafood, meat—from game animals including deer and the hare (Greece never was to harbor rabbits) as well as from domestic stock—plus vegetables, how did Mycenaeans consume their wheat and barley? Because ovens are not normally found at Bronze Age sites, specialists debate whether or not they baked bread or simply relied on porridge.[48] As Chadwick mentions, the question is resolved by tablet reference to a "baker's" trade *(artopoqoi)*. In any case, it would be inconceivable that people with such strong connections to the Near East would not have similarly evolved baking flat bread on a stone at the hearth, perhaps under a slightly domical cover, or even turning a *pithos* on its side to make a rudimentary oven like the one we see in an archaic Boeotian terra-cotta (fig. 51).[49] Husked wheats, of course, and barley do not produce light, leavened loaves. It is probably innate conservatism and love of tradition that enshrines the barley cake in classical Greek ritual of sacrifice and feasting. Another aspect of ritual conservatism forces me to believe that the herbs and spices which proliferate in Linear B were used to flavor breads. At religious sanctuaries throughout the later Greek world, where sacred stories preserved the memory of the earliest heroic days of the founding of their cults, certain offices bear names that speak of aboriginal roles as herb gatherers and spice grinders who are in charge of preparing special cakes to share with their particular divinity or divinities.[50]

At the very dawning of Hellenic civilization all the elements are present to provide a well-balanced "Mediterranean diet" equal to that which current nutritionists recommend for twentieth-century health.[51] In the stratified and administratively complex Mycenaean culture of the thirteenth century B.C. we seem to read in its relics and Homeric afterglow that the rulers and their nobles overemphasized protein from animal flesh, leaving a truly favorable regimen to those of lower estate (and presumably to rural dwellers far from a

51.   *Terra-cotta model of a woman baking in a vessel turned on its side. Boeotia, fifth century B.C. Berlin Museum*

palace center, who were able to poach or snare birds and small mammals, and to shore dwellers supplementing their provisions with the same denizens of the sea relished by their betters).[52] Perhaps if the privileged had had access to refined bread wheat instead of emmer and barley, they would have been as nutritionally deprived as a medieval elite, with its high-status manchet loaves of whitest wheat instead of humbler, darker, and coarser fare.

Given the lack of recipes, any conclusions about how the Mycenaeans may have prepared the ingredients discussed so far must be deduced from two sources. First, from the classification of different vessels rendered by both name and ideogram in the palace archives. The variety of those apparently employed in culinary use reveals a degree of sophistication reaching far beyond the cauldron and the spit.[53] Broad, shallow "boiling pans" with handles for suspension are distinguished from huge tripod cauldrons and from mere "cooking bowls"; ladles are in good supply. Second, we are able to rely on archaeological finds, thanks to Minoan/Mycenaean devotion to fixed hearths. There are even some identifiable kitchens, in contrast to Greek houses of historical periods where portable braziers could make any area into a cooking space. Portable hearths, *escharai*, were not, of course, neglected by pre-Greek cooks, and graves were sometimes furnished with a *batterie de cuisine* that visually enhances the range of possible cookery techniques. A burial in the Late Minoan II Tomb of the Tripod Hearth at Zafer Papoura in Crete (fig. 52) also yielded bronze vessels that Chadwick termed "relatives" of Mycenaean types; another included what Evans identified as a "frying pan," although there is some question as to whether it might not be a lamp.[54]

An important discovery in the Minoan palace at Zakro in Crete provides reliable evidence of the culinary use of aromatics. A series of miniature vessels in the kitchen seems to indicate that spices were not solely employed to produce perfumes and scented oils.[55]

52. *Late Minoan II cooking vessels in the Tomb of the Tripod Hearth. Zafer Papoura, Crete, ca. 2000 B.C. (After Sir Walter Evans,* Palace of Minos, *II, fig. 398)*

Scholars offer differing explanations for the collapse of the aristocratic Mycenaean society, so vigorous in its sensibilities and so structured in its dynamics. For some it simply speaks to the inevitable decay that occurs in a stratified civilization with a limited economic base. For others it may signal a sudden onslaught that left the principal centers looted and burned. If this was due to the "sea peoples" who upset many regimes in the eastern Mediterranean at the beginning of the twelfth century B.C. or to waves of immigrant Greek tribes — the Dorians in their so-called return of the sons of Herakles — it would still not explain why many of the sites were abandoned rather than rebuilt. One group argues from climatology studies that a sustained drought brought disaster to Mycenaean husbandry and agriculture with its rather limited range of crops, leading to the depopulation of the palatial centers and destruction of their social order. Surely all these pressures and more must have contributed to the trauma that created in Greece the "dark ages" from the twelfth to the eighth century, marked by a cultural impoverishment that even seems to have wiped away any knowledge of writing until the Phoenician alphabet was introduced in the middle of the latter century.[56]

There are advocates also of cataclysmic explosions caused by grain storage and the dust this entails when it is constantly handled (at Pylos there were designated "sweepers"); its explosive potential may have been enhanced by dry air from a putative drought. (From inventories the destruction of Pylos has been placed in the spring months because no grain harvest appears and the sheep have not yet been shorn.) Van Leuven points to instances of supernatural blasts in Greek myths as manifestations of catastrophes similar to an American grain elevator explosion that was heard seventy miles away; for him, a clue to the destruction of Mycenaean Thebes may lie in the divine lightning that killed Semele, whose name, meaning "earth" in traditional etymology, seems to indicate that she was a personification of grain.[57] Van Leuven's argument compares the cataclysm with violent grain elevator destructions in the United States during the summers of 1977 and 1978. Indeed, a panel of the National Academy of Sciences reported in the summer of 1982 on reforms to prevent dust explosions in the nation's storage facilities, which OSHA numbered at more than four hundred at the time, with two hundred fatalities.

The demise of Mycenaean civilization comes increasingly these days to seem less abrupt and irrevocable than theories like Van Leuven's would have it. Displacement, impoverishment, and decay in standards of consumption there may have been, but daily living was sustained even among refugees in migration, and we see their artifacts slowly transformed from aristocratic

53. *Minoan vase with octopus, ca. 1500 B.C. Heraklion Museum, Crete*

costly bronze to weapons of iron, from pottery expressing metal in its shapes and admiration for marine motifs borrowed from a Minoan repertoire (if perceived with an already Greek sense of logical design; see figs. 53 and 54) to the geometric harmonics of the eighth century (fig. 55). Mycenaean citadels became the acropolis centers of civic and/or religious life in classical Greece; the sanctuaries, as at Eleusis, preserved their numinous cultic power; and ethnic bondings ultimately brought dispersed Greek tribes into pan-Hellenic worship and/or fraternal athletic competition at centers like Delos, Delphi, or Olympia (where Herakles is said to have founded the games in 776 B.C.).

For the Greeks themselves, Homeric poetry and most mythology captured

54. *Mycenaean goblet decorated with marine motives, from Nestor's Palace at Pylos. Thirteenth century* B.C. *(After a watercolor by P. D. Jong)*

55. *Early Geometric Vase, ca. 740* B.C. *Munich, Museum für Kleinkunst*

the vividness that the Mycenaean remote past held for an ordinary citizen of any city-state, whether Dorian in the Peloponnesos or Ionian in Attica and the far reaches of Asia Minor. The alimentary heritage was acknowledged, too. Some educated Greeks of the late fourth century, considering legends of the heroic past that contributed the basic materials of traditional literature and drama, would accept the theories of the learned mythologist Euhemeros. This authority who lived circa 340–260 B.C. developed a rationalized interpretation of myths in which the gods were considered to have been historical personages. He was quite certain that Hellenic gastronomy owed its origins — just as the Greeks owed their letters, those *Kadmēia grammata* — to Kadmos, the grandfather of Dionysos, subject to cult reverence in Thebes as its legendary founder. According to Euhemerus, Kadmos, the brother or cousin of Europa, was a chef who taught the arts of eating to the king of Sidon in Phoenicia. Absconding with the flute girl Harmonia (which brought them both into roles in the Samothracian mystery religion), they wended their way to Boeotia and to parentage of Semele (and immortality in Euripides' *Bacchae*). In alternative ancient chronologies the date for the founding of Thebes by Mycenaean Cadmus (as his name is rendered in English, he of the dragon's teeth story) is calculated anywhere from 1518 to 1285 B.C. The classical Greek alphabet did derive from a Phoenician source, but we have no examples of its archaic letters before the eighth century B.C.[58]

SACRED AND PROFANE IN EATING RITUALS

Food and commensality — eating and drinking shared with fellow citizens, with the gods, with long-departed heroes or ancestors, and in hospitality offered to visitors or wayfarers — were central to the Greeks' definition of their political, religious, and personal selves. In private confraternity or in public congregation, taking sustenance together appears to be the socializing cement of civic organization.[59] Using a collective ceremony of dining to bind a sociopolitical structure was as true for a Spartan in Laconia as for an Athenian in Attica, or for a Greek in Miletos in Asia Minor. And the concept served for them all to define those of either Ionian or Doric heritage and civilization set against "barbarians" of other races (whose speech sounded like the onomatopoeic "baa(r)-baa(r)" bleating of sheep to Hellenic ears). The "others" lived to the north and drank undiluted wine or, worse, beer; they used butter instead of oil from olives or other seeds and nuts, and might even practice a cannibalism that the Greeks had renounced far back in their own mythical past.[60]

Contemplate a paramount institution of communal life in the *polis*, the political vitality of a city-state, whatever its constitutional persuasion. From perhaps as early as the Geometric period (eighth century B.C.), an executive committee of sorts, a prytany of citizens — aristocrats at first, but ultimately representatives of all male property owners — served on twenty-four-hour duty for specified terms to transact city business and to receive foreign embassies and important communications. At the expense of the state, they ate together in prescribed fashion at or near their *prytaneion*, which held the communal hearth dedicated to the goddess Hestia. Athens in classical times was exceptional in distinguishing a *prytanikon* for this function, while their prytaneion apparently was reserved for privileged guests and those who, like athletes, had brought special honor to the state. The fifty men of the prytany, with six to ten officials, dined together in the *tholos*, a round building with an attached space for cooking, next to the *Bouleuterion*, or Council House.[61] (See fig. 56, a plan of the Agora.)

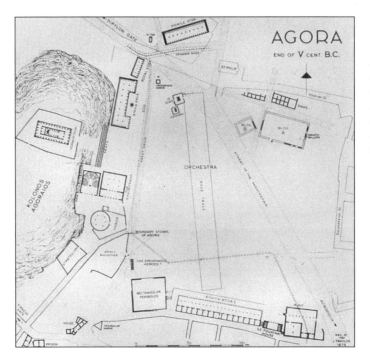

56. *Plan of the Athenian Agora in the fifth century B.C. Tholos (the circular structure) and Bouleuterion are at lower left.*

A truly ideological application of communal eating appears in Crete and Sparta, strongholds of the primordial Dorian usurpation of Mycenaean power. In Athens, coming of age at eighteen or nineteen might mean introduction to the *symposion* we shall discuss shortly, into a socializing ritual among adult men with a mature mentor (and lover). In militaristic Sparta and Crete, males were raised from childhood in cohorts of age group rather than with the family, and a youth's rite of passage to manhood entailed admittance to a communal mess *(syssitia)* sponsored by an older citizen. In Sparta this could be one's father or, more normally, one's *erastēs* (lover). In Crete a curious pseudo abduction culminating in two months withdrawal into the wilderness by *erastēs* and *eromenos* (the loved youth) preceded initiation to the commensality of male bonding. Select Spartan youths did not have the support of a more mature companion while from seventeen to nineteen they served a *krupteia* (a secret, *i.e.,* kryptic band), withdrawing from the community to live by their wits — including theft — in the countryside and to terrorize the subject helots (likened to serfs) by nighttime assassination and mayhem. It all sounds rather like Green Beret training or particularly severe sessions of Outward Bound, but the *kruptoi* evidently survived individually, each on his own.[62]

Thus hardened and disciplined for the Spartan military machine, a twenty-year old could look forward to living the next ten years with his messmates, forced to use lessons gained from subterfuge in order to consort with family or a wife (save for approved conjugal visits for necessary procreation). The metaphor of eating together in the *syssitia* seems as powerful as the sexual interrelationships binding one generation to the next in the most intimate social engineering.[63]

Spartiates enjoying full citizenship in the common mess contributed a fixed monthly donation of barley, wine, cheese, and figs, plus a modest amount of accompaniments (*opsonia,* or "side dishes") equivalent in value to 10 Aeginetan pence.[64] Although Spartans were famous for the simplicity of their diet, messmates also made voluntary donations to the *eranos* (Greek for a pot-luck meal, or a kind of picnic) that might include a bit of pork, dried fish, and the rewards of the hunt; probably also the olive oil into which they dipped barley cakes in a second postprandial session.

It is easy to understand why "Spartan" survives in our language and many others as an adjective defining sober restraint. Athenaeus preserves the comment of a Sybarite entertained at a Lacedaemonian mess: "It is no wonder that

Spartans are the most brave of all; for any sensible person would choose to die ten thousand deaths rather than share in such limited fare" (IV, 138d; cf. XII, 518e). Indeed, their famous 'black broth," which must have been made with blood of the animal that produced the stock, was evidently a frequent butt of ancient joking and satire.[65] But Spartans took pride in their dietary ethos. After the defeat of Xerxes at Plataea in 479 B.C., wishing to dramatize the superiority of his troops to the Persian, Pausanias had one of the enemy's extravagant feasts prepared, then a Spartan one for instructive comparison.[66]

If we find Spartan abstemiousness uncongenial to our interest in good food, an advantage of their dietary concerns stands out in today's emphasis upon a healthy Mediterranean diet. With an imperative to raise effective hoplites, or foot soldiers, Lacedaemonians seem to have surpassed other ancient peoples in developing the best possible nurture for their children, not only for the boys, but — quite unlike the norm — for the girls as well. Girls shared a nutrition calculated to make the young lean and tall, a similar system of education, and athletics that were considered as important for them as for the warriors in training (scandalizing other Greeks at the very idea of revealing young daughters naked in public).

Counterweight to such extraordinary freedom, as well as to women's rights in Laconian law, emerges in the Spartan devaluation of the family in favor of the state. As Oswyn Murray puts it: "The actual marriage ceremony expressed the subordination of women to male society; it took the form of ritual seizure of the woman, who then had her head shaved, and was dressed as a man to await the bridegroom in a darkened room."[67] Then, too, a wife could be lent to another man or shared with a brother.

Subordination of the individual to the state assumed radically different patterns in Attica, at least in their classical form of the fifth and early fourth centuries B.C., marked by certain institutions we celebrate today as the origin of Western democracy. Yet one of these institutions began as an arrogant display of aristocratic dominance and privilege. Notwithstanding its origin, the Greek *sumposion* [68] — literally, a session of "drinking together" — always held a ritual component. It developed from an archaic prerogative of social status, and as regalement of bodily self to become a classical feast of reason. As such it offers insight into the tradition of our own phenomenon called a symposium, providing a mode of philosophical discourse for Plato and Xenophon (not to mention Athenaeus), initiating a literary genre called "Table Talk" that has inspired over centuries essayists as diverse as Plutarch and Hazlitt, as well as contributing a format for modern scholarly interchange (alas, without the requisite potions nor the consortial pleasure of reclining two to a couch).

Some aspects of the *sumposion* are comparable to the Spartan *sussitia*, namely (speaking of Athens), male bonding within a military elite before democratic initiatives brought hoplite service to all citizens under fifty-nine, and a rite of passage that introduced youths (ephebes) at nineteen or so to adult homoeroticism.[69] The symposium is a major theme of decorated pottery of the Archaic period (600–480 B.C.) which served its needs — see figures 57 and 58 of red-figured ware, with pictorial elements reserved in the red of the clay matrix allowing interior details to be more freely drawn than was the case in the earlier black-figured vessels on which inner contours had to be incised (cf. fig. 43).

Although the custom of reclining for the banquet and the "second table" symposion, following when the deipnon (dinner) came to a close, had been borrowed from the Near East,[70] Greeks put their own mark on the proceedings.[71] First of all, one is struck by the private, intimate sense of *euphrosyne* ("good cheer," what the French mean by *esprit*) rather than oriental arrant display — despite the obvious sociopolitical statement of constituting an elite. In contrast to the vast public banquets we will encounter among Hellenistic kings, an early sense of close companionship and trust is expressed architecturally in spaces that allow for five to seven couches *(klinai)* as a norm; these small chambers are multiplied if more diners must be accommodated, in a sanctuary, for example.[72] A symposiarch (ruler of the drinking party) is elected to determine the proportion of water to wine in a great krater, or mixing bowl (often half and half or even three parts water to one of wine — but remember that the wine is both thick and sweet) as well as to name how many servings will be drunk, what entertainment presented, or what games played.

The event opens and is punctuated by appropriate addresses to the gods, evading the hubris Greeks decry in Persian autocrats who seem to have invented a reclining posture at meals to flaunt their regal power. In addition to invoking divine blessing on the affair, the participants do not forget the Muses; music and poetry flourish from the beginning, and, by late classical times, revivals of earlier dramatists were sometimes featured.[73] All sorts of diversions punctuate the festivity, including word games, riddling, and the special play of *kottabos*, said to have been invented in Sicily, wherein contestants flicked the last drops of wine in their cups at a target (in one variant, a metal bowl which might give out a satisfying ping to perfect aim). Servings of

57.   Symposion. *Early fifth century B.C. Attic red-figured drinking cup* (kylix) *by the Foundry Painter. Cambridge, Corpus Christi College*

58.   Symposion. *Early fifth century B.C. Attic red-figured kylix by Makron. The man at left raises his drinking cup as in the game,* kottobos. *Munich, Museum für Kleinkunst*

delicacies to complement the wine and sustain one's thirst include cheese, honey, dried fruits and nuts, roasted chickpeas, and various cakes flavored with poppyseed, sesame, and linseed.[74]

Although its message embodies the aristocratic control of the city, and its associated *kōmos* (a rowdy, drunken parade through the streets) has been termed a "spit in the eye of the community" by Oswyn Murray, the archaic heyday of the symposion corresponds to a period of ostentatious display among those in the circle of the Athenian tyrant Peisitratos who manipulated his way to power in 546 B.C. The participants seem to flaunt their brotherhood and hedonist existence as if aware of threats to their ascendancy that would culminate in popular rebellion in 510 B.C., the assassination of Peisistratos' son and heir, and the democratic reforms of Cleisthenes in 507.

Whatever one thinks of the rule of the Peisistratids, it brought Athens into the "big time," for the tyrant encouraged all the arts, importing Ionian poets, natural philosophers (the first "scientists" of intellect, not experiment), and fashions from the Ionian Greek cities of Asia Minor, where a more sophisticated cultural life had developed in proximity to Phrygia, Lydia, and other enlightened centers of the Near East, themselves under the influence of expansionist Persia.[75]

This era in the life of Athens provides a spectacular instance of the interface I continually find between the culinary and the visual arts. Though Oswyn Murray believes the custom of reclining at festive banquets began in the eighth century B.C., it is first represented in vase painting of the late seventh with the culmination of oriental influence in this regard. Figure 59, an Early Corinthian krater in the Louvre, depicts Herakles at the House of Eurytos in a story from the Homeric cycle. The scene is visualized in current fashion with the diners reclining rather than seated in a manner proper to those heroes of bygone days. Under one handle, the cook and his assistant hack at a haunch of meat.

What a contrast between this noble repast, at which the daughter of the king is not out of place as she aids in dispensing the hospitality of the house, and the licentious vision of a late Archaic sympotic feast where proper women had to be banned in favor of *hetairai* or courtesans (fig. 60). It is the proliferation of "gilded youth" in Peisistratean Athens, cultivation of the pleasure principle, and importation of Ionic manners and dress to which Attic sculpture of the last third of the sixth century responds with superabundant pattern, exquisite opposition of textures, and contrapuntal rhythms of shapes and lines. The head of an aristocratic rider displaying a barber's artifice — and likely

59. Herakles Banqueting at the House of Eurytos. *Early Corinthian krater, ca. 625–600 B.C. In this drawing, the vignette under one handle of the* mageiros *butchering meat appears at left of the middle zone which introduces a battle on the opposite side of the krater. Paris, Louvre*

60. Symposion with Hetairai. *Red-figured stamnos by Smikros. Brussels, Musée Cinquantenaire*

perfumed ointments as well (fig. 61), or an Acropolis maiden (*korē*, fig. 62) pulling at her diaphanous Ionic underchiton to enhance her shapely legs and buttocks while her himation (mantle) is slung across one shoulder to complicate the richness of its folds, both stand in strikingly different aesthetic purpose from the famous Kore 679 (fig. 63). The latter disciplines the swelling curves of her body beneath a sober woolen garment (a *peplos*, the simple open tube with its upper third folded over upon itself and fastened at the shoulders); she is sprightly in her animation without any hint of the flirtatious sensuality of her Ionic peers.[76]

This sculptural comparison between sober restraint and opulent intricacy metaphorically encodes the opposition between Attic and Ionic approaches to style in another medium, cookery. A host of references indicate that Ionians, like their Lydian neighbors, were known for luxurious indulgence at the table. One Lydian preparation in particular is often singled out in numerous

61. The Rampin Horseman. *Head of an archaic marble horseman from Athens, ca. 530 B.C. Paris, Louvre*

62. *An archaic Maiden, or* kore, *ca. 520–10 B.C. Athens, Acropolis Museum (no. 682)*

63. Kore no. 679, *ca. 540 B.C. Athens, Acropolis Museum*

sources[77] and is also associated with self-indulgent Ionians by Menander: "Ionians bloated by wealth, make their chief dish *kandaulon* and foods which provoke desire."[78] Its name, *kandaulos*, or *kandylos*, resonates with provocative allusions. But first let us look at its ingredients as cited in Athenaeus (XII, 516d) after Hegesippus of Tarentum: boiled meat, grated bread (crumbs that make Gulick translate the dish in every passage of this text as "pilaf," in the face of thickening by bread that could not be gratable if it were soft), Phrygian cheese, anise, and fatty broth *(zōmos piōn)*, although it is made clear that at least three variants of this stew were known. Its richness is palpable, summoning up reminiscence of unctuous Mesopotamian ancestors. Yet its most beguiling historical ramifications concern hints that the constituent meat may once have been dog, an ingredient that would account for its infamous reputation in the literature.

From Sardis, the capital of Lydia and its paradigmatically wealthy King Croesus, excavators have uncovered about thirty ritual meal deposits from different contexts, each consisting of knife, serving dish, wine vessel with drinking cup, and a jug which held the body of a puppy (now a skeleton, obviously). The scholar who has made a detailed study of these deposits, Crawford Greenewalt, argues that the dinners represent offerings to the Lydian divinity Kandaulas, whose name comes from an epithet meaning "puppy choker." He wonders, on analogy with the way in which chicken has replaced squirrel in American Brunswick stew, whether the "meat" of that notorious Lydian/Ionian stew should not be viewed as the ritual transformation of an original ingredient to one more suited to human sensibilities.[79] However this may be, the contrast between the Peplos Kore and other Acropolis Maidens in Ionic dress serves as a metaphoric equivalent of Attic compared to rich East Greek fare during the Archaic period. Moderation in all things remains a guiding principle in the classical age of Athens' imperial grandeur, inflecting a sensitivity to subtle refinements in architecture and ideal forms distilled from the vagaries of nature in all the arts.

In the realm of foodways, this vision of the underlying geometric structure, this gift of abstracting the essence of the visible world, will take the shape of Plato's puritanical recommendations for his idealized *Republic* (VIII, 559e) where unnecessary luxuries and anything more than simple food and condiments required for health are to be considered hurtful to body and soul.[80] By his day, Attic style in fine dining had become characterized as a service of many tidbits; instead of casseroles of multiple ingredients, the sources joke that one dined characteristically at Athens on lots of little "appetizers,"[81] though, as we shall see, the fourth century brought expanded possibilities to the typical menu.

To return to the archaic symposium, self-referential sympotic poetry, initiated by such lyricists as Alcman, Alcaeos, Anacreon, and Semonides, embodies individual creativity in elegiac song. By the late Archaic age, under the tempering onslaught of Persian expansionism, one poet—an Ionian philosopher who became a displaced person in the West, Xenophanes[82]—emphasizes the underlying sacred aura in the symposium. He rhapsodizes on the purity of its rituals, from first ablutions with sweet, cold water and fragrant incense to the central altar wreathed in flowers and godly virtue of speech, ending with moral suasion toward moderation in drinking (so that one does not cease to do honor to the gods and, if he be not old, may reach home without the aid of a servant). We are already at a classic threshold of the subsequent Platonic stress on self-control and temperate conduct for ideal citizens, a symposion of sages come together less in sensual refreshment for the body than in a feast of reason for the soul.[83]

HESTIATORIA (HEARTHS SHARED WITH THE GODS)

All religions seek some mode of communion with the divine. For the ancients, food represented a channel of communication in a multitude of ways, whether in a humble familial context or a formal religious one involving the entire populace. The Greeks appear marvelously ingenious in devising ways to share sustenance with the gods, all the while retaining the portion most favored by humans for themselves.

For the Greek city-state, the sacred character of the prytany's common hearth *(koine hestia)* is dramatized by an imperative that citizens take some of its fire with them when they set out from a home *polis* to found new colonies in Africa and the western Mediterranean during the late eighth and seventh centuries B.C.[84] Not merely politics, but all religious experience found expression in the ritualized consumption of food and drink. A group of modern scholars has investigated the complexity of cult and ritual—of expiation of mutual blood guilt reaching far back to bonds forged among the first hunters, if one follows Walter Burkert—to help us understand Greek animal sacrifice as well as other sacred communications with divinities.[85]

Each god or goddess, each minor deity or nymph, every heroic being from a legendary past who might receive homage, had his or her favorite food. Worshippers must surely have relished festivals when the cult addressed one who preferred sweet smoke rising from an altar where a thighbone of a special animal, wrapped in folds of its fat, was laid upon the sacrificial fire. The diet of Greeks, like that of other ancient folk, was principally based on grains; the meat shared on these occasions could well be a rare taste of animal flesh for ordinary citizens.

Collective eating shapes Hellenic dietary systems in every time period, including our own when hospitality rules as forcefully as it did for Odysseus in each encounter as a castaway or ungrateful guest. In a social order which made little distinction between the religious and the secular, which dedicated its theater and poetry as well as its athletic contests to specified divinities, feasting became a worshipful and revelatory act. But it would lead us too far afield to consider all the varieties of sacrificial meals held for major public festivals[86] or in *hestiatoria* (banqueting halls) at important sanctuaries,[87] or those shared in more private religious associations[88] or in connection with funerary rites.[89] So-called funeral banquets depicted in late classical reliefs do aid in identifying some bread shapes mentioned in the sources, such as the *omphaloi* (mounded navels) and pyramids (fig. 41), while molded offering tables and models of breads or cakes (fig. 64) help us to visualize the fare in many cases.

64. Clay models of food offerings include cakes from a sanctuary of Demeter and Kore at Acrocorinth. (Photo by N. Boukadis)

Inscriptions from different cities and periods document regulations governing disparate ceremonies as well as the distribution of participants' shares.[90] Yet other evidence will lead us closer to both cookery and taste of the classical age of Greek gastronomy.

FOOD AND DRINK IN CLASSICAL GREECE

The separate states of the classical Greek world were each known for idiosyncrasies of diet. Dwellers in remote and forested Arcadia were thought of as still eating the acorns that served early humankind as food, establishing a metaphor for the Golden Age that echoes in Latin and Renaissance poetry.[91] Boeotians, regarded as dreadful gluttons by their Attic neighbors, were ridiculed for consuming untoward foods like wild weasels, foxes, moles, otters, and cats, in addition to indulging in their prized but costly exports: fat geese and the giant eels they harvested from Lake Copais (today filled in with the most fertile soil in the Theban area).[92] The country folk of Megara were given to pork and cabbage, and we have already encountered their abstemious overlords, the Spartans (who knew how to give fighting men the most efficient high energy nutriment, as we learn from Thucydides' history of the Peloponnesian War when Lacedaemonian equivalents of modern "frogmen" swam underwater to troops cut off at Sphacteria towing skins filled with honey and poppyseed as well as bruised linseed).[93]

By all accounts, however, the palm in gastronomy went to the famed chefs of Sicily and Magna Graecia, and theirs were the compendious (lost, alas) cookbooks that instructed lesser mortals in all the arts of the table. As was already noted, their preeminence was due to the quality of ingredients where, alongside the bounty of the sea, climate and soil were so blessed; to adventurous colonist ancestors who sired palates open to innovation; and to the glitter of tyrant's courts at Syracuse and wealthy entrepreneurs elsewhere providing the purse. But even Archestratos admired Athenian cheesecake and the wonderful honey from Mount Hymettos, which, then as now, made all Attic pastries esteemed.[94]

Fierce Thessalians, breeders of horses in their northern plains, were believed to be insatiable eaters and fond of voluptuous foods. They invented the *mattyē*, which came to mean any rich delicacy, but survives in at least one recipe from its many varieties: a wild game bird—a pheasant would do admirably—is killed through its mouth to thrust directly into the brain, then hung unplucked (and presumably ungutted) to retain its blood and to permeate and tenderize the flesh. Next it is seasoned and cooked in a fatty broth made from a guinea hen and "baby cockerels that are just learning to crow." Vinegar is added (or a bunch of unripe grapes in summer—thus anticipating the medieval use of verjuice), and it is served either smothered in stewed vegetables (if one accept Gulick's reading *lachana*) or with a kind of pasta, *laganon*, if you accept my argument to be made below. (Then again, it might have included both vegetables and "noodles.") [95]

Thessalians also made a better groat "pudding" than other Greeks according to some critics. This *chondron* of wheat groats, swollen with lamb broth in one variant, and incorporating (toasted) pine nuts, had many variations. A recipe that represents a complicated use for the molded *chondron* may be found in the appendix; after it is cooked and sautéed in hot honey, it becomes *thrion*. [96] All Greeks in whatever part of their world were ingenious in utilizing their grains. Some statistically minded investigator calculates that Athenaeus mentions more than seventy-two kinds of bread or cake in his report of the gastronomers' lore. [97] Cooking methods determine the categories: oven bread, brazier bread, spit bread, bread baked in the ashes, *artos* baked on hot coals— also of course, whether it is leavened or not, and special shapes like those used ritually at Syracuse in honor of Demeter and Persephone which represented female genitalia. [98] Further distinctions reflect its grain: different wheats— bolted to varying degree—as well as barley, spelt, millet, or more rare rye and rice (ancients knew a red-grained species from east Africa before Alexander the Great brought knowledge of the oriental seed). [99]

The importance of seafood in the diet—above all in Attica—may be estimated by a bit of Greek etymology. *Sitos*, the word for "grain" or "meal," or in earliest days "bread," came to signify "food" in general, as opposed to drink. All that accompanied it was called *opson*, a word derived from a verb *(epsō)* meaning "to boil" or "to stew" (those familiar with Chinese foodways will think of the distinction between *fan*—rice and its cognates—and *ts'ai*, or everything else that goes with it). In Attic Greek, *opson* came to mean "fish"— hence modern Greek for the finny tribe, *to psari*.

We can assemble condiments from a passage in Athenaeus that quotes a comic playwright's characters. [100] A cook-caterer in one play calls for seasonings he will need: sesame seeds, crushed raisin, fennel, dill, mustard, kale or cabbage *(kaulon)*, silphium, coriander, sumac, cumin, capers, marjoram, horn onion (related to leek), garlic, thyme, sage, must, heartwort *(seseli,* an umbelliferous genus) rue, and leek. A second fragment has a querulous hired cook natter about what he is missing, including equipment such as a well rope, kneading trough, or wood for the fire; he lacks vinegar, anise, oregano, fig leaves, oil, almonds, garlic, must, horn onion, bulbs, cumin, salt, and eggs.

Among the flavor elements cited, a modern Greek homemaker would likely substitute grape leaves for the fig leaves to wrap victuals, but sorely miss New World tomatoes and peppers, as well as spices then still rarely imported from distant lands (pepper, cloves, ginger and galingale, cardamom, cinnamon). It would take until around the birth of Christ before Arab traders gave up the secret of sailing to India and South Asia by exploiting the dependable monsoon winds that permitted regular sea commerce with the Mediterranean world.[101] Caravan routes were something else again, and brought exchange that led a Han Chinese emissary to learn wine-making in the third century B.C., but spices came from different climes.

Herodotos' fantastic tale (III, 110–111) of methods of harvesting cassia and cinnamon (in "Arabia!") shows how exotic south Asian spices were to classical Greeks.[102] The seekers gather at a shallow lake, protecting themselves from bat-like creatures by disguising themselves with ox-hides and other skins. Cinnamon sticks are carried by great birds to their nests on the tops of inaccessible crags; Arabians cut dead oxen and asses into large chunks and set them below the mountains, tempting the birds to this bait. The birds (who sound like the ancestors of Sinbad's Roc) carry the meat back up to their nests, which break under the added weight, so cinnamon sticks and pieces can be gathered at the base of the aeries.

Modern Greeks who dine on one of the ancient meals that I plan for special events always find it a major deprivation to do without freshly ground pepper or, above all, lemon for their fish. In antiquity, before different kinds of pepper became commonplace—or even after, for those who could not afford it—myrtle berries were used to contribute pungency and to bring out the flavor of food.[103] In place of lemon, ancients used sumac—varieties with red fruits not to be confused with white-berried "poison sumac"—much as our own Appalachian dwellers long ago discovered its pleasant acidity and lemony savor.[104]

For the first time in Western history, it seems, seasonings, aromatics, and condiments (*hēdusmata*, as the Greeks called them) joined basic nutrients in a philosophic structure of dietetic lore. A new Hellenic vision of the relationship between body and mind—soul, if you will—in the human animal raised dietetics to primacy in Greek medicine, unlike Egyptian and other Near Eastern cultures that accorded privilege in this realm to pharmacology and surgery.[105] An entirely new science had its roots in the Greek quest for understanding the individual's relationship with cosmic order, embracing also climate, seasons, and winds, all involved with keeping the body healthy for the proper life of the soul. "By diet the Greeks meant a man's entire mode of living, the relation between sleep and being awake, between exercise and rest, and, of course, also, the choice of food, the quantity to be consumed, evacuations, and all other factors that constitute a man's life and must be under control if the individual is to be not only healthy but also strong and beautiful."[106]

It was Empedocles (the philosopher of South Italy active about 444 B.C.) who defined the four constituent elements of all matter—air, water, fire, and earth. These elements, according to medical theory, found their expression in four essential humors of the human body: blood, phlegm (as a thickened equivalent of water), yellow bile, and black bile. Whoever wrote the treatise, *The Nature of Man,* in the Hippocratic collection (Erasistratos, the Hellenistic sage?) with its vision of perfect health resulting from the balance and blending of these substances, set down a humoral doctrine that would prevail for millennia, underwritten by the authority of Aristotle.[107] The treatise developed coordinated temperaments or types of people in whom one of the humors characteristically dominates. Theophrastos in the fourth century had already written on melancholy, ruled by black bile, as the creative constitution of genius if moderated by a balance of opposites: hot and cold; moist and dry.[108] The way was opened to assign these qualities to foodstuffs in calculated degrees in order to counter any surplus or deficiency in one's humors that could cause disease.[109] Hygiene as a holistic pattern of life, with exercise and food calibrated to a wide variety of factors including age,[110] nevertheless laid stress upon moderation as an overarching principle and harmonious reconciliation of extremes.

It is precisely such consummate balance and harmonizing of opposites—of stability with active rhythms, of compositional rules and symmetries with their apt evasion, of solid volumes with an ineluctable power of line—which is the glory of Greek art and architecture of the stage we term "classical." Rules or conventions regulate fifth-century reliefs like the Parthenon frieze in which sculptors were bound by isocephaly (all figures, seated or standing, human or animal, have their heads at the same height, filling the relief); landscape is generally eliminated; and there is an ideal surface plane that every form must respect as soon as it emerges from others overlapping it. Rules or principles of counterpoise center fifth-century statues in their own gravity, with head closing, by its turn to the weight-bearing leg, a cadence of movement set up throughout the body by relaxation of the other. These self-imposed limits or restraints, within which exquisite refinement can operate, invite comparison with politics — that Greek invention. Just so the citizen submitted to *eunomia,* the common good established in law, and because this was done by the citizen's own free will, it ultimately exalted the individual and his contribution to the democratic body.

SPECIALTIES

The point has come to consider the vexed question of ancient pasta. Today at least there is enough responsible writing on food history to have laid to rest a persistent fable that Marco Polo brought noodles back from China, although his only surprise at "pasta" (not at a loss for the word) he met on his trip was encountering noodles made not of flour but of breadfruit growing on trees.[111]

There are two schools of scholarly thought concerning the beginnings of simple (i.e., flat varieties, not extruded hollow types) pasta-making. One follows an Arabist, Andrew Watson,[112] who argues that it was the Arabs who invented pasta, introducing what has become the national dish to Sicily and South Italy in their conquests of the ninth century A.D. The Arabs certainly did bring reformed methods of farming to North Africa and Europe, as well as many new products, including sugar cane, eggplants, spinach, and a broad range of citrus fruits to supplement the citrons known in antiquity from Persia. But many scholars, myself among them, argue that noodles and lasagna, whoever invented that first (inevitable?) preparation of flour and water, sometimes with added egg or other ingredients, were already well known to Greeks and Romans. Our case has been enormously advanced by modern paleobotanical research[113] which proves that durum wheat, the gluten-rich, "heavy" wheat required for good pasta, was grown from an early date and is one of the reasons that much Greek and Roman bread was very dense.[114] It was durum wheat that made Greek *semidalis* — semolina. For Watson, durum wheat was not an important crop before the medieval period.

Even so, the only widely read author on cookery outside the academic community who seems to have the right explanation is Patience Gray; in *Honey from a Weed*[115] she announces the discovery of those who live in Apulia and other Italian provinces once the heartland of Magna Graecia[116] (one I made for myself in May 1995) of the etymological proof needed to supplement botanical evidence. This involves two ancient Greek words: *laganon,* plural *lagana;* and *itrion, itria.*[117] When one learns that the Arabic word *itrijah,* found in Aramaic and Hebrew cognates, means "noodle," it is difficult not to see a derivation from the Greek, originally connoting "ribbon." In the Salentine peninsula and the region around Taranto, the dialect preserves *lagana* for the rolled out square of dough used by housewives to be cut into pasta, and *tria (itria)* survives in the local dish, *tagliatelle*, cooked just as in ancient Greece with chickpeas and wild arugula (rocket). Part of the pasta is reserved to be browned in oil in final assembly of the specialty[118] as in a recipe preserved in Athenaeus (XIV, 647e) that incorporates lettuce juice to make green pasta.

The "waters" of the pasta invention controversy were somewhat muddied by one Italian archaeologist who supplemented linguistic evidence with that of an artifact represented in an Etruscan tomb. The rock-cut supports of the Tomba dei rilievi at Cervetri are decorated with reliefs of objects of all kinds, some for warfare, others of household equipment. One seemed to be an ancient *spianatoia*, a board for rolling out pasta, complete with a little bag of extra flour hanging from one handle. Alas, definitive study of the reliefs has now identified the object as a gaming board precisely like one shown on an Etruscan mirror being used by two competing Greek heroes.[119] This does not negate Etruscan knowledge of pasta, however, and at least one museum devoted to history of the genre holds that they even rolled flat noodles about metal needles to fashion macaroni (much as medieval and Renaissance cooks would anticipate extruded manufacture of spaghetti at a later date).[120]

A word on the uses of pasta by Greeks and Romans. The "ribbons," as we met them earlier in the *mattyē* were seemingly partially dried and broken up to add to stewed dishes as a form of thickening. And the chickpeas with *tria* and greens I so relished in Apulia as atavistic Western Greek fare are matched by Horace's supper dish of chickpeas with leeks and *lagani*.[121]

Greek taste ran to the sharp and even sour as we learn from Athenaeus on vinegar, "the one condiment Attic writers call 'delight'" (II, 67c–f) and from literary references to a favored sauce called *hypotrimma*,[122] of many ingredients both sharp and acerbic. Pickled fish, called *garos*,[123] that gave rise to the fish sauce *garum* which, in Roman hands, makes some people shudder, was much appreciated with other pickled delicacies given to provoke appetite — turnips and radishes dressed with vinegar and mustard, for example. Also, a banquet dish *par excellence* is served with a sauce of vinegar and precious silphium juice (replaced in our recipe in the appendix by tincture of asafoetida); this is the famous *mētra* (Latin *matrix*), the boiled womb of a sow, preferably one which had just been miscarried, stuffed like the Scottish haggis with grain and other ingredients.[124] Some connoisseurs recommended additional seasonings, such as cumin or harsh rue.

Because vegetarianism [125] plays such a prominent part in Greek philosophy and the morality of food, we must pay further attention to their vegetables, beyond what has emerged concerning legumes, bulbs, and other field fare, including blite and amaranth (the *horta* still dominant in peasant diets today). The range of pot herbs, both wild and cultivated, found in Theophrastos (his book VI, for example) far outnumbers the forage plants praised by our own Euell Gibbons and Marvin Harris. Diokles, the physician we met earlier, advises the best wild vegetables for boiling: [126] beet (meaning both red and white chard with their modest roots), mallow, sorrel, nettle (forget the sting; the young tender leaves are indeed delicious in early spring); orache (do not believe texts which speak of "spinach") [127]; bulbs (of hyacinth, asphodel, iris, and the like), truffles, and mushrooms. Lettuces and cabbage, each in several varieties, but not headed, were exploited both cooked and raw. Translations often make it seem that squashes and pumpkins were substantial contributions to Greek fare, but the family of these New World products was represented by marrows, bottle gourds *(lagenaria)*, cucumbers, and a species of watermelon.[128] Celery, with white, red, or particolored stalks,[129] was gathered wild or grown to make wreaths for particular occasions. Another vegetable which in antiquity looked strikingly different from our own version is the carrot. The "red" carrot is a creation of early modern gardeners, while the ancient root was as colorless as the parsnip—or possibly on occasion purple-black.[130]

Two vegetables require a bit more attention: artichokes and asparagus, both of which Theophrastos (VI, iv, 2 and 10) places among plants that are wholly spinous in nature. *Asparagos* seems to be a term that covers a variety of plants, judging from Matron's Attic dinner with its echoes of Homer in which he bundles together "bulbs" and "asparagos" as categories. Likewise, Athenaeus speaks of numerous types beyond wild species divided between swamp and mountain asparagus. We hear of sown varieties growing to enormous size, twelve feet in the case of a Libyan example and twenty cubits in that of another prodigy. Pliny will later complain of asparagus grown at Ravenna of which three stalks make a Roman pound. As for the artichoke, this exists in two main species evolved from a common thistle: *kaktos* (or "cactus") as *Kynara cardunculus*, cardoon, and *Cynara scolymus*, artichoke. The flowering heads look similar as they are reproduced in Roman mosaics (compare fig. 65, Antioch, and a detail from a North African mosaic, fig. 66). Athenaeus says the *kaktos* peculiar to Sicily is called *carduus* by the Romans—that is, the cardoon, which was a favorite vegetable of our colonial ancestors

65.   Hors d'oeuvres *(gustatio)*. *Detail of Mosaic of The House of the Banquet, Antioch, Syria.* *(See also fig. 87)*

and is today difficult to procure except in some Italian markets or — at exorbitant price — in certain specialty grocers.[131]

Greek wines [132] become another specialty topic thanks to a continuing tradition of doing what we would call violence to the beneficent soul of the grape. Dilution with water is one thing, but a tendency to mix in different additives seems quite another to our sensibilities, even though strainers that serve this process may beguile our eyes. We have already met Homer's Pramnian wine doctored with barley meal and cheese — the wine representing a type rather than designating geography, for classical sources attribute it variably to sites on the Aegean islands, Lesbos or Ikaros, and in Asia Minor, Ephesus as well as Smyrna.[133] This heroic, long-lasting wine was treated to make a restorative potion. Other treatments were intended to achieve various purposes from

66. Cardoon, or artichoke. *Detail of mosaic from El Djem (see also below, fig. 87). Tunis, Bardo Museum. (Photo by Mary Taylor Simeti)*

sweetening a harsh wine, enhancing or transforming its bouquet, to altering its color.

Additives for color remind us that ancient wines of the first rank were never the deep rich hue of fine burgundy (*pace* Homer's "wine-dark sea") and whites predominated among the *grands crus*. Modern techniques of fermenting the skins of black grapes to strengthen color in premier must of the first pressing (and as we know today, to supply important antioxidants) were not employed by classical vintners.[134] Saffron could be added to obtain a golden hue, but Greeks are thought not to have been very sensitive to color, since a fourth-century author mentions only three categories: dark or red, white, and yellow (Athenaeus, I, 32d), while Romans who cite him add one or two further distinctions of hue.[135] Still, the Greek writer was a physician recommending red for bodily growth, white as a diuretic, and dry yellow as a better aid to good digestion; he might be expected to think only in terms of general categories.

Greeks surely were, however, sensitive to bouquet and savor, as any reader of lyric poetry can attest. Although much of the adulteration of wine occurs in support of preservation or in correcting acidity—Forbes gives turpentine, pitch, resin, chalk, gypsum, lime prepared from marble or sea-shells, as well as seawater—other additives were felt to enhance particular vinous qualities. Seawater, regularly added to the fine vintages of Lesbos, Chios, and Cos, was explicitly valued for enhancing their bouquets *(anthosmias).*[136]

The northern Aegean island of Thasos, with rockbound coast and pine woods that remind down-East folks like me of Maine, produced wines that were among those most sought-after in antiquity. Curious fates of historic preservation permit us even to read the Thasians' substantial regulations concerning export of their famous product: all the way from trademark protection (stamped on a shipping amphora's handle) and prohibition of preharvest speculating down to embargos on Thasian ships carrying any "foreign" wines to selected mainland ports.[137] Yet this source of one of the greatest wines Greek vineyards had to offer (in a class with those from Thrace, Magnesia, those islands already mentioned—Lesbos, Chios, and Cos—as well as Toronē and Mendē on the Chalcidic peninsula) served wine in its prytaneion flavored by a lump of spelt dough kneaded with honey.[138] The acclaimed Mendaean wine, incidentally, brought Dionysos himself as a character in New Comedy to exclaim that it was fine enough to cause the gods to wet their soft beds.[139]

Other modifications of wine include smoking, chilling with an admixture of snow, spicing, perfuming with flower extracts or grains of anise and pomegranate, and straining through a cloth impregnated with myrrh, all methods to be adopted by the Romans, although they learned their actual viticulture from the Etruscans.[140] Dioscurides (A.D. 40–80) wrote of other methods of flavoring wines beyond additives for medicinal purposes. He warned of sweetening by boiled-down must or wine, which seemed to produce symptoms we recognize today as lead poisoning, because the reduction was best accomplished in leaden vessels.[141] Dioscurides also speaks of all the fruit wines, the use of honey potions and various herbs used to flavor wine (germander, lavender, betony, thyme, marjoram, and a fennel-dill-parsley combination) as well as to promote abortion if adulterated with hellebore or drugged sleep if treated with mandrake.

Our emphasis on additives must not allow us to forget that from the seventh century until the second B.C., when Romans began to dominate the wine trade, Greek commerce was responsible for implanting the pleasures of the grape in peoples of the West in Spain and Gaul. From the Greek port of Massilia (Marseilles) up the Rhone Valley and expanding into the hinterland, archaeology traces the trade amphoras with their handle stamps that document the fateful diffusion of Dionysos' fermented nectar among the Celtic ancestors of today's preeminent oenophiles.

The long history of the Greek experience does not come to a close but begins to be transformed in the course of the fourth century, culminating in the conquests of Alexander and a succeeding age when Greek civilization is disseminated more widely than ever before but requires a different adjective to describe it — no longer Hellenic, but Hellenistic. It is an age of kingdoms rather than city-states, of polyglot and cosmopolitan cities, of spiritual ferment and of increasing interaction with the rising power of Rome. Transformations in its modes of eating will be the topic of the next chapter.

5 Hellenistic Transformations

Antiochus . . . daily held receptions for large crowds at which, aside from heaps of food that was set forth or wasted, each person carried away from the hearth fires whole creatures of land, of air, of sea — enough to fill a cart; and with all this also honey-cakes and wreaths of myrrh and frankincense with pressed fillets of gold man-size in length. (Athenaeus XII, 540c) [1]

IT IS SUCH LAVISH hospitality and conspicuous consumption that I wish to make the centerpiece of this short epilogue to the Hellenic Experience. In considering the opulence of royal Hellenistic courts, which emulated the magnificence of Persian monarchs whom Greeks of the classical period had scorned for their barbaric luxury, we will meet standards set for all time to come in respect to flaunting riches and power. For the successors of Alexander the Great, their propagandist banquets and spectacles also served to cement loyalties among their followers and the public as well as demonstrating the blessings of fortune the gods bestowed on one of their own, a deified or semidivine ruler.

In the course of the fourth century, profound change begins to transform Hellenes' perceptions of what had previously been considered their supreme values in life. That suppression of individual concerns to the needs of the body politic that had characterized the high classical *polis* progressively gives way to a dominating self-interest, although — or perhaps because — it was sited in a wider and more universal political context. We can read the new mind-set in so many phenomena of fourth-century life, beginning even before the rise of Macedonia and the conquests of Alexander who, before his untimely death in 323 B.C., would unite under the hegemony of Hellenism all of the eastern Greek world as well as nearer Asia and Egypt.

The growing subjectivism of the fourth century is strikingly displayed in novel attitudes toward religion and the gods.[2] Divinities who promise personal salvation in the beyond and those who may heal one's mortal husk enjoy a powerful upsurge in their cults. Among international sanctuaries, those of Asklepios and his medical progeny see expansive development at sites such as Epidauros and the island of Kos (fig. 67), prepared to welcome hordes of

67.   *Reconstruction by the Italian excavators of the Sanctuary of Asklepios on the island of Kos. Fourth century B.C.*

68. Masked Actors in a Scene from Comedy. *Mosaic from Pompeii copying a third-century original by Dioskoureides of Samos. Naples, National Museum*

worshippers to miraculous cures in their incubation rites. At Delphi, earthy Dionysos in his role as rescuer from Hades (or at least a divinity whose wine can make you forget its gaping mouth) joins the empyrean cult of Apollo to share the latter's original temple for half the year.

In no realm are the dynamics of change that will shape the infrastructure of the Hellenistic world more discernible than in new forms among the arts. Austere themes of human destiny that had been set forth in tragedy are replaced by theatral melodrama, while Middle Comedy already exploits the foibles of lower-class characters who foreshadow the buffoonery of New Comedy and Greco-Roman *farceurs* (fig. 68). Coordinated harmonics of proportion and movement in the visual arts give way to uncertain rhythms and disturbed emotions, even pathos in the works of a sculptor like Scopas (fig. 69). Austere decorum no longer governs the representation of the goddess Aphrodite when Praxiteles renders his famous Cnidian statue shockingly

69. *Male head in an expressionistic style associated with the sculptor Scopas. Fourth century* B.C. *From the pediments of the Temple of Athena Alea at Tegea. Athens, National Museum*

70. *Grave relief of* Ampharete and Her Grandchild. *Attic, end fifth century* B.C. *Athens, Kerameikos Museum*

nude and develops a technique of marble carving that gives the illusion of soft-est flesh and melting gaze. Idealized depictions of types of people—the phi-losopher, the statesman, the athlete, the military leader—give way to more in-dividualized renderings worthy to be termed portraiture.

Until sumptuary laws ban their production, in Attica a rich series of grave reliefs with increasingly affective subject matter punctuate the development of funerary art (fig. 70). Accompanying the shift from public preoccupations to those in the private sphere is an emphasis on privileged consumption. This is especially marked in the richness and variety of decorated wares in gold and silver, or in bronze gilded in imitation of gold, for household use. Strainers and vessels of metal for the symposion are of an order of calculated beauty and opulence quite different from earlier ceramics (figs. 71, 72).

For our culinary purposes, we must note transformations that anticipate the Hellenistic "fusion" cuisine that will result from Alexander's conquest of the vast Persian empire in Asia and his expedition to India. (His cohorts studying exotic flora and fauna may be closely compared to the scientists and scholars who made up Napoleon's mission in Egypt.) True, many of Alexan-der's reporters seem to relate "tall tales" of Indian marvels such as gold-mining ants with foreparts of lions, people who sleep in their own monstrous ears, and oysters a foot long.[3] Here is one source of natural wonders that will absorb the imaginations of medieval people.

More realistic encounters on Alexander's expedition to India were with hitherto unknown plants such as mango, banana, oriental jujube, and huge jackfruit in the tamarind family, or a new type of minuscule "fig," from expan-sive banyan trees. The troops were introduced to "wool that blossoms on cer-tain trees" (cotton) or "reeds that produce honey, though there are no bees" (sugar cane),[4] and they discovered other sources of spikenard, cinnamon, and cassia or new forms of terebinth, cardamom, and rice (known earlier solely in a red variety from Ethiopia valued for medical use). Efforts to cultivate spice trees and other flora in the west had success only if the climate was congenial for the transplants: rice in the marshes of Babylonia and, elsewhere in the Seleucids' Syrian realm, the Bactrian peach tree and the "Persian apple" (medlar), offset by failed attempts at nard and cinnamon.[5] Because Alexan-der's triumphal return from the East seemed to echo Dionysos' Indian *thiasos*—and his men had been excited to visit Nysa, which they knew the god had founded in honor of his nurse, and the mountain called Meros[6]—a spe-cial aura may have surrounded efforts to introduce in the West grapes from those parts (which we know to be of a different strain than *Vitis vinifera* like

71. Kylix in gilded bronze from a late fourth-century tomb at Vergina. Salonika, Archaeological Museum

other oriental vines).[7] Among Alexander's successors, Ptolemy II in Egypt, seeking to improve native varieties, saw to plantings of tried and true vines from Thrace, figs from Chios, pomegranates, perhaps even apricots.[8]

But efforts to acclimatize new plants and to import exotic foodstuffs began much earlier. The very writers of cookbooks and comedies we have been considering via Athenaeus are fourth-century witnesses to the dynamics of culinary change. On the other hand, the long travail of the Peloponnesian Wars between Athens and Sparta and their allies during the last third of the fifth century had everywhere, but above all in Attica, disrupted the mutual dependence of the city and the agricultural countryside, either immediate or that which belonged to allied neighbors. Orchards and vineyards had been burned and farms laid waste. Athens, more than ever, had to increase grain imports from the Black Sea region, and, by the time of her defeat by the Macedonians at Chaeronea in 338 B.C., "was in effect already showing some of the essential features of the typical Greek city of the Hellenistic period, above all, a chronic tendency to food crises, and a dependence on wealthy and generous individuals, *[euergetai]* whether those benefactors were residents or outsiders."[9]

The enrichment of an entire class of entrepreneurs and professionals during the fourth century appears as one more trend that eventually shaped the social structure of Hellenistic kingdoms where a wealthy, generally Greek, elite lived a cosmopolitan life of luxury among a native population bound to

72. Dionysos and
Ariadne. *Gilt bronze krater,*
late fourth century B.C.,
from a Macedonian royal
Tomb at Vergina. Salonika,
Archaeological Museum

the ways and sustenance of their forefathers. But every citizen at least bene-
fited from the munificence — generated through ego or enforced by public
office — of *euergetai* who provided public banquets and tried to keep up with
the spectacular diversions provided by deified rulers in dynasties founded by
the Diadochi, the successors of Alexander who divided up his empire.

Alexander initiated the Hellenistic disposition toward excess with his
adoption of Persian dress and oriental ways. The later moralist Stoic Seneca
would not forgive him, despite his glory, because he had put to death Callis-

thenes for censuring his un-Hellenic behavior. Classical Greeks had almost refused to believe the luxury of Persian rulers' modes of living,[10] but Alexander tried to emulate the extravagance of their court rituals and banquets, the profligacy of their gifts. Returned from India and Persia to his restored seat at Babylon, his expenses each day for himself and his court seemed, to one writer cited by Athenaeus, more costly than even those entailed by the famous golden plane trees under which Persian rulers had held forth with their vine made of gold from which hung clusters of emerald-and-ruby grapes.[11]

A famous exemplar of Hellenistic prodigality and Macedonian immoderation in the matter of banquets is the "bachelor party" that marked the marriage of one Caranos, related by Hippolochos as an eyewitness in a letter to a disciple of Theophrastos (summarized by Athenaeus, IV, 128–130e).[12] Nothing could better represent the underlying motivations for spectacular entertainment and generosity unless it were the *potlatch* ceremony of Northwest-coast Indians. A similar reciprocity and gift exchange in what economists would describe as a redistributive economy made for a network of power alliances—not without a competitive edge—among the Greek rulers in their cosmopolitan world. Their prestige demanded lavish hospitality and liberality, seemingly in conscious emulation of their heroic ancestors immortalized in Homer as well as the erstwhile Great Kings of Persia.[13]

Caranos—or, if my speculation is correct, the power-mad Ptolemy Ceraunos, a sort of Hellenic Richard III, who briefly gained Macedonia by plotting against Seleucos, marrying his step-sister Arsinoë, the widow of Lysimachos, to gain legitimacy and then murdering her two princes—put on a banquet that Hippolochos describes as "surpassing in sumptuousness any ever given anywhere" (Athenaeus III, 126e). Textual questions make it uncertain whether the guests were twenty or one hundred and twenty,[14] but the latter would not be out of keeping with third-century ideals of celebration.

Hippolochos' description is more obsessed with the extraordinary monetary value of the "take-home baskets" of Greek custom which we call "doggie bags" than with details of the culinary delights of the occasion. As gifts, everyone received a spoon of solid gold required for one dish, plus multiple gold tiaras (changed like Renaissance tablecloths with each course), double-jars (half silver and half gold) of perfume, individual platters of bronze, of gold, of silver, of crystal, not to mention cups of precious material, and—most tantalizing of all to an archaeologist who would love to see one—bread baskets plaited of ivory to hold all this bounty afterward.[15] In keeping with Macedonian custom,[16] wines of premium vintage were drunk unmixed until a final "stirrup cup," including one round drunk from six-pint *skyphoi!* Guests understandably sobered up in apprehension at the thought of robbers as they wended their way homeward with wealth enough to purchase land, houses, or slaves galore.

What of the food served to accompany such magnanimous gifts? and together with beguiling entertainment by prized jugglers, musicians, jesters, naked female flame-swallowing acrobats, dancing girls attired as Nereids and Nymphs, a hundred-man chorus to sing the wedding hymn, human candelabra miming Pans, Herms, Erotes, and Diana's nymphs? The list of spectacles does not end here; it must even include a diversion that would have seemed scandalous to an Athenian of the old school. Mummers acted out the sacred wedding procession of Dionysos and the wife of Athens' archon-king in celebration of the last day of the god's major religious festival in Attica, the Anthesteria.

The guests consumed an array of fowl, both domestic and wild, ranging from geese, chickens, ducks, and doves to pigeons, turtledoves, partridges, and the like, as well as hares and kids. These entrées were followed by more elaborate fare: for each diner a silver platter heaped high with a whole roast pig lying on its back to disclose its belly stuffed with countless small birds (thrushes, fig-peckers, and ducklings) and with pulse porridge poured over eggs, oysters, and scallops. Next came another roast kid on its own large platter—presumably the earlier young goats and hares were disjointed in a sort of ragout—followed by all sorts of baked fish on crystal platters nestled in silver surrounds accompanied by Cappadocian loaves (a "soft," delicate bread made with a little milk and oil and salt for leaven, according to Athenaeus III, 113b–c). After further entertainment, revealed when the linen walls of the room (undoubtedly a dining tent or pavilion) were drawn back, huge roast boars pierced by silver spits were served each diner, followed by all kinds of desserts, then by flat cakes—Cretan, Samian, and Attic varieties among them—put up individually in elegant boxes to carry home. We can marvel that the guests were able to stagger homeward, and the thought comes to mind that the Greeks invented the word *boulimia*, irresistible "foddering" in "ox-hunger." But still, we should remember that each participant shared his platters with an entourage of slaves backing him up.

Other spectacular manifestations of the largesse of a Hellenistic *basileus* stand out in ancient literature, some of relatively private indulgence, others of public openhandedness broadly cast. Worthy of notice is a festival orchestrated by Ptolemy II Philadelphos (the epithet based on his marriage in good old Egyptian custom to his sister, Arsinoë II—that indomitable woman we met as the widow of Lysimachos and transient wife of another brother, Ptolemy Ceraunos, until she had to escape his infamy). Alexandria's population witnessed a procession that is calculated to have taken perhaps three or four days to accommodate all the floats and marchers in the parade.[17]

The panoply stuns us by the thousands of participants and by the very weight of gold, silver, and jewels used to garnish the exotic sights that included a contingent of 150 men with trees sheltering rare animals and birds. There were parrots, peacocks, guinea hens, pheasants, and fowl from Ethiopia; strange sheep and cattle from distant sources, lions, leopards, and other African felines, camels laden with spices, elephants, antelopes, teams of ostriches, two thousand hunting dogs of rare breeds, bears, a giraffe, and even a rhinoceros. Among divisions honoring various divinities the text from Kallixeinos of Rhodes (Athenaeus V, 197c–203b) describes in greatest detail the cortege of Dionysos.

We are amazed at the vision of precious accoutrements and the costumes of devotees, both men and women, gotten up as hordes of satyrs, silenes, bacchants, and actor members of the "guild of Dionysos." But it is the description of gigantic floats that truly boggles the mind. They carried such wonders as, under a canopy hung with cult objects, vines, ivy, and fruits, a fifteen-foot tall statue of the god himself pouring wine from a golden goblet into a gold krater that could hold one hundred and fifty gallons (of interest to oenophiles are his bowls filled with cassia and saffron, implying that these were additives for the wine). Another carried an automaton of the god's nurse Nysē, crowned with gold ivy and jeweled clusters of grapes, twelve feet in height, although seated, an image that rose repeatedly to pour a libation of milk from her golden *phialē.*[18] There was a giant wine press filled with grapes being trodden by sixty satyrs singing a vintage song while new wine poured out along their line of march (and this took place in winter, meaning clever storage of this impressive harvest!). Still another cart bore a wineskin stitched from leopard pelts that held 30,000 gallons, trickling out along the way. The parade also boasted a float representing Dionysos' triumphal return from India, and, perhaps most beguiling to think of, a cart drawn by five hundred men representing a deep shadowy cavern in which lay the infant Dionysos, watched over by Hermes and some nymphs, while two fountains gushed forth wine or milk, adding to the delectation of spectators who were also able to catch various kinds of doves, their flight hampered by fettered feet, released along the route.

73.   Reconstruction by Studniczka (1914) of the dining pavilion of Ptolemy II

An equally famous symposion at the palace regaled special guests in a splendid pavilion with a hundred golden couches (this tent could hold one hundred and thirty). An outmoded reconstruction, figure 73,[19] gives some idea of its appearance without providing any idea of its central circular canopy or the elaborateness of its furnishings with statues, paintings, textiles, oriental rugs, and quantities of precious metals. For the first time we meet an element of display set out on a dresser or credenza that will be featured in many a formal "power" dinner in the future, becoming standard at noble banquets in medieval and Renaissance custom. An empty *klinē* is arrayed before the company to hold a wealth of gold vessels studded with gems, and the narrator does not attempt to describe them all, merely asserting their incredible weight: equal to ten thousand silver talents (calculated as nearly three hundred tons by Gulick)!

As with the dinner of Caranos, space for the diners' retinues was reserved on three sides, in a portico outside the column supports, which were shaped as Bacchic *thyrsoi* and palm trees. But we are not told, alas, of the wonderful viands that were to be shared, except for one dish that turns up elsewhere in

Athenaeus. At III, 100f, a friend of Theophrastos is quoted on the subject of silphium [20] and refers to an obviously famous *mētra* (stuffed sow's paunch or womb) served with vinegar and silphium "at Ptolemy's symposion." Which Ptolemy? there were fourteen in all, if one counts the son of Caesar and Cleopatra, but the date fits only the first, Ptolemy Soter, founder of the dynasty, or our Ptolemy II Philadelphos. In any case, this adds to the evidence that show-feasts of Hellenistic leaders included delicacies of established Hellenic tradition, dishes of complex flavor and subtle composition, not merely the whole roasted beasts attesting the hunting prowess of the host or to the vast herds of conquered monarchs. In the appendix you will find a recipe based on a Roman adaptation that shows a sophisticated *matrix*, a haggis as it were, blending many flavors — of onions and garlic, of poached brains, of livers, of aromatics — with the nutty savor of toasted grain, to be bathed with a titillating combination of vinegar-and-asafoetida sauce. This is a cuisine that knew the luscious pungency of truffles, even though Theophrastos and others believed that autumn thunderstorms were responsible for their growth.[21]

Clearly, other perfumes lingered in the air — not least the flower petals drifting on the floor of Ptolemy's pavilion, a special winter boon of Egypt's climate. I think of medieval sweet rushes characteristically spread on the floor of the great hall, much needed to cover the odor rising from careless refuse from both dining trestles and dogs. The work of an artist of Hellenistic Pergamon named Sosos, *The Unswept Floor*, frequently copied in later Roman mosaic for dining room pavements (figs. 74, 75)[22], provides some idea of potential discards at such a well-attended feast: eggshells, the feet of various fowl, nutshells, fishbones, and all sorts of peelings and unchewable bits.

Ptolemy's banquet and similar events described by astounded recorders illustrate the importance of gorgeous mise-en-scène to fully express a propagandist purpose. For us today, however, such status-enhancing hospitality represents a novel feature of Hellenistic culture and individual Gestalt. A new perception of space is not so much an awareness of widened geographical horizons in the Greek *koinē* ("commonality," symbolized by international predominance of the Attic dialect) as it is an aspect of expanded psychological boundaries. This takes on a physical dimension in visual arts of the Hellenistic period, known for incorporating the dynamics of spatiality.

Let us consider a few trends that may be applied to comparable phenomena in the festal/culinary sphere. Sculpture, above all, exploits new spatial conceptions, with autonomy relinquished in favor of environment: sculptural groups become organized in such a way as to interact across actual air and

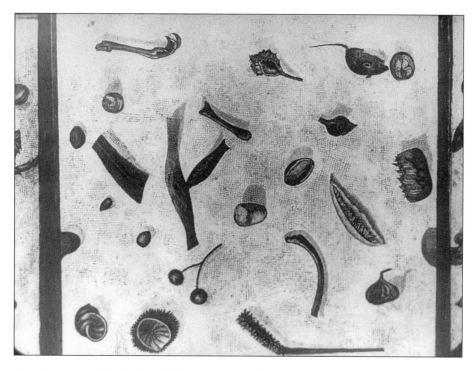

74. *Roman mosaic inspired by a Hellenistic prototype,* The Unswept Floor, *by Sosos. Vatican Museum (from the Lateran collections)*

75. Unswept floor. *Fragment of a Roman mosaic floor from a Tunisian villa. Tunis, Bardo Museum.* (Photo Mary Taylor Simeti)

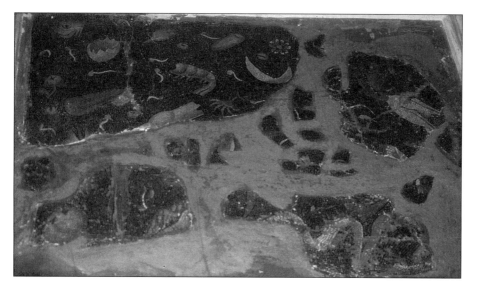

76. Victory from
Samothrace, *ca. 200*
B.C. Paris, Louvre

space. The Victory of Samothrace may be dramatically installed at the head
of a grand staircase today in the Louvre, but this is nothing compared with her
original ambiance (fig. 76).

Excavations in Samothrace revealed the statue's setting on a high escarp-
ment overlooking one of the main approaches to the Sanctuary of the Great

Gods.[23] The bow of the ship, on which she has just fluttered down, emerged from between huge natural boulders, to be reflected in a large basin fitted out to hold a constant supply of water, thus simulating the sea. This stagecraft enhanced the sense of a caught moment, while the illusion made for an ancient kind of virtual reality. In a comparable exploitation of real air and space that cannot be separated from the work of art, writhing-serpent legs of Giants in the Pergamon Altar "Battle of the Gods and Giants" refuse to be contained within the relief and invade the actual space of visitors climbing the steps (fig. 77).

77. Altar of Zeus from Pergamon, ca. 180 B.C., as reconstructed in the State Museum, Berlin. The view shows one side of the staircase and part of the Great Frieze of the Battle of the Gods with Giants

From critical discussions of lost paintings and a few modest survivals in the funerary sphere we know something of the illusionary effects famed artists achieved in pigment as well as perspectival construction of pictorial space, the beginnings of fictive architectural prospects best known from wall frescoes in Pompeii. Pliny (*NH*, XXXV, 112) writes of an entirely new genre of easel painting created in the Hellenistic period by *rhuparographoi*, painters of "sordid" or ignoble subjects. He names one, Piraiikos, who painted *opsonia*, meaning ordinary still-lifes of things to eat, rather than honorable *xenia*, or renderings of gifts offered to the gods and honored guests. Copies of both kinds of Greek still-life are found among Pompeian frescoes (figs. 78), some of them depicted within the shuttered collectors' cases that protected prized antique panels that would have been painted in encaustic (wax-based medium). Often they strike one with apt combinations of ingredients for a recipe: a brace of thrushes with a handful of chanterelles, for example.[24]

Fruits, nuts, a rabbit here, a songbird there, these evocations of succulent yet dainty edibles stand against the weighty flagrancy of all the whole roast beasts or extravagantly seasoned dishes of palatial show-feasts. They embody a more idyllic view of pastoral life found in the poet Theocritos versus historical realism or overwrought emotion in heroic legends revived by Alexandrian playwrights. Beside the spectacles considered above set Theocritos' Idyll XV, with a festival of Adonis where a singer pictures green bowers laden with sweet-smelling dill, service of rare dainties, and sweetmeats of the finest white flour mixed with honey and oil and molded into delicate images of birds and small creatures. The contrast exemplifies rococo versus baroque, in the terminology of historians of Hellenistic art attempting to characterize the arts in which a once unitary voice is now replaced by contending sentiments and diverse forms of expression.

Illusion enters into cookery as well. Clever chefs must have been ingenious to use up the considerable leftovers from grandiose feasts, even after doggie bags had been carried away. As one cook in a comedy reports satirically: "I am preparing a stew by reheating a fish, mixing in half-consumed remnants, moistening it with wine, slinging in some innards seasoned with salt and silphium, some cut-up sausages, adding a slice of gut, and a pig's snout well soused with vinegar; so you will all agree that the morning repast is better than last evening's wedding fare."[25]

There is yet one more facet of Hellenistic life and our food history upon which we should cast our eyes. It is related in strangely comparable ways to our own multicultural but unified world. I do not of course refer merely to

78.   *Roman still-lifes from Pompeii or Herculaneum. Naples, National Museum. On the left, moray eels are included; at right, thrushes with chanterelles*

the dichotomy between "haves" and "have-nots"—sadly, ever present in all phases of human history so far—but to a retrospective tendency of culture in mature, especially urban, educated societies that leads to what Erwin Panofsky used to call "the grandfather law." His concept of reaction against the basic values, taste in literature and the arts, and political stance of one's parents to find fresh impetus in selected *mores* of one's grandparents was formulated to highlight action–reaction in generational exchange. More complex revivalism is a hallmark of our contemporary culture (decade following decade in nostalgic progression), joined with an exoticism that includes a sophisticated appropriation from other ethnic traditions. Just such phenomena characterize the latest phases of Hellenistic art and civilization. We recognize revival styles most readily in sculpture: archaistic versions of hair and drapery patterns that originated in the sixth century B.C.; various reinterpretations of High Classical Athenian masters adapted to make political statements about stability, about leadership and power (on the part of a dynasty of the Pergamene kingdom, for example); and an entire antiquizing repertory of earlier artistic modes popular in the Greco-Roman world of the first century B.C. This corresponds, on the one hand, to what I have termed Hellenistic "fusion cuisine" at the beginning of this chapter: willingness to accept elements from the multicultural melting pot in Hellenistic centers.

79. Old Market-woman. *Second century B.C. The live fowl she carries above her bucket is much damaged. New York, Metropolitan Museum of Art*

On the other hand, the correspondence entails such phenomena as the revival of characteristic foods and food practices from earlier epochs. Take the Hellenistic "hero reliefs" created in both votive and funerary contexts (fig. 41). The diner—sometimes two—semireclines on his *klinē* with a table set before him bearing symposial fruits and sweetmeats in a formula in honor of the dead that goes back to archaic horizons. A chthonic serpent may be present to share in the meal if the protagonist is a semidivine hero, but in any case this view of eternal delectation in the hereafter generally includes cakes that are as venerable as the image itself. The pyramid and the omphalos — the latter summoning up an image of the "navel" stone of the earth at Apollo's sanctuary at Delphi, to equal the numinous geometry of the former — are revivals on several levels of meaning.[26]

The sheer magnitude and complexity of information that must now apply to foodstuffs and their preparation makes for a new genre of culinary literature. The work of Artemidoros, a grammarian and lexicographer from Tarsus in the first century B.C., anticipates the Roman devotion to systematizing knowledge established by earlier Greek philosophers and scholars. His *Opsartutikai glōssai,* a lexicon of cookery, is a major source for Athenaeus.[27] Artemidoros also apparently wrote a treatise on kitchen plants, which raises another interesting point about Hellenistic learning as it relates to our subject. Scientific botanical research (such as that conducted by Aristotle, his disciple Theophrastos, and their authorities) gives rise to illustrated herbals that incorporate folklore and accumulated medical advisories.[28]

With the consolidation of their power in the West, climaxing in their occupation of Syracuse in 212 B.C. up to the final destruction of Carthaginian power in 146 B.C., Romans become active players in the Hellenized eastern world. First they arrive as businessmen usurping a leading role in the wine, slave, spice and other trades, then as subjugators progressing from the conquest of Macedonia and Greece (148–146 B.C.) to the end of their civil wars and the battle of Actium in 31 B.C., which turned Ptolemaic Egypt into an imperial province.

From what we have viewed as a few selected instances of Hellenistic excess, is it not understandable that the plain-living Romans of the Republic were often seduced by the glamorous, self-indulgent life led by Greeks who held power in the lands of Aexander's triumphs? If the great Alexander could enact the role of Dionysos, is it surprising that Mark Antony caroused in Athens with all the trappings of the same divinity? If Alexander and his companions learned in India (as still practiced today in some of its cuisine) to scatter gold leaf upon desserts,[29] is it difficult to understand how readily the Roman general would fall under the spell of Cleopatra VII and her ultimate flourish of Ptolemaic extravagancy? Athenaeus (IV, 147f–148), *per* the historian Socrates of Rhodes, tells of her coming to Antony in Asia Minor, arranging for him and his officers a four-day banquet and symposium, each day more lavish than the last. All the ingenuity of Hollywood in recreating regal splendor never matched the tales of golden, jeweled vessels, precious weavings, sumptuous presents (a king's ransom of their very couches and the sideboards carried away by the guests), and a drift of roses upon the floor a foot and a half deep!

The prodigality of Cleopatra has fascinated later ages. The fame of one meal with Antony resonates in Pliny's work on natural history, is passed on to the Middle Ages and John of Salisbury by the Late Antique writer Macrobius, and is visualized by classicizing painters of the seventeenth and eighteenth centuries as well as by illustrators of books that narrate the story (fig. 80). Let us call it the "Feast of the Pearl" at which Cleopatra bet Antony (whom she loved to tease, judging from the story that she once stopped him only at the last moment from floating petals from his symposial crown in his wine—flowers she had caused to be poisoned as a practical joke on one who was careful to have every bit of food proved by a taster) that she could spend ten million sesterces on a single meal! [30] Disbelieving Antony lost the wager when she removed one of her earrings—a pair that Pliny called the largest pearls in the whole of history—dissolved it in a vessel of vinegar, [31] and drank

80. Cleopatra and the Pearl. *Woodcut from the 1483 edition of Boccaccio's* De claris mulieribus *("Of Famous Women")*

CLEOPATRA •ANTONIVS •

it down. She was stopped from doing the same with the second pearl, said to have been cut in two after her death to end up in the ears of the statue of Venus in Agrippa's Pantheon in Rome.

Before we turn to Roman gastronomy, let us reflect on what the Latin heirs of an international and universal world order created by Alexander encountered during the last three centuries B.C. Before the age of Empire initiated by Octavian (raised to "August[us]," thus assuring his succession in the East to the deified status of Greek Hellenistic kings), Rome itself was still a relatively small, homogeneous and provincial city compared with the polyglot megalopolitan centers whose elite cultures we have briefly considered above. Its transformation is our next concern.

6 Ancient Rome

"CROWNED WITH GARLANDS, bathed with essences, and clad in the convivial robe; the luxurious Roman reclining on his couch, partook of the brains of peacocks and pheasants, the tongues of nightingales, and the roes of the most delicious fish. The annals of the empire, are almost the annals of gluttony." These words from the culinary authority in Georgian England, Richard Warner,[1] may be enhanced for modern readers by powerful images from cinema. Fellini's *Satiricon* (1969) or the television rendering of Robert Graves' *I, Claudius* merely confirm a general consensus that the decline and fall of ancient Rome was brought about by indulgence in deadly sins, licentiousness and gourmandizing.

Our own guru in matters of cookery and gastronomy, M. F. K. Fisher—for all her knowledge and mastery in presenting her judgment—was not above making use of attitudes that may be traced back to early Christian ideologues. She writes, apropos the presumed difficulty of digestion in a reclining position (which was, after all, only for more or less formal occasions): "the Romans found the capacity of their sated stomachs infinitely enlarged [through use of emetics]. . . . Twice as much could be eaten! . . . *Vomitoria* came into being. . . . Their insides heaved too often. Quacks and honest physickers could not help. Rome grew dyspeptic."[2] Continuing, Fisher castigates the use of a fish sauce *(garum)* that we will deal with shortly, a condiment of undeservedly infamous reputation.

At this point, when we have looked at Hellenic traditions of gastronomy and the *grande cuisine* Romans inherited from Greek neighbors in southern Italy and Sicily, I hope that the reader will not be so quick to condemn Roman cuisine. I have orchestrated ancient dinners to which celebrants brought feathers for supposed authenticity, thinking of those putative vomitoria (which simply means "exits" in Latin and has no other architectural relevance, *pace* M. F. K. Fisher).[3] Everything Romans learned of gourmandizing came from Hellenic practice and Greek literature on gastronomy. Also, the Italian archaeologist Eugenia Salza Prina Ricotti—who has written one of the best books on Roman cookery—has made a scholarly specialty of studying Roman service quarters and kitchens.[4] She argues persuasively that the Campanian type of cooking "range" came about because people who early dwelt in cities like Pompeii and Herculaneum wished to emulate the refined cuisine of their Greek neighbors in Naples and to the South. One cannot produce fine sauces cooking over bright flames in large cauldrons; what was needed was a layer of glowing charcoal and various devices to control the position of a pot (see figs. 81, 82).

What irony for a people who truly believed in their divine mission to bring the benefits of their morality to the decadent fleshpots of the Hellenistic East, as well as to the unenlightened denizens of lands that classical civilization had never reached! Like Britons of the nineteenth century or Americans of the twentieth, Roman confidence in the justice of the imperious conquest of their world was predicated on the validity of their "family values" ruled by Concord and Piety, on their statecraft governed by law and jurisprudence (which are not the same), and on their superiority in civic virtue dominated by temperance and frugality.[5] The Romans' visions of themselves were shaped by nostalgic allegiance to such Republican ideals throughout the vast expanse and duration of an Empire brought into being by the military capacity to create and sustain Peace in their "new world order." Satire arose as a novel literary form in part because of that moral stance—not to mention the powerful role that food habits can play in matters political. Disaffected writers of the first and second centuries A.D., Stoics and Epicureans among them, contribute to the denigrating view of Roman cuisine and food consumption among early modern and contemporary judges. Juvenal, Martial, and Seneca above all, then authors who reflect political antipathy to "bad," self-indulgent emperors like Vitellius, Commodus, Elagabalus, all have fed the literature that demeans Roman culinary art.

81. TOP: *Pompeii, Kitchen of the Villa of the Mysteries, showing cooking "range" and rare small oven for baking cakes.*

BOTTOM: *Vaison, France, Kitchen of the House of the Messii. Compare the openings for large cauldrons or spits. (Photo by Elsbeth Dusenbery)*

For *art* it surely was.[6] Just as Roman city plans underlie most of the major cities of western Europe; just as, long after the demise of Empire, its roads and bridges, water supply, and science of agriculture fostered the well-being of dwellers in lands it had once conquered; so its modes of cookery endure in numerous dishes at which none of us look askance. Today's paella of the Iberian peninsula, the cassoulet of southern France and Perigord, the bouillabaisse or cioppino of the Mediterranean littoral, and the tian of Provence stand out among regional relics of Roman kitchen-craft. The very names affirm their ancestry etymologically even if many of these dishes have incorporated products from the New World like the tomato. The Roman *patella* has seen its median *t* drop out over the ages; *tian* is the Provençal remnant of one classical word for a frying pan, *teganum*.

It is not merely supposed debauchery or monstrous gluttony among the elite of the Empire that arouses negative estimates of Roman cookery. Ever

82.   *Pompeii, House of the Vettii, close view of the cooking surface with culinary equipment. The space beneath the cooking surface is for storing fuel.*

since it was called a "destructive cuisine" by an eighteenth-century aestheti-cian,[7] critics have seized upon every clue in Roman literature as well as reci-pes from the single surviving cookbook of antiquity — of which more anon — in order to uphold the opinion that Roman cuisine delighted in letting no original taste survive its ministrations without being transformed, masked, or incorporated in a radically different concoction.[8] It is true that Latin literature provides instances of cooks' ingenuity at culinary disguise. Two come to mind in comic context: Martial's Caecilius (*Epigrams*, bk. XI, xxxi) who could make gourds into every kind of dish from hors d'oeuvres to dessert so skillfully that you would think you were eating things like beans and lentils, or mushrooms, a tuna, blood sausage, even sweet cakes; Trimalchio's cook, whom he called Daedalus because he was such a wonder-worker (Petronius, *Satyricon*, LXX, 2), could make anything, from fish to game birds and fowl, out of parts of a pig.[9] Yet such *tours de force* make for perennial tales in the history of gastron-omy, equivalent to a Greek chef, Soterides in the second century B.C., meet-ing the desire of King Nicomedes of Bithynia for an anchovy in the midst of winter, far, far from the sea, by creating the satisfactory fish from a turnip![10] We will meet others in the Middle Ages and in more recent times.

Before arguing against many pejorative views of an alleged passion for disguise on the part of Roman cooks, let me first summarize what modern philological research makes of the precious recipe book mentioned above, setting out as well what we can establish about its author. The cookbook in question purports to be the work of one Marcus Gavius Apicius who lived at the time of Tiberius. With the discovery in the fifteenth century[11] of ninth-century manuscript copies of this work, a problem about the very name of its writer was initiated. Because the division of the title page of one manu-script (Vat. Urb. lat. 1146) abbreviates and breaks the lines of its majuscules thus: INC(I)P(IT)/API/CAE, humanists interpreted his name as Apitius Caelius. In this form it came down through many of the printed editions that began toward the end of the century, until the modern Teubner edition of 1922. Other scholars[12] worked out problems with a text that can scarcely be con-sidered the Latin of a contemporary of Tiberius, the famous gourmet Apicius, named as a symbol of high living by numerous later authors, both pagan and Christian.

There is now general agreement about *De re coquinaria* by the Apicius who lived in the early first century A.D. Possible allusion in titles of dishes to per-sonalities of the second or third century (Commodus, Elagabalus, et al.)[13]

aside, this cookbook must have been put together from various sources by some Late Antique compiler—the phenomenon is one with which we are all too familiar today. In the fourth or even early fifth century, striving to preserve gastronomic tradition, the compiler snobbishly labeled each of his ten books with up-scale Greek titles; plucked from Apicius' earlier works selections from a general book on cookery and another, more specialized, on sauces; incorporated parts of Hellenic handbooks on agriculture and dietetics; and published the whole under the cachet of Apician reputation for extravagant eating.

How Apicius gained this reputation comes down to us in many anecdotes. His credentials as a great trencherman are assured by Seneca's tale of his suicide. Discovering that he had spent a million sesterces on his kitchen, he took stock of his finances. When he found that his assets totaled ten million sesterces, he poisoned himself out of fear of no longer being able to dine in his accustomed fashion.[14] That Apicius was far from beggared in what he thought of as straitened circumstances, is clear when we consider that the average annual salary for a Roman soldier up through the second century A.D. was 900 sesterces.[15] Seneca marvels at the idea of someone doing away with himself when faced with a sum most people only dream about.

Apicius' fastidious taste, ingenuity of invention, and spendthrift excesses are related by sober scholars like the elder Pliny, while censorious Christian writers like Tertullian in the second century A.D. or Saint Jerome in the fourth still treat his name as a synonym for notorious gluttony.[16] We learn that he created a dish from the crests of living cocks; poultry parboiled before cleaning or plucking in order to seal in the full savor of fat and juices; mullet suffocated in a sauce (the costly *garum* we have yet to consider) "made of their fellows"—in a pun that names at the same time the "allies'" corporation that made the finest grade, as well as a fishpaste concocted of their livers; and a sort of on-the-hoof marinade when pigs were made to die in a state of sated ecstasy by a sudden ministration of wine sweetened with honey (*mulsum*, a Roman aperitif, as we will discover). The well-fed swine of Pliny's description illustrate a further Apician inspiration which enshrines his fame in the Italian language. Foie gras had long been known, thanks to Pompey's father-in-law, one of the Scipios, but Apicius not only refined the idea of engorged liver, but invented a method of fattening pigs on dried figs. The special flavor imparted to pork liver as a result of being "figged" (*ficatum*) ultimately came to be applied generically to all liver (*fegato* in Italian).

The story I like best in Apician literature concerns a "shaggy-dog" anecdote. At his summer home near Minturnae, our gourmand heard of extraordinarily large prawns—bigger than the local variety that rivaled even the lobsters of Alexandria—to be found off the coast of Lepcis in Libya. Straight away, heedless of the warnings of its captain about a great storm, Apicius hired a ship to take him to Africa. After days of peril from bad weather, he and the crew neared the Libyan coast and small native craft swarmed out to meet them. Their mission being explained, the largest crustaceans these vendors could muster merely raised contemptuous looks from Apicius. Without even putting ashore at the hard-won landfall, he commanded the captain to return to Minturnae.[17]

Another story concerns an unusually huge mullet brought to the Emperor Tiberius; it weighed four and a half Roman pounds. Wishing to test the ardor of conspicuous gourmets of the day, the ruler had it put up at auction in the market, where it fetched 5,000 sesterces, with Apicius as second bidder.[18]

We are able to meet Apicius more directly in *De re coquinaria* since so much of its advisories on sauces and a few recipes are specifically attributed through the name of the resulting dish: *Sala Cattabia Apicianum* (a sort of composite salad mold), *Patina Apiciana, Minutal Apicianum* (a fricasse of sorts, often created from leftovers, ancestor of medieval salmagundis), *Conchicla Apiciana* (apparently a pulse concoction, the ancestor of French cassoulets, rather than, as some would have it, a dish prepared or served in a specialized shell-like receptacle),[19] and *Ofellae Apicianae* (literally, "morsels," but in a chapter devoted to "gourmet" treats).[20] Let us look at some Apician prescriptions.

First let us consider a serious charge, the falsification and disguise of ingredients. Suggestions for "salsum sine salso" (salt-fish without salted fish) in book IX on seafood (cap. xiii, nos. 441–443)[21] are simply substitutes for a rather costly hors d'oeuvre, and no. 443, touted as an aid to digestion, surely comes from a dietetic/medical source rather than from Apicius. Number 441 will not surprise a modern hostess in its use of cooked, ground livers of hare, kid, lamb, or chicken seasoned with salt, pepper, and a bit of oil to mold into the form of a fish, extra virgin (hence green) olive oil sprinkled over it.

Probably the most egregious instance in Apicius' repertoire is an anchovy casserole without anchovies (bk. IV, ii, 12, no. 132).[22] For this, a mousse is made of cooked, minced fish, eggs, a little oil and fish-sauce seasoning called *liquamen*, with pepper and rue. Pressed into the pan, this is topped with a sea anemone (*urtica marina*, modern French *ortie de mer*, which some translate "jellyfish"), then gently steamed so as not to incorporate the topping into the underlying mixture, until the mousse is set and sea creature opaque. It is served sprinkled with more pepper. Apicius adds: "At table, no one will know what he is eating," and you may well feel, "a good thing, too!" But let us not forget comparable deceptions practiced in one of the greatest cuisines in the world: Chinese "mock duck" and a hundred other artful imitations created by Imperial chefs over the centuries to test their craft or to titilate Buddhist palates jaded by vegetarianism. Nor would that sea anemone or jellyfish faze any oriental diner or those of us willing to try anything once.

Several items in the recipe just cited testify to Apicius' *grand goût.* The elder Pliny, who died in retirement, a victim of Vesuvius in A.D. 79, tells us (*NH,* XII, chap. xiv) that pepper newly imported from India was becoming a popular seasoning in his day for those of refined (and costly) tastes. Early in the first century, when Apicius flourished, its use would mark an extravagant table; pepper appears in almost every one of the recipes which derive from his records.

Typical also is his specification of *liquamen.* Apicius never refers to ordinary *garum,* his fish sauce of preference being this more delicate variant, the name of which better reflects their process of manufacture: liquefaction. Post-Vietnam and with an influx of southeast Asians, few Americans can any longer shudder at what we have come to know and/or use as *nuoc-mam, nampla, patis,* or, once again citing superiority in aesthetics of savor, Chinese "fish gravy." For those in Great Britain to understand *garum/liquamen* takes only a moment's recollection of the anchovy sauce of Victorian tables or a glance at the ingredients in their Worcestershire — a long-term descendant of Roman occupation, it seems. *Allec,* the residue from its production, will be familiar in its modern form as *Patum Piperum, The Gentleman's Relish,* whether enjoyed as breakfast treat or as dinner savory.

No other ingredient of ancient Roman cookery has elicited more disdain, even revulsion, than this fish condiment used in lieu of salt for refined cuisine like that of our gourmet. Paeans of praise and gratitude for Neptune's gift — a familiar concept to anyone who learned in first-year Latin the startling fact that English "salary" derives from the Roman word for salt, reflecting its significance as army ration as well as spice of wit and life — were too basic to engage Apicius. *Liquamen* is his status seasoning; salt is the exception in genuine recipes.

We are able to look at *garum* a bit more objectively than M. F. K. Fisher, without her urge to dramatize what Pliny (*NH,* XXXI, xliii, 93) wrote about the way it was produced. "With hand over nose, and a piece of ice on tongue, look at *garum* [this is pure Fisher not Pliny, who calls it a choice liquor (*liquoris exquisiti genus)*] . . . Place in a vessel all the insides of fish . . . salt them well. Expose them to the air until they are completely putrid. In a short time a liquid is produced. Drain this off." Pliny is responsible for the blood and guts, assisted by what the *Geoponika* (a compendium of ancient agricultural and other advice, mostly Greek, assembled about A.D. 900) calls the best *garum — himation*, made by taking entrails of tuna fish and its gills, juice and blood, adding sufficient salt, and leaving it in a vessel for two months "at most."

But how misleading to state that those innards were to turn putrid! Precisely because so much salt was utilized to macerate entire fish, or larger ones cut up, they did not putrefy in vats exposed to the sun. Rather, they fermented and liquefied for two or three months (scarcely a "short time") until a clear fluid rose to the top, while the residue became the *allec* already mentioned. Processors added wine and/or herbs to the basic mixture, while different *officina* run by middle men continued to refine and season their own brands at sites in the Hellespont, on the coasts of Dalmatia, or in such cities as Pompeii (Fig. 83), Lepcis Magna in Africa, and Clazomenae in Asia Minor.

Of refined and seasoned fish sauces, Eugenia Salza Prina Ricotti illustrates a comparative table of ingredients for *oxyporum* and for Worcestershire. *Oxyporum:* vinegar, honey, *liquamen*, pepper, ginger, dates, cumin, rue; Worcestershire: vinegar, molasses, liquid from salting anchovies, red pepper, ginger, tamarind, onion, soy sauce, shallots, garlic.[23] *Hydrogarum, oleagarum, oxygarum* and *oenogarum* resulted from an admixture of water, oil, vinegar or wine respectively. *Garum piperatum* is self-explanatory as another ready-made seasoning.

Gargilius Martialis, about A.D. 240, gives a recipe for *oenogarum* repeated in a Carolingian manuscript.

> Take fat-fleshed fish (salmon, eel, shad, sardines) with dried herbs and salt. In a deep, solid vessel holding 26–35 liters, layer in the bottom very aromatic herbs, both cultivated and wild ones (dill, coriander, fennel, parsley, clary, rue, mint, lovage, pennyroyal, oregano, betony, agrimony, [etc.]. Next place a layer of salt two fingers deep. Keep filling the vessel in these alternate layers and cover closely with a lid. Leave for seven days untouched. Then for twenty consecutive days stir the mixture right down to the bottom. At the end of this period, gather the liquid that rises to the top.

In the ninth-century variant, the mixture is also subjected to reduction by boiling, and it is clear from archaeological evidence of *garum* factories at Lixus on the Mauretanian coast or Cotta in North Africa, for example (fig. 84), that heat played some role in concentration during production. Study of a dynasty of *garum* vendors at Pompeii would seem to indicate that "jobbers," like one Umbricius Scaurus and his family, treated the industrial product variously and put it up in small containers *(urcei)* for sale, carefully labeled.[24]

Such labels of Pompeian and other *urceorum* confirm what Pliny and many literary sources say about the finest grades of *garum* or *liquamen:* that mackerel made the type most sought after. An epigram by Martial affirms Pliny's exclamation that scarcely any other liquid save unguents and perfume were so highly valued as *garum:* "Receive this noble sauce made from the first blood of a mackerel, breathing still, an expensive gift" (XIII, 102). We have already met the same author's pun concerning *garum sociorum, garum* of the allies.[25] Manufactured in the fisheries of New Carthage on the east coast of Spain, this commanded the highest price. Near modern Cartagena (the ancient Carthago Nova) the modern city of Escombreras preserves the Latin name for mackerel *(scomber)* to remind us of the cartel—made up of men of equestrian rank holding hereditary rights—whose industry dominated an export trade.[26]

Few modern writers have a positive word to say about the taste of *garum,* though Mrs. Fisher disingenuously mentions *nuoc-mam.* In 1866, H. C. Coote[27] was willing to wonder what it tasted like and to cite several passages in Apicius which make it clear that *garum/liquamen* did not turn out brutally salty. The most revealing passage (*De re coquinaria,* IX, viii, 5, no. 429) directs one to infuse salted sea urchins in the best *liquamen* in order to make them taste just like fresh ones straight out of a holding-tank.[28] There is also the evidence of a non-Apician advisory (I, vi, no. 7) recommending a technique for treating *liquamen* that had become overly salty with age by adding a pint of honey and seasoning with pitch(?)[29] or, alternatively, using freshly pressed grape juice (must). Coote concluded that the flavor of the fish sauce was "a nuance that recalled to the jaded Roman the healthy ozonic [*sic*] air of the fresh and tonegiving seas of Baiae and Tarentum." He adds that we can comprehend how it gave spirit to food by reading Apicius bk. IV, ii, 25, no. 145, where a dish of spring onions with a centerpiece of raw salt fish is sprinkled with honey, a little vinegar, and boiled-down grape juice; "if it seems insipid, add [more] *liquamen.*"[30]

In any case, *garum* was not the invention of the Romans, but one more refinement taken over from the Greeks. Archaeological exploration of Mediterranean sites where the ancient industries of *salsamenta* produced salt

83. Establishment of a garum *processor, Pompeii.*

84. View of a Roman factory for fermenting garum, *Cotta, Algeria.*

fish, fish pickle *(muria)*, *garum*, and *allec* dates many of them long before Latin expansion. Besides, Athenaeus cites passages from Greek authors from the fifth century B.C. down to fourth- and third-century comic poets (II, 67c, from Aeschylus, Sophocles, Plato Comicus, et al.). One classical scholar goes so far as to argue that the Greek invention, using as Pliny records a fish called *garos* (otherwise not identified among Hellenic fishes), was carried by the Indian expedition of Alexander the Great into southeast Asia, the ancestor of *nuoc-mam* and cognates.[31]

Aside from disguise and the problem that some people still feel about *garum*, we may return to other charges against Apicius and thus against Roman cuisine in general. A perennial criticism from food writers is an alleged welter of ingredients of contrasting, self-defeating tastes. "Patina à la Apicius" (IV, ii, 14, no. 134)[32] has notably been derided as evidence of indiscriminate taste. Its directions are to take pieces of cooked sow's udder, of fish, of chicken, tiny fig-peckers *(beccafichi*, the tiny birds beloved of Italian and French cuisine which are eaten whole, ungutted, all but the beak and feet daintily set aside), cooked breasts of thrushes (some translate turtledoves), and "quaecumque optima fuerint." Taken as "any good thing that comes to mind," this behest means one thing—and some of the cooked ingredients could be leftovers—but the sense is profoundly altered if we translate "take any other thing that seems best [at the market, understood]." Then the recipe would simply be following recommended practice of our finest chefs, or any sensible cook in the home.

It is worth pursuing this *patina* because, in my interpretation of ancient forms of pasta *(tracta, laganum)*, it so resembles a rich lasagna, particularly Bolognese *lasagne imbottite* with its astounding variety of meats. All the above, except the minute fig-peckers, are to be chopped and cooked with an added sauce, itself composed of pepper and lovage ground in a mortar, moistened with *liquamen*, wine, and a reduced, sweetened raisin juice *(passum*, equivalent to modern Italian *sapa)* and heated to thicken with wheat starch *(amulum)*. Raw eggs are to be stirred into olive oil and used to bind the entire mixture and sauce. Next, in a special bronze saucepan (called *patella* at this juncture, indicating that *patina* is the more generic term) which was illustrated in the original document,[33] it is layered, enriched by whole peppercorns and pine nuts *(nuclei)*, added alternately with *laganum* (I translate fresh broad lasagna; Flower and Rosenbaum read "oil-cakes"), ending with the pasta pierced by a hollow reed straw and sprinkled with more pepper. Plainly, further cooking is implied by this last point, designed to distribute the sauce, and by the special pan. Worth adapting today with less of that novel pepper and replacing the oil/egg mixture with tomato sauce, a New World gift to us which ancient Romans lacked. The dish is especially good when you take whatever good thing you happen to enjoy.

One *patina* that is recommended in the cookbook might indeed make a purist shrink. It uses asparagus, a favorite vegetable among all Romans, whether gathered in the countryside or purchased as an expensive cultivated variety. Pliny (*NH*, XIX, xix, 54) railed against the luxury market of his day that developed products beyond the reach of ordinary purses; even vegetables like kale and asparagus were now grown too thick and large for a poor man's table, though asparagus had been something Nature allowed anyone to gather at random ". . . now we see artificial kinds and, at Ravenna, three stalks weigh a pound. What monstrous gluttony!" In the Apician recipe (bk. IV, ii, 6, no. 126),[34] you are to crush this spring delicacy in a mortar, add wine and pass it through a sieve. Next, into the mortar go pepper, lovage, fresh coriander, savory, onion, wine, *liquamen,* and oil. Combine purée and seasonings in an oiled shallow pan and break eggs over it on the fire to set the mixture. Serve with finely ground pepper sprinkled over the *patina.* If this seems like doing violence to one of the first fresh delights of spring, let us also remind ourselves that one Latin idiom for "quick as a wink" was "quicker than it takes to cook asparagus."

Sala Cattabia Apicianum (IV, i, 2, no. 118)[35] is a fairly complicated mold to be served cold, yet it is no more dependent on heady spices or a principle that food should taste like what it was not than many a modern hostess' one-dish treat for a summer buffet. Its name reflects the particular pan used *(catabus* or *caccabus)* and the fact that the mold might be chilled by packing it in salt, although Apicius recommends snow in keeping with his willingness to incur the expense of sending to the mountains for this indulgence.[36]

In a mortar combine celery-seed, dried pennyroyal, dried mint, ginger, fresh coriander, stoned raisins, honey, vinegar, oil and wine. Line a mold with pieces of Picentine bread [Pliny tells us of this specialty made of malted spelt grits and raisin juice] and arrange in alternating layers chicken meat, kid's *glandulas* [sweetbreads?],[37] Vestine cheese [a hard cheese from the vicinity of Rome], pine nuts, cucumbers, and finely chopped dried onions. Pour the dressing over the top and chill before serving.

Another recipe in the same chapter has the bread used to line the mold soaked in vinegared water, then squeezed out; still another specifies a hollowed-out loaf of "Alexandrian" bread with its soft part similarly soaked.

Fricassee à la Apicius (IV, iii, 3, no. 173)[38] is a *minutal* (a dish of cut-up pieces) composed of oil, *liquamen*, wine, bulb-leeks, mint, small fish, tiny meatballs, testicles of cocks, and *glandulas* of suckling pig. While it cooks, a sauce is made by crushing pepper, lovage, fresh coriander or its seed, and moistening this with *liquamen*, a little honey, and some of the cooking liquor. Following the general rule for a *minutal*, when the combined mixture boils up, *tracta* are broken into it to thicken (for some interpreters these are crumbled bits of pastry, for me they are noodles which we already encountered in Grecian cookery; recall that in Latin *trahere* means "to draw out"). This reaffirms a Roman taste for the combination of fish with meat and, of course, its cocks' testicles explain why the recipe bears the name of a gourmet. Yet we should not register too much surprise when contemporary modifications of *nouvelle cuisine* are not above unexpected marriages between or among parts of animals, birds, or fish and exotic vegetables.

Still another Apician composition in every sense of that word is a *conchicla* that bears his name (V, iv, 2, no. 203).[39]

> Take a clean earthenware saucepan to cook dried peas [by the usual method]; add various meats, including Lucanian sausage [a favorite type for which an earlier section of the cookbook gives a recipe], tiny pork meatballs, and a shoulder of pork [*petaso*, cured as ham]; crush pepper, lovage, oregano, dill, dried onion, fresh coriander and moisten with *liquamen*, then blend with wine and more *liquamen*. Add this to the saucepan and finally add olive oil, pricking the mixture all over so the oil is absorbed down into the peas.

Is this not equivalent to a cassoulet Toulousaine or Perigordienne with its beans incorporating preserved duck, different pork products, and what have you, right down to the "pricking" that seems to echo in the choice of many French cooks to break up the crust occasionally as the cassoulet cooks? Does any one of the seasonings offend your sense of taste?

It is probably Apicius' sauces that receive the most opprobrium, though many are quite simple. If a sauce intended to be served cold with boiled boar requires nineteen or so ingredients,[40] consider any respected sauce recommendation in, for example, *Larousse gastronomique.* It will not be difficult to find a good number with a multitude of ingredients if one counts every least addition down to the salt and pepper. Apicius simply enumerates without quantities and with very scant clues to procedure.

One sauce for roast meat (VII, v, 4, no. 274) [41] does take a modern reader aback. It specifies 6 scruples [one twenty-fourth of an ounce in a scruple; let's call it a pinch] each of pepper, lovage, parsley, celery-seed, dill, asafoetida root, hazelwort, galingale, caraway, cumin, and ginger, together with a *hemina* [one cup] of *garum*, 1/2 gill of oil, and a "modicum" of pyrethrum. Some of these herbs require a special sort of gardener friend nowadays, and pyrethrum, your old-fashioned pharmacist will inform you — if your inquisitive nose does not — is an important ingredient in many insect powders (because it *can* be ingested by pets and small children without ill effect). On the other hand, this particular contribution to *grand goût* does not even stem from Apicius. Its careful listing of quantities and a preponderance of rather sharp spices demonstrate that our Late Antique compiler of the Apician handbook copied this one from a Greek or Roman medical treatise on dietetics. We must forgive him, because recipes of the kind are one factor that assured survival of genuine Apician fragments which make up much of his manuscript. They served the needs of medieval monks who transcribed it in their search for prescriptions that might ensure good digestion, and they explain why subsequent editors of Apicius tended to be physicians. The latter include Hummelberg, editor of an edition printed in Basle in 1542, Jacques Dalechamp (Lyon, 1583), as well as Martin Lister, Queen Anne's doctor (London, 1705).

Rome-bashing is much more entertaining than attempting to discover the historical and sociological truth of Latin food systems and cooking. And ancient authors thought so, too. [42] That is the trouble. Gastronomic excess and jaded appetites were a more inviting topic for satiric poets than the harsh reality of old-fashioned, unadorned fare preferred by Stoics, influential men like Seneca, or Pliny and his nephew at the height of Imperial splendor. Seneca, with his intimate knowledge of elegant dinners given by the Emperor Nero in his "Golden House" where one dining room had a domed ceiling that appeared to turn in imitation of the heavens and constellations (fig. 85) [43], complains petulantly in a letter of the manner in which chefs serve up complicated mixtures that might as well be ready-chewed for the diner. [44] This is in keeping with his nostalgic recall of the dark, moldy bathing rooms of Republican worthies or the stinking kitchen areas in their villas. The younger Pliny, associate of the emperor Trajan and governor of one of his provinces, writes a

85. *Rome, Golden House of Nero. View of the great polygonal dining room, which had a celestial dome.*

86. *The last meal of Priests of the Isis Temple, Pompeii, A.D. 79, as preserved in the National Museum, Naples. Bread, nuts, dates, and lentils would also have made for a Roman middle-class supper.*

letter (I, 15) rebuking a friend who missed supper with him to dine elsewhere. He lists the pleasures of the table he had prepared: "a lettuce and three small snails apiece, with two eggs, olives, beets [meaning red chard], marrows and shallots" plus barley water and some sweet wine as beverages. Even if only the appetizers, there is nothing very extravagant about them and "a hundred of such dainties," although some pains and expense were taken to see that the wine was cooled by snow.

Pliny's *cena* is typical in its hors d'oeuvres. The Latin equivalent of our "soup to nuts" expressing in shorthand a dinner menu, translates as "from eggs to apples," underlining normal dessert courses (*secundae mensae* or *bellaria*) of fruit and/or nuts. There are practically no sweets in Apicius, merely an omelet (*ova melita*) of honeyed eggs; a kind of French toast served with honey; stoned dates filled with pine nuts, rolled in coarse salt and heated in honey (delicious if one toasts the *pignoli*, uses Kosher or canning salt and the rosemary honey the Romans favored); a few custards, and wheat dishes (bk. VII, cap. xiii).

We may reconstruct an analogous menu in its entirety by referring to a mosaic from an elegant Roman villa excavated in a suburb of Antioch in Syria (fig. 87).[45] Reading from the right we see the normal sequence of courses, in this case set out for an intimate dinner for two on silver platters of alternately round or rectangular shape; garlands and loaves of bread are ready to hand. The first course (*gustatio*) consists of eggs in their eggcups, accompanied by small spoons (*cochlearia*) and a little container for sauce, with two pig's feet — undoubtedly pickled — and what seem to be artichokes.[46] The entrées (*primae mensae*) follow: a fish, then ham on a round platter (*lanx*), and two further dishes that have been badly damaged, but at least one of them seems to have been of fowl. There may have been fruit in the lacuna, but the meal concludes with an elaborate dessert: a round layer cake of some type that may be better represented by a fresco from a first-century villa not far from Pompeii at what is probably ancient Oplontis (fig. 88). There is nothing in this repast, however elegant, to arouse opprobrious comments about gourmandizing — or even about multifarious ingredients overwhelming natural flavors.

How many people today recognize Roman vegetarian impulses represented by Pliny the Younger's menu? Who believes in the constraint of an Epicurean diet followed by so many upper-class citizens, vegetarians like the followers of Pythagoras, but for different reasons? The very name of Epicurus summons up visions of Greek love-feasts in the third century B.C. — open even

87. Antioch, Syria. Mosaic floor in the dining room of the House of the Banquet. Third century A.D. (See also fig. 65)

to women and slaves and wrongly taken to belie the foundations of his philosophy. Through one of his most famous disciples, Lucretius (ca. 99–55 B.C., author of *De rerum natura*), he taught the Romans that there was no afterlife; that one must positively cultivate the senses to relish life on this earth, but that true pleasure derives from the savoring of it, from restraint and temperance in all things, from acceptance even of pain in order to win tranquillity of soul — to put Epicurean tenets in a simplistic nutshell. The skeleton at Trimalchio's banquet in Petronius' *Satyricon* reflects the Epicurean practice of reminding diners to relish their least significant daily pleasures, for death awaits (see fig. 89).[47] But nothing else about that most famous of literary dinners has anything to do with usual Roman practice.

Petronius' novel is a satirical thrust at nouveaux-riches freedmen, that is, ex-slaves, who had enriched themselves by clever entrepreneurial feats in the marketplace that would be demeaning to patricians. It pokes fun at Trimalchio's lack of true sophistication in matters of food and wine, at the debauched atmosphere and gross tastelessness of presentations for show, and the host's comments on their cost: a roast hare outfitted with wings to masquerade as Pegasus, a punning Zodiacal offering of tidbits,[48] and a wild sow stuffed with living thrushes. Trimalchio brags of his wine, of the famous vintage when Opimius was consul in 121 B.C. The Romans did date their vintages by consular years, but we know, as did every contemporary of Petronius almost two hundred years later, that the Opimian was no longer drinkable even if diluted with water; Pliny (XIV, vi, 55) says the surviving few were reduced to the consistency of honey with a rough flavor of overripeness predominating to the point of bitterness, though they could be used to season other wines in small quantities. Trimalchio's boast is one more know-nothing gaffe of a would-be oenophile showing off the cost of his cellar.[49]

88. Detail of a fresco, Villa at Oplontis (Torre Annunziata). The dessert torte on its tray helps restore the final course of the Antioch mosaic, although it is decorated with less fruit.

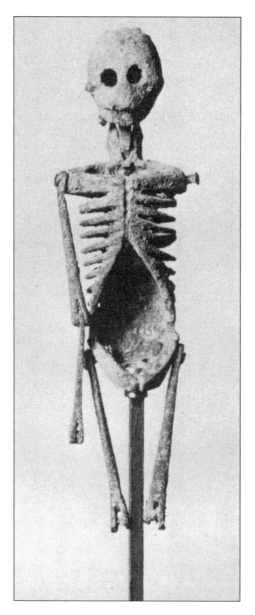

89. Larva convivialis. *Roman bronze miniature skeleton as a banquet memento mori. Dresden Museum*

Outside of satirical literature or political propaganda, forget Apicius' flamingo tongues or heels of camels, and equally outrageous delicacies favored by that mad "sun-god" emperor, Heliogabalus, or, again, Vitellius' special compote of rare aliments from every part of the Empire.[50] That emperor, so briefly triumphant among contenders for rule after the death of Nero in

A.D. 68, is said to have beggared anyone whom he honored by his command presence at a feast that could not cost less than 400,000 sesterces — and he could attend three of these gargantuan meals a day, taking emetics to do justice to the fare. Here is one source for the misapprehension that induced vomiting was common practice!

Chance has preserved for us the menu for a formal *epulum,* the type of official banquet given at the time of a priestly inauguration attended by Caesar in the period 71–63 B.C.[51] For the appetizer course *(gustatio)* are proffered: sea urchins, oysters, and two other kinds of mollusk, a thrush on asparagus, black and white chestnuts, a fatted hen, and an oyster-mussel ragout.[52] Entrées fall into three categories: shellfish and other marine creatures including various types of mollusk; purple murex fish garnished with fig-peckers and a fattened bird wrapped in pastry; and a game course consisting of more fig-peckers, roast loins of doe, and a game pie. The main course features roast game, hares, duck, boiled teal, a boar's jowl, a fricassee of fish and one of sow's udder, udders served alone, a meal pudding and Picentine bread. When one considers that only one large meal a day was eaten, at noon in the country or in late afternoon/evening for city-dwellers, as well as the fact that guests selected from such a wide variety of choices offered simultaneously in *fercula* ("courses," literally "bearings," the same word used for the litters on which prisoners and booty were borne in triumphal processions), the elegance and range of these dishes in a formal *convivium* is far from overwhelming. Our Victorian ancestors would scarcely raise an eyebrow.

No dessert course is recorded, and the literary evidence from all antiquity hardly hints at excesses in this sphere to compare with Carême's architectural creations or elaborate confections which crowned banquets in the nineteenth century. Caesar's contemporary, Cicero, was able to view such *convivia* as more worthy of esteem than Greek symposia on which Roman after-dinner serious drinking and conversation was modeled. To his perception,[53] Roman practice was more civilized in combining food and drink instead of indulging in pure drinking contests. His judgment was to bear fruit among later Renaissance Ciceronians, humanists who would enthusiastically revive his concept of conviviality in their intellectual sodalities.

In the annals of Roman gastronomy there appears one meal that rivals the dinner of Trimalchio for *parvenu* ostentation. At the same time it helps us learn that the aesthetic encountered in Archestratos and Greek gourmet tradition, with its emphasis on care taken in the selection, geographic and otherwise, of each ingredient, still ruled among a Latin elite whom the host wished to emulate. I speak of Horace's Satire II, viii, a poem setting out the *cena* of Nasidienus and what at first reading might seem the equivalent of Apicius' sensitivity of palate in the latter's concern for the manner in which mullets, pigs, and other creatures had been bred or put to death. But that is precisely the comic aspect of a "ludicrous meal" that established a formula to echo down through European literary history.

Nasidienus' meal is ridiculous just because this upstart is trying to impress the wealthy patron of Horace, Maecenas, who joins his five other guests and has brought two of his "parasites" (hangers-on for favors). Through every course, each dish is accompanied by a commentary that parodies true refinement of taste and enhances the vulgarity of touting its expensiveness (all recounted by one of Horace's friends who was present). The *gustatio* centers on an entire cold roast boar, a signal item of conspicuous consumption in a period of Augustan relative sobriety.[54] But what the new-rich amphitryon prides himself on is that the boar from Lucania was caught when a gentle south wind was blowing, while the apples that soon follow were picked on the waning of the moon. The wine he offers comes from far-off Chios, of such quality that seawater did not need to be added as usual for tang, also prized Caecuban from the marshes of Campania, yet Nasidienus asks Maecenas if he would prefer from his cellar an Alban or Falernian (the latter highly regarded and so rich in alcohol that Pliny says it could be lit with a spark). The fish course next displays even more fake-sophisticate *goût:* a lamprey swimming as if alive in a great circular platter, surrounded by *scampi,* in a sea of sauce incorporating the finest, extra-virgin olive oil, roe from that special mackerel of Spanish *garum* fame, Italian wine aged for five years, white pepper, and vinegar from the fermentation of Lesbian wine. The lamprey was caught pregnant, just before spawning; just after, Nasidienus explains, it would not be the same quality at all. The second course, following a comic disaster worthy of a Marx-brothers film, presents meat servings of massed delicacies such as foie gras, legs of crane, fore-rack of hare, blackbirds cooked rare with only their breasts seared, and breast of squab—all with copious commentary.

What is the societal context that makes this dinner party the archetype for a literary *topos,* the ridiculous meal? Maecenas' shadows (*umbrae*), who are dismayed at the small size of their wine cups, prefigure those who will eat a meal in medieval literature that is patently above their station in life. The pretensions of Nasidienus are dramatically revealed when, in the midst of dinner, the regal purple hangings fall down and shower everything with dust as the majordomo breaks quantities of glassware. The order of the conviviasts on the

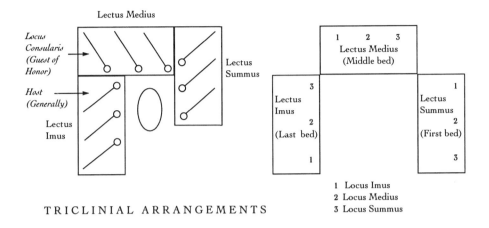

TRICLINIAL ARRANGEMENTS

Lectus Medius

Locus Consularis (Guest of Honor)

Host (Generally)

Lectus Imus

Lectus Summus

1 2 3
Lectus Medius
(Middle bed)

3
Lectus Imus
2
(Last bed)
1

1
Lectus Summus
2
(First bed)
3

1 Locus Imus
2 Locus Medius
3 Locus Summus

90.   *Diagram of the prescribed order of couches in a Roman triclinium.*

triclinial couches does not follow normal protocol (figs. 90 and 91). But more than all these abnormalities, one has to comprehend the historical background and hierarchic organization of Roman life. What we have already scanned shows how potent excess in dining could be as a political or social symbol, but there is much more to the story of Latin absorption of Greek ways. There is need, too, to understand class differences that grew ever more categorical in almost a thousand years of Roman history from the expulsion of its Etruscan kings in 509 B.C. to the fall of the Western Empire to Odoacer in A.D. 476.

Originally, the soldierly pastoralists who came to dominate their neighbors had a very simple diet. Farinaceous and leguminous, it was to continue throughout Roman history as basic nutrition for the lower classes, although country-dwellers could gather wild greens and fruits in season as well as grow root vegetables and *holera* (pot herbs) in their garden plots. The earliest grains in use consisted of hulled varieties that had to be roasted to break down encasing glumes and free the heads of barley, spelt, einkorn and emmer wheat. Happily, such a process guarantees the presence of carbonized grains in excavations like those which have revealed Iron Age burials in the Roman Forum. There one can read the contents of funeral meals buried with its primitive hut-dwellers.[55] None of the cereals identified would make good bread — especially without leaven — so it is not surprising that the ancestral "staff of life" was porridge, *puls* — made of barley or *far* (emmer) or, again, spelt grits — subsequently called *alica,* to become as nostalgically political a symbol as apple pie is for Americans who wish to summon up the good old days. Time has substituted New World maize for *polenta,* which meant hulled barley in ancient Latin. The sacral significance of all these gifts of Ceres is highlighted by one Latin legal term for marriage: *confarreatio,* a rite in which each partner sprinkled farro (our current fad in Tuscan-inspired cookery).

The transformation from a simple subsistence agriculture was not fully realized until the third century B.C. The austerity of their diet was a positive boon to soldiers of the Republic who, like Cincinnatus, left the plow to follow the leaders who conquered first Italy and eventually their entire world. As we were reminded in the dreadful tragedy of a defeated British army at the beginning of World War II, trying to win its way to safety in India through Burma, pursued by Japanese who knew how to forage things to cook with a ration of rice carried in their packs, Roman military might gained from each soldier's ability to cook up in his helmet his ration of *far,* extended by whatever serendipitous extra fell into his hands. Each had his basic homespun diet at hand "just like home" in contrast to Brits starving in the midst of jungle

91.   *Triclinium in the House of Julia Felix, Pompeii. This photograph shows a dining area with background step-fountain installed after the house was made over into a semipublic meeting establishment.*

plenty, not being trained to exploit it and dreaming only of beef and Yorkshire pudding.

THE POLITICAL AND SOCIAL FRAME

The potency of gastronomy as a sociopolitical metaphor reflects certain tensions in Roman society that we can begin to document from the early second century B.C. Conflict between a conservative pride in native agrarian roots and attitudes open to new, even foreign, modes of living and thought invests ideals of social harmony and political control that took hold throughout the expansion and duration of Roman power. If it went back far enough in time, a once-detested culture could be made acceptable to even the most diehard traditionalists. Roman Republican patricians sent their boys off to Etruscan mentors for schooling in manners and matters of empowerment, and Maecenas boasted of his Etruscan forebears (forget Tarquin and Lucretia and the expulsion of Rome's Etruscan overlords in 509 B.C., it was like coming over in the Mayflower).

In fact, tension starts to build in the third century B.C., as subsistence farming decays and Rome brings Magna Graecia under its sway. It erupts vividly with reaction to the sack of Syracuse in 212 B.C. Watching a rich booty of elegant bronze statues coming to replace native baked clay images that seemed rude in comparison, Cato the Censor (239–149 B.C.) bemoaned this invasion of Hellenic artistry and taste: "the vanquished have conquered us, not we them," a sentiment echoed by the poet Horace about two centuries later.[56] Sicily and South Italy, as we have seen, represented one of the gastronomic flesh-pots of Hellenic culture. Cato would have appreciated the American World War I refrain: "How're you goin' to keep them down on the farm after they've seen Paree?"

Cato—whose name Marcus Porcius ("porky") reflects the geoponic pride of Republican aristocrats who took names of gens or family from agricultural products (for example, the Pisones, peas; the Fabii, beans; or Lentulus, lentil, the augur of Caesar's day)—could not stand those Greek philosophers becoming active at Rome, reserving a particular hatred for Hellenic physicians and their newfangled medicine that was replacing good old Roman home remedies. Yet he seems not to have been averse to foreign influences if these did not represent subversion of traditional frugality, sobriety, and care for the land. His major work, *De re agricultura,* on agriculture and farm management, parallels that of Mago the Carthaginian, which the Roman Senate considered to be so authoritative they ordered the work translated after the conquest of Carthage in 146 B.C.[57]

In 202 B.C., Cato, the author who, in the estimate of contemporary critics, first gave authentic Latin voice to prose, encountered the first Latin poet of note, Quintus Ennius (239–169 B.C.), when both were serving in Sardinia.[58] They became fast friends, and Cato sponsored Ennius to settle in Rome. Despite his opposition to the ways of the Greeks, Cato seems to have set up Ennius—born in Oscan territory in Hellenized Apulia and thus trilingual—as a translator of Greek plays and teacher of the language; he even studied it himself according to Plutarch (perhaps the better to counter those medical "quacks" and philosophers). Soon Ennius, writing an epic sequel to Homer that traced the arrival of Aeneas in Italy with subsequent events up to his own day, won the affection of the Scipios and, equally, of M. Fulvius Nobilior, who took him off to campaigns in Aetolia circa 189 B.C. as poet annalist of this general's heroic deeds.

Ennius' friendship with his benefactor, Cato, waned however. By writing a parodic imitation of Archestratos' great verse advisory on gastronomic delicacies, Ennius flaunted his upbringing in the South of Magna Graecia and engaged in activity that could be seen as furthering Hellenic excesses in luxurious dining. Unhappily, his *Hedyphagetica* ("Fine Eating") reaches us solely by reputation and in one quoted fragment,[59] and the same is true of his *Satires*, which also in part dwelt upon dining themes, or his comedies, which surely did not avoid Greek conventions of the cook as signal comic character.[60] Together with C. Lucilius (born ca. 180 B.C.), a contemporary satirist, he created a poetic satire tradition that would come to influence an entire body of early Empire work by authors using foodways to attack the foibles of society in their era: the satires of Horace, Persius, and Juvenal, for example, which are such a precious source of information on eating, menus, and social mores.[61]

For the Roman historian Livy, it was a scandal of 186 B.C. that marked the full flood of Hellenic luxury and dissipation to corrupt Latin morality. In Bacchanalian cult observance, chaste Roman matrons and others reached such an intolerable level of participation in divine frenzy that the Senate was forced to enact a ban on imported rites of Dionysos, the Greek version of their own more estimable god of fertility and wine, Liber Pater.[62] To combat cosmopolitan threats to the political ideal, the Senate promulgated a series of sumptuary laws in the course of the second and first centuries B.C. designed to limit the number of participants at private dinners, how much one might spend for such parties, or to forbid serving exotic creatures such as ostriches or parrots imported from Africa (in one instance, even dormice, which were often fattened at home in *gliaria* (fig. 92).[63]

None of this seems to have done much to moderate a flow of alien delicacies and new cultural values inspired by late Republican conquests of lands once held by either Carthaginians or Greeks. A potent sign of changes in the economy of Italy herself lies in a remark in Pliny (*NH*, XVIII, xxviii, 107) that there were no public bakeries (figs. 93, 94) in Rome before the war against Perseus in Macedonia (171–168 B.C.). This marks the transformation from simple home baking in ashes on a hearth by a basically rural population to the need to serve the burgeoning proletariat of the capital, urban folk living in multilevel apartment houses without anything more than a brazier on which to cook.[64] Landowners realized that, despite the risk of bad harvests, rewards could be great if one added vines to produce more wine than they needed to serve a growing city clientele who appreciated fine vintages.

Entrepreneurs arose to satisfy increasingly sophisticated tastes of those who would indulge themselves, if they were not tied by politics and philosophy to reactionary precepts that harked back to puritanical lifestyles of patrician ancestors.[65] We learn of C. Sergius Orata (whose cognomen came from his favored fish, golden bream, *aurata*) making a fortune because he began seeding oysters (fig. 95) at the sea resort of Baiae around 108 B.C., and he enhanced the value of his real estate at the Lucrine Lake by constructing *piscinae* to cultivate exotic fish for snobbish Republican palates.[66] Comparably, a prefect of Rome, L. Licinius Murenae, won his cognomen by raising lam-

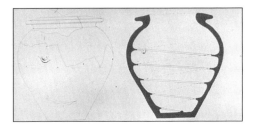

92.   *Vessel for raising dormice. Rome, National Museum*

preys *(murenae)*, at his country estate and introducing the delicacy to the city.[67] We have already realized through an Apician anecdote how expensive this passion for seafood could be. Roman literature is rich in tales of famously high prices paid for a prize catch and Diocletian's price edicts at the beginning of the fourth century reveal fish as more costly than the Roman favorite meat, pork.[68]

It appears that by the late Republic, if their social decorum did not allow for crass money-making, nevertheless many patricians were exploiting the possibilities of nurturing seafood and rare birds for the tables of connoisseurs. As with Varro's aviary, they might combine pleasure with profit in the process of self-indulgence in the delights of nature (which Romans always preferred cultivated, displaying the hand of man, rather than threateningly wild and untended).[69] Varro describes his *plein-air* dining retreat, its resident ducks, and

93.   Funerary Monument of Eurysaces, the baker, near the Porta Maggiore, Rome. First century B.C. The frieze represents the progress of work in his bakery, while the entire structure imitates the ovens.

94.   Seventeenth-century drawing after a Roman relief of a bakery (pistrinum). *The relief is in Bologna, Museo civico archeologico*

the clever bird "theater" that allowed one to enjoy their songs while consuming their companions.[70] This was more successful than a more ambitious project of Lucullus, and foreshadows one outdoor dining spot at the Younger Pliny's famous Tusculan villa where a stream floated dainties to the hand of a diner.[71]

The degree of self-indulgence by a sober military leader like Lucullus (ca. 106–56 B.C.) has brought enduring fame. His name comes down to us proverbially to epitomize voluptuous dissipation at table. As a general in far-off Pontic regions beyond the Black Sea he had been the very incarnation of old Roman frugality and disciplined lifestyle, keeping his troops in the field during harsh winters rather than permitting them the relative luxury of seasonal quarters in some populated venue. Upon return to Italy, however, bringing

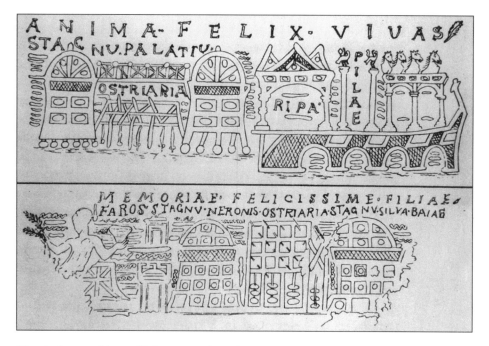

95. *An Oyster-seeding establishment, at a shore where fresh water meets the sea. Drawing after the decoration on a glass ampulla in the Corning Museum of Glass. After Brothwell,* Food in Antiquity.

96. Sea Creatures.
*Mosaic from Pompeii.
Naples, National Museum*

with him the cultivation of cherries from the Pontus,[72] his values appear to have been completely altered by the time he spent in the East and the wealth he amassed there. Contemporaries thought his estates (plural) more likely to be swept rather than hoed (i.e., endowed with marble pavement rather than soil to cultivate). His dining triclinia were so numerous that a secret code informed his chefs of the amount that might be spent for an evening's hospitality. His enemy, Pompey, and Cicero, with more traditional values, are said to have met him by chance one day, demanding that he invite them to partake of "pot luck" without giving notice to the cooks. They wished to discover whether he sustained his renowned opulence when dining alone,[73] and if he could truly keep to Sulla's sumptuary law then in force. They were astounded by the viands set before them when Lucullus employed the subterfuge of telling his majordomo: "we will use the Apollo dining room," code for a stunning amount to be expended. Whatever his indulgences, we should all thank him for acclimatizing cherries so that Roman horticultural gifts could develop their cultivation in a wide realm of Roman hegemony — and ultimately beyond to North American shores.

People of rank, without losing "face," might well turn their hands to a theoretical and philosophical side of the new interest in cookery as an art rather than as service industry, to paraphrase Livy *(ars* versus *ministratio).*[74] A few stand out in the literature, cited by the elder Pliny for developing fresh varieties of fruits or vegetables as well as improving a species and the methods of utilizing it. Take, for example, a friend of Caesar and the young Octavian (later Augustus), Gaius Matius. Of equestrian rank, he turns up in Columella and Pliny[75] as the inventor of topiary pruning of arbors, a specialist at grafting fruit trees, and author of three recipe books: *The Cook; The Preparer of Seafood;* and *The Maker of Pickled Foods.* He appears to have been a sort of equivalent to Martha Stewart at the end of the Republic, publishing advice on how to entertain elegantly without violating heredity or good manners. Apicius includes a pork and meatball casserole with noodles — *tracta* — that uses the "Matian apples" which took their name from his horticultural acumen.

The conflicted absorption of foreign ways during the late Republic, as well as contact with a multitude of "others" over hundreds of years of Imperial domination, helps us understand why food habits became for Romans such a political symbol and metaphor to be used in public discourse. It certainly helped Octavian's cause in the civil war against Mark Antony that the latter could be pictured as violating every Latin behavioral code — not by dallying in Egypt with Cleopatra necessarily, for Caesar had also been captivated by her, but by gross indulgence in wasteful gluttony and impious conduct. With his companions he had celebrated himself as a new Dionysos in a drunken brawl at the god's theater in Athens. Stories of profligate living multiplied to shock people back home: Cleopatra's trick of dissolving a costly pearl in her wine (fig. 80); or eight entire boars being roasted in preparation for their dinner, just so *one* of them would be done to Antony's taste when they decided to eat.[76]

Yet there is much more to the societal situation of Rome than this underlying dichotomy between conservative ancestral values and multicultural embrace of changing patterns of life, or, for that matter, than the opposition between high culture and what we might term the vernacular. Alimentary models are extraordinarily difficult to construct for ancient Rome without myriad qualifications. In the course of the Empire, food habits probably became even more varied than in melting-pot America which now appreciates unfamiliar ingredients from all over the globe and decries former tentatives in "ethnic" foods like chop suey or run-of-the-mill spaghetti sauce. We have seen how the Roman rhetoric of power adopted an ideal of frugality and restraint in matters of conduct. It tended also to proclaim an egalitarian doctrine in matters of state or ritual. *Noblesse oblige* on the part of the elite, in addition to the state dole of grain, oil, sometimes meat, to deserving households, made for distribution of special bounty to everyone on the occasion of festal days, religious games *(ludi)*, or notable events in the career of a leader (fig. 97).[77]

Thus the urban proletariat enjoyed many an opportunity to escape the usual lack of variety and artistry in diet. City-dwellers' regular fare was based on a *bollito* prepared on a brazier—the *puls* we have already met, of grains or pod legumes that echo down in our own word for them, pulses. They could spice up the contents of the pot with that old allium trinity, leek–onion–garlic, and other vegetables in season, and also run out to a local cook-shop to pick up a bit of sausage or salt fish. Background color in a series of detective novels by Lindsey Davis, set in Flavian times and starring an impecunious private eye named Marcus Didius Falco, gives a well-researched idea of ancient fast food and "takeout" that seems his habitual fare (figs. 98, 99). All sorts of sweets and snacks such as roasted chickpeas were also hawked by street vendors.

The variety and complexity of economic and social conditions that qualified nourishment in Rome informed mandates of healthful living for the privileged who followed theories first framed by Hippocrates, then developed by Hellenistic sages such as Erasistratos. These sought to establish that you are

97.   Often published under the title, A Bakery Shop, *this fresco recently has been interpreted as representing the distribution of the bread dole* (annona). *Fresco from Pompeii, Naples Museum*

what you eat (without aid of our growing knowledge of the role of nutrition in brain chemistry, or, indeed, awareness that the brain is the seat of nervous functions).[78] The physician Galenus of Pergamon wrote in the second century A.D. a fundamental treatise on medicine and diet that would prove the authoritative guide for medieval and Renaissance health professionals. As we shall see, his work provided during the Middle Ages a schema for ordering a human organism in concert with the entire natural world and cosmos.[79] Galen, receiving from earlier Greeks a doctrine of bodily humors equated with four qualities and four primary elements of creation, expanded the concept of allied human dispositions. To his four primary temperaments (sanguine, phlegmatic, choleric, and melancholic), corresponding with earth, water, fire, and air, he admitted composites which could at the same time

98. Thermopolium, *or take-out shop. Ostia, second century* A.D. *The counter at the entrance has an arched reservoir for water, offered for hand-washing.*

combine dry with either warm or cold, moist with either hot or cold, and similar gradations. He conceived as well a notion of a temperament that fitted no norm, an "idiosyncratic" disposition peculiar to one individual.[80] The selection of proper ingredients of diet to counter one's proclivities or illness became increasingly vexed.

Despite the myth of equality among citizens, and clearly marked paths of upward mobility, Roman society was organized in a hierarchic system of clan and class, from slave or freedman and plebeian, to knight of the equestrian order and the senatorial elite. Inevitably, structures of cuisine and convivial dining reflect the same social distinctions, if we exclude an entire free-floating class of *liberti*. These freedmen, since they were able to engage in commercial activities to a degree that would be demeaning to most patricians, were often exceedingly wealthy and given to conspicuous consumption, like Tri-malchio of the famous Petronian banquet or, in real life, the brothers Vettii, who owned one of the most elaborate houses in Pompeii (fig. 82).

We have already met many examples of food used as a marker of status. A rich Latin literature uses dining and cookery as analogy and metaphor to open our vision to an intricate network of social obligations: entertainment demanding reciprocity; sharing and hospitality that may highlight either friendship or subjugation; extravagant spectacle countered by virtuous frugality and abstemiousness.[81] Formal public *epulae*, meals shared with a divinity in his or her temple, or state sacrifice had to maintain an illusion of equality, though portions were actually distributed with careful attention to rank.[82] On the other hand, in civic and trade associations ("colleges"), as well as societies of initiates in mystery religions such as those of Dionysos/Bacchus, Isis, or the

99. *Take-out counter for hot and cold foods, a thermopolium in course of excavation. Pompeii*

Persian sun-god Mithras, any departure from fraternal fair shares — among the human participants at least — might solely involve ritual status, officiating priest(s), perhaps compared with congregants. Even so, most adherents probably belonged to relatively the same class.

It was the Christians, from the late first century proselytizing among the underprivileged, who truly embraced an egalitarianism that had only occasionally flourished in the past, as with Epicurus three centuries earlier. For Christians, imagery of a banquet, ambiguously blending the funeral meal of pagan tradition with the celestial feast to come, replicated a sacrament of the eucharist in which they could share the body of Christ in bread and wine, modeling how gentiles mystically partook of their god of wine, fertility, and afterlife.

The patronage system *(clientela)* by which aristocratic Romans, in assuring their own political power, dispensed favor, economic support, and sustenance to as many clients as they could afford, engendered caustic passages in Latin satire. These picture for us a subservient aspect in hospitality. Juvenal (Satire v) expresses the abasement of Trebius, a parasite — ignominious descendant of the Greek *para sitos* standing as witness at an altar of sacrifice or serving the *polis* in the prytaneion — at a dinner party of a mean host. As each dish appears, he contrasts what Virro is served to its pale imitation plunked down before the client: a measly shrimp versus a lobster, to mention only one. It was quite polite to take extra food home in one's napkin *(mappa)*, but in this case what food! moldy coarse bread? oil that might as well be left over from lamps, suspect fungi (instead of truffles), and other disappointments served on a minuscule crust instead of the bread trenchers often used by Romans as plates.[83]

When it came to the Emperor, of course, inequality was a given, and someone like detested Domitian might humiliate or even terrify senators with impunity. I think of Dio Cassius' tale of his Black Banquet on a funereal theme with grave stelae as "place cards," abominable foods of ebony hue served by blackened youths to mournful music, and his guests' fears that they were to be added to the ruler's murder victims when sent home with escorts from the imperial household rather than their own servants.[84]

Another aspect of an emperor's feasts opened a gulf between an increasingly exalted host and participants who became an audience and were invited to be overwhelmed by spectacles rivaling those of Hellenistic kings. It was the custom, following dictates of hospitality and largesse, to send baskets of food *(sportula)* home with guests or to distribute them widely at special festivals in seeming lack of regard to social distinctions, thus preserving that myth of equality which makes *hospes* in Latin able to designate either host or guest. But these actually held lesser viands for less important citizens.

From Greeks and Etruscans who taught them to recline at formal affairs, the Romans had developed their concept of the perfect private *convivium* using three couches, or *klinai,* in a prescribed arrangement, three diners to a couch according to rank (fig. 90). Hence the name of one or more formal dining rooms in the upper-class *domus* and villa: *triclinium.* The scheme mirrors Varro's witticism: "dine with at least the [three] Graces, or, at most, the [nine] Muses." Intent upon preserving a triclinial, three-couch ideal, Imperial architects developed cunningly differentiated dining spaces that could multiply the basic unit many times over. Apsidal dining areas of Hadrian's Villa at Tivoli announce elaborate designs of later antiquity, brought about by a gradual rise of court ritual and awe-inspiring majesty surrounding the person of the emperor. Responding to semicircular spaces like that of the main fountain apse of the Canopus at Tivoli, arcuate, *sigma* (C-shaped as the S in late Greek writing) couches came largely to replace the three-couch arrangement.[85] Guests reclining in a series of triconch apses, increasingly remote from the head apse, such as those at the Lausa Palace in Constantinople, must have felt demoted to the position of spectators "in the audience," so to speak. Although they did feast, their situation presages masses of invited lookers-on who would not dine, but stand and observe ceremonial dinners of the future hosted by European rulers.

Outside of the capital and environs, in other parts of Italy and in more distant provinces less guidance exists to the social dialogue in regard to food habits. We know of the Roman passion for *otium,* leisure and relaxation pursued in villa and country estate where careful management could contribute to gastronomy without bringing scorn for one's gluttony. On great farm holdings *(latifundia)* life must not have been very different from that on pre–Civil War plantations in our Deep South; the diet at least was comparable. Every part of the pig but the squeal was favored, because cattle were too important for motive power—the ox who shares your labor in the field is not to be eaten[86]—while sheep and goats were valued for wool, hair, and milk. The meat of swine had an additional advantage which made it *the* animal protein of choice, since its flesh preserved best in the meat safe *(carnarium)* where butcher's products smoked over the kitchen hearth (fig. 100). Lamb seems to have been second in preference; because ewe's milk was considered best and most nutritious, nursing offspring were culled early.[87]

100. *Relief of a pork butcher. Third century A.D. Villa Albani, Rome. The background inscription speaks of his meat as "always fresh or juicy," ebria being the Latin from which we derive our "inebriated." Note the variety of cuts and innards.*

Other similarities to southern plantations abound in vegetables and methods of cooking them. For keeping qualities, root vegetables and their greens, both cultivated and wild, are high on the list — especially turnips and beets, that is, red and white chard, to which *beta* generally refers in Latin, not our large globular roots developed in later centuries. A particularly striking comparison resides in mustard or turnip greens cooked with bacon and dressed with vinegar, as well as a kind of black-eyed pea, regular peas, and beans.[88] But what was the relationship of landowner to neighbors of differing backgrounds and class? to his farm manager? to surrounding natives? to local administrators for the state?[89] Latter-day patricians in Roman Gaul exhibited a generalized sort of racism in looking down upon the Gallic love for the three B's: butter, beer, and bacon (perennial appreciation for the hams of Gaul and Belgium as opposed to more heavily salted Italian products notwithstanding).[90]

Concerning the slaves' lot we are better informed, at least for the late Republic and early Empire. Agricultural writers such as Cato, Varro, and Columella tell of the distasteful diet of slaves on those estates requiring their labor. Their wine *(lora)*, which lasted only three months from the time of vintage, was obtained by soaking skin and seeds, the marc, in water and pressing it. Winter wine for Cato's servants was an unpalatable mixture of 10 "quadrantals" of must with 2 each of sharp vinegar and boiled-down must, and 50 of fresh water; after stirring three times daily for five days, 64 *sextarii* of aged seawater were added before sealing ten days later. Cato says this "wine" would last until the summer solstice and then any left over would make a "sharp, excellent vinegar." Amen.[91] In general, rations of wine — as of all nutrients — were larger during summer months in light of heavier work demands, and slaves of the chain gangs received the largest allotment of wine and food, some indication of the ancients' attitude that the fruit of the vine was necessary in undertaking heavy work.[92]

Bread for slaves and other unfortunates was rough and dark, of lesser quality even than *panis secundarius*, second to that made from the finest grade of flour *(siligo)* — and undoubtedly more healthy; much of it in the earlier periods was made of barley. Cato calculated 3 *modii* of grain as the monthly allotment for slaves with light, household duties, compared with 5 or 6 *modii* for the chain gang.[93] As accompaniments, what Romans termed *pulmentaria*, Cato provided windfall olives preserved in salt while they lasted, then *allec* residue from *garum* or vinegar, besides inferior olive oil, salt, and all-important figs, in season or dried in winter.

From a Pseudo-Virgilian poem that gives a vivid picture of the life of a humble peasant, it is clear that the basic diet of the protagonist, Simulus, differed little from the sustenance of slaves (or his own African one sharing his abode), although we are given an inventory of the plants in his kitchen garden. We watch him rise in the morning, stoke the fire, mix and bake his country loaf on the hot stones, and prepare a *moretum* of salted cheese, mixed with pounded garlic, oil, a little vinegar, and a bit of celery, green coriander, and heady rue. Margaret Visser calls this a pesto, yet cheese is the prevailing element rather than the herbs, though the concept is similar, especially as a lost work of the same title, *Moretum,* has a recipe that incorporates ground almonds, equivalent to pine nuts in pesto.[94]

Another segment of society deserves at least a passing glance, because its members surely aided in the spread of multicultural foodways and Mediterranean habits into northern Europe and Britain. The diet of legionaries and auxiliary troops has been investigated in archaeological digs at military encampments in various settings throughout the Empire.[95] From numerous sites in Britain, from Novaesium (Neuss) and Vindonissa (Windisch) on the Germanic frontier, to Dura-Europos in far-off Syria, evidence comes from food remains (bones of fowl, game, and other animals; nuts, seeds, and grains; shells, if near the sea), supplemented by labels and graffiti on imported amphoras, by extraordinary preservation on strips of wood of garrison ledger accounts, and soldiers' letters in Britain, as well as, in the dry climate of Egypt, papyrus correspondence from recruits writing food requests to their families.[96] The last often bring to mind today's students away at school writing home for a favorite delicacy, though the ancient requests are strikingly different: radish oil, the grain *tiphe* [teff], for example, and the exchange includes desiderata from the home folks such as special bread or cakes.[97]

In the field, Roman soldiers had to rely on the standard grain issue and a "refreshing" beverage called *posca* made by adding vinegar to water — said to be especially salutary in hot weather and recommended by Napoleon's surgeon-general when French troops served in Egypt. It was his vinegar allotment that the centurion used to moisten the sponge at the Crucifixion; was this compassion or further torment?[98] The story was quite different in garrison quarters. Studies have been made of the various tasks, including KP, distributed among soldiers in collecting sustenance for themselves and their animals from the local populace.[99] Some were designated as hunters in appropriate territory, others were herdsmen and butchers, while still other cadres made cheese, brewed beer, or baked bread. The standard of eating was certainly well beyond that of ordinary dwellers in the teeming city of Rome, where the proletariat had to be sustained by the grain dole *(annona)* or by distribution of staples — "bread and circuses" to keep them under control.[100]

At Neuss, grains identified include rice, a luxury import from eastern Africa used in antiquity for thickening sauces rather than as a staple. A beguiling hint of military concern for the well-being of soldiers comes from one excavation on the cold, wet, northern *limes* in Scotland: discovery of a labeled amphora of wine infused with horehound, lending immediate color to an age-old receipt from Dioscorides (V, 488) for chest congestion.[101] In Britain, after the governing bureaucracy and the legions withdrew in 410, many soldiers settled down with native wives or concubines to form new allegiance to an unknown future in a land where Roman horticultural genius had transplanted vines and fruit trees native to very different climates.

WINE

For those who read French it is superfluous to add a section on Roman wines, vintages, the *grands crus*, changes in oenophiles' preference at different periods, and various additives used more liberally by Romans than Greeks to alter consistency or taste. Jacques André's 1958 commentary on Pliny, of which book XIV is devoted to wine, and recent work by a younger scholar, André Tchernia, make every other study of the topic obsolete.[102]

We have already encountered that loathsome wine substitute concocted for slaves, and have considered the Opimian vintage of 121 B.C., which Trimalchio thought possible to drink. Of a host of wine names we know from Pliny and other writers, it is impossible to think that any one has survived today, even if grapes are grown in the same district. But I like to use an Italian white made from trebbiano grapes as my substitute for the ancient, simply because its name summons up a Trebulan wine Pliny recommends among those from Campania. Other appellations are names to conjure with in imagination as later writers have kept them reverberating down through the centuries.[103]

Above all, probably, stands the famed Falernian, of at least three domains including a Massic from the estate of L. Cornelius Sulla Faustus, the son of the dictator Sulla (Pliny, *NH,* XIV, viii, 61). Unlike other wines, Falernian was said to be so rich and heavy that one could make it flame.[104] Another gem of the late Republic and early Empire, Caecuban, disappeared when Nero drained the salt marshes near Amyclae at the start of a project to build a ship canal from Baiae to Ostia to replace Pozzuoli. The Setinian was especially appreciated by Augustus and the Julio-Claudians, while the Nomentanum, Alban, or Surrentine claimed their own adherents. As well we can dream of imports from Greece; but would we relish the wines of Cos and Chios, which were regularly treated with seawater to stabilize them?[105]

To us it may seem a sacrilege to adulterate fine imported wine with seawater. Yet it becomes less shocking when one reads in advisories by Cato or late antique Palladius how that seawater was treated and also when one learns from Pliny that Lesbian wines gained the desired savor of the sea naturally from its own soil. Cato's recipe takes seventy days (compared with six years in Palladius' report of his uncle's treatment) to ready seawater for making a Roman imitation of Coan. The water had to come from the open sea on a calm, windless day, and it was to be put into successive storage jars slightly open to evaporation, first for thirty days, then twenty apiece, leaving any residue behind at each remove. With harvest, grapes were soaked in this for three days before pressing so they swelled and absorbed the tang of salt water—if far from the sea, the substitute was salt added to fresh water.[106]

Other additives seem even less appealing to a modern palate: chalk and plaster to lighten red wine, myrrh and anise to perfume it, and likewise all sorts of aromatic herbs, cinnamon, saffron, bitter almond—all this aside from medicinal wines or those made from fruits and other substances. Some appreciated wines that had been smoked to enhance the color, others the addition of wormwood *(artemisia)*, that in later times would be used to make the infamous distilled liquor, absinthe. From the Greeks, Romans learned to enjoy resinated wines like those of Marseilles. Pliny's directions for the proper resin with which to line wine amphoras gives the impression that most vintages probably tasted to some degree of pitch. To go into the various additives introduced in the course of viticulture or when wines were diluted with hot or cold water at serving, strained through further aromatics, would entail a chapter in itself.

Our interest is in cuisine and the contribution of wine to cookery. Unlike modern French practice in which it is usual to deglaze a pan with wine, then reduce it for final napping of a dish, Roman cooks utilized precooked wine and must boiled down in varying degrees. Just as we have seen in the case of *garum* mixtures, one might well compare the Chinese concept of ready-made sauces arrayed to hand. In addition to *liquamen* and other prepared seasonings, both wine and must in diverse reductions are absolute requisites in any attempt to recreate an ancient banquet. Many a recipe from Apicius requires *defrutum* as a finishing touch, what the French refer to as *vin cuit*. This is must reduced anywhere from half to a third of its initial volume, while *sapa* is more concentrated, to one-third of its quantity (Pliny, *NH*, XIV, xi, 80). *Passum* is fortified in sweetness and alcohol by drying fully ripe grapes, often on the vine, and then soaking them in fresh must for a time before pressing and fermenting. Described by Columella (XII, 39) and Palladius, *passum* is comparable to a "muscatel" cited by Pliny.[107] *Caroenum*, also a frequent ingredient, is wine boiled down to the same relative consistency as *defrutum*. Also useful is a Roman aperitif, *mulsum*, which entails mixing honey into dry white wine for preprandial imbibing.

It is fascinating to discover the manner in which this concentrated sweetness, the result of boiling down juice of the grape, enhances the flavor of a dish one might expect to have a quite different balance of flavors (notably those cooked in *liquamen* or *garum* like the chicken recipe in the appendix). And this brings us back to the question of *taste* and an aesthetic of Roman food.

ANCIENT TASTES AND ITALIAN CONTINUITY

Everyone asks how ancient Roman fare may be supposed to compare with modern Italian cookery, speaking, of course, solely of the home country and not major differences once found in distant provinces such as Egypt or what is today Armenia. In a typical upper-class household the basics were those which sustain the modern kitchen: virgin olive oil that connoisseurs could regionally locate, as they could even more precisely their wine; varieties of excellent crusty bread, often herb-flavored by devices that included Cato's prescription for placing bay leaves under the loaves in baking (and remember that *focaccia,* now a supermarket staple, is the descendant of the ancient flat bread baked on the hot stones of a hearth, *focus* in Latin); different sorts of sausage characterized by topical specialties; comparably diverse cheeses from very fresh to hard grating types;[108] fruits and vegetables predominant in the culinary repertoire. It was essentially a classic Mediterranean diet missing a few items much in favor today: no spinach for dishes *alla Fiorentina,* though many substitutes from orache and *blitum* (blight) to chard and *bietole;* no eggplant, also a later gift from the Arabs; above all, no tomatoes or capsicum peppers, which today proclaim Italian creativity in exploiting these natives of the New World; and a dearth of citrus fruits, save citron,[109] to achieve the *agrodolce* flavor relished by ancient Romans as much as by contemporary Italians (though plenty of vinegars and *agresto,* the juice from unripened fruits).

Continuity, however, impresses in the proclivity of ancient dwellers in Italy to gardening. If you think that Italian markets today offer a stunning assemblage of olives, read Pliny (*NH,* XV, iv–vi, 13–23), who names more than thirty varieties, including a white one. We who suffer under a modern reduction in product diversity—think only of countless strains of apple that have vanished in the drive for yield and shelf life—must envy the produce that tempted a shopper in an ancient market (fig. 101). Again, Pliny (XV, xvi, 53–56) astounds us by differentiating more than forty kinds of pear of various shapes, sizes, colors, and degrees of sweetness or acidity. Figs, such a fundamental staple of nutrition for slave and patrician alike, also came in numberless variety, local types being supplemented by imports from eastern provinces and from Africa (ibid., xix–xxi, 68ff.).

101. Relief depicting a greengrocer's stall. Third century A.D. The wicker basket below the trestle table must hold small animals — rabbits or chickens? Ostia Museum

Species of vegetables manifest comparable diversity. Jacques André counts fifty-four cultivated and forty-three wild ones in the Roman repertoire.[110] Many of them are strangers to us nowadays, or we know them in different guise, like carrots which, as we have said, the ancients had in different hues but not in orange. There seems only a single reason to regret mallows, the fiber of which was so difficult to digest that Cicero complained of having diarrhea after one meal featuring them (in a letter to Gallus, *Ad fam.* VII, 26, complaining that sumptuary laws prevented the host from serving anything but highly seasoned vegetables and fungi). But think of our colonial ancestors using marsh mallows to make soothing gobbets to ease sore throats with the plant's slippery ooze; do you prefer our artificial, sugary treats that borrow the name? Unless you shop in oriental foodstores or own your own garden, it is next to impossible to cook the wealth of small shoots from the host of plants that Romans gathered from their plots or in the wild: peas, hops, grapes, bugloss, giant fennel, and countless species in the cabbage and lettuce families, among them.

In the seasoning of their foods, the people of old lacked the sharp bite of hot red peppers so prized by Italian cooks in recent times. But, despite the expense, they did increasingly enjoy pepper, both the regular dried berry, white and black, as well as "long pepper" and melegueta pepper from Africa ("grains of Paradise" to the Middle Ages).[111] If one could not afford the real thing, ground pepper adulterated with juniper berries, with which dealers tried to cheat unwary shoppers, might even have been welcome, or myrtle berries could serve as a substitute, or, alternatively, the mustard seeds that Romans already knew how to turn into a condiment (this has never gone out of favor in diverse admixtures).[112] Dusting freshly ground pepper on Apicius' pear tart (see the appendix) is a palate-refreshing bonus that I can recommend, one that meets Roman anticipation of a robust tang in the final notes of proper dinner. Other finishing touches among the fruits and nuts that capped a meal are less easy to come by legally. The seeds of *cannabis sativa*, like poppy seeds, were sometimes served grilled with honey.[113]

In defending Apicius, I have already dealt with aspects of the Roman use of herbs and spices. It is important to bear in mind their importance in a quest for complex flavor when cooking facilities were themselves so rudimentary (figs. 81, 82). Although one might grill or spit-broil on a small scale, sauté as well over a *bancone* of hot charcoal, in the majority of households everything was cooked by immersion in water, by boiling, or at best by braising. All segments of society had access to native herbs, of course, and their use accords with modern Italian cuisine save a few exceptions. Asafoetida we first encountered in considering Greek use of silphium; it is left to Arab and Indian cuisine today except for those who wish to follow Apicius, who uses it as a refined substitute for garlic, which he disdained as strongly as did Horace.[114] Nor is rue any longer appreciated by our contemporaries, and the ancient reliance on a wide variety of plants in the mint family is generally curtailed. Pennyroyal *(puleium)* is difficult to find in markets nowadays, save, perhaps, in Britain, and most people in Italy or elsewhere grow catnip for feline friends, though *nepeta* was standard in the ancient kitchen.[115] The odds-on favorite of the past, leaf coriander, or Chinese parsley and Hispanic *cilantro*, has come to enliven American flavors of late, thanks to the influence of Asian and Latin American cookery.

Spices, because of their transport — always the most expensive item in the cost of any product in antiquity—were less widely accessible. Not everyone could be as profligate as Apicius or the Ostrogoth who excerpted his text at the beginning of the sixth century. Vinidarius gives a staggering list of roots, seeds, nuts, and dried fruits and leaves every kitchen should have in stock, from saffron and spikenard to ginger and cardamom. Two spices are conspicuous by their absence: cinnamon and cloves. Although both were imported from the East, these medieval favorites were used in ancient times medicinally and in perfumes, including those from cinnamon or cassia to cover the smell of burning flesh at special cremation ceremonies.[116] The spices of choice were milder, the so-called sweet spices, cumin, anise and, above all, coriander.

Insofar as it is possible to reconstruct the aesthetic of a cuisine that evolved in a context surpassing the multiculturalism of the Hellenistic world, we can insist upon at least a few basic principles that Roman culinary arts shared with contemporary visual and literary ones. They all participate in the arts of persuasion and manipulation so early mastered by Romans, whose genius lay in statecraft and law, unlike the Greeks, whose gifts rested in philosophy. Little wonder that rhetoric was developed by Romans beyond Hellenic suasive formulations, that their public monuments communicate social and political messages through a rhetoric of vision. To empower representation for its new task, expanding beyond delight or instruction to psychological control, Romans developed artistic and gustatory means to convince by a principle they termed *decor*.[117] This Latin word may summon to mind English derivatives such as decoration, but the original expressed "fittingness," or appropriateness of a choice of *style* to the subject at hand—whether in oratory, literature, architecture, other works of art, or, I feel certain, menu-building and gastronomy. In the fifth century, Macrobius would write: "This dinner of ours has combined the moderation of the heroic age with the good taste of our own; it is sober yet elegant, carefully planned without being lavish"—this from the age of so-called Late Antique decadence!

Roman architects, painters, and sculptors, just like the orators and the literati, always match their renderings in subtle differentiations to pragmatic purposes of the work, to the message it must convey, and to the nature of their audience. In sharp contrast to Greek imagery, which expressed contemporary events by way of metaphor (the contest with Persians by mythical battles of gods against giants or of Lapiths with centaurs, heroes with Amazons, for example), a documentary impulse drives Roman historical relief as well as other art, more dependent upon Hellenic example, by which they brought pure abstractions such as Piety, Virtue, Honor, Harmony, Clemency, and the like into graphic actuality. This realism then can be extended to the visual field surrounding human enterprise if that makes the image more powerful in political or religious impact. Sculptors had to be able to "speak" differing languages of style in one and the same monument, counterparts to the categories of style set forth in handbooks on rhetoric: the "Grand," or elevated; the "Elegant," or florid; the "Plain"; and the "Low," or forcible.[118] Examples abound. Augustus' Altar of Peace dedicated to the new world order he had established, designed to endure a thousand years, employs four contrasting styles of relief for differing content from mythology to personified concepts of propaganda, virtual actuality of its dedicatory processions, and a solemn climax in the frieze of the altar itself (where each figure has the significance of a ritual sign, isolated from its fellows and frontally presented to the gaze of any spectator).

In architecture as well, a surface vocabulary of columns and lintels borrowed from the Greeks repeatedly translates for the eye the actual construction by arches and vaults, which Hellenic architects generally had spurned in favor of self-revelatory trabeate systems. In buildings that had to express a conservative bias in favor of age-old tradition (not unlike American community banks once erected in classical style), Etruscan habit was raised to fresh eloquence for religious structures, founded with auguries and rituals inherited from former rulers. A Roman temple—so unlike a Greek one that invites access to its platform from every side—aggressively takes possession of the space before it, not unlike a Roman hegemonic gesture of command which speaks so vividly of the power of leader, general (emperor in later days), the *ad locutio* pose with right arm taking possession of the masses that has been assumed by demagogues ever after. It is raised high on a podium that makes it inaccessible from any side but the façade, awe-inspiring in its deeply shadowed porch with many sturdy columns that may oppose an illusory series of supports girdling the rest of the shrine in relief. Physically dominating precinct and exterior altar in the name of a divinity, houses of the gods contrast with public structures which dominate by vastness of interior space, particularly those like the Pantheon of propaganda purpose.

Sensitivity to *decor* and other rhetorical principles of purpose must have contributed substantially to gastronomic enjoyment in addition to those sociopolitical factors we have already considered. There is ample literary and visual testimony to a sensitivity of palate expressed in Roman poetry and painted still-life (fig. 102). This cultivated taste is implicit also in the concern for good farm management and the pleasures of horticulture and animal husbandry. Instead of the quotation with which this chapter began, I give you the

102.   Roman still-lifes from Pompeii or Herculaneum. Central elements (left to right): a hare with grapes, a rock lobster (langouste) with clams, and cuttlefish beside a galinule. Naples, National Museum

admiring judgment of John Milton, writing his essay on ideal education for Britain's seventeenth-century youth:

> After the evening repast, till bed time [religion and the story of scripture]. The next step would be to the Authors on Agriculture, Cato, Varro, and Columella, for the matter is most easie, and if the language be difficult, so much the better . . . and here will be an occasion of inciting and enabling them hereafter to improve the tillage of their Country, to recover the bad Soil, and to remedy the waste that is made of good.

There are lessons here for modern environmentalists. I was astonished to find, on a guided tour of the Rodale experimental farm, that the most up-to-date methods for reducing pesticides, for improving topsoil, and for developing new sources of human nutrition could be replicated in the writings of those ancient agronomists.

7 The Early Middle Ages

FROM THE FIRST CENTURIES of Christianity, as it spread from a small cult appealing to the least privileged members of society to engage a pagan elite, we are able to discern a fundamental dichotomy that affects cooking and eating during the so-called Middle Ages. Body and soul; feasting and fasting; relishing God's bounty yet evading sins of the flesh like gluttony—how was one to reconcile a classical tradition of concern for bodily health and dietetics, or of gentile and Jewish ritual dining in spiritual fellowship, with a new ascetism that could ultimately lead to saints sustained by mystical visions rather than food?[1] The conflict was made more acute by the reliance on nourishment for the soul, represented most strikingly in the Early Christian *agapē* (love feast) and liturgically in the Eucharist.

In no comparable historical period do we sense so strongly in human affairs another duality: strength of custom set against the vitality of change. Tradition versus innovation, to look solely at cookery, is still represented today in what was once Gaul, by ancient Roman dishes such as cassoulet, bouillabaisse, or Provençal tian (minus its New World tomatoes). At the same time the modern Frenchman enjoys his gifts from "barbarian" Germanic tribes of long ago: his *bon bock*, on the one hand, and his butter-based pastries and

sauces on the other. Tacitus, in the first century A.D., elaborated Caesar's succinct observation about the Germanic diet: milk, cheese, and meat. In his *Ger-
mania* (book 23) Tacitus describes the barbarians subsisting on wild fruits,
nuts, and seeds to accompany their game (*recens*, not even hung to tenderize it
in a Roman manner); their *lac concretum*, which probably means milk curds,
but could also refer to butter and cheese; and finds their immoderate use of
beer (the ubiquitous drink of fermented grains) an indulgence that should
make it easy to conquer them. By the fifth century, when such beer-abusing
northerners are in full possession of Gaul, a cultivated survivor of classical
civilization will still snobbishly look down upon uncouth Burgundian neighbors stinking of onion, leek, and the rancid butter with which they dress their
hair (Sidonius Apollinaris, bishop of Clermont in Auvergne, in his letters).[2]

During the slow interpenetration of two entirely different ways of life and
thought that took place over the centuries from about A.D. 300 until the age
of Charlemagne just before and after the year 800, we meet the decay of Roman political and intellectual life but discover an infusion of fresh vigor and
imagination. Those cultures which had flourished throughout antiquity outside the boundaries of the "civilized" classical world, migrant survivals of Paleolithic hunting and gathering societies, developed an entirely contrasting society and an art based, not on the natural appearance of things, nor on human
representation, but a mobiliary art founded upon animal forms transfigured
by a will focused on their supranatural realities (fig. 103). We can expect Germanic tribes, even while slowly filtering into Roman territories, joining its
armies, and coming to enjoy its beguiling luxuries, to go on loving their spit-
roasted meats and cauldrons of stew thickened with barley or oats. As the cultivated Old Guard of Gallo-Romans long assimilated to villa living retreated
slowly to the southern reaches of Gaul, a more sophisticated gastronomy was
still kept alive by much of the agricultural and viticultural wisdom of the past.
From Decimus Magnus Ausonius, serving the Empire at the end of the fourth
century, to the poet Bishop Venantius Fortunatus at the court of Merovingian
kings in the sixth, these aristocrats and poets sustained gourmet traditions of
wining and dining. Ausonius' praise of the wines of his native Bordeaux region — especially those made by the Medulorum living in Médoc — and of the
succulence of its oysters is not mere culinary chauvinism. A letter to a friend
assesses an impressive number of oyster species despite Ausonius' disclaimer
of connoisseurship; and his catalogue of the fish in a tributary of the Rhine included in his romantic nature poem *Mosella*, speaks more of gastronomic than
scientific interest.[3]

103. Hybrid Beast *(lion, griffin, and serpent)* Attacking a Horse. *Scytho-Siberian gold plaque, fifth–fourth century B.C. St. Petersburg, Hermitage*

A word here should be devoted to the alleged slow destruction by barbarians of vineyards that classical civilization once fostered far from the natural home of *vitis vinifera.* Celtic peoples had long since learned from Greek settlements at the mouth of the Rhone how to enjoy the fermented fruit of the vine. There is nothing to suggest that Germanic tribes had not also come to respect the gift of Dionysos/Bacchus[4] during their gradual infiltration preceding the violent incursions after the collapse of Roman political power during the fifth century. Actually, in Norse myth, the chief of the gods, Odin, lends special reverence to wine by being the only resident of Valhalla to drink it. What was destroyed during the so-called Dark Ages was an international system of trade and communication that had once sustained large-scale agriculture and commerce in vintage wines. Gradually vast estates gave way to smaller holdings and what we might almost call subsistence farming compared with that which had gone before. Wine-making became the province of the small landowner, of the noble on his holdings, and of the monk in one of the developing monastic communities — all for private and local consumption.

It should also be noted at this point that the devotion to exotic spices from the Near and farther East fostered by classical Mediterranean culinary arts met a rather different fate. Since they could not be produced locally, and because those who could afford spices continued to demand them, they increasingly became status luxuries for a small elite. A late fifth-century Ostrogothic version of Apicius, by one named Vinidarius, insists upon basic inventories of herbs and spices for the well-stocked larder. This author, anthologizing his source, gives an almost incredible catalogue that nevertheless had to be familiar to his readers. Of "seeds" *(de seminibus)* he lists poppy, rue, and its berries, laurel (bay) berries, dill, celery, fennel, lovage, rocket (arugula), coriander, cumin, anise, parsley, caraway, and sesame; these preceded by saffron, pepper, ginger, *laser* (asafoetida), myrtle berry, *cariofilium* (clove carnation), costmary, cardamom, spikenard (but he also names identical *Spica Indica*), and *addena*.[5] Spice-hungry eaters in the West were served by Byzantine traders through their outposts in Ravenna (a role late- and postmedieval Venice would usurp) and in Sicily until the Arab conquests of the seventh and eighth centuries. But even pepper was a precious commodity to the Venerable Bede in Anglo-Saxon England when, on his death bed in 735, he called for his pitifully few "valuables" to distribute to fellow monks: some grains of pepper and incense, together with vestments for which he would have no further use.[6]

THE HIBERNO-SAXON REVOLUTION

From the slow decline of a classical worldview with its cultivated refinements of thought and life, from the gradual acculturation of "barbarians," we must turn to the vitality and creativity of peoples alien to Mediterranean civilization. Even though their ideas about food and cookery remain impenetrable, we need to consider Celtic descendants in Wales and Ireland because, once converted by Saint Patrick from 432, they became ultimately a vehicle for the spread of Christian piety and conventual living throughout the British Isles and thence in Europe. With the ardent zeal of new believers in a geographical area that had always lain outside Roman colonization, in other words, in a cultural vacuum (where exciting new directions or syntheses so often enliven human history), the Irish created a dynamic, original art that was unlike anything that had existed before. By the seventh century it had united centuries-old Celtic tradition with the "animal style" of migratory Germanic tribes. The result has all the impetuous sweep of Celtic spiral ornament plus a fantastic maze of abstracted animal parts interlaced in endless tangles of strap-work (fig. 104).[7] This is calligraphy of infinite expansiveness, though disciplined by

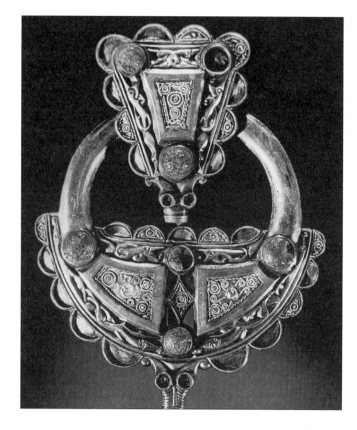

104. Hiberno-Viking Pseudo-Penninsular brooch (detail). Early ninth century A.D. Silver with gold and amber. Found near Roscrea, County Tipperary.

a latent geometry of equal complexity, that must be experienced over time by a deciphering eye. Applied to the new Gospel books rather than to its native metal, it creates magical pages to enhance the mystery of the Word — a sacred rebus, as it has been called — to the illiterate catechumen being instructed in hidden meanings within the evangelists' message. Deciphering initial letters and phrases in a manuscript like the famous Book of Kells (fig. 105), we enter a visual equivalent to the urgent scrambled language of James Joyce (who constantly refers to its "whipplooplashed," "upandinswept" enlacements and even claims in one reversal of time to have produced it).[8]

Without the classical tradition that concentrated on representing the human form, Irish *scriptoria* excel, as one would anticipate, in depiction of animals. Their artists inventively portray the established symbols of the four Evangelists: the Lion for Mark, chronicler of the Resurrection, because folk legend held that the lion's roar could bring a cub back to life; the Ox, an animal of sacrifice from time immemorial and holy to ancient Celts, for Luke in

105. The Book of Kells. *Hiberno-Saxon manuscript, mid-eighth century A.D. The compound initial reads,* Liber generationis *. . . Trinity College Library, Dublin*

allusion to his story of the Passion of Christ; the Eagle for Saint John, because its flight can be read as a sign of the Ascension stressed in his Gospel). But poor Matthew, given human form to typify his emphasis on the genealogy of Christ, becomes a mere field for ornament, inarticulate in mankind's modes of expression (fig. 106).

The sacro-magical evasiveness of Irish representation embodies age-old Celtic mythology as well as a folklore familiar to us in stories of fairies and leprechauns. Indeed, early Irish literature and its Celtic forebears from Gaul and Wales can tell us a lot about the foods consumed by these people. We read of

106. The Book of
Durrow. *Hiberno-Saxon*
manuscript, ca. 700 A.D.
The symbol of Saint Matthew
is shown. Trinity College
Library, Dublin

supernatural swine that reconstitute themselves each time they are roasted
and eaten, coinciding with the boar motif so prominent in Celtic and Gallo-
Roman art, with pig bones and joints of pork discovered in pagan funerary deposits in Britain and Ireland.[9] Divine and otherworldly auras mantle other
creatures, including fabulous salmon and trout among the fish, and certain
fruits and nuts associated with them — above all the apple and the hazelnut.[10]
There are tales of a hazel tree growing beside a well into which its nuts fall to

bestow supernatural wisdom on a salmon. These reflect Celtic veneration of the hazel *(coll* and derivatives like *cuill)* that is confirmed by Gaelic philology, some names of Celtic heroes, and by archaeological discoveries of ritual deposits in extraordinarily deep wells at various sites in Britain.[11]

The other half of our Hiberno-Saxon (Irish and Anglo-Saxon) equation centers on marauding Germanic pirates who decided to settle among the Britons during the latter part of the fifth century after the protective Roman legions withdrew and Latin administration of the territory slowly decayed. To the villas (the deserted ones now given over to poachers) and peasant farms of the countryside they brought a new type of dwelling. It featured a central hearth *cum* living area for people and beasts, a prototype of the medieval great hall for manor and castle alike.[12] Their language, similarly to Celtic, helps to discriminate various foodstuffs; one can tell which fruits and vegetables were eaten long before Roman horticulture brought unfamiliar ones to northern climes. Celtic *fin,* for example, derives from Latin *vinum* (cf. *winberige* for *grape* in Anglo-Saxon), as does *piris* for pears. The Anglo-Saxon word *aeppel* is another matter, distinguishing both sweet *(swite)* and sour *(surmelst) apulder* varieties without any connection to Latin vocabulary. Like the Celts, they drank cider and, presumably, fermented honey potions such as mead and metheglin—wild bees are said to have swarmed in Britain in huge numbers before so much of its forests were cut down for the purpose of ship-building during the reign of Elizabeth I. Among vegetables, the words for leek—and remember that this is a national badge for Celts in Wales—and garlic *(leac, gar-leac)* are pure Anglo-Saxon, while Latin *pisa* gave the name for peas *(pyse).* Members of the brassica, or cabbage, family also took their names from the Latin, as did turnips, radishes, and various herbs (cress, parsley, mint, rue, and sage).[13]

Throughout the sixth and seventh centuries, the religious leadership of the Irish effects a conversion to Christianity of vast populations and a steady spread of monasticism from Ireland, first to the North with the founding by Saint Columba of Iona in 557, from there to Northumbria and the Abbey of Lindisfarne in 635, to Jarrow and Wearmouth, and on to Burgundian and Frankish sites across the Channel. A countercurrent of Benedictine monasticism from Italy led to a papal mission of Augustine to Britain in 597, yet reconciliation of the Celtic/Saxon Church with Roman Catholicism in the matter of calculating Easter and in many aspects of liturgy was not accomplished until the Synod of Whitby in 664. Insular creativity, however, affects not only the artistic substructure of all future medieval art by its unconstrained linear

107. Norman Feasting after the Battle of Hastings. *The Bayeux Tapestry, twelfth century. Bayeux, Cathedral Treasury*

energy and expressiveness, but also underlies a synthesis of barbarian and classical culinary practices which characterizes the Middle Ages.

Missionary zeal was even able to civilize those wild Viking invaders who harassed Ireland, all Europe even into the Volga basin, from about the end of the eighth century until they settled down in Normandy as pious Christians beginning in the tenth. How those Normans came to conquer England and portions of the Byzantine Empire is another story. Fascinatingly, it is a story that determines how we speak of certain foods today; most striking is an echo of the ruling-class Norman consumption of meat that made its mark upon Anglo-Saxon peasants' speech after 1066. The conquerors' field rations, as shown in the famous Bayeux Tapestry made for William the Conqueror's half-brother, Bishop Odo, to decorate his palace, may have differed little from those of their roving past (fig. 107). But our Saxon-derived names for food animals like sheep, cattle or calves, boars or pigs, contrast sharply with those for their prepared flesh: beef *(boeuf)*, veal *(veau)*, pork *(porc)*, and mutton *(mouton)*, all via the French elite.

THE CAROLINGIAN AGE

The united missionary fervor of Hiberno-Saxon monks spread Christianity onward to the Continent, where we must consider their spiritual and intellectual leadership as background for the so-called Carolingian Revival—of learning, of the arts. They must also have spread their own brand of spirituality in terms of cultivating the fruits of the earth and in producing numinous ornament to glorify ritual objects and books. This is what strikes the observer most forcefully when considering two aspects of life in monastic communities in the Age of Charlemagne. On the one hand, a devoted efficiency in horticulture and husbandry; on the other an enduring love — covertly pagan, barbarian — of metal worked so it reflects light to the utmost, of lustrous jewels and enamel, joined always with that Celtic linear excitation which rediscovered its natural home in Frankish Gaul.

Alcuin (Ealhwine), the leading intellectual light and educator in Carolingian Europe until his death in 804, came from York, in Britain. A direct heir of Bede through a disciple, Egbert, who was one of his teachers, he is called by one biographer of Charlemagne "a man more skilled in all branches of knowledge than any other person of modern times. . . . His teaching bore such fruit among his pupils that modern Gauls or Franks came to equal the Romans and the Athenians." [14]

Such emulation of the classical past is the watchword of the Carolingian *renovatio*, its "renewal" given the seal of approval of the Western Church when Pope Leo III crowned Carolus Magnus Holy Roman Emperor on Christmas day in 800. Emperor Charles the Great (768–814), upon consolidating politically his subdued domains (ignoring here for the moment external threats from Arab expansion during the seventh and eighth centuries that his grandfather, Charles Martel, had kept from engulfing Merovingian France at the Battle of Tours in 732),[15] could challenge the "Ruler of the Romans," as the Byzantine Emperor in Constantinople called himself, and vividly express a renascence of classical civilization and hegemony in the West. His coinage announced RENOVATIO ROMANI IMPERII, renewal of the Roman Empire, and his domination unites Late Antique ideas of majesty invested in the Emperor with his Teutonic forebears' concept of *munt*, or divine power inherent in the leader protecting his kingdom.

Renascence, renewal, and revival are terms justifiably used to characterize the impact of the Emperor's reforms during his lifetime and well into the ninth century, as they survived the break-up of his realm among his heirs. Compare an Evangelist portrait in the Gospel Book of Charlemagne (fig. 108) with the Hiberno-Saxon one previously reproduced in a confrontation that is a textbook favorite among historians of art. Modeled on a classical author portrait, modeled in light and shade to give a full three-dimensionality to the figure and spatiality to his surroundings, this "illumination" shows us how artists were now indeed able to *illuminate* biblical messages, to make the human figure articulate, to instruct by visual narration.

Another focusing monument for understanding Carolingian art is a Psalter housed today in the Library of the University of Utrecht in Holland but written and illustrated at Rheims in the 820s to 835 (fig. 109). Its inspired penwork, as sensitive as that from a seismographic stylus, carries all the passion of Hiberno-Saxon renderings, but its models both in script and illustration were Late Antique manuscripts. The Psalter's excited drawings interpret poetic metaphors with literal-minded renderings of daily life. These and copies made in England during the eleventh and twelfth centuries have sometimes been used to illustrate Anglo-Saxon activities and artifacts—farming, vintaging, outdoor cooking, dining, and tablewares, for example. But its

108. Coronation Gospels of Charlemagne. *Carolingian Manuscript, ca. A.D. 800. Evangelist Mark is shown.* Vienna, *Schatzkammer*

109. The Utrecht Psalter, End of *Psalm 18 Carolingian manuscript, Rheims style, 820s A.D. Utrecht, Cathedral Library*

multiplicity of sources scattered in chronological time make it safer to rely upon archaeological and documentary evidence.

For our purposes, it is fortunate that Charlemagne, activated by ambition, but under the tutelage of Alcuin and of Einhard, another heir to Anglo-Saxon learning, determined to systematize every aspect of the administration of his realm. This affected the selection of artistic models, agriculture, planning and governance of new monasteries and convents, the very diet of his court and, by extension, the health of his peoples. We are provided with documents of many kinds, including manuscripts that copy most of what has been preserved to us of Latin literature as well as the relics of classical scientific works on astronomy, agronomy, geography, medicine and the like (fig. 110). The two master-copies that give us Apicius, the only surviving cookbook from the vast culinary literature of antiquity, date from the ninth century, as we have seen (fig. 111). Undoubtedly, it was the few medical recipes in that Late Antique compilation that justified some gourmet abbot's choice of text.

Carolingian records include advisories against treading out a vintage in dirty bare feet and other admonitions designed to serve the populace in newly prosperous towns and villages. For Frankish nobles are mandated great new hunting preserves and *vivaria* that had not been seen since Roman days. The Emperor's joy in hunting never ceased, even when as an old man his doctors recommended that he give up spit-roasted game for simmered meats and stews. A cartulary, *De villis*, gives Charlemagne's instructions for running his estates. A complete plan (fig. 112) for a monastery from St. Gall, Switzerland, provides insight into the daily life in an ideal convent through explanatory notations—the fruit trees are named in its orchard, the herbs in the garden, for example. The Abbot Irminon of St.-Germain-des-Pres outside Paris kept an account book of the abbey's estates that is equally informative. Einhard's biography of Charlemagne and the works of Alcuin and Theodulf of Orleans are additional sources, together with such post-Carolingian reflections of the life of the ruler as the biography by a Monk of St. Gall (Notker the Stammerer, it seems) and various *chansons de geste* of a later Age of Chivalry, including *Huon de Bordeaux*.[16]

More authentic is Hincmar of Rheims' description of the organization of Charlemagne's court, *De ordine palatii* (882), which helps define the role of servitors such as the seneschal (whom we would call the majordomo) and the butler/steward *(buticularius)*.[17]

From all of this documentation as well as from the letters and poetry of the major players on the scene—whose convivial ideas are reflected in nicknames both serious and playful: Flaccus, Homer, David (the psalmist, applied to Charlemagne)—what do we glean of the actual diet and cookery of the Carolingian renaissance? Just as in ancient times, or for that matter down to the Revolution in France, the basic nutrition of the common people was founded on grains. Now, however, in addition to the various kinds of wheat, barley, and millet, other cereals native to cold climates became important, notably rye and oats. Rye was from this point on one of the marks of peasant fare in the North, leading to dreadful outbreaks of ergotism ("Saint Anthony's Fire") like the one that carried off thousands at Limoges in 943.[18] In Britain and Scotland, hearth cakes of oats were favored; think of the famous anecdote about King Alfred the Great of Wessex (r. 871–899) being scolded for letting them burn on the hot stones in that age-old process that gives us bannocks and scones. For those of us engaged in the American passion for fashionable food imports, it is interesting to note that this is the point in history when we can first document French *fougasse*, Italian *focaccia*, though in the early Middle Ages it was cooked under the coals. Where ovens were available in palaces, village, or monastic communities there was leavened bread, each consumer

110. Astrological Treatise of Aratus. *Carolingian manuscript, ca. A.D. 800. The Constellation Perseus, showing the revival of antique learning and artistic style.* University Library, Leiden

111. OPPOSITE: *Carolingian manuscript of Apicius from the ninth century A.D. New York, Medical Society Library*

provided with the appropriate grain in the hierarchy according to his or her station in life. As in ancient Rome, the finest bread was the whitest bread, of *similago, symilla,* the most thoroughly bolted variety of *triticum vulgare;* spelt does not seem to have been as important a crop at this time, except for brewing.[19] Barley continued to be the most widely consumed grain for those at the low end of the social ladder.

Just as in works of art, Roman and barbarian traditions coalesced in the preparation of porridge as part of the meal—barley for the poor countryman's mainstay, wheat for the tables of the monk or of the wealthy. Here we meet the *frumenty* that is de rigueur with game right down into the nineteenth century, the *farro* that is even yet a feature of autumn menus in Tuscany (look back at ancient Latin *far*). Porridge frequently introduced a meal. Other "appetizers" included salads of mallow or other kitchen-garden herbage, and of hop shoots.

This leads us to consider a vexed problem concerning the hop vine (Lat. *lupulus*). It is widely held that it was not until at least the thirteenth or fourteenth century, at the hands apparently of Flemish brewers, that hops were added in the brewing process to produce "true" beer. But, were the hops ordered in quantity for the Carolingian Abbey at St. Germain used medicinally or for brewing? This is a question for specialists, and, happily, the congress held at Nice in 1982 produced an answer (although it was less informed on the history of brewing in antiquity). An article by Léo Moulin, drawing on linguistic evidence as well as documents of Carolingian and post-Carolingian capitularies, attributes the invention of beer to the ninth century and to the Benedictine order.[20] Of course, by *beer* he means the brew to which hops have been added for both flavor and preservation, as opposed to *cervisia* (modern French *cervoise*, from a root word of ancient Gaul) and all the beers we have met from antiquity up to now. Romans had eaten the tendrils of hops, *lupus salictarius*, as a wild delicacy (Pliny, *NH*, XXI, l, 86), but it was northern

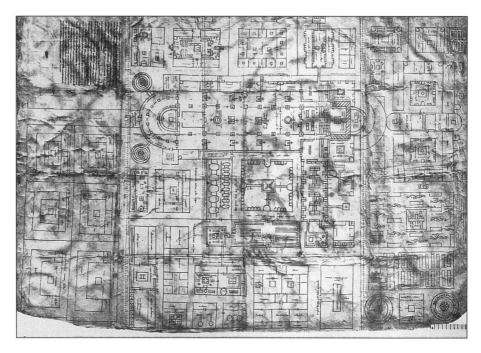

112. *Carolingian plan for a monastery, ca. A.D. 820. St. Gall, Switzerland, Chapter Library*

peoples in what are today Finland, Latvia, and Estonia who cultivated and relished the vine.[21] The Abbot Adalhard at Corbie, in a statute of 822, specifies *humolone* (hops) in a context that involves brewing *cervisia*.[22] It seems clear that the barbarian brew continued to be improved without applying the name "beer" *(beura)*, to it.

The plan of the Abbey of St. Gall (fig. 112) shows three separate breweries for making *cervisia*, each sharing space with a bakery in a mode we have come to expect ever since studying Pharaonic Egypt. Beer and bread are not merely appropriate companions in terms of the workplace, but also in terms of consumption. It has been pointed out that meals like those in monasteries, so heavily based on bread and *companaticum* (that which goes with the bread) dominated by dried legumes, would necessarily require vast quantities of liquid for digestion. And as everywhere throughout the medieval period when water near towns was generally of suspicious purity, the drink of preference was beer or wine — even for small children — right up into early modern times.

Because the series of books, A History of Private Life,[23] is so widely read, we must look a little closer at nutritional aspects of the high carbohydrate/ high fiber diet it depicts in medieval monasteries. A study on the early Middle

Ages in this work is written by Michel Rouche, based upon his own earlier article on alleged famines in the Carolingian epoch. He had argued that, thanks to a psychological mind-set,[24] the perception of hunger was stronger than the reality of drought, hunger and pestilence cited in a letter of 829 from Charlemagne's son and successor, Louis the Pious, to a Council of bishops. The normal diet was so extraordinarily high in calories as well as filling, that one felt deprived when his expectation had to be lowered! Rouche calculates that the *normal* diet for peasant and monk alike provided "some 6000 calories, twice what is now considered necessary for the average active man." Feast-day "gullet-stuffings" warded off hunger caused by unbalanced diets, not from starving, while flatulence took its toll in "ubiquitous belches and farts."

Working with Abbot Adalhard's *Statuta* for the Abbey at Corbie with its account of annual rations for a community that varied between 350 to 400 souls a day (yet sometimes only 300 depending on the results of hospitality) and other later documents, Rouche calculates that each individual "loaf" of bread weighed about 1.70 kilograms. If each pauper harbored in the monastery was given three and a half rolls of that weight, it was indeed a lot of grain. He admits that figures throughout are suspect, since later copyists who preserved Carolingian sources for us often made arithmetical mistakes in dealing with Roman numerals—not to mention that they confused their terms, as witness "pounds" cited for measures of wine. Yet Rouche prefers to follow modern writers on weights and coinage rather than estimates of 12 ounces per loaf put forward by early commentators on the Roll of St. Germain by Abbot Irminon.[25]

The paupers at Corbie, like the vassals who were provided with five rolls (and the frugal abbot mentions that his monks received either larger or smaller loaves according to their appetites so as to avoid waste), were expected to move on to the next charitable harbor. Takeout was clearly practiced. In the chapter on Rome, we saw that calculations of ancient Roman caloric intake often assume that people really ate each item in menus preserved to us. Similarly, I do not believe that medieval people were so well-cushioned with fat nor all monks of such Falstaffian proportions as the figures just discussed would make them appear.[26]

A letter requested by Charlemagne from a then-current abbot of St. Benedict's foundation, Monte Cassino, gives a more Spartan picture of the monastic pulmentarian diet.[27] In the sixth century, Saint Benedict had prescribed two cooked dishes daily (i.e., meatless stews or other *pulmenta*, which Rouche translates as *purées*, to accompany bread) and a third prepared from dried legumes reconstituted in water. But Charlemagne's respondent, Theodemar, says that in his day the limit of two cooked dishes is adhered to only on the "lean" days, Wednesday and Friday. Other days see three cooked preparations except for a few fast days when the brothers are nourished solely by bread and "herbs" from the garden, while on Sundays and feast days a fourth *pulmentum* is added, and, at Christmas and Easter week, a fowl. At dinner, *prandium* at mid-day, they relish a cup of wine, because "we have so much of it here" in South Italy.

This regimen reminds us that Catholicism enlarged upon traditional lean or *maigre* days in the course of the seventh century. The proscription against eating the flesh of creatures of the earth based upon the Lord's sentence on Adam after the Fall (Genesis 3:17–18) was extended from Wednesday and Friday to Saturday and the eve of feast days. The fast days of Lent, established to recall Christ's sojourn in the wilderness, were gradually expanded to forty.[28] One must keep in mind, however, that medieval fasting rules did not restrict those with means from exploiting other water creatures than fish. Legitimized by their lifestyle were otter and beaver, even porpoises and whales among the mammals (the first whale of record, salted down for meat and *craspois*—its blubber, or fat—was captured off the coast of Bordeaux in 875).[29] During this period such casuistry also permitted the use of fetuses of rabbits, which had never set four feet upon the cursed ground. (One suspects that the rabbits' propensity for devouring the fruits of labor in gardens helped in this regard.)

Unless they lived in an abbey like that at Corbie, where Adalhard's records cite 600 swine (evidently raised for sale, for salting down for guests and workers, for making sausages, and for lard and *petit salé*) in annual consumption, monks generally led vegetarian lives. But their cereals and pulses were well seasoned with produce from the herb garden as well as with imported spices. One of the Corbie records tells of a trip to market at Cambrai to acquire exotics such as pepper, cinnamon, galanga (galingale, or laos, from a root related to ginger), cloves, and mastic.

The herb garden indicated in the plan of St. Gall clearly served a medicinal function for the infirmary as well; its beds are labeled: lily, roses, *fasiolo* (on which bean see more below), gladiolus, rosemary, fenugreek, sage, rue, cumin, mint, costmary, lovage, fennel, *sisimbria* (garden cress), and *saturegium* (savory).[30] Its gardener lived next to another, larger kitchen garden and orchard *cum* cemetery to the south of the cloisters reserved for the ill and for novices. The fowl-keepers also dwelt nearby, together with their charges,

113. Detail of the plan of St. Gall showing the cemetery with fruit trees, each labeled

geese and hens raised for their eggs, for feast days, and probably for the abbot's separate kitchen and honored guests.

That St. Gall garden, its cemetery/orchard so efficiently uniting pragmatic fertilization with hope of resurrection[31] symbolized by spring-flowering fruit trees, joins other documents in filling out our picture of early medieval foodways (fig. 113). At least fourteen varieties (possibly fifteen if we accept an abraded inscription deciphered in the nineteenth century) of fruit and nut trees are labeled in the plan: apples, pears, plums, service trees *(sorbus domestica)*, medlars, bay laurels, chestnuts, figs, quinces, peaches, hazels, almonds, mulberries, and walnuts, plus, seemingly, *pignoli*-bearing pines. Pines are plausible by virtue of the fact that they are among the trees specified for Charlemagne's estates in his cartulary, *De villis.* Much has been made in the literature of the fact that figs, laurel, and bearers of edible chestnuts and pine nuts are basically Mediterranean; for some scholars their presence is evidence of a prevailing Carolingian literary classicism in both the plan and the inventory of *De villis.* Yet it seems most unlikely that Charlemagne would specify purely hypothetical rules for governing his estates and tenants. With care, these flora are able to grow in non-Mediterranean climates. I have cooked with leaves of a flourishing bay tree that grows in a London garden much loved because it is the legacy of Henri Frankfort, who was as knowing a gardener as he was an archaeologist. I have known as well a fig tree that grew in Brooklyn, though it is uncertain whether its fruit or those in the St. Gall plan would succulently mature without propagation by a special wasp; Gerard's *Herbal* of 1597 advises, too, that the fig must grow beside a warm wall and be protected from the north or northeastern winds (certainly the case in the St. Gall plan).[32]

While the catalogue testifies that ancient arboriculture had not declined, citrus fruits beginning to be cultivated in Spain with the triumph of Arab gardening practices do not, of course, appear. Already it may have been important to pulverize almonds and dilute the crushed nuts to produce the milk that would serve later medieval cooks with substitute *laiterie* on lean days when no animal products might be used. There is as yet, however, little evidence that "cold" raw fruit was thought to be unhealthy, an opinion that would subsequently prevail from medieval dietary theory into modern times, according to the humoral system of medicine. Charlemagne's biographers tell us that the emperor enjoyed a bit of fruit after his midday meal before retiring for a nap.

Nowadays when we think "monastery" in connection with fruit orchards or herb gardens, liqueurs and cordials come inevitably to mind. At the time the plan of St. Gall was created, the process of distilling alcohol was known only to Arab alchemists (as its name from kohl—not to mention the word chemistry—announces). It would later spread through their influence from North Africa (the Maghreb) and Sicily to the premier medical school of the Middle Ages at Salerno—of which we will hear much more in the next chapter. The first widely circulated treatise on the topic, written by Arnold of Villanova, comes, naturally, out of Islamicized Catalonia about 1300.[33] Remember, nonetheless, what refreshing drinks or wines can be made from every one of the fruits in Carolingian orchards; perry, from pears, was a medieval favorite, and not only was wine made from mulberries, but their juice was added for color to must and made into "murrey" for sauces and puddings.

In no Carolingian monastery was the population of monks and secular laborers or visitors (at St.-Germain-des-Pres, Abbot Irminon expected 140 a day, so it may have been a case of sheltering pilgrims) dependent solely on an orchard and a garden. Outlying vineyards, orchards, and fields of grains, of staple root vegetables—above all the favorite turnips, onions, and leeks—of ever-present lentils and chickpeas, all these extended a monastery's resources, aided by substantial contributions from even more distant tenancies. St. Gall records cite 30 pounds annually delivered from only two of its distant holdings, while it could rely on imports of lemons, olives, pomegranates, and dates from allied southern brethren at the great monastery of Bobbio in Lombardy.[34] Drying kilns assured a year-round supply of fruits and condiments such as raisins.[35]

All but one controversial entry for the St. Gall kitchen garden, *magones*, appear in *De villis*, and our lists of Carolingian herbs both medicinal and culinary is enhanced by Walahfrid Strabo's poem on the cultivation of gardens at his abbey of Reichenau.[36] He joins lyrical sensitivity to changing seasons and to the particular qualities of each plant listed (twenty-three of them) with hard-headed instructions on raised beds, fertilizer, and gardening lore for growing plants from seeds or cuttings. The same flowers appear in all these documents: roses, lilies, gladioli *(Iris germanica)*, to be used in medicine, but probably adding their essences and color to pottages as well. Since the good old Roman taste for stewed bulbs survived—or was stimulated by Carolingian revival of Apicius—perhaps lilies made for a special treat in season.[37]

There is substantial agreement on the most favored herbs, and we surely concur in the case of sage, fennel, chervil, pennyroyal, lovage, mint, and celery; even horehound and rue or our old friends from Roman cookery, catnip *(nepeta)* and asafoetida. Clary *(salvia sclarea)*, a substitute for sage, is used nowadays only by fans of Henry Beston or by forager disciples of Euell Gibbons (in Pennsylvania it grows wild as an escapee from eighteenth-century gardens). Most of us are strangers to agrimony *(agrimonia eupatoria)*, betony *(stachys betonica)*, or an artemisia, *abrotanum* (southernwood, which must have been particularly valued for its ability to keep moths out of monks' habits). A different artemisia, *absinthium*, or wormwood, will be a culinary familiar only through derivatives like Vermouth and Pernod. Walahfrid also devotes a section of his poem to *papaver* (poppy), while two beds in the St. Gall kitchen garden are devoted to this somniferous plant, if the commentators on the plan are correct in their interpretation of *magones* as a different variety of poppy. I take it rather as something Sorrensen dismisses: a type of carrot, with its name related to Italian dialect *majugola;* his etymology leads him to cognate German *Mohn.* Strabo includes in his poem *beta* (meaning red chard, just as in ancient contexts) and radish, as at St. Gall, but writes not one edifying word about mundane lettuce, cabbages, leeks, garlic, shallots, and the like.

Walahfrid's long segments on the *cucurbita* (cucumbers and gourds) cannot at this date relate to New World pumpkins and squashes, but his *pepones* (from the Greek for melon) seem to be either a type of marrow or, possibly, watermelons, already known to antiquity. In their book on ancient food, Don and Patricia Brothwell deal in exemplary fashion for the nonscientist with the confusing identities of 90 genera and 750 species of Cucurbitaceae, but as we have seen in considering Roman texts and foodways, the problem persists in being vexed.[38] Similar questions about the species involve those "beans" twining up the wall of the herb garden of the St. Gall plan for an ideal monastery. They cannot represent varieties that would come centuries later from the Americas (kidney, lima, and the French, or string bean, among them). Despite the label, they were undoubtedly not of the family Phaseolus, but some form of Dolichos, in other words a bean with a black eye, not unlike the cowpeas of the American South.[39] The fava, or broad, beans inherited from ancient gardeners joined the field crops.

Given the monastic repertory of herbs for flavoring foods and wines, given also an enduring connoisseurship in honey and the possibilities offered by various nuts, there is no need to feel sorry for monks with their vegetarian diet. Some idea of the subtleties of taste they enjoyed is gleaned from a recipe for *oenogarum* worthy of ancient Rome. A ninth-century manuscript from Echternach recommends:

Take fatty fish like salmon, eels, shad, or herring and mix them with salt and fragrant dried herbs (like anise, coriander, fennel, parsley, pepperwort, endive, rue, mint, watercress, privet, pennyroyal, thyme, marjoram, betony, or agrimony) in a solid, well-pitched vat. Layer the herbs, fish and salt two fingers deep in that order, the fish to be left whole if they are small or cut in pieces if large. Repeat these layers to the top, and then cover and leave undisturbed for seven days. Next, for twelve days more, stir the mixture daily, being certain to reach the bottom. To make the sauce, collect all the liquid from the vat and mix it with good wine in the quantity of two *sextarii* to two and a half of wine. Add four bunches each of anise, coriander and pepperwort as well as a fistful of fenugreek seed, thirty or forty grains of pepper, and some costmary, cinnamon and cloves, the latter pulverized. In an iron or bronze pot, then boil down the mixture, adding a half pound of purified honey, until reduced to one *sextarius*. Strain until clear, cool and keep in a well-pitched bowl for seasoning viands.[40]

Diet and cookery gained additionally from animal products such as eggs and various kinds of milk. Walter Horn's magisterial study of the St. Gall plan points out that the geese sharing accommodations with the chickens were useful in more ways than eggs and feathers allow us to imagine because of their propensity for snacking on garden pests and vermin. As for that old barbarian love of *lac concretum*, cheeses were not limited to freshly made types. Testimony as to well-aged varieties comes from an anecdote told in the biography of Charlemagne attributed to Notker. A bishop whom the Emperor unexpectedly visited on the sixth day of the week was hard put to serve his ruler, since he had not been able to order fish in advance, so he served up a fine cheese, "white with cream." But when the Emperor began to cut away its rind, the bishop asked, "Why do you do that? You are throwing away the best part." Charlemagne chewed it questingly and found it "like butter," then asked for two cart loads to be sent to him at the palace each year. When the host wondered how he would test the quality of so much cheese, he was advised to cut each in half, inspect, then reunite it with a skewer and *store* it in his cellar. Some food historians interpret this story as evidence that Camembert had been developed by Carolingian days; others speak out for Brie, which does seem more plausible, given that it is well-documented in the late Middle Ages and that the part of France where its production centers today is on a direct route from Paris to Charlemagne's court at Aachen (Aix-la-Chapelle).

If the regimen of monasteries in early medieval times begins to seem healthful, satisfyingly varied and seasoned (with a discernible heritage of Roman *agrodolce*, sweet honey melded with fruit and herb vinegars), in other words, too beguiling for the austere life of a monastic community, your opinion was shared by St. Bernard of Clairvaux (1090–1153), the austere architect of Cistercian reforms. By his day, abbeys like the Bendictine wonder at Cluny had become extraordinarily wealthy, ruling over far-flung dependencies both monastic and secular. The feudal system, nascent in Carolingian

114. *Sandstone capital decorated with the type of "monster" Saint Bernard decried. Twelfth century. Philadelphia, University Museum of the University of Pennsylvania*

times, now constituted the stabilizing structure of every aspect of life in a development that saw numerous initiatives for economic growth and social order in the course of the eleventh century. Inventions like the horse collar[41] and improvements in water mills enhanced productivity. Urban growth led to the differentiation of craftsmen, merchants, and other town-dwellers from various types of peasant, while a fixed system of heraldry came to identify aristocratic genealogies. So striking is the transformation wrought in building churches and monasteries once millennial fears of the year 1000 had passed, that the period of eleventh and twelfth centuries, before the birth of Gothic architecture, has been given the style-name Romanesque.

The militant Church expressed its unalloyed power in crusades — the Second preached by Saint Bernard at Vezelay in 1146 — and in churches no longer wooden-roofed and subject to devastating fire, but vaulted à la ancient Rome. To attract lucrative trade from hordes of worshippers on the roads of pilgrimage, cathedrals in urban centers sprouted hosts of chapels with additional altars and relics radiating from their eastern sanctuary. The art of large-scale stone sculpture was revived, lavished above all upon portals and capitals (fig. 114). Against the figurative capitals of church and cloister, especially those with carvings copied from Byzantine textiles or fantasized bestiaries, Saint Bernard launched tirades of opprobrium for their distraction from the proper meditative life. He railed equally against the luxuries that had usurped the abstemious regimen appropriate for conventual living. At Cluny the monks might not eat meat, but their fish were luxury species served with elegant sauces, and eggs—what metamorphoses ingenuity was able to devise! (Remember that eggs and other animal products were forbidden during Lent.) Monks were charged, too, with having become oenophiles in some monasteries where tastings of several varieties of wine might precede a meal. What gastronomic excess led everywhere to dead birds being served up in their plumage as if they might fly once again!

Bernard's outrage rings out alike for sculptured fantasies and culinary diversions:

> eyes are feasted with relics cased in gold. . . . The Church's walls are dazzling, but her poor are needy . . . in the cloister, under the eyes of the Brethren who read there, what profit is there in those ridiculous monsters, in that marvelous and deformed comeliness, that comely deformity? To what purpose are those unclean apes, those fierce lions, those monstrous centaurs, . . . Many bodies are there seen under one head, or again, many heads to a single body.

Compare: "What pain and care were not taken to disguise (eggs), to turn them, to make them soft, to make them hard, to chop them? Here they are fricasseed, there they are cooked over the fire; they are stuffed, they are scrambled, and at times their parts are separately served."[42] The austere regime at Bernard's foundation at Cîteaux permitted no meat or fish, no eggs or milk products, and but two meals daily of coarse bread plus vegetables seasoned with oil. Other reform orders were even more severe; Carthusians followed a similar diet, but instituted three days of fasting on bread and water each week.[43]

Feast days, however, brought the bounty of the land and its waters to less restricted tables: birds and game in season, shellfish, crayfish, and fish from streams and estuaries—the favorites being eel, tench, and pike—and herring, from the sea, which lent itself well to preservation by air-drying or salting. Served with sauces of an acidic base gained from vinegar or juice of unripe fruits balanced by honey and herbs, others of wine and spices, early medieval cuisine already sketched the outlines of the cookery we will meet in loftier social contexts, both aristocratic and bourgeois, during the waning of the Middle Ages. The fourteenth century brings what we have lacked since the end of antiquity, manuals of cookery and actual recipes, from every European country.

8 Late Gothic International Style

BLAW MAUNGERE, brawne bruse, bruet or brewet, caudell, fermente or frumenty, frettoure, gyngaudre, graspeys, leche lardys, mawmene, mortruys or mortrew, payne foundow, sotylte, vyaund ryall.[1] These names of medieval dishes do not need to be italicized. They are all given in *English*—albeit Middle English, selected from menus or recipes of the fourteenth and fifteenth centuries. Directions for making some of them appear in our Late Gothic banquet described in the appendix. All represent the cuisine of an elite that relied on costly imported spices and a kitchen endowed with more than the minimal cauldron of lesser folk. They introduce us to conspicuous consumption in the waning Middle Ages,[2] as flamboyant as the like-named style developed by French Gothic architecture in this very period.

To represent any period in the Age of Chivalry from the First Crusade of 1099 to the Hundred Years' War between Britain and France in the fifteenth century, artists illustrating fairy tales, children in school plays, adults in masquerade, and actors in medieval stage presentations, or the metatheater of "creative anachronism," all picture or don the garb of noble courtiers (with an occasional odd peasant or nun) of a time about 1400, give or take twenty-five years.

115.   *Calendar illumination for* April. *Limbourg Brothers,* Très riches Heures, *created for the Duke de Berry, ca. 1415. Chantilly Museum*

Fashion decreed tightly laced waists for men shod with such exaggerated pointed toes *(poulaines)* that they might have to be tied to their wrists to permit walking. Court dress for ladies shared with the men exceedingly pendent sleeves, while elaborate headdresses — like the pointed cone, or *hennin,* from which veils could dangle — rose over temples and foreheads shaved to extend their sway. So ostentatious in its materials, so exaggerated in its cut and outline, was the dress of an era historians of art call the "Late Gothic International" period, it has captured our imaginations unto the present day (figs. 115–16).[3] These very elaborations express the unrestrained imagination of the lords and ladies themselves, creating costumes that summoned up a nostalgic picture of a vanishing feudal culture certain of its prerogatives and confident in its ideals of chivalry and courtly love.

They were not yet aware, or, at least, refused to believe that their way of

116. May. *Limbourg Brothers,* Très riches Heures *for the Duke de Berry. Chantilly Museum*

life was in its final days. It was as if outrageous consumption and display, the accoutrements of power, could fend off an assault upon their citadel of privilege by a growing class of wealthy merchants and craftsmen able and ready to ape their standard of living. Long centuries—from the tenth until the Black Death that wiped out half the population of Europe in 1348–49—saw urban growth and the expansion of trade and industry that brought concomitant increase in activities and sensibilities of a different communal value than the dynamics of manor or village life in the earlier Middle Ages.[4] Immediate local horizons were broadened by pilgrimage, crusades, or other travel, and, closer at hand, the parochial was undermined by widely attended festivals and fairs.[5] Society developed new cohorts and fresh sentiments that led, by the twelfth century in the Ile de France and by the thirteenth century elsewhere, to an enhanced unity of belief, purpose, and effort that marked the concerted drive to

117. St. Bartholomew
(detail of head). French
High Gothic, thirteenth
century. Chartres, South
Transept Portal. This
represents the Gothic
"classical" synthesis of
naturalism and the
spiritual.

build a High Gothic cathedral. The long-term commitment and effort required to compete in such a realm of ambition marks the High Gothic synthesis, in classic terms, of form and content, of artistry and faith (fig. 117).

But the period of the Late Gothic that we are about to consider could
scarcely still be characterized as one of confidence and harmony. Even the
underpinnings of faith, the eternal verity of a unified Christendom, were rup-
tured by the Great Schism following the enforced papal sojourn at Avignon
from 1305–78, a schism marked by contending popes and ecclesiastical loyalties until the Council of Constance reestablished Rome as the central seat of
Christianity in 1417. Religious piety cannot help but be transformed under
such strife and the assault of war, recurrent famines, and the terrible plague
of the mid-fourteenth century that vastly overshadowed sporadic earlier out-
bursts. This is not to mention the perennial dangers of smallpox and "Saint

118.   TOP: *English Gothic* Tomb of a Knight, *ca. 1260. Dorchester Abbey. This is unusual in depicting the deceased as an active figure rather than quietly sleeping.*

119.   ABOVE: *Late Gothic* transi, *or tomb figure, of Guillaume de Harcigny, 1390s. Laon, Musée Archéologique*

Anthony's Fire" (ergotism, from peasant consumption of coarse bread made from rye contaminated by mold) that caused torment everywhere.[6]

A profound change is expressed in the morbid fascination with death (figs. 118–19). A new sense of suffering and pain undergone even by Christ, his Mother, and other holy figures (fig. 120) brought stronger personal response to the sacred, initiating a more intense mystical devotion mediating dogma and ritual. This is the age of the passion of Saint Thomas à Kempis, not the lofty universals of Saint Thomas Aquinas. Nobles found themselves still

120. *Late Gothic*
Vesperbild, *or* pietà, *ca.*
1330. Bonn, Rheinisches
Landesmuseum

inspired by Godefroy de Bouillon, hero of the First Crusade, and the dream
of recapturing Jerusalem. But the thirteenth century had seen the Fourth
Crusade take (and sack!) Christian Constantinople in 1202–4 and, then, after King Louis IXth's futile Seventh and Eighth crusades, the fall of the last
Christian stronghold in the Holy Land in 1291. Yet fading knighthood appears to have been more and more obsessed by empty codes of chivalry and
honor while less and less aware of Islamic menace spreading into the Balkans
and Central Europe. With the fall of Constantinople to the Turks in 1453,

Philip the Good of Burgundy, at Lille in 1454 (at a feast we will consider shortly), called for a crusade to recapture the Golden City on the Bosphorus. But he seems to have been playacting, putting on an appropriate show to simulate outmoded rites of fealty.

If the aristocratic behavior, dress, and manners of the Late Gothic period around 1400 enacted a vain attempt to hold back the clock, and to stem burgeoning middle-class ambition to emulate noble lifestyles, class self-consciousness led equally to curious fascination with the life of simple peasants and other least members of society. Altarpieces commissioned by wealthy donors reveal new iconography stressing the humble origins of the Holy Family, and scenes of the Nativity depict Joseph preparing soup in the kind of tripod pot that was often the only cooking vessel for a peasant household (figs. 121, 122).[7]

121.   Konrad von Soest, Nativity, ca. 1400. Panel of an altarpiece, Parish Church, Niederwildungen, Germany

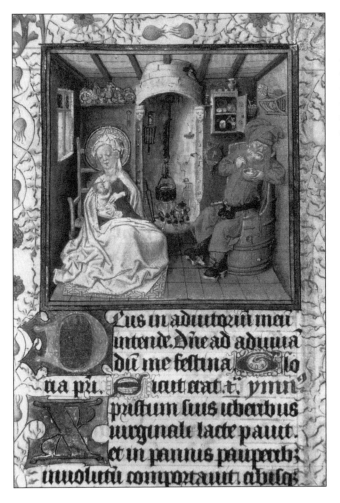

122. The Holy Family
at Home. *From the Hours
of Catherine of Cleves,
Dutch, early fifteenth
century. J. Pierpont
Morgan Library*

Calendar illustrations in prayer books of the time contrast the activities of
peasants working the fields or slaughtering hogs (November) with scenes of
feasting in the castle of their noble lord (January). The *Très Riches Heures* illuminated for Jean, Duke of Berry (brother of the king of France) by Pol Limbourg and his two brothers in about 1416 (figs. 123 and 124) contains famous
examples of such juxtaposition: the duke at table set against peasants huddled
indoors at a fire to fend off February's chill blasts. Each illumination is executed with telling Late Gothic joy in minute observation, whether of nature or
details of daily life and human artisanry at opposite ends of the social scale. To
the beehives and household of the peasants is contrasted the great hall of one

125. Calendar illumination for January. *Limbourg Brothers,* Très riches Heures *of the Duke de Berry*

of the duke's chateaus, hung with a tapestry of knightly combat, bright with a roaring fire that requires a screen to diffuse its warmth, boasting a dresser or credenza to display gorgeous gold and silver plate and a trestle table laid with (we know) cloths in several layers, as well as Berry's golden *nef,* a ship-shaped vessel to hold his essential seasonings, salt, pepper, and possibly the powdered horn of a "unicorn" as a proof for poison (see fig. 125, a *nef* of the period).[8]

As he signals his chaplain and perhaps his personal physician to approach, the duke is served by elegant officers of his household, all high-born aristocrats honored to serve a king's brother. One on the left tests the wine, while the panterer in charge of the bread (source of our "pantry") cuts the square trenchers *(tranchoirs)*[9] that will be set one upon another as service plates to gather up any juices. Before the table, two specially trained carvers

124. February. Très riches Heures *of the Duke de Berry*

(*écuyers tranchants*), prepare for duty. The entire scene breathes an air of extravagance and power, but this need not mean that Jean de Berry was the less devout. Philip the Good of Burgundy (1419–1467) was renowned in his own day for high living and indulgence in ways of the flesh that would have been branded deadly sins of gluttony and pride — at the very least — in earlier times or in the habits of one less nobly blessed. Yet we are told of his piety as well, of four days a week and vigils before special holy days spent praying and subsisting on bread and water.[10]

This was an age in which paradox and the coupling of incongruities such as worldliness and asceticism need not surprise us. To fin-de-siècle artifice and excess the nobility might join the pleasures of playing at the pastoral life. Outdoor picnics of hunting parties (fig. 126) became the rage, but they seem far different from their idealized inspiration in earlier poetry like the *Dit de Franc*

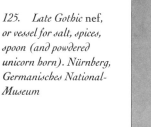

125. Late Gothic nef, *or vessel for salt, spices, spoon (and powdered unicorn horn). Nürnberg, Germanisches National-Museum*

Gontier of Philippe de Vitry (1291–1361), Bishop of Meaux. His hero delights in nature — sweet-smelling grass, a babbling brook, shade from green leaves, and a clear fountain of water to drink — as he dallies with his love over a peasant meal of crusty dark bread, coarse salt, fresh cheese and curds, garlic, onions, and scallions, plus fruits and nuts. Such a sylvan vision is replaced in

126. A Hunt Picnic. *Miniature in the* Hunting Book of Gaston Phoebus, *early fifteenth century. Paris, Bibliothèque National*

the early fifteenth century by imagery from gorgeous fabrics and colors of precious stones to express the delights of an April day in the verses of Charles d'Orléans.[11]

CULINARY SOURCES

The conspicuous consumption of the Late Gothic nobility and a class of competing rich urban dwellers serves food history supremely well. Manuscripts of recipes by and for chefs in court kitchens proliferate throughout Europe.[12] They begin to match the refinements which had already characterized Arabic cookbooks from tenth-century Baghdad and Mozarabic Spain.[13] Not only are we provided with documents from Italy, Denmark, Germany, and England (where the master cooks of Richard II, "acounted the best and ryallest vyaund[ier = eater] of alle cristen [k]ynges," produced the celebrated *Forme of Cury*).[14] We also have from France in the 1390s a splendid opportunity to compare a royal cookery book with a household advisory — a *Ménagier* which, happily, does include menus and recipes—that was produced by an elderly Parisian burgess of means to instruct his teenaged bride.[15] What is more, it is finally possible to deal with real personalities, even though the "Goodman of Paris" remains anonymous.

The royal French cookbook, known in several variant manuscripts, goes under the title *Le Viandier*, by Taillevent.[16] Taillevent, "Jib-sail," was the nickname for one Guillaume Tirel, bestowed—and apparently retained with pride—on a man of darting quickness and flexibility.[17] A rubbing of his tomb-stone in the Museum at St. Germain-en-Laye (fig. 127) shows that he was

127. Taillevent and His Wives. *Rubbing from his tomb cover in the Museum of St.-Germain-en-Laye. Note his coat-of-arms, with culinary emblems.*

knighted for his service to the royal house of Valois. Born about 1313–15, he was dead by 1395, after a long career that began with an apprenticeship in the Normandy kitchen of Louis Count d'Evreux, whose daughter Jeanne d'Evreux was joined, in 1326, in a short-lived marriage to Charles IV, King of France. The Cloisters of the Metropolitan Museum of Art holds her precious Book of Hours, illuminated by Jean Pucelle in a style that shows the artist's acquaintance with the latest developments in Italian pictorial art.[18] Since young Taillevent went off to Paris in service to Jeanne, one wonders whether he, too, discovered new influences from the Mediterranean to modify his provincial, feudal expertise in spit-roasting and handling game. It is certain, in any case, that his talents were recognized after 1328 by the new Valois king, Philip VI, under whom he rose to *queux* (chef) in 1347. Because we have an inventory of staples in the kitchen of the widowed queen, it is possible to reconstruct typical supplies of spices ready to Taillevent's hand in the 1330s.[19]

By 1359–61 Taillevent was chef and sergeant-at-arms for the Dauphin, the Duke of Normandy, following him to Paris when he was crowned Charles V in 1368, and becoming in turn *premier queux* by 1373. With the accession of Charles VI, Tirel continued his career, next becoming the equivalent of what we would term *maitre d'hôtel*, to end his days as head of all provisioning for the court (cited as such in 1381, 1388, and 1392).[20] For the first time since Apicius, we meet a cook who gained fame (and knighthood) through his profession. His influence endured longer than among contemporaries. In the mid-fourteenth century (before the first printed edition of the *Viandier* about 1486)[21] an allusion to Taillevent's cuisine, albeit a characteristically caustic one, appeared in François Villon's *Grant Testament*. Like a medieval "Mrs. Beeton"—a nineteenth-century classic on household management republished and brought up to date until contemporary editions show scant resemblance to her original recipes—Taillevent's work sustained its authority. Cookbooks bearing his name and the glamour of "grant Cuysinier du Roy" continued to be printed down to 1604. And a noted Paris restaurant today bears his name, just as another memorializes Archestratos.

Tirel himself, it has been suggested, was not above appropriating material handed down by others. A *Viandier* manuscript in Sion is written in a script that is dated by its editor to the second half of the thirteenth century or, at latest the very first years of the next, in other words, before Tirel's birth.[22] Other French manuscripts of a different tradition antedate the *Viandier*, which is lost to us in the original according to the *stemma* worked out by Scully for its family of extant manuscripts.[23] From Anglo-Norman England a collection of twenty-nine recipes survives, dated at the end of the thirteenth century, headed *Comment l'en deit fere viaunde e claree*.[24] From the end of the thirteenth century or the beginning of the next, a treatise that shares some general aspects with the *Viandier* tradition was composed with forty-six dishes: *Enseignemenz qui enseingnent a apareillier toutes manieres de viandes*.[25]

Meaningfully, the *Enseignements* joins two early fourteenth-century Latin texts in the same manuscript — from the library of the Duke of Berry no less.[26] At least one of them, *Liber de coquina*, has been attributed to a circle of the House of Anjou holding court at Naples.[27] The international character of court culture is pointed up by other versions of the two texts from Italy,[28] where newly founded dynasties ruling over individual city-states were eager to emulate the lifestyle of Europe's feudal aristocracy. But Italy has its own fourteenth-century survivors, among them compendia from two cities, Venice and Florence, which demonstrate that republican circles may be equally enamored of noble perquisites in dining and rituals of power.[29]

Very provocative data are coming to light for Florence through the research of Allen Grieco, carrying on the work of Curzio Mazzi at the end of the last century by exploiting archives that record purchases and resultant menus over a period from 1344 to 1428 for the table of the Signoria, the priors who governed the city before the Medici came to power.[30] His preliminary results highlight a weekly cycle of meals that alternate between simple repasts and those of marked refinement, punctuated by banquet occasions when important visitors or foreign dignitaries were to be entertained. The earlier medieval differentiation of "fat" days from "lean" (when no meat or animal products such as milk, cheese, butter and eggs might be consumed) seems to have been modified at this *mensa della Signoria*. Wednesdays, Fridays, and Saturdays, as we have seen, were regularly *maigre;* here Wednesday was marked by an "unassuming" meal, but it did include meat.[31] Otherwise, an emphasis on more lavish fare for Sundays and Thursdays conforms with long-standing tradition and with practice elsewhere. More far-reaching in hierarchical implications is the signorial appetite for an aristocratic diet, above all for poultry and a conspicuously elite dish: blancmange made with costly capon, ground almonds, pine nuts, sugar, and cloves.[32] Contemporary sumptuary statutes in Florence reveal something of the tensions between the view of food as a requisite status symbol and the demands of a pious life that must avoid excess in fashion and gluttony or other pleasures of the flesh.

A propriety in observing established alimentary boundaries between social classes also marks our second major document in Late Gothic France, the

Ménagier.[33] Writing about 1393, this elderly townsman is wealthy enough to employ a majordomo, a housekeeper, and a battery of servants; to enjoy his horses and falconry; and to be well connected to government functionaries and minor gentry. Yet in his section on cookery and entertaining (which is a lesser portion of the whole compendium), he simplifies a recipe borrowed from Taillevent with a comment that it is too complex and not suitable for a bourgeois, nor even for a simple knight. Again, he mentions but avoids empirical advice on cooking snails, since they are "for rich people."[34]

The author of the *Ménagier* instructs his fifteen-year-old bride in all the necessary skills for tending the household and a substantial garden in a benevolent tone that Eileen Power characterized as "so kindly, so affectionate, so full of indulgence for her youth."[35] Today's feminists will find it "patriarchal" in the extreme, because all his prescriptions for a happy home and his wife's deportment are designed to assure his comfort and pleasure (or that of her second husband, whom he is realist enough to foresee, lest any shortcomings redound to his own dishonor). With cautionary tales borrowed from didactic literature of the period he instructs his child-bride in religion and morality. For her edification he includes a disquisition on the seven deadly sins with their countering virtues, modeled essentially on Frère Laurent's *La Somme le Roy* of 1279.[36]

A section on the five branches of gluttony—itself but one of two categories of "sins of the mouth" *(pechiez de bouche),* the other of which is an unwary tongue—seems of sufficient interest, given our topic, to justify a brief discussion at this point. The Goodman shares the opinion of his day that gluttony is not merely overeating and drinking to excess. It is also sinful to eat or drink when one is not hungry or thirsty; to eat before the proper time or having said one's "hours" (prayers), and ever before the hour of *tierce* (the liturgical hour ending at nine A.M.);[37] to gobble up food so greedily that one is at risk of choking; or to indulge in food and drink that is overly elaborate or costly while ignoring the needs of the poor, like the fabled rich man whose soul was lost because of his selfishness towards the begging leper Lazarus (fig. 128).

Judging from what remains, the fourteenth century witnessed everywhere a considerable production of manuscript originals and a proliferation of copies of treatises on cookery. After all, one must suppose that these are merely fortuitous survivals of works that saw active use in the hands of "executive" chefs, those who could read, in addition to lords of the manor or castle, and were subject to more than the usual perils endangering the written

128. The Story of Dives and Lazarus *(The Rich Man and the Beggar who will enter into the Kingdom of Heaven, though denied charity by the other). Frieze of the entrance portal of the Romanesque Church at Moissac. The arcades below depict the death of Dives and his punishment in Hell.*

word.[38] In terms of reception, it is clear that late medieval cookbooks are addressed to professionals who have no need for explanations of specialized cooking vocabulary ("parboil" before roasting, for example) and are able to use their own judgment about proportions. What we might call vernacular cookery was carried on in ordinary households without benefit of written guidance, but through an oral tradition handed down from mother to daughter over generations — the reason for survival even today of many ancient Roman practices in the homespun cuisine of European provinces where they once held sway.

We have not yet exhausted cookery manuscripts from the fourteenth century, the early side of the focus date of 1400 for Late Gothic International culture. To Germany of the thirteenth century is attributed, by the late Rudolf

Grewe, an original reflected in Danish manuscripts of the fourteenth.[39] For others the prototype was clearly French.[40] However that may be, Germany is splendidly represented by a mid-fourteenth-century manuscript from Würzburg's episcopal court, *Das Buch von guter Spise*, with ninety-six upscale recipes that focus on made dishes and condiments while enhancing our Gothic repertory of fritters and foccace *(fladen)*.[41]

Last but not least, another variant of fourteenth-century cuisine is represented by a Catalan work, the *Libre de Sent Soví*.[42] Its author purports to be a cook who had worked for the king of England, though his recipes display a distinctly Catalan flavor, especially the *mig-raust* or "half-roasted fowl" in a sweet-sour sauce of almonds and spices that echoes as "mirause Catalan" in European culinary literature down through the sixteenth century.[43] Catalan cuisine is also responsible for an early specialized collection of recipes for confections, undoubtedly under the influence of the neighboring Mozarab virtuosity with sugar.[44] Renaissance Italy was to be particularly affected by the sophistication of Catalan and Aragonese court cookery after the united House of Barcelona took over the rule of Naples in 1443.[45]

On into the fifteenth century, the pace of Late Gothic culinary writings accelerates. Copies and variants of the favorites proliferate, first in manuscript and finally, by the second half of the century, in the revolutionary multiple issues permitted by printing.[46] Still within international-style originality stands a revealing French treatise from the princely household of Arnaldo I, Duke of Savoy (later Pope Felix V, 1440–49), written by his head chef, Maistre Chiquart Amiczo.[47] A *Livre fort excellent de Cuysine tres-utille et proffitable . . .*, printed at Lyons in 1542 and thereafter under varying titles until the end of the century, was once thought to go back to the fourteenth century in origin.[48] England produced a formidable series of manuscripts through the fifteenth century, including 127 verse recipes of the *Liber Cure Cocorum*, said to date from the reign of Henry VI (1421–69).[49]

Despite varying degrees of regional characteristics in all the cookery treatises and compilations of the high Middle Ages, the roster fully expresses a cosmopolitan court and ecclesiastical culture that knew no national boundaries.[50] "International" is a fitting rubric for a time when the noble houses of Europe were linked by kinship—so narrow that the Holy Roman Emperor was at once the uncle of Charles V of France and the father-in-law of Charles's English enemy, Richard II—and forced to adjust to rapid changes in society. It was a time when artists of every persuasion, including chefs, could gain wide reputation and be summoned to serve first one court, then another, and when commodity trade allowed an elite to escape dependence on solely local comestibles. The English may have made more of a presentation dish with the entire head of a boar — still a feature of Christmas celebration at one Oxford College — than did their continental brethren. The French may have preferred to season their foods with "grains of Paradise" (meleguetan pepper),[51] which Moroccans today call "desert nutmeg," more frequently than with the pepper favored by English and Italians.[52] Southerners like the Catalans and Italians seem to have been devoted to a heavier hand with sugar than their counter-parts in the North — and not merely because sugarcane was grown in their area, for the most prized was imported from Cyprus. Germanic cooks already displayed a fondness for cabbages, sour and otherwise, as well as for meats cooked with fruits and berries. The Goodman of Paris instructed his wife on the German antipathy toward fish perceived as undercooked: if a French chef cooked carp for both Frenchmen and Germans, the Germans would send theirs back to be redone.[53] Lard and butter were constant as fats in rec-ipes, though olive oil more commonly made an appearance in Mediterranean countries — yet not so frequently as one might expect.[54] These and a host of regional modifications cannot, however, conceal a commonality in basic culi-nary procedures and results.

THE MEDICAL BACKGROUND

Our figure 129 is taken from a twelfth-century manuscript copying Byrht-ferth's *Manual*,[55] a compendium, or *summa*, of knowledge in the realm of Nat-ural History, including ways in which the structure of the macrocosm, the universe of the Lord's creation, might be correlated with the microcosm, the human body. Such schemata represent the mind-set of the Middle Ages to a most significant degree because they were fundamental to education, to the mode in which scholars were taught to think, making symbolic arithmology visually explicit.

In this relatively simple example, the four elements, reading from the top clockwise, consist of earth, water, air, and fire; they are conjoined with direc-tions of the compass and the winds and are integrated into the surrounding arcs of the zodiac and a calendar of the months, including notations of each solstice and equinox, the four ages of man (infancy and childhood, adoles-cence, youth, and old age calibrated to spring, summer, autumn, and winter),

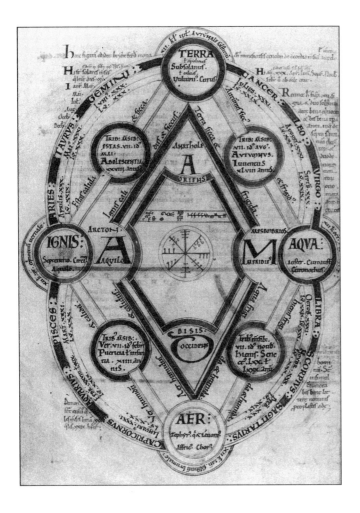

129. *Diagram of some quaternities: the humors and correlates. Twelfth-century English manuscript illustrating the Anglo-Saxon* Manual *of* Byrhtferth.

and—most important for our nutritional lore stemming from Galen—the qualities of both elements and seasons (whether hot or cold, moist or dry, and a sliding scale thereof).

We have already been introduced to the humors of the body as well as to their associated temperaments. Accumulated doctrine—embodying the researches of physicians from Galen to such medical men as Anthimus, doctor to Theodoric, the Ostrogothic ruler of Italy at the end of the fifth and early sixth centuries; Simeon Seth, medical director for a tenth-century Byzantine emperor; and Seth's contemporary, Constantinus Africanus, the learned Arab physician who, in the eleventh century, became a leading light of the medical school at Salerno in Italy—embraces all their dicta about what constituted physical well-being and how to preserve good health by eating wisely, and found increasingly detailed prescription and systematic order in the course of the Middle Ages. It is this quality of system and order that is the hallmark of the entire period we call the Middle Ages. But there is a very important difference from the way we define concepts of the kind and our medieval forebears did. For them, ordering principles were not rationally derived by humans but were qualities preordained in the Creation. The Bible specified God's postulates: everything was brought into being by application of number, weight, and measure.[56] It is therefore most appropriate for us to speak of the scholastic *system, orders* of chivalry within the feudal *system,* the *system* of a Gothic cathedral, or the *ordo* of the ecclesiastical mass. As we shall see, the same principles of system and order govern the menus and cookery[57] that characterize meals for the three estates into which society was divided, following God's inviolable design: the aristocracy, the clergy, and the "other," with their constituent classes. They are precepts strongly revealed in elite gastronomy of the period upon which we are focused, the "waning of the Middle Ages," or the Late Gothic International Style prevailing before and after 1400.

In a larger sense, literary historians have frequently considered the shorthand methods by which authors of the fourteenth and fifteenth centuries could give a reader any character's precise location on a scale of hierarchic social class by simply alluding to the item(s) of food he or she was eating. Chaucer is a notable example, expanding the method from class to personality. By what economy of means he tells you of social pretensions on the part of guildsmen (who have brought their own cook to make dishes such as blancmange [blamensyr], which demanded a lavish hand with capon, almonds, rice, sugar, and similar signs of an elite diet). Again, take the Franklin[58] among his pilgrims to Canterbury, in contrast to the straightforward persona and homely domesticity of the Wife of Bath or the vision of a farm widow's impoverished dignity in "The Nun's Priest's Tale"—each a complete portrait if one only considers the clues of their normal fare and the utensils they used to partake of it.[59] The "Grotesque Feast" of the *Prima Pastorum,* a fourteenth-century tale of pastoral life, has been shown to encode the "grotesqueness" of a meal shared by two shepherds through a device of simply mixing dishes or ingredients from both lordly and peasant food habits in a manner most incongruous—at least for its original audience.[60]

The medieval quest for order and system affected, not merely the social hierarchy of diet, but every aspect of alimentary culture. The manner in which menus were structured has been minutely analyzed by Jean-Louis Flandrin

ɑɒiutoꝛ coꝛum ꞇ pꝛotectoꝛ coꝛum est.
ꞅui timent ꝺominum sperauerunt

130.   *Four bas-de-page miniatures from the* Luttrell Psalter. *English, ca. 1340. In sequence, the miniatures depict the preparation and serving of a dinner. London, The British Library*

in a comparative study of French and English custom in the fourteenth and fifteenth centuries.[61] Whereas previous scholars often stressed merely a disordered profusion of dishes without a reasoned balance of flavors and textures or a particular order of sequence, Flandrin demonstrates that in each country the succession of courses (*cours* in Britain; *assiette* and *mès* or, plural, *mets,* in France) followed a specific logic. He finds that there may be more services in a French aristocratic banquet, but there are more component dishes in each one of the English. What is more, Flandrin has been able to work out some rules by which the distribution of dishes among the different courses seems to have been settled in France, although he has yet to explore their "logique gastronomique" in depth. The rules he discovers in England involve a precedence, or rank, assigned to individual dishes within the first, second, or third service; these suggest to him that, after being set out on the table all together, they were then taken up in turn to be passed around by servitors. When he discerns signs of ranking in a French menu — particularly in the case of large roasts and venison requiring the arts of the carver — the same sort of service is suggested. If he is correct about a ranking system in British menus,

131. Regal Feast Held for Noble Women in a Great Hall. *Woodcut by Michael Wolgemut from an incunable, Stefan Fridolin's* Der Schatzhalter, *printed in Nuremberg in 1491.*

it suggests that a greater proportion of game and spectacular roasts might have been served there. Does this already represent the proverbial "roast beef of Old England," foreshadowing a certain envy expressed by Gallic visitors in the seventeenth and eighteenth centuries?[62]

Systematic aspects of cuisine and culinary logic can be detected right down to what might be termed a microscopic level, in the detail of a cook's repertoire of sauces. To casual investigators and readers of their histories, it is a given that medieval food was heavily and exotically seasoned with spices and herbs thanks to a lack of refrigeration and a need to cover the taste of tainted or salt-preserved meat.[63] Writers more scholarly than journalistic counter such popular assumptions, justly putting forward sociopolitical motives for the display of one's wealth and status by being able to afford costly spices, as well as for medical reasons stemming from humoral doctrine. Besides, since there are few clues to proportions in recipes, we cannot know with how heavy a hand cooks added their seasonings.[64]

What may be termed the late medieval spice system has been investigated from a point of view at once social and psychological by Bruno Laurioux,[65] who discovered a set of complex symbolic values, including the sexual, in aromatics imported from a fabled Orient "contigu au Paradis." Using account-books, tariff regulations, and other commercial documents to supplement scanty culinary treatises, he traces the evolution that transformed tastes and trade from the Apician tradition to the great diversity of aromatics privileged in the High and Late Middle Ages. National differences are also revealed in his statistics, but most important for our present concern with medieval *system* is his observation that the theory of the humors must explain a difference noted between winter spices and those of summer. Sauces in the winter employ hot, dry spices — mustard, ginger, pepper, cinnamon, and clove in quantity — while these are largely abjured during the heat of summer, just as wine and vinegar may be replaced by verjuice (Italian *agresto,* of unripe fruits), lemon or pomegranate juice, and rose water.

Such a seasonal foundation of medieval spice theory is but the least part of a complex science that has been brought to light by specialized research into sauce-making, first adumbrated by a historian of science, Lynn Thorndike, and furthered by the medievalist and food historian, Terence Scully.[66] Using other *regimena* together with a sauce book and the medical *Regimen* from which it derives (attributed to Maino de' Maineri, a Milanese physician of the fourteenth century who taught at Paris for a time and died about 1364), Scully has been able to reconstruct the variables that governed the selection of a sauce to accompany a particular viand.

The meats, fowl, and seafood of Maineri's handbook of health, listed according to their mode of cooking—whether roasted, boiled, fried, or baked in a pastry—are each accorded a proper sauce or, in some cases, alternative sauces. Minute analysis permits Scully (arguing from the medical to the gastronomical) to propose that "culinary art in the Middle Ages tended to be less a matter of inspiration than of science, a science which relates in some respects to the rational operation of the scholastic method, and in others to a sort of rudimentary organic chemistry whose rules concerning the interaction of elements are not less rigorous."

Before looking at the minutiae of sauce-making, we must review the authority enjoyed in the Middle Ages by the Galenic tradition of the humors, itself derived from a long line of classical theorists traceable back to the fifth century B.C. and Empedocles' definition of four elements in the visible world, followed by the Hippocratic doctrine of four associated qualities with their humors. This, as we have seen, was developed through Platonic and Stoic macrocosmic/microcosmic theory into Galen's formulation of the temperaments. Medieval people placed particular confidence in the humoral precepts disseminated by the most prestigious health center of the day, the School of Salerno.

From its tenth-century founding in the dark days of the Saracen invasions, which saw the sack of St. Peter's as well as the advent of Arabic science, the School at Salerno was the preeminent European institution for medical research and teaching. It was surrounded by a special aura long after other medical centers, like Montpellier, had come to share its influence on diet and the care of one's mortal husk. Manuscript copies of its *Regimen Sanitatis Salernitanum* proliferated in the fourteenth and even fifteenth centuries. Most books on medieval cookery, including this chapter, are illustrated with its miniatures of merchants selling or householders cooking a particular ingredient analyzed as to its quality, cold or hot, moist or dry—and in what degree from one to four (figs. 132–34).[67] Today we can gain some further idea of the renown of Salerno and the prestige of its handbooks by reference to the Mother Goose rhyme in which old Dame Trott preserves popular reclame for Trotula, an early teacher and healer devoted to women's complaints.[68]

It is within this context that one must view the sauces and other prescriptions of Maino de' Maineri and of such older contemporaries as Arnaldus de

132. Cooking Ricotta. Tacuinum sanitatis *(Manual of Health). Fourteenth century. Rome, Biblioteca Casanatense*

133. Tacuinum sanitatis, *another ingredient. Here the women are preparing* testiculi *for a dish that will also be a favorite in Renaissance Italy: a ragout based on cock's combs and testicles garnered when capons are castrated. Rome, Biblioteca Casanatense*

134. Tacuinum sanitatis. *In this miniature the cooks are making and drying pasta. Rome, Biblioteca Casanatense*

Villanova. One then gains a clear understanding of the frequent wording in recipe books of the Late Gothic. When modern cookbooks would "add" or "mix," the medieval cook is directed in whatever language to "temper" an ingredient or mixture with another. One must moderate the temperature and moisture to balance the qualities of the food in question, but also bring it into harmony with the temperament of the person for whom it is destined. Manifestly, this is dietetic practice which favors the most powerful in any group of diners. How did the phlegmatic wife of a choleric husband fare? Set beside his fiery disposition, how was her nature (demanding a warm and dry diet) reconciled with nourishment both cool and moist to make temperate his preponderance of yellow bile? Also, little wonder that a person of rank had a personal physician in attendance at meals, just as Maino de' Maineri served the Visconti in Milan, as well as Andreas Ghini de' Malpighi of Florence, the Bishop of Arras, from 1331–33.

From Maineri, let us examine prescriptions for capon or pheasant, as interpreted by Scully. I have chosen these two fowl because their almost ideally temperate qualities in both warmth and humidity made them universal favorites for entertainment menus.[69] It must be borne in mind that moist and dry in whatever degree are characteristics secondary to dominant hot/cold parameters. Male creatures are by nature hot and dry, female cold and moist. But when animals or fowl are castrated, like the capon, their heat is moderated, and they retain a youthful moistness that has not been dissipated in sexual activity. A sauce for this bird or a naturally moist pheasant need have very little countering action, save to account for seasonal differences between summer and winter. We know that, to a degree, boiling as opposed to roasting ultimately removes, while high heat sears and seals in vital juices of meat — the contrast between bouillon and "drippings." But in the Middle Ages, boiling in water was, of course, seen as moisturizing, spit-roasting as drying. The moderate nature of capon and pheasant meant they could well sustain either method of cooking in contrast, say, to beef, which was more regularly subject to boiling.[70] Beef, as the coldest and driest of all meats — being the *char* of a neutered male or ox, if not a female — was rendered digestible by boiling, and recipes indicate that most roast meats were first parboiled, just as Taillevent recommends plumping chickens initially by hot water.[71]

Maino's fowl, if boiled in summer weather, might profit either from a cool and very slightly moist juice of sorrel or of vine stock added to their own bouillon, or from a "white" sauce — made of ground almonds and sugar — instead of a green one, each only very slightly warm and moist to the first degree. In winter cold, on the other hand, as with many viands, their warmth had to be enhanced by warmer spices that were also dry as well as by optional warm, dry herbs like sage, hyssop, and parsley.

Being temperate in nature, both capons and pheasants might appropriately be baked in pies, and Maino sets out all the alternatives to maintain a requisite balance. Roasted, the birds call for a different strategy. The white sauce used for the boiled dish must now be modified to counter drying heat by the addition of garlic and ginger, moist and warm to a higher degree. For summer, fewer spices need be used, and cold, dry verjuice (of sour fruit or grapes) replaces any wine (warmer and drier) that might be used in winter to prepare the crushed almonds.

One begins to grasp something of the calculations that went into planning sauces that complied with preventive medicine of the day and to recognize the desire of highly placed personages to have a doctor or two in attendance at mealtime! One also understands why the humoral system ruled pathological as well as "psychological" science. Otherwise it might be difficult to comprehend the medieval explanation for dogs' susceptibility to rabies: this melancholic complaint comes from its "disordered" life, eating any kind of thing, sleeping indoors beside a hot fire, next out in the cold.[72]

Yet humors and "complexions" were not all there was to healthful diet. Alchemists and astrologers had their contribution to make to wholesome nutrition. An alchemist is responsible for an experiment reported in an early fourteenth-century text attributed to Duns Scotus. It sustained the alchemical notion that inanimate stones and minerals also possessed humors by showing that milk resolves into phlegm (whey), blood or sanguine (butter), melancholia (cheese), and choler (those remains which disappear in boiling).[73] Astrologically speaking, it was important for an individual to know the therapeutic value of foods in a context of planetary and zodiacal influences both general and personal.[74]

The role of spices being crucial to neutralizing dangers that arose from the nature of diverse foods, it is easy to understand the role of apothecaries[75] in blending ready-made "powdours" as digestive aids and the presence of special kitchen boys to handle braying of spices to make "powdour douce," or "pouldre blanche," which appear in our English, French, and Italian sources.[76] It seems particularly fitting that the spiced wine concoction that capped formal dining should be dedicated, as it were, to the master physician of antiquity, Hippocrates, whose name is still today invoked in the oath of newly fledged doctors. "Hippocras" or "ypocras" was strained through a long inverted cone

135. Straining Hypocras. *Illustration from a fifteenth-century manuscript depicting the "sleeve of Hippocrates." Modena, Biblioteca Estense*

of finely woven fabric called "Hippocrates' sleeve" (fig. 135). Recipes vary slightly, but red wine was always simmered with cinnamon, ginger, and sugar, to which pepper and grains of Paradise were usually added, and perhaps red coloring from sandalwood.

For those who might view the medieval passion for spices and herbs as monstrous excess, it should be remembered that the phenomenon is one further example of the classical tradition. Galen's exemplary medical text included a quotation that was to have repercussions down to the nineteenth century. He quoted a poem attributed to Andromachus of Crete, physician to

Nero, prescribing his formula for theriac, said to derive from a formula devised by the Hellenistic king Mithridates VI as an antidote against poison. Its original forty-five ingredients grown to hundreds, it was believed to combat not only poison but all disease, and it was compounded as a favorite nostrum until the end of the eighteenth century in many European cities, under the supervision of municipal administrators — not unlike our FDA's oversight of vitamin supplements today.[77]

THE LATE GOTHIC KITCHEN AND CUISINE

Glastonbury Abbey in England or Fontevrault in France, in Viollet-le-Duc's reconstruction, bring the Late Gothic monastic kitchen vividly alive in our imaginations. Woodcuts in some of the earliest printed books show that in more modest establishments professional cooks might be favored with more practical equipment than the gigantic fireplaces of monasteries and palaces or the limiting chimneys of ordinary folk (figs. 122, 132). Everything could very well be cooked on a spit, in a hanging cauldron, or in vessels amid the coals, if the chef were provided with a waist-high platform for charcoal akin to the good old Roman *bancone*.

Richard II of England was said by chroniclers to have had 2,000 cooks in his kitchens and 300 servers, but he was, of course, famous for his extravagance and hospitality, purportedly feeding at one time as many as ten thousand guests at his court, as befitted a paragon of Late Gothic stylishness and conspicuous consumption.[78] What is probably a more realistic picture of royal kitchen staffs is found in Taillevent's: 48 personnel directly occupied in cookery, plus 30 of the *paneterie* ("pantry") in charge of breads and the like, 15 to manage the *fruiterie* and conserves, 13 *maistres d'hostel* in supervisory positions over workers and equipment, and 38 *échansons*, or cup-bearers, for wines and other beverages. It must be held in mind that these and similar records do not take account of noble servitors who directly served their lord at table.

In vast royal or monastic kitchens, how did the head *queux* control such hordes of underlings? In his fifteenth-century memoirs, Olivier de la Marche, drawing on his life at the court of the dukes of Burgundy centered at Dijon, paints an image of their head chef, his main tasks done, sitting between the fireplace and the "buffet" so he can oversee everything going on in the kitchen and holding a long wooden spoon *(louche)* with which to test dishes and beat the "enfants de cuisine" (the young apprentices, that is) back to their chores. All of his duties for Charles the Bold are outlined by Olivier, the majordomo:

how the chief cook is elected, how he watches over the sugar and spices, how he surveys the work of his domain, and all the details of service.

Olivier outlines the responsibilities of the duke's other minions as well. It is normal to find that fruiterers are in charge of all illuminating devices from small candles to large *flambeaux,* a further example of medieval systematic logic: wax is made by bees who feed upon the flowers of fruit trees, among others. Notice that it is the *rôtisseur* who takes charge of the cuisine if the chef is away or ill, indicating his rank in command of the kitchen hierarchy (the fourth, if one counts two patrician equerries who supervise these matters). This highlights the fact that spit-roasting was privileged in noble establishments. As one would expect, medieval inventories and wills, not to mention archaeological finds, all confirm that lesser households would not need large spits for haunches of meat and fowl. But it has also been found that even small spits and grills are quite rare in certain geographical contexts, in Provence for example.[79]

Clearly, a vast proportion of all European cooking was accomplished by boiling or simmering brouets (or brewets) and stews like potages, hochepots, and caudles. Keep in mind, however, that the humble housewife, limited to a hanging cauldron or a three-legged bronze pot sitting among the coals, had a bit more flexibility in her cookery than we might expect. Different preparations could be suspended in a cloth and by a cord into the simmering stew (origin of the British pudding-bag), and she might well possess a toasting or waffle iron and a long-handled utensil for frying or pan-baking when coals were heaped over its cover. She would not have the specialist to cope with the fire on whom a court chef could rely, someone not merely to lay it properly and ignite it, but wise in the cooking qualities of different woods — even more complex lore than that our grandmothers were forced to master with their iron ranges ("pie wood" is still a term in New England for cherry, which burns with a very hot, quick flame). But both the court and the vernacular cook would have welcomed use of the terra-cotta *couvre-feu* that preserved embers for the following day, safeguarded the premises from unwanted fire, and gave us our word "curfew."

We have already encountered some ceremonial aspects of service in Jean of Berry's Great Hall, but his prayer-book miniature (fig. 123) depicted him dining alone, not seated at "high table" — or more accurately, at a portable trestle board, hidden beneath a sequence of three to four cloths for as many courses — and raised on a dais with other noble guests. Rigid protocol governed every aspect of formal banquet feasting. The dresser (*dressoir, dressouer*), or credenza, which displayed cold dishes and wines while vaunting the lord's gold and silver plate and precious vessels rose in stages strictly prescribed in number: in France, five for a ruling prince or a queen, four for a princess, three for a countess, and so forth down the line of titles.[80] A flamboyant representative of fourteenth-century precious objects is a table-fountain in the Cleveland Museum (fig. 136) executed in silver gilt and enamel with an architectural vocabulary of castellated towers, vaults, crockets, filigree tracery, gargoyles and fantastic animals.[81]

Niceties of etiquette flourished during the fourteenth century to culminate in refinements of the international style. The use of spoons for more liq-

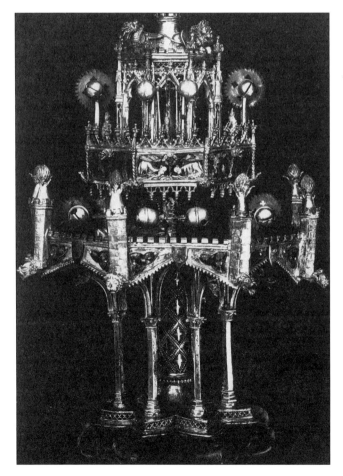

136.   *Late Gothic table fountain. French, fourteenth century. Cleveland Museum of Art*

uid dishes developed to ease courtesy-book advisories about putting one's lips to the bowl *(écuelle)* shared, like the wine chalice *(hanap)*, with a partner. Forks, of course, except for two-pronged instruments for cooking or carving, were not to come into general use before the sixteenth — even in some contexts seventeenth — century. This despite a few fastidious souls like the Byzantine princess who married the Doge Orseolo II of Venice in the eleventh century and stunned the Italians by her affectations: her eunuch had to gather dew for her to wash in, because water was too harsh; he cut her food into tiny pieces for her to eat with a little gold, two-tined fork.[82] Gradually individual nappery appeared to supplement a huge communal napkin that had previously, together with the overhang of a tablecloth, done service for the high table.

For late medieval noble dining, men no longer had to use their own knives to slice off portions from roasts passed about by servitors. Again, international-style ostentation brought new heights to carving, which became a virtuoso performance in the court spectacle that the banquet had become.[83] The *écuyer tranchant* we encountered at the Duke of Berry's January dinner was well matched by his counterparts elsewhere. An entire specialized vocabulary of verbs for carving came to be applied to each species of fauna. A sample of them in English will put to rest the notion put forward by some writers on medieval food habits that such words as "smite" or "hew" for "cut" and "hack" for "chop" reflect the crudeness of the times. "Dysfygure that pecocke," "spoyle that henne," "alaye that fesande [pheasant]," "splatte that pyke," "splayce that breme," "breke that dere," "dysplaye that crane," "wynge that quayle," "barbe that lopster," and "undertranche that purpos [porpoise]" are not the most ingenious modes of "unhingeing" meat or getting proper "lesches" (slices) from it.[84] A comparable medieval sense for system and order is to be found in the special counting vocabulary for plural animals that puts to shame our paltry survivors such as "pride of lions" or "gaggle of geese."

MENUS AND COOKERY

Wine-lovers will be disappointed that extant menus for so many regal feasts of the Late Gothic do not follow the custom of modern banquets in listing the wines for each course. Household accounts may list purchases for a particular entertainment, but they rarely indicate what dish a particular vintage is meant to complement. The medieval appetite for sweetness meant that wines from Greece and especially Cyprus were much appreciated. Both France and Italy produced native wines for local consumption as well as export, while England's Roman heritage had become a casualty of slight changes in climate and a decay in the art of viticulture.

Already in the twelfth century, Peter of Blois could denigrate British wine as more fit "to be sieved rather than drunk."[85] Yet one of the most poetic oenological appreciations of the Middle Ages is to be found in the same century in the *Natural History* of Alexander Neckham:

> Good wine should be as clear as the tears of a penitent, so that a man should see distinctly to the bottom of his glass; its color should represent the greenness of a buffalo's horn; when drunk it should descend impetuously like thunder, sweet-tasted as an almond, creeping like a squirrel, leaping like a roebuck, strong like the building of a Cistercian monastery, glittering like a spark of fire, subtle as the logic of the schools of Paris, delicate as fine silk and colder than crystal.[86]

Of course, from 1152 until 1453 and the arrival of Joan of Arc, England occupied, by right first of marriage, then of conquest, much of western France. Thus the wines of Gascony — the clarets of Bordeaux that have ever since dominated British cellars — came to be the favorites across the Channel.

Eustache Deschamps (born in 1346 at Vertus in Champagne) in his *Miroer* (Mirror) *du mariage* gave the palm to Burgundy and the wine of Beaune in his listings of *crus* from all regions of France, as well as Germany, Spain, and Portugal — not one from Italy, despite his travels there![87] He enumerates in verse the wines which should be at hand for any good mistress of a household:

> Vins d'Auxerre et de Bourgogne,
> De Beaune et de Gascogne,
> Vin de Chably, vin de Givry,
> Vin de Vertus, vin d'Irancy,
> Vin grec et vin muscadé
> Verjus veut avoir et vin gouais.[88]

Vineyards on all the hills that surround the Paris basin enjoyed a good reputation in the Middle Ages: côtes de Chaillot, Montmartre, Belleville, Ménilmontant, and Sainte-Geneviève. Gottschalk reports several score *clos* as well as others in neighboring communes such as Argenteuil and Suresnes. Even after World War II it was still possible to trace at various sites in the city

remnants of what had once proved a flourishing viticulture until urban expansion progressively swallowed them up.[89]

Beverages other than wine continued in popularity: cider and cervoise in
France, beer and ale in England above all, where these were even considered
the most healthful drink for small children.[90] Perry, fermented pear juice, was
also widely appreciated. A relish for honey preparations such as mead and
metheglin was more characteristic of English palates, where drinking them
could be a statement of historic allegiance—a good old Anglo-Saxon preference over Norman wine.[91] For the French peasant there was also traditional
piquette, sour wine, a descendant of *posca,* the potion that served Roman soldiers in the field.

Turning to other ingredients of medieval menus and cuisine, we have already considered one of the myths that abound in popular imaginings, the
alleged misuse of spices. Another embraces the notion that vegetables were
not held in high esteem, that meat and, for fast days, its alternative, fish, dominated upper-class tables just as cereals did the lower. Nothing could be further from the truth. Misapprehension of the actual situation comes about
through understandable neglect on the part of medieval communicants—ma-
jordomos and other chroniclers of courtly feasts, who laid stress on elaborate
main dishes rather than on their accompaniments in documenting menus (*es-
criteaux,* in France), and authors of cookbooks, who tended to concentrate on
the most challenging viands in addressing culinary professionals.

The author of the *Ménagier de Paris* includes a treatise on gardening that
supplements the medieval literature on health, plants, and herbal lore as evidence for the importance of fruit and vegetable produce.[92] Both he and the
Viandier indicate what such crops meant to their tables: not merely the perennial onions and leeks with their botanical family, but purées of legumes and
root vegetables, as well as many more fruits than most modern cooks use
for tarts and stewed dishes. Quinces, medlars, mulberries, wardens (a kind
of large pear), elderberries, barberries, and a host of other "berries" seldom
figure in our present-day recipe books, yet are constants in those of the
Middle Ages.

Granted that testimony to the dangers of eating melons or other fruits is
readily found in medical texts. But the opposite is true when one requires
their cold, moist influence to bring down fevers. And no one is able to view
the sensuous imagery of medieval poetry and pictorial renderings of the enclosed garden *(hortus conclusus)* that symbolizes the Virgin Mary without recognizing the love of fruits shining forth.[93] Even the lower classes were able to

relish apples and cherries, while the patrician garden could now boast, thanks to the Arabs, citrus fruits to supplement the citron cultivated since Roman times. Lemons and bitter oranges — Seville oranges, or *bigarades* — are featured now in Late Gothic cookery sources. We are told of Eleanor of Castille's ornamental *bigarade*, planted upon her marriage to Charles III of Navarre (ruling from 1397), a cherished tree that passed into the gardens of the Constable de Bourbon and was forfeited to Fontainebleau in 1522. Known as "le grand Connétable," it lived on at Versailles until 1858.[94] In menu-planning, "dangerous" melons and other fruits could be assigned to the beginning of a meal so they might stimulate the appetite and open a path to digestion, while hot, dry spices to follow would counter any harmful effect. But more acid fruits such as apples and pears were suitable to join heavy cheese at the end of a meal, helping to press down the vapors of food that one had consumed.[95]

Our Goodman of Paris distinguishes three kinds of cabbage (*choulx*): a white one, called *cabus*, spring cabbages of pointed heads, and a "Roman" type, though courtly Taillevent only mentions the lowly cabbage among his *potaige* vegetables with leeks, chard, peas, turnips, and fava beans. Understandably, Late Gothic cookery manuscripts tend to privilege meat dishes — dramatic evidence, in a period when about 180 days a year required abstention from flesh or animal products, of the elite environment in which they flourished. Even so, those of the most encyclopedic character often begin with vegetables and herbs; the *Liber de coquina* of the Angevin court at Naples, for example, includes forty-three recipes, considerably more than for fish.[96]

Many greens that have fallen out of commerce today — or are in the course of being rediscovered in mesclun — were favored by medieval cooks: smallage, purslane, blite, lamb's lettuce, and the like. A salad in the *Forme of Cury* is typical:[97] parsley, sage, garlic, shallots, onions, leeks, borage, fennel, cresses, rue, rosemary, mints, and purslane to be washed and picked over, torn and mixed with oil, lastly vinegar and salt applied. You might well decide to add a variant to the menu in the appendix, remembering that the Arabs had long since contributed spinach to the repertoire (fig. 137, from *Taccuinum sanitatum*) and that spicy nasturtium leaves or its velvety flowers (seasonally packaged in British supermarkets, why not in ours?) make an authentic addition.

Perhaps the most egregious error that keeps turning up in otherwise unremarkable books is that Marco Polo brought a knowledge of noodles from China on his return to Italy in 1292. (Readers of chapter 4 will already be aware of this error.) We have encountered Greek and Roman *lagana* and *tracta*

137. Gathering Spinich. Tacuinum sanitatis. *Fourteenth century. Rouen, Bibliothèque municipale, MS. 3054*

as well as the essential distinction between simple forms of pasta cooked fresh and that which can be dried and readily stored: *pastasciutta.* There seems to be general agreement that it was the Arabs who developed dried types from the ninth century A.D.[98] The earliest Italian reference to dried "maccheroni" appears to be an inventory of 27 February 1279, in a Genoa archive citing a *bariscella plena de macaronis.*[99] Among commodities traded by a Tuscan merchant a generation later appears dried vermicelli, called *tria* from the Greek via Arabic[100] (cf. fig. 134). While fourteenth-century recipes from Italy include lasagna, vermicelli, ravioli, and other filled types of pasta, the last often fried, in Northern Europe the generic term is *maccharoni,* or *macrows,* as in this recipe from Richard II's *Forme of Cury:* "Take and make a thynne foyle of dowh [dough], and kerve it in pieces, and cast hem on boillyng water, and seeth it wele. Take chese, and grate it, and butter, cast bynethen, and above as losyns, and serve forth" (*FC* 92). "Losyns" means lasagna as *FC* 49 makes clear: "Loscyns" are to be seethed in broth, then layered two or three times with grated cheese and "powder-douce" [cinnamon, ginger, nutmeg]. It must be noted that directions specify white bread flour, a roller to flatten the "thin foil" of dough, and that this must be dried hard before boiling.

Some account must be taken of the extraordinary range of fish that make up upper-class menus on fast days. What a challenge to the cooks to vary savors and modes of presentation in order to tickle appetites when ten to a dozen different water creatures could be required for each of three courses! At the end of the Advent fast preceding Christmas, the hero of *Sir Gawain and the Green Knight* is welcomed at a baronial castle and offered "a fair feast" of hospitality:

> Soon up on good trestles a table was raised
> and clad with a clean cloth clear white to look on;
> there was surnape, salt cellar, and silvern spoons.
>
> . . . .
>
> soups they served of many sorts, seasoned most choicely
> in double helpings, as was due, and divers sorts of fish;
> some baked in bread, some broiled on the coals,
> some seethed, some in gravy savoured with spices
> and all with condiments so cunning that it caused him delight.[101]

The fourteenth-century author omits other treatments in the cook's repertoire, roasted and glistening in clear jelly, or *estouffé*, smothered in onions,[102] not to mention various concoctions of ground fish (which include blancmange when a *maigre* day forbade the use of chicken or capon and meat broth to temper bread).[103]

It is possible to trace a general progression through three courses of a fish-day banquet: from introductory dishes such as salt herring, fried whitings, crabs, trout, and a codling (young cod) poached with "herbage," accompanying a major fish, served in pastry, perhaps, and with a special sauce, on to more serious accomplishments with such prized delicacies as lamprey, sturgeon, pike or luce, eels (often prepared *renversées*—flesh turned out—with a rich sauce), salmon, all handsomely garnished with shellfish or flora, culminating in roasts that may include lobsters and porpoise.

For the underprivileged who could not raise carp and other freshwater fish in their moats or ponds and who lived a distance from the sea, fast days meant reliance on various kinds of preserved fish. Herring might well have become hateful to ordinary folk during Lent, as literary plaints attest. These plentiful fish from the Channel and the Baltic were handled by a guild incorporated in 1394 of dealers in salted or pickled fish and smoked "red" herring. Until 1536, when they united into a single Fishmongers' Company, the salt fish merchants were distinguished from those who dealt in "stockfish," which came from farther afield off Norway and Iceland, and were simply air dried for longer keeping.

You may understand why today's *baccalà,* or dried codfish, is so expensive in reading the Goodman of Paris' notice to his wife (notice 194 on cod [*morue*]):

> . . . et l'en veult icelle garder .x. ou .xii. ans [one wishes to keep it ten or twelve years!], l'en l'effondre et luy ote l'en la teste, et est seichee a l'air et au soleil, et non mye au feu ou a la fumee [only dried in air and sun, never at a fire or smoke]. Et ce fait, elle est nommee *stofix.* Et quant l'en l'a tant gardee et l'en la veult mengier, il la couvient batre d'un maillet de boiz bien une heure, et puis mectre tremper en eaue tiede bien .xii. heures ou plus; [not two hours soaking as often quoted, but twelve or more, in warm water, after beating it for one] puis cuire, et escumer [skim] tresbien comme beuf; puis mengier a la moustarde ou menger trempee au beurre.[104]

Given the equipment the medieval cook had to work with, the sophistication of his technique is striking. The range of both cooked and uncooked sauces in Late Gothic treatises vies with Apician recipes in number and exceeds him in sophistication and in the use of many more spices — above all cinnamon and nutmeg (the latter popularized by Arab traders after the crusades). They are characteristically thickened by pounded bread steeped in broth, wine, or verjuice (of unripe grapes, sorrel, apples, gooseberries, or other acid fruit), by eggs, by finely ground almonds, or other nuts, including chestnuts. But there are recipes for making *amydon,* wheat starch, to use as liaison, following the traditional method recommended by ancient Roman sources.[105]

The complexity of contrasting flavors bears comparison with the intricacies of Late Gothic vaulting ribs and tracery — at least in England and France, unlike Italian classicality which did not permit these charged linear networks into built architecture, merely into the fantasy architectural framing of altarpieces. Another aspect of the cuisine of Late Gothic International style that is consonant with all the other arts is a richness of texture and, above all, color. To the single melodic line of early medieval Gregorian chants and secular music of troubadours, the *ars nova* brought polyphonic sonority and embellishment, culminating in the works of Guillaume Machault, the court composer of Charles V, and other French and Flemish musicians.

The symbolic value of effulgent light and reflective color has long been understood as central to Gothic architecture and sculpture (though this is often forgotten by nonspecialists admiring sculptures that time has robbed of paint and gilding).[106] Though the kaleidoscopic play in church interiors of resonant deep reds and blues of High Gothic stained glass had been much reduced by the end of the fourteenth century, that same sense of ornate color-play affected the Late Gothic table. International-style objects for the table, glittering with silver, gold, brightly hued enamels and jewels, express the same luxury as multicolored dishes (called *"party"* in the *Ménagier*) and shim-

138. Presenting the Peacock. *Detail of a miniature in the* Histoire du Grand Alexandre *(The Romance of Alexander the Great). Late fourteenth century. Paris, Petit Palais*

mering jellies made red by sandalwood ("saunders" in English manuscripts) or alkanet, blue by heliotrope or mulberries, green by parsley and other herbs, and yellow by saffron. At a dinner given by an archbishop described in an allegorical work of the 1370s, two or three *potages* (I remind you that these were more thick stews than soups in modern use of the French term) are praised for their different colors and for being strewn with sugar and red pomegranate seeds.[107] "Endoring" of meats and pies and gilding of the feet and beaks of such birds as swans and peacocks (fig. 138), roasted then reassembled in their skin and feathers (*rivestu* or *rivestiti* in Italian) as if alive, is but another aspect of the same taste for luster and radiance.

At risk of a diversion, I cannot resist an example of the "speaking presence" represented by such dishes. There is a minstrel's song of the swan performed at an earlier period on the Feast of St. Martin (November 11):

Once I was white as snow
by far the fairest high and low
Now I'm darker than a crow.

Refrain: Alas, alack, I am black,
to repeat burned to a crisp.

Once I swam upon a lake
all my beauty wide awake
I was a pretty swan.

On the water I should lie
bare below the airy sky
Not spiced with peppercorn

How the searing fire burns
as the spit turns and turns
So to table I must go.

Laid out on a silver platter
I liked flying high much better
than the teeth of hungry eaters.[108]

These spectacular masterpieces—and anyone who has duplicated the feat of presenting a peacock in full plumage can attest to its difficulty even with the

139. Adoration of the Magi. *From the* Strozzi Altarpiece *by Gentile da Fabriano, 1423. Florence, Uffizi. A focusing monument of the International Style illustrating Late Gothic infatuation with the naturalism of plants and animals and with its opposite, the artificiality of gorgeous raiment.*

use of modern equipment [109] — introduce another facet of the extravagance of the waning Middle Ages and of that predominance of the sense of sight that Huizinga brought forth in his interpretation of the epoch. As he noted, this principle invests literature in its prolixity and love of embroidered detail, just as painters (fig. 139) relish capturing exotic minutiae of the three Magi and their retinues, of costly fabrics, and of phenomena of light.

The special presentation of peacock or pheasant, with fanfare, at the last stage of a feast introduces another feature of medieval display. Unsurpassed virtuosity on the part of the chef was brought into play by the custom of ending each course of a grand dinner with a special dish intended to surprise and delight both host and guests. Called a *sotiltie,* or *soteltey* in England, in France it is termed *entremets,* or *entremez,* [110] in Italy *intermezzo,* after the late antique *intermissum.* "Subtlety" well describes many of these presentations which simply play upon a time-honored tradition of skillful deception in making something look like what it is not. *Layt lardé,* "fried milk," for example, results when milk is simmered with eggs and made to curdle by the addition of wine or verjuice (for a fish day), then drained overnight and pressed firm so that it can be sliced and treated as if it were meat — not unlike Japanese fried bean curd (tofu), *atsu-age* or *nama-age.*[111] A favorite invention was the "cock-entrice," or "cokagrys," which added a fanciful creature to the ranks of nature. The fore-part of a large capon (cock) was sewn to the hind-quarters of a suckling pig (grys) after stuffing with a farce; the newborn beast was then parboiled, roasted, and "gilded" with an egg glaze.[112]

Yet these showpieces came to represent all the imaginative excess of the waning Middle Ages, bringing down the wrath of Chaucer's Parson. Under censure of the sin of pride he includes that of the table: "in excesse of diverse metes and drynkes, and namely [particularly] swich manere bake-metes and dissh-metes, brennynge [burning] of wilde fir and peynted and castelled with papir, and semblable wast, so that it is abusioun for to thynke."[113] Mention of the wild fire summons up a visual image: frequently the beak of the peacock or other *rivestito* held a piece of camphor that was lit to spew out flames. "Castelled" recalls that in many an elaborate construction of a castle the fourteenth-century spread of gunpowder was used to good effect. With this development we enter a magical realm in which all the arts and crafts participate, where painters and sculptors are to be collaborators with confectioners and pastry chefs.[114]

Elaborate *pièces montées,* molded in marzipan or baked as "coffins" — stiff medieval pastry made with hot water and salt, strong enough to include many sorts of surprises — evoke the reality of "four-and-twenty blackbirds baked in a pie."[115] The entertainment value of such sleights-of-hand with pastry and accessories in other media, up to and including live actors, led to fierce competition among kitchen staffs and their masters, an intensified gusto for surprise that was to shape later Renaissance and baroque intervals in feasting. The competitive aspect is explicit in a famous series of banquets held at Lille in 1454.

With Constantinople in the hands of the Turks as of May 1453, Christian knights convened at Lille to consider how to counter this renewed threat of Mahomet II and his hordes. At the Council, the last flower of feudal aristocracy, the Knights of the Golden Fleece, vied with one another in hosting grand banquets for the delectation of both participants and spectators. One of those who took part — literally as well as figuratively — in the council, Olivier de la Marche in the company of Duke Philip the Good of Burgundy,[116] records the events in order to lend "lasting renown" to such "great and honourable achievements." To plan his spectacle, Philip set up a committee of his counselors, including Nicolas Rolin, his prestigious chancellor of Burgundy and patron of Jan Van Eyck, and his majordomo, or seneschal, Olivier himself.

Tables displayed set pieces that included a full-rigged ship, a fountain with a statue of Saint Andrew in a meadow surrounded by trees, the castle of Lusignan with the fairy Mélusine, a scene of a bird hunt near a windmill, and an artificial forest populated by wild beasts. The ancestry of that fountain is instructive. You will recall the fantastic fountain of Ptolemy II's Dionysiac procession in chapter 5. Medieval fancies may have been captured by reverberations coming down in literature from that marvel of Alexandrian technology, but inspiration lay closer to hand.

Fabulous tales of travel and imagined wonders are among the most popular secular food for the mind during the Middle Ages. Stories by Louis IX's emissary to the Mongols, William of Rubruck, in circa 1253, told of a silver fountain at the palace of the Great Khan at Korakoram that dispensed from four different spouts wine, *kumiss* — the fermented mares' milk still drunk today by horsemen of the steppes — mead, and rice wine (fig. 140).[117] This glorious object had been created for the Mangu Khan by a French goldsmith, Guillaume Boucher, and it is in France that it bore ceremonial descendants.

In Avignon in 1334 a *festa* offered to Pope Clement VI included a fountain dispensing five different wines,[118] and during the Entry of Charles VIII into Vienne in 1490, a real fountain structure set at a crossroad — representing the choice between Virtue and Voluptas — gave forth red or white wine, and the option of a sugared drink or a sour one.[119]

But let us return to Philip the Good's Feast of the Pheasant, in progress. "Personages" both mechanical and alive took part in the kind of entremets that had grown out of inventive dishes to mark the end of a course or to honor a special guest: a church holding an organ and a performing choir, while an orchestra of twenty-eight musicians emerged from a pie! In this case the pheasant was brought into the hall in its natural plumage, living still, for vows to be sworn upon it, according to custom, by Knights of the Golden Fleece roused by Philip's exhortations to follow him on a new crusade to liberate Constantinople (which never did take place). And Olivier de la Marche rode in upon an "elephant," enacting the Captive Church led by a huge conqueror

140.   *Illustration from J. Pinkerton,* A
Collection of Voyages and Travels
*(1808–14), vol. 7. This image recreates
in eighteenth-century style William of
Rubruck's thirteenth-century description
of the Great Khan's fountain dispensing
four different beverages, created by a
Gothic Parisian goldsmith.*

wearing a Turkish turban. We are in a society that will have to requisition the
services of entire Guilds of Painters from every Flemish city when Charles the
Bold is wed to Margaret of York at Bruges in 1468; Olivier tells of a Tower
forty-six feet high on that occasion and a whale that made "a very fine entremets, for there were more than forty persons in it."

I think it has become clear why in England the word "sotelty" was altered,
once the concept grew to involve such ambitious undertakings. "Pageaunt"
came to distinguish these amplified interruptions in the flow of service from
the kitchen, precursors of the masques and orchestrated festivities that will
necessitate a Master of Revels for feasts and occasions of state. It all began
with the extravagant consumption of International Gothic Style, and we are
witness to the beginnings of secular theater to supplement religious drama
and political tableaux vivants of medieval life of the street.[120]

If fifteenth-century entremets might be expected to outstrip those of the
inspiring International Style, forget it. Taillevent's master, Charles V, hosted
a famous example of the genre, one continually depicted in articles and books

on medieval dining. The special occasion was Twelfth Night, 6 January 1378, and a state dinner for the Holy Roman Emperor Charles IV of Bohemia, who had come to Paris with his son, Prince Wenceslaus of Luxembourg, to visit his nephew-godson. The event is described for us in Froissart's *Grandes Chroniques de France* — wondrously illuminated in one manuscript copy (fig. 141) — as well as by Christine de Pisan.[121]

More than eight hundred guests were invited, though we are shown only the high table set at one end of the great hall, which is draped with cloth-of-gold. Each royal person has his own canopy of velvet with golden fleur-de-

141. Twelfth-Night Feast, *staged in 1378 by King Charles V in honor of Emperor Charles IV and King Wenceslaus (from Froissart's* Chronicle of France). *The entremet represents the siege of Jerusalem by Godfrey de Bouillon and Richard the Lion-Hearted in 1099; Peter the Hermit stands in the boat. Note that each ruler has his own* nef. *Paris, Bibliothèque Nationale*

lys, each his own golden *nef*. They are flanked by three churchmen, but we are told that the high table (of marble!) was shared by four: the archbishop of Rheims, and the bishops of Brunswick, Paris, and Beauvais. Because the aging emperor grew tired, plans for four courses of ten pairs of dishes were curtailed to three. Obviously the entremès could not be omitted. Presented in two "scenes," which are brought into one by the miniaturist, it enacts a capture of Jerusalem. I say *a* capture because the leaders of the crusaders who were drawn into the hall in a ship "piloted" by Peter the Hermit are Godefroy de Bouillon—who did, indeed, take Jerusalem in the crusade of 1099—and Richard the Lion-Hearted of the abortive campaign of the next century. They scale a tower defended by "Saracens" who have been taught to call out in Arabic.

This vivid "happening" and that of Philip the Good in the succeeding century manifest an intimate union of fine dining, exciting entertainment, self-aggrandizement, and political purpose—political because each seized the occasion to make a rousing call for a renewed crusade to recapture the Holy Land. In a subsequent volume I will follow ever more costly and grandiloquent propaganda cuisine in the Renaissance, making these medieval enterprises pale in comparison. But the ostentation of the International Gothic style already opens to our gaze a gulf that will continue to widen between courtly and ecclesiastical patterns of consumption and display, imitated by a burgeoning middle class of entrepreneurs, as against the hard-scrabble diet of the rural peasant or urban laborer.

The fare of the English farm worker was, by the fourteenth century, the envy of the Continent. Yet Langland tells us of staple aliments and their seasonal variation: Piers the Plowman has no penny "to buy poletes, or grys" (pullets or suckling pigs), but ekes out "twey grene cheeses, And a fewe cruddes [curds] and craym, and a therf cake [oat cake] and a lof of benes and bren [bread of chickpea or bean flour and bran]." No salt bacon and cabbage with penny-ale for the Plowman that could supplement his oat cake in season, nor wheat bread and fresh meat that might follow a good harvest.[122]

Glazed chestnuts and acorns may turn up on the tables of the upper classes as *amuse-gueules* at the final *boutehors* (or English reresupper) after a banquet, but for Italian mountain-dwellers they are the staff of life, along with cheese and polenta of millet or fava beans.[123] Such discrepancies will take center stage during the Renaissance and Early Modern periods, when the politics of food becomes insistent. In the meanwhile, poorer folk must continue to feast in their imagined gustatory utopia, the Land of Cockaigne or Cuccagna,

Boccaccio's country of Bengodi, where everything good to eat and drink makes up the landscape, the grapes on the vine are always ripe and staked up by sausages, and exotic spices may be plucked from any tree.

There is much more that could be worked into my thesis concerning the unitary message of all the arts—the culinary not excepted—in the period before and after 1400. And a major part of any discussion about cookery has scarcely been mentioned. That is: how did it *taste?*

A practical exploration of this question, together with annotations on topics neglected in this chapter, may be found in the menu and recipes of the section in the appendix dealing with the International Late Gothic period.

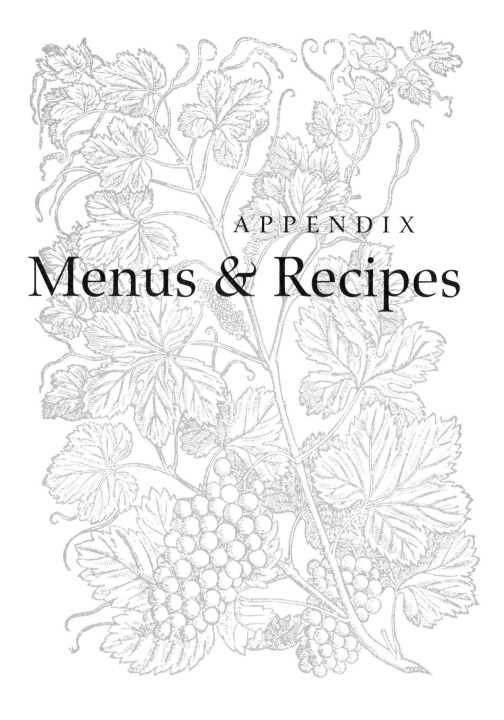

APPENDIX

Menus & Recipes

❧ A PREHISTORIC REPAST

This meal is based on early agricultural communities in the Near East, particularly Anatolia, and what I observed at Çatal Hüyük. You may fill out your menu with foraged foods, checking in such sources as Sturtevant's *Edible Plants of the World* (1972) or others in the general bibliography to learn whether your plant is native to the area chosen.

As you realize, the recipes that follow are pure invention, and techniques executed in a modern kichen — or even at a campfire — differ radically from neolithic practice.

Unless otherwise noted, recipes will serve about 6 people.

Menu

Spelt bread or *porridge*
Millet cakes
Fermented honey drink, Sumac lemonade
Salad of wild herbs
  Goosefoot *(Chenopodium album)*, lamb's lettuce, cress, sour grass
  (sorrel), dandelion, alfalfa sprouts
Baby wild boar
Smelts (or other "fry"), *Frog legs, Snails*
Lentils or *Lupine*
Onions baked in ashes or *Chufa (Cyperus esculentus) tubers*
Wild plums or *Crab apple purée, Black mulberries (Morus nigra), Nuts*

A note on ingredients: The oldest ancient spelt was not *Triticum spelta*, but *Triticum monococcum* (*kussemeth* of the Bible, one-grained wheat), Lesser spelt. It is now possible to buy "kamut," marketed by one producer as "an ancient Egyptian wheat," in specialty stores.

Campanula rapunculus, rampion (roots and leaves) would be another appropriate vegetable.

For lupine, use *Lupinus luteus* not wild lupine *L. perennis*; dried Italian lupini "beans" are a good alternative to lentils.

For verjuice, see the note below on p. 309.

❧ BREAD BAKED IN ASHES

1 cup wheat berries

1 egg

2 tablespoons melted lard

2 cups water

salt

bay leaves (optional)

Cover wheat berries with salted water and boil 2 to 2-1/2 hours until water is absorbed and wheat berries are tender. (The proportion of water to wheat is 2 to 1, as with rice, and other ingredients can also be increased proportionately.) Combine the wheat, egg, and melted lard. Drop by cooking spoonfuls on sheets of foil in the smoothed hot white ash of fireplace or barbecue (at a stage when you would use the heat for making popcorn). Cover with another sheet of foil, rake ashes over the foil, and bake for about 20 to 30 minutes. This bread is improved by placing a large bay leaf under each cake before dropping the batter. It may also be baked for 20 to 30 minutes on a cookie sheet in a 350-degree oven.[1]

❧ SMELTS: Prehistoric peoples probably did not gut such small fry, but you may wish to do so; leave head, tail, and fins however. These would grill well on the barbecue, like most dishes in this menu. But I suggest dusting them with crushed, salted pistachio nuts and quickly pan-frying them in hazelnut oil (often available at coffee-bar outlets). Serve garnished with caper buds or seeds (imported from Spanish sources).

❧ FROG LEGS

6 pairs of frog legs

1/4 cup lard

1 cup sliced onions

2 cloves garlic, minced

bouquet garni of parsley, fennel, and celery or lovage tops

1 cup boiling water or vegetable stock

In a deep, heavy pot, melt the lard and sauté the onions and garlic until lightly browned. Add frog legs, bouquet garni, and boiling water or stock. Reduce heat, cover and simmer about 15 minutes or until tender. Remove legs and lightly brown them under the broiler; serve with bowls of the braising liquid.

❦ SNAILS: Snail shells turn up rather consistently in excavations at prehistoric sites; undoubtedly they would simply have been tossed into a fire and fished out "grilled." But you will probably not wish to purge and clean a batch of live snails. Instead, purchase enough canned snails, packed with their shells, to serve 4 to each guest.

Reduce by boiling 1 cup grape juice (preferably from wild grapes, but bottled white grape juice or verjuice will do) to 1/3 cup. Put a few drops into each shell and put snails into them, sealing the opening with a bit of soft goat cheese or whipped cream cheese from a batch that has been mixed with a crushed clove of garlic and chervil. Heat them in a hot oven (400 to 425 degrees) for 10 minutes.

❦ BABY WILD BOAR: French *marcassin* is available from Ottomanelli, Butchers, in New York. Alternatively, use venison or more mundane butterflied leg of goat or lamb. This recipe is based on a 6-to-8 pound roast, opened broadly to be rolled and tied around seasoning ingredients.

Marinate the young boar overnight in hard cider[2] and 1/3-quantity malt vinegar with cut-up onion, garlic, crushed juniper berries and seeds of black mustard and cardamom (the plant of which is a cress).

When ready to cook, season the meat with salt, black mustard seed, and coriander seed, crushed in a mortar. Also place along its center a dried fennel stalk, parsley, fresh coriander, and a medium onion, chopped and sweated with 2 large cloves of minced garlic. Roll and tie the roast. Rub outside with more garlic and/or insert slivers of it into the flesh at numerous spots. If you choose to substitute venison, you may wish to bard or lard the roast at this point with fat back or salt pork. In any case, rub it with safflower oil. Roast for 15 to 20 minutes in an oven preheated to 500 degrees; add chopped root vegetables — onion, turnip, parsnip, wild carrot (Queen Anne's Lace, if you can distinguish it from poisonous look-alikes such as hemlock).[3] Lower heat to 325 and continue cooking, covered, 1/2 hour to the pound, basting regularly with the reduced marinade (if venison or lamb, preferred rare, 12 minutes per pound for the first, 12 to 15 for lamb, neither covered).

❦ LENTILS: Cook lentils in boiling salted water about 20 minutes or until they are tender but not mushy (no need for presoaking if you have the quick-cooking type). For each cup of lentils fry 1/4 cup of finely diced salt pork; mix these and their rendered fat into the cooked lentils, with 2 finely chopped scallions and fresh chervil or minced parsley.

❦ ONIONS BAKED IN ASHES: You may take this literally if barbecuing or cooking at a fireplace. Otherwise, sprinkle each peeled onion with sea salt and ground black mustard and enclose it with a smashed clove of garlic inside a leaf from a grape vine or fig tree (alternatively use canned grape leaves from Greece, but rinse them carefully and cut the salt on the onion — the result will be rather different). Rub the outside with walnut oil. Set onions on a baking sheet and bake in a preheated 400-degree oven until leaves are charred and onions soft, depending on size, from 30 minutes to 1 hour.

❦ SPELT BREAD: Spelt is a hulled wheat that the ancients had to char in order to husk its kernel. Traditionally grown by Pennsylvania Dutch farmers, it is today becoming more available in the form of both groats and flour.

For groat porridge, presoak the grain — in other words treat it as you would dried beans — and give spelt long cooking in salted water and final sweetening with honey to taste. For bread, you may make a primitive flat bread by mixing spelt flour with duck or pork fat and making small balls to flatten on a hot griddle, or the following sourdough product.

Prepare a starter by keeping 1 cup of milk (goat or sheep milk preferred) at room temperature for about 24 hours. Stir in 1 cup flour and let stand in a warm place until the mixture smells sour and raises bubbles (from wild yeasts in the air — this will take anywhere from 3 days to 5 or more, depending on the season).

The night before baking, add 1 cup starter to 6 cups spelt flour or a mixture of spelt and whole wheat flour; then add lukewarm water to mix, 1 cup at a time, until a thick, paste-like batter is formed; beat thoroughly. Let stand overnight covered with cheesecloth.

Next day, return a cup of this sponge to your starter to replenish it for future use (and store in refrigerator now). To the remainder in the bowl fold in 3/4 cup safflower oil, 1 tablespoon salt, and gradually work in up to 8 cups of spelt flour (or, again, a mixture with whole wheat flour) until dough comes away from the sides of the bowl, though it will still be slightly sticky. Place on a floured surface to knead for about 8 to 10 minutes, adding more flour as necessary. Shape 2 or 3 loaves and place in oiled baking pans; slash tops. Allow to rise for 2 to 3 hours. Bake in a preheated 425-degree oven for 20 minutes, then lower heat to 350 and continue baking for about 80 minutes, or until bread sounds resonantly hollow when thumped.

❦ MILLET CAKES

> 2 cups whole wheat flour
> 3 cups millet, cracked with a rolling pin
> 1/2 cup sheep ricotta
> 1/2 cup safflower oil
> 1/3 cup herb honey
> 1 cup roughly crushed and toasted pistachio nuts
> 2 teaspoons sea salt
> water

Stir together safflower oil and honey. Add whole wheat flour, millet, ricotta, pistachio nuts, and sea salt. Stir in water until mixture holds together. Shape in patties and bake on an oiled cookie sheet at 350 degrees for about 30 to 35 minutes.

❦ SUMAC LEMONADE: In autumn, be certain to use the fruit of staghorn or squaw bush sumac with brilliant foliage and *red* berries; POISON sumac has white berries. Bruise the clusters of berries slightly and steep in water until the liquid turns a pinkish color; strain. A bit of honey may be added for sweetener. This also makes a satisfactory tea by heating the "lemonade," but steeping the fruits in boiling water would bring out a different, more bitter flavor.

❧ DINNER IN ANCIENT EGYPT

Menu

Hors d'oeuvres
Breads
Baked broad beans with lentils
Grilled fish
Roast duckling or goose
Preserved duck gizzards
Melukhiya stew with lotus root
calf's hoof and shank or *sheep's head*, optional
Carob pudding
Fresh fruits (figs, dates, grapes, etc.), or a *Compote*

A note on ingredients: The dried beans, *ful* or Egyptian small brown fava beans, may be found in Middle Eastern or Greek markets. If unavailable, use dried broad beans or pigeon peas, black eyed peas, and the like (Japanese adzuki beans look similar but are too sweet in flavor).

Melukhiya (also spelled "Melokhia") is likewise available in Middle Eastern stores, either chopped frozen, looking like spinach, or in dried crumbled leaf. (When I brought some home from Egypt it was at first taken by an airport "sniffer" dog for marijuana!) Calf's hoof and head were banquet fare for our colonial and Victorian ancestors, but today you will need a cooperative butcher or wholesale market.

Lotus root will be found in Chinese shops either as dried or sometimes fresh slices — the dried will require considerable presoaking in water (started at boiling point).

Carob (St. John's Bread) will be found not in the pod, but as powder, in health stores where it is considered a substitute for chocolate — it is interchangeable with cocoa ounce for ounce in recipes.

To make clarified butter (similar to Indian ghee), I use Paula Wolfert's method,[4] heating 1 pound unsalted butter mixed with 3 tablespoons of cracked wheat over very low heat for about 2 hours, until butter makes a clear oil separated from the sediment, which should be discarded (or used for other purposes). Store in sterilized jars. By this method Egyptians and other ancient peoples could keep butter without refrigeration.

❦ BEVERAGES: Wine, beer, and/or water boiled for a few minutes with aniseed (1 teaspoon per cup), then strained and optionally sweetened with honey.

❦ HORS D'OEUVRES

Raw vegetables: Choose from among those mentioned in chapter 2 (including chufa if your locale and the season is right), and serve with a dip made from yogurt, thickened with cream cheese, seasoned with crushed garlic and dill. Cooked lentils and/or chickpeas dressed with safflower oil, malt vinegar, and nigella (black cumin, available in Middle East markets) form another option.

Fresh calves' liver: Serve raw, cut into small cubes, and marinated in dry white wine mixed with a few drops of vinegar (ratio one teaspoon vinegar to 1/3 cup wine) and a grated onion, 2 minced cloves of garlic, salt, and nigella seeds. Refrigerate in marinade for at least 2 hours, stirring occasionally. Serve on toothpicks.

Boutargue can be produced at home from other fish roes than grey mullet — especially cod and shad. The process relies on getting them to lose their moisture through salting and drying without allowing them to release their moisture so quickly that individual eggs within the membrane (which must be intact) separate and the whole tends to crumble. The final product must be compactly firm. I follow Claudia Roden's process,[5] turning off the oven after each use, even more often than she recommends, plus applying a weight during times the roe is sitting on absorbent paper. A variant is also worth experimenting with if you have a smoker; I have had fine results with mine.

❦ BAKED BEANS WITH LENTILS

1 pound beans (*ful hamam* preferably)
1 onion
2 cloves garlic
1/3 cup split lentils
boiling water
ghee or safflower oil
salt
seasonings

Pick over beans and cover with 3 to 4 times their measure in boiling water; soak 12 hours or overnight.

A New England bean pot or something similar makes a perfect cooking vessel. In the bottom place a cut-up onion that has been sautéed in ghee or safflower oil and 2 cut cloves of garlic. Add the beans and see that they are just covered with more boiling water, if needed. Add split lentils to act as thickening. Cover closely and bake in a slow oven (300 to 325 degrees) for 2 to 2-1/2 hours (see note), adding boiling water as needed. When water is absorbed and beans are soft, add 1/2 teaspoon of salt and 2 tablespoons of safflower oil. Serve accompanied by little dishes holding garlic crushed with salt, minced coriander or parsley, sliced scallions, and ground cumin, so that each person may season his or her own.

Note: Time given is for modern treated beans, different varieties may take significantly longer. Modern Egyptians usually serve the beans partially mashed; we don't know about the ancients.

❦ GRILLED FISH: (Unless it is barbecue time, or you have a top-of-the-stove grill, this means broiling for most of us.) Buy a whole, firm-fleshed fish (see the following note). Preheat the broiler and grease the rack well. You may wish to split the fish, remove its backbone and reassemble (or, alternatively, broil it skin-side down without turning).

Rub fish with 2 garlic cloves brayed in a mortar to a paste with 1/2 teaspoon salt. Brush well with ghee and dust lightly with flour. Broil 4 to 6 inches from the heat, following the general rule of 10 minutes for each inch of greatest thickness; for a whole fish, include turning the fish once, and baste occasionally with more ghee. When crisply browned and yielding to the touch, serve sprinkled with a few drops of herb vinegar and minced coriander leaves.

Note: It is now possible to buy in fish markets a variety of a Nile fish, *Tilapia nilotica,* often still cultivated today. Mullets[6] are also very appropriate, ocean perch arguable. Avoid salmon, which never made its way into the Mediterranean. For our purposes, I would also consider catfish sufficiently akin to bottom-feeders in the Nile. Dried or smoked fish might also be used with different cooking procedures, but only cod is generally available in this form (after the usual soaking, it may be spread with ghee and broiled under a low flame).

❦ ROAST DUCKLING

    1 duckling, approximately 4-1/2 to 5 pounds
    1 medium onion, quartered
    garlic
    sea salt
    fresh coriander
    pomegranate juice for basting, and seeds for garnish
    flour

Remove extra fat at the vent (an Egyptian would save this to render cooking grease for other dishes). Rub the duckling outside and in with a cut clove of garlic; also rub the interior with sea salt. In its cavity place the onion and some leaves from a bunch of coriander. If the duckling is very fat, prick its breast in a few places. Place on a rack in an open roasting pan and cook in a 325-degree oven about 25 minutes per pound, basting occasionally with drippings and pomegranate juice. For the last 15 to 20 minutes, if the duck is not crisply browned, dust with flour and raise heat to 350. Serve garnished with pomegranate seeds.

❦ MELUKHIYA STEW WITH LOTUS ROOT: You may substitute frozen, chopped turnip greens for Melukhiya, recognizing that both taste and a lack of slightly gelatinous texture will be very different. Melukhiya acts the part of cut okra in many Southern stews, as a thickening as well as flavoring agent.

    1 package chopped melukhiya, thawed (or substitute 1/2 cup crushed dried leaves)
    1 disjointed rabbit
    2 onions, chopped
    8 cloves of garlic
    4–6 slices dried lotus root, reconstituted (see above, note on ingredients)
    3 teaspoons ground coriander
    2–4 tablespoons ghee or safflower oil

salt and ground mustardseed to taste

2 cups water

In a heavy pot, fry onions, 2 minced cloves of garlic, and lotus root until golden in 1 or 2 tablespoons of ghee or safflower oil; remove, and brown a disjointed rabbit in the remaining oil; season with salt and ground mustardseed. Return vegetables to the pot and add about 1 cup of water (or beer or wine). Simmer covered until rabbit is tender—about 40 minutes to 1 hour. Add 1 cup boiling water and melukhiya and continue simmering for 10 to 15 minutes. Add a final seasoning of 6 cloves of garlic crushed with salt and 3 teaspoons ground coriander, then fried in 2 tablespoons ghee or oil. Add to the simmering stew and continue cooking for 2 or 3 minutes.

❦ PRESERVED DUCK GIZZARDS:[7] You will need enough rendered duck or goose fat to keep air from reaching the gizzards in a preserving jar; it may be stretched by clarified butter (Egyptian ghee; see note on ingredients above or any comprehensive cookbook if you need directions for clarifying).

1/2 pound duck gizzards

2 teaspoons coarse sea salt

1 teaspoon minced garlic

1 tablespoon chopped fresh coriander

2 teaspons minced shallots

1/2 teaspoon dried marjoram

1/2 teaspoon cumin

1 bay leaf, crumbled

1/4 teaspoon crushed peppercorns (preferably melegueta pepper from Morocco)

Remove fat from duck gizzards. Toss with the remaining ingredients and refrigerate over night in a covered dish.

Next day, rinse and dry gizzards and place in an ovenproof earthenware dish with a lid; add rendered duck or goose fat to cover. Cook about 2-1/2 hours in an oven preheated to 225 degrees, until tender. Ladle some of the fat into a sterile jar, allowing it to congeal. Layer in the gizzards, adding more fat over each layer with each addition; finish with fat. Store in the refrigerator until needed; use within 2 to 2-1/2 weeks.

The gizzards may be sliced, fried up and used with a salad of greens (chickory frisé, lamb's quarters, unheaded lettuce, or foraged greens, like nettles). Or, they may be reheated in some of their fat and used to stuff figs in a compote of mixed stewed fruits. Use your ingenuity.

🌿 CALF'S SHANK OR HEAD: If you choose head, consult any early American or nineteenth-century cookbook; a modern recipe is found in Irma Rombauer, *The Joy of Cooking*. The following recipe is adapted from Claudia Roden.[8]

> 2 shanks with hooves attached
> hot oil or ghee for browning
> salt
> boiling water to cover
> 1 large onion, chopped
> 2 bay leaves
> 1 cup dried chickpeas, soaked overnight and drained
> sweet-sour sauce

Clean shanks carefully and parboil, removing the scum that would otherwise rise in your stew. Brown the feet and shins in hot oil or ghee in a large stew pot. Salt and cover with fresh boiling water, adding the onion, bay leaves, and chickpeas. Simmer gently until tender, roughly 4 hours.

Serve with a sweet-sour sauce made from vinegar heated with appropriate honey, a few raisins, and ground black mustardseed. For elegance, you may bone the shin and arrange slices of the hoof around the platter. Strain and clarify any remaining juices while simmering with beaten egg white, and you will have a fine calves' foot jelly or flavoring to add to future dishes.

🌿 CAROB PUDDING

> 1/2 cup ghee
> 1/2 cup honey
> 2 jumbo eggs, beaten
> 1/4 teaspoon salt
> 1 teaspoon rose water (*not* the type used in cosmetics)
> 1 cup whole wheat flour
> 1 teaspoon baking soda
> 3/4 cup carob powder
> 1/2 cup sour milk
> raisins or pine nuts (optional)

Combine ghee and honey; to this mixture, add eggs, salt, and rose water. In a separate bowl, stir together whole wheat flour, baking soda, and carob powder; gradually incorporate sour milk. Combine the two mixtures. Optionally raisins and/or pine nuts may be stirred in. Pour batter into a greased, floured cake pan and bake at 325 degrees for 25 to 30 minutes or until a toothpick comes out clean.

❦   FUNNEL BREAD: This recipe is based on the depiction in fig. 19 and on Pennsylvania Dutch methods of making funnel cakes.

>   3 cups whole wheat flour
>   1/4 cup wheat bran
>   1 teaspoon baking soda
>   1/2 teaspoon cream of tartar
>   4 eggs
>   1 cup honey
>   1/3 cup oil or melted ghee
>   milk

Sift whole wheat flour; resift with wheat bran, baking soda (replacing Egyptian *natron*), and cream of tartar (I feel Egyptian wine-making would familiarize them with this tartrate). Beat eggs until light and mix with honey; add oil or melted ghee. Stir in sifted ingredients and add enough milk to make a dough soft enough to flow steadily through a funnel in a continuous spiral into deep fat heated to 375 degrees. Fry until lightly browned, turning over once. This is a sweet bread comparable to a doughnut in flavor.

❦   FLAT BREAD

>   2 cups whole wheat flour
>   1 teaspoon salt
>   warm water

Mix flour with salt. Make a well in the center and deftly stir in 3/4 cup warm water. (As with pancake batter, it is not necessary to get every small lump out of this dough.) Cover with a damp, not wet, dish towel and leave for about 7 to 8 hours unrefrigerated.

When ready to bake, flatten golf-ball size balls of the dough shaped in floured hands, mark the tops to resemble the flat breads in fig. 21, and slap onto a wok (Chinese oil-drum type, not the stainless or other imitations) that has been overturned and then preheated on a gas burner until a drop of water dances on its surface. (Again, like cooking pancakes, keep wiping this "tandur" surface with the corner of a paper towel dipped in ghee.) Cook briefly, turning once, and stack in a 200-degree oven until there are enough to serve hot.

❦ MESOPOTAMIAN RECIPES

These recipes for an ancient Mesopotamian dinner are based on the few scattered records from Mari and the three southern Babylonian cuneiform tablets in the Yale collections published by Jean Bottéro. In addition, Bottéro's articles in the *Reallexicon der Assyriologie,* plus the culinary glossary in his *Textes culinaires Mésopotamiens* (1995) have immensely aided my speculative reconstructions, together with Mrs. Grieve's *Modern Herbal* (and others). If not totally authentic, the suggested ingredients are at least not anachronistic. For the rest, I must admit that my interpretation may seem to fulfill a circular argument about culinary style by relying in numerous ways on cooking procedures in a Near East of far-from-uninterrupted tradition. In the absence of any clues to ancient menu-building, I give you a number of dishes from which you can develop your own.

A note on ingredients: If you are not a bread-maker, you may wish simply to use any modern flat bread from pita to Afghanistani *naun* — even plain, store-bought pizza or focaccia.

A few hints from my friends Claudia Roden and Paula Wolfert: the propensity of yogurt, unless made from goats' milk, to curdle when cooked can be countered by first mixing egg white with it — for full directions, see Roden, *A New Book of Middle Eastern Food* (1985).

A substitute for the pomegranate molasses (Arabic *dibs rumman*) bought in Middle Eastern groceries can be made at home by boiling down six cups of pomegranate juice mixed with 1 cup of sugar to produce 2 cups of molasses. The sophistication of cooking procedures in recipes interpreted by Bottéro indicates to me that professional cooks in ancient Mesopotamia would have developed a comparable product from their pomegranates. Paula Wolfert's *The Cooking of the Eastern Mediterranean* (1994) has these instructions, and also ones for freezing pomegranate seeds when they are in season in autumn and for pressing their juice rather than buying it in bottles.

❦ BEVERAGES: Serve beer (Akkadian *sikâru*) and *ayran,* the modern Middle Eastern refreshment that does seem of ancient tradition (preferably with sheep or goats' milk yogurt): to 1 pint of yogurt, beaten, whip in about 3/4 to 1 pint of cold water; add salt and crushed dried mint to taste and serve chilled.

❦ BREAD *(Ninda):* This would have been for the most part tossed on the inner face of a tandur oven.

Unleavened Bread
1 pound whole wheat flour
1 teaspoon salt
6 ounces lukewarm water

Combine flour with salt; add lukewarm water; mix and knead into a smooth dough. Let rest in a warm place for 2 or 3 hours, covered with a dampened cloth. Form bits of dough into small balls and roll these out on a lightly floured surface to the size of small pita breads. Cook on a greased cast-iron skillet as you would pancakes, a minute or two on each side. Stack in a 200-degree oven until all rounds are cooked.

Like other ancient peoples, Mesopotamian bakers relied on ambient wild yeasts in the air, on sourdough leaven, and on carbonate of soda (Gk. *nitron*).

Leavened and Seasoned Flat Bread
1 pound whole wheat flour
2 teaspoons baking powder
1/2 teaspoon salt
2 teaspoons dried minced onion
1 teaspoon dried coriander leaf
1/2 teaspoon ground coriander seed
1/2 teaspoon ground cumin
3–4 tablespoons vegetable oil
water

Stir together whole wheat flour, baking powder, and salt. Add dried onion, coriander leaf, coriander seed, and cumin. When seasonings are thoroughly incorporated, add vegetable oil. Make a hole in the center of the flour and gradually mix in about 2 cups of water, until a soft dough is formed that pulls away from the sides of the bowl. On a floured surface, knead the dough thoroughly; divide into eight or nine pieces, and pat out into rounds about 1/4-inch thick. Cover with a clean cloth and let stand for half an hour. Bake in a 500-degree oven on preheated and lightly greased cookie sheets until lightly browned, about 10 minutes.

❦ SALAD

chicory
arugula (Akkadian *egengeru*)
fenugreek shoots (*warqu,* "verdure")
sliced hearts of palm (optional)
1 clove garlic
honey

dressing
1/3 cup safflower oil
2 or 3 tablespoons garlic vinegar
1/4 teaspoon salt
1/4 teaspoon powdered sumac

About three to four days ahead, start to sprout 1 cup of fenugreek seeds (see the following note). Wash and dry greens. Combine with sprouts and (optionally) a small tin of sliced hearts of palm. For dressing, mix safflower oil, garlic vinegar, salt, and powdered sumac. Rub a wooden salad bowl with a cut clove of garlic and a drop or two of honey.

Like all salads, appearance is enhanced by flowers as garnish: whole nasturtium flowers are my favorites. Nasturtium leaves would also be alternative salad ingredients, as would wild greens such as purslane or knotweed.

Note: To sprout fenugreek seeds, first soak in hot water for 5 to 8 minutes, changing the water four times and swishing them around with your hands. Discard any that float. Soak overnight for 12 hours in ordinary tap water; drain. Spread in a layer not more than 1 inch thick in the bottom of a large flower pot. Arrange for good drainage by raising the pot on some blocks above a tray or some other container; put a dish cloth over the top and cover with a weighted foil pie plate. Place in a warm, dark place and water every four hours throughout the day — the point is to keep the seeds moist but not allow standing water in which they will rot.

LAMB STEW (Akkadian *me-e puhâdi*)

1/4 pound "streaky" salt pork, cut in small cubes
3 pounds boney lamb parts, such as shanks, breast, or shoulder
3–4 cups chopped onions
4 cloves garlic, minced
6 shallots, minced[9]
2 leeks, cleaned and cut crosswise, including much of the green
seasonings: salt, ground coriander, cumin, crushed juniper berries, and sumac
vegetable or meat stock
fresh coriander leaves or mint
"oil-cake" (use crushed sesame breadsticks)
fresh yogurt cheese (see note)
1 egg white
toasted pine nuts or hazelnuts for garnish

In a heavy pot render the fat from the salt pork and brown thoroughly. Remove and reserve. In the rendered fat, over high heat, brown lamb parts; remove and reserve. In the same fat and drippings sauté the onions, garlic, shallots, and leeks. Return lamb and salt pork to the pot and season with salt, ground coriander, and cumin, a few crushed juniper berries, and sumac. Add enough boiling stock—vegetable or meat—to cover and simmer for about 1-1/2 hours. For the last half hour of cooking, add fresh coriander leaves or mint to the stew. When meat and cooked-down vegetables are placed in their serving dish, thicken the residue with crumbled "oil-cake" and fresh yogurt cheese beaten with the white of an egg. Serve with this sauce, garnished with toasted pine nuts or hazelnuts.

Note: Make fresh yogurt cheese by draining plain yogurt overnight in a colander lined with muslin or a triple thickness of cheesecloth. A cast-iron deep kettle with a cover makes an ideal cauldron.

PIGEON SURPRISE: Akkadian *issûru,* refers to domestic fowl; you may also use quail or, if necessary, small Cornish game hens. Chickens seem not to have been known to early Mesopotamian cooks.

4 pigeons (squab), 6 quail, or 2 game hens
ghee
1 chunk fat back[10]
1 cup milk diluted with 1/4 cup water

bouquet garni: stalk of fennel, of rosemary, and laurel (bay leaf), tied together with
   fresh coriander
1/2 teaspoon dried rue (optional) [11]
1 onion, sliced
a few shallots
2 cloves garlic
1 large leek
mint and nigella (black cumin seeds, a pepper substitute), for garnish

pastry
1 to 1-1/4 pounds fine-grained semolina flour
1/2 cup safflower oil
1/2 cup melted butter
1/2 cup scalded milk
nuoc nam or other fish sauce
finely minced shallots, garlic, and dried leek flakes

Split "pigeons" and remove their innards and clean carefully (if game hens,
you will only find heart, liver, and gizzard). In the bottom of a heavy iron pan
melt 1 tablespoon of ghee; in this sear the split fowl and their pluck, the latter
cut up into small pieces. Salt and remove to a terra-cotta casserole (preferably a
French *marmite* or a Romertopf).[12] Add fat back, watered milk, bouquet garni,
and dried rue, if available. Bring the casserole to a simmer and add onion, a
few shallots, and the garlic, crushed together with a large leek. Roast in a
350-degree oven, covered, until liquid is reduced and fowl are tender, about
45 minutes.

Meanwhile, prepare pastry for presenting the birds: mix safflower oil,
melted butter, and scalded milk. Gradually work in the semolina flour while
moistening the dough with fish sauce, and incorporating the shallots, garlic, and
dried leek flakes. Do not overmix after a soft ball is formed. Divide dough into
two parts, one a bit larger than the other. Take the larger and pat it out to cover
a lightly floured, flat oven-proof dish large enough to serve the birds, making a
circle and raising its edge as much as possible. Pat out the second batch on a
floured baking sheet to the same diameter. (The original recipe adds more garlic, crushed leek, and shallots to the bottom crust.) Bake both at 350 until firm
and lightly browned.

Finally, assemble lower crust, add the cooked birds and their innards, with
as much of their sauce as clings to them; sprinkle with mint and nigella. Cover

with the second crust and serve. Strain any residue in the casserole, "deglazing" with a bit of milk, and serve this sauce separately.

MOLD OF BULGUR AND GREEN WHEAT: Green wheat is *freekeh* in modern Syria, and may be obtained from Middle Eastern grocers or specialty importers.

1 cup green wheat
1 cup coarse grain bulgur
4 tablespoons ghee
1 medium onion, minced
4 cups rich stock
1/2 teaspoon salt
2 eggs, beaten
1/2 cup pine nuts or pistachios
date sauce (see below)
dates for garnish

Pick over green wheat and wash it in several changes of water (until the water runs clear); mix with bulgur. Heat ghee in a sauté pan and use to cook the onion over a slow fire without browning. Add the wheats and stir for a minute or two to coat the grains. Add stock and salt; cover and cook until liquid is absorbed, about 30 minutes. When almost cool, add eggs and pine nuts, and pack into a greased mold. Bake in a preheated 325-degree oven for about 30 minutes, or until firm. Unmold on a platter and serve with date sauce. Decorate with a few reserved dates.

For the date sauce, mash stoned fresh dates and simmer in pomegranate juice with a tablespoon or so of honey until a syrupy sauce is obtained.

RED CHARD (Akkadian *alûtu*?): Separate stalks and leaves while washing thoroughly. Cook in very little water with salt and a sprinkling of dried onion flakes, no longer than 10 to 15 minutes. Arrange in a greased baking dish together with sprigs of dill. Sprinkle with vinegar. Dot with goat cheese (slivers of Boucheron, if cost is no object, but soft varieties that imitate Montrachet will serve) and bake at 325 degrees until cheese melts and is lightly browned.

For dessert, serve poached and spiced fruits such as figs, quince, sickel pears, crab apples cooked with dilute honey and a touch of rose water. If you make your own yogurt, flavored with honey, fruits, etc., this would also make an acceptable dessert. The following pastry is documented by name and inventory at Mari (see Bottéro, *Textes*, p. 22f.).

❦ MERSU

> 2 cups whole wheat flour
> 1 teaspoon salt
> 1/2 cup safflower oil
> 1/4 cup water
>
> ### *filling*
> stoned fresh dates
> raisins
> "terebinth" (i.e., pistachio) nuts
> nigella seeds
> cumin and coriander seed
> dried minced garlic

Sift flour and salt into a bowl. Pour in safflower oil mixed with water. Lightly stir into a soft ball. Roll out on a floured surface under a pastry cloth or waxed paper so the dough will not stick to your roller. With a pastry cutter cut into four-inch rounds; on each place a stoned fresh date, a few raisins, pistachios, a few nigella seeds, a sprinkle of ground cumin and coriander seed, and 2 pieces of dried minced garlic [*sic*]. Fold up into a pouch and bake at 425 degrees until nicely browned and firm. Apple slices might also be used, or other appropriate fruits. Since this dough is difficult to work with, you may wish to use quadruple sheets of phyllo (sometimes spelled "filo") pastry.

A GREEK *DEIPNON*

Although there is much that is traditional in modern Greek fare, you must forget today's affection for tomatoes, eggplants, peppers, and lemons — also for a preprandial liquor such as ouzo. If trying for authenticity in other respects than food, you will wish to entertain only a small group and save the bulk of your wine-drinking for the "second table," a symposion with platters of nibbles and sweetmeats.

Garlands of flowers are de rigueur for decorations plus optional wreaths of greenery (even of flat-leaf parsley or lovage) to crown the guests' heads. A bowl or bowls of scented water and cloths for hand-washing before the party begins are requisites that will continue to be appreciated throughout the forkless meal. Greeks did not sit about a groaning board. Though you may not wish or be able to recline, small portable tables will be more authentic than a table with your major dishes set out upon it. You will need willing young servers (even flute girls and acrobats?) to keep a flow of presentations coming before your eager guests.

This is an eclectic feast coordinating favorites from culturally distinct Hellenic cities and periods, Archaic to Hellenistic. A few ingredients may be difficult to find if you do not live in a polycultural metropolis, but mail order has opened every possibility to the contemporary cook.

A note on ingredients: I am not able to provide more than one recipe for breads and rolls, or to emulate all those fine shapes we learn from the sources. Focaccia-style flat breads are an important convenience for the diners; semolina rolls or wholemeal sourdough bread seem fitting, or the coarse, country-style loaf presented below.

Bulbs (*Muscari comosum* — what South Italians call *lampascioni;* modern Gk. *volvi*) are imported from Greece, put up in glass jars by Krinos and other packers.

For fish sauce *(garum),* substitute Chinese or Southeast Asian types.

ᎈ BEVERAGES: Ancient Greeks, after an opening libation to a god or gods, did not consume much wine with their food. You might like to save serious drinking for later and serve honeyed water *(hydromel)*, even touched with mild vinegar *(oxymel)*, or unfermented must with a bit of honey added—needless to say, the honey should be an import, preferably Hymettan the bees make from thyme, available in Greek markets or specialty shops.

ᎈ PROPOMA (Appetizers)

Lamb meatballs (modern Gk. *kephtedes)*
1 pound lean ground lamb
2 cloves finely minced garlic
2/3 cup chickpea flour
2 teaspoons ground cumin
1 teaspoon toasted mustard seeds brayed in a mortar
1/4 cup minced coriander leaves or parsley
sea salt and pepper to taste
1 egg

Bind all of the other ingredients with the beaten egg. Shape and brown in hot olive oil.

Stuffed figs: Use fresh figs if in season, or imported dried ones that are packed moist—not the hard ones air-dried on strings. Remove stems and carefully open a pocket in each; fill with a mixture of cracked or bulgur wheat cooked in chicken stock and seasoned with sesame oil, dill, mint and coriander or parsley, and plumped currants (which take their English name from Greek Corinth—say "currant" quickly—where a "currant grape" was a viticultural specialty). *Or* if you are using very dry figs, fill them with a mixture of chopped almonds, pistachios, and hazelnuts and simmer until tender in a light syrup of honey and water. (These will be difficult to eat with one's fingers as an hors d'oeuvre and might better be introduced as a side dish with the pork below.)

Walnuts toasted with a honey/wine glaze: The ancients thought of these as the "acorns of Zeus" in reference both to humans' original food and to presumed resemblance to the sexual "glands" of the god (a word play that comes out better in the Latin for the nut: *juglans)*. Toast walnuts in a 325-degree oven on a baking sheet in one layer, with or without removing their skins, after dipping in the glaze. (You may wish to save these for the symposion.)

To supplement these, choose among store-bought possibilities: blood sausage, smoked eel, roasted chickpeas, various olives, bulbs (volvi — see note on ingredients), smoked mackerel, and the like, since this will aid in presenting a satisfying variety while sparing the cook. I sometimes include a Chinese sausage, because sausages were so popular in ancient Greece and I believe the chunky bits of pork fat and slightly sweet savor would have suited ancient palates. The love of shellfish may prompt you to include oysters on the half-shell, so long as you and your guests are not accustomed to drowning their taste of the sea in "seafood sauce"; just serve with a drop of *garum* (see note on ingredients) and a sprinkling of powdered sumac (available at an Iranian grocer or restaurant).

❦ *ZŌMON* (Soup): Lentil soup was a favorite. In Athenaeus reference is made to combining bulbs (erroneously termed "little onions" by some food writers) with lentils for a winter soup "like ambrosia." You may add these as final garnish if you have a source for Greek imports.

> 1 cup lentils
> 1 small onion, diced
> 1 large parsnip, peeled and diced
> 1 tablespoon extra-virgin olive oil
> leaves from the top of 2 celery stalks (or lovage, if available)
> fresh thyme and parsley
> flour (optional)
> 1-1/2 quarts hearty meat stock
> 1 teaspoon ground coriander seed
> sea salt and freshly ground pepper to taste

Soak lentils overnight unless they are the quick-cooking variety. In 1 tablespoon extra-virgin olive oil, sweat onion, celery leaves or lovage, parsnip, 2 sprigs of fresh thyme, and the same of parsley. Add the drained lentils and simmer gently over a slow fire, covered, for about 15 minutes. Add 1-1/2 quarts of hearty meat stock (a goat broth by preference, but any other homemade broth) and continue cooking until lentils are soft. Put through a sieve and reheat with the addition of the ground coriander seed, sea salt, and pepper to taste (preferably brayed in a mortar). For a thicker soup, either use more lentils or blend in a tablespoon of flour when the vegetables are first simmering.

❦ *ARTOS* (Bread): Shaped as a mound *(omphalos)*, like a country loaf, this bread is best while still warm, but also delicious when no longer fresh if dipped in buttermilk and fried in hot olive oil, then served with honey as a breakfast dish, or even dessert.

    2 cups stoneground whole wheat flour
    1 cup barley grits or flaked barley "pilaf," as sold in supermarkets
    1-1/4 cup cultured buttermilk
    warm water (optional)
    1-1/2 teaspoons sea salt
    3/4 teaspoon baking soda
    1/2 teaspoon cream of tartar
    olive oil, for dipping

Sift together the flour, sea salt, baking soda, and cream of tartar (the Greeks knew about using the tartar that was a by-product of wine fermentation). Thoroughly mix in the barley grits (to be found in breakfast cereal section of healthfood stores). Make a well in the center of the mixture and gradually stir in the buttermilk. If the dough seems too thick, you may add a tablespoon or two of warm water.

Mound the dough on a floured baking sheet and cover with an inverted heat-proof bowl (a French terra-cotta casserole works as perfectly as a baking *cloche*). Do not delay putting into your preheated oven; bake at 400 degrees for approximately 30 minutes, then lower the heat to 350 degrees, uncover, and finish the loaf with an additional 10 to 15 minutes to slightly brown its crust.

Serve with little dishes of olive oil for dipping.

❦ *MĒTRA* (Stuffed Sow's Womb, or Matrix): The secret of this dish is to use a more available stomach from pig or sheep and treat it like a Scottish haggis.

    1 pig or sheep stomach
    1 cup cracked wheat
    pine nuts
    2 calves' brains
    1 onion, minced
    2/3 pound ground pork, or Italian sausage, removed from its casing
    minced pork liver or lamb's kidney (optional)
    2 tablespoons fish sauce

aniseed, rue, asafoetida leaf, fennel seed, and freshly ground pepper, to taste
1 egg, beaten
stock or water to cover the matrix
vinaigrette (see below)

Toast cracked wheat in a 250-degree oven; at the same time toast a handful of pine nuts until golden brown. In vinegared water, blanch two calves' brains until firm; trim off their membranes and chop. When cooled, mix wheat with nuts, brains, onion, ground pork or Italian sausage—you have to get your hands into this!—and, if desired, a bit of minced pork liver or a lamb kidney. Moisten with fish sauce and season further with aniseed, dried rue, asafoetida leaf, fennel seed, and freshly brayed pepper. Bind with a beaten egg.

Fill the stomach 2/3 full, allowing for swelling of the wheat. Tie tightly at the top, with 2 small metal or hard plastic straws inserted to allow steam to escape. Poach in simmering water or, preferably, stock, for about 2 hours, pricking the bag all over with a needle when it begins to swell, so it will not burst.

Serve with a vinaigrette made from balsamic vinegar mixed with a little extra virgin olive oil, red wine, and asafoetida.

❦ *TEUTHIS ŌNTHULEUMENĒ* (Stuffed Squid): This recipe is adapted for squid of modest size from Sotades (Athenaeus, 293c) rather than of the two-foot long type used by Alexis (326d).

1 pound small squid
fennel seed
salt
Italian sweet sausage
finely chopped greens, such as kale or mustard, blanched or cooked
olive oil
marjoram
dry white wine

Clean squid by cutting between body and head, removing cartilage from body and sharp beak from mouth. Rub skin from body and chop tentacles and "wings" plus all of head save the eyes. These are prepared much more simply than those we tend to copy from modern Italian or Greek recipes.

Combine the chopped appendages, fennel seed, salt, some Italian sausage (about a handful, removed from casing and sautéed into crumbles), and chopped greens. Stuff squid and place in one layer in a greased baking dish;

brush with olive oil, sprinkle with marjoram and about 1/4 to 1/3 cup of dry white wine. Bake at 350 degrees for 30 minutes.

❦   CHOIROS HEMIEPHTHOS KAI HEMIOPTOS: Whole Pig, Half-boiled and Half-roasted (adapted from Athenaeus, IX.381b–d).

1 suckling pig, weighing 15 pounds or more
2 pounds chitterlings (pigs' small intestines, available fresh or frozen at stores catering to cooks from the South)
separate marinades for pig and chitterlings (described in the body of the recipe)
meat stock
flour
oil
cut-up vegetables (onion, garlic, celery, fennel, moistened with olive oil)

stuffing
1 large chopped onion
garlic cloves
2 bay leaves
1 stalk of chopped celery
10 peppercorns
a few sprigs of parsley
1 cup vinegar
enough boiling salted water to cover chitterlings
1 pork liver
olive oil
2 teaspoons dried mint
sea salt, freshly ground pepper, onion powder
fresh sage leaves

Clean and wash both the piglet and the chitterlings thoroughly. Overnight, soak the chitterlings in a nonreactive pan with a cut-up onion in half water, half garlic white wine vinegar to cover. Separately marinate the pig in dry red wine with 8 cloves of minced garlic.

The next day, dry the pig and rub inside and out with cut cloves of garlic; salt and pepper the inside and fill the cavity with prepared chitterlings (the cook in Athenaeus gutted and bled his pig through a small incision in one shoulder, thus having to cram it through its mouth!)

For the stuffing, place drained chitterlings in a pot with the onion, 4 chopped garlic cloves, the bay leaves, chopped celery, peppercorns, and a few sprigs of parsley. Add vinegar and pour over boiling salted water to cover; simmer for 1-1/2 hours. Drain and cut into small pieces. While chitterlings are cooking, cut up the pork liver and sauté the pieces in olive oil, seasoning them with sea salt, freshly ground pepper and onion powder. Combine liver, cooked chitterlings — generously peppered — 2 teaspoons dried mint, 10 sliced garlic cloves, and a clutch of fresh sage leaves.

Tightly sew up the stuffing in the cavity and arrange the pig in a deep roasting pan (or large fish poacher) on its side, using weights to steady it. In a separate pan bring a meat stock (I recommend stock I make to have on hand for Chinese cooking, made from pork and chicken bones — with garlic, always more garlic, which makes the happiest marriage with any swine product) diluted with some of its marinade to a boil. Pour it around the piglet to a level that covers half the pig, being careful not to submerge the sewn incision. Simmer gently for 1-1/2 to 2 hours.

Remove from broth and, when cool enough to handle, dry it and salt and pepper it all over. Make a paste of flour and oil, plus more of the marinade, and coat the boiled half of the pig; carefully oil the exposed half; cover both ears with foil. Arrange the animal as you wish to present it, crouching in the same (now drained) pan in which it was poached on a bed of cut-up vegetables. Roast in a preheated oven at 500 degrees for 20 to 30 minutes, then lower temperature to 325 for continued cooking while occasionally brushing the exposed side with your stock mixed with a bit of oil and vinegar.

An idea from Roberta W. Smoler, *The Useful Pig* (1990), inspired me to baste with a "brush" (baton) made from the top of the fennel, sprigs of fresh oregano and coriander, tied together. Roasting will take a further 2 hours or so, since the "roasted" side already began to cook in the first stage of this process. Remove caked paste from the "boiled" side (some may have cracked and fallen off, in any case). Let rest for at least 20 minutes. Garnish appropriately.

Note: It is not necessary to cut up the chitterlings, but my experience with stuffing a 102-pound wild boar with great strings of Italian sausage taught me that people's sensitivities do not condone such realism.

On the other hand, if the sleight-of-hand boasted by the ancient chef is too onerous, you may prefer to follow a simpler recipe cited in Athenaeus: whole roast pig stuffed with scallops and oysters!

❦ LAGŌS PHOINIKOBALANOS (Hare with Date Sauce): The dates, called "Phoenician acorns," are not difficult for today's cooks to find, but we must substitute rabbit (which the Greeks did not have) for the hare.

1 whole rabbit, about 2 pounds (fresh or defrosted)
honey, capers, and red wine

Stuffing
1/2 cup chopped walnuts and almonds, mixed
4 or 5 chicken livers
2 minced garlic cloves
1/2 teaspoon ground mustardseed
olive oil
Salt and pepper

Sauce
20 or so pitted dates, fresh if possible
2/3 cup each fish sauce and red wine, reduced by boiling to 1/3 of its original
   volume
1 tablespoon finely minced onion
1/2 teaspoon mint
1/2 teaspoon ground sage

Sauté chicken livers and garlic cloves in olive oil, chop finely, and combine with walnuts, almonds, and ground mustard seed to make stuffing. Salt and pepper the rabbit cavity and fill with the stuffing; sew closed.[13] For the sauce, mash dates; combine with the fish sauce and wine, minced onion, and sage.

Place rabbit in an oven-proof casserole; pour sauce over. Cover and roast at 350 degrees for about 1 hour, checking occasionally to see if more liquid should be added; uncover near the end of cooking time if you wish to further brown the rabbit. Remove to a heated platter and garnish appropriately. Deglaze the casserole with 1/2 to 2/3 cup unreduced red wine mixed with 1 teaspoon honey and 2 teaspoons capers, cooking off all the residue to pour over your dish.

❦ THRIA (Filled Fig Leaves): Instead of fig leaves, you may use preserved grape leaves in jars from Greek markets. Cook barley groats (or bulgur wheat) in lamb stock to make a thick pilaf, adding some crisply rendered dice of salt pork and pine nuts. Cool and add half of a poached calf's brain; mix in honey and mizithra Greek cheese (or ricotta), enough to make the mixture hold its shape if molded; bind with egg. Shape by spoonfuls into ovals and wrap each in a fig or grape leaf (if you do not know how to do this, tucking in the ends to make a neat package, look at the diagram in any good modern Greek cookbook).

Heat in aromatic honey (rosemary or thyme preferred), diluted with pomegranate juice if available (or juice from unripe grapes—verjuice if you have an up-to-date specialty source). Garnish with toasted pine nuts.

❦ GONGGULIDES (Turnips): Alternatively, use rape turnip, kohlrabi (cf. Athenaeus IX. 369c). Remember that the rutabaga or "swede" is not a turnip known in antiquity, nor before early modern gardeners developed it.

> 1 pound white turnips
> 1/4 cup olive oil
> raisins
> 3 tablespoons red wine vinegar
> 1/4 cup water
> 1 generous tablespoon thyme or rosemary honey
> 1/2 teaspoon ground mustard
> toasted pine nuts or chopped hazelnuts

Trim and peel turnips (if mature; young ones need only be scrubbed), reserving all tender leafage. In boiling salted water parboil turnip and turnip tops about 5 minutes. Drain. Heat olive oil in a skillet; add turnip slices and sauté briefly until lightly browned. Blend together the vinegar, water, honey, and ground mustard, and add to skillet, together with the turnip leaves and a handful of raisins. Reheat and adjust seasonings and serve sprinkled with toasted pine nuts or chopped hazelnuts.

❦ KRAMBĒ (Cabbage): Headed cabbages were developed by the Celts, it appears. Athenaeus (IX, 369) discusses various types of Greek cabbage. The most authentic variety available today is apt to be kale.

> 1 bunch kale
> 2 tablespoons extra virgin olive oil
> 1 large clove garlic, minced
> salt and pepper to taste

Wash kale thoroughly, remove tough stems and tear large leaves in several pieces. In the water clinging to the leaves steam until tender, about 10 minutes.

Heat olive oil and garlic in a large skillet. When garlic starts to color, add drained kale, salt, and pepper; keep tossing until leaves are covered with oil and crisped bits of garlic well distributed.

Among other possible vegetables are chard (white and red), leeks, cardoons and artichokes, parsnips, cucumber, zucchini squash, radish, sea kale, broad beans, black-eyed peas, and greens such as dandelion, arugula, nettles, ramps, purslane, mustard.

❦   TRAGĒMATA: These are "desserts" for the second table, or symposion; "tidbits," as it were, with a punning play on the "nibbles" of a goat *(tragos)*, though the word derives from the verb "to eat." Here you are on your own as to choices among nuts, fruits, cheese etc., guided by our chapters on Greece. A few sweetmeats are suggested below.

Plakous kudoniata (Quince flat cake)

2 or 3 quinces, thickly sliced
sweet wine, such as Greek Mavrodaphne, water, and honey for poaching
1 teaspoon coriander seeds
1 teaspon fenugreek seeds
4 cups fresh recotta cheese or mizithra
1 cup aromatic honey
4 eggs, well beaten
1/2 cup fine semolina flour
toasted almonds

Poach quinces in wine mixture with coriander and fenugreek. Do not over-cook unless you wish a texture approaching jam; about 10 minutes, depending on ripeness of the Cydonian apple, as the ancients called it. Drain and cool.

Stir together the cheese, honey, eggs, and flour. Pour into a greased shallow baking pan or deep pie plate. Distribute fruit over the top and bake approximately 1 hour in an oven preheated to 350 degrees. Garnish with toasted almonds.

Gastris (Honey Nut-cake)

This recipe was adapted from Chrysippos of Tyana via Athenaeus XIV, 647.

1-1/2 cup white sesame seeds
1/4 cup each blanched almonds, hazelnuts, and walnuts
2 tablespoons poppy seeds

2 teaspoons peppercorns
1-1/2 cups of aromatic honey
1/4 cup water

Spread sesame seeds on a cookie sheet and place in a preheated, 350-degree oven for a few minutes to lightly toast them. Crush them in a mortar, being careful not to go so far as to make them release their oil; set aside. On the same sheet, toast the blanched almonds, hazelnuts, walnuts, and 2 tablespoons of poppy seeds. While still warm, rub walnuts and hazelnuts in a dish towel in order to free some of their skins. Bray nuts in a mortar with the peppercorns (or, if you insist on using modern conveniences, pulse them in a food processor until crushed but not giving up oil). Set aside.

Have ready 3 square cake pans 8 inches by 8 inches, lined with well-oiled wax paper. Boil honey and water until mixture reaches the soft ball stage when a bit is dropped into a cup of cold water. Working quickly, combine 1 cup of the honey with the crushed sesame and spread thinly in two of the pans. Mix remaining honey with crushed nuts, poppy seeds, and pepper; spread on bottom of third pan. Let all cool and congeal. Remove from the pans, peel away wax paper and make a "sandwich" by placing the dark nut mixture between the two sesame confections.

⚘ A CONVIVIUM IN ANCIENT ROME

A fine antidote to pervasive ideas of Romans' debased gluttony and libertine ways, even if you opt for as much authenticity as possible (i.e., reclining in triclinial style with no more than nine participants and wearing proper costumes; appropriate entertainment). Avoid calling attention to Trimalchio's banquet or to the hilarious disaster of a Roman meal hosted by the pedantic doctor in Tobias Smollet's *Peregrine Pickle*! In any case suitable tableware (no forks, of course) and squares of stale bread for individual plates are fun; for serving dishes, I have used the pottery receptacles that go under flower pots as substitutes for ordinary Roman household ware.

A note on ingredients: You must prepare a number of cooking aids well ahead of time in order to have them available in labeled containers. *Caroenum:* by boiling, reduce a bottle of red wine to half its volume. *Defrutum:* reduce fresh unfermented grape juice *(must)* to one-third volume. *Liquamen:* use *Nuoc mam,* Philippine *patis,* or Chinese fish sauce.

⚘ GUSTATIO: Hors d'oeuvres should be served with a Roman apértif, *mulsum,* made by mixing honey into dry white wine. Note that this is an item for economizing; I recommend a cheap but nonetheless good wine from Romania (Premiat or Cuvée St.-Pierre, Momessin, from the Rhone Valley).

⚘ FERCULUM PETRONIANUM (Service à la Petronius): This is especially effective if you have a round table large enough to display images of 12 zodiacal signs above each platter of hors d'oeuvres, which pun upon their names or myths.[14]

Cancer (Trimalchio's birth sign, given a crown of flowers at his *cena*). Use crab claws for an extravagant feast, *crab* apples pickled for a more modest play on words.

Leo (an African fig). This is a difficult one; since varieties of olives — over thirty including "white" ones are described by Latin agricultural writers — are not otherwise present, set them out here.

Virgo (womb of an unfarrowed sow). I have made an Apician recipe for a sheep's stomach, available in Puerto Rican markets. Otherwise I use tiny hard-boiled quail eggs with an Apician dipping sauce (see below, Dipping Sauce 2).

Libra (scales holding tarts and cakes). A good spot to provide your crackers, a high-fiber content variety. I include a small antique bronze scale discovered at a flea market in Salonika years ago.

Scorpio (a Mediterranean scorpion fish, the French *rascasse*). For an exotic meal, poach freshwater crayfish. In New England you may acquire a sculpin or so. Otherwise, play on "sting" with any hot, pickled vegetable — again, no peppers, though.

Sagittarius (Bull's eye). I tried this *once* with the eyes of a calf, a delicacy in some cultures; not a success. Use pickled onions of comparable size, either the ones imported from England or, best, Greek volvi, equivalent to the "bulbs" eaten in antiquity. Alternatively, play on the rabbit carried by the archer in late antique zodiacal illustrations; see Apicius for recipes.

Capricorn (Lobster). Play on the goat with a strong goat cheese, boucheron, for example, if rock-lobster tails are too much for the budget; no *Homarus americanus!*

Aquarius (Goose). A goose-liver paté or confit; you may think up your own pun.

Pisces (Two mullets). Fresh sardines or deep-fried smelts, dressed *à l'escabèche.*

Aries (Chickpeas, *cicer arietinus* in Latin because of the little projection like a horn at one end). Use roasted chickpeas from any Italian market or dress cooked ones with a marinade, garlic, and parsley.

Taurus (Piece of beef). Beef tartare or slices of beef tongue or small veal tongues (fresh), simmered in stock with bay leaf, onion, garlic, and spices. Alternatively, ox-tails, braised.

Gemini (Kidneys and sheep testicles — mountain oysters in our parlance). Sautéed kidneys.

❦ DIPPING SAUCE 1: For cucumber, celery, romaine lettuce (Antiquity did not know our headed lettuces), and appropriate items above, mix together:

1 tablespoon honey
2 tablespoons wine vinegar

2 teaspoons *liquamen* (see above, note on ingredients)

a pinch each of rue and pennyroyal or *nepeta* (catnip).

Use the following sauce with hard-boiled eggs and crudités, being careful to avoid anachronistic vegetables: no broccoli, for example, or New World string beans, tomatoes and peppers; squash only of the marrow family, but some new-comers to the supermarket such as taro *(colocasia)* would be authentic.

🝔 DIPPING SAUCE 2

3 garlic cloves, crushed (or 3 drops of tincture
   of asafoetida and a pinch of dried leaf)

1 tin anchovy fillets, with their oil

2 tablespoons olive oil

1 tablespoon flour

1/2 cup wine vinegar

up to 1/2 cup retsina (Greek resinated wine)

freshly ground pepper

In a mortar, bray anchovies and flour to a smooth paste. Sauté garlic in olive oil briefly; add the anchovy mixture and slowly incorporate the vinegar, stirring until smooth and thickened. Season with pepper and gradually add the retsina, stirring at the simmer for about 15 minutes. Cool and serve.

🝔 SALSUM SINE SALSO (Salt Fish without Salt Fish — a paté): Cook chicken livers in olive oil, seasoning with salt, pepper, cumin, and either boiled-down wine (to half-volume) or the same simmered with raisins to make a sweet liquid equivalent to modern Italian sapa (this to balance but not overwhelm the saltiness). Grind livers with walnuts and olive oil (proportion 1/4 cup oil to about 1/2 pound chicken livers, but depending on how much of the wine has been incorporated) — in other words, enough oil to achieve a proper texture. Press into a fish-shaped mold and, when unmolded, sprinkle with extra-virgin olive oil (so that the greenish tint carries out the "fish" concept).

MENSA PRIMA

❦ EMBRACTUM BAIANUM (Delights of Baiae): Baiae was a seaside resort.

4 pounds mussels
2 pint-sized containers shelled oysters
roe from 2 pounds sea urchins (see note)
1/4 cup toasted pine nuts
1 stalk of celery
6 peppercorns, crushed
coriander
cumin seeds
rue (if unavailable, substitute chervil or marjoram)
4–6 chopped fresh dates
olive oil
liquamen
white wine
green coriander, for garnish

Steam open the mussels in 1/4 cup white wine; when shelled, mince these, together with 2 containers of shucked oysters poached for a few minutes in their own liquor, and the roe from the sea urchins.

Toast pine nuts in a 250-degree oven until golden brown, then chop and combine with the seafoods and a finely chopped stalk of celery. In a mortar crush peppercorns and equivalent amounts of both coriander and cumin seeds; add a pinch to 1/4 teaspoon of rue. Combine with seafood mixture, together with chopped fresh dates (Apicius specifies "Jericho" date) to a proportion that seems right for your taste, remembering you wish to balance the sea flavors, not overwhelm them. Moisten all with olive oil, *liquamen,* and a sweet wine (made by reducing white wine, boiled with sultana raisins) mixed for sweet-salty harmony—about 1/4 to 1/3 cup in total.

Serve cold, if desired in individual shells. It also is possible to serve hot: bake in a gratin dish for 10 to 15 minutes at 350 degrees. In either case, garnish with green coriander.

Note: Sea urchins are available spring and fall in Italian fish shops. When you break open each *testa* you will note the cartilaginous "mouth," called "Aristotle's lantern" because the Greek philosopher and naturalist was the first to describe this feature, and because it does resemble an old-fashioned lantern. The orange, star-shaped roe or gonads may be lifted out easily.

❦ IN LOLLIGINE FARSALI (Patella of Stuffed Squid)

2 pounds squid, cleaned and skinned
olive oil
liquamen
1 egg, beaten

filling

the squids' tentacles, minced
3 crushed cloves of garlic
1/2 cup chopped scallions
1 cup fresh bread crumbs
1/2 cup minced green coriander
1 teaspoon celery seed
1/2 cup minced calves brain, poached in vinegared water and with membrane
    removed (optional)
1 teaspoon peppercorns pounded in a mortar

sauce

1/2 cup white wine
1 teaspoon honey
1 tablespoon fish sauce
olive oil
freshly brayed pepper
a pinch of rue (if unavailable, substitute oregano)

Combine ingredients to make the filling. Moisten with 1 tablespoon each of olive oil and of *liquamen* and mix with the beaten egg. Stuff squid 1/3 to 1/2 full; fasten with toothpicks. Place in a shallow oiled pan.

Mix sauce and pour over the squid, arranged in one layer. Bake at 350 degrees for 35 minutes.

❦ CONCHICLA DE PISA (Cassoulet of Dried Peas)

1 pound whole dried peas (green or yellow)
2 leeks
bouquet of coriander
1 small chicken
water mixed with wine, sufficient to cover chicken
1/4 cup *liquamen* (or 1 teaspoon salt)

bouquet garni of dill, coriander, savory, and 1 leek

1 small smoked pork shoulder

lovage (or substitute celery tops)

1 tablespoon caraway seed

8 peppercorns

1 calf brain, parboiled in vinegared water, with membrane removed.

1 *lucanica* dried sausage from an Italian market (see note below)

meatballs

1/2 pound fresh Italian sausage (hot or sweet), removed from casing

cumin, dried onion, and ground ginger

1 beaten egg

sauce

pepper, oregano, and dried onion flakes, pounded in a mortar

lovage or celery tops

fresh coriander

liquamen

red wine

olive oil

Soak dried peas overnight if necessary (follow packager's directions) and cook with leeks and coriander for 1 hour.

Simmer chicken in water, wine, and *liquamen* to cover, with the bouquet.

Cook pork shoulder with lovage, caraway seed, and peppercorns (a tea ball to enclose these is welcome) until the meat easily comes off the bones.

Parboil the calf brain in vinegared water and remove the membrane.

Cut *lucanica* sausage in pieces.

Form meatballs from the fresh Italian sausage mixed with cumin, dried onion, ground ginger, and the beaten egg. Fry in olive oil.

In a mortar, pound pepper, oregano, dried onion flakes, lovage or celery tops, and fresh coriander; moisten with *liquamen;* mix these seasonings with 1 cup red wine. In an earthenware casserole layer the ingredients, alternating the meats, in bite-size pieces, with this sauce. Over the final layer float enough olive oil to glaze the top of the vessel. Bake the casserole in a preheated 350-degree oven for at least 1 hour, poking the oil down with a straw as a crust forms on the top during cooking.

Note: Apicius specifies Lucanian sausage, from South Italy, in his recipes, though *lucanica* is today a northern product.

🌿 PULLUS FRONTANIANUS (Chicken à la Fronto)

> 1 frying chicken cut in pieces, or 2 pounds chicken legs and thighs.
> 2 leeks, cleaned and cut in rounds
> 1 teaspoon ground dried savory
> 1/4 cup olive oil for sautéeing chicken
> 1 small bunch dill
> 1 small bunch coriander
> 4 ounces pine nuts
> 2 to 3 tablespoons *garum* or to taste
> 1/3 cup *defrutum* (see above, note on ingredients)
> freshly ground pepper

Brown the chicken in the oil without seasoning. Set pieces in one layer in an oiled baking/serving dish, scattering leeks, pine nuts, chopped herbs among them. Sprinkle with the *liquamen* and savory. Bake at 350 degrees for 30 minutes or until tender. Finish with *defrutum* and pepper.

🌿 PATINA DE ASPARAGIS (Asparagus Patina)

> 1 pound asparagus
> 1/4 cup wine (rosé or vernaccia)
> 1 small onion
> 2 or 3 medium eggs
> peppercorns, lovage, coriander, savory to taste
> olive oil, sweet wine, and *liquamen*

Make a purée of asparagus (by braying in a mortar if you wish to be authentic) and 1/4 cup of wine, reserving some tips for garnish. Bray in a clean mortar the pepper and herbs (quantity to your judgment; half the fun of Roman cookery is the continual tasting and estimating of cumulative effect). Grate the onion or put through a food mill. Add with the spices to the purée and mix in a mixture of reduced sweet wine and *liquamen,* plus a bit of oil—enough to moisten the purée but not to turn it soupy. Put all the mixture into a greased oven-proof, shallow dish; garnish with reserved asparagus. Beat eggs as for scrambling and pour over the purée when it is thoroughly heated in a 325-degree oven, pushing it to make uneven pools to receive the eggs; continue baking until eggs are set. Sprinkle with freshly ground pepper and serve.

SECUNDA MENSA

❦ DULCIA THEBAICAE (Stuffed Dates in Honey): Toast pine nuts in a slow oven until they color. Take fresh dates, stone them and refill cavities with the toasted nuts, about two to a date. Roll in coarse canning or kosher salt. Heat a skillet full of honey (thyme or rosemary preferred) in which the dates may be spread in one layer; honey should be about 1/2-inch deep. Heat dates through and serve warm.

❦ SAVILLUM (Cato's Cheesecake)

24 ounces cream cheese (or mix half and half with fresh ricotta)
3 to 4 tablespoons wholewheat flour
1/2 to 1/3 cup honey (herb preferred)
2 eggs, separated
poppy seeds (variation: toasted almond slices)
additional honey

Mix cheese, flour, honey, and yolks, whipping as much air into the mixture as possible (by hand). Beat the egg whites into soft peaks and fold into cheese mixture (Cato specified only 1 egg and there is no mention of trying to lighten the cake by this means). Pour into a greased spring-form pan (or an oiled earthenware serving dish, unglazed). Bake at 350 degrees for 45 minutes to 1 hour, testing with a straw until done. Turn off oven, remove cake and pour warm honey over and sprinkle with seeds or nuts; return to the cooling oven for 5 or 10 minutes.

❦ PATINA DE PIRIS

6 pears of a firm variety
red or white wine to poach pears (may be mixed with water for economy)
honey
3 or 4 beaten eggs
1/2 teaspoon ground cumin
2 teaspoons olive oil
1 teaspoon *liquamen*
2 tablespoons reduced wine, sweetened by simmering with raisins
pepper, freshly ground in a mortar

Poach pears until tender; peel and core; reserve two for decoration of the dish. Purée four pears with remaining ingredients, adding eggs and oil last. Pour into a greased pie dish and decorate top with slices of remaining pears arranged in a slightly overlapping circular pattern; glaze top with honey mixed with a little oil. Bake in a 375-degree oven about 20 to 25 minutes.

Note: You may wish to bake a bread from Cato's repertoire, but guests will be happier with any good wholemeal loaf (or semolina). Plates may authentically be focaccia to be eaten before dessert with all its soaked in sauces. Remember that you eat with your fingers; provide a handsome basin of water perfumed with rose water or spices.

A LATE GOTHIC FEAST

If you wish to truly match the number of different dishes that were the norm for extravagant feasts of the waning Middle Ages, supplement this more modest assemblage with recipes from Black, Brown, Hieatt and Butler, Kosman, Sass, or Scully (see the bibliography). I have had to include a few basic preparations *de luxe* — no festive board could be imagined without the ancestor of blancmange, and the evening must finish off with hypocras — but I have otherwise tried not to replicate recipes worked out by authors readily accessible in English.

You will scarcely — at least for a private dinner party — wish to include as many dishes as were borne in to Late Gothic diners. Nor will you wish to make distinctions among your guests so that those "below the salt" receive fewer and less pretentious ones. Otherwise, be as authentic as your means permit: use some exotic basin and ewer to hold sweet-scented water for hand-washing before the meal and at intervals between courses. Display special metal plate and ceramic objects on a sideboard or credenza. Use three layers of table-cloth — one to be removed after each service. Provide large napkins and no forks. However, a few sharp knives may be placed strategically, as well as spoons for especially liquid provender. Serve your wines in metal goblets *(hanaps)*, one to each couple (they may wish to drink from opposite sides, and will surely observe medieval courtesy-book admonitions about wiping their lips carefully before imbibing). The same goes for shared bowls of brewet or pottage, a reason to seat husbands and wives or dating pairs together rather than in the usual manner. Use pared bread a few day old to cut trenchers to lay upon your place-plates of either wood or pewter — no porcelain!

Whether you plan three or five courses, you will want to present a special dish, extravagantly garnished, and/or performance as entremés, intermezzo, sotelte. You may discover that you have performers among youngsters who are, in any case, willing to dress up and play servitors; employ one of them also to sound a trumpet or to pipe in the major dish of each course.

A note on ingredients: In specialty shops of large cities it is now possible to purchase *verjuice;* there is also *agresto* in some Italian markets. You may make your own, even if you do not own a vineyard or crab apple trees. Mix some cider with a mild cider vinegar for an approximation of the unripe apple type; for grape-derived verjuice, use white grape juice mixed with a bit of white wine vinegar.

Almond milk will take a bit more work. Care must be taken not to grind almonds to the point that will render oil. A blender works well for this task, as it does for grinding rice into a fine rice flour for certain dishes or to thicken the almond milk. In the last blancmange of fish that I made for a Renaissance dinner, it was advantageous to leave the almond milk unstrained in order to enhance the texture of the fish purée. The liquid (brought just to the boil before removing from the fire) to soak the pulverized almonds may be water, fish stock or white wine; proportion 4 or 5 ounces of ground almonds to 1 cup of liquid. Soaking may take anywhere from 15 to 30 minutes (least satisfactory), to overnight (it freezes also). If made in large enough quantities for a "lean" or Lenten meal, any left over may be used in Middle Eastern cookery, and it makes a splendid flavoring for homemade ice cream.

While this menu is not a *recreation* of a particular banquet (that would try the soul and hands of any modern domestic cook), it represents a selection from one served Henry V at Windsor. Recipes assume a dinner for ten or twelve, but remember that guests select from the presentations and that not every dish serves that many diners more than a taste. The style is English, with only three courses, each ending with a "sotelte," then a "reresupper" to follow in your [with]drawing room. It is also English in beginning straight off with roasts and main dishes. If you wish to be more continental, start with a compote of fruits such as cherries and berries, or melon (the most "dangerous" because it is so cold and moist in the humoral system) and build up to the chief roast. Serve wholemeal bread or rolls, and good wines (bordeaux preferred to burgundies).

I.

Grosse Chare, Vyaund Ryall
Capoun of haut grece
Pease Chewetys, Frettoures
A Sotelte (Gyngerebred)

II.

Moustarde Brewette, Venyson with Frumenty,
Saumon Rosted
Salat, Cryspes, Porcellys
A Sotelte (Qualys in Pye)

III.

Creme de almaundys, Perys in syruppe,
Crustade, Blamanger
A Sotelte (Cokentrice)

EXPLANATION:

I. The large piece of meat might be beef or lamb; I give the latter. The royal viand is a condiment prepared with meat, wine, honey, spices. Pease puddings may be made individually or as a single large one. Fritters are made with a thin batter like Japanese tempura (if made of slices of apple, they should come in the final course according to medieval beliefs about dietary health). The sotelte gingerbread should be a highly decorated castle or house. Alternatively sotelties were made to look like some edible that they were not, like Apicius' "fish" made of chicken liver.

II. Mustard broth uses prepared Dijon mustard, no longer made as in the Middle Ages of the must that gives it its name. If the cookery involved is daunting, forget the venison and frumenty (boiled wheat) and order the piglet(s) already roasted whole from a Latino market. The salmon and crisps are self-explanatory. For the sotelte you make a salt pastry, thick and solid, from which to build a deep pie—you may prefer another surprise inside; I have found it difficult to acquire live quail except in breeding season, and they are messy if released untethered.

III. The cockentrice is an elaborate finale, made of the front half of a capon and the rear half of a piglet, but this means guests may take some samples home and that you can rest from your labors with plenty of leftovers for the morrow.

If less meat and more vegetables are desired, cook up root vegetables or cabbage, leeks, and onions and season with favored cinnamon, sugar, and ginger. Spinach braised in oil appears in Richard II's cookbook; season it with freshly grated nutmeg and a pinch of ginger. (I also use "grains of Paradise," bought in Morocco, but these are rare in this country.)

❦ GROSSE CHARE: Roast either a baron of beef or a large leg of lamb (mutton) by your usual method. During summer, and if you have a skilled assistant, spit-roast a whole lamb outdoors, as the Greeks do at Easter. Serve with cameline sauce, one of the most widely used of medieval sauces.

❦ SAWSE CAMELYNE

1/3 cup currants
1/3 cup hazelnuts (filberts)
1/8 teaspoon peppercorns
1/4 teaspoon ground cloves
1/2 teaspoon ground ginger
1/2 teaspoon ground mace
1 teaspoon cinnamon
a pinch of salt
3 tablespoons toasted bread crumbs
dry red wine
vinegar

In a mortar, bray the currants, hazelnuts, and spices. Soak the bread crumbs in 2/3 cup dry red wine to which a tablespoon of wine vinegar has been added. Combine with spice mixture and serve as an accompaniment. If you are fortunate enough to have melegueta pepper, these "grains of Paradise" should also be used in addition to pepper.

❦ VYAUND RYALL

meat from 1 cooked chicken, finely minced

saffron

1 cup raisins, simmered in sweet wine (malmsey or port) and honey

1 cup stoned dates, coarsely chopped

1/2 cup currants

pine nuts

ground cloves, cinnamon, and mace to taste

chopped blanched and toasted almonds

1 cup pear or quince preserves

conserve of pine nuts cooked with apples

powdered ginger

salt and/or sugar

pastry shells, prebaked

Put minced chicken through a fine sieve and color it strongly with saffron soaked in hot water. Grind raisins and simmer in enough sweet wine and a bit of honey to make a thick syrup; set aside. Chop stoned dates, mix in currants, a handful of pine nuts, and season with ground cloves, cinnamon, and mace to your taste; moisten with more wine and bring to a boil. Remove from the fire and add the raisin syrup, chopped blanched and toasted almonds, and pear or quince preserves, plus a conserve of pine nuts cooked with apples; season with powdered ginger and cinnamon. Bring to a boil once more. Remove from fire and check seasoning; you may find that it needs a little salt to bring out the spices, possibly sugar as well if your wine was not sweet enough. Cool. Bake large tart shells of simple pastry. Fill with the chicken and arrange some of the fruit and nut mixture on top, allowing the yellow chicken purée to show. Serve cold as accompaniment to the roast.

❦ CAPOUN OF HAUT GRECE

1 fat capon, approximately 6 pounds

fresh herbs, including parsley, hyssop, sage, rosemary, and thyme

salt and pepper

sauce

liver of the capon

goose fat (or available substitute)

1 onion, sliced

sugar
1/2 teaspoon ginger
1/2 cinnamon
1/2 cardamom
1/3 cup toasted bread crumbs
2 tablespoons verjuice (or 1 of tarragon vinegar)

Take fresh herbs and crush them with your hands; stuff them into the cavity of a fat capon with salt and pepper. Roast following your preferred method. While it cooks, lightly sauté its liver in a bit of fat (goose preferred), so that it is still pink inside; in the same fat brown slices of onion, sprinkled with a bit of sugar. Bray liver and onions in a mortar with ginger, cinnamon, and cardamom, and bread crumbs; add verjuice. When capon is done, mix the crushed liver, seasonings and thickener (bread crumbs mixed with vinegar being the normal liaison in the Middle Ages) into the fat and drippings in the roasting pan; bring to a boil, scraping up all brown bits, to make the sauce. Depending on the amount of fat rendered by the capon, you may wish to add a bit of wine in this final deglazing.

The peas to make the following pudding-pies may be fresh or dried. Terence Scully claims that medieval French "peas" were still white peas as in Apicius, but early fifteenth-century English sources make it clear that late Gothic "pease porridge hot and cold" was made from green peas. He is quite right in stressing that a light purée of peas was one of the *fonds* of French Gothic cuisine, together with beef broth and almond milk. Dried peas must, of course, be soaked before being used in this recipe, but it is excellent for the fresh new peas of early summer.

❧   PEASE CHEWETYS

1 peck of peas, shelled
homemade chicken broth
parsley
1 teaspoon dried mint
2 tablespoons dried onion flakes
2 tablespoons sugar
summer savory (fresh if in season, otherwise dried)
bread crumbs
2 eggs

1 prebaked pie shell, or several small ones
pea sprouts, for garnish

Cook peas briefly in chicken broth (depending on age from the garden, for 3 to 10 minutes). Reserve 1-1/2 cups of the peas and bray the rest in a mortar with a few sprigs of parsley, mint, onion flakes, sugar, a few leaves of summer savory (if indeed it is summer), and enough bread crumbs to make a satisfactory purée. Add more broth as necessary and 2 eggs, beaten into the purée. Add the reserved whole peas and fill the pie shell (or shells). pre-baked (or several small ones) With present concern about salmonella, you may bake these at 375 degrees for 15 minutes or so. Garnish with pea sprouts and set forth, cold or hot.

🌿 FRETTOURES: Make a batter using the recipe given below for crespys, but thinned to resemble the coating for tempura. These fritters may be of fruit, root vegetable, or assorted herbs, spiced appropriately, dipped in the batter, and deep fried. If using carrots, turnips, or parsnips, you may wish first to parboil slices briefly.

🌿 GYNGEREBRED: This is quite different from what we call gingerbread today, and more akin to a dense Middle European honey cake.

1 loaf stale bread, grated and dried
8 ounces wildflower honey
1 tablespoon ginger
2 teaspoons cinnamon
2 teaspoons ground aniseed

Make a *stiff* paste by grating the bread, then sieving it to make the crumb fine (depending on the loaf, you may need more than 1 loaf); add crumbs to the honey, brought to a boil, together with the spices. Let this simmer to reduce water content in the honey. To cool, place "gingerbread" in well-greased molds (if you have the parts for a house, fine) or roll out on waxed paper to shape into an appropriate sotelte.[15]

🌿 MOUSTARDE BREWETTE

chicken stock
salt and white pepper
light cream mixed with egg yolks

Dijon mustard
minced chives or nasturtium leaves and flowers for garnish

Prepare a rich chicken stock with extra amount of onion; strain and cool. Reheat, adjusting seasoning with salt and white pepper. Thicken by adding light cream mixed with egg yolks (proportions: 1/2 the quantity of soup; 1 yolk to every cup and a half of cream), putting a bit of the warm broth into the egg/cream mixture before incorporating the entire mixture. Do not permit the soup to boil. When ready to serve, add enough Dijon prepared mustard to color. Garnish with minced chives on individual servings, or with nasturtium leaves and flowers for a tureen.

The medieval cook would spit roast venison, usually after parboiling it. My adaptation is based on preferring it medium rare and using an oven. It would have been served with cameline or pepper sauce and accompanied by frumenty. Since the first course already introduces a comparable sauce, I suggest a different fruit-based one not unlike today's Cumberland. Although I normally marinate a venison roast, this does not seem to have been the practice in medieval England or France.

❦ VENYSON

1 venison roast, approximately 6 pounds
1/2 pound salt pork
salt, pepper, powdered ginger
butter
fat back or bacon (optional)
red wine for basting
2 or 3 bay leaves plus 5 or so juniper berries (optional)

sauce
currant jelly
red wine vinegar
toasted bread crumbs (optional)

Lard venison roast (loin, haunch, leg, or whatever) with lardons made from salt pork rolled in salt and pepper and powdered ginger. Rub exterior with the same seasonings (also some softened butter if the meat has no surface fat — in the latter case, you may wish to bard it, using fat back or strips of bacon). Roast uncovered in an oven heated to 475 degrees for 20 minutes; lower heat to 325 and continue to roast basting with red wine, for a total of 18 to 20 minutes per pound (lower figure is for for roast with bone in). For extra flavor, once heat is lowered and basting wine and drippings accumulate, place bay leaves and crushed juniper berries in the bottom of the roasting pan. Have it carved immediately (i.e., do not let the roast stand to let juices retreat, especially if it is a cut with any fat on it).

Over low heat, melt 2 tablespoons or more of currant jelly into the drippings, adding enough red wine vinegar to make a sweet-sour sauce; adjust seasoning and add toasted bread crumbs if thickening is desired.

❦ FRUMENTY

> 1 medium onion, chopped
> 2 tablespoons butter
> 1 cup cracked wheat (see note)
> 2-1/2 cups hot meat stock, or beef bouillon
> 1 teaspoon salt
> 1/2 teaspoon ginger
> 1/2 cup rich milk
> 1 teaspoon saffron threads
> 2 egg yolks, beaten

Sauté the onion gently in the butter. Lower heat and add cracked wheat, hot meat stock, salt, and ginger; cover closely and simmer until liquid is absorbed. Meanwhile, warm milk and soak saffron threads in it, off the heat, for 15 minutes or longer; combine with egg yolks. Add a few tablespoons of the hot frumenty to the egg/milk mixture, then combine both mixtures. Serve warm. (If it must wait, it will thicken further, but may be reheated with the addition of a little more milk.)

Note: For authenticity use cracked wheat rather than kasha (made from buckwheat—which is not wheat, despite its name) or bulgur (which *is* wheat, parboiled and dried by a special process).

❦ SAUMON (Salmon) ROSTED: In a culture of open fireplace cookery, "roast" may be grilled on a gridiron rather than turned on a spit; hence you will want sufficient salmon steaks. Season them with salt and pepper and dot with butter; broil, turning once, a total of about 8 minutes. The usual sauce suggested combines wine, cinnamon, minced onion, verjuice or vinegar, and powdered ginger, brought to a boil and poured over the fish as arranged in a serving platter.

Also good for fish is an uncooked *verde sawse* ("green sauce") in which the color comes from finely minced fresh herbs such as parsley, mint, sage, and thyme (the last two as substitutes for dittany and pellitory, unless you have a superbly stocked herb garden), brayed in a mortar with a bit of ground ginger, mixed with vinegar and/or verjuice and white wine.

There are infinite variations, with and without fine crumbs, with or without heating of ingredients, with or without straining the sauce, and with or without the addition of saffron.

❦ CRESPYS: "Crisps" are the medieval equivalent of our potato chips; it may seem *de trop* for our fat-avoiding cuisine that medieval recipe manuscripts suggest that they be served with "fritters," likewise deep fried — and generally in lard. Leaven in the original recipe was *barm*, the froth that forms on the top of fermenting ale or beer; we use commercial yeast.

> 3 cups flour
> 1/2 cup sugar
> 1 teaspoon salt
> 1 cup milk
> 1 cake compressed yeast
> 4 extra-large eggs, whites only
> sweet wine
> fat for deep-frying
> powdered sugar

Sift together flour, sugar, and salt. Scald milk and use some of it to proof the yeast. Whisk the eggwhites until just frothy. Gradually incorporate the flour mixture; add the milk and yeast. Finally, add enough sweet wine to make a pancake-like batter. Heat deep fat until smoking and let the batter run through your fingers according to the original directions, or dribble from a spoon to fry until crisp, turning once. Drain on paper towels and sprinkle with confectioner's sugar.

❦ SALAT: The salad is simply dressed with oil, vinegar, and salt. Finely slice a fennel bulb and place in a bowl, mixing in a teaspoon of fennel seeds. Add a small sliced onion, 2 minced cloves of garlic, 4 shallots, sliced, a large (carefully cleaned) leek sliced crosswise and a handful of purslane (a delicious "weed" — I use some that I pickle when I find it). Mix these with your hands and let them sit together in a cool place for at least an hour. When ready to serve add fresh herbs, "picked small with thyn hand": parsley, sage, borage, mint, cress, rosemary, and rue (not everyone will relish the last named). Dress with your own vinaigrette — a bit of walnut oil is a fine addition.

🌿 SOTELTE (QUALY PYE): Medieval cofynes (coffins: "pastry shells") to hold surprises can be simulated by modeling a thick salt pastry pie of the needed depth and diameter. The secret is to bake a separate small (true) pie as a stopper for a hole cut in the bottom. Through this one can introduce the birds, unharmed, at the last moment — or animal rights activists can devise mechanical jumpers to leap out when the top crust is removed. The real stopper/pie is to placate your disappointed guests.

🌿 CREME DE ALMAUNDYS: For this "custard," which may become a cawdell of added richness by incorporating eggs, you will make almond milk (in quantity) at the same time for the Blamenger, according to the directions above (p. 309). In essence, this uses the almonds strained from the "milk," a nice bit of economy in an otherwise royal menu!

To ground almonds remaining when all the liquid has been pressed from them by twisting tightly in cheesecloth or muslin, add white wine, enough to make the mass slightly liquid again, together with sugar and powdered ginger to taste. Bring this to a boil, adding rice flour as thickening, mixed as you would cornstarch with a few tablespoons of the wine (proportions 1/2 cup to a quart of almond mixture). When it seems thick enough to shape on a platter, remove from the heat and color with saffron or another agent (you may cheat with food coloring rather than sandalwood, etc.). Garnish with pomegranate seeds if in season (or if you providentially keep them in your freezer). Another cheat: I find a dash of almond extract an enhancement in some cases.

🌿 PERYS IN SYROPPE

pears, as many as guests to serve
red wine and water, mixed half and half for poaching
1 stick cinnamon
6 whole cloves

syrup (for 4 to 6 pears)
2-1/4 cups sugar
2 tablespoons honey
1 cup red wine
verjuice

Seville (bitter) orange peel or lemon zest
powdered ginger
egg yolks (optional)

Poach firm pears in a mixture of half red wine and half water to which a stick of cinnamon and 6 cloves have been added. You may leave pears whole or pare and slice them. Prepare a syrup by boiling sugar and honey dissolved in the red wine, as it thickens add some verjuice and strips orange peel or lemon zest (either would have been great delicacies in late Gothic times) carefully cleaned of the inner white substance. When it is quite thick, mix in some powdered ginger to taste (one medieval variant adds raw egg yolks at this point, which you are not advised to do). Pour this syrup over the pears in an earthen baking/serving dish. To serve warm, place the dish in a 250-degree oven up to 1 hour. If you have left the pears whole, partially pared perhaps, candied violets can be a nice garnish.

❧   CRUSTADE: This is an open custard tart which may contain dried fruits, such as dates, raisins, or currants, nuts, or fresh fruit in season — berries, for example. Modern mincemeat (no longer made commercially with meat) is also a possibility. A *Crustad Lumbard* even held marrow balls, rabbits, and small birds with the dates, or fish on fast days. Another variation could produce a cheese cake. Use your ingenuity.

Prepare a large pastry shell or individual small ones. Make a rich custard beating eggs and sugar together until light (proportion: 7 or 8 eggs to 1-1/2 cups sugar for a quart of light cream). Add light cream and spices — or you may use almond milk instead, or part cream and part almond milk. Spices would include ground cinnamon, cloves, ginger, mace, cardamom, and saffron (if all of them, use about 1/4 to 1/2 teaspoon each) and 1/2 teaspoon salt. Pour over your chosen filling and bake at 400 degrees for 10 to 12 minutes, then lower heat to 350 and continue cooking until a toothpick comes out clean, about 25 minutes (small tarts will take less). Garnish with edible flowers.

❧   BLAMENGER

a capon, or combination of capon and chicken breasts (see variants below)
2 cups almond milk
clarified poaching broth from capon
rice flour
sugar to taste

dried galanga root ("galengale," the milder relative of ginger, Indonesian *laos*)

white pepper

butter

parchment paper

Variant 1

1 capon, approximately 6 pounds

salt and pepper

bay leaf and 1 small onion (optional)

chicken broth for poaching

Season inside of capon with salt and freshly ground pepper; you may include a bay leaf and a small onion as well. Truss and poach in chicken broth (preferably homemade), at a simmer — if in the oven, bring to a boil and place in the center of a 325-degree oven — for about 2 hours or until legs move easily. You may wish to use a trick of Julia Child's: cover the breast with double layers of cheese-cloth, allowing the ends to soak in the broth as a self-basting device to keep the white meat moist.

Variant 2

Poach in homemade chicken stock the breast of a capon or two large whole chicken breasts.

In either case, when cool shred the white meat finely with the grain — one Italian recipe advises that the shreds should be as fine as hair! — or purée it. Reserve.

To 2 cups almond milk (this will be especially good if you have used goat's milk to make the almond cream above) add some of the clarified poaching broth. Proportions are difficult to advise: you do not want to alter the whiteness that gives the dish its name, merely a subtle hint of the fowl's flavor, since a breast is the least tasteful part of the bird. Meanwhile, make rice flour from whole rice grains (in a mortar, if you control kitchen serfs who are sufficiently enthusiastic) or in a blender. You will need approximately one third to half the quantity of almond milk.

In a heavy saucepan heat the almond milk with sugar to taste (remembering the sweet tooth of the Middle Ages) and several slices of dried galanga root. Add the rice flour, stirring until thickened. Incorporate the capon or chicken purée. Season with white pepper.

Pack into a well-buttered terrine (with a strip of buttered parchment paper down its length and extending at either end, if your terrine is not spring-form but ceramic) and bake until solid in a 350 degree oven.

To serve, garnish extravagantly with candied violets, other flowers, or a design of fresh herbs.

Note: for fast days — or if you simply desire more fish in this menu — the same dish is made with any firm, white-fleshed fish (pike preferred by Gothic diners). The last batch I made was of fish and took an inordinate amount of time to "set," a point to be remembered when you do not have any egg to assist the process (because yolks would add color).

❦ COCKENTRICE: Compare the half-roasted, half-boiled pig of our Greek banquet. One way of accomplishing this compound beast is given in a recipe by Madeleine Pelner Cosman in her section on soteltees and entremets (*Fabulous Feasts*, p. 200). After you have prepared this forepart of a large capon sewn to the hind part of a piglet, you may reverse the order with the remaining halves to have another *mischling* ready for a future dinner if you have space in your freezer.

As a final "cup" from the table, or *issue* as French and court English termed it, you will wish to serve Hippocras now and for the rere-supper to follow. At the latter various "comfits," or sugared tidbits like almonds should appear, above all, candied anise seeds to sweeten the breath.

❦ HIPPOCRAS: The drink, similar to our own spiced wines, took its name from the long apothecary's bag through which it was strained, so-called in honor of Hippocrates.

Mix a spice powder in which cinnamon predominates, using half as much ginger, grain of Paradise (optional), a quarter as much nutmeg, mace, cloves, galingale, and cardamom. Mix an ounce of this spice powder with approximately 6 ounces of sugar (making what was called "the Duke's powder") and combine with 1 quart of red wine. Bring to a boil and simmer gently for 10 or 15 minutes. Strain through clean muslin. May be served cool or hot. Stopper closely if it is to be kept (after about a week it will ferment because of the sugar).

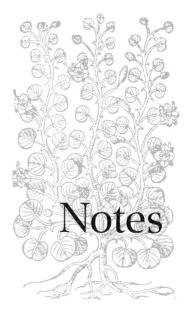

Notes

ABBREVIATIONS

AJA	*American Journal of Archaeology*
ANRW	*Aufstieg und Niedergang der römischen Welt*
BCH	*Bulletin de correspondance hellénique*
CIL	*Corpus inscriptionum latinarum*
FGC	*Comicorum Atticorum Fragmenta.* Ed. T. Kock
FGH	*Die Fragmente der griechischen Historiker.* Ed. F. Jacoby
JdI	*Jahrbuch des deutschen archäologischen Instituts*
JHS	*Journal of Hellenic Studies*
JRS	*Journal of Roman Studies*
MAAR	*Memoirs of the American Academy in Rome*
MGH	*Monumenta Germaniae Historica*
Migne	Jacques Paul Migne, *Patrologiae cursus completus seu Bibliotheca. Series latina.* 221 vols. Paris, 1864–1904.
RE	*Paulys Realencyclopädie der classischen Altertumswissenschaft neue Bearbeitung . . . unter Mitwirkung zahlreicher Fachgenossen hrsg. von G. Wissowa . . .* Stutgart: J. B. Metzler, 1894–1972.
TAPA	*Transactions and Proceedings, American Philological Association*

INTRODUCTION

1. To my knowledge, the first modern scholar to concentrate on a nutritional system as the basis of human institutions and relationships was Audrey I. Richards, who stated: "I have tried to show that just as the fundamental drive of sex is shaped by human codes and customs, which regulate the whole relation of man to woman, the legal status and functions of parenthood, the laws of exogamy, and the subsequent education and upbringing of the child; so also this *reproductive system* is paralleled in the nutritional sphere, the two great physiological needs often being fulfilled by the same institution, since the family is the starting-point for the formation of all subsequent ties. The analysis of social institutions on the basis of such fundamental biological needs is therefore the end to which the Functional method of anthropological study leads." *Hunger and Work in a Savage Tribe* (London, 1932), 213.

2. Reay Tannahill, perhaps better known as a novelist, is also an outstanding chronicler of both food and sex: see her *The Fine Art of Food* (1968), *Food in History* (1973; rev. ed. 1988); and *Sex in History* (1980).

3. Cited in K. C. Chang, *Food in Chinese Culture: Anthropological and Historical Perspectives* (New Haven, 1977), 3.

4. *Physiologie du goût* (Paris, 1825); translated by Arthur Machen as *The Physiology of Taste, or, Meditations on Transcendental Gastronomy* (New York, 1960), 3. Brillat-Savarin's writing on the "science of gastronomy" and the pleasures of the table are as fresh today as they were in Napoleonic France. An essay on the turkey includes his adventure on a wild turkey hunt in Connecticut on a trip to the new United States in 1794 and makes for "must" reading.

5. For a very accessible lay discussion, see the how-to book by an MIT scientist, Dr. Judith J. Wurtman, *Managing Your Mind and Mood Through Food* (New York, 1988), with bibliography. For a survey of some of the nutrition fallacies that affect New Age adherents, see Jack Raso, M.S., R.D., *Mystical Diets: Paranormal, Spiritual, and Occult Nutrition Practices* (Buffalo, N.Y., 1993).

6. See for example Mary Douglas, *Purity and Danger: An Analysis of Concepts of Pollution and Taboo* (New York, 1966), though there is a vast literature on such topics in both anthropology and sociology, not to mention philosophy and religion. On Jewish dietary laws and Christian interpretation of Biblical proscriptions, see chap. 3, n. 18.

7. The 1878 listing of his nostalgic menu is given a Missouri context in Evan Jones, *American Food: The Gastronomic Story* (3d ed.; Woodstock, N.Y., 1990), 114–15. For Twain's full nostalgic text, see *The Writings of Mark Twain* (New York, 1869–1909), 4:258–66, castigating European coffee, bread, butter, beefsteak. He waxes poetic at thoughts of an American *breakfast*: ". . . a mighty porterhouse steak an inch and a half thick, hot and sputtering from the griddle; dusted with fragrant pepper; enriched with little melting bits of butter of the most unimpeachable freshness and genuineness; the precious juices of the meat trickling out and joining the gravy, archipelagoed with mushrooms; a township or two of tender yellowish fat gracing an outlying district of this ample county of beefsteak; the long white bone which divides the sirloin from the tenderloin still in its place; and . . . a great cup of American home-made coffee, with the cream a-froth on top, some real butter, firm and yellow and fresh, some smoking-hot biscuits, a plate of hot buckwheat cakes, with transparent syrup." How far calorie, fat and cholesterol conscious Americans have come!

8. In *Mainstays of Maine* (New York, 1944), the chapters on eels; on Baked Bean Saturday (103ff.); on Codfish Chowder (113ff.); and on the clambake (158ff.): "When I say clams, I mean clams. I don't mean what New Yorkers miscall clams . . . little-necks or cherry-stones. Those round bivalves are nothing but quahogs."

9. See the essay, "Wine and Milk," in *Mythologies*, trans. A. Lavers (New York, 1983), 58–61.

10. Announced in "Le triangle culinaire," *L'Arc* (Aix-en-Provence), no 26 (1965): 19ff. and in the 4-volume *Mythologiques* (1964–72), available in an English translation by John and Doreen Weightman as (vol. 1) *The Raw and the Cooked*, (vol. 2) *From Honey to Ashes*, (vol. 3) *The Origin of Table Manners*, and (vol. 4) *The Naked Man* (Chicago, 1969–78).

11. "Pour une psycho-sociologie de l'alimentation contemporaine," *Annales ESC* 16 (1961): 977–86; Enquêtes ouvertes, p. 979: "Qu'est-ce que la nourriture? Ce n'est pas seulement une collection de produits, justiciables d'études statistiques ou diététiques. C'est aussi et en même temps un système de communication, un corps d'images, un protocole d'usages, de situations et de conduites. Comment étudier cette réalité alimentaire, élargie jusqu'à l'image et au signe?"

12. See especially, "Deciphering a Meal," *Daedalus* 101, no. 1 (1972): 61–81. In this essay she develops upon lexical categories applied to food elements by Michael Halliday in "Categories of the Theory of Grammar," *Word, Journal of the Linguistic Circle of New York* 17 (1961): 241–91. See also A. Lehrer, "Semantic Cuisine," *Journal of Linguistics* 5 (1969): 39–56.

13. See his *The Civilizing Process*, vol. 1, *The History of Table Manners (Sociogenetic and Psychogenetic Investigations)* [1939], trans. Edmund Jephcott (New York, 1978) and vol. 2, *Power and Civility* (New York, 1982), and the related work, *The Court Society*, trans. Edmund Jephcott (New York, 1983).

14. See his *The Origins of Courtliness: Civilizing Trends and the Formation of Courtly Ideals, 939–1210* (Philadelphia, 1985). Jaeger rightly places much emphasis on the revival of ancient ethics and moral codes in medieval humanism of the late eleventh and twelfth centuries.

15. Marvin B. Becker, *Civility and Society in Western Europe, 1300–1600* (Bloomington, Ind., 1988).

16. *The Rituals of Dinner: The Origins, Evolution, Eccentricities, and Meaning of Table Manners* (Toronto, 1991).

17. *Adventure of Ideas* (New York, 1933), 13–14.

18. Kenneth M. Craig, "Pieter Aertsen and *The Meat Stall*," *Oud Holland* 96 (1982): 1–15 (p. 6). Although elements of the picture's symbolic meanings had been recognized earlier, all were brilliantly synthesized in this article, wherein Craig argues convincingly that the painting, now in Uppsala, Sweden, was probably commissioned by the Antwerp Guild of Butchers.

19. There is a host of books on principles of Chinese culture. Outstanding among those which deal historically with cuisine are K. C. Chang, *Food in Chinese Culture* (see above, n. 3); E. N. Anderson, *The Food of China* (New Haven, 1988); and Frederick J. Simoons, *Food in China: A Cultural and Historical Inquiry* (Ann Arbor, 1991). One of the best for discussion of gastronomic aesthetics is by Hsiang Ju and Tsuifeng Lin, *Chinese Gastronomy* (New York, 1969).

20. Food historians and professionals are engaged in working out the details of such borrowings in individual cases, often reported in the pages of the periodical *Petits Propos Culinaires*, founded by Alan and Jane Davidson, or in the annual *Proceedings* of the Oxford Symposium on

Food and Cookery and comparable symposia. Relevant instances of misattribution and copying will be considered when appropriate.

CHAPTER ONE

1. See Grahame Clark, *Economic Prehistory: Papers on Archaeology* (Cambridge, 1989), 349 on late glacial period evidence: amber and shells for adornment found at Mezhirich in the Ukraine which had to have been brought from a distance of 350 to 500 kilometers (km); a special flint from a site in Poland used over a radius of 180 km; and the obsidian of the Zagros Mountains, in the latter case, citing J. E. Dixon, J. R. Cann, and C. Renfrew, "Obsidian and Early Cultural Contact in the Near East," *Proceedings of the Prehistoric Society*, 32 (1966): 30–72. See also below on Çatal Hüyük and obsidian trade with the Levant from Anatolia.

2. See Clark, *Economic Prehistory*, chap. 1: "Bees in Antiquity." In this essay reprinted from *Antiquity* 16 (1942): 208–15, Clark discusses exploitation of both honey and bees' wax in prehistoric Europe and points to an intermediate stage in the domestication of bees when people improved on nature by enlarging holes in trees in order to attract nests and fitting them with the means to extract their honey easily.

3. Harold McGee, *On Food and Cooking: The Science and Lore of the Kitchen* (New York, 1984), 206. It should be noted that these "Lake" dwellings are no longer considered to have been in the water, but on shore, their piles sunk into marshy ground for sounder footings.

4. See J. Mellaart, *Çatal Hüyük: A Neolithic Town in Anatolia* (London, 1967); preliminary reports were issued in *Anatolian Studies* from 1962, but ceased when work was suspended after 1964 and a scandal which saw revocation of his permit to dig by the Turkish government. Only about one acre of a thirty-two acre site has been explored, although the British under Ian Hodder have now (1994) undertaken a fresh campaign, first of conservation, which may lead to new findings and expand into other quarters.

5. J. Mellaart, "A Neolithic City in Turkey," no. 14 in Lamberg-Karlovsky's *Old World Archaeology: Foundations of Civilization: Readings from Scientific American* (San Francisco, 1972), p. 120 (reprinted from *Scientific American*, April 1964).

6. In one instance the beaks of such vultures are applied to the walls of a shrine and, built up around them in clay, are what are taken as female breasts (see fig. 6). Our reproduction of one painting represents a flock of them or, possibly, human dancers dressed as vultures.

7. "First Impressions of the Çatal Hüyük Plant Husbandry," *Anatolian Studies* 14 (1964): 121–23. Helbaek identified *Vicia noeana* as well as *V. ervilia*, a bitter vetch, in a cultivated form. The tiny seeds, or "peas," may not appear very palatable to us, but can be eaten in soups or dried to grind and combine in flours. Other species of vetch have been found in prehistoric sites, as well as in Middle-Kingdom Egypt, Ashur, and Troy; see R. J. Forbes in C. Singer et al., *A History of Technology*, vol. 1 (London, 1954), 362.

8. See F. E. Zeuner, *A History of Domesticated Animals* (London, 1963), passim. Note that he is one of the specialists who sees the taming of dogs as another initiating phenomenon, whereas others find the evidence very problematic at best, distorted in part by remnants of nineteenth-century concepts of the canine as friend and companion in the hunt, rather than as a competitor. For a just estimate, at a popular level, of some of the factors that must be considered, see

D. Brothwell and P. Brothwell, *Food in Antiquity: A Survey of the Diet of Early Peoples* (New York, 1969), 39ff. Cf. S. Davis and F. Valla, "Evidence of Domestication of the Dog 12,000 Years Ago in the Natufian of Israel," *Nature* 276 (1978): 608–10; the "puppy" in a child's burial in the Jordan Valley could as readily be seen as a pet orphaned wolf pup, so difficult is it to distinguish at this stage the morphology of animals descended from a common ancestor. On general problems and methods of distinguishing wild from domestic specimens of animals, see Gil Stein, "Herding Strategies at Neolithic Gritille: The Use of Animal Bone Remains to Reconstruct Ancient Economic Systems," *Expedition* 28 (1986): 35–42.

9. This secondary agriculture is a major argument against a theory put forward by Jane Jacobs, although she uses Çatal in support of her idea expressed in *The Economy of Cities* (New York, 1969). In opposition to all other hypotheses about the origin of agriculture, she believed that cities and towns gave rise to domestication of plants and animals and that farming and herding subsequently moved off to the countryside, all developing from barter and markets; see Charles B. Heiser Jr., *Seed to Civilization: The Story of Man's Food* (San Francisco, 1973), 17.

10. *T. aestivum* is thought by some to have come about through gene mutation in *T. spelta;* spelt is a club wheat that is just now becoming a staple of supermarket grains, thanks to our appetite for grains of the "nutrition pyramid." Others believe that it is a hybrid of *T. dicoccum,* and a wild grass. In any case, Çatal is one of the very earliest finds of it, though it must have been brought into cultivation elsewhere: near the Caspian? Northeast Anatolia? See Renfrew's essay in P. J. Ucko and G. W. Dimblebey, *The Domestication and Exploitation of Plants and Animals* (Chicago, 1969).

11. *Çatal Hüyük,* 224.

12. See Daniel Zohary and Maria Hopf, *Domestication of Plants in the Old World: The Origin and Spread of Cultivated Plants in West Asia* (Oxford, 1988), 129; see also p. 13 for their discussion of founder crops they term "selfers," because they are self-pollinating; this "first wave" to be cultivated in the ninth millennium are emmer, einkorn and barley, the pea, lentils, chickpeas, bitter vetch, and flax. Their self-pollination kept them from exposure and reversion to their wild ancestors.

13. *Çatal Hüyük,* 224. Once people have moved from porridge to baking bread, beer is almost the inevitable result. For the process, see chapter 2, below, and figs. 20 and 21.

CHAPTER TWO

1. *Corchorum olitorius,* eaten hashed and stewed in broth with onion, garlic, and coriander. The evidence of Pliny *Natural History* (cited hereafter as *NH*), book XXI, chapter cvi, section 183, stresses medicinal use, but indicates that it was eaten at Alexandria. See W. J. Darby, P. Ghalioungui, and L. Grivetti, *Food: The Gift of Osiris* (London, 1977), 2:671f. At least one authority, G. Schweinfurth (1873) argued that the *corchorum* (melukhiya) was abundant in earliest times as a wild forage plant, just as in other regions of Africa. It is in season during spring and summer, but in today's markets may be purchased at other times of year either frozen or dried; the latter is especially useful to thicken soups, thanks to a gelatinous quality comparable in effect to okra. A modernized recipe for its use may be found in Michelle Berriedale Johnson, *The British Museum Cookbook* (London, 1987), 38f.; also, with good advice on using fresh, dried,

or tinned, in Claudia Roden, *A Book of Middle Eastern Food* (New York, 1972), 111–14 (spelled *melokhia*—vowels are just as evanescent in modern Arabic as in ancient Egyptian).

2. The entire book II of his *History* is devoted to Egypt, its geography, its religion and the life of its people.

3. *Geography*, XVII; this passage i.3 (C787).

4. For modern survival, see Martin Bernal, *Black Athena: The Afroasiatic Roots of Classical Civilization* (2 vols., London, 1987).

5. In *Moses and Monotheism* (*Works*, ed. J. Strachey et al., London, 1966–74), vol. 23. See Carl E. Schorske, "Freud's Egyptian Dig," *The New York Review*, 27 May 1993, pp. 35–40. When a selection of Freud's collection of antiquities traveled to Philadelphia from the Freud Museum in London in 1989, the Egyptian works were particularly impressive, above all a representation of Isis holding the infant Horus. See the catalogue, with an introduction by Peter Gay: *Sigmund Freud; His Personal Collection of Antiquities*, SUNY/Freud Museum (London, 1989).

6. Max Waehren, *Brot und Gebäck im Leben und Glauben der alten Ägypter* (Bern, 1963), passim. In ancient Egyptian *tannurim* is equivalent to Akkadian *tinûru* or Old Testament *tannur*. For an excavated example, see G. Lerche, "Khubz Tannur: Freshly Consumed Flat Bread in the Near East," in *Food in Perspective: Proceedings of the Third International Conference on Ethnographical Food Research, Cardiff, Wales, 1977* (Edinburgh, 1981), 179ff.

7. For collections of sayings and songs, see W. Guglielmi, *Reden, Rufe und Lieder auf altägyptischen Darstellungen der Landwirtschaft, Viehzucht, des Fisch-und Vogelfangs vom Mittleren Reich bis zur Spätzeit* (Bonn, 1973). This comic-strip type of speaking characters reaches its most rich stage in Theban graves of the New Empire.

8. In several versions of the "Song of the Harper," originally written beside a tomb image of the New Empire, the musician sings of the fleeting joys of this world, of putting aside all cares until the day one passes into the land that loves silence. See [Georg] A. Erman, *Life in Ancient Egypt* (Dover books ed. 1971, from the 1894 English translation), pp. 386f. Herodotos, II, 78, tells of the practice of carrying about after dinner a carved and painted image of a corpse in its coffin to remind each guest of the transitoriness of pleasure; this is a theme we shall find taken up in little bronze skeletons distributed at Epicurean feasts in Roman times.

9. Analysis of literary and pictorial evidence regarding consumption of pork, with bibliography, is included in chapter 4 of Darby, Ghalioungui, and Grivetti, *Gift of Osiris*, 1:171ff. For Herodotos (II, 47) there was no hesitation in stating that swine were considered unclean animals among the Egyptians of his day (ca. 485–ca. 425 B.C.). But there is ample visual documentation for pigs among Old Kingdom reliefs and tomb paintings of the Middle Kingdom and New Empire. A disputed scene from a Seventh-Dynasty tomb at Saqqara, which shows two men tending an animal that one feeds from his own mouth, represents a pig, in my opinion (see Darby et al., fig.4.4). A Theban village for workmen of the Ramessid period revealed many pig bones and skulls in trash heaps (ibid., p. 188), as I have reconfirmed at the Dokki Agricultural Museum in Cairo. On problems of pork consumption in the Near East and discussion of Jewish ritual avoidance, see below, chap. 3, n. 18.

10. See J. E. Manchip White, *Ancient Egypt* (New York, 1952; Dover paperback ed., 1970), 89.

11. Panofksy, rather than Egyptologists, was the first to explore the contrast between

Greek systems of proportion and the scheme used by Egyptian sculptors. See Erwin Panofsky, *Meaning in the Visual Arts: Papers in and on Art History* [1939] (Garden City, N.Y., 1955), 57ff.

12. If this sketch is not artistic "doodling," the foods on the table could be explained by the necessity of representing them in the formal, discrete form in which they appear in banquet scenes to make certain that there are no ambiguities in the catalogue. In any case, evidence of the duck cannot be explained away.

13. W. B. Emery, "A Funerary Repast in an Egyptian Tomb of the Archaic Period," issued by Leiden's Nederlands Instituut voor het Nabije Oosten (Scholae Adriani de Buck memoriae dicatae, no. 1, 1962). An intact New Kingdom tomb of the architect, Kha, and his wife found at the workers' village at Deir el-Medina, next to the Valley of the Kings where they labored, was excavated by the Italians under E. Schiaparelli during the period 1903–6; a table of bread offerings displayed flat and triangular shapes, some with leavening, and one molded in the shape of a gazelle; vegetables included onions, chickpeas, lentils, beans, peas, leeks, and cucumbers, and I must admit that many of the greens had been sliced up as if for the pot. Seasonings noted were cress, cumin, juniper, and a container of what was considered to be fruit purée; baskets held figs, grapes, dates, and doum palm nuts. See the exhibition catalogue, *L'alimentazione nel mondo antico: Gli Egizi* (Rome, 1987), pp. 69–71. These materials are now in Turin.

14. The *nabq* (*Zizyphus spina Christi*) or *nabk* berry was clearly popular and grew prolifically in the Nile Valley as well as other parts of North Africa. Theophrastos discusses it (*Enquiry into Plants*, IV, iii, 3): "the fruit is round and red, and in size as large as the fruit of the prickly cedar or a little larger; it has a stone which is not eaten . . . but the fruit is sweet, and, if one pours wine over it, they say that it becomes sweeter and that it makes the wine sweeter." For full treatment of the fruit and sources, see Darby et al., *Gift of Osiris*, 2:702ff. A related species is the Chinese jujube.

15. See Ahmed Zaky and Z. Iskander, "Ancient Egyptian Cheese," *Annales du Service des antiquités de l'Égypte* 41 (1942): 295–313 for the chemical analysis of the contents of two jars found by Emery in a First Dynasty tomb. Their conclusion was that the substance in question was a sort of fresh cheese; from another jar with a label they suggested a name for cheese (*srt*), but this has been questioned (W. Helck and E. Otto, *Lexikon der Ägyptologie*, vol. 3, col. 289, s.v. "Käse"; followed by Darby et al., *Gift of Osiris*, 772–75). Both of the last passages take Pliny's (*NH*, XI, xcvi, 239) assertion that "barbaras gentes" do not know cheese-making, only curds of soured milk, to apply to the Egyptians; I believe the passage is intended to refer to curd-loving "genuine" barbarians among the Germanic tribes, not to simply any foreign races.

16. J. D. S. Pendlebury, *Tell el-Amarna* (London, 1935), 111. Commonly kitchens were separated from the villa proper, while in townhouses they frequently are to be found on the topmost story, leaving the middle floors as the coolest retreat for the family over workshops on the ground floor; see E. Baldwin Smith, *Egyptian Architecture as Cultural Expression* (New York, 1938), 204 and pl. LXVI, 4, a drawing after a painting in the Theban tomb of Thutnufer.

17. Almost every funerary offering of food includes a haunch of beef, usually the right foreleg, evidently a sacrificial portion. On meat cuts, see H. E. Winlock, *Models of Daily Life in Ancient Egypt from the Tomb of Meket-Re at Thebes* (Cambridge, Mass., 1955), apropos serving maidens bearing containers of meat and beer. An excellent study of chicken and their eggs is to be found in F. J. Simoons, *Eat Not This Flesh: Food Avoidances in the Old World* (Westport, Conn.,

1981), chap. 5; see also Darby et al., *Gift of Osiris*, 1:297–309. There is much evidence that the original motivation for domestication was not economic but religious, involving the cock's crow at reappearance of the sun and the fertility symbolism of the egg. We will find also that in Greece the major early use of these fowl was for divination.

18. For both two-row and six-row barley, the latter predominating in historic Egypt, see Darby et al., *Gift of Osiris*, 2:479–89; R. J. Forbes, *Studies in Ancient Technology*, vol. 3 (Leiden, 1955), 87f. For a scientific discussion of beer production, still using barley, although with the addition of hops from the early modern period on, see McGee, *On Food and Cooking*, 470ff.

19. The onomasticon, which lists more than 40 items that begin with "flour" and share a determinative indicating various kinds of pastry, bread, or cake, was published by A. H. Gardiner, *Ancient Egyptian Onomastica* (London, 1947), 2:228. In general, see Helck and Otto, *Lexikon der Ägyptologie*, vol. 1, s.v. "Backen," cols. 594ff.; see also "Brot," col. 871, where the sacral character of the favored bread baked in a triangular mold is underscored by its name, *benben*, which otherwise defines the primeval mound of the creation of the earth from chaos by Atum, at Heliopolis, that is likewise replicated in the top of obelisks (ibid., col. 694). The Egyptian dictionary by [G.] A. Erman and H. Grapow, *Wörterbuch der ägyptischen Sprache* (Berlin, 1957), 6:31, under "Brot," listed 57 distinct names; see P. Montet, *Everyday Life in Egypt in the Days of Ramesses the Great* (Philadelphia, 1981), 85ff. For baking molds, see E. Strouhal, *Life of the Ancient Egyptians* (Norman, Okla., 1992), pp. 126ff. and fig. 135.

20. One of the best discussions of date cakes and associated sacral aspects of the palm is to be found in an article by M. A. Beauverie, "Sur quelques fruits de l'ancienne Égypte exposés au Musée de Grenoble," *Bulletin de l'Institut français d'archéologie orientale* 28 (1930): 393–405. This points out that Bedouins can subsist on a diet of dates and camel's milk, so nutritious are dates. For both dates and the doum fruit *(Hyphaene thebaica)*, see Darby et al., *Gift of Osiris*, 2:722–33. Desiccated examples of the latter from funeral context displayed in the Dokki Museum reveal a fruit the size of a large peach; the doum palm seems not to be widespread or cultivated today in Egypt, at least in my observation.

21. For a scientific examination, see F. Filce Leek, "Teeth and Bread in Ancient Egypt," *Journal of Egyptian Archaeology* 58 (1972): 126–32, pls. 28–32, including his hypothesis that gritty bread was the reason Pharaoh imprisoned his chief baker with Joseph, and subsequently beheaded him (Genesis 40).

22. This is splendidly illustrated by one of an impressive number of models of estate activities from the Middle Kingdom tomb of Mekhet-Re in the Metropolitan Museum; see Winlock, *Models of Daily Life*, figs. 22, 23, 77 and relevant text; the granary model, Winlock's fig. 20, is apropos. In rock-cut tombs of the Middle Kingdom the carved reliefs of the Old Kingdom were replaced by wooden models to serve the same function of provisioning the afterlife of the deceased.

23. Darby et al., *Gift of Osiris*, 1:125, as well as Hellmut Brunner, *Lexikon alte Kulturen* (3 vols.; Mannheim, 1990–93), s.v. "Trunkenheit"; on various names for beer, see Helck and Otto, *Lexikon der Ägyptologie*, vol. 1, s.v. "Bier." For the process, Forbes, *Ancient Technology*, 3:65–72.

24. Herodotos II, 37 conflicts with a later passage (II, 77) that states there are no vines in Egypt; he speaks of wine brought daily for the priests' meals and the adjective applied specifies

"of the vine" *(oinos ampelinos)*. Syrian and Palestinian wine jars have been found in New Kingdom excavations.

25. On viticulture and its product, see Darby et al., *Gift of Osiris*, vol. 2, chaps. 14 and 15 (the latter dedicated to different vintages); older literature includes H. F. Lutz, *Viticulture and Brewing in the Ancient Orient* (Leipzig, 1922), somewhat outdated. Egyptians staked their vines in order to make veritable arbors of their foliage; in certain cases they are thought to have even used columns to create an architectural framework for the vines in an ideal hypostyle hall symbolizing the cosmos: earth, earthly realm of the growing plants, a vault painted with stars (as in some of the tombs): see Manfred Bietak, "Ein altägyptischer Weingarten in einem Tempelbezirk (Tell el-Dab'a)," *Anzeiger der österreichischen Akademie der Wissenschaften*, phil.-hist. kl., 122 (Vienna, 1985), 267–78, and his references.

26. Berkeley, Calif., 1977; this delightful essay by the present head of Egyptology at Brown University is highlighted in our text for obvious reasons.

27. L. Lesko, *King Tut's Wine Cellar*, 31. His comparative material includes labels from Pendlebury's excavations at Amarna as well as Malkata, the western Theban palace-city of Amenhotep III.

28. Darby et al., *Gift of Osiris*, 2:597f. gives a listing of what is known of wine classifications. The "green eye" would be opposed to Horus's "white," or milk. One gets the impression that most of the Egyptian wines were "whites," unless skins went through a delayed secondary pressing in a *must* sack after the initial stomping in a vat; for an informed discussion of white versus red, see L. Lesko, *King Tut's Wine Cellar*, 17f.

29. The atmosphere is admirably brought out by Barbara S. Lesko, "True Art in Ancient Egypt," in *Egyptological Studies in Honor of Richard A. Parker* (Hanover, N.H., 1986), 85–97, in her discussion of secular love songs, the Egyptian sense of humor revealed in their love of puns and homonyms, and their love of nature, which was often expressed in a most delicate anthropomorphizing way. Her bibliography leads to articles on the Song of the Harper from the famous papyrus, Harris 500, including Michael V. Fox, "A Study of Intef," *Orientalia* 46 (1977): 400–403, and Edward F. Wente, "The Egyptian 'Make Merry' Songs Reconsidered," *Journal of Near Eastern Studies* 21 (1962): 118–28).

30. Fine examples in the Metropolitan Museum are reproduced in its *Bulletin* for Spring 1973.

31. On agriculture and animal breeding, [G.] Adolf Erman's *Life in Ancient Egypt*, chap. 17, is still a useful, compact text.

32. Darby et al., in *Gift of Osiris*, vol. 1, chap. 6, consider all aspects of netting, raising, and preparing fowl, including the process of preserving them by pickling; sacral and medicinal use is also mentioned. Some were also drawn and salted, then hung, as Herodotos reported. See the illustrations in Hilary Wilson, *Egyptian Food and Drink* (Aylesbury, 1988), 39–41; Wilson states that eggs were also used from such birds as pelicans.

33. A list in Alfred Lucas, *Ancient Egyptian Materials and Industries* (London, 1962), gives in addition to ox or goose fat that of hippopotamuses and other wild creatures. Since olive oil had to be imported until at least the Nineteenth Dynasty, and was not cultivated widely until Greek propagation of the Ptolemaic period, oils came from a variety of plants, as will be discussed below.

34. Darby et al., *Gift of Osiris*, 2:776ff. considers oils; cf. Helck and Otto, *Lexikon*, vol. 2, cols. 5522–55, s.v. "Öle," where sesame oil is said to be documented from Dynasty XVIII; according to Alfred Lucas (ibid.), sesame oil makes a late appearance. Pliny (*NH*, XV, vii, 30) remarks on the remarkable esteem in which Egyptians hold the radish *(Raphanus sativus L.)* because of abundant oil they make from its seed.

35. Darby et al. assemble much conflicting evidence about identification of fish species, acceptance and avoidance of certain varieties, and different means of catching and preparing them, with bibliography (see *Gift of Osiris*, vol. 1, chap. 7).

36. Textual evidence is ambiguous and derives from late Greek and Roman authors. Darby et al. (*Gift of Osiris*, vol. 1, chap. 8) details some of it, including Aelian's (X, 21) description of a village in which people are overjoyed with happiness when their children make a meal for the crocodile god, countered by revenge torture killings by villagers on the other side of the Nile who ultimately eat it; also Pliny's account of Egyptian rodeo-like riding of the beasts (*NH*, VIII, xxxviii, 93)!

37. The most full account of the myth of Isis and Osiris comes down to us from the first century A.D. (Plutarch, "On Isis and Osiris," *Moralia*, 351c–384c) but is amply verified by the Pyramid Texts and other ancient Egyptian documents. See John Gwyn Griffiths, *The Origins of Osiris* (Münchner ägyptologische Studien, vol. 9 [Berlin, 1966]). An exhibition at the University of Kansas Museum in 1977 saw a useful publication by Eugene Larkin, *Isis and Osiris* (museum publication no. 88).

38. See Darby et al., *Gift of Osiris*, 1:373, which suggests that *batarekh* may be equivalent to the Coptic *pi-tarikh;* if the Copts best represent ancient Egyptians, as some believe, this would push manufacture back before travelers' citation of the delicacy beginning in the sixteenth century A.D. In any case, I would place knowledge much earlier, during Byzantine occupation of Egypt (sixth and early seventh centuries), since *boutargue* is well documented for Byzantium/Constantinople. The argument of L. Keimer, "La boutargue dans l'ancienne Égypte," *Bulletin de l'Institut française d'Égypte* 21 (1938–39): 215–43, following Oric Bates, "Ancient Egyptian Fishing," *Harvard African Studies* 1 (1917): 265, is convincing that visual evidence dates from the Old Kingdom.

39. There is only one doum palm in the upper rank of trees, reflecting the modern lack of a species once prolific in Egypt. The persea and sycamore fig are instructively discussed by Pliny (*NH*, book XIII); he compares (xvii) the persea *(Mimusops Schimperi)* to a pear, but enclosed in a shell and a rind like an almond, though where an almond has a kernel, this has a "plum" *(prunus)*. Pliny (xvi) denies the carob *(ceratonia)* to Egypt, following Theophrastus, the Greek botanical writer of the third century B.C.; but there is ample evidence of its presence from at least the Middle Kingdom: there are dried pods of this "locust-bean," traditional food of Saint John in the desert, in el Dokki Agricultural Museum. See also Darby et al., *Gift of Osiris*, 2:699–701; in the British Museum fragment reproduced (my fig. 28), I think I see its dangling pods on the tree at lower left.

40. See especially, Wilson, *Egyptian Food and Drink*, 50f. and his illustration 54, a drawing after the tomb of Nakht at Thebes, of the Empire period.

41. Judging by seeds in the Dokki Agricultural Museum as well as etymological evidence that ancient *bddw-k* agrees with the modern Arabic, Coptic, and Hebrew name for *Citrullus*

vulgaris, the melon of choice was watermelon (see Wilson, ibid., 24; Darby et al., *Gift of Osiris,* 2:717f.). On the other hand, this was denied by one authority: L. Keimer, *Die Gartenpflanzen im alten Ägypten* (Hamburg, 1924), 2:18, 33. The squash-family gourds in representations of funerary offerings resemble English marrows or oversized zucchini. Cucumbers are depicted in such a way as to emphasize their botanical kinship with the squashes, being curved and rather swollen at the opposite end from the stem.

42. See Darby et al., *Gift of Osiris,* 2:644–51 for discussion and bibliography on papyrus and edible sedges. Readers of Euell Gibbons will think of his "super-market of the swamps," the common cat-o'-nine-tails (*Stalking the Wild Asparagus* [Putney, Vt., 1962], 55ff.; also, in connection with the sedge *Cyperus esculentus L.,* his recipes for chufa cookies and pudding in *Stalking the Healthful Herbs,* Field Guide Edition [New York, 1970], 265f). I agree with Darby et al. (2:668) that identifications of asparagus in tomb reliefs are rather to be recognized as bundles of papyrus; these mislead commentators like M. Toussaint-Samat (*A History of Food* [Oxford, 1992], 701), who has Egyptians offering asparagus to their gods.

43. For *Lactuca sativa,* see Darby et al., *Gift of Osiris,* 2:675ff.; Helck and Otto, *Lexikon,* vol. 3, col. 938f. (R. Germer). M. Detienne, in *The Gardens of Adonis: Spices in Greek Mythology* (Princeton, N.J., 1977), has explored the semiotic value of Adonis' death in a field of "lettuce." A fine, popularized account of the opposition between different views of lettuce and sexuality is to be found in the section, "For and Against Sex," in a chapter entitled "Lettuce: The Vicissitudes of Salad," in Margaret Visser, *Much Depends on Dinner: The Extraordinary History and Mythology, Allure, and Obsessions, Perils and Taboos of an Ordinary Meal* [1986] (New York, 1988), 192–223.

44. For informed discussion of the etymological origins of the Arabic term for this dish of beans, *ful mudammas,* see letters from Peter Heine, Russell Harris, Charles Perry, and Eva Kurtze in *Petits Propos Culinaires* 43 (1993): 47–48. *Mudammas* (also written *medames*) refers to the method of long baking, originally under the ashes overnight. None of the *ful* I had for breakfast in Egypt were made of fava beans, however, and this was probably true in antiquity; see the following discussion of this "Egyptian bean."

45. Theophrastos calls it *kuamos,* comparing it with the lotus, meaning the white variety. See Darby et al., *Gift of Osiris,* 2:638–41 on the confusion with colocasia. For all the legumes, see ibid., pp. 682–93, citing Ludwig Keimer and Victor Loret on the identification of the black-eyed pea *(Vigna sinensis).* Peas themselves seem to be attested from the Middle Kingdom only.

46. For a list of spices and herbs, see the summary in Darby et al., ibid., chap. 20, based on both archaeological finds and linguistic evidence, much of the latter speculative. On Egyptian medicine from the earliest great vizier and architect of King Djoser's Third-Dynasty pyramid complex at Saqqara, Imhotep, who received divine honors in later times for his achievements as a physician, see Henry E. Sigerist, *A History of Medicine* (New York, 1951) vol. 1, part 3.

47. See Darby et al., *Gift of Osiris,* vol. 1, chap. 10. The evidence for salt avoidance by the priests depends upon Plutarch (46–120) in his *Isis and Osiris,* and in *Moralia* ("Table Talk," IV, x, 684–85).

CHAPTER THREE

1. The cuneiform tablet which partially preserves the Sumerian myth of the Flood begins with a creation story just as Genesis does; see the translation by Samuel N. Kramer in James B. Pritchard, ed., *Ancient Near Eastern Texts Relating to the Old Testament*, 2d ed. (Princeton, N.J., 1955), 42–44, or in idem, *The Ancient Near East: An Anthology of Texts and Pictures* (Princeton, N.J., 1958), 28–30. The hero, Ziusudra survives in his huge boat the Flood of seven days and seven nights, opens a window to receive the rays of the sun god, Utu, and makes sacrifice of an ox and a sheep. An Akkadian text and derivatives includes the Deluge account in the epic of Gilgamesh and is much more extensive and even more closely related to Genesis; see Pritchard, *Anthology*, 40–75.

2. See for example, M. P. Charles, "An Introduction to the Legumes and Oil Plants of Mesopotamia," *Bulletin on Sumerian Agriculture* 2 (1985): 40.

3. In H. Frankfort and H. A. Frankfort, et al. *Before Philosophy* (Harmondsworth, 1949; pbk. ed. of *The Intellectual Adventure of Ancient Man* [Chicago, 1946]), 137. The quote is from the epic of Gilgamesh in Old Babylonian version, from a cuneiform tablet at Yale (IV:7–8).

4. For the fascinating story of cuneiform decipherment and discovery of the role played by the Sumerians, see chap. 1, "Archaeology and Decipherment," in S. N. Kramer, *The Sumerians: Their History, Culture, and Character* (Chicago, 1963); for an easily accessible discussion of cylinder seals as well as development of cuneiform writing from its pictographic roots in the period 3200 to 2800 B.C., see Hans J. Nissen, *The Early History of the Ancient Near East* (Chicago, 1988), 74–90. The sequential nature of the devices incised into cylinder seals often generated for obvious reasons compositions that rely upon repeated elements, a hybrid beast for example, who meets his counterpart, confronted or addorsed, ancestor of heraldic design through the ages.

5. Henri Frankfort in his Pelican History of Art volume, *The Art and Architecture of the Ancient Orient* (Baltimore, Md., 1954), 51–55, beautifully expresses both the technique of those "congenital carvers," the Egyptians, as well as the modeling qualities and the dominance of the cylinder and the cone in Mesopotamian sculpture.

6. Any basic text on architecture will explain the principles of arch and vault construction; H. W. Janson's *History of Art* (3d ed. [New York, 1986], p. 66, fig.78), includes notice of Egyptian building with mud brick when a structure was not intended to express eternal duration, and illustrates a New Kingdom vaulted storage facility.

7. See Solomon H. Katz and Mary Voigt, "Bread and Beer: The Early Use of Cereals in the Human Diet," *Expedition* 28 (1986): 23–34. An archaeological chemist on the staff of the University of Pennsylvania Museum has analyzed residues on Mesopotamian potsherds from the fourth millenium B.C. that yield evidence of beer consumption earlier than elsewhere—see R. H. Michel, P. E. McGovern, and V. R. Badler in the British scientific journal *Nature* 360 (5 November 1992), p. 24.

8. In relation to the problems of salinization of the soil in Lower Mesopotamia, my colleague, Richard Ellis, has pointed out that barley is more tolerant of salts than wheat.

9. *Philadelphia Enquirer*, 1 March 1990; S. H. Katz and F. Maytag, "Brewing an Ancient Beer," *Archaeology* 44 (July/August, 1991): 24–31. Fritz Maytag was the brewer, owner of Anchor Brewing Co. in San Francisco, who had joined the reported tasting at the University Museum. About a hundred barrels were produced under Sol Katz's stimulus and advice, using a

honey-barley bread and a mash of water, dates, and malted barley, and were first tested at a micro-brewers' convention in San Francisco. The nineteenth-century tablet with its hymn to Ninkasi is reproduced by Katz and Maytag in their article in *Archaeology* and translated in a sidebar on p. 29.

10. See Lutz, *Viticulture and Brewing,* 128ff. for the inn or tavern keepers and indications that their establishments were often brothels. The relevant regulations in the code of Hammurabi, nos. 108–111, translated in Pritchard, *Anthology,* 149f. It is interesting to note that payment for drink was in an equivalent amount of grain. For a comprehensive study of Mesopotamian brewing, see Louis F. Hartman and A. Leo Oppenheim, *On Beer and Brewing Techniques in Ancient Mesopotamia* (Baltimore, 1950).

11. In a chapter on food and drink at Mari, an upper Mesopotamian kingdom in what is today Syria, Stephanie Dalley suggests that communal drinking from a large container necessitated drinking tubes to avoid ubiquitous "big bulbous bugs," that hover about liquids today in Iraq (*Mari and Karana: Two Babylonian Cities* [London, 1984], 89). William Younger (*Gods, Men and Wine* [London, 1966], 73), argues, not very persuasively, that because divinities are often seen using these siphons, they symbolize the other world, but at the same time he takes the liquid as wine and the tubes as indication that wines were not racked. For the tube from Ur, see Leonard Woolley, *Ur Excavations,* vol. 2: *The Royal Cemetery (Text),* p. 81; pp. 90–91 for two others in gold and in silver; pls. 193–94, 200 illustrate Early Dynastic seals which represent drinkers using such tubes.

12. A. Finet, "Le vin à Mari," *Archiv für Orientforschung* 25 (1974–78): 122f.; the date of the Palace archives is the 18th century B.C.

13. Pritchard, *Anthology,* Gilgamesh, Tablet II, iii, 19–21 (Old Babylonian Version of the Epic).

14. See Marvin H. Pope, "A Divine Banquet at Ugarit," in *The Use of the Old Testament in the New: Studies in Honor of William Franklin Stinespring* (Durham, N.C., 1972), 170–203; also idem, "Notes on the Rephaim Texts from Ugarit," in *Essays on the Near East in Memory of Jacob Joel Finkelstein, Memoirs of the Connecticut Academy of Arts and Sciences,* vol. 19 (New Haven, 1977), 104f., elaborating on the connection with a tradition of drunkenness at funeral feasts in particular.

15. See A. Salonen, "Die Ofen der alten Mesopotamer," *Baghdader Mitteilungen* 3 (1964): 100–124.

16. Jean Bottéro is the authority on Mesopotamian cuisine; his articles in the *Reallexicon der Assyriologie* on various topics from cooking (s.v. "Küche"), to every aspect of food and drink are summarized in more accessible form in English: "The Cuisine of Ancient Mesopotamia," *Biblical Archaeologist* (March 1985): 36–47; see his p. 38 for over 300 bread varieties, shapes [apparently votive] molded of human anatomical parts, and bread or cheese(?) molds from Mari, ca. 1780 B.C. Some of the molds are illustrated in vol. 7 of the photographic documentation of the French excavation: A. Parrot, *Mari* (Paris, 1953), pls. 87–91. For the Hittites, using the Sumerian character for bread (*ninda*) and derivatives, see especially H. A. Hoffner, *Alimenta Hethaeorum: Food Production in Hittite Asia Minor* (New Haven, 1974), chap. 6.

17. On the phenomenon in medieval Arabic culture and today, see Charles Perry, "The Fate of the Tail," *Proceedings, Oxford Symposium 1994,* (Totnes, Devon, 1995), 150–53.

18. F. J. Simoons, *Eat not This Flesh,* devotes chap. 3 and its notes to the question of the pig;

he puts to rest any notion that reasons for historical avoidance could include knowledge of trichinosis or be based on the "dirty habits" of swine wallowing in mud and their own excrement and urine (pigs being exceptionally clean animals when not penned, although since they have no sweat glands they do have to keep their skin damp to cool themselves). Marvin Harris makes some of the same points in a chapter on "Pig Lovers and Pig Haters," in his *Cows, Pigs, Wars and Witches* (New York, 1974), and other writings such as *Cannibals and Kings* (New York, 1977). For him the compelling reasons, however, are economic: by the time the Hebrews settled down in the Middle East, the forests so necessary for shade and food for pigs were disappearing and swine became competitors for agricultural products as well as a luxury food. Inconvenience and expense cannot completely explain dietary prohibitions in Deuteronomy and Leviticus. An essential factor is brought out by Mary Douglas in *Purity and Danger* (see above, Introduction n. 6), and it is echoed in a more extended study by Jean Soler in *Annales ESC* (1973) (translated as "The Semiotics of Food in the Bible," in F. Forster and O. Ranum, eds., *Food and Drink in History* (*Selections from the Annales*, vol. 5), 126–38.

19. Although in an outdated text, lists of identified Mesopotamian fish are to be found in William Radcliffe, *Fishing from the Earliest Times* [1921] (Chicago, 1974), 376f. For an example of fish included among temple offerings in the period of Hammurabi, see R. Marcel Sigrist, "Offrandes dans le Temple de Nusku à Nippur," *Journal of Cuneiform Studies* 29 (1977): 169ff.

20. See for example Hartmut Waetzoldt, "Knoblauch und Zwiebeln nach den Texten des 3 Jahrtausend," *Bulletin on Sumerian Agriculture* 3 (1982): 23–56.

21. Jean Bottéro has published numerous articles on a vocabulary written on 24 tablets with one food section of about 800 entries which he interprets as indicating the variety in Mesopotamian diet; he also deals with recipes, primarily a group of tablets at Yale University. See his "The Cuisine of Ancient Mesopotamia" *Biblical Archaeologist* (March 1985): 36–47; "La plus vielle cuisine du monde," *L'Histoire* 49 (October 1982): 72–82; and *Textes culinaires Mésopotamiens* (Winona Lake, Ind., 1995).

22. See D. J. Wiseman, "A New Stela of Assurnasirpal II," *Iraq* 14 (1952): 24–39; the stela is attributed to 879 B.C. The list includes the trees in the royal orchard outside the city, corresponding to the Assyrian passion for collecting exotic trees and plants for their gardens. For their botanical nomenclature, see R. Campbell Thompson, *A Dictionary of Assyrian Botany* (London, 1949), as well as his *The Assyrian Herbal: A Monograph on the Assyrian Vegetable Drugs* (London, 1924).

23. Wiseman, "A New Stela," 30, translating *nuḫurtu*. For a discussion of asafoetida in Roman cookery, see below, chap. 6. On cardamom, or cardamon, see M. Stol, "Cress and Its Mustard," *Jaresbericht van het vooraziatisch-egyptisch Genootschap*, no. 28 (1983–84) (Leiden, 1985), 24–32 discussing variants in the cress family and, p. 28, Assyrian *kuddimmu* or cardamom; in Babylonian, *saḫlû*.

24. Dalley, *Mari and Karana*, 83. Of course, we cannot know whether these were used in cooking or possibly as in Han China for sweetening one's breath.

25. "Cuisine of Ancient Mesopotamia," 42. In the German Dictionary of Akkadian, on the other hand, *samidu(m)* is defined as meal of an indeterminate grain. Dalley, *Mari and Karana*, also affirms that *samidu(m)* is unidentified.

26. XVI, i, 14. Strabo claims to know a Persian song that enumerates 369 uses for the

palm tree, and he notes Mesopotamian use of sesame as the basic oil (as will be indicated below).

27. See H. W. F. Saggs, *The Greatness that was Babylon: A Sketch of the Ancient Civilization of the Tigris-Euphrates Valley* (New York, 1988), 172–76 for a survey of food and drink; on the apricot, *armmanu*, see p. 495. See also Gerlinde Mauer, "Agriculture of the Old Babylonian Period," *Journal of the Ancient Near Eastern Society* 15 (1983): 63–78, s.v. Note that D. Zohary and M. Hopf, *Domestication of Plants in the Old World*, 159, speak of the apricot and the peach, originating in East Asia, as latecomers to the Near East; this refers to *cultivated* species, of course. They note that Greeks received peaches from Persia by ca. 300 B.C., although Romans did not cultivate them until the first century A.D.

28. *Everyday Life in Babylonia and Assyria* (London, 1965), 465, in a section on the fruits of Mesopotamia; he equated Akkadian *karshu* with the Greek *kerasos*, cherry, but Akkadian dictionaries do not confirm this. Cf. Thompson, *Dictionary of Assyrian Botany*, 307–8, on Sargon's discovery of what he interprets as a very fragrant variety, *Prunus Mahaleb L.* (the morrella).

29. For *šamaššammu(m)*, "grain of the oil-tree," see Thompson, *Dictionary of Assyrian Botany*, 101, "cultivated from the earliest times," citing C. Luerssen, *Medicinisch-pharmaceutische Botanik*, 2:1010; J. N. Postgate, "The 'Oil Plant' in Assyria," *Bulletin on Sumerian Agriculture* 2 (1985): 144–51, confirms the linguistic evidence and discusses why the seed is not found in archaeological deposits while linseed is (the latter is generally processed by being roasted, sesame seed is first soaked and less likely to survive); see in the same issue of the *Bulletin*, W. Van Zeist, "Pulse and Oil Crop Plants," pp. 33–37, and Dorothea Bedigian, "Is Se-gis-i Sesame or Flax?," pp. 159–71.

30. M. Lichtheim, *Ancient Egyptian Literature* (Berkeley, Calif., 1973), 1:222–35, gives a translation of the Tale of Sinuhe, or at least all of it that has been preserved. One translator, Gustave Lefebvre (*Romans et contes égyptiens de l'époque pharaonique* [Paris, 1949]), interprets the tree-oil in this passage as olive oil. This would highlight a distinction between olive oil in the Levant as compared to sesame in Lower Mesopotamia.

31. Indeed, one translation (Lefebvre, *Romans et contes égyptiens*, 12), reads that there was milk in every dish cooked.

32. Alexandra Hicks, of the University of Michigan — reported in *People* magazine in April or May 1988, in an article by N. Geeslin and S. Avery Brown, of New Haven.

33. For discussion of the Roman *garum* and its similarity to oriental *nuoc-mam, nam pla*, or *patis*, see below, chap. 6.

34. My paraphrase makes use of Bottéro's translations into both English ("Cuisine of Ancient Mesopotamia," 43f.) and French ("La plus vieille cuisine," 80).

35. Bottéro, "La plus vieille cuisine," 78.

36. For consideration of the funerary banquet and *theoxenia* in Greek religious life, see chap. 4.

37. Interestingly, Elinor Ferris Beach, in "The Samaria Ivories, *Marzeah*, and the Biblical Text," *Biblical Archaeologist* 56 (1993): 94–104, calls attention to this oracular passage, because she identifies a number of ivory plaques found at Samaria as revetments of such couches, used in a religious celebration, the *marzeah*. It seems to me that the context, mourning the ruin of Joseph, already bears a funerary meaning.

CHAPTER FOUR

1. For an interesting discussion of this exploration of their past and its artifacts, see Rhys Carpenter, *The Humanistic Value of Archaeology*, Martin Classical Lectures, no. 4 (Cambridge, Mass., 1933), 7f.

2. The fragments are edited in H. Lloyd-Jones and P. Parsons, *Supplementum Hellenisticum* (Berlin, 1983), 46–75, and may be sought out in one English translation by using the index to the Loeb edition of Athenaeus, edited by C. B. Gulick, from which the selections derive. A new translation with introduction and extensive commentary is to be recommended: John Wilkins and Shaun Hill, *Archestratus. The Life of Luxury: Europe's Oldest Cookery Book* (Totnes, Devon, 1994), with bibliography. On Archestratos himself, s.v. Wellmann, *RE*, 2,1; also Enzio Degani, "On Greek Gastronomic Poetry, I," *Alma mater studiorum* (Bologna, 1990), 51–63. The latter takes certain phrases as criticism of Syracusan cuisine in a manner I do not find convincing; I read these as "don't follow such-and-such a practice of those among us at Syracuse who do thus-and-so" (in reference to putting cheese and vinegar on certain fish—which he otherwise recommends for those which are either tough or fatty).

3. *UP: University Publishing*, Food issue (Fall 1979): 28, in Dillon's column on Greek cookery, "Last Words."

4. See H. Dohm, *Mageiros: Die Rolle des Kochs in der griechisch-römischen Komödie* (Munich, 1964); also A. Giannini, "La figura del cuoco nella commedia greca," *Acme* 13 (1960): 135–216. Emily Gowers (in *The Loaded Table: Representations of Food in Roman Literature* [Oxford, 1993], 78ff.) considers the "metatheatrical potential" of the cook as comic character, with special reference to his activities as analogy for the processes of the poet.

5. Athenaeus IX, 378. Elsewhere (VII, 292e, for example) the cook's learnedness is stressed; Gulick translates *sophistēs mageiriskos* as "cook-professor." Among outstanding experts are cited: Agis of Rhodes as the perfect grill-master for fish; Euthynos, renowned for his way with lentils; Nereus of Chios, whose conger-eel could please the gods; and Aphthonetos, who invented sausages (Athenaeus IX, 379e). But general cookbook authors of fame included Mithaecos of Syracuse, cited by Plato (*Gorgias*, 518), who spent some time at the court of the Sicilian ruler, Dionysus II.

6. Note Athenaeus IV, 172c where the *dēmiourgos*—with feminine article and adjective accompanying this masculine noun—rivals the chef by preparing roast thrushes and bits of meat to go with her honey cakes for dessert ("second table" or *tragēmata*). Menander wrote a play with the title, *Dēmiourgos* (Kock, *FGC*, 3:34).

7. In addition to Athenaeus IV, 146f–147, XIV, 643a–e, and passim, see Dalby, "The Banquet of Philoxenos," *Petits Propos Culinaires* 26 (1987): 28–36. He is sometimes confused with Philoxenos of Leucas, another famous trencherman who may have written on the same topic; cf. David A. Campbell, *Greek Lyric*, vol. 5 (Cambridge, Mass., 1993), who attributes our banquet to the latter.

8. Matron is the subject of Enzo Degani's second study "On Greek Gastronomic Poetry, II," *Alma mater studiorum* (Bologna, 1991), 164–75. His *Attic Banquet* may be found in Athenaeus IV, 134d–137c. Gulick's edition footnotes the Homeric passages that are parodied.

9. Athenaeus XIV, 648d–e in which the speaker loves flat cakes (*plakounta*) made of this fine meal; q.v. Greek index to Gulick. For a recent text subsuming earlier literature on wheats

of antiquity, and discusson of *amulon,* see R. Sallares, *The Ecology of the Ancient Greek World* (London, 1991), particularly chapter 3. This is an especially important work, marshaling evidence of durum wheats in antiquity—the "heavy" wheat opposed to this light, hexaploid bread wheat in question—and in countering criticism of A. M. Watson's *Agricultural Innovation in the Early Islamic World: The Diffusion of Crops and Farming Techniques, 700–1100* (Cambridge, 1983), which champions Arab cultivation of durum wheats and invention of pasta.

10. Athenaeus XIV. This particular passage is confusing; see Gulick, 6:471, notes. His translation does not explain the relation of marrow to the word *amulos;* for Gottschalk (*Histoire de l'alimentation et de la gastronomie depuis la préhistoire jusqu'à nos jours* [Paris, 1948], 1:136), the item is a brain. Campbell (see above, note 7) translates "custard," correcting *amu(y)los* to *mu(y)elos* as a reference to beestings, the first milk of sheep or goats after giving birth, used for dessert because it was thought too rich for young animals.

11. A maidservant says "we'll soon be eating this concoction," in anticipation of a banquet: ingredients work out as various kinds of fish, limpets, salt fish, cornel berries, leftover brains seasoned with silphium and cheese, honey-basted thrushes, blackbirds, doves, pigeons, chickens, hare, and hashed "wings" in reduced must (lépadotémachosélachogáleokránioleípsanodrímypotrimmatosílphiotýromélitokátkechymenokíchlepikóssyphopháttoperísteraléktryonóptokepháliokínklopeleíolagoíosiraíobaphétragalópterygon).

12. The Greek words for safflower *(knēkos)* and for tawny yellow *(knēkós)* differ only in accent; I follow Gulick in reading "saffron-yellow" here.

13. For the antiquity of these traditions about heroes and references to representations from the seventh and sixth centuries B.C. as well as Pindaric editing, see D. S. Robertson, "The Food of Achilles," *Classical Review* 54 (December 1940): 177–80.

14. Julie M. Hansen, "The Palaeoethnobotany of Franchthi Cave," *Excavations at Franchthi Cave, Greece,* ed. T. W. Jacobsen (Bloomington, 1991), fasc. 7.

15. In the first century A.D., Plutarch labors under a similar misapprehension (*Moralia,* "Table Talk," VIII, 8, 730), leading to moralistic musing on the wastefulness of eating fish.

16. In the Homeric passage in question, the cooking process depends on interpretation of two words: Patroclos casts down a *mega kreion.* This big meat thing is translated "chopping block" by some; by others (and by me) as a big cauldron suiting the preposition *en* that places the meat in it, rather than on it, for parboiling, so to speak. Also, translation of the *Iliad* into Latin renders *caccabum ingentem,* "a mighty vessel" See Marcel Detienne's arguments and citations as he maintains the structuralist opposition between the two methods of cookery, using the same Caeretan pot; for him only the Titans reversed the order by first boiling the baby Dionysos (M. Detienne and J.-P. Vernant, *La cuisine du sacrifice en pays grec* (Paris, 1979).

17. For Bronze Age and Homeric food, the best older text is K. F. Vickery, *Food in Early Greece* [1936] (Chicago, 1980); see more recently, Gerda Bruns, "Küchenwesen und Mahlzeiten," *Archeologia Homerica,* vol. 2, pt. Q (Göttingen, 1970), with bibliography; the contemporary cooking equipment is discussed by Siegfried Laser in vol. 2, pt. P of the same serial. See also A. D. Keramopoullos, "Mykēnaïka," sec. A., "Ichthyophagia"; sec. B., "Ornithon Historia," in *Archaiologikon Deltion,* vol. 4 (1918), 88–101 on the eating of fish and fowl by Homeric heroes. The question is newly addressed by James Davidson in John Wilkins, ed., *Food in European Literature* (Exeter, 1996), 57ff.

18. Because I have taken part in New York University's excavations at the mystery

sanctuary of the Great Gods on Samothrace, my thoughts turn to salt-cellars inscribed with the letter theta, standing for *theōn*, dedicated to those gods; see J. McCredie's report on the 1962–64 campaign in *Hesperia* 34 (1965): 116, pl. 35c. Throughout antiquity ritual meals were part of the ceremonial here, in a context that included a replica of the entrance to a Mycenaean bee-hive tomb; see my article "Identity with Mycenaean Ancestors in Cult Meals at Ancient Greek Sanctuaries," *Proceedings, Oxford Symposium 1991* (London, 1992), 50–53 and note 50 below.

19. See Sallares, *Ecology*, 401. The famed hunting-knife sheath from the Shaft Graves at Mycenae is inlaid with a lion hunt in Minoan style, and Sallares gives a reference for bones uncovered in Late Helladic IIIb context at Tiryns.

20. See J. Chadwick, *The Mycenaean World* (Cambridge, 1976), 127–30, who also points out improvements for grazing cattle and sheep after the forests disappeared; in Crete wild goats were important as well. See also below, our discussion of acorns from vast stands of oak, the tree sacred to Zeus, which represent *Ur*-nurture in Greek and in other tradition-oriented societies, like the Amerindian.

21. Sallares, *Ecology*, 15f.

22. See Chadwick, *The Mycenaean World*, 32. As one of the team that deciphered Linar B script and proved it an early form of Greek, Chadwick's discussion of the etymology of products listed in the inventories is particularly valuable. A most useful contrbution is appendix I in Emily Vermeule's *Greece in the Bronze Age* (Chicago, 1964), a listing of known plants and animals compared with a Homeric text; there is also a list of spices and condiments (n. 5 to chap. 6, on p. 341). On Syrian and Palestinian connections in general, see L. R. Palmer, *Mycenaeans and Minoans: Aegean Prehistory in the Light of the Linear B Tablets* (New York, 1962), 113.

23. Vermeule, *Greece in the Bronze Age*, 181. A rich vocabulary of herbs and spices does not necessarily reflect cookery, of course; many may have been used in the manufacture of perfumes and scented oils; cf. Chadwick, *The Mycenaean World*, 119 and C. W. Shelmerdine, *The Perfume Industry of Mycenaean Pylos*, SIMA Pocketbook, no. 34 (Göteborg, 1985). But see also J. T. Killen, "More Mycenae Tablets," a review of Chadwick, *The Mycenaean Tablets*, III (*Transactions of the American Philosophical Society* 52, 7) 1962, in *Classical Review*, 14 (1964): pp. 171–73, apropos West House at Mycenae.

24. At least, there are two types of ending on the word for olive (Chadwick, *The Mycenaean World*, 121f.). A great debate about olive cultivation, as opposed to exploitation of it in the wild, involves paleobotanists who dispute Colin Renfrew's triad of agricultural conquests that brought Myceaean civilization into being: wheat, the vine, and the olive. While vines cultivated from wild grape seeds are readily distinguished by specialists, the same is not true of the olive; the change from Mesolithic to Middle Helladic of the second millennium may be gradually charted. For most recent discussion and bibliography, see Julie Hansen, "Agriculture in the Prehistoric Aegean: Data versus Speculation," *AJA* 92 (1988): 39–52; she establishes that the vine was added to the agricultural repertoire in the early Bronze Age (third millennium B.C.).

25. Singer et al., *A History of Technology*, 1:358f.; 2:122.

26. Chadwick in M. Ventris and J. Chadwick, *Documents in Mycenaean Greek*, 2d ed. (Cambridge, 1973), 221–31.

27. See further discussion in our chapter on Rome, as well as pp. 117, 134 for "gourmet" Greek uses. In detail: A. C. Andrews, "The Silphium of the Ancients: A Lesson in Crop Control," *Isis* 33 (1941): 232–36; C. H. Coster, "The Economic Position of Cyrenaica," in *Studies in*

Honor of Allan Chester Johnson, ed. P. R. Coleman-Norton (Princeton, 1951), 3–26 [p. 11f.], citing Charles Daremberg and Edmond Saglio, *Dictionnaire des antiquités grecques et romaines d'après les textes et les monuments . . .* (5 vols.; Paris, 1873–1929), IV, 2, 1337ff. and *RE*, IIIa, cols. 103ff.; and Alice Arndt, "Silphium," *Proceedings, Oxford Symposium 1992* (London, 1993), 28–35.

28. Arndt, "Silphium," p. 33. The Hippocratic corpus (*peri nousōn*, IV, 34) speaks of unsuccessful attempts to transplant silphium in Attica and Ionia (Sallares, *Ecology*, 352. Other ancient sources: Theophrastus, III, ii, 1 and VI, iii, 1–7; Arrian, *Anabasis of Alexander*, III, 28, 6–7; Pliny, *NH*, XIX, 41–42. Similar species grew elsewhere in Bactria and in what is now called the Hindu Kush, but none so prized as the Cyrenaican variety. I assume that the silphium plant could be employed just as one uses its relative, asafoetida: dried leaves (delicious as a salad herb I find), ground dried root, and inspissated juice.

29. K. F. Vickery (*Food in Early Greece*, 51), accepts Sir Arthur Evans' linguistic deduction in *The Palace of Minos at Knossos* (4 vols.; London, 1921–35), 1:284–85.

30. Vermeule (see above, n. 22), lists mint, marjoram, pomegranates, parsnips, bees and their honey, beer. Vickery cites Greek words which seem to originate in the pre-Greek Aegean as those for celery, cucumber, chicory, garlic, leek, pumpkin (meaning either gourds or colocasia), rampion, water parsnip, peas, and chickpeas (*Food in Early Greece*, 51).

31. *Works and Days*, line 41. Elsewhere (lines 585–94) he supplements the bulbs and mallow of a poor Boeotian farmer with more serious fare, sounding like an early Greek Omar Khayyam, sitting under the shade of a rock instead of a tree to escape the heat of summer "with wine, a barley cake, goat's milk curd, the meat of a young heifer and of baby kids." Theophrastos (*Enquiry into Plants*, VII, xiii, 3), writes of asphodel's uses for food: the stalk may be fried, the seed roasted, and the bulb, above all, cut up with figs.

32. Chadwick notes that the date tree may grow in Crete, but its fruit will not ripen (*The Mycenaean World*, 121). The evidence for almonds is not linguistic, but a find from Phaistos (Ventris and Chadwick, *Documents*, 129).

33. It is also rendered *kuparo, -ero,* or *-airo*; in classical Greek *kupeiron*, botanically, *Cyperus rotundus*—listed among aromatics used for perfumes by Theophrastos (*Plants*, IX, vii, 3). In Pliny *cypirus* is rendered as "gladiolus bulb" by the Loeb translator. Compare Chadwick in his second edition of Ventris and Chadwick, *Documents*, 223–24, with his *The Mycenaean World*, 120. Cf. *chufa*, a sweet rush documented above in chapter 2.

34. Note that pulses—beans, lentils, and other legumes—do not leave archaeological traces so readily as cereals that are parched or flora with pips or seeds, as is pointed out by Anya Sarpaki, "The Palaeoethnobotanical Approach: The Mediterranean Triad, or is it a Quartet?" in Berit Wells, ed., *Agriculture in Ancient Greece: Proceedings of the Seventh International Symposium at the Swedish Institute of Athens, May 1990* (Stockholm, 1992), 61–76. Sarpaki argues rightly that one must add pulses to the trinity of vine, wheat, and olive as touchstones of Bronze Age civilization; we have seen how vital they were in the transition from foraging to agriculture.

35. See Hans Helbaek, "Late Cypriote Vegetable Diet at Apliki," *Opuscula Atheniensia* 4 (1962): 171–86; charred vegetable remains found in a house burned toward the end of the thirteenth century B.C. included wild radish, fava bean, vetch, lentil, two kinds of both barley and wheat, almond, olive, coriander, grape pip, and several "weeds," including pimpernel and neslia.

36. On chickens, see F. E. Zeuner, *Domesticated Animals* (see above, chap. 1, n. 8), 443–55;

Vickery, *Food in Early Greece,* 67, a summation; Sallares, *Ecology,* 233 and 320, with 460, n. 326, including further bibliography. Sallares notes that Caesar's *Gallic Wars* tells of Britons reluctance to eat the strange new bird, keeping it for amusement (*De bello gallico* V, 2, 4–5).

37. A. D. Keramopoullos, "Mykēnaïka," *Archaiologikon Deltion,* 88–101. Part A is devoted to arguments against scholars who speak of Homeric heroes eating fish only in dire necessity; part B, "Ornithōn istoria," discusses the hen and the goose. A later Greek called the cock "the Persian bird" (Kratinos in Athenaeus, IX, 374), apparently not because it was still exotic, as Keramopoullos implies, but because it "wakes us up from our beds at all hours." For consecrated eggs placed about tombs at Thebes, see p. 99f. In early reverence for eggs, we must remember that fowl seemingly laid but once a year like other birds when first brought into domestication, just as cows lactated only after giving birth.

38. Vickery (*Food in Early Greece,* 69), following Evans, notes that the sign for honey in the Cretan system seems close to the Egyptian hieroglyph for it.

39. Chadwick, *The Mycenaean World,* 124–26.

40. *Odyssey,* X, 235; *Iliad,* XI, 638f., on Nestor's cup. Is Pramnian chosen by Homer because of familiarity resulting from his supposed birth in Smyrna? It could be an Asia Minor wine, reflected in the legends that Dionysos' cult came to Greece from Phrygia (?). But see below, p. 119. The ritual potion of the Eleusinian Mysteries, *kykeon,* originated when Demeter refused to break her fast with meal mixed into wine, accepting it with water and pennyroyal, a variety of mint (Homeric Hymn to Demeter, verses 49, 200f., 208ff.). On varying interpretations of the Eleusinian drink and its meaning, see A. Delatte, *Le Cycéon breuvage rituel des Mystères d'Éleusis* (Paris, 1955) and, especially, N. J. Robertson's commentary in appendix IV of *The Homeric Hymn to Demeter* (Oxford, 1974). Thalia P. Howe is one classicist at least who has tried something similar, using a sweet wine to cook barley groats, then adding grated Parmesan at the end; served with wild duck, she found it as successful as wild rice; "Linear B and Hesiod's Bread-Winners," *TAPA,* 89 (1958): 48, n. 16.

41. Zohary and Hopf, *Domestication of Plants* (see chap. 1, n. 12), 139: "The boundary between the cultivated grape vine clones and the wild forms is blurred by the presence of escapees and secondary derivatives of hybridization . . . the pre-agriculture distribution of the wild vine has probably been blurred by 'weedy' forms occupying secondary habitats." They point out that even acid wild grapes are perfectly suitable for making wine.

42. See Chadwick's argument against Evans in Ventris and Chadwick, *Documents,* 131.

43. *The Mycenaean World,* 99–100.

44. Ibid., 124; one issue to several people is recorded from Pylos.

45. See the examples excavated at Sparta in the Mycenaean settlement about Menelaos' palace, described in R. M. Dawson, "Excavations at Sparta 1910, Part 2: The Mycenaean City near the Menelaion," *Annals of the British School at Athens* 16 (1909–10), 9–10, pl. 3. One was stamped with a seal in nine places.

46. For bibliography and notice of Paul Aström's analysis of material found in tomb offerings at Dhenia in Cyprus, see Bruns, "Küchenwesen und Mahlzeiten," pp. 8 and 9 n. 57. On the general use of resin in antiquity, Singer et al., *A History of Technology,* 1:299f. For the Greek historian Plutarch, pitch in wine jars not only added bouquet but also vigorous body ("Table Talk," V, 3, 676). Sir Moses Finley has suggested that "in the retsina regions of the ancient world there was a somewhat higher life expectancy (and therefore a somewhat higher

percentage of the elderly) than in the sapa regions," sapa being the grape must in which raisins were soaked to make it extrasweet, then greatly reduced by simmering. He believed that sapa became life- and fertility-threatening because it was reduced in lead vessels; see his "The Elderly in Classical Antiquity," *Greece and Rome* 28 (1981): 156–71 [p. 158].

47. "The Mycenaean Age, The Trojan War, The Dorian Invasion, and Other Problems," in *Lectures in Memory of Louise Taft Semple 1961–65* (Prnceton, 1967), 23. The tall, footed wine goblets, numbering 2,853, smashed from their shelves when fire destroyed the Palace of Nestor in the period archaeologists label LH IIIB.

48. A review of the evidence by a scholar who opts for both individual banquet porringers and a communal serving basket from which bread was handed around to the diners is found in the article previously cited by Thalia Howe (above, n. 40).

49. Ventris and Chadwick, *Documents*, 130; see Vickery, *Food in Early Greece*, 50, citing nomads of modern Greece who bake in a tripod pan over hot coals using a stone or pottery cover to which he compares certain examples discovered in Crete (Harriet Boyd Hanes, *Gournia Vasiliki, and other Prehistoric Sites on the Isthmus of Hierapetra* [Philadelphia, 1909], p. 30, pl. 2, nos. 34, 39, 40, 41, 43).

50. At Delos, for example, townspeople working in the Sanctuary of Apollo served as "barley-magicians," and "rounders" (makers of sacral barley cakes and the breads shaped like *omphaloi:* high, rounded loaves), while others were called "cumin-sprouters"; see Athenaeus, IV, 172f–173a; cf. herb breads at the ancient shrine of Athena at Lindos (Athenaeus IV, 131–33), and Bober, "Cult Meals," 52.

51. One interesting analysis of Mycenaean nutrition, with reference to societal contexts, is by Pia de Fidio, "Dieta e gestione delle risorse alimentari in età Micenea," in *Homo edens: Regimi, miti e pratiche dell'alimentazione nella civiltà Mediterraneo,* ed. O. Longo and P. Scarpi (Verona, 1989), 193–203. A recent book by Nancy Harmon Jenkins subsumes all the scientific and dietetic advisories on the Mediterranean Diet in a beguiling recipe book—*The Mediterranean Diet: A Delicious Alternative for Lifelong Health* (New York, 1994).

52. See W. Lord Taylour, *The Mycenaeans* (New York, 1964), 125, on fish bones found at Mycenae and Thebes, as well as abundant mollusk shells found at Bronze Age sites.

53. See Ventris and Chadwick, *Documents*, chap. 9, secs. 4–7, and, for inventories at major sites, their diagram, fig. 16, on p. 324.

54. Ibid., 325; cf. Evans, *Palace of Minos*, 4:861, fig 843. For Late Helladic fixed and portable hearths, see Vickery, *Food in Early Greece*, 88 (citing evidence from Korakou and Mycenae) and Bruns, "Küchenwesen und Mahlzeiten," sec. 5. Mabel Lang's reports from Pylos include discussion (in *AJA* 62 [1958]: 189) of two tablet entries with a "rimmed" portable hearth (? *a-pi- qo-to*) that would suit grilling on wooden spits for which stands have been unearthed, but the adjective is taken as perhaps descriptive of a table or fittings to a tripod cauldron by Chadwick (Ventris and Chadwick, *Documents*, 341, 499). Her second piece of equipment is described as *i-to-we-sa*, a portable hearth provided with "feet" [*(h)istoFessa*].

55. Nikolas Platon, *Zakro* (New York, 1971), 203f. See Ventris and Chadwick, *Documents*, 442, with additional commentary to pp. 225f., on a review by J. T. Killen of Mycenaean spice tablets (*Classical Review*, 14 [1964]: 171–73) which points out that some spices are not aromatic and holds that all plants listed were used to season food rather than perfumes.

56. For a balanced summary, see Chadwick, *The Mycenaean World*, 177–79 (Pylos'

destruction), and his chap. 11; Sallares, *Ecology*, 15f.; Per Alin,"Mycenaean Decline — Some Problems and Thoughts," in K.-H. Kinzl, ed., *Greece and the Eastern Mediterranean in Ancient History and Prehistory* (Berlin, 1977), 31–39. On the drought theory, R. A. Bryson, H. H. Lamb, and D. A. Donley, "Drought and the Decline of Mycenae," *Antiquity* 48 (1974): 46–50. Individual sites are discussed in final excavation reports.

57. See J. V. van Leuven, "Prehistoric Grain Explosions," *Antiquity*, 53 (1979): 138–40, with bibliography. Notice of the scientific report on elevator dust is to be found in the *New York Times*, 8 July 1982.

58. For modern analysis of the Cadmus myth and consideration of all the interpretations and archaeological issues, see Ruth B. Edwards, *Kadmos the Phoenician: A Study in Greek Legends and the Mycenaean Age* (Amsterdam, 1979); on the ancient sources concerning the date of Thebes' founding, p. 167f.

59. All forms and structures of communal eating are considered historiographically in P. Schmitt-Pantel, "Banquet et cité grecque: Quelques questions suscisitées par les recherches récentes" *Mélanges de l'École française de Rome* 97 (1985): 135–58. Her *La Cité au Banquet: Histoire des repas publics dans les cités grecques* (Rome, 1992), develops extended analysis of every manifestation in a valuable addition to Oswyn Murray's unitary and synthetic concentration on one form, the *symposion* proper (see below, n. 69). See also her collaboration with François Lissarragues: "Partage et communauté dans les banquets grecs," in *La Table et le partage* (Paris, 1986).

60. See above, p. 81f. and note 13. In historic times Pelops' ivory shoulder was one of the relics displayed at Elis (see Pliny, *NH*, xxvii, 34). The story of Thyestes was the subject of dramas by Sophocles and Euripides, preserved in solely a few fragments, as well as in a tragedy by Seneca. Cf. Itys served up as meat before his father, Tereus, by Prokne; Alkamenes, a follower of Pheidias, is thought to have carved a moving sculpture in the Acropolis Museum of this mother contemplating the dreadful deed as the boy clings to her, unknowing.

61. The distinction was first argued by E. Vanderpool, "Tholos and Prytanikon," *Hesperia*, 4 (1935): 470–75; see P. Schmitt-Pantel, "Le repas au prytanée et à la tholos dans l'Athènes classique. Sitesis, trophē, misthos: Réflexions sur le mode de nourriture démocratique," *Annali dell'Istituto orientale di Napoli* 2 (1980): 55–68; Frederick Cooper and Sarah Morris, in "Dining in Round Buildings" (*Sympotica: A Symposium on the Symposion*, ed. Oswyn Murray [Oxford, 1990], 66–85), elaborate on the distinction between the more democratic and modest meal in the *tholos*, where fifty members of the prytany, with six to ten officials, dined seated, and the "aristocratic" repast in the *prytaneion*, where guests reclined on couches in symposiast fashion (pp. 75–79), making the *tholos* emerge as "the first politically designed building in Western architecture."

62. On the Spartan *agōgē* (educational system, entered in one's seventh year at the age of six), its various stages and *krupteia*, see Robert Garland, *The Greek Way of Life from Conception to Old Age* (London, 1990), dealing with Greek age-classing, both male and female, as a means of structuring society in variant ways; see also the still basic work by M. P. Nilsson, "Die Grundlagen des spartanischen Lebens," *Klio* 12 (1912): 308–40, and G. Cambiano, "Becoming an Adult," in *The Greeks*, ed. J.-P. Vernant (Chicago, 1995), 86–119. On the *sussitia* specifically, as well as *andreia* of Crete, see also Mario Lombardo, "Pratiche di commensalità e forme di organizzazione sociale nel mondo greco: Symposion e Syssitia," in Longo and Scarpi, *Homo edens*, 311–26; Oswyn Murray, *Early Greece* (2d ed., Cambridge Mass., 1993), 175–79; and Sallares,

Ecology, 130, 172–74, 189f.; and bibliography on symposia cited below in n. 69. For a New History study which stresses the institution of *sussitia* in socioeconomic terms, dealing with statistics on mess dues and contributions in a context of redistributing food to reinforce the dependent status of helots, see Thomas J. Figueira, "Mess Contribution and Subsistence at Sparta," *TAPA* 114 (1984): 87–109.

63. A passage in Athenaeus (XIII, 561e) reflects a belief that because success in warfare depends on the friendship *(philia)* of the men drawn up in battle-line, Spartans offered preliminary sacrifice to Eros.

64. Athenaeus IV, 141c; see also 138c–143a, for discussion of Spartan meals, festivals, and abstemiousness. Another ancient source for customs of the Lacedaemonians is Plutarch's life of Lycurgus, the leader whose reforms established these regulations. Figueira, "Mess Contribution," points out that olive oil is conspicuously absent, and suggests it was part of voluntary contributions made from the rent-in-kind each Spartan received from his agricultural plot *(kleros)* worked by a helot slave.

65. Gottschalk, *Histoire de l'alimentation,* 1:143, cites a Mme Dacier in the eighteenth century who, enamored of ancient Greece, had a vision in which she discovered the recipe; when she tried it out on six members of the Academy, the effect was disastrous.

66. Athenaeus, IV, 138b–c, the occasion being the one which stimulated the Sybarite's observation. Elsewhere, Athenaeus' companions react disbelievingly to tales of Persian rulers' predilection for whole roast oxen or huge fowl like the *phenax* (ostrich?) (ibid., 130f–131a).

67. *Early Greece,* 176. Apparently, after all that same gender "companionship," it took a little role-playing to develop bisexual or heterosexual proclivities.

68. From Hug's article for *RE,* ser. 2, VII, cols. 1266–70 and Mau on origins in IV, 61ff. (1931) to current scholarship on the part of Oswyn Murray and others, this phenomenon seems to dominate popular representation of Greek protocols in dining.

69. The dominant authority on sympotic history and interpretation is Oswyn Murray; most important of his writings in English are "The Symposion as Social Organization," in *The Greek Renaissance of the Eighth Century B.C.: Tradition and Innovation* (Stockholm, 1983), 195–99; "The Greek Symposion in History," in *Tria Corda: Scritti in onore di Arnaldo Momigliano,* ed. E. Gabba (Como, 1983), 257–72; "Nestor's Cup and the Origin of the Symposium," *AION Archeologia, Storia, Antichità* 16 (1994), and the introduction to *Sympotica: A Symposium on the Symposion* (see above, n. 61), which includes a full bibliography to 1990. On the ephebes' introduction to sympotic customs, see Jan N. Bremmer, "Adolescents, Symposion, and Pederasty," in the last named, pp. 135–48. For discussion of some points of Murray's theories that are problematic, especially his treating in unitary terms a phenomenon which embraced a wide range of different practices in time and space, see Lombardo, "Pratiche di commensalità," 311–26.

70. For the process and antecedents, see J. M. Dentzer, "Aux origines de l'iconographie du banquet couché," *Revue archéologique* (1971–72): 215–58, and his *Le Motif du banquet couché dans le Proche-Orient et le monde grec du VIIème au IVième siècle avant J.-C.* (Paris, 1982). According to Hegesander (Kock, *FGC,* 2:118; Athenaeus I, 18) Macedonians were not allowed to recline at meals until after they had killed a wild boar without a hunting net.

71. For the visual documentation, see François Lissarrague, *The Aesthetics of the Greek Banquet: Images of Wine and Ritual* (Princeton, 1990). See also idem, "Around the *Krater:* An Aspect of Banquet Imagery," in Murray, *Sympotica,* 196–209.

72. One study of various banqueting rooms and the arrangement of couches which permits identification of these spaces archaeologically is Christoph Börker, *Festbankett und griechische Architektur* (Xenia. Konstanzer althistorische Vorträge und Forschungen, 4), 1983; see also Birgetta Bergquist, "Sympotic Space A Functional Aspect of Greek Dining-Rooms," in Murray, *Sympotica*, 37–65.

73. On the music and songs, see Luigi Enrico Rossi, "Il simposio greco arcaico e classico come spettacolo a se stesso," in *Spettacoli conviviali dall' antichità classica alle corti italiane del '400: Atti del VII Convegno di Studio, Viterbo, 27–30 Maggio 1982* (Viterbo, 1983), 41–50, stressing that all nonchoral poetry was for private context in the symposium, the change to public performance coming with the end of the archaic period. Also in the same volume: Mario Torelli, "Gli spettacoli conviviali di età classica: Documenti archeologici su possibili fatti genetici e sviluppi," pp. 51–64, for historical transformations in dance and the kōmos; Carlo Corbato, "Symposium e teatro: Dati e problemi," pp. 65–76, emphasizes the theatral quality of some sympotic entertainment and cites fourth century recitations from earlier playwrights (good bibliography on *skolia*, or the intricately communal songs, p. 67, n. 5).

74. See J. M. Edmonds, ed., *Lyra Graeca* (Loeb Classical Library, 1928), vol. 1: Alcman, no. 138 (from Athenaeus, bk. V) on the significance of these last three seasonings. Athenaeus XIV, 642f. lists sweetmeats at "second table," i.e., symposion, including cannabis in expanded servings of *chondros*, beans, frogs, whelks; on cannabis seed as an after-dinner treat in many cultures, see Bober, "The Infamous Herb of 'Joyous Perfection': *Cannabis sativa* in Cooking," *Proceedings, Oxford Symposium 1992*, 48–55.

75. A good general survey of the history and culture of the Eastern Greeks from the Iron Age to the Roman conquest is J. M. Cook's *The Greeks in Ionia and the East,* Ancient Peoples and Places, ed. Glyn Daniel, no. 31 (New York, 1963).

76. My colleague, Brunhilde Ridgway, believes that the Peplos Kore represents a goddess rather than a votary, and that the sculptor was inspired by an earlier cult image of a more primitive type; see her *The Archaic Style in Greek Sculpture* (Princeton, N.J., 1977), 100 and passim.

77. For the sources, ranging from the fourth century B.C. to Byzantine times, see Crawford H. Greenewalt, Jr., *Ritual Dinners in Early Historic Sardis* (University of California Publications. Classical Studies, no. 17) (1978), 52ff., n. 57. According to the *Oxford Classical Dictionary*, a rich Lydian sauce called *karuke⁻* was made of blood and strong spices, giving rise to the adjective *karukinos* ("blood red"); this in turn, incidentally, explains the "gravy-makers of Delphi" *(karukopoioi)* who served the meat of sacrifice with similar sauces (Athenaeus IV, 173c–d).

78. Menander, *Trophonios,* quoted in Athenaeus 517a. We must especially regret the loss of this play of Menander's, because Trophonios was a legendary cult hero whose claim to glory came from his eating capacity.

79. *Ritual Dinners*, 53, on the basis of a suggestion by W. C. Kohler connecting stew with the god, as well as a prehistoric Lydian king Candaules (of the Herodotos story, I, 7, 12). On cynophagy in antiquity in general, see also p. 31, n. 1 for bibliography.

80. Compare Socrates' discussion of the analogy between cookery masquerading as medicine, and flattery in rhetoric pretending to serve justice, each false and deceitful, neither deserving to be called an art (*Gorgias*, 462–65, 518).

81. For example, Athenaeus IV, 131f–132, 134a–d, 137c,d,f, the latter passage noting that

each little dish was served separately before guests rather than being presented together in more impressive style.

82. Born ca. 570–60 B.C. and, by his own testimony, living into his nineties at the court of Hieron in Syracuse (478–67 B.C.); see J. H. Lesher, *Xenophanes of Colophon: Fragments, A Text and Translation with a Commentary* (Toronto, 1992). His works are also included in the Loeb Library edition of *Elegy and Iambus,* vol. 1, ed. J. M. Edmonds (Cambridge, Mass., 1931).

83. Lesher's notes and commentary (*Xenophanes of Colophon,* fragment 1, pp. 47–54) admirably elucidates the didactic nature of Xenophanes' banquet (preserved for us by Athenaeus, XI, 462c), and a detailed appreciation of the fact that it is not profane but entails new moral ideas of a "philosophical *thiasos*" is to be found in Leon Defradas, "Le Banquet de Xénophane, *Revue des études grecques* 75 (1962): 344–65.

84. The background for expansion of the Greek world through colonization is variously interpreted by historians. Some emphasize demographic data (explored in the works of Sir Moses Finley in concert with interclass tensions), others stress capitalist enterprise on the part of certain elites (e.g., Chester G. Starr, *The Economic and Social Growth of Early Greece, 800–500 B.C.* (New York, 1977). For varying motivations as well as geographical variation, see John Boardman, *The Greeks Overseas: Their Early Colonies and Trade* (Harmondsworth, 1980). For gustatory history, a fascinating footnote alleges evidence of male colonists marrying native women with very different food habits, so that wives and husbands kept each to his or her traditional diet: Jean Rouge, "La Colonisation grecque et les femmes," *Cahiers d'histoire* 15 (1970): 307–17.

85. Outstanding among such studies are W. Burkert, *Homo Necans: The Anthropology of Ancient Greek Sacrificial Ritual and Myth* [1972], trans. P. Bing (Berkeley and Los Angeles, 1983); also Marcel Detienne and Jean-Pierre Vernant, eds. *La cuisine du sacrifice* (see above, n. 16). For considerations of the indissoluble link between sacrifice and social cohesion in partaking of the flesh as traditional survival into modern Greek village life, see M. Detienne ("Il coltello da carne"), J.-L. Durand ("Figurativo e processo rituale"), and Stella Georgoudi ("Presso i Neogreci: fare il kourbani"), in "Cibo, carneo, sacrificio e società in Grecia," *Dialoghi di archeologia,* n.s., 1 (1979): 6–35.

86. For Attic festivals themselves, see Herbert W. Parke, *Festivals of the Athenians* (Ithaca, N.Y., 1977), and Erika Simon, *Festivals of Attika: An Archaeological Commentary* (Madison, Wisc., 1983).

87. Among the most important studies: A. Frickenhaus, "Griechische Banketthäuser," *JdI* 32 (1917): 114–33; Ernest Will, "Banquets et salles de banquet dans les cultes de la Grèce et de l'Empire romain," in *Mélanges d'histoire ancienne et d'archéologie offerts à Paul Collart,* ed. Pierre Ducrey et al. (Lausanne, 1976); Georges Roux, "Salle de banquet à Delos," in *Études déliennes, BCH* Suppl. (1973): 525–54 and *BCH* (1981): 41–61; M. S. Goldstein, "The Setting of the Ritual Meal in Greek Sanctuaries, 600–300 B.C.," Ph.D. diss., University of California, Berkeley, 1978; and articles by F. Cooper and S. Morris, R. A. Tomlinson, N. Bookadis, and B. Bergquist in Murray, *Sympotica.* The article by Nancy Bookadis, "Ritual Dining in the Sanctuary of Demeter and Kore at Corinth," is particularly significant because of the extraordinary number of dining complexes (some 52!) dating from the 6th to the 2d century; their kitchens and built-in couches are preserved and the excavations on the Acrocorinth have yielded many clay models of foods and offering plates (including our fig. 64).

88. On some Attic *orgeōnes* (the members of certain hereditary devotees of a particular

minor divinity, hero, or heroine), see William Scott Ferguson, "The Attic Orgeones," *Harvard Theological Review* 37 (1944): 61ff. (a decree specfying division of the sacrifice is reproduced on pp. 73ff.), and see also Arthur Darby Nock, "The Cult of Heroes," ibid., pp. 141–73, interpreting the decree.

89. See R. N. Thönges-Stringaris, "Das griechische Totenmahl," *Athenische Mitteilungen* 80 (1965): 1–99 and a study of Etruscan tomb representations which subsumes their Greek background: Simonetta de Marinis, *La tipologia del banchetto nell'arte Etrusca antica* (Rome, 1961). Oswyn Murray, in all his writing on symposia, upholds the idea that Greek reliefs of "funeral banquets," like the one in fig. 41, are votive reliefs depicting heroes. He argues that the prominence of banquet scenes in Etruscan tombs marks their emphasis on the aristocratic life of the symposion, borrowed from the Greek social code.

90. A noted example from Mykonos at the end of the third century B.C., records regulations for sacrifices at festivals throughout the year: specifications for animals, budgetary details, share given the slayer, etc. (W. Dittenberger, *Sylloge Inscriptionum Graecarum,* 3d ed. [Leipzig, 1915], 615). From 335 B.C. we have the rules governing distribution of meat at the Attic Panathenaic festival (ibid., 271).

91. Elsewhere these continued to represent the good old foods of uncorrupted humans and the temperate life: see Plato, *Republic* II, 372d, where the simple meal will culminate with a "second table" of figs, peas, and beans, and the roasting of acorns and myrtle berries at the fire. Harry Levin's *The Myth of the Golden Age in the Renaissance* (Bloomington, Ind., 1969), p. 29 and passim, highlights the poetic ancestry and emblematic value of acorn-eating.

92. Aristophanes, *Acharnians* 878.

93. Book IV, xxvi, 8.

94. Archestratos in Athenaeus, II, 101e. Samian cheesecake, however, gained distinction for its individual ones imitating a woman's breast: see Athenaeus, III, 115a, calling them *kribana,* after Alcman.

95. Diners in Athenaeus devote some time to the discussion of *mattyēs, mattuēs* (XIV, 663–664). The recipe stems from Artemidoros, *A Glossary of Cookery,* 663d, but a fifth-century lexicographer defines *mattuēs,* as a bird and the *lagana* strewn about in its broth. For my interpretation of *laganon* (which Gulick in every case translates as "wafer bread," hence "crumbled" in this instance) see below, p. 116f.

96. Athenaeus, III, 126c, cf. 57b. Our recipe is adapted from Georges Blond and Germaine Blond *Histoire pittoresque de notre alimentation* (2 vols.; Ottawa, 1961)—with a free historicism that is indeed "picturesque," after Pollux. See appendix, p. 52.

97. For a major passage on breads, see Athenaeus, III, 109b–116a.

98. Athenaeus, XIV, 647, on these *mulloi;* the practice was undoubtedly more widespread. Molded breads and cakes include also the famous *kribanai* baked in the shape of the female breast (Athenaeus, XIV, 646), of which the most famous were a specialty cheesecake of Samos. Compare "Minni di Virgini," pastries made still at the Monastery of the Virgins of Palermo and another convent of cloistered nuns at Itria di Sciacca; for recipes, see June di Schino, "The Waning of Sexually Allusive Monastic Confectionery in Southern Italy," in *Proceedings, Oxford Symposium 1994,* 70. The custom of shaping substitutes for sacrificial animals we met in the Near East is sustained in Greece as well.

99. McGee, *On Food and Cooking*, 237.

100. Book IV, 170a–c; Koch, *FGC*, 2:343 and 362. Pollux, *Onomasticon*, VI, 66 quotes the same list from Alexis, with minor changes: no garlic, but *annison* (anise), which means that the fourth item, *anēthon*, which can mean either dill or anise, was probably the former; no *seseli*, which is either heartwort or amaranth, but pepper in its place.

101. See, for example, Lionel Casson, "Rome's Trade with the East: The Sea Voyage to Africa and India" (chap. 8) and "Cinnamon and Cassia in the Ancient World" (chap. 11), in his *Ancient Trade and Society* (Detroit, 1984), with reference to earlier literature; also his *The Periplus Maris Erythraei* (Princeton, N.J., 1989), 12.

102. In book II, 112, Herodotos tells of equally "strange" ways in which gum mastic is produced in the beards of billy goats. This resinous exudation from a shrub *(Pistacia lentiscus)* is supplied to Greek cooking today from only one source on the island of Chios. It is difficult to believe that this *lēdanon* was more exotic in antiquity. When gathered, mastic hardens to a clear crystalline substance that must be ground to sweeten breads, cakes, and sweets (nowadays, also chewing gum and a distilled liquor, *masticha*): see Aglaia Kremezi, *The Foods of Greece* (New York, 1993), 36, 38.

103. Tannahill, *Food in History* (2d ed. [1988], p. 87) asserts that pepper was common in Greece by the fifth century B.C., citing Hippocrates' recommendation of its medicinal use as well as Theophrastos in the fourth, but much in the Hippocratic corpus postdates Hippocrates himself; use spread very slowly before the first century A.D. Plutarch, *Quaestiones convivales*, VIII, 9, 733, says many older people in his day couldn't tolerate it. The pepper favored in antiquity was the relatively milder "long" pepper. For a general overview of the ingredient, see Toussaint-Samat, *History of Food*, 490–85.

104. E. Lewis Sturtevant's *Edible Plants of the World* (New York, 1972), lists eleven species of sumac used in different parts of the world from Asia to Persia and Turkey, the Mediterranean area, and North America. In the United States, *Rhus glabra* is called the vinegar tree. For the introduction of lemons first to Mesopotamia through Alexander the Great's transplantation of Asian plants, then to the wider Mediterranean world, see S. Tolkowsky, *Hesperides: A History of the Culture and Use of Citrus Fruits* (London, 1938); p. 100ff. combats the literature stemming from Gallesio and de Candolle which holds that lemons and oranges were unknown in the West before Arabs brought the first trees from India. Wilhelmina F. Jashemski has excavated roots of espaliered lemon trees in Pompeii and considers some of the same representations in painting and mosaic cited by Tolkowsky, confirming introduction in the course of the first century A.D. But no ancient author mentions any citrus but the citron (see below chap. 6, n. 9).

105. Ludwig von Edelstein, "Antike Diätetik," *Die Antike* 7 (1931): 255–70 (subsumed in *Ancient Medicine, Selected Papers*, ed. O. Temkin and C. L. Temkin [Baltimore, 1967]) points out the origins of this mind-set in doctrine that stems from Pythagoras, noting that dietetic resources, dominant in the Hippocratic corpus, are omitted in the oath taken by those who now receive the M.D. One hopes that increasing emphasis in our medical education will come to be placed on nutrition and dietetics as we continue to learn about their pathological implications.

106. Henry E. Sigerist, *A History of Medicine*, vol. 2: *Early Greek, Hindu and Persian Medicine* (Oxford, 1961), 236. Preserved fragments of a fourth-century regimen by Diokles of Carystos stress exercise and the advice to lie still in the mornings until sleep fully departs the body (ibid.,

238ff). This anticipates the modern medical caution reported in the media in 1986: be slow to awake and rise because statistics indicate most heart attacks occur at that point of transition in the morning.

107. Aristotle's doctrine of the elements and his extension of opposites into the realm of cooking anticipate for a modern reader the contrapositions of the structuralists: active heat and cold, passive moist and dry applied to the elements (chap. 1) and boiling versus roasting (a better cook then Lévi-Strauss, since he recognizes that boiling is more drying through drawing out the juices) and scalding opposite both (chap. 3); see *Metaphysics* and *De generatione et corruptione*.

108. *Problemata*, XXX, 1—see Sigerist, *A History of Medicine*, 2:324.

109. See the discussion below, chaps. 6 and 8, in relation to Roman and medieval foodways.

110. *On nutriment* (*peri trophēs*, 41), in the Hippocratic corpus, recommends different ways of preparing foods for variant age groups, whether youths, those in their prime, or elders. Robert Garland (*The Greek Way of Life*, 5–6) considers this in the context of general Greek regulation of society by age classes.

111. *Il Milione*, cap. cxlvii (of the island of Fansur in Indonesia): "Qui hae una grande maraviglia: ch'egli hanno farina d'albori, che . . . hanno la buccia sottile, e sono tutti pieni dentro di farina; e di quella farina si fanno mangiari di pasta assai e buoni"; Toussaint-Samat, in *History of Food*, cites the passage in her discussion of pasta through history, but does not go into the Hellenic background. For a well-researched article dealing with pasta, although leading to different conclusions from my own, see Charles Perry, "The Oldest Mediterranean Noodle: A Cautionary Tale," *Petits Propos Culinaires* 9 (1981): 42–45.

112. Watson, *Agricultural Innovation* (see above, n. 9).

113. A useful critical survey of a great deal of specialized literature to replace outdated texts on wheats (e.g., Naum Jasny, *The Wheats of Classical Antiquity* [Baltimore, 1944]) is found in Sallares, *Ecology*, 316–26.

114. Pliny, *NH*, XVIII, xxvii, 105, on "Parthian" bread (also called "water bread" because high liquid content made it spongey and full of holes), is sometimes interpreted to imply that this was distinctively able to float.

115. (New York, 1987), 105–7, "Origins of Pasta," apropos a recipe for *laganelle*. With a scholar's instinct she looked up the word *lagano* in the Gerhard Rohlfs's authoritative dictionary, *Vocabolario dei dialetti salentini* (2d ed., 3 vols.; Galatina, 1976).

116. Luigi Sada, "Spaghetti e compagni" (*Appunti di gastronomia*, no. 1 [1990]: 16–35) is fundamental to the discussion of both ancient and medieval pastas of the region he knows so intimately (his books on Pugliese cookery are classics in the field). His compromise entails an Arab invention of *dried* pasta as opposed to fresh.

117. The former is translated in Gulick's edition of Athenaeus as "wafer-bread" or, in one instance, "pan-cake"; the latter as "sesame cake," "seed-cake," "thin cake," and "meal-cake." Athenaeus also in one case (III, 113d) speaks of *artolaganon* (translated "wheat-wafer") with a little wine, pepper, milk, and a bit of oil or lard, while *kapyria*, called by the Romans *tracta*, are made by a similar mixture; baked, this might produce something like a matzo. When Aristophanes writes *lagana pettetai* (*Ecclesiazusai*, 843) it may be translated "wafers are baking," but *pettō* more generally means "cooking" and "boiling." The Roman equivalent is *laganum*, the apparent origin of *lasagna*.

118. In Puglia not only does the dialect and many foodways speak of the Greek heritage, but a group of villages in the area about Maglie speak *griko,* derived from ancient Hellenic speech rather than from Italian. See the appendix for an adaptation of *cicere e tria.*

119. P. Mingazzini, "Gli antichi conoscevano i maccheroni?" *Archeologia classica* 6 (1954): 292–94; cf. H. Blanck and G. Proietti, *La Tomba dei rilievi a Cervetri,* Studi di archeologia pubblicati dalla Soprintendenza archeologica per l'Etruria meridionale, no. 1 (Rome, 1986), 27; eleven lines divide the surface transversely.

120. C. Perry, "The Oldest Mediterranean Noodle," 42f., decrying the claim of the Museo Storico degli Spaghetti in Campodassio, Liguria, based on finds "in Etruscan kitchens" of iron pieces like knitting needles.

121. *Satire,* I, vi, 115–16: "inde domum me / ad porre et ciceris refero laganique catinum" [when I return home to my dish of leeks and chickpeas and lasagne].

122. Cited in the Hippocratic treatise on diet (ii, 56; iii, 80) and by Galen. The name implies pounding, and clearly among its many compounded ingredients were green herbs brayed in a mortar like "pesto"; see Pollux, *Onomasticon,* VI, 71.

123. Athenaeus, book II. Another word for fish pickle is *tarichos;* Gulick notes that *garos,* when distinguished from the former, seems to refer to the fishpaste eaten in Greece today [*tarama,* preserved gray mullet roe]—I would think it just the opposite, judging by linguistic tradition, although the roe is on the way to becoming boutargue like that we met in Egypt. On *garum,* see below, chap. 5.

124. Discussed in Athenaeus, III, 100c–101c, with a quote from Archestratos and other authors. It seems clear from one of them, Sopater, that the *vulva eiectita* was valued for its fetal contents (it is termed *kallikarpos,* "well-fruited," "fecund"; also "cheese-like").

125. For a comprehensive history of vegetarianism, East and West, in supremely readable form, I recommend Colin Spencer, *The Heretic's Feast: A History of Vegetarianism* (London, 1993). The chapter on Pythagoras and his inheritance is a very useful synthesis of much recondite material.

126. Athenaeus, II, 61c.

127. For example, Forbes, writing in Singer et al., *A History of Technology,* 2:120. On the difficulty of interpreting ancient names of genera, with specifc reference to Cucurbitaceae (gourds, wild watermelon, etc.), see Sallares, *Ecology,* 483, n. 117.

128. On melons, see Zohary and Hopf, *Domestication of Plants,* 167–68. The watermelon (*Citrullus lanatus*) was cultivated in Egypt at least from the second millennium B.C. Among the Cucurbitaceae, the melon (*Cucumis melo*) was also brought into cultivation relatively early in "Southwest Asia or Egypt" from wild forms that Zohary insists are native only in the Himalyas and adjacent areas eastward. Including both muskmelons and chate melons, the variables in the species may make it difficult to separate latter curved forms from cucumbers in Egyptian representations.

129. Theophrastos, VII, iv, 6; alexanders (*olusatrum*) or "horse-celery" was also used. Our own celery is a development of seventeenth-century horticulture; the ancient was more like smallage.

130. Alfred C. Andrews ("The Carrot as a Food in the Classical Era," *Classical Philology* 44 [1949]: 182–96), on purple carrots is now considered out of date by many scholars, who find the purple carrots of Afghanistan evolved without playing any part in the development of

European varieties (see Sallares, *Ecology*, 470, n. 397, with bibliography). Theophrastos (IX, xv, 5) does apply the adjective "blood-red" to *Daukon*, but the text is corrupt, and philologists believe the epithet belongs to another vegetable which has dropped out; however, at IX, xx, 2, he praises *Daukon* from Achaia that has a black root.

131. On the "artichoke" and cardoon, Athenaeus II, 70b–71f; Theophrastos, VI, iv, 10–11, a distinction being made from the stalk on which the artichoke head grows.

132. Among the best general works, see R. Billiard, *Le vigne dans l'antiquité* (Lyons, 1913); R. Dion, "La viticulture dans l'antiquité grecque," *Revue des deux mondes* (1952): 465–86; Mario Fregoni, *Origini della vite e della viticoltura: Contributo dei popoli antichi* (n.p., 1991).

133. Athenaeus, I, 28f, 30b–c,d and 31d–e. H. Warner Allen (*The Romance of Wine* [New York, 1932], 220–22) argued that Pramnian was probably like Tokay, made from grapes left to ripen on the vine until they almost become raisins, giving up a small quantity of their juice by their own weight before treading. This from adjectives used by Dioscurides, *protropos* and *prodromos* ("urged forward," "leading," in regard to wine, "self-propelled" or "squeezed"). William Younger (*Gods, Men and Wine* [see above, chap. 3, n. 11], 97f.) picks up on the concept of Pramnian as "raisin wine." Similar flow from unpressed grapes is recorded in the same Athenaeus passage for vines of Mytilene, but this would make a sweet, heavy wine and a fragment (Kock, *FGC*, 1:539, Ath. 30c) quoted from Aristophanes suggests that Pramnian was hard and dry to Athenian taste, "contracting the eyebrows as well as the bowels." Note, however, a late antique listing of grape varieties that includes Pramnian as type (Macrobius, *Saturnalia*, chap. 20, 7.

134. A. D. Fitton Brown, "Black Wine," *The Classical Review*, n.s., 12 (1962): 192–95. On the Greek perfection of earlier arts of viticulture—and on trade errors that eventually undermined the economic advantages of Greek wine exporters—see R. J. Forbes, in *Studies in Ancient Technology*, 3:111–20. He praises Theophrastos' observations on viticulture, not only in his *Enquiry into Plants*, but "even more fully" in *Causes of Plants* (also translated as *On the Life of Plants*), book III, 11–16.

135. Fitton Brown, "Black Wine," 193. Pliny (*NH*, XIV, 80) translates and adds black (*niger*), while Galen supplements *xanthos* and *eruthros* to Mnesitheus of Athens' *melas, leukos*, and *kirros*.

136. Athenaeus, I, 32a; the proportion is given as one pitcher of seawater to fifty of wine. For treatment by Romans to gain the effect of Chian or Cos wines, and special pains taken in gathering the water, see below, p. 185f. and note 106.

137. François Salviat, "Le vin de Thasos, amphores, vin et sources écrites," *BCH* Supplement 13 (1986), *Recherches sur les amphores grecques*, ed. J.-Y. Empereur and Y. Garlan (École française d'Athènes, Colloque internationale de Septembre 1984) for a discussion of the decree *I.G.* XII Suppl. 347, with bibliography. It dates from the end of the fifth century. See also Forbes, *Studies in Ancient Technology*, 3:112.

138. Theophrastos, *Concerning Odors* (Loeb edition of *Enquiry into Plants and Minor Works* . . . 2:372), 51, quoted in Athenaeus, I, 32a, saying that the wine had a wonderfully delightful quality flavor from being thus specially seasoned. The context is imparting fragrance or sweetness to wines by admixture of perfume such as rosewater. In the same passage he goes on to discuss the blending of wines. Perhaps the Thasians served their prytany new wine rather than their

aged vintages (cf. Athenaeus I, 29c, praising Thasian of many years). Forbes (ibid.), however, does not believe that Greek wines were ever older than four or so years.

139. Athenaeus, I, 29e, attributed to Hermippus.

140. See Pliny, *NH*, XIV, 98ff. on artificial wines. Note that for the Greeks chilling with snow entailed either direct admixture or use of a special vessel, a *psykter*, floated in the mixing krater.

141. *De materia medica*, V, 6–7; see J. R. Riddle, *Dioscorides on Pharmacy and Medicine* (Austin, Tex., 1985), 144, citing Jerome O. Nriagu, *Lead and Lead Poisoning in Antiquity* (New York, 1983), 350.

CHAPTER FIVE

1. "Antiochou . . . [h]upodochas epoieito kath' [h]ēmeran ochlikas; en [h]ais chōris tōn analiskomenōn kai ekphatnizomenōn sōreumatōn [h]ekastos apephere tōn [h]estiatorōn [h]olomelē krea chersaiōn te kai ptnēnōn kai thalattiōn zōōn adiaireta eskeuasmena, [h]amaksan plēpōsai dunamena; kai meta tauta melipēktōn kai stephanōn ek smurnēs kai libanōtou sun andromēkesi lēmniskōn chrusōn pilēmasin plēthē." Gulick makes the point in his notes to the passage that what I render as "hearth fires" implies a method of cooking that is a barbecueing. The Seleucid king he names is Antiochus VII Euergetes; since the text specifies the Antiochos who fought against the Mede Arsaces, this could with better reason refer to the Seleucid ruler of Syria who was successful in his campaign, Antiochos III, the Great, of the later third century B.C.

2. Among the most perceptive considerations of fourth-century society and *mentalité*, succinctly but admirably expressed, are those of Blanche R. Brown in her study of the sculptures of the Temple of Asklepios at Epidauros, *Anticlassicism in Greek Sculpture of the Fourth Century B.C.* (New York, 1973; see especially her last chapter, "*Polis* and the People"), and of J. J. Pollitt in his survey of art criticism in antiquity, *The Ancient View of Greek Art* (New Haven, 1974), 29–31.

3. Pliny (*NH*, XXXII, xxi, 63) echoes the writers of Alexander's expedition and compares the *tridacna* oyster of his own day that took three bites to consume. For the lost observations of Nearchos, who led the sea contingent back from India, and of others, Arrian's *Indica* (Loeb Library edition, ed. P. A. Brunt, vol. 2), Theophrastos (*Enquiry into Plants*), and Strabo's *Geography*, bk. XV, are the best sources. On the medieval tradition of Alexander's purported letter to Aristotle on the marvels of India, see Lynn Thorndike, *A History of Magic and Experimental Science* (New York, 1923), chap. 24, 1:555 and n. 2.

4. Strabo, *Geography*, XV, i, 20, quoting Eratosthenes of the Alexandrian Library. In XV, ii, 10, he mentions silphium at the borders of Bactria.

5. The Seleucids had succeeded in rice cultivation in Lower Syria and Babylonia by the time Rome conquered them (ibid., XV, i, 18). On the royal botanical garden experimenting with fruit trees in Ptolemaic Egypt, see T. C. Skeat, *Greek Papyri in the British Museum*, vol. 7, *The Zenon Archives* (London, 1974), no. 59156.

6. Arrian, *Anabasis*, V, 1, 3–7.

7. Edward Hyams, *Dionysus: A History of the Wine Vine* (London, 1987), 250, points out that

Bactria (partly modern Afghanistan) at the north of India was indeed one of the original sources for wild vines. On oriental species, cf. his p. 232. On Seleucid attempts to acclimatize new vines, see Claire Préaux, *Le monde héllenistique* (Paris, 1987), 2:477, and n. 1 to Strabo, XV, iii, 11.

8. Préaux, *Le monde héllenistique*, 476; Préaux makes the point that newly acclimated plants tended to be of the luxury variety, except for new varieties of early wheat that could facilitate two harvests a year. Strabo speaks of an Indian grain, smaller than wheat, called *bosmoron;* judging by its name it should be a fodder plant, but Strabo (XV, i, 18) says it was roasted when threshed and workers were made to swear not to carry any away unroasted, to prevent the export of seed. What was this grain? akin to teff?

9. Peter Garnsey, *Famine and Food Supply in the Graeco-Roman World: Responses to Risks and Crisis* (Cambridge, 1988), 163. Cf. Dominic Rathbone, "Grain Trade and Grain Shortages in the Hellenistic East," in P. Garnsey and C. R. Whittaker, eds., *Trade and Famine in Classical Antiquity* (Cambridge Philological Society, suppl. 8; Cambridge, 1983), 45–55. "On Hellenistic *euergetism,* munificent charity, and its origins, see Paul Veyne, *Bread and Circuses: Historical Sociology and Political Pluralism* (London, 1990), [abridged from *Le pain et le cirque* (1976)], chap. 2, secs. 3, 4, and 5.

10. For example, Dikaiopolis in Aristophanes' *Acharnians* (lines 86–89) cannot believe the assertion of ambassadors returned from the Persian court that they were served whole roast oxen *(ek kribanou bous).*

11. Phylarchos in Athenaeus XII, 539d, going on to report a dining pavilion with space for 100 couches, supported by golden uprights that seems to be based on tales of Alexander's mise-en-scène for the wedding for himself and many of his Macedonians who took Persian brides when Alexander added the daughters of Darius and of Artaxerxes to his polygamy (Athenaeus XII, 538b–c and others).

12. Often quoted, but best considered by Andrew Dalby, "The Wedding Feast of Caranus the Macedonian by Hippolochus," *Petits Propos Culinaires* 29 (1988): 37–45. There was a Caranus among the companions of Alexander, but I find myself wondering whether scribal error masks the name Ceraunos ("Thunderbolt"), the occasion being the ill-starred wedding of Ptolemy Ceraunos with Arsinoë II when he succeeded in usurping the Macedonian throne (281–80 B.C.)

13. As early as Herodotos, Greeks marveled at the munificence of Xerxes in gift-giving on his birthday (*Histories,* IX, 110, i) and Athenaeus (IV, 146b–c), comparing Euhippos on Alexander, cites historians who reckoned that the Great King, being accustomed to dine with 15,000 retainers, spent 400 talents per banquet (a sum Gulick evaluated as $600,000 in 1960s dollars).

14. It seems to me that the discrepancy might be explained by the fact that each diner was accompanied by slaves who stood behind his couch and to whom foods were handed back in profusion. If each brought six such servitors and bodyguards for their return, the second number could also be explained.

15. My colleague Richard Hamilton is working on inventories of temples on the sacred island of Delos from the fourth through the second centuries B.C. In one instance, two items called "a basket of Ptolemy" are listed. No indication of which Ptolemy, but ivory and precious

metal baskets and "bread-racks" mentioned in the description of Caranos' banquet give assurance that such mundane objects were worthy of dedication among the treasures of deities.

16. Macedonians were famous among the Greeks for their intemperance and love of unwatered wine. For questions of Macedonian symposia, see Eugene N. Borza, "The Symposium at Alexander's Court," *Archaia Makedonia: Ancient Macedonia* (Thessalonika, 1983), 45–55 and R. A. Tomlinson, "Ancient Macedonian Symposia," *Archaia Makedonia: Ancient Macedonia* (Thessalonika, 1970), 308–15.

17. The estimate of E. E. Rice, *The Great Procession of Ptolemy Philadelphus* (Oxford Classical and Philosophical Monographs) (Oxford, 1983), assuming that it did not continue after darkness.

18. Rice (ibid., 63f.) points out the fondness for mechanical inventions of the type of these activated statues, citing Ktesibos' ingenuities and the snail made for Demetrius of Phaleron that left a trail of mucus as it moved along (Polybius XII.13.11).

19. For more recent reconstructions than this one by Studniczka (*Abhandlungen der sächsischen Akademie der Wissenschaften* [1914]: 1–188), see Eugenia Salza Prina Ricotti, "Le tende conviviali e la tenda di Tolomeo Filadelfo," in *Studia Pompeiana et Classica in Honor of Wilhelmina Jashemski*, ed. R. I. Curtis (New Rochelle, N.Y., 1988), 2:199–239, with other modern bibliography. She places the pavilion in the context of Xerxes' domical *ouraniskos* in imitaton of the heavens, set in a square field with recesses on three sides. One should follow the symbolism as well in Karl Lehmann, "The Dome of Heaven," *Art Bulletin* 27 (1945): 1–54.

20. See also above, p. 89 and note 28. Archestratos recommends cumin for a *mētra* in addition to vinegar and silphium (for which we must substitute asafoetida).

21. Theophrastos I, 6, 9 is cited in Athenaeus' (II, 62) discussion of *[h]ydna*, apparently subscribing to the connection with thunder.

22. Attribution of the lost original is due to Pliny, *NH*, XXXI, 184. On the interpretation of different fragmentary mosaic copies, the most famous of which came with Lateran collections to the Vatican, see Klaus Parlasca, "Das pergamenische Taubenmosaik und der sogenannte Nestor Becker," *JdI* 78, no. 1 (1963): 256–93 and in opposition to his funerary interpretation, H. Meyer, "Zu neueren Deutungen von Aserōtos Oikos und kapitolinischem Taubenmosaik," *Archäologische Anzeiger* 92, no. 2 (1977): 104–10. Examples besides the Lateran are found in Aquileia, and from Oudna and El Djem in Tunisia; L. Foucher, "Une mosaïque de triclinium trouvée à Thysdrus," *Latomus* 20 (1961): 291–97, pls. XVII–XVIII (note his identification of okra, p. 293).

23. In the New York University campaign of 1949 we also unearthed one hand of the Nike; a gift was made of it to the Louvre.

24. Professor Rolf Winkes of Brown University has convinced me that those still-lifes set out on paired stone steps as in our illustrations do represent recipes for particular dishes. *Xenia* may also show gift offerings of hospitality not to the gods, but to house-guests who are invited to fix food for themselves on a portable brazier.

25. Axionicus in "The Chalcidian": Koch, *FGC* 2:415, Athenaeus, III, 95c.

26. On the dual significance of the stelai and close analysis of various examples, see Rhea A. Thönges-Stringaris, "Das griechische Totenmahl," *Athenische Mitteilungen* 80 (1965): 1–99; on the "standard" cakes in ancient bibliography, ibid., p. 19. For the *puramous* of roasted wheat

soaked in honey used as prizes in religious vigil, Athenaeus XIV, 647c after Iatrokles; also III, 114b for their sesame seed ingredient.

27. See the article in Pauly-Wissowa, *RE*, 2:1, col. 331f. (#31 of the name); Athenaeus I, 5b; III, 111c; IV, 171b; IX, 387c,d; XIV, 662d–f, and 663c,d, for example.

28. On this point, Charles Singer, "The Herbal in Antiquity and its Transmission to Later Ages," *JHS* 47 (1927): 1–52, p. 3f. on Nikander and the Alexandrian School ca. 200 B.C.; p. 5 on Mithradates VI, himself a herbalist, and the source for an antidote against poison, the medieval "mithradate" or theriac.

29. See Athenaeus IV, 155d (*FHG* 2:476, "Agatharcides") on symposion nibbles encased in gold that was removed to eat things like figs, raisins, or nuts, and then wantonly tossed aside.

30. Pliny, IX, lviii, 119; Macrobius, *Saturnalia*, III, xvii, 15–18; John of Salisbury, *Polycraticus*, VIII, 7, 732c–d (vol. 199 in Migne).

31. H. Rackham, the editor of the Loeb Library edition of Pliny, noted that no vinegar strong enough to dissolve a pearl exists—that Cleopatra must have swallowed knowing the jewel could be recovered later. However, B. L. Ullman produced a witty and learned article about his experiment proving a pearl *will* dissolve if pulverized and noting the alleged strength of Egyptian vinegar (Pliny, XIV, 103 and Athenaeus II, 67c) as well as the efficacy of its lime as an antacid after Antony's and Cleopatra's indulgence; see "Cleopatra's Pearls," *The Classical Journal* 52 (1957): 193–201.

CHAPTER SIX

1. *Antiquitates culinariae; or, Curious Tracts Relating to the Culinary Affairs of the Olde English* [1791] (London, 1981), iv.

2. Essay, "Garum," in the collection, *Serve it Forth*, originally published in 1937, but appearing in numerous collected editions from 1954 to the present.

3. This does not mean that no one used emetics, just as the Greeks or other peoples of antiquity had resorted to them (see chapter 2, on Egypt, for example). The idea that Romans particularly indulged was probably picked up in secondary sources from the biography of the despicable Emperor Vitellius written by Suetonius (and later Latin authors), cap. XIII, then generalized and repeated in derivative literature. Cicero, in a letter to his friend Atticus, says something similar about Caesar (xiii, 52).

4. *L'arte del convito nella Roma antica* (Rome, 1983), is her general study; but it is her article on the kitchens of Pompeii and Herculaneum which discusses this point: "Cucina e quartieri servili in epoca romana," *Rendiconti Pontificia Accademia Romana di Archeologia* 1978/79 (1980–81): 238ff. My figure 81 reveals the contrast between a Pompeian *bancone* and an arrangement for receiving large cauldrons over direct flames at the House of the Messii, Vaison, France.

5. Often expressed in terms of conquest never undertaken for its own sake, but only to come to the aid of the oppressed. Cicero's *Tusculan Disputations* puts the values well (I, i, 2): "Nam mores et instituta vitae resque domesticas ac familiares nos profecto et melius tuemur et lautius, rem vero publicam nostri maiores certe melioribus temperaverunt et institutis et legi-

bus" (For morality, and the regulations of living, of the management of household and family, are truly upheld by us in a better and finer manner [than the Greeks, whom he has just admitted to excel in abstract studies, but not in Roman pursuits of engineering, law and war]; and unquestionably our ancestors duly established in affairs of government better practices and laws).

6. Livy, XXXIX, vi, 7–9, speaks of banquets becoming increasingly elaborate and extravagant in the first decades of the second century B.C., when the cook gained new status instead of being a lowly slave and his service came to be considered an art ("et quod ministerium fuerat, ars haberi coepta").

7. C. F. von Rumohr [a disciple of Hegel], *Geist der Kochkunst* [attributed to his cook, Joseph Koenig] (Stuttgart, 1822), now available in an English translation by B. Yeomans (London, 1993). Against his criticisms of Roman cuisine—that everything was drowned in sauces with too many ingredients, that no ingredient was permitted unless made unrecognizable: Jean-François Revel (*Culture and Cuisine: A Journey through the History of Food* [New York, 1982], 56), notes that they seem unjust if one thinks of Chinese arts of culinary surprise; yet he still apparently subscribes to the idea that natural savors were concealed.

8. Even authors of the best English translation of that surviving cookbook, Barbara Flower and Elisabeth Rosenbaum [Alföldi], *Apicius: The Roman Cookery Book* (London, 1958) [cited hereafter as Flower and Rosenbaum], write (p. 19): "the Romans abhorred the taste of any meat, fish or vegetable in its pure form. There is hardly a single recipe which does not add a sauce to the main ingredient which changes the original taste radically."

9. Philip Murray has produced a witty poetic translation of Martial, XI, 31: "Dinner at Milo's," *Arion* 2 (1963): 75f., together with several other selections.

10. Athenaeus, *Deipnosophists*, I, 7, d–e, after Euphron.

11. Augusto Campana discusses the discovery and diffusion of knowledge of Apicius in "Contributi alla biblioteca del Poliziano" (*Poliziano e il suo tempo: Atti del IV convegno internazionale di Studi sul Rinascimento, September 1954* [Florence, 1957]), 98–217. Poggio Bracciolini discovered a manuscript at Fulda in 1417, but it was not brought to Italy until 1455, when Enoch of Ascoli obtained it; the second ninth-century manuscript (now Vatican, Urb. lat. 1146) came into the hands of the Duke of Urbino. There are numerous copies after these, made during the fifteenth century; Angelo Poliziano collated both manuscripts (fragmentary autograph in Leningrad), and another Vatican example, Vat. lat. 6337, is said to derive directly from his own copy.

12. See the bibliography, primary sources. The first discrimination of the various prototypes that are used by the Late Antique compiler was worked out by E. Brandt, *Untersuchungen zum römischen Kochbuch* (*Philologus* 19, no. 3 [Leipzig, 1927]). The recipe numbers used in my text are those of Schuch, as in the Guégan translation of Apicius and that of Flower and Rosenbaum.

13. Elagabalus (emperor executed A.D. 222) has been taken as the subject of a recipe à la Varius because of a family name from his father, Varius Marcellus, as well as his reputation for gluttony and extravagant cuisine: see, for example, Revel, *Culture and Cuisine*, 49. However, the recipe might more plausibly refer to L. Varius Rufus, a poet of the Augustan period who was a friend of Virgil, Horace, and Maecenas; he may well be the Varius who participated in Horace's 'Feast of Nasidienus' (see below, p. 166f.).

14. Seneca, consolation of his mother, *Ad Helviam*, 10, 8. The most valuable survey of all references to Apicius is to be found in the edition of his work by Jacques André, *Apicius: L'art culinaire* (Paris, 1965) [cited hereafter as André]. References in Pliny include: *NH*, VIII, lxxvii, 209; IX, xxx, 66; X, lxviii, 133; XIX, xli, 137, 143. A scholiast to Juvenal, *Satires*, IV, 23 wrote: "Apicius auctor praecipiendarum cenarum, qui scripsit de iuscellis" (that Apicius was the author of preparing dinners, who wrote [also, a book] on sauces). Athenaeus, I, 7a, 647c, muddied waters that have made some authors speak of three Apicius figures.

15. My authority for this is my colleague, Darby Scott.

16. Pliny, in one passage, does apply the word *gurges* to Apicius. For Tertullian, see *Apologia*, iii, 6 in Migne, ser. 1, vols. 1–2 (1884). Isidore of Seville in his seventh-century dictionary, gives Apicius grudging admiration as the *fons et origo* of Roman cookery, praising his inventiveness: *Originum* XX, i, 1: "coquinae apparatum Apicius quidam primus composuit."

17. This anecdote comes from Athenaeus; might it be apocryphal? like his story of confused chronology that Apicius—active in the period of Tiberius (Emperor A.D. 14–37)—devised a special packing that enabled Trajan, in the early second century A.D., to receive fresh oysters while on campaign in distant Parthia. If such anachronism merely reflects some device à la Apicius, or attributed to his savoir faire, it could of course be true.

18. Seneca, *Epistle* XCV, 42. On the Republican and Early Imperial "craze" for such mullets, see A. C. Andrews, *Classical Weekly* 42 (1948–49): 186ff. By the later Empire, Galen's advice that their quality was better when they were small had carried the day. Seneca elsewhere, and Galen as well, testify to the gastronomic diversion produced in the days of conspicuous consumption: because these fish went through kaleidoscopic changes of color as they died, hosts entertained their guests by enclosing them in glass vessels to watch the changing hues as they expired before being cooked.

19. See Joan Liversidge, "Roman Kitchens and Cooking Utensils," in Flower and Rosenbaum, 36, with the note by the authors on p. 133. There seems no reason to serve a dish of legumes in a shell-shaped vessel; I prefer to stick with the *Thesaurus linguae latinae* and most Latin dictionaries in deriving the name *conchicla* from the word for a bean with its pod *(conchis)*; peas and beans were not so systematically distinguished in antiquity when "bean" *(fabia)* could also be *phaseolus* or *dolichos* (the latter today supplanted by New-World "field peas," "black-eyed peas").

20. One might think of "offal" in this connection. but several recipes in this category refer to "boning" as well as "skinning" the pieces.

21. André, nos. 430–432.

22. The *patina* uses fish called *apua* which can be any of a variety of small fish, including anchovies. In André's edition the recpe is no. 139.

23. *L'arte del convito*, 233. She translates into Italian passages from the *Geoponika* (XX, xlvi, 1ff.) and Gargilius Martialis (lxii), pp. 225f.

24. See especially Robert I. Curtis, "The Garum Shop of Pompeii (Reg. I.xii.8)" *Croniche Pompeiane* 5 (1982): 5–23. For inscriptions on the vials, see *CIL*, 4:172ff., 2574–76. Curtis argues that production of *garum* rather than mere seasoning of it might have been carried on at Pompeii, downplaying any potential stench; cf. a report in the *New York Times*, 12 September 1977, on the pervasive odor engulfing an entire area around a Vietnamese site where *nuoc-mam* was fermented.

25. See above, p. 150; the pun has led many translators of Martial to make his passage about Apicius read not "of the allies," but "sauce made of its fellows."

26. On *garum* see the bibliography, in particular M. Ponsich and M. Tarradell, *Garum et industries antiques de salsaison dans la Méditerranée occidentale* (Bordeaux, 1965), which subsumes earlier studies.

27. "Some Account of the Cuisine Bourgeoise of Ancient Rome," *Archaeologia* 41 (1866): 283–324.

28. "Echinis salsis liquamen optimum admisces, et quasi recentes apparebunt, ita ut a balneo sumi possint." Flower and Rosenbaum (and André, where the recipe is no. 419) translate this in terms of their consumption "after the bath," i.e., as an appetizer to begin the daily *cena*); cf. Coote, p. 319.

29. The text is corrupt. Brandt and others propose to read *picas* (pitch), while others, including André, restore *spicas* meaning 'spikenard.'

30. André's edition, no. 152. For a succinct discussion and accurate assemblage of citations on *garum/liquamen*, see his *L'alimentation et la cuisine à Rome* [1961] (2d ed., Paris, 1981), 195–98.

31. C. Jardin, "Garum et sauces de poisson de l'antiquité," *Rivista di Studi Liguri* 27 (1961): 70–96; as supporting evidence he makes much of the popularity of Iskander as a name for Malay boys in souvenir of the great conqueror.

32. André, no. 141.

33. Brandt, *Untersuchungen zum römischen Kochbuch,* 126, was the first to point this out; see also Flower and Rosenbaum, 101.

34. André, no. 133.

35. Ibid., no. 126.

36. Wealthy Romans also frequently included ice and snow storage spaces in their villas; for a vault apparently used as such at Hadrian's Villa at Tivoli, see Salza Prina Ricotti, *L'arte del convito,* fig. 82, and p. 158 citing Martial (*Epigrams,* V, lxiv), on summer snow used to cool Falernian wine; this conclusion is based on her archaeological study in *Les cryptoportiques dans l'architecture romaine* (Rome, 1973), 246–48, pl. 13.

37. André, *L'alimentation,* 115, n. 21, takes *apri glandulas* in an epigram of Martial as the filet mignon; W. A. Ker, in the Loeb edition, translates: "the kernel of a boar." But, cf. Leslie D. Johnston in *Classical Philology* 49 (1954): 244–49, and the convincing argument of O. J. Todd, "Frustum Porcinum," *Classical Philology* 47 (1952) that 'sweetbreads' is meant by *glandulae* (as in Pliny, *NH,* XI, lxvi, 175: "Tonsillae in homine, in sue glandulae" [man has tonsils, the pig glands]).

38. André, no. 167.

39. Ibid., no. 196.

40. Bk. VIII, i, 8: Mix pepper, lovage, cumin, dill seed, thyme, oregano, a little asafoetida, a good measure of rue [rocket] seed; add wine, a few pot herbs, onion, hazelnuts or toasted almonds, dates, honey, vinegar, a little more wine, color with boiled-down grape or fig juice; add *liquamen* and olive oil.

41. André, no. 271; bk. VII, v, 2 also evidences its source by precise quantities.

42. Emily Gowers's *The Loaded Table* (Oxford, 1993), deals with poetic texts, especially satire, that seem to encode their own stylistic message in the meals which they describe.

43. Actually a circular platform on which the diners slowly revolved, much like some of our tower restaurants today; one can make out its outline in the center of the floor of this octagonal, complex space. Suetonius (Nero, 31) tells of the main banqueting hall revolving night and day like the heavens, but in modern literature the motion is sometimes mistakenly attributed to the ceiling: see William L. MacDonald, *The Architecture of the Roman Empire* (New Haven, 1982), 1:42 and pls. 29–34 for the octagon. For a reconstruction, P. Mingazzini, "Tentativo ricostruzione grafica della 'coenatio rotunda' della Domus Aurea," *Quaderni dell'Istituto di Storia dell'Architettura*, fasc. 31–48 (1961): 21–26.

44. *Epistulae morales*, ed. R. M. Gummere (Loeb Classical Library [1971]), vol. 3, no. 95, a letter that expresses his puritanical, Stoic disgust with such delicacies as oysters and *garum*; in line 26f. he speaks of a *patina* composed of many ingredients (it sounds like Apicius' "Delights of Baiae," for which see our recipe appendix): "People mix many flavors into one, so the dinner table takes over the work of the stomach. Next I anticipate food being served already chewed since the cook performs the task of teeth. . . . No vomited food could be so much of a mishmash."

45. Doro Levi, *Antioch Mosaic Pavements* (Princeton, 1947), 1:127ff., from the House of the Buffet Supper. The courses of the meal are set out on a semicircular table of a type that responded to a sigma-shaped couch for diners that became ever more popular during the Empire, until it became the form of choice in late antiquity.

46. The mosaic is of a late period in the third or early fourth century A.D. when we might expect an artichoke to have been developed from the thistle. For earlier Romans the *cardui* of choice would have been cardoons, a favored vegetable in colonial America now difficult to find outside of Italian markets.

47. Faya Causey Frel, "A *Larva Convivialis* in the Getty Museum," *The J. Paul Getty Museum Journal* 8 (1980) reproduces two skeletons in bronze (Munich and Dresden [our fig. 89]); she notes others in bronze, one in wood in Berlin, and a silver example in Naples.

48. Salza Prina Ricotti, "Il ferculum dello Zodiaco," *Rendiconti Pontificia Accademia Romana di Archeologia* 55–56 (1983–84): 245–64, discusses the 'showpiece' that might have been used to present this complex dish (*Satyricon*, bk. xxxi), together with cognate archaeological material; her figures 12–14 give hypothetical reconstructions with all the delicacies ranged around a celestial hemisphere. For ways to incorporate the punning viands, see the menu and recipes in our appendix.

49. Pliny's passage goes on to estimate the inflation rate of the Opimian vintage, so famous that its name was given to all wines produced by that exceptional summer's heat, which 'cooked' the juice in the grapes, regardless of region or type of vine. See H. C. Schnur, "Vinum Opimianum," *Classical Weekly* 50 (1952): 122–23. On wine cellars in Roman villas, see H. Thédenat, *Pompei* (Paris, 1928), 104.

50. *Vitellius*, 13. The *patina*, called 'the Shield of Minerva,' featured brains of peacock and pheasant, blended with lamprey roe, nightingale's tongues and other exotic ingredients. According to Pliny (*NH*, XXXV, 165) it cost a million sesterces and one needed a special oven for it. It is not imperial propaganda *per se* that we should resist, showing off the breadth and diversity of foodstuffs from every corner of the realm, but the particular ingredients chosen to denigrate Vitellius. See Aulus Gellius, VI, xvi (*The Attic Nights of Aulus Gellius*, ed. J. C. Rolfe (Loeb

Classical Library [1960], vol. 2), quoting a satire of Varro and castigating the gluttony that constantly searched out new flavors and dainties from everywhere: "a peacock from Samos, a woodcock from Phrygia, cranes from Media, a kid from Ambracia, a young tuna from Chalcedon, a lamprey from Tartessos, cod from Pesinus, oysters from Tarentum, cockles from Sicily, a swordfish or sturgeon *(helops)* from Rhodes, a pike from Cilicia, nuts from Thasos, dates from Egypt, acorns from Spain."

51. Macrobius, *Saturnalia,* III, xiii, 12, apparently hosted by Lentulus.

52. Cf. Apicius IX, xiv, no. 444, *embractum Baiaenum* ("delights of Baiae"), and our recipe appendix.

53. Like the passage quoted in our note 5, this passage (*de senectute,* 45) embodies Cicero's political and social conservatism; cf. a letter (*Ad familiares,* IX, 24, 3). John D'Arms has written appreciatively of the more egalitarian aspects of Roman conviviality as well; see his "The Roman *Convivium* and the Idea of Equality," in *Sympotica,* ed. Oswyn Murray (see chap. 4, n. 61), 308–20.

54. According to Suetonius, II, *76–77,* Augustus disliked rich foods, was abstemious at dinner parties (accepting only a slice of bread dipped in cold water, or a slice of cucumber or heart of lettuce, or an unripe apple!), and as host, gave dinners of but three courses — or, "at most six." Today we read of his modest table habits and preference for coarse bread, farmer's fresh cheese, and small fishes with knowledge of his canny political enactment of wrapping his new powers in the fiction of a return to time-honored moral principles of the republican past. But Suetonius (70) also cites an equally politicized charge of Mark Antony's supporters concerning a private banquet at which Augustus appeared as Apollo in portrayal of the twelve Olympian gods and goddesses at dinner, introducing novel debaucheries. The extravagance of Nasidienus' wild boar is underlined by a notice in Pliny (*NH,* VIII, lxxviii, 210) and Varro of how recent was the origin of serving one entire; the first to do so was P. Servilius Rullus, moneyer in 89 B.C.

55. H. Helbaek, "Vegetables in the Funeral Meals of Pre-urban Rome" (appendix I in E. Gjerstad, *Early Rome,* 2:287–94), discusses the finds from tombs of these early Romans in the Forum Romanum. In addition to the grains named, plus millet, he identifies fava bean and grass-peas; seeds of white beam (a tree related to the rowan and bearing red berries), indicated to him that "the Iron Age cook was able to flavour the insipid farinaceous food" even before Etruscans brought cultivation of the grape.

56. Horace, *Epistles,* II, i, 156.

57. Pliny, *NH,* XVIII, v, 22. Varro (*Rerum rusticarum,* I, i, 10) reports versions of Mago in Greek as well as Latin. The dates of Mago are uncertain (see Klotz,"Mago," no. 15, in Pauly-Wissowa, *RE,* 27, col. 506f.) but the weight of opinion now rests on third century B.C.

58. The earliest biographical material on Cato is to be found in Polybius, the Greek historian of the second century B.C.; Plutarch devotes one of his *Lives* to him. Modern literature includes Francesco della Corte, *Catone Censore: La vita e la fortuna* (Florence, 1969), and Alan E. Astin, *Cato the Censor* (Oxford, 1978).

59. Apuleius, *Apologia,* 39.

60. See especially H. Dohm, *Mageiros: Die Rolle des Kochs in der griechisch-römischen Komödie* (Munich, 1964).

61. For Emily Gowers, *The Loaded Table*, these writers are less to be read as clues to dining habits than as exemplars of the manner in which food is manipulated to express personal aesthetics and encode each author's literary style and personality.

62. Livy XXXIX on the investigation; cf. A. Bruhl, *Liber Pater, origine et expansion du culte dionysiaque à Rome* (Bib. Écoles françaises, clxxv [1953]), 82ff.

63. For example, the Lex Orchia of 182/1 B.C., the Lex Fannia of 161 stipulating the amount of money that might be spent on ordinary days or for special holidays like the Saturnalia, the Lex Didia of 143 reaffirming such restrictions — an indication perhaps that they had not been stringently enforced? — the Lex Aemilia of 115 on imported animals, certain seafood, and dormice (repeated in 78 B.C.); the Lex Licinia of 97 B.C. updated the Orchia, while a Sullan law permitted a special sum of 200 sesterces for a nuptial banquet and defined the weight of meat and charcuterie that could be served (by the time of Augustan inflation banquet expenses on occasion of marriage were raised to 1,000 sesterces). All this we learn from a report of Aulus Gellius (*Attic Nights*, II, 24). A persuasive argument by Guido Clemente ("Le legge sul lusso e la società romana tra III e II secolo A.C.," in *Società Romana e produzione schiavistica*, vol. 3 [Bari, 1981]) holds that the intent was not to combat social change, but to utilize it by deemphasizing private luxury in favor of public prodigality as sops to the lower classes.

64. For this important change, see Joan M. Frayn, "Home-baking in Roman Italy," *Antiquity* 52 (1978): 28–32. It is striking that in Ostia, the port city of Rome, only three or so chambers that can definitely be established as kitchens have been found in apartment houses of the Imperial period: see James E. Packer, *The Insulae of Imperial Ostia* (*MAAR*, XXXI), 1971, who allows only the Casa delle volte dipinte.

65. Such ancestors became almost legendary — and were already worshipped in family cult observance and flaunted at funerals of those of rank by clan members outfitted in costume and mask to enact them.

66. Pliny *NH*, IX, lxxix, 168: "before the Marsian war," 91–88 B.C.; cf. Columella, *De re rustica*, VIII, xvi, 5ff., who goes on to recommend turning a country estate to profit by installing fishponds, since the moral sense concerning delicacies has been blunted by his day in the first century A.D. John D'Arms has elucidated in several of his writings the benefits of adding fish-raising ponds or oyster beds to one's seaside villa, see especially, *Commerce and Social Standing in Ancient Rome* (Cambridge, Mass., 1981).

67. Pliny, *NH*, IX, lxxix, 170, going on to speak of one villa owned by Lucullus near Naples where he built a fishpond at greater expense than for the house, cutting a channel through a mountain to reach the sea and causing Pompey to compare him to Xerxes because the Persian king had once cut passage for his fleet through Mount Athos.

68. Cato was already astonished that fish cost more than an ox, according to Plutarch (*Quaestiones conviviales*, IV, iv, 668). For Diocletian's price controls, see S. Lauffer, *Diokletians Preisedikt* (Berlin, 1971), section 4, 1a and 4, 5; cf. 5, 1, 2 (most expensive of all are the oysters, 6).

69. A revealing study of Roman attitudes toward nature emerges in a study of the poet Statius by Zoe Pavlovskis, *Man in an Artificial Landscape* (Leiden, 1973).

70. See A. W. Van Buren and R. M. Kennedy, "Varro's Aviary at Casinum," *JRS* 9 (1919): 59–66; *Rerum rusticarum*, III, v, 8–17. For a summary of modern reconstructions, see Bertha Tilly, *Varro the Farmer* (London, 1973), 112–16, 283–89. One strolled or dined within netted

colonnades filled with birds, refreshed by running water in which ducks swam freely, while a domical pavilion sheltered a revolving table with everything at hand for the diners (within the dome, the morning star by day or evening star by night circled to provide the hour). In a preceding passage one of Varro's friends discusses how Lucullus tried to combine business with pleasure in such an *ornithon* at one of his villas, but diners were put off by the odor of so many bird droppings.

71. *Letters* bk. V, vi (vol. 1, p. 390 in the Loeb edition); his *stibadium*, or semicircular dining bench, is fronted by a marble basin of water and a fountain opposite, the complex arranged so that larger serving dishes filled with hors d'oeuvres may be placed about the margins, while smaller offerings sail about in imitation of little ships and waterfowl. A recent commentary subsumes earlier bibliography on Pliny's letters: Reinhard Fortsch, *Archäologischer Kommentar zu den Villenbriefen des jüngeren Plinius* (Mainz, 1993). In English: Helen Tanzer, *The Villas of Pliny the Younger* (New York, 1924), or, with more emphasis on the beguiling lifestyle, G. Bret Harte, *The Villas of Pliny the Younger, a Study of a Roman Gentleman* (Boston, 1928).

72. According to Pliny (*NH,* XV, xxx, 102), "Before the victory of Lucius Lucullus in the war against Mithradates, that is down to 74 B.C., there were no cherry trees in Italy. Lucullus first imported them from Pontus, and in 120 years they have crossed the ocean and got as far as Britain; but all the same no attention has succeeded in getting them to grow in Egypt." Pliny goes on to the varieties, naming at least six.

73. Plutarch's Life is the main source for information about Lucullus, including an anecdote about his dining alone; when he was served too modestly for his taste, Lucullus called his steward to complain and was told that it had not seemed necessary to put on a grand dinner and entertainment when there were to be no guests; "What, you did not know that tonight Lucullus was to dine alone with Lucullus?" This riposte may well have inspired Jefferson's well known *bon mot* about dining with himself.

74. Bk. XXXIX, vi, 9.

75. Columella, V, x, 9; XII, iv, 2: "C. Matius [et al.] quibus studium fuit pistoris et coqui nec minus cellarii diligentiam suis praeceptis instuere"; xlvi, 1: "ille enim propositum fuit urbanas mensas et lauta convivia instruere. libros tres edidit . . . Coci, et Cetarii, et Salgamarii." Cf. Pliny, *NH,* XII, vi, 13; XV, xv, 49. One wonders whether his instruction in cellar-keeping is not confused in Columella's second passage (*cetarii,* seafood sellers, for *cellarii*). A scholar once suggested that the person called Catius in Horace, *Satires,* II, iv, who delivers a hilarious lecture on cookery, is a parody of Matius: see A. Palmer, *The Satires of Horace* (London, 1891), 314. Pliny mentions his topiary and fruit trees; Apicius' recipe no. 168 is named for him.

76. Athens: Athenaeus, IV, 148b–c; the boar story is related in Plutarch's biography, after Philotas, liv. See above p. 158, and n. 54 on Rullus for a whole boar being proverbial for costliness at this period.

77. The grain of the *annona,* or *alimenta,* established in the late Republic, was later distributed in the form of loaves of bread, another sign of the demise of home baking. The often-reproduced Pompeian fresco interpreted as "The Seller of Bread" is discussed by Klaus-Peter Goethert ("Il panettiere—Zur Geschichte einer Fehldeutung," *Festschrift für Nikolaus Himmelmann* [Mainz, 1989], 385–88) as an aedile and two assistants engaged in distributing the *annona.*

78. For Aristotle and most Greek philosophers it was the heart which served these func-

tions of the senses. An exception was Alcmaeon, who is regarded as the founder of physiology by many historians of science; see Sigerist, *A History of Medicine* (see chap. 4, n. 106), 2:101f.

79. See chap. 8, pp. 243–46.

80. See George Sarton, *Galen of Pergamon* (Lawrence, Kans., 1954), 52ff. as a succinct account. The humors of the body—blood, phlegm, yellow bile, and black bile—were considered under Greek medicine, see above, p. 115.

81. Perceptive discussion of various aspects are to be found in the writings of John D'Arms, the work previously cited and "Control, Companionship, and *Clientela:* Some Social Functions of the Roman Convivial Meal," in *Échos du monde classique/Classical Views* 28 (1984): Studies in Roman Society, 327–48.

82. See M. Isenberg, "The Sale of Sacrificial Meat," *Classical Philology* 70 (1975): 271–73; John Scheid, "Sacrifice et banquet à Rome: Quelques problemes," *Mélanges-École française de Rome, Antiquité* 97 (1985); and Bruce Lincoln, "Of Meat and Society, Sacrifice and Creation, Butchers and Philosophy," and Carlo Santini, "Il lessico della spartizione nel sacrificio romano," in *L'uomo* 9 (1985): 9–19 and 63–73, on an altar in a market, the sale of meat from sacrifices, and especially the interconnection of banquet ritual and religious life.

83. On this "divisive dinner," see the close reading by Emily Gowers, *The Loaded Table,* 211–19.

84. After being suitably terrorized, the guests were brought back to a more enjoyable repast. This banquet gave birth to a historical series of imitators from the Renaissance to the nineteenth century; see my article, "The Black, or Hell Banquet," *Proceedings, Oxford Symposium 1990,* 55–57.

85. Actually the *sigma* couch, or *stibadium,* has a venerable tradition which goes back to ritual dining of worshippers at Greek sanctuaries, where the earliest forms were simply straw or foliage—ultimately cushioned—set out on the ground. For development of late antique ceremonial, see in general Sabine MacCormack, *Art and Ceremony in Late Antiquity* (Berkeley and Los Angeles, 1981); in specific reference to dining, Irving Lavin, "The House of the Lord: Aspects of the Role of Palace Triclinia in the Architecture of Late Antiquity and Early Middle Ages," *Art Bulletin* 44 (1962): 1–27, and Lise Bek, "Quaestiones conviviales: The Idea of the Triclinium and the Staging of Convivial Ceremonial from Rome to Byzantium," *Analecta Romana Institut Danici* 12 (1983): 81–107.

86. Romans seem even to have kept cows from calving, never breeding for milk production and depending upon goats and sheep for cheese-making; see André, *L'alimentation,* 151. Note that in the *Satyricon* Trimalchio's cook is able to make anything out of pork, from fish to chicken (70, 1–2).

87. On animal husbandry, as well as all aspects of Roman farming, see K. D. White, *Roman Farming* (Ithaca, N.Y., 1970); on sheep, pp. 301–12.

88. The recipe I have in mind, granted, is from late antiquity, but must surely reflect earlier practice: Anthimus (doctor to Theodoric, who flourished in the late fifth and early sixth century), *De observatione ciborum,* lii.

89. In certain areas, exemplary studies have been accomplished to answer such questions. See John D'Arms, *Romans on the Bay of Naples: A Social and Cultural Study of the Villas and Their Owners from 150 B.C. to A.D. 400* (Cambridge, Mass., 1970), passim.

90. On preservation methods for all kinds of meats, see André, *L'alimentation,* 141–43. He

cites a report not available to me of excavations at Nora in Sardinia which confirms a passage on salting meats in the *Geoponika* (xix, 9, 5) that enhances salting by drying, then resalting and insulating the pieces in grape seeds *(marc).*

91. Cato, *De re agricultura,* CIV; this was called *vinum familiae,* 'family' being taken as the *entire* household much as during the Italian Renaissance when this might mean hundreds of people. André, *L'alimentation,* 163, takes the conversion from quadrantal (8 *congii,* or roughly 2 cups) and *sextarii* as 260 liters of must to 52 each of reduced must and vinegar, 1,300 of fresh water and 35 from the sea.

92. André, as a Frenchman, takes particular note of this (ibid., 169).

93. A *modius* yielded 25 or 26 Roman pounds of bread, and it was in loaf form that it was distributed for those slaves who were unable to bake their own; cf. Antonietta Dosi and François Schnell, *A tavola con i Romani antichi* (Rome, 1984), 139–47 on nomenclature of bread according to types of flour and baking methods.

94. *Moretum,* 87–118 (ed. E. J. Kenney, *The Ploughman's Lunch: Moretum* [Bristol, 1984]); the lost work is cited by Macrobius (André, *L'alimentation,* 155). Ovid also refers to the mixture of cheese with pounded herbs as an old-time food, while Columella (XII, lix) gives a more complex recipe that is modernized by Salza Prina Ricotti (*L'arte dell'convito,* p. 289), as *formaggio condito,* with three others. For Margaret Visser's substantial discussion and further references, see her "Moretum: Ancient Roman Pesto," *Proceedings, Oxford Symposium 1992,* 263–74.

95. Roy W. Davies expands an article on military diet in *Britannia* 2 (1971): 122–42 into an authoritative contribution, "The Daily Life of the Roman Soldier," to *ANRW,* vol. 2, 1 *Principat,* 299–336 (food, 318ff.). For an example of how revealing the excavation of a military sewage ditch may be in terms of faecal matter and pollen, see J. H. Dickson and C. A. Dickson, "Flour or Bread in a Roman Military Ditch at Bearsden, Scotland," *Antiquity* 53 (1979): 47–51; in addition to seeds of figs and cereal grains, there was some evidence of flavoring with coriander and opium poppy seed (botanical analysis even yielded traces of the beetles that infested grain stores). See also, D. J. Breeze and Brian Dobson, *Hadrian's Wall* (London, 1978), 186; for an earlier period, J. Harmand, *L'armes et le soldat à Rome de 107 à 50 avant notre ère* (Paris, 1967), 193f.

96. For quartermaster stores and records on wood found at Vindolanda, see R. E. Birley, *Vindolanda, a Roman Frontier Post on Hadrian's Wall* (London, 1977). The Egyptian letters are summarized in Davies' article in *Britannia,* 134ff., after Michigan papyri published by C. C. Edgar, A. E. R. Boak, and J. G. G. Winter from 1931ff.

97. Of course, the finds do not preserve a true exchange among family members, simply generic requests from either population. *Tiphe,* the grain associated with Ethiopia nowadays, is currently enjoying a revival together with quinoa and amaranth.

98. Mark 15:36; Luke 23:36, taking the intention as torment; cf. André, *L'alimentation,* 172f. For another aspect of the mobility and ease of transport that this entailed: a modest amount of vinegar rather than a hundred times more wine.

99. Davies (see above, n. 95) calculates the annual need for grain as 2,032 tons per legion and 635 of barley for the horses.

100. For a modern evaluation of "circus" and festival in Roman political and social life, see Paul Veyne, *Bread and Circuses* (London, 1990), an abridged translation of Veyne's *Le pain et le cirque* (Paris, 1976).

101. R. E. Birley from excavations at Carpow, Perthshire, communicated by D. R. Wilson and R. P. Wright in *JRS* 53 (1963): 166, inscription no. 51 (on an amphora of the mixture), dating at the beginning of the third century A.D. For Neuss, see K. H. Knoerser, "Römerzeitliche Pflanzenfunden aus Neuss," *Novaesium* 4 (1970).

102. See Jacques André, ed., *Pline l'ancien: Histoire naturelle* (Paris, 1958); André Tchernia, *Le vin de l'Italie romaine* (École française de Rome, 1986). Tchernia's study began as a doctoral dissertation on amphora-handle stamps, but developed in true French regard for wine into a detailed investigation of all the features noted in my preceding sentence. There are of course numerous specialized studies, for which see the bibliography; in English there are two very readable, reliable general works with significant attention to antiquity: Edward Hyams, *Dionysus: A Social History of the Wine Vine* (London, 1965), 1987 and William Younger, *Gods, Men, and Wine* (London, 1966).

103. A sixteenth-century doctor believed that he could name the ancient wines corresponding to Italian ones of his own day—Alessandro Trajano Petronio, *de Victu Romanorum et de sanitate tuenda libri quinque . . .* (Rome, 1581; Italian ed., 1592).

104. There is still a white wine today bearing the name of ancient Falernum, but there is no reason to suppose that the grape is the same. The Massic among these Vesuvian wines is praised by Horace in several odes: III, xxi, its mellowness; II, xix.

105. Apparently the water was heated—see Horace, Ode III, xix, an invitation to a drinking bout in which the dilution specified by the drinking master will be by three or nine cups ("cyathi").

106. *De re agricultura*, CXII; Palladius' uncle kept the seawater three years before decanting and reducing it to two-thirds volume, closing it up again for three more years and then giving it another reduction to one-third. Note that in no case was it allowed to become stagnant, *pace* authors such as Giacosa (*A Taste of Ancient Rome* [Chicago, 1992], 194) to Cato CIV; his "old" simply refers to the process indicated above. Dosi and Schell (*A tavola con i Romani*, 182f.) discuss the seawater and other additives.

107. Palladius XI, xix; Pliny *NH*, XIV, xi, 82, also as "bee-wine," *apianum* (though 'muscatel' in modern languages derives from flies drawn to the sweetness of the grapes) comparable to fine *passum* from Crete.

108. The sixteenth-century antiquarian, Pirro Ligorio, writes in his Turin manuscripts (vol. 2, fol. 109f.) of ancient Roman cheeses still extant in modern days, gleaning their praise from the Poet Martial. These include Vestine and Trebulan from Sabine territory, and Luna from old Etruscan territory. The area of Parma was always a cheese-making center, and its inhabitants insist upon unbroken continuity of its production.

109. Wilhelmina F. Jashemski believes that it is possible to identify lemon-tree roots in casts taken at the House of Polybius at Pompeii ("The Gardens of Pompeii, Herculaneum and the Villas Destroyed by Vesuvius," *Journal of Garden History* 12 [1992]: 102–25, p. 109 on the espaliered potted plants in question). These might well be citron trees (?), treated as Pliny describes them (*NH*, XII, vii, 16). Domenico Casella has also recognized lemons among Pompeian still-lifes, just as he finds an even more problematic pineapple in one fresco (see his arguments, "La frutta nelle pitture pompeiane," in *Pompeiana: Raccolta di studi per il secondo centenario degli scavi di Pompei* [Naples, 1950], 355–86). Cf. Berthold Laufer, "The lemon in China and elsewhere,"

Journal of the American Orientaal Society 54 (1934): 43–160; this native of India is not supposed to have been cultivated even there before the 4th century A.D., later migrating westward with the Arabs.

110. *L'alimentation*, 48. His section on vegetables is particularly valuable, dealing even with the vexed question of identifying mushrooms the Romans consumed regularly, a difficult task before scientific taxonomic classification.

111. On pepper, see Pliny, XII, xiv, 26–27. A section on pepper appears in M. Toussaint-Samat, *History of Food*, 490–95. The milder white pepper, paradoxically, represents the seed of the ripe berry, decorticated, while the black is the dried immature fruit. On the spice trade of the Roman Empire, see J. I. Miller, *The Spice Trade of the Roman Empire, 29 B.C. to A.D. 641* (Oxford, 1969).

112. Trade histories of Dijon mustard insist upon the origin of production in that Burgundian city during Roman days, though it is more likely that Gallo-Roman cooks ground their seeds to need, as they did other spices. H. Gault and C, Milhaud, *Guide gourmand* (1970), 287, àpropos Dijon, write of Romans bringing the use of mustard to Gaul and note that Palladius, the son of a fourth-century prefect in the province, gives the first recipe. This is not quite accurate since Columella, in the first century, gives a different recipe than Palladius, who brays his mustard seeds and mixes them with honey, Spanish olive oil, and strong vinegar. Columella (*De re rustica*, XII, lvii) moistens the pounded mass of seeds, to which a few live coals have been applied, with sharp white vinegar, and substitutes crushed pine nuts and almonds for olive oil. Present Dijon mustard uses a medieval verjuice (acid juice of unripened grapes or other fruit) in place of vinegar.

113. Pliny speaks of the poppy seeds among such 'nibbles,' (*NH*, XIX, lv, 168); while Galen (XII, 8) attests to consumption of the hemp seeds. On uses of cannabis in cookery, see my article, "The Infamous Herb of 'Joyous Perfection:' *Cannabis sativa* in Cooking," *Proceedings, Oxford Symposium 1992*, 48–55, with bibliography.

114. Horace's Epode III, addressed to his patron and lover, Maecenas, is a notorious example of violent expression of distaste for the after-effect of eating "noxious" garlic, which elevated Romans apparently left to the lower classes. Gowers, *The Loaded Table*, chap. 5, devotes a special section to analysis of the poem and to "love-hate" relationships to the bulb.

115. I recommend a good variety (not Hertz) for a salad herb, especially if a few drops of tincture of asafoetida are in the dressing.

116. Pliny (*NH*, XII, xli, 83) cites authorities testifying to the enormous quantity Nero used at the funeral of Poppaea; in xliiff., he recalls the fantastic stories told by Herodotos about the origin of cinnamon and cassia, knows that they are false, and goes on to discuss the nature and qualities of these spices. According to him, a massive root of the shrub was to be seen in the Palatine Temple to Divus Augustus, while Vespasian dedicated crowns of cinnamon embossed with gold in the Temples of the Capitol and his own Temple of Peace (xlii, 94), all testimony to its exotic character.

117. For the importance of this principle, decorum, in the Italian Renaissance — gleaned not only from writers on rhetoric, but importantly from Vitruvius, *On Architecture,* see my introduction to Phyllis Pray Bober and Ruth Rubinstein, *Renaissance Artists and Antique Sculpture* (Oxford, 1986), pp. 37–40. On particular effects applied to the representation of divinities, see

Eugene Dwyer, "Decorum and the History of Style in Pompeian Sculpture," *Studia Pompeiana et Classica,* ed. R. I. Curtis (New Rochelle, N.Y., 1988), 105–25.

118. I use the categories of Demetrios, a Greek writer of the third or first century B.C., rather than the more generic types given by most writers in Latin: low or plain, middle or forcible, and high or florid; for Macrobius (*Saturnalia,* V, 1, 7), they are the copious, the short, the dry, and the florid or ornate.

CHAPTER SEVEN

1. On these topics, especially as they involve female saints, see Caroline Walker Bynum, *Holy Feast and Holy Fast: The Significance of Food to Medieval Women* (Berkeley and Los Angeles, 1987) and her bibliography.

2. *Poems and Letters,* ed. W. B. Anderson (2 vols.; Loeb Classical Library, 1936–65).

3. *Opere . . . ,* ed. A. Pastorino (Turin, 1971), Letter IX, to Paulus on oysters; as for his famous poem on the Moselle, Sister M. J. Byrne, *Prolegomena to an Edition of the Works of Decimus Magnus Ausonius* (New York, 1916), 31, pointed out that his friend Symmachus wrote Ausonius of his incredulity about the fish species cited (Epistle XIV in the *MGH,* vol. 6, pt. 2) and many of them are, indeed, marine creatures; remarks on Bordeaux appear in his *Ordo Urbium nobilium,* no. 20, and Epistle IX, 21 ("non laudatia minus nostri quam gloria vini"). A general view of the way in which these patricians seem to ignore the catastrophic changes taking place around them is vividly presented in Eileen Power's classic *Medieval People,* first published in 1924.

4. For a recent assessment, see T. Unwin, *Wine and the Vine: An Historical Geography of Viticulture and the Wine Trade* (London, 1991), 144ff., "Viticultural Continuity and Survival." O. Brogan in his study, "Trade between the Roman Empire and Free Germans" (*JRS* 26 [1936]: 195ff.), notes that trade goods included barrels of wine and that wine merchants had probably crossed the Rhine before the time of Augustus, preceding a development of the Rhenish and Moselle vineyards of the middle and late Empire (p. 218).

5. On the Vinidarius-compiled excerpts, see M. E. Milham, "Toward a *Stemma* and *Fortuna* of Apicius," *Italia medioevalia e umanistica* 10 (1967): 260; they are reproduced in full in her edition of Apicius (Teubner, 1969).

6. See the Venerable Bede, *Ecclesiastical History of the English People,* ed. B. Colgrave and R. A. B. Mynors (Oxford, 1969), 415–19.

7. Still one of the best books on the topic is Françoise Henry, *Irish Art in the Early Christian Period (to 800 A.D.)* (Ithaca, N.Y., 1965).

8. Joyce suggests that the Tiberiast duplex or manifest of ALP inspired the *Tunc* page in the Book of Kells (*Finnegans Wake* [New York, 1944], 122). See Joseph Campbell and Henry M. Robinson, *A Skeleton Key to Finnegans Wake* (New York, 1944), for full consideration of the interplay between Joycean and early Irish art.

9. Anne Ross, *Pagan Celtic Britain* (London, 1967), 308ff. discusses the magical swine of Derbrenn, of Mucca Shlangha and the like on the basis of Gaelic epics that I am unable to read in the original.

10. Ibid., 28, 34, 337f., for examples. The yew *Eo Mugna,* that bore three crops yearly (apples, blood-red nuts that may have been hazel, and acorns), is especially intriguing.

11. Ibid., 28, citing the hazelnuts and objects from the well at Ashill, Norfolk, among others.

12. G. E. Burcaw, *The Saxon House: A Cultural Index in European Ethnography* (Moscow, Idaho, 1979), 99f., considers the relationship with a "Black Kitchen" type among the Balto-Slavs with its central hearth and chimney.

13. This linguistic material is taken from Thomas Wright, *The Homes of Other Days: A History of Domestic Manners and Sentiments in England* (London, 1871). A useful article by Patricia Lysaght, tracing changes in Irish diet through the ages, confirms many aspects of food preference in the period 700–900, including the love of milk and milk products such as curds, the privileged role of apples, etc. See her "Continuity and Change in Irish Diet," in A. Fenton and E. Kisbán, eds., *Food in Change: Eating Habits from the Middle Ages to the Present Day* (Edinburgh, 1986), 80–89.

14. Notker "the Stammerer" (a monk of St. Gall, writing long after the death of Alcuin, ca. 884), *Gesta Karoli Magni;* see *Two Lives of Charlemagne,* trans. Lewis Thorpe (Baltimore, 1969), 22 and 94. Thorpe points out the anachronism that makes Bede Alcuin's mentor in this text, Bede dying just about when Alcuin was born in 735; I believe the error stems from a desire to connect the outstanding intellect of an earlier century with the next.

15. And also ignoring continuing incursions by Vikings, or disruptions to life in the following period of the break-up of his realm among his heirs, when famine was a problem during the ninth century.

16. For the general reader, one of the best recreations of the life of the period is the classic by Eileen Power, *Medieval People,* first published in 1924, in which chap. 2, "The Peasant Bodo," utilizes all these materials. In French there are interesting summaries in Blond and Blond, *Histoire* (see chapter 4, n. 96) and A. Castelot, *L'histoire à table* (Paris, 1972).

17. Edited by Th. Gross and R. Schieffer in *MGH, Fontes iuris Germanici antiqui,* vol. 3 (2d ed. 1980); on the formative stages in Carolingian times of the courtly ideal that he studies from its Ottonian heirs until the Gothic period, see C. Stephen Jaeger, *The Origins of Courtliness: Civilizing Trends and the Formation of Courtly Ideals, 939–1210* (Philadelphia, 1985), esp. pp. 19ff. The studies he cites by Josef Fleckenstein are the most important for understanding Charlemagne's courts.

18. Tannahill (*Food in History,* p. 101) gives a succinct account of the disease, various medieval epidemics, etc., citing G. E. Carefoot and E. R. Sprott, *Famine on the Wind: Plant Diseases and Human History* (1969), who place the earliest recorded outbreak in the Rhine valley during A.D. 857.

19. For an excellent article on breads — their sizes and weights, composition, and modes of preparation — see A. M. Bautier, "Pain et patisserie dans les textes médiévaux latins anterieurs au XIIIe siècle," in Denis Menjot, ed., *Manger et boire au Moyen Age* (Nice, 1984), 1:33–65.

20. "La bière, une invention médiévale," in Menjot, *Manger et boire,* 1:13–31.

21. Cited by Moulin (ibid.), after a thesis by W. Rinckenberger on modern hop culture in Alsace.

22. J. Semmler, ed., *Le Moyen âge* 68 (1962): 91–123, 233–69, vi; Leon Levillain, *Le Moyen âge,* 13 (1900): cap. xv. See Moulin, ibid., 19.

23. General editors, Philippe Ariès and Georges Duby, (Cambridge, Mass., 1987–91), 5 vols.

24. "La faim à l'époque carolingienne: Essai sur quelques types de rations alimentaires," *Revue historique* 250 (1973): 295–320; the letter, *MGH*, II, Concilia (1906), ed. Werminghoff, vol. 2, p. 599. See also Ariès and Duby, *A History of Private Life,* 1:444–47.

25. A. H. Longnon, *Polyptyche de l'Abbaye de Saint-Germain des-Pres* (2 vols.; Paris, 1886–95); B. Guerard, *Polyptique de l'Abbé Irminon* (3 vols.; Paris, 1844).

26. Rouche's revised study, "Les repas de fête à l'époque carolingienne," in Menjot, *Manger et boire,* 265–96, elicited a rebuttal from J.-C. Hocquet, "Le pain, le vin et la juste mesure à la table des moines carolingiens," *Annales ESC* 40, no. 1 (1985): 661–86. In this "Polemique" with a response from Rouche (p. 687f.) and an afterword by Hocquet (p. 689f.) the counterargument to Rouche's supposed diet of 6,000 to 9,000 calories is recalculated to modest, healthful rations. It is important to note that *pulmentum* is corrected from Rouche's etymology: not akin to Italian *polenta* and thus a purée, but more like a *minestra,* or stew (n. 88).

27. Cited by Rouche, "Le faim à l'époque carolingienne," 301. *MGH*, Epist. Kar. aevi, II (1905), cc. 510ff.

28. See C. Bynum, *Holy Feast and Holy Fast,* 37–45.

29. The *craspois* became the *lard de Caresme* for medieval France, while the salted flesh lost popularity in the Gothic period; see "Baleine" in Castelot, *L'histoire à table.*

30. Lorna Price, *The Plan of St. Gall in Brief: An Overview Based on the Work by Walter Horn and Ernest Born* (Berkeley and Los Angeles, 1982), 33, considers this medicinal garden adjacent to the infirmary. Her translation of *saturegium* is "pepperwort," of *sisimbria,* "cress." On pp. 66–69 she reproduces in detail and discusses both orchard and kitchen garden for the monastery as a whole.

31. This is underlined by two short poems, one written flanking the central cross: "Among the trees of the soil, the most sacred is always the cross / On which the fruits of eternal health are fragrant"; the second, around the perimeter: "Around this (cross) let rest the dead bodies of the brethren / And through its radiance may they attain again the realm of heaven"; see W. Horn and E. Born, *The Plan of St. Gall,* 2:211.

32. The analysis relied upon in the Horn and Born text, as well as its epitome, is W. Sorrensen, "Gärten und Pflanzen im Klosterplan," in *Studien zum St Galler Klosterplan,* ed. Johannes Duft, Mitteilungen zur vaterländischen Geschichte, 42 (St. Gall, 1962), 193–227. Cf. Horn and Born, *The Plan of St. Gall,* 2:211f., on the orchard. For figs in medieval and Renaissance England, see F. A Roach, *Cultivated Fruits of Britain: Their Origin and History* (Oxford, 1985), 201f. Konrad Hecht, *Der St Gallen Klosterplan* (Sigmaringen, 1983), also stresses the plants that could not grow in the northern climate as evidence for the plan's genesis in the South, even if adopted as a result of the Aachen reform synod of 816–17.

33. On the Catalan Arnaldus, the most accessible study is that of H. E. Sigerist, ed. and trans., *The Earliest Printed Book on Wine* (New York, 1943); although Arnaldus wrote ca. 1300, his work on the Salerno School and distillation first appeared in printed form in the first years of the sixteenth century; his collected *Opera,* already revised, I used in a British Library copy (Lyon, 1520). A succinct account of distillation is to be found in McGee, *On Food and Cooking,* 431ff., noting that Aristotle apparently recognized only pure water as the distilled essence of either seawater or wine.

34. Horn and Born, *The Plan of St. Gall,* 2:208; Sorrensen, "Gärten und Pflanzen."

35. Horn and Born, *The Plan of St. Gall*, 2:212, though the primary use must have been for parching barley and other grains ("locus ad torrendas annonas," according to the label).

36. See G. E. Fussell, *The Classical Tradition in West European Farming* (Rutherford, N.J., 1972), 51. Walahfrid studied with Rabanus Maurus at the monastery of Fulda; he was tutor to Charles the Bald and died in 849 as Abbot of Reichenau. In addition to *De cultura hortorum*, his works include other verse, the preface to Einhard's Life of Charlemagne, and glosses on the Bible. The quality of his horticultural knowledge is attested in a note added by Barthius to the *MGH* text that his canto on the *cucurbita* (gourds and cucumbers) has never been surpassed.

37. A warning for those who may wish to try cooking bulbs: those sold commercially in this country are generally treated with toxic pesticides. You may safely purchase imported Greek hyacinth bulbs or gather wild ones with careful attention to a good field guide to edible plants; all the Iris family is poisonous, for example.

38. *Food in Antiquity*, 125ff. (see chap. 1, n. 8). See also, McGee, *On Food and Cooking*, 184f.; Sturtevant, *Edible Plants of the World*, 169ff., on *Citrullus vulgaris*, watermelon.

39. Sorrensen, "Gärten und Pflanzen," 226; Sturtevant, *Edible Plants*, 425 argues from Albertus Magnus' thirteenth-century text (*De vegetabilibus*, ed. Jessen [1857], 118, 167, 515) which describes *faseoli* of many colors with a *maculam nigram* in loco *cotyledonis*.

40. Horn and Born, *The Plan of St. Gall*, 2:183f.; see J. Lestocquoy, "Épices, médecine et abbayes," in *Études merovingiennes* (Paris, 1933), 182ff.

41. Before this invention, full horsepower could not be utilized, obviously, because the animal would choke on the harness; this is one of the reasons that earlier peoples plowed with oxen.

42. The comparison is put forward engagingly by Henry Kraus in his *Living Theatre of Medieval Art* (Philadelphia, 1967), 174f., from which I have used his translation from Bernard's *Apologia* concerning the eggs.

43. Gottschalk, *L'histoire de l'alimentation*, (see chap. 4, n. 10), 1:279f.; his note 381 summarizes a manuscript by a tenth-century monk of St. Gall listing blessings for various foods (*Benedictiones ad mensam*) which categorizes types of bread and other aliments from fish, game, and fowl to cheeses and fruit.

CHAPTER EIGHT

1. *Blaw maungere* (also blamanger, blamang), is blancmange, but, unlike our own, a mixture of white meat of poultry or fish, with ground almonds, spices, and sometimes rice; *brawne bruse* is a pickled meat dish, in this case of the "umbles" or innards of swine; a *brewet* is a broth or food cooked in a broth; *caudell* is a made dish thickened with eggs to a soft custard; *frumenty* continued to be favored into the early nineteenth century, a dish of boiled hulled wheat generally served as accompaniment to venison; *frettoure* is a fritter; *gyngaudre* is a spicy fish dish originally made with green sauce of herbs; *graspeys* are probably "cryspis," or crêpes; "leche" means "slice," in this case of milk and bacon set by eggs; *mawmene*, or *mawmenny*, derives from the Arabic *ma'muniyyat*, and is a sweet dish of pieces of meat, spices, wine and sour grape or fruit juice; *mortrews*, as their name suggests, were originally made in a mortar of ground meat or fish mixed

with almond milk and thickened by bread and/or egg yolks to set when heated at the fire to a sort of molded mousse; "pain fondue" would be the French equivalent of *payne foundow*, fried bread in a sweet sauce of wine, honey, raisins, and spices; "soteltes" or "subtleties" were complex *pièces montées*, or showpieces that ended each course of a meal—also such surprises as "twenty-four blackbirds" flying out of a pie, or enactments by human actors (the French equivalents are *entremets*; the Italian, *intermezzi*); *viand ryall* is a dish of fish equivalent to mawmene for fasting days (for a recipe with chicken, see our appendix).

2. The classic formulation is still that by Johan Huizinga, *The Waning of the Middle Ages*, first published in Dutch, in 1919; an amended English translation appeared in 1924; in this chapter references are to an Anchor paperback edition (1954) of a St. Martin's Press publication of 1949.

3. Art-historical validation for the term was eloquently argued by the late Erwin Panofsky, *Early Netherlandish Painting, Its Origins and Character* (Cambridge, Mass., 1953); see also chap. 3 in his *Renaissance and Renascences in Western Art* (Stockholm, 1960), and subsequent paperback editions.

4. See M. M. Postan, ed., *The Cambridge Economic Life of Europe*, vol. 3: *Trade and Industry in the Middle Ages* [1952] (2d ed., with Edward Miller [Cambridge, 1987]).

5. For England as a type case, see Ellen W. Moore, *The Fairs of Medieval England: An Introductory Study* (Montreal, 1987).

6. In addition to the Hundred Years' War, peasant rebellions and sporadic famines in the North, compare as an Italian example, the catastrophes experienced by Florentines in the course of the first half of the fourteenth century, as narrated by Giovanni Villani (*Cronache* [Padua, 1841]): conflict between the Black and White political parties, followed by banishment of the Whites; a devastating fire in 1304; siege by the Emperor Henry VII in 1312; defeat of the Guelphs and repressive political control in 1315; defeat at the hands of Lucca in 1325; famine in 1329; a catastrophic flood in 1332; smallpox epidemic in 1335 that carried off 2,000 children; portents of more disasters to come in the eclipse of 1333 and comet of 1339—the latter a year of runaway inflation that placed food out of the reach of many; and an outbreak of the plague in 1340 that killed 15,000 people.

7. Some of such scenes are reproduced in Bridget Ann Henisch, "Unconsidered Trifles: The Search for Cookery Scenes in Medieval Sources," in *Current Research in Culinary History: Sources, Topics, and Methods*, (Cambridge, Mass., 1986), 110–21.

8. Our illustration manifests the symbolism of the royal instrument, equating the health and safety of the ruler with the "ship of state." For examples in the Victoria and Albert Museum, London, see Charles Oman, *Medieval Silver Nefs* (London, 1963). *Nefs* held salt, spices, and other table necessities in addition to objects believed to detect poison, not only a piece of "unicorn horn" (narwhal tusk), but "serpent's tongue" (shark's tooth) as well; they were kept locked. For a discussion of Berry's table, see Manuel Nuñez Rodriguez, "El ritual de mesa en la miniatura *le bon repas* del duque de Berry," in Menjot, *Manger et boire*, 2:33–41.

9. Medieval use of *pain tranchoir* for plates continues an ancient Roman practice we know from Virgil (cf. his *quadrae*). In a noble household like that of Berry, the trenchers—at least four slices deep and carefully pared from specially baked rather than slightly stale bread—would rest upon a metal underplate. After a meal they would be fed to the dogs (though if the sauces

were especially delicious. I imagine some lesser mortals could not have resisted eating them!) or they made part of the distribution an almoner gave to the poor.

10. Coexistence of piety and worldliness in Philip and as a sign of the times is considered by Huizinga, *The Waning of the Middle Ages,* 180f.

11. A translation of Vitry may be found in ibid., 130; that of Charles d'Orléans in Panofsky, *Early Netherlandish Painting,* (Icon edition), 69.

12. Outstanding in the bibliography on the earliest European manuscripts are: Bruno Laurioux, "Les premiers livres de cuisine," in *La cuisine et la table: 5000 ans de gastronomie* (Paris, 1962), 51–55; idem., "Les livres de cuisine en Occident à la fin du Moyen Âge," in *Artes mechanicae en Europe médiévale: Actes du colloque du 15 octobre 1987,* ed. R. Jansen-Sieben (Brussels, 1989), 113–26; Alain Girard, "Du manuscrit à l'imprimé: le livre de cuisine en Europe aux XVe et XVIe siècles," in *Pratiques et discours alimentaires à la Renaissance,* ed. J.-C. Margolin and R. Sauzat (Paris, 1982), 107–17; and J.-L. Flandrin and Odile Redon, "Les livres de cuisine italiens des XIV et XV siècles," *Archeologia medievale* 8 (1981): 393–408. Papers given at a conference held in Montreal in 1990 contain much material: see Carole Lambert, ed., *Du manuscrit à la table: Essais sur la cuisine au Moyen Age et répertoire des manuscrits médiévaux contenant des recettes culinaires* (Montreal, 1992). This includes Constance B. Hieatt's survey of her work assembling English manuscripts, Anglo-Norman and over fifty in Middle English: "Listing and Analysing the Medieval English Culinary Recipe Collections: a Project and its Problems," 15–21. A team in Paris, at the Centre de Recherches Historiques, is working under the direction of Jean-Louis Flandrin to gather and analyze all extant materials into a data base of early culinary treatises.

13. A bibliography written in A.D. 988 already includes more than ten culinary items; see Claudia Roden, "Early Arab Cooking and Cookery Manuscripts," *Petits Propos Culinaires* 6 (1980): 16–27. Fundamental is Maxime Rodinson, "Recherches sur les documents Arabes relatifs à la cuisine," *Revue des Études Islamiques* (1949): 95–165.

14. British Library, MS. Add. 5016. Earlier editions by Samuel Pegge *(The Forme of Curye* [London, 1790], reprinted in R. Warner, *Antiquitates culinariae)* are superceded by the study of a cognate group of fourtenth- and fifteenth-century manuscripts by Constance B. Hieatt and Sharon Butler, *Curye on Inglysch: English Culinary Manuscripts of the Fourteenth Century (Including the Forme of Cury)* (Early English Text Society, ss 8; London, 1985).

15. *Le Menagier de Paris,* ed. Georgine E. Brereton and Janet M. Ferrier (Oxford, 1981; cited hereafter as Brereton and Ferrier)—an exemplary edition in the original archaic French, with introduction, notes and a glossary, replacing that by Jérôme Pichon of 1846, *Le Mesnagier de Paris, traité de morale et d'économie domestique composé vers 1393 par un bourgeois parisien* (reprint, Geneva, 1970). For a translation into Middle English, see Eileen Power, *The Goodman of Paris* (London, 1928).

16. The manuscripts are edited, collated, with commentary and glossary, together with an English translation of the most complete version (Vatican, Regina 776), by Terence Scully, *The Viandier of Taillevent: An Edition of all Extant Manuscripts* (Ottawa, 1988). In this exemplary work he also gives an assessment of medieval culinary theory and practice, his view of the *Viandier* among early cookery books, and adapts four recipes for a modernized menu. An earlier edition by J. Pichon and G. Vicaire, *Le Viandier de Guillaume Tirel dit Taillevent* (Paris, 1892), was based on a manuscript in the Bibliothèque Nationale (fonds français, 19, 791), with some reference

to other versions in the Mazarine Library in Paris and in Archives at Saint-Lô (destroyed during World War II). They did not discuss the importance of a "Viandier" in the Archives cantonales du Valais, Sion, Switzerland (S.108, a parchment roll with the title and two recipes on the verso cut away) — see below, notes 22, 23.

17. For a concise biography, see Liliane Plouvier, "Taillevent, la première star de la gastronomie," *L'histoire* 61 (1983): 93–94, as well as editions of *Le Viandier*. See also Barbara Berkhout, "Taillevent, Cuisinier du Roi," *Gourmet* (February 1968), 16ff., which includes several of his recipes adapted for modern cooks.

18. A facsimile edition, with an introduction by James J. Rorimer, was published by the Metropolitan Museum as *The Hours of Jeanne d'Evreux, Queen of France, at the Cloisters* (New York, 1957). Since Charles the Good died in 1328, the tiny prayerbook must date between their betrothal in 1325 and 1328.

19. Cited by Alfred Franklin, *La vie privée d'autrefois: La cuisine* (reprint of 1888 edition, Geneva, 1980), 45f.: "3 bales of almonds, 6 lbs. pepper, 23-1/2 lbs. ginger, 13-1/2 lbs. cinnamon [cassia bark probably], 5 lbs. 'grains of Paradise' [melegueta pepper; Franklin interpreted this as cardamom], 3-1/2 lbs. cloves, 1-1/4 lb. saffron, 1/2 lb. long pepper, 1-1/2 quarterons of 'massis' [= macis, mace; mastic?, queries Franklin], 1/2 quarteron cassia buds, 46 lbs. rice, 20 lbs 'amidon' [wheat starch descended from ancient Roman *amulum*], 3 quarterons 'espit' [spikenard or 'aspic' = *Lavandula spica*], 5 lbs. 'commun' (cumin), 20 lbs. sugar in 4 loaves"; all the equipment is also inventoried.

20. The documents are compiled in appendixes to the first modern edition of *Le Viandier* by Jérôme Pichon and Georges Vicaire, *Le Viandier de Guillaume Tirel dit Taillevent* (Paris, 1892). Note that a *Supplément* was published the next year in order to incorporate an important variant manuscript in the Vatican; a reprint of both volumes, ed. Sylvie Martinet, Geneva, 1970.

21. Printed editions of the fifteenth and sixteenth centuries take up cols. 815 to 828 in Vicaire, *Bibliographie gastronomique* (1890). The first, without place or date, are ascribed to 1486 (Paris, Caillot?), 1488 and 1490 (each Lyon, Mathius Huss?): see Philip Hyman and Mary Hyman, "Les livres de cuisine et le commerce des recettes en France aux XVe et XVIe siècles," in Lambert, *Du manuscrit à la table* (1992), 59–68. Their work is very important in showing both the authority held by Taillevent (as well as the Italian Platina) in the sixteenth century and the manner in which publishers falsified their editions by incorporating other material under such august names.

22. Paul Aebischer, "Un manuscrit valaisan du *Viandier* attrbué à Taillevent," *Vallesia* 8 (1953): 73–100 (on the date of the Gothic script, see p. 74).

23. *Viandier*, 12–17, after already pointing out that no one of the surviving copies is preeminent and justifying his decision to reproduce all variants in his edition; Scully hypothesizes an original standing behind the Valais example and a putative lost version that would have been the source for two further branches of the family tree, one leading to the Mazarine copy, the second to that in the Bibliothèque Nationale and to the latest, augmented (by Tirel emending his own text?) and best, in the Vatican. Of course this enhances a late thirteenth-century stylistic context for the 'Taillevent' tradition.

24. Edited by Constance B. Hieatt and Robin F. Jones, "Two Anglo-Norman Culinary Collections Edited from British Library Manuscripts Additional 32085 and Royal 12.C.xii,"

Speculum 61 (1986): 862–66; Scully considers the *Viandier* among early cookery books, commencing with this one, on pp. 25–30. Note that *claree* (French *cleret, clairet, claret*) refers to the clarity and smoothness of a mixture; it is here used in the sense of "ragout" I take it, although in other usage of the time it means spiced wine.

25. Paris, Bibliothèque Nationale lat. 7131, fols. 99v–100r [the first portions are (A) "Tractatus de modo praeparandi et condiendi omnia cibaria," and (B) "Liber de coquina"]: see the *Répertoire* of early manuscripts assembled by Hieatt, Lambert, Laurioux, and Prentki as an appendix to *Du manuscrit à la table* (1992), no. 104. Pichon and Vicaire edited this in their edition of Taillevent (see n. 16), 213–26; it appeared also as appendix 1 in Grégoire Lozinski, *Bataille de Caresme et de Charnage* (Paris, 1933). Cf. L. Douët-D'Arcq, "Un petit traité de cuisine écrit vers 1306," *Bibliothèque de l'École des Chartes* 21 (1860): 216–24.

26. See Marianne Mulon, "Les premiers recettes médiévales," *Annales ESC* 19 (1964): 933–37 (reprinted in J. J. Hémardinquer, ed., *Pour une histoire de l'alimentation* (1970), 236–40. The doctoral dissertation of Carole Lambert, "Trois réceptaires culinaires médiévaux: Les *Enseignemenz*, les *Doctrine* et le *Modus*" (University of Montreal, 1989), has not been available to me.

27. Mulon, "Les premiers recettes médiévales" (1970), 237; the *Liber de coquina* includes an invocation to an Angevin prince and is filled with North French allusions such as "caseum de Bria" (Brie cheese), or dishes "ad usum Franciae." The court culture of Naples in the Late Gothic was already prefigured in the reign of Robert of Anjou, 1309–43.

28. Both are included in Paris, Bib. Nat., 9328; Mulon, "Les premiers recettes," (1964), 934; Lambert, *Du manuscrit à la table, répertoire* no. 106, dated about 1380–90. Carmello Spadaro di Pasanitello has found a Vatican manuscript (Palatino lat. 1768, which I have not seen) that he believes to be the source for these Italian manuscripts. It collates very strongly with the "Angevin" one, but he has not yet, to my knowledge compared details of recipe instructions; see "La fonte vaticana dei primi libri di cucina italiani," *Appunti di gastronomia* 5 (1991): 5–13.

29. The Tuscan manuscript, dated in the fourteenth century by its original editor (F. Zambrini, *Il libro della cucina del secolo XIV* [Bologna, 1863; reprinted 1968]), is now dated at the very end of the century or beginning of the fifteenth, see Emilio Faccioli, *Arte della cucina: Libri di ricette, Testi sopra lo scalco Il trinciante e i vini dal XIV al XIX secolo*, 1:19 and the text of MS 158 of the University of Bologna Library reproduced on pp. 21–57. Like other manuscripts in question it too gives evidence of being a recension of earlier materials. The Venetian collection, *Libro per cuoco* (Biblioteca Casanatense cod. 225), was first published by Ludovico Frati, *Libro della cucina del secolo XIV* (Livorno, 1899); reedited by Faccioli, *Arte della cicoma*, 61–105. This last cookbook is notable for unusual precision in giving quantities and proportions of ingredients as well as cooking times.

30. See Allen J. Grieco, "Classes sociales, nourritures et imaginaire alimentaire en Italie (XIVe–XVe siècles)" (diss., Paris, École des Hautes Études en Sciences Sociales, 1987).

Grieco gives a tantalizing foretaste of the culinary ambition of the Signoria through their day by day account books, see "From the Cookbook to the Table: A Florentine Table and Italian Recipes of the Fourteenth and Fifteenth Centuries," in Lambert, *Du manuscrit à la table*, 29–38. Curzio Mazzi analyzed expenses in precious detail from May, 1344 to the end of April the next year as well as for January and February, 1477, in "La mensa dei Priori di Firenze nel secolo XIV," *Archivio storico italiano* 20 (1897): 336–68; the texts are reproduced on pp. 355ff.

31. The second chapter of Caroline Walker Bynum's *Holy Feast and Holy Fast* (see chap. 7, n. 1) is devoted to the historical background for her theme. She points out (p. 7) that Wednesday and Friday fasts emerged very early, perhaps even by the second century, but that later in the West Saturday was added to Friday while Wednesday often dropped out. For detailed material on fasting, see J. A. MacCullough, "Fasting" in *Encyclopedia of Religion and Ethics* (1908–27), 5:759–65, and other sources cited in Bynam's note 11.

32. Grieco, "From the Cookbook to the Table," 34f. Cf. Bruno Laurioux, "Table et hiérarchie sociale à la fin du Moyen Age," in Lambert, *Du manuscrit à la table*, 87–107; p. 92, citing Grieco on the Florentine table in a discussion of *volaille* as privileged food in the social scale.

33. Known in three manuscripts copies of the fifteenth century: Paris, Bib. Nat., fonds français 12477; Brussels, Bibliothèque Royale, 10310–10311; and a copy of the first-named, Bib. Nat., nouvelles acquisitions françaises 6739. The latest, definitive publication by Brereton and Ferrier (1981, see above, note 15) is based on fr. 12477 with variants noted in the apparatus. Interestingly, the author twice comments on meals at the Duke of Berry's residences. II, iv.3 (Brereton and Ferrier, 171) is a signal example of provisions calculated for distribution according to the social scale: a distinction between pages and ordinary "varlets" in dividing their portion of *boeuf*, the muzzle.

34. Brereton and Ferrier, xxiif.; the comment on Taillevent's recipe: "il y a trop affaire et n'est pas ouvrage pour le queux d'un bourgoiz, non mye d'un chevalier simple," and snails "sont pour les riches gens" (II, v, no. 364 and 257).

35. *Medieval People*, 127; chapter 5 of this work is devoted to "The Ménagier's Wife."

36. Brereton and Ferrier, xxxivff., with special reference to Gluttony.

37. I believe that he refers to the dinner hour, not what we might term breakfast. Medieval people rose with the sun for the most part and partook of a very modest breaking of the overnight fast, akin to the wine or sometimes beer, plus or minus a croissant, that a modern French worker consumes standing at a local *zinc*. Dinner was normally between ten A.M. and eleven, although often later at a lordly court, supper being the early evening repast.

38. Scully (*Viandier*, p. 9) points out that the Valais roll of the *Viandier* was a functioning cookbook, much rubbed and spattered with grease.

39. R. Grewe, "An Early XIII Century Northern-European Cookbook," in *Current Research in Culinary History*, Culinary Historians of Boston (Proceedings of a Conference at Radcliffe College, June 1985) (Cambridge, 1986), 27–45. See also the Danish bibliography in Scully, *Viandier*, 330

40. See Bi Skaarup, "Sources of Medieval Cuisine in Denmark," in Lambert, *Du manuscrit à la table*, 39–43 (p. 40, with the opinion that the *Urtext* for both Copenhagen manuscripts, one transmitted through a Low German translation, was French and earlier than other European survivors).

41. Munich, Universitäts-Bibliothek, *2° Cod. MS. 731, first edited by Maurer-Constant, *Bibliothek des literarischen Vereins in Stuttgart*, vol. 9 (1844); Hans Hajek, ed., *Das buch von guter spise. Aus des Würzburg-Münchener Handschrift neu herausgegeben* (Berlin, 1958). See the full bibliography given as *répertoire* no. 80 in the appendix to Lambert, *Du manuscrit à la table*, 345. An Italian edition with a valuable commentary does not appear there: Anna Martellotti and Elio Durante, *Libro di Buone Vivande: La cucina tedesca dell'età cortese* (Fasano, 1991).

42. Known in two manuscripts, one of which Rudolf Grewe dated to the fourteenth

century: *Libre de Sent Soví (Receptari de cuina)* (Barcelona, 1979). See also his "Catalan Cuisine, in an Historical Perspective," *Proceedings, Oxford Symposium 1981*, 170–78, for the context at a period of wide Catalan presence and commerce throughout the Mediterranean, for the Roman and Arabic heritage.

43. The famed natural historian of the second half of the sixteenth century, Ulisse Aldrovandi, citing Platina's cookbook of 1475, even includes a recipe for the "delicacy" as well as another "white food [of the] wealthy Catalan people" in a chapter on chickens in his *Ornithologiae, hoc est, De avibus historiae libri XII* (3 vols.; Bologna, 1599–1603), vol. 2, bk. xiv For a translation, see L. R. Lind, *Aldrovandi on Chickens, The Ornithology of Ulisse Aldrovandi (1600)* (Norman, Okla., 1963), 416–17. The recipe appears not only in Platina but in a Neapolitan manuscript of the late fifteenth century in the J. Pierpont Morgan Library, New York (B19), and in Platina's source, Maestro Martino's work of mid-century. Later Renaissance Catalan works, such as Roberto da Nola's *Libre del Coch* (probably of the 1470s, first printed 1520) may reflect further Late Gothic interchange between Catalonia and Italy in matters culinary: see Barbara Santich, "Influence italienne sur l'evolution de la cuisine médiévale catalane," in Menjot, *Manger et boire*, 2:131–40.

44. See Luis Faraudo de Saint-Germain, "Liber de totes maneres de confits: Un tratado manual cuatrocentista de arte de dulcería," *Boletín de la Real Academia de Buenas Letras de Barcelona* 19 (1946): 97–134. On this book as the first work on confiserie independent of medical texts, and on the importance of Arabic tradition, especially at Cordoba, see Liliane Plouvier, "La confiserie européenne au Moyen Âge," *Medium Aevum Quotidianum* (1988): 28–47 (p. 47).

45. Although Grewe tended to exaggerate the Catalan regional style in Late Gothic International Europe, it is true that both Borgia Renaissance popes, Calixtus III (1456–58) and Alexander VI (1492–1503) brought many Catalans to Italy.

46. For analysis of the widespread effects of the invention of printing in the 1450s, see Elizabeth L. Eisenstein, *The Printing Revolution in Early Modern Europe* (Cambridge, 1983).

47. Edited by Terence Scully, first in "*Du fait de cuisine par Maistre Chiquart (1420),*" *Vallesia* 40 (1985): 101–231, then independently and in translation: *Chiquart's "On Cookery": A Fifteenth-century Savoyard Culinary Treatise* (New York, 1986).

48. See Brereton and Ferrier, liii, for Pichon's misapprehension that the author of the *Ménagier* relied on the *Livre fort excellent*. Like compilations by Pierre Pidoulx (*La Fleur de toute cuysine*, printed 1543, and *Le Grant Cuysinier de toute cuysine*, 1560 et. seq.), all reflect the *Ménagier* and Taillevent.

49. British Library, Sloane 1986, first edited by R. Morris, *Transactions of the Philological Society*, Supplement (1862); see for the various families of manuscripts, Lambert, *Du manuscrit à la table*, 333–41 (the *Liber* no. 63).

50. Jean-Louis Flandrin has addressed this question, upholding the unity of diverse cuisines, although noting regional modifications in taste; he inventories thirty-seven recipes for blancmange in "Internationalisme, nationalisme et régionalisme dans la cuisine des XIVe et XVe siècles: Le témoignage des livres de cuisine," in Menjot, *Manger et boire*, 75–91. Apropos a late thirteenth-century Anglo-Norman work, a courtesy book and French-English vocabulary list in verse by Walter of Bibblesworth, Constance Hieatt, on the contrary, finds that "more than half of the most frequently repeated recipes [in fourteenth- and fifteenth-century English

and French collections] are in fact peculiar to one country or the other"—*Acts of Interpretation* (1982) p. 219f. (see Bibl.)

51. Paul Beichner ("The Grain of Paradise," *Speculum* 36 (1961): 302–7), finally put to rest the assertion in many studies that this spice, *Afromomum melegueta*, was a kind of cardamom.

52. An explanation may be sought in part in realities of trade and politics. Pepper was the most significant item in the Venetian spice trade, while sea trade with England was dominated by Italian cities such as Genoa and southern ports. Pepper was so important a commodity that it was used in place of coinage as a medium of exchange; for this and fluctuations in its value, see Jacques Heers, "Il commercio nel Mediterraneo alla fine del sec. XIV e nei primi anni del XV," *Archivio storico italiano* 113 (1955): 157–209.

53. See sec. 178, p. 233, 14f. in Brereton's and Ferrier's edition of the Ménagier. The Goodman says the Germans warn the French of great danger in eating carp so lightly cooked—were they considering parasites?

54. See J.-L. Flandrin, "Le goût et la nécessité: Sur l'usage des graisses dans les cuisines d'Europe occidentales (XIVe–XVIIIe siècle)," *Annales ESC* 38 (1983), p. 385 on relatively low percentages of olive oil consumption even in Italy. Olive oil was especially useful for fast days when meat products were eschewed: butter, lard and clarified pork fat *(sain* or *saindoux)*.

55. MS. Ashmole 328 in the Bodleian Library, Oxford; the Early English Text Society, publishes this original work of an Anglo-Saxon monk in 1011 (vol. 177 [1929]). Our illustration comes from a twelfth-century copy in St. John's College, Oxford (MS. 17). A sampling of the arithmological symbolism of the text establishes the medieval mind-set as to inherent system in Creation and further explicates our diagram: the number 12 as a product of 3×4 or 4×3 refers to the creation of the world because of its four quarters (N, S, E, and W) and the four elements; 3 refers to the Trinity, 4 to the Evangelists or to the four orders (of the two righteous classes and the two reprobate [Apostles are in the first group and they are twelve in number]) . . . ; there are four kinds of ground into which seed is cast [described]; $12 \times 6 = 72$, or just so many hours in three days that Our Lord spent in the tomb. And so through the properties of every number.

56. Namely, a passage in the Wisdom of Solomon, 11:21: ". . . omnia in mensura et numero et pondere disposuisti"; for even more complex reasoning on elemental numbers revealing Divine Truth hidden in Scripture, see Harry Bober, "*In Principio:* Creation before Time," in *Essays in Honor of Erwin Panofsky,* ed. Millard Meiss (Princeton, 1960), 13–28.

57. Although flawed by structuralist oppositions, see on Italy and France: Grieco, "Classes sociales." See also Bruno Laurioux, "Table et hiérarchie sociale," 87–107.

58. See Joseph A. Bryant, "The Diet of Chaucer's Franklin," *Modern Language Notes* (1948): 318–25.

59. See Muriel Bowden, *Commentary on the Prologue of Chaucer's Canterbury Tales* (New York, 1948), p. 187 on the five guildsmen. It has been pointed out that the coarse Summoner of unfortunates to the ecclesiastical court eats strong-smelling and pungent food accompanied by equally robust red wine. Aside from literary studies, Madeleine Cosman scans Chaucer with a sharp eye for "Character by Food Habit" and "Food and Social Class," 103–107 in her *Fabulous Feasts: Medieval Cookery and Ceremony* (New York, 1976).

60. A. C. Cawley, "The 'Grotesque Feast' in the *Prima Pastorum*," *Speculum* 30 (1955): 213–

17. For Germany, see George Fenwick Jones, "The Function of Food in Medieval German Literature," *Speculum* 35 (1960): 78–86.

61. "Structure des menus français et anglais aux XIVe et XVe siècles," in Lambert, *Du manuscrit à la table,* 173–92, using 29 menus from the *Ménagier* and 13 from British Museum, Harley 279 (after T. Austin, *Two Fifteenth-Century Cookery Books* [London, 1888]) plus 8 published by Richard Warner, *Antiquitates Culinariae* (see chap. 6, n. 1).

62. An article on the beef of Old England by Constance B. Hieatt ("The Roast or Boiled Beef of Old England," *Book Forum* 5 [1980]: 294–99) bears out the predominance of beef over other meats in the diet of the English as compared to other medieval populations. Eileen Power, in an early study of communities of nuns in Britain, discovered the ox as chief meat at Barking Abbey (*Medieval English Nunneries* [Cambridge, 1922]).

63. Many responsible writers counter these prevalent ideas, but in particular note Lorna J. Sass, "Religion, Medicine, Politics and Spices," *Appetite* 2 (1981): 7–13 and Bruno Laurioux, "De l'usage des épices dans l'alimentation médiévale," *Médiévales* 5 (1983): 15–31. To these articles, add that of T. Peterson, "The Arab Influence on Western European Cooking," *Journal of Medieval History* 6 (1980): 317–41, though his topic is different.

64. Recommended readings include Sass, "Religion, Medicine, Politics and Spices" and Laurioux, "De l'usage des épices." C. B. Hieatt and S. Butler (*Pleyn Delit: Medieval Cookery for Modern Cooks* [Toronto, 1978]), argue in their introduction that, like chefs of today, those of the Middle Ages applied their spices with moderation. This is not fully convincing in the light of documents like the *Ménagier* in which the Goodman of Paris recommends the amount of spices to purchase for a dinner offered to forty guests: "One lb. of powdered columbine ginger; Half a lb. of ground cinnamon; 2 lb. lump sugar; One oz. saffron; A quarter lb. of cloves and Grain of Paradise [melegueta pepper] mixed; Half a quarter lb. of long pepper; Half a quarter lb. of galingale [galangan, or laos powder]; Half a quarter lb. of mace; half a quarter lb. of green bay leaves": Eileen Power, *The Goodman of Paris*, 241, quoted by Bridget Ann Henisch, *Fast and Feast: Food in Medieval Society* (University Park, Pa., 1976), 106. For the same occasion, the after-dinner *boutehors* [see below, p. 265] required "candied orange peel, 1 lb.; Citron, 1 lb.; Red anise, 1 lb.; Rose-sugar, 1 lb.; white confits, 3 lbs.," and he noted that little remained of the spices afterward. It should be noted that, had he been of the aristocracy rather than a rich bourgeois, the Goodman would have had a kitchen boy whose sole task would have been to grind the spices to powder in a mortar.

65. In "Table et hiérarchie sociale." The late Gothic represents merely a small part of his survey of the use of spices from the end of antiquity; much of it concerns the Carolingian period.

66. Thorndike, "A Medieval Sauce Book," *Speculum* 9 (1934): 183–90; Scully, "The *Opusculum de saporibus* of Magninus Mediolanensis," *Medium Aevum Quotidianum* 54 (1985): 178–207. To Thorndike we owe the attribution to Maineri of both *Regimen* (formerly ascribed to Arnaldus of Villanova) and the Naples sauce book that echoes one of its chapters; he gives biographical information on Maino, a medical astrologer at the court of the Visconti in Milan and a friend of Petrarch. Scully includes further material in his edition of the *Viandier* of Taillevent, pp. 20f. and notes.

67. For an accessible survey in English, see Luisa Cogliati Arano, *The Medieval Health Hand-*

book Tacuinum Sanitatis (New York, 1976). The original was the work of an Arabic physician of eleventh-century Baghdad, Ibn Botlan, called "Ellbochasim" in the Latin derivatives. These, all illustrated in Gothic International Style. are preserved in libraries at Rome (Casanatense), Paris, Vienna, Rouen, and in the New York Public Library. The Vienna manuscript, from the Cerruti family of Verona, is reproduced in facsimile with translation by Judith Spencer, *The Four Seasons of the House of Cerruti* (New York, 1984).

68. See for example the entry "Trotula" in the *Enciclopedia Italiana*, vol. 34, p. 415. She lived about 1100, but the volume on gynecology and obstetrics attributed to her was printed in the sixteenth century: *De mulierum passionibus ante et post partum* (Strassburg, 1544; Venice 1547 et seq.).

69. Thus, as Scully (in *Medium Aevum* [1985]) cites in his note 76, Averroës, the great Arab polymath, opined that pheasant was the best of all fowl for eating, an esteem echoed by Aldobrandino of Siena, the Italian medical authority of the end of the thirteenth century.

70. Scully, ibid., 182: "boiling a meat, or any food, will tend to render it more moist without greatly increasing its natural warmth; roasting will both warm and dry a meat; frying— which always implies frying in oil or in lard—warms moderately and humidifies; baking in pastry is considered to warm moderately without greatly altering the natural moisture of the meat." Cf. *Viandier*, 22f.

71. Thus, the title of Constance Hieatt's article cited above (n. 62): "The Roast, or [rather] Boiled Beef of Old England."

72. William de Marra of Padua, in a fourteenth-century manuscript in the Vatican (Barberini 306) cited by Lynn Thorndike, *A History of Magic and Experimental Science* (New York, 1934), 3:534.

73. Thorndike, *History of Magic,* 8; the experiment stems from Avicenna, the great Arabic teacher and philosopher (980–1037) whose interpretations of Aristotle and work on medicine were major influences in the medieval West.

74. Thorndike (ibid., 228–30) gives an interesting example from Augustine of Trent, bishop of that city from 1336 to 1347. He gives instructions, dietary and otherwise, for avoiding disease when the constellations of the year 1340 prevail; especially if one is under the domination of Saturn (which ruled melancholia): abstain from fruit and raw vegetables and eat no leguminous plants, such as beans. The zodiac was held to govern the external anatomy of humans, while the planets dominated the viscera, with the moon, as it affected tides, causing humoral fluids to increase or decrease. For an informed discussion of this science and representations of a *homo signorum* ("zodiac man") in the Duke of Berry's prayer book and elsewhere, see Harry Bober, "The Zodiacal Miniature of the *Tres Riches Heures* of the Duke of Berry—Its Sources and Meaning," *Journal of the Warburg and Courtauld Institutes* 11 (1948): 1–34.

75. Sugar, used inordinately to modern taste by all who could afford it, was also sold by apothecaries, since it was considered a spice of universal medical value. Its nature, according to the Salernian scheme of things, was warm in the first degree, humid in the second; the best kind was white and had been clarified; in usefulness it purified the body, being good for the chest, the kidneys, and the bladder; its dangers of causing thirst and bilious humors might be neutralized by sour pomegranates: "Effects: Produces blood that is not bad. It is good for all temperaments, at all ages, in every season and region" (Vienna MS. fol. 92). Honey, in contrast,

was considered warm and dry in the second degree, though it was seen to purify and to cause thirst. Sugar was sold in the conical loaves in which it was molded during the refining process, so nipping off an amount from the solid and pounding it in a mortar added one more chore for the kitchen boy who ground spices. On the various types and grades of sugar, see Balducci Pegolotti, *La pratica della mercatura,* ed. Allan Evans (1936), 362ff. At least twelve varieties of sugar appear in fourteenth- and fifteenth-century commerce.

76. See L. Sass, "Religion, Medicine, Politics and Spices," p. 10 and her references. The sweet powder blending cinnamon, ginger, cloves, she compares to Indian curry powder as a variable mixture according to personal taste. A powder "du duc" that appears in the *Ménagier* (II, v, 317—Ypocras, using the above as well as grains of Paradise, nutmeg, and galingale) and other sources has been thought to be a scribal error from *douce,* but it appears with enough frequency in different languages as to make it seem legitimate. *Pouldre blanche* of French manuscripts was composed not of "white" spices, but of nutmeg, ginger, and cinnamon — I think because one kind of ginger was called *blanc, de Mesche* (from Mecca).

77. An account of *theriaca Andromachi* may be found in Charles Singer, "The Herbal in Antiquity, " *Journal of Hellenic Studies* 47 (1927): 1–52 (p. 18f.), with the lore that theriac became "treacle" in English and, when it was abandoned as medicine, the word was transferred to molasses, thus explaining our grandfathers' spring tonic of sulphur and molasses. Mithridates' panacea was based in large part on venomous substances from poisonous snakes.

78. See Warner, *Antiquitates culinariae,* p. xxxii after Harding; neither he nor the chronicler indicate that these figures might refer to special occasions such as the twelve days of Christmas and their extra "free-loaders" celebrating at court.

79. B. Laurioux, "Table et hiérarchie sociale," 93 and n. 26 cites important bibliography to support his statement that only privileged classes owned equipment for rôtissage. See also G. Bresc-Bautier, H. Bresc, and P. Herbeth, "L'equipement de la cuisine et de la table en Provence et en Sicile (XIVe–XVe siècles): Étude comparée," in Menjot, *Manger et boire,* 2:51f.

80. Alfred Gottschalk, *Histoire de l'alimentation,* (see chap. 4, n. 10), 328f. discusses the *dressoir* and other aspects of dining ceremonial; B. Laurioux, "Table et hiérarchie sociale," is more thorough-going.

81. William M. Milliken, "A Table Fountain of the Fourteenth Century, " *Bulletin of the Cleveland Museum of Art* 12 (1925): 36–39; exhibition catalogue, William D. Wixom, *Treasures from Medieval France* (Cleveland Museum of Art, 1966), no. VI-18; also *Fastes du Gothique* (exhibition, Grand Palais, 1981–82), no. 191.

82. Reported by Peter Damian in his *Opusculum,* cap. 11, *ca.* 1050; see Curt Sigmar Gutkind, *Das Buch der Tafelfreuden aus allen Zeiten und breiten gesammelt* (Leipzig, 1929), 160. On the history of the instrument, see Pasquale Marchese, *L'invenzione della forchette . . . dai Grechi ai nostri forchettoni* (Soveria Mannelli, 1989) and a review article, Stefano Ludovisi, "Forchette e compagni," *Appunti di gastronomia* 4 (1991): 57–60.

83. Bridget Ann Henisch's *Fast and Feast* (see above, n. 64), is a splendid survey of food preparation and presentation. This text cannot begin to match her rich detail on every aspect of kitchen, table, and manners — on carving, see pp. 179, 197, and (citing carvers on the hunting field so skilled that they refused to turn up their sleeves in confidence that they would spatter no blood on their clothing), 200.

84. For the full vocabulary, see Frederick J. Furnivall, *Early English Meals and Manners* [1868] (New York, 1969), with courtesy books: *Modus cenandi, The Babee's Book,* Hugh Rhodes and John Russell, and Wynken de Worde's *Boke of Kervynge,* printed in 1508.

85. Henisch, *Fast and Feast,* 118–19, citing Edward Hyams, ed., *Vineyards in England* (London, 1953), 33–35 on a change to colder and wetter summers during the fourteenth century, and E. M. Carus-Wilson, *Medieval Merchant Venturers* (London, 1967), 267f., on Peter of Blois and other critics. See also Hyams, *Dionysus,* chap. 6, on the retreat of viticulture in England and Germany and his theory of climate change.

86. Rendered into modern English by Thomas Wright, *The Homes of Other Days,* (see chap. 7, n. 13), 90.

87. Gottschalk, *Histoire de l'alimentation,* 1:310f; his entire section on wine and other drinks is particularly useful (pp. 304–22 and documentation, pp. 387–95). Especially interesting is his reprint of a 1395 ordonnance of Philip the Bold, from the Dijon archives. This forbids any *vigneron* to introduce "inferior" gamay grapes into Burgundian vineyards: it may give abundant wine but it "est plein de très grand et horrible amertume, et devient tout puant" [language modernized by Gottschalk]. Deschamps may have neglected Italian wines, but vernaccia ("Vernage") was much appreciated in Britain.

88. Ibid., 311; note that the final line is devoted to purely cooking products of the grape: verjuice and "strong" wine *(gouais)*.

89. Ibid., 388–90, with listing of each *clos* and notes on scattered vines throughout Paris in our own day.

90. Proportion of wine drinking to that of beer or ale is gained by statistics for England in 1309: 354 taverns vending mainly wine as against 1,330 brew shops producing and selling ale and beer; Peter Clark, *The English Alehouse: A Social History 1200–1830* (London, 1983), 21. Clark traces not only the social, economic and political role of the alehouse, ancestor of the modern pub, but the change culminating in the fifteenth century that brought hops to beer, thanks to Netherlandish replacement for earlier preservation and flavoring by spices.

91. See Cosman, *Fabulous Feasts,* 76 on the chauvinist cycles that brought mead periodically into fashion and their potential influence on a fourteenth-century literary revival of Anglo-Saxon techniques and themes. Her section on beers and ales is especially valuable for data on fraud on the part of ale-makers and tavernkeepers in matters of production and measure, as well as on regulations to control the trade.

92. Brereton and Ferrier, xli–xlii. They point out rightly that even certain of his flowers were grown for culinary purposes: violets in one of his recipes for omelettes — as well as for garnishing — and roses for rose water and *succre rosat.* Cf. Cosman, *Fabulous Feasts,* 48.

British Museum MS. Sloane 1201, English, XVth century, begins (fols. 1r–v, 2) with a list of plants necessary for a garden, giving them first alphabetically, then categorized as to use: organized for potage, for sauces, for the "coppe," for salad, for distilling, also for "favour & beauté," concluding with root vegetables (parsnips, turnips, radishes, carrots, galingale, eringoes, and saffron). Those for potage alone number about forty-eight, remarkably few of them familiar herbs.

93. A symposium held at Dumbarton Oaks provides a full spectrum of papers edited by Elisabeth MacDougall: *Medieval Gardens* (Washington D.C., 1986). A thirteenth-century trea-

tise by Piero de' Crescenzi, *Liber ruralium commodorum,* gives an idea of the quality of gardening lore in relation to alimentary and medicinal plants. Allen J. Grieco examines late fourteenth- and fifteenth-century Italian poetry concerned with fruits in an article revealing for their classification (36 fruits divided into 3 groups of 12, or 30 in 10s, 21 in 7s — our medieval system and arithmology again!): those eaten whole, stoned fruit of which one eats the exterior flesh, and those like oranges, pomegranates, and nuts of which the interior is edible ("Savoir de poête ou savoir de botaniste? les fruits dans la poésie italienne du XVe siècle," *Médiévales* 16–17 (1989): 131–46).

94. Gottschalk, *Histoire de l'alimentation,* 1:287.

95. The idea that melon was particularly dangerous, especially if one followed it with water rather than wine, came down from Galen; cf. a hygienic manuscript from Namur in which monks are warned off all fruit as generating putrefaction and corrupting humors. It considers cheese in very dire terms — unless one use it medicinally, after dinner — because it is hard to digest, generates melancholia, clouds the mind ("cerebrum obnubilat virtutem intellectuam debilitat"), and weighs down the entire body. Indeed, all milk products and eggs are looked at with a jaundiced eye; see L. Elaut, "The Walcourt Manuscript: A Hygienic Vademecum for Monks," *Osiris* 13 (1958): 184–209. For the persistence of these ideas in the Renaissance, see J.-L. Flandrin, "Médecine et habitudes alimentaires anciennes," in *Pratiques et discours alimentaires à la Renaissance,* ed. J.-C. Margolin and R. Sauzat (Paris, 1982), 88–89.

96. See Mulon, "Les premiers recettes médiévales" (1970).

97. Recipe no. 78 in Hieatt and Butler, *Curye on Inglysch.* MS. Sloane 1201 in the British Library lists (fol. 2), among plants for salad, buds of alexanders and primroses, flowers of violets and borage, dandelions, daisies, chives, red fennel, rocket, nettles, chickweed, among others.

98. A forthcoming book by Clifford Wright will subsume most earlier bibliography. Note two important sources for the medieval West: an issue of *Médiévales* (vols. 16–17 [1989]) is given over in large part to the topic of pasta, under the rubric "Contre Marco Polo: Une histoire comparée des pâtes alimentaires," including "La constitution d'une nouvelle catégorie culinaire? Les pâtes dans les livres de cuisine italiens de la fin du Moyen Age," pp. 51–60, by Odile Redon and Bruno Laurioux; and articles by Massimo Montanari and J.-L. Flandrin. Luigi Sada contributes "Spaghetti e compagni" to *Appunti di gastronomia* 1 (February 1990), 16–35, stressing the role of Apulia, Sicily and Genoa in diffusion of *tria* (the dried product, from Arabic *al-itrija* and ultimately, Greek — see above, chap. 4, "Specialties.").

99. Massimo Alberini, *Storia del pranzo all'Italiana* (Milan, 1966), 43, based on G. Alessio, "Storia linguistica di un antico cibo rituale: I maccheroni," in *Atti della Accademia Pontiniana,* n.s., 8 (1958–59): 261–80. Alberini notes that, as in many early references, "maccheroni" probably means "gnocchetti." In our later Gothic manuscripts from Italy, the word refers rather to tubular pasta, since directions are painstakingly to wrap dough about a straw or a metal bodkin and then cut it, or to roll and cut it first before poking holes through each piece. In the North the term is used very loosely.

100. Balducci Pegolotti, *La pratica della mercatura,* 297.

101. Translated by J. R. R. Tolkien (Boston, 1975), pt. 2, stanza 37, p. 47. The surnape is the second-cover cloth.

102. See, for example, "estouffiz," p. 207, line 23, p. 223, line 6 in Brereton and Ferrier, *Ménagier,* and elsewhere. Within a few pages, Bridget Ann Henisch (*Fast and Feast,* 128, 129, 131) covers an appetizing range of fish cookery that does more than justice to the topic.

103. A Neapolitan manuscript of the fifteenth century in the Morgan Library, Bühler 19, has three recipes for *biancho mangiare* plus a very simple one for Lent: cooked fish, almonds, and bread soaked in pea broth brayed together in a mortar, in place of rice cooked in almond milk, sugar and other spices found in fourteenth-century receipts for either poultry or fish blancmange.

104. Note that the mustard with which to eat the stockfish when boiled was not made according to today's formulas. The *Ménagier* also recommends dishes eaten *au moust,* which better represents the *must* (unfermented grape juice) that gives the condiment its name.

105. See for example Pliny, *NH*, XVIII, vii, 17, *amulum,* which Apicius used to thicken sauces.

106. For the deep philosophical and religious beliefs which fostered the symbolic value of light as transcendant reflection of the superessential light of the godhead, see E. Panofsky, *Abbot Suger on the Abbey Church of St. Denis* (Princeton, 1946), for architecture; and, for painting, Millard Meiss, "Light as Form and Symbol in Some Paintings of the Fifteenth Century," *Art Bulletin* 27 (1945): 43–68, reprinted in his collected essays, *The Painter's Choice: Problems in the Interpretation of Renaissance Art,* part 1, 1.

107. See B. Laurioux, "Table et hiérarchie sociale," 97; a quote from Henri de Ferrières, *Les Livres du roy Modus et de la reyne Ratio,* ed. G. Tillander (Paris, 1932), 2:33: "deux ou trois peres de potages de diverses coulours, lesquiex esoient chucrés et dessus semez de grains de poumez de grenades," and the viands were the most "rich" it was possible to find.

108. From the rendering by Angel Flores, ed., *Medieval Age* (London, 1963), 88.

109. Barbara Wheaton describes her achievement step by step for those who might like to try a peacock in "How to Cook a Peacock, " *Harvard Magazine* (November–December, 1979): 63–65; I am grateful to William Milliken for calling my attention to her article. A pheasant has so far been sufficient for my talents.

110. On *entremets* and their development from dishes to be eaten to tasks for carpenters and painters, see A. Lafortune-Martel, "De l'entremets culinaire aux pièces montées d'un menu de progande," in Lambert, *Du manuscrit à la table,* 121–39. B. Laurioux, in the same volume considers the variables in use of the term, demonstrating its place in the hierarchy of honor ("Table et hiérarchie sociale," 94–98).

111. The Goodman of Paris includes this *lait* in his section on *entremés, fritures, dorures* ("glazings," which often used real gold leaf rather than egg wash); the *Viandier* includes two recipes, in one of which it is made to emulate bacon (nos. 200 and 201 in Scully). In Britain, Leche Lumbarde can appear as a sotelte if the compound of dates, currants, sugar, wine, and spices is treated to look like a "slice" or slices of meat. The term *Lumbarde* applied to various custards and other dishes is rendered by most writers on medieval cookery as "in the manner of Lombardy"; this queried by J.-L. Flandrin ("Les Livres de cuisine italiens," 407), as simply an alternative way of referring to a rich dish, since all Italian bankers were called Lombards. The modest art of illusion involved seems comparable to musicians of the period writing a composition in ideographic form. Whether a Chantilly manuscript (MS. 564, formerly 1047) was copied in France or Italy circa 1400, the music of a secular rondeau is laid out in the shape

of a heart: see Isabelle Cazeaux, *French Music of the Fifteenth and Sixteenth Centuries* (Oxford, 1975), 3, n. 3.

112. Madeleine Cosman, among others, gives a recipe for accomplishing this marvel (*Fabulous Feasts*, 200).

113. *Canterbury Tales*, ed. A. C. Cawley (New York, 1992), "The Parson's Tale," lines 1113–20. The *Forme of Cury* gives directions for making castles (Warner, *Antiquitates culinariae*, no. 189; see also Hieatt and Butler, *Curye on Inglysch*, no. 197): "Take and make a foyle [crust] of gode past with a rollere of a foot brode, & lynger by cumpas [longer proportionately]. Make iiii coffyns of the self[same] past, upon the rollere the gretenesse of the smale of thyn arme, of vi ynche deepnesse. Make the gretust in the myddell. Fasten the foile in the mouth upwarde, & fasten thee other foure in every syde. Kerve out keyntlich [properly] kyrnels [battlements, crenellations] above in the manner of bataillyng [embattling] and drye hem harde in an ovene, other [or] in the sunne. In the myddel coffyn do a fars [farce, filling] of pork, with gode poudour [powder, i.e., ground spices] and ayren [eggs] rawe with salt, & colour it with safroun; and do in another creme of almaundes; and helde [hold, keep] it whyt. In another, creme of cowe mylke with ayren; colour it red with saundres [sandal-wood]." For another farce he suggests figs, raisins, apples and pears; then one "as to fritters blanched" to be colored green. It is baked well and served forth with "ew ardaunt," convincingly interpreted by Hieatt and Butler as aqua vitae, so the castle will indeed be flaming. An example given by Chiquart (Scully, *Chiquart's "On Cookery,"* no. 10 and notes) is an even larger and more elaborate chateau with numerous roasted animals, a boar's head and a piglet among them, breathing fire as well as living actors.

114. Henisch engagingly summarizes English sotelties (*Fast and Feast*, 228ff.), although most of her references are to the fifteenth century.

115. This is not difficult to accomplish on a modest scale. Birds or any other creatures that will create a sensation by jumping about (frogs, rabbits) or flying are not, of course, baked. A large pie shell of requisite depth is baked blind with a hole in the bottom stopped by a regular pie (a reward to guests after the surprise if you do not make it of the shortening-less medieval dough) through which the birds are introduced just before the "unveiling." I learned that one should not use quail, because of the quantity of their droppings when frightened or startled.

116. *Mémoires*, ed. H. Beaune and J. d'Arbaumont (Paris, 1883–88), 2:340–81; Olivier even played a part in one allegorical enactment. Also described in the *Chroniques* of Mathieu d'Escouchy, ed. G. du Fresne de Beaucourt (Paris, 1863), 2:116–237. O. Cartellieri, *The Court of Burgundy: Studies in the History of Civilization* [1929] (London, 1972), 139–53. I am grateful to Jeffrey Chipps Smith for having shared with me his special knowledge of documents in Lille Archives and Philip the Good's official program for his feast (Paris, Bib. Nat., MS. fr. 11594) as well as bibliography on the occasion, deriving from his work on the patronage of Philip (1419–67) initiated in his dissertation at Columbia University (1979).

117. See J. Pinkerton, ed., *A General Collection of Voyages and Travels* (1808–14), vol. 7: "The Remarkable Travels of Wm de Rubruquis into Tartary and China." A century later (purportedly in 1422–36), Jehan d'Outremuse of Liège wrote as "Sir John Mandeville," making his way to the Holy Land and Cathay. His adventures, set down originally in French or Anglo-Norman, were so popular that over 300 manuscripts survive, including variants in every European language; see *The Travels of Sir John Mandeville*, trans. and with an introduction by

C. W. R. D. Moseley (Harmondsworth, 1983), 10–11. A copy of this in one *Livre de merveilles* (Bib. Nat. fr. 2810) belonged to Philip the Bold. For illustrations from manuscripts, see M. Letts, *Sir John Mandeville: The Man and His Book* (London, 1949). On the forgery, see also Arthur P. Newton, *Travel and Travellers of the Middle Ages* (New York, 1968), p. 160.

118. This intermezzo came as the fifth among nine; see E Casanova, "Visita di un papa avignonese a suoi cardinali," *Archivio della Società Romana di Storia Patria* 22 (1899): 361–81; reproduced on pp. 238–40 of the publication of a conference that took place at Viterbo in 1982; see chap. 4, n. 73.

119. See Jacques Heers, *Fêtes, jeux et joustes dans les sociétés d'Occident à la fin du Moyen-Âge* (Montreal, 1982), 24f.

120. On the street theater, see George R. Kernodle, "Renaissance Artists in the Service of the People: Political Tableaux and Street Theaters in France, Flanders and England, 1380–1650," *Art Bulletin* 25 (1943): 59–64; his article includes the tableaux of the 1468 wedding of Charles the Bold. Cf. Huizinga, *The Waning of the Middle Ages*, 315f. on tableaux at entries of monarchs in which sirens, goddesses, and other figures of classical mythology, as well as Adam and Eve, posed in the nude, indicating medieval lack of prudery in such matters.

121. Grandes Chroniques, Paris, Bib. Nat., MS. fr. 2813, fol. 473v; Laura H. Loomis, "Secular Dramatics in the Royal Palace, Paris 1378, 1389 and Chaucer's Tregetours," *Speculum* 33 (1958): 242–55, comparing the Franklin's Tale and wondering if Chaucer's diplomatic tour in France brought him to witness; she gives an account in English. For Christine de Pisan, *Le Livre des Faits et Bonnes Meurs du Sage Roy Charles V*, ed. S. Solente (2 vols.; Paris, 1936–41). See also M. Thomas, "La visite de l'empereur Charles IV en France d'après l'exemplaire des "Grandes Chroniques" exécuté pour le roi Charles V," in *Congrès international des bibliophiles, Vienne, 1969* (1971), 85–89, and Raoul Manselli, "La festa nel Medioevo," in *Atti del VII Convegno di Studio, Viterbo, 27–30 Maggio 1982* (Viterbo, 1983), 219–41 (with texts in an appendix that includes the Avignon banquet cited above).

122. D. Chadwick, *Social Life in the Days of Piers Plowman* (New York, 1922), 59, citing A VII, 268, B VI, 283, and C IX, 305.

123. The description comes from Folengo (Merlin Cocai), *Il Baldo*, ed. G. Dossena (2 vols.; Milan, 1958), bk. XII, lines 498–501, showing sixteenth-century persistence of a diet we met in prehistory and which survives today in some areas as a reminder of the verity of Greek and Roman myths about the original food of humankind. See G. Cherubini, "La 'Civiltà del castagno in Italia alla fine del medioevo," *Archeologia medievale: cultura materiale. insediamenti. territorio* (Florence, 1981): 247–80.

APPENDIX

1. Throughout this appendix temperatures are given in degrees Fahrenheit.

2. I calculate that any juices pressed from wild apples would have naturally fermented from equally wild yeasts. If you have the inexpensive license from the Federal Government, use home-made wine from elderberry, wild cherry (*Prunus avium*, not native to North America), or dandelion in place of the cider—it is also possible to cheat and use a dry red wine.

3. I stress this because carrots seem to have been transformed more completely under cultivation over the centuries than many others of their tribe (think white? think blackish? red? but not orange and not the triumph of early-modern gardening acumen, celeriac).

4. *The Cooking of the Eastern Mediterranean* (New York, 1994), p. 385.

5. *A New Book of Mediterranean Food* (London, 1985), pp. 90–91.

6. Called goatfish in Caribbean and Atlantic waters: see Alan Davidson, *Mediterranean Seafood*, 2d ed. (Baton Rouge, 1981), 92f. In the Middle East, whole red mullet are grilled ungutted.

7. Adapted from Paula Wolfert, *Paula Wolfert's World of Food* (New York, 1988), 29.

8. *A New Book of Mediterranean Food*, pp. 312–13.

9. I am freely interpreting these as Bottéro's *samidu*, untranslatable, but another of the favored garlic/onion/leek family of *alliacae*, their Near Eastern origin assured by their name in Palestine, "onions of Ascalon."

10. The original piece of fat would likely have been from fat-tailed sheep, the type still bred for cooking lard in Middle Eastern countries, often with tails so large that they must be supported by little carts.

11. This strong herb *(sibburratu)* is specified in Bottéro's reading; available from certain herb gardens and a few old-fashioned pharmacies, if not from your own garden.

12. This step may seem unnecessary, but it preserves a Mesopotamian distinction between the first step accomplished in a bronze cauldron and the second, longer cooking procedure in clay.

13. If you are very ambitious, you may follow Paula Wolfert's technique for boning a rabbit first, so that you will be able to serve it as a galantine (*World of Food* [New York, 1988], p. 209).

14. My own are wonderfully realized woodcuts by Eleanor Robbins of Cambridge, Mass.

15. For a castle subtlety made from cheese pastry, see Constance B. Hieatt and Sharon Butler, *Pleyn Delit: Medieval Cookery for Modern Cooks* (Toronto, 1979), 156–58.

Bibliography

PRIMARY SOURCES
Ancient and Classical

Aelian (Claudius Aelianus; Early third century). *On the Characteristics of Animals.* Translated by
A. F. Schofield. 3 vols. Loeb Classical Library. Cambridge, Mass., 1958–59.

Alcman. In *Lyra Graeca.* Edited by J. M. Edmonds. Vol. 1, pp. 44–135. Loeb Classical Library.
Cambridge, Mass., 1928.

The Ancient Egyptian Book of the Dead. Translated by R. O. Faulkner; Edited by Carol Andrews.
Rev. ed. London, 1985.

Anthimus (5th–6th centuries A.D.). *De observatio ciborum.* Text and commentary, Shirley H.
Weber (diss. Princeton 1923), Leiden, 1924; now translated by Mark Grant. Totnes, Devon, 1996.

Apicius, Marcus Gavius (1st century A.D.). *De re coquinaria.* [Excerpted and combined with
household and medical advisories in Late Antiquity.]

    Apicii Decem Libri qui dicuntur De re coquinaria et Excerpta Vinidario conscripta. Translated by
M. E. Milham. Bibliotheca Teubneriana, Akademie der Wissenschaften zu Berlin.
Berlin, 1969. [The definitive modern edition in Latin, with full critical apparatus.]

    Glossarial Index to De Re Coquinaria of Apicius. Études et commentaires de la Centre Na-
tionale de la Recherche Scientifique, no. 58. Paris, 1965.

    André, Jacques. *Apicius "L'art culinaire" De re coquinaria* [1965]. New ed. Paris, 1974. [A
magesterial edition by the author of the most useful commentary on Pliny's *Natural
History* (see below). Essential reading, for its corrections of earlier translations and
studies.]

    Brandt, Edward. *Untersuchungen zum römischen Kochbuche.* Philologus, Supplement 19, 3.

Leipzig: Teubner, 1927. [Attribution of the various sections; renumbering of recipe paragraphs.]

Edwards, John. *The Roman Cookery of Apicius. A Treasury of Gourmet Recipes and Herbal Cookery.* Point Roberts, Wash., 1984. [A free English translation, modernized and interspersed with historical tidbits.]

Flower, Barbara, and Elizabeth Rosenbaum. *Apicius. The Roman Cookery Book*, London, 1958. [The translation and commentary is the most accessible to English-speakers. (The parallel Latin, and some footnotes of suggested recipes that started me on this novel career.) A more recent edition has been published by Mrs. Rosenbaum-Alföldi in Germany.]

Giarratano, Cesare, and Friedrich Vollmer. *Apicii Librorum qui dicuntur De Re Coquinaria quae extant.* Leipzig: Teubner, 1922. [The first truly critical edition after those of Renaissance humanists.]

Guégan, Bernard. *Les dix livres de cuisine d'Apicius.* Paris, 1933. [Translation and commentary by a noted gastronome, of value for speculation based on knowledge both of culinary practice and classical literature.]

Schuch, C. T. *Apici Caeli De Re Coquinaria Libri Decem* [1867]. Heidelberg, 1974. [The first modern edition to begin study of the text, including the Excerpts by Vinidarius. Arbitrary numbering of the paragraphs.]

Vehling, Joseph Dommers. *Apicius: Cookery and Dining in Imperial Rome* [1936]. New York, 1977. [An English translation by a chef who is not a Latinist. (Roman fish sauce *[garum]* is simply rendered "stock!") Contains a useful bibliography of editions and commmentaries.]

Archestratus of Gela *vel* Syracuse. *Supplementum Hellenisticum.* Edited by H. Lloyd-Jones and P. Parsons, 46–75. Berlin, 1983.

Aristotle. *Metaphysics* and *Oeconomicus.* Edited and translated by H. Tredennicks and C. Armstrong. 2 vols. Loeb Classical Library. Cambridge, Mass., 1935.

———. *On Sophistical Refutations; On Coming-to-Be and Passing-Away.* Translated by E. S. Forster. Loeb Classical Library. Cambridge, Mass., 1955.

Arrian. *History of Alexander and Indica.* Edited by P. A. Brunt. 2 vols. Loeb Classical Library. Cambridge, Mass. [1929–33], 1976.

Athenaeus (ca. 200 A.D.). *The Deipnosophists.* Text and translation by C. B. Gulick. 7 vols. Loeb Classical Library. Cambridge, Mass., 1927–50. [In Roman Egypt, the title might be rendered "The Gastronomers at Dinner."]

Aulus Gellius (2d century A.D.). *The Attic Nights of Aulus Gellius.* Edited by J. C. Rolfe. 3 vols. Loeb Classical Library. Cambridge, Mass., [1927], 1961.

Campbell, David A., ed. *Greek Lyric.* 5 vols. Loeb Classical Library. Cambridge, Mass., 1982–1993.

Cato, Marcus Porcius (234–149 B.C.). *On Agriculture.* Text and translation by W. D. Hooper, revised by H. B. Ash. Loeb Classical Library. Cambridge, Mass., 1934.

———. *De l'agriculture de Cato.* Edited and translated by Raoul Goujard. Paris, 1975. [Includes extensive commentary.]

Celsus, Aulus Cornelius (1st century A.D.). *De medicina.* Translated by W. G. Spencer. 3 vols. Loeb Classical Library. Cambridge, Mass., [1935–38], 1971.

Columella, L. Junius Moderatus (1st century A.D.). *On Agriculture.* Text and translation by H. B. Ash and E. S. Forster. 3 vols. Loeb Classical Library. Cambridge, Mass., [1940 et seq.], 1977.

The Complete Greek Dramas. Edited by J. Whitney Oates and Eugene O'Neill, Jr. 2 vols. New York, 1938.

Davies, W. V. *Egyptian Hieroglyphs.* Berkeley and Los Angeles, 1987.

Dio (Cassius Dio; early 3d century A.D.). *Dio's Roman History.* Edited by Earnest Cary. 9 vols. Loeb Classical Library. Cambridge, Mass., 1944f.

Dioscorides, Pedanios (ca. 40–80 A.D.). *De materia medica libri quinque.* Edited by M. Wellmann. Berlin, 1907–14; reprint, 1958.

———. *Dioscorides on Pharmacy and Medicine.* Edited by John M. Riddle. History of Science series, no. 3. Austin, Tex., 1985.

The Egyptian Book of the Dead. Edited by Thomas G. Allen. Chicago, 1960.

Edmonds, J. M., ed. and trans. *Elegy and Iambus.* 2 vols. Loeb Classical Library. London, 1931.

Ennius, Quintus (d. 169 B.C.). *Hedyphagetica.* In *Remains of Old Latin,* vol 1. Edited by E. H. Warmington. Loeb Classical Library. Cambridge, Mass., 1961.

Erman, [Georg] Adolf, ed. and trans. *The Ancient Egyptians: A Sourcebook of Their Writings.* New York, 1966.

Galen (Claudius Galenus; 2d century A.D.). *De sanitate tuendi. De alimentorum facultatibus. De bonis malisque sucis. . . . De Ptisana.* Edited by Konrad Koch et al. Corpus medicorum Graecorum. Leipzig: Teubner, 1923.

———. *Peri kraseōn (De temperamentis Liber III).* Edited by George Helmreich. Stuttgart, 1904; reprint, 1969.

Gargilius Martialis, Quintus (3d century A.D.). *De hortis.* Opuscula philologica 1. Bologna, 1988.

Guglielmi, W. *Reden, Rufen und Lieder auf altägyptischen Darstellungen der Landwirtschaft, Viehzucht, des Fisch-und Vogelfangs vom Mittleren Reich bis zur Spätzeit.* Thübingen ägyptische Beiträge, 1. Bonn, 1973.

Herodotos. *Histories.* Edited and translated by A. D. Godley. Loeb Classical Library. 4 vols. Cambridge, Mass., 1926–.

Hesiod. *Theogony, Works and Days.* Translated by R. Lattimore. Ann Arbor, 1959.

Hippocrates. *Du Regime.* Edited and translated by Robert Joly. Paris, 1967.

———. *Hippocratic Writings* [1950]. Edited by G. E. R. Lloyd and translated by J. Chadwick et al. New York, 1978.

Homer. *The Iliad of Homer.* Translated by R. Lattimore. Chicago, 1951.

———. *The Odyssey.* Edited and translated by A. T. Murray. 2 vols. Loeb Classical Library. Cambridge, Mass., 1946.

Horace (Quintus Horatius Flaccus; 65–8 B.C.). *Satires, Epistles and Ars Poetica.* Edited by H. R. Fairclough. Loeb Classical Library. Cambridge, Mass., [1926], 1978.

———. *Odes and Epodes.* Edited by C. E. Bennett. Loeb Classical Library. Cambridge, Mass., 1939.

———. *The Odes of Horace.* Edited and translated by Arthur Palmer. 4th ed. London, 1891.

Juvenal (Decinus Iunius Juvenalis; 60–100 A.D.). *Satires* (with Persius). Edited by G. G. Ramsay. Loeb Classical Library. Cambridge, Mass., [1918], 1959.

Lichtheim, Miriam. *Ancient Egyptian Literature: A Book of Readings.* 3 vols. Berkeley and Los Angeles, 1973–80.

Livy (Titus Livius; 59 B.C.–A.D. 17). *Ab urbe condita.* Edited by Benjamin O. Foster. 13 vols. Loeb Classical Library. London, 1919 et seq.

Lucian of Samosata. (ca. 120–90 A.D.) *Convivium.* In *Luciani Samosatensis Opera.* Edited by Charles Jacobitz. 3 vols. Leipzig: Teubner, 1881–84.

———. *Lucian.* With an English translation by A. M. Harmon. 8 vols. Loeb Classical Library. London, 1913 et seq.

Macrobius, Theodosius Ambrosius Aurelius (4th–5th centuries A.D.). *Saturnalia.* Edited and translated by H. Bornecque. 2 vols. Paris, 1937.

———. *Saturnalia.* Translated by Percival V. Davies. New York, 1969.

Manetho. *Manetho.* Edited by W. G. Waddell. Loeb Classical Library. Cambridge, Mass., 1940.

Martial (M. Valerius Martialis; ca. 40–105 A.D.). *Epigrams.* Edited by Walter C. A. Ker. 2 vols. Loeb Classical Library. Cambridge, Mass., [1919], 1968.

Menander. *Menandri reliquiae selectae.* Edited by F. Sandbach. Oxford, 1972.

———. *The Plays of Menander.* Edited and translated by L. Casson. New York, 1971.

Oppian. *Cynegetica, Halieutica.* In *Oppian. Colluthus. Tryphiodorus.* Edited and translated by A. W. Mair. Loeb Classical Library. Cambridge, Mass., 1928.

Ovid (Publius Ovidius Naso; 43 B.C.–17/18 A.D.). *Ovid's Fasti.* Translated and edited by James G. Frazer. Loeb Classical Library. Cambridge, Mass., [1931], 1976.

XII Panegyrici Latini. Edited by Emil Baehrens. Leipzig, 1974.

Petronius Arbiter (d. 66 A.D.). *Satyricon* (with Seneca's *Apocolocyntosis*). Edited by M. Heseltine. Loeb Classical Library. Cambridge, Mass., [1913], 1969.

———. *Petrone Latin et François, traduction entière, suivante le manuscrit trouvé à Belgrade en 1688.* [Edited by M. Nodot.] 2 vols., Amsterdam, 1756.

Pindar. *Odes.* Edited and translated by J. E. Sandys. Loeb Classical Library. Cambridge, Mass., 1915.

Plato. *Laws.* Edited by R. G. Bury. 2 vols. Loeb Classical Library. Cambridge, Mass., 1952.

———. *Republic.* Edited by Paul Shorey. 2 vols. Loeb Classical Library. Cambridge, Mass., 1930.

———. *Symposium.* Edited by W. R. M. Lamb. Loeb Classical Library. Cambridge, Mass., 1953.

Pliny the Elder (Gaius Plinius Secundus; 23–79 A.D.). *Natural History.* Edited by H. Rackham. 10 vols. Loeb Classical Library. Cambridge, Mass., 1938ff.

———. *Pline l'ancien: Histoire naturelle.* Edited by Jacques André. 13 vols. Paris, 1958. [Commentary is especially valuable for book 14: "Des arbres fruitiers: La vigne."]

Pliny the Younger (G. Plinius Caecilius Secundus; 1st–2d centuries A.D.). *Letters.* Translated by W. Melmoth, and edited by W. M. L. Hutchinson. 2 vols. Loeb Classical Library. Cambridge, Mass., 1915.

Plutarch (ca. 45/50–125 A.D.). *Plutarch's Lives.* Translated by B. Perrin. 10 vols. Loeb Classical Library. Cambridge, Mass., 1914–.

———. *Plutarch's De Iside et Osiride.* Edited by J. G. Griffiths. Cardiff, 1970.

———. *Plutarch's Moralia.* Edited by H. B. Hoffleit and translated by P. A. Clement. Loeb Classical Library. Cambridge, Mass., 1969. [*Quaestiones convivales* ("Table Talk") is included in vols. 8 and 9.]

Pollux, Julius (ca. 130–188 A.D.). *Onomasticon.* Edited by Erich Bethe. 3 vols. Stuttgart, 1967.

Seneca (Lucius Annaeus Seneca; 4 B.C.–65 A.D.). *Ad Lucilium: Epistulae morales.* Edited by R. M. Gummere. 3 vols. Loeb Classical Library. London, 1917–25.

Simpson, William K., ed. *Literature of Ancient Egypt: An Anthology of Stories, Instructions and Poetry.* New ed. New Haven, 1973.

Strabo. *The Geography of Strabo.* Translated by H. Leonard Jones. 8 vols. Loeb Classical Library. London, 1917–32.

Strauss, Leo. *Xenophon's Socratic Discourse: An Interpretation of the Oeconomicus.* Ithaca, N.Y., 1970.

Suetonius (Gaius Suetonius Tranquillus; A.D. 69?–121? or later). *Lives of the Roman Emperors.* Edited by J. C. Rolfe. 2 vols. Loeb Classical Library. Cambridge, Mass., [1914], 1924.

Theophrastus. *Enquiry into Plants.* Edited and translated by A. Hort. 2 vols. Loeb Classical Library. Cambridge, Mass., 1916.

———. *De causis plantarum.* Translated by Benedict Einarson and George K. K. Link. 3 vols. Loeb Classical Library. Cambridge, Mass., 1976–90.

Varro, Marcus Terentius (116–27 B.C.). *On Agriculture* (with Cato). Loeb Classical Library. Cambridge, Mass., 1943.

———. *Peri edesmatōn.* In F. Buecheler, ed. *Petronii Saturae et Liber Priapeorum et Varronis Menippearum Reliquiae.* Berlin, 1922.

———. *De lingua latina: La langue latine.* Edited by Pierre Flobert. 2 vols. Paris, 1985.

Virgil (Publius Vergilius Maro; 70–19 B.C.). *Georgics.* Edited by H. B. Fairclough. Loeb Classical Library. Cambridge, Mass., [1916], 1935.

——— (Pseudo-Virgil). *Moretum.* In *Appendix Vergiliana.* Translated by J. J. Mooney, *Minor Poems.* Birmingham, 1916; 2d, rev. ed., 1920.

Xenophanes of Colophon. *Fragments.* Translation and commentary by J. H. Lesher. Toronto, 1992.

Xenophon. *Oeconomicus.* Edited by E. C. Marchant. Loeb Classical Library. Cambridge, Mass., 1965. *See also above* Strauss (1970).

———. *Symposium.* Edited by O. J. Todd. Loeb Classical Library. Cambridge, Mass., 1961.

Early Medieval and Gothic Periods

A Collection of Ordinances and Regulations for the Government of the Royal Household. London: Society of Antiquaries, 1790.

Anon., *Sir Gawain and the Green Knight.* Edited by J. R. R. Tolkien and E. V. Gordon. Oxford, 1925. 2d ed. revised by Norman Davis, 1967; transl. Tolkien, Boston, 1975.

Anon. (ca. 1290–beginning 14th centuries). *Enseingnemenz qui enseingnent a apareiller toutesmanieres de viandes* . . . Paris, Bibliothèque Nationale, MS. lat. 7131. [Includes two other treatises, *Tractatus de modo praeparandi et condiendi omnia cibaria* and *Liber de coquina.*]

See Marianne Mulon, "Deux traités inédits d'art culinaire médiéval" (1970), and Carole Lambert, ed., *Du manuscrit à la table* (1992), no. 104 in *Répertoire des manuscrits.*

Anon. (14th century). *Le grand cuysinier de toute cuysine.* Ms. lost. Printed under variant titles, Paris, 1540–66.

Anon. [The cooks of Richard II] (ca. 1390). *The Forme of Cury.* MSS. British Museum, Add. 5016 et al.

Pegge, Samuel, ed. *The Forme of Cury.* London: J. Nicols, 1780.

Richard Warner. *Antiquitates culinariae: Tracts on Culinary Affairs of the Old English* [London, 1791]. London: Prospect Books, 1983.

See also Constance Hieatt and Sharon Butler, *Curye on Inglysch* (1985).

Anon. [A burgher of Paris, ca. 1393, advice to new young bride]. Paris, Bibliothèque nationale, fonds fr. 12477 et al.

Pichon, Jérôme, ed. *Le Ménagier de Paris.* Société des Bibliophiles françois. 2 vols. Paris: Crapelet, 1846.

Power, Eileen, ed. *The Goodman of Paris . . . A Treatise on Moral and Domestic Economy by a Citizen of Paris.* London: Routledge, 1928. [An abridged translation of the Pichon edition.]

Brereton, Georgine E., and Janet M. Ferrier. *Le Ménagier de Paris.* Edited, translated, and with commentary. Oxford: Oxford University Press, 1981.

Anon. (ca. 1430). MS. British Museum, Harley 279.

Margaret Webb. *Early English Recipes Selected from the Harleian MS. 279 of about 1430 A.D.* With an introduction by Sir Stephen Gaselee. Cambridge, 1937.

See also Thomas Austin, *Two Fifteenth-Century Cookery Books* (1888).

Anon. [Bills of fare, recipes] (late 15th century). MS. British Library, Sloane 1201.

See Thomas Wright, *The Homes of other Days* (1871), which includes two menus; and, for the recipes, Hieatt and Butler, *Curye on Inglysch* (1985).

Anon. (Veneto, 14th century). *Libro per cuoco.* MS., Rome, Biblioteca Casanatense, cod. 225.

Ludovico Frati, ed. *Libro di cucina del secolo XIV.* Livorno: R. Giusti, 1899; reprint, Bologna, 1970

See also Emilio Faccioli, *Arte della cucina* (1966).

Anon. (Angevin court at Naples, end 13th–early 14th centuries). *Liber de Coquina.* MS., Paris, Bib. Nat. 7131, part B, 96v–99v.

Marianne Mulon, ed. "Deux traités inédits d'art culinaire médiéval." *Bulletin philologique et historique (jusqu'à 1610) du comité des travaux historiques et scientifiques (1968).* (1970): 1:369–435.

Anon. (Tuscan, 14th century). *Libro della cucina.* MS., Bologna, Biblioteca Universitaria, no 158 [at end].

F. Zambrini, ed. *Il Libro della cucina del secolo 14.* Bologna: Romagnoli, 1863.

See also Emilio Faccioli, *Arte della cucina* (1966), 1:19–37.

Anon. (14th century). *Ein Buch von guter Spise.* Munich, Universitäts-Bibliothek, cod. MS. 731

Hans Hajek, ed. *Das buch von güter spise. Aus der Würzburg-Münchener Handschrift neu herausgegeben.* Texte des späten Mittelalters, ed. W. Stammler and E. A. Philippson, no. 8. Berlin, 1958. [For attribution, see E. Schroeder, ed., *Die Gedichte des Königes vom Odenwalde* (1900).]

Anon. (early 15th century). *Liber Cure Cocorum.* MS. British Library, Sloane 1986.

Edited by Richard Morris. *Transactions of the Philological Society,* Supplement. London, 1862.

Anon. *A Noble Boke off Cookry ffor a Prynce Houssolde or eny other Estately Houssolde* (Library of the Earl of Leicester, Holkham Hall, MS. 674). Edited by Robina Napier (Mrs. Alexander). London: E. Stock, 1882.

Anon. *Küchenmeisterei* [Nurnberg, 1482; Augsburg, 1507, et seq]. Edited by H. Wegener. Leipzig, 1935.

Anon. (end of 15th century, old English). Untitled MS., Cambridge, Magdalene College, Pepys 1047.

> Gerald A. J. Hodgett, ed. and trans. *Stere Hit Well: A book of medieval refinements, recipes and remedies from a manuscript in Samuel Pepys's library.* Cambridge: Cornmarket, 1972. [Facsimile.]

Anon. (13th century). *De Quaresme et de Charnage,* MSS. Paris, Bib. Nat., fr. 837 (also 1593, 2168, 19152, 25545).

> Grégoire Lozinski, ed. *La bataille de Caresme et de charnage.* Bibliothèque de l'École des Hautes Études, vol. 262. Paris: H. Champion, 1933.

Albertus Magnus (1193–1280). *De vegetabilibus libri VII; historiae naturalis, pars XVIII.* Edited by E. Meyer and Karl Jessen. Frankfurt am Main, [1857] 1982.

Aldobrandino da Siena. *La régime du corps de maître Aldebrandin de Sienne, Texte français du XIIIe siècle.* Edited by Louis Landouzy and Roger Pépin. Paris: H. Champion, 1911.

Arnaldus de Villanova. *Liber de vinis.* [MS. early 14th century]. Edited and translated by Henry E. Sigerist as *The Earliest Printed Book on Wine (1478).* New York, 1943.

Ausonius. *Opere.* Edited by A. Pastorino. Classici latini, ed. Italo Lana. Turin, 1971.

> See also Sister M. J. Byrne. *Prolegomena to an Edition of the Works of Decimus Magnus Ausonius.* New York, 1916.

Balducci Pegolotti, Francesco, *La pratica della mercatura* (MS., Florence, Riccardiana 2441). Edited by Allan Evans. Publication no. 24. Cambridge, Mass.: Medieval Academy of America, 1936; reprint 1970.

Bartholomaeus Anglicus (mid-13th century). *De proprietatibus rerum. On the properties of things, John Trevisa's translation of Bartholomaeus Anglicus.* 2 vols. Clarendon 1975.

> See also selections in Robert Steele, *Mediaeval Lore from Bartholomew Anglicus.* With a preface by William Morris. London, 1924.

Bede, The Venerable (8th century A.D.). *Ecclesiastical History of the English People.* Edited by B. Colgrave and R. A. B. Mynors. Oxford, 1969.

Byrhtferth (Anglo-Saxon monk of Ramsey Abbey, ca. 950–1000). *Manual.* [Oxford, St. John's College, MS. 17, ca. A.D. 1110]. Edited by S. J. Crawford. Early English Text Society. London: Oxford University Press, 1929.

> G. F. Forsey, "Byrhtferth's Preface." *Speculum* 3 (1928): 505–22.

Chaucer, Geoffrey. *Canterbury Tales.* Edited by A. C. Cawley [1958]. New York, 1992.

Christine de Pisan. *Le livre des faits et bonnes meurs du sage Roi Charles V.* Edited by S. Solente. 2 vols. Paris, 1936–41.

d'Escouchy, Mathieu. *Comment les entremes, joustes et veux furent fais aux banquets des ducs de Bourgoinge et de Clèves* (MS., Baluze 10319 [Fr. 5739]). Published in G. du Fresne de Beaucourt, *Chroniques de Mathieu d'Escouchy,* 2:116–237. Paris, 1863.

Frederick II Hohenstaufen. *De arte venandi cum avibus* [Vatican MS. Pal. lat 1071]. Edited by Reinher Hausherr. 6 vols. Stuttgart, 1977–79. See also the facsimile edition with commentary by Carl A. Willemsen (Graz, 1969).

Geoponika. (10th century). *De re rustica, libri XX.* Edited by Cassiano Basso. 4 vols. in 2. Leipzig, 1781.

Guy de Chauliac. *Inventarium seu collectorium in parte cyrurgicali medicine* (1363; Middle English translation, MS. Paris, Bib. nat., anglais 25).

> Margaret S. Ogden, ed. *The Cyrurgie of Guy de Chauliac.* Early English Text Society, no. 265. London: Oxford University Press, 1971.

Isidore of Seville. *Isidori Hispalensis episcopi. Etymologiarum sive originum libri XX.* Edited by W. M. Lindsay. 2 vols. Oxford, 1911.

Mandeville, Sir John. (Early 15th century, compiled by Jehan d'Outremuse of Liège). *The Travels of Sir John Mandeville.* Harmondsworth: Penguin, 1983.

Marche, Olivier de la. *Mémoires.* Edited by H. Beaune and J. d'Arbaumont. 4 vols. Paris, 1883–88.

Neckham, Alexander [12th century]. *De natura rerum libri duo* (de utensilium nominibus, et al.). In Thomas Wright, ed., *A Volume of Vocabularies.* [London], 1882.

Notker "the Stammerer." *Two Lives of Charlemagne.* Translated and with an introduction by Lewis Thorpe. Baltimore, 1969.

Platearius, John, the Younger (beginning of the 12th century). *De simplicis* from *Circa instans.*

> See Robertson, "Circa instans" (1982); also Paul Dorveaux, *Le livre des simples medicines, traduction française du Liber . . . circa instans de Platearius* (Paris, 1913).

Russell, John. *Boke of Nurture* (15th century; by a marshal and usher to Humphrey, Duke of Gloucester). MS., British Library, Harley 4011.

> F. J. Furnivall, ed. *Early English Meals and Manners.* Early English Text Society, no. 32a. London: Oxford University Press, 1863; also an independent ed. of 1894.

Sidonius, C. Sollius Modestus Apollinaris (ca. 430–482). *Poems and Letters.* Edited by W. B. Anderson. Loeb Classical Library. 2 vols. Cambridge, Mass.: 1936–65.

Taillevent (pseud. of Guillaume Tirel). *Le viandier* [Sion: MS. Archives cantonales de Valais, S.108; Paris: Bibliothèque Mazarine, 3636; Bibliothèque Nationale, fonds fr. 19, 791, et al.; printed eds. from 1490 to 1604]. (Tirel died ca. 1395, but the Valais manuscript dates from the late 13th century, indicating that what is attributed to the chef of King Charles V incorporates much earlier material.)

> Pichon, Jérome, and Georges Vicaire. *Le Viandie de Guillaume Tirel dit Taillevent.* Paris: Tchner, 1892.

> Martinet, Silvie, ed. and trans. *Le viandier de Taillevent.* Geneva, 1967. [Includes commentary.]

> Scully, Terence. *The Viandier of Taillevent: An Edition of all Extant Manuscripts.* Ottowa: University of Ottowa Press, 1988.

Wernher der Gartenäre. *Helmbrecht,* [Bavarian/Austrian, ca. 1260–1274].

> Linda B. Parshall, ed. and trans. *Wernher der Gartenäre: Helmbrecht.* Garland Library of Medieval Literature, ser. A, vol. 18. New York: Garland, 1987.

William of Rubruck [13th century]. "The Remarkable Travels of Wm. de Rubruquis into Tartary and China." In vol. 7 of J. Pinkerton, *A General Collection of the Best and Most Interesting Voyages and Travels in All Parts of the World.* 17 vols. London, 1808–14.

Wynkyn de Worde (15th century). *Boke of Kervynge.* Edited by F. J. Furnivall in *Early English Meals and Manners.* Early English Text Society, no. 32a. London, 1863. [Also included in Early English Text Society, no. 4, together with Caxton's *Noble Boke of Curtasye,* and *The Babees Book.*]

SECONDARY SOURCES
Prehistory, Egypt, and Mesopotamia

Adams, R. M. *The Evolution of Urban Society: Early Mesopotamia and Prehispanic Mexico.* Chicago, 1966.

Adams, R. M., and H. J. Nissen. *The Uruk Countryside: The Natural Setting of Urban Societies.* Chicago, 1972.

L'alimentazione nel mondo antico. 4 vols. Exhibition catalogue, Ministero per i beni culturali e ambientali. Rome: Istituto poligrafico e Zecca dello Stato, 1987.

Amiet, Pierre. *The Art of the Ancient Near East,* trans. J. Shepley and C. Choquet. New York, 1980.

Baines, John, and Jaromir Malek. *Atlas of Ancient Egypt.* London, 1979.

Baker, Herbert G. *Plants and Civilization.* Fundamentals of Botany series. Belmont, Calif., 1965.

Bates, Oric. "Ancient Egyptian Fishing." *Harvard African Studies* 1 (1917): 199–271.

Beach, Elinor Ferris. "The Samaria Ivories, *Marzeah,* and the Biblical Text." *Biblical Archaeologist* 56 (June 1993): 94–104.

Beauverie, M. A. "Sur quelques fruits de l'ancienne Égypte exposés au musée de Grenoble." *Bulletin de l'Institut français d'archéologie orientale* 28 (1930): 393–405.

Beck, Martinus A. *Atlas of Mesopotamia.* London, 1962.

Bettinger, Robert L. *Hunter-Gatherers: Archaeological and Evolutionary Theory.* New York, 1991.

Binford, Sally R., and Lewis R. Binford, eds. *New Perspectives in Archaeology.* Chicago, 1968.

Birket-Smith, Kaj. *The Paths of Culture: A General Ethnology,* trans. K. Fennow. Madison, 1965.

Bottéro, Jean. "The Cuisine of Ancient Mesopotamia." *Biblical Archaeologist* (March 1985): 36–47.

———. "Getränke." *Reallexicon der Assyriologie und vorderasiatischen Archäologie.* Part 3. Berlin, 1966.

———. "Gewürze." *Reallexicon der Assyriologie und vorderasiatischen Archäologie.* Part 3. Berlin, 1966.

———. "Konservierung." *Reallexicon der Assyriologie und vorderasiatischen Archäologie.* Part 6. Berlin, 1966.

———. "Küche." *Reallexicon der Assyriologie und vorderasiatischen Archäologie.* Part 6. Berlin, 1982.

———. "La plus vieille cuisine du monde." *L'Histoire* 49 (October 1982): 72–82.

———. *Textes culinaires Mésopotamiens: Mesopotamian culinary Texts.* In *Mesopotamian Civilizations,* ed. Jerold S. Cooper, vol. 6. Winona Lake, Ind., 1995.

Braidwood, Robert J. "The Agricultural Revolution." In *Hunters, Farmers, and Civilizations,* ed. C. C. Lamberg-Karlovsky. San Francisco, 1979.

———. "The Origin and Growth of a Research Focus: Agricultural Beginnings," *Expedition* 28 (1986): 2–7.

Braidwood, Robert J., and Bruce Howe. *Prehistoric Investigations in Iraqi Kurdistan.* Studies in Ancient Oriental Civilization, no. 31. Chicago, 1960.

Brothwell, Don. *The Bog Man and the Archaeology of People.* Cambridge, Mass., 1987.

Brothwell, Don, and Patricia Brothwell. *Food in Antiquity: A Survey of the Diet of Early Peoples.* Ancient Peoples and Places series, ed. Glyn Daniel, no. 66. New York, 1969.

Brothwell, Don, and Eric Higgs, eds. *Science in Archaeology: A Comprehensive Survey of Progress and Research.* New York, 1963.

Bulletin on Sumerian Agriculture 1984–. [Vol. 1 has articles devoted to cereals.]

Callen, E. O. "Diet as Revealed by Coprolites." In *Science in Archaeology,* ed. Don Brothwell and Eric Higgs. New York, 1963.

Charles, M. P. "An Introduction to the Legumes and Oil Plants of Mesopotamia." *Bulletin on Sumerian Agriculture* 2 (1985): 39–61.

Civil, Miguel. "A Hymn to the Beer Goddess and a Drinking Song." In *Studies Presented to A. Leo Oppenheim,* 67–69. Chicago, 1964.

Clark, Grahame. *Economic Prehistory: Papers on Archaeology.* Cambridge: Cambridge University Press, 1989.

Cohen, Mark Nathan. *The Food Crisis in Prehistory: Overpopulation and the Origins of Agriculture.* New Haven: Yale University Press, 1977. [Controversial.]

Cole, Sonia. *The Neolithic Revolution.* 5th ed. British Museum of Natural History, no. 541. London: British Museum of Natural History, 1970.

Coles, Bryony. *Anthropology for Archaeologists.* London: Duckworth, 1981.

Contenau, Georges. *Everyday Life in Babylonia and Assyria.* New York, 1954.

Cowan, C. Wesley, and P. J. Watson, eds. *The Origins of Agriculture: An International Perspective.* Smithsonian Series in Archaeological Inquiry. Washington D.C., 1992.

Crabtree, Paul J., Douglas Campana, and Kathleen Ryan, eds. *Early Animal Domestication and its Cultural Context.* MASCA Research Papers in Science and Archaeology, vol. 6, supplement. Philadelphia, 1989.

Dalley, Stephanie. *Mari and Karana: Two Babylonian Cities.* London, 1984.

Darby, William J., Paul Ghaliounghi, and Louis Grivetti. *Food: The Gift of Osiris.* 2 vols. London, 1977.

Dixon, J. E., J. R. Cann, and C. Renfrew. "Obsidian and the Origins of Trade." In *Hunters, Farmers, and Civilizations,* ed. C. C. Lamberg-Karlovsky. San Francisco, 1979.

Ehrenberg, Margaret. *Women in Prehistory.* Norman, Okla., 1989.

Ellis, Maria de Jong. "An Agricultural Administrative Archive in the Free Library of Philadelphia." *Journal of Cuneiform Studies* 29 (1977): 127–150.

Emery, Walter B. "A Funerary Repast in an Egyptian Tomb of the Archaic Period." Nederlands Instituut voor het Nabije Oosten, *Scholae Adriani de Buck memoriae dicatae,* no. 1 (Leiden, 1962), 13–17.

Erman, [Georg] Adolf. *Life in Ancient Egypt* [1894]. Dover reprint, New York, 1971. [Out of date, but contains useful drawings of details.]

Figulla, H. H. "Accounts concerning Allocations of Provisions for Offerings in the Ningal-Temple at Ur." *Iraq* 15 (1953): 88–122.

Finegan, Jack. *Archaeological History of the Ancient Middle East.* New York, 1979.

Finet, André. "Le vin à Mari." In *Trade in the Ancient Near East,* ed. J. D. Hawkins. Rencontre Assyriologique internationale, no. 23, 1977. [Abstract of an article in *Archiv für Orientforschung* 25 (see chap. 3, n. 12).]

Flannery, Kent V. "Early Pig Domestication in the Fertile Crescent." In *The Hilly Flanks and Beyond,* ed. Linda S. Braidwood and Robert J. Braidwood. Chicago, 1983.

———. "The Ecology of Early Food Production in Mesopotamia." *Science* 147 (1965): 1247–56.

Fox, Michael V. "A Study of Intef." *Orientalia* 46 (1977): 400–403.

Frankfort, Henri. *The Art and Architecture of the Ancient Orient.* Baltimore, Md., 1955.

Germer, Renate. *Flora des pharaonischen Ägypten.* Mainz am Rhein: P. von Zabern, 1980.

Gilbert, Robert I., and James H. Mielke, eds. *The Analysis of Prehistoric Diets.* Orlando, Fla., 1985.

Gould, Richard A., ed. *Explorations in Ethnoarchaeology.* Albuquerque, 1978.

Groenewegen-Frankfort, H. A. *Arrest and Movement: An Essay on Space and Time in the Representational Art of the Ancient Near East* [1951]. Cambridge, Mass., 1987.

Hartman, Louis F., and A. L. Oppenheim. *On Beer and Brewing Techniques in Ancient Mesopotamia.* Supplement to the *Journal of the American Oriental Society,* no. 10. Baltimore, 1958.

Hartmann, Fernande. *L'agriculture dans l'ancienne Égypte.* Paris, 1923.

Hawkins, James D., ed. *Trade in the Ancient Near East.* 23d Rencontre Assyriologique Internationale. University of Birmingham, July 1976. London, 1977.

Heidel, Alexander. *The Gilgamesh Epic and Old Testament Parallels.* Chicago, 1946.

Heiser, Charles Bixler. *Seed to Civilization: The Story of Man's Food.* San Francisco, 1973.

Helbaek, Hans. "First Impressions of the Çatal Hüyük Plant Husbandry," *Anatolian Studies* 14 (1964): 121–23.

Helck, Wolfgang, and Eberhard Otto. *Lexikon der Ägyptologie.* 7 vols. in 14. Wiesbaden, 1976–92.

Henry, Donald O. *From Foraging to Agriculture: The Levant at the End of the Ice Age.* Philadelphia, 1989.

Herre, Wolf. "The Science and History of Domestic Animals." In *Science in Archaeology,* ed. Don Brothwell and Eric Higgs. New York, 1963.

Higgs, Eric S. *Papers in Economic Prehistory.* 2 vols. London, 1972–75.

Higgs, Eric S., and M. R. Jarman. "The Origins of Agriculture: A Reconsideration," *Antiquity* 43 (1969): 31–41.

Hoffner, Harry A., Jr. *Alimenta Hethaeorum: Food Production in Asia Minor.* New Haven, 1974.

Hole, Frank. "Pastoral Nomadism in Western Iran." In *Explorations in Ethnoarchaeology,* ed. Richard A. Gould. Albuquerque, 1978.

Hole, Frank. "Evidence of Social Organization from Western Iran, 8000–4000 B.C." In *New Perspectives in Archaeology,* ed. Sally R. Binford and Lewis R. Binford. Chicago, 1968.

Hopf, Maria. "Frühe Kulturpflanzen aus Bulgarien." *Jahrbuch des römisch-germanischen Zentralmuseums* 20 (1973): 1–55.

Hugonot, Jean-Claude. *Le jardin dans l'Égypte ancienne.* New York, 1989.

Jacobsen, Thorkild. "Mesopotamia." In H. Frankfort et al., *The Intellectual Adventure of Ancient Man.* Reprint, with revised bibliographies. Chicago, 1946.

James, Edward Oliver. *Sacrifice and Sacrament.* London, 1962.

Jensen, Lloyd B. *Man's Foods, Nutrition and Environments in Food Gathering Times and Food Producing Times.* Champaign, Ill., 1953.

Katz, Solomon H., and Mary M. Voigt. "Bread and Beer: The Early Use of Cereals in the Human Diet." *Expedition* 28 (1986): 23–34.

Katz, Solomon H., and Fritz Maytag. "Brewing an Ancient Beer." *Archaeology* 44 (1991): 24–33.

Keimer, Ludwig. "La boutargue dans l'ancienne Égypte." *Bulletin de l'Institut française d'Égypte* 21 (1938–39): 215–43.

———. *Die Gartenpflanzen im alten Ägypten: Ägyptologische Studien* [1924]. 2 vols. Reprint, Hamburg, 1984.

———. "Pavian und Dum-Palme." *Mitteilungen des deutschen Institutes für ägyptische Altertumskunde in Kairo* 8 (1939): 42–45.

Kemp, Barry J. *Ancient Egypt: Anatomy of a Civilization.* New York, 1989.

Kenyon, Kathleen. *Archaeology in the Holy Land.* 3d ed. New York, 1970.

Kramer, Samuel Noah. *The Sumerians: Their History, Culture and Character.* Chicago, 1963.

Laclant, Jean, "Le rôle de l'allaitement et du lait d'après les textes des Pyramides." *Journal of Near Eastern Studies* 10 (1951): 123–27.

Lamberg-Karlovsky, C. C., ed. *Hunters, Farmers, and Civilizations: Old World Archaeology: Readings from Scientific American.* San Francisco, 1979.

———. *Old World Archaeology: Foundations of Civilization: Readings from Scientific American.* San Francisco, 1972.

Lee, Richard B., and Irven DeVore, eds. *Man the Hunter.* Chicago, 1968.

Leek, F. Filce. "Teeth and Bread in Ancient Egypt." *Journal of Egyptian Archaeology* 58 (1972): 126–32.

———. "Further Studies." *Journal of Egyptian Archaeology* 59 (1973): 199–204.

Lefebvre, Gustave, ed. and trans. *Romans et contes Égyptiens de l'époque pharaonique.* Paris: A. Maisonneuve, 1949.

Lerche, Grith. "Khubz Tannur: Freshly Consumed Flat Bread in the Near East." In *Food in Perspective: Proceedings of the Third International Conference on Ethnological Food Research, Cardiff, Wales, 1977,* ed. A. Fenton and T. M. Owen. Edinburgh, 1981.

Lesko, Barbara. "True Art in Ancient Egypt." In *Egyptological Studies in Honor of Richard A. Parker.* Hanover, N.H., 1986.

Lesko, Leonard H. *King Tut's Wine Cellar.* Berkeley, Calif., 1977.

Levey, Martin. "Food and its Technology in Ancient Mesopotamia: The Earliest Chemical Processes and Chemicals." *Centaurus* 6 (1959): 36–51.

Lucas, Alfred. *Ancient Egyptian Materials and Industries.* 4th ed. Revised and enlarged by J. R. Harris. London, 1962.

Lutz, H. F. *Viticulture and Brewing in the Ancient Orient.* New York, 1922.

MacKay, Alastair I. *Farming and Gardening in the Bible.* Emmaus, Pa., 1950. Reprint, Old Tappan, N.J., 1970.

MacNeish, Richard S. *The Origins of Agriculture and Settled Life.* Norman, Okla., 1992.

Manniche, Lise. *An Ancient Egyptian Herbal.* Austin, Tex., 1989.

Mateescu, Corneliu N. "Remarks on Cattle Breeding and Agriculture in the Middle and Late Neolithic on the Lower Danube." In *Dacia: Revue d'archeologie et d'histoire ancienne* 19 (1975): 13–18.

Mauer, Gerlinde. "Agriculture of the Old Babylonian Period." *Journal of the Ancient Near Eastern Society* 15 (1983): 63–78.

Mellaart, James. *Çatal Hüyük: A Neolithic Town in Anatolia.* London, 1967.

——. *Excavations at Hacilar.* Occasional publications of the British Institute of Archaeology at Ankara, nos. 9–10. Edinburgh, 1970.

Mertz, Barbara. *Red Land, Black Land: Daily Life in Ancient Egypt.* Rev. ed. New York, 1978.

Milano, Lucio. "Alimentazione e regioni alimentari nella Siria preclassica." *Dialoghi di archeologia,* n.s., 3. Milan, 1981.

Montet, Pierre. *Everyday Life in Egypt in the Days of Ramesses the Great* [1925]. Reprint, with a new introduction by David B. O'Connor. Philadelphia, 1981.

Oppenheim, A. Leo. *Ancient Mesopotamia: Portrait of a Dead Civilization.* Rev. ed. Chicago, 1977.

——. "Cuneiform Texts." In *Glass and Glassmaking in Ancient Mesopotamia.* Corning, N.Y., 1970.

Parrot, André. *Mari.* Collection des Ides photographiques, no. 7. Neuchâtel, France, 1953.

——. *Mission archéologique de Mari.* Vol. 2, *Le Palais.* Institut français d'archéologie de Beyrouth, nos. 68 and 69. Paris, 1958.

Parrot, André, and Georges Dossin, eds. *Archives royales de Mari.* 17 vols. Paris, 1950–.

Pendlebury, J. D. S. *Tell el-Amarna.* London, 1935.

Perkins, Dexter, Jr., "Fauna of Çatal Hüyük: Evidence for Early Cattle Domestication in Anatolia." *Science* 164 (1969): 177–79.

Plankoff, Alexandre, trans. *The Shrines of Tut-ankh-amon.* Edited by N. Rambova. New York, 1955.

Pope, Marvin H. "A Divine Banquet at Ugarit." In *The Use of the Old Testament in the New: Studies in honor of William Franklin Stinespring,* ed. J. M. Efird. Durham, N.C., 1972.

——. "Notes on the Rephaim Texts from Ugarit." In *Essays in Memory of Jacob Joel Finkelstein.* Memoirs of the Connecticut Academy of Arts and Sciences, no. 19. Hamden, Conn., 1977.

Postgate, J. N. "The 'Oil Plant' in Assyria." *Bulletin on Sumerian Agriculture* 2 (1985): 144–51.

Price, T. Douglas and James A. Brown. *Prehistoric Hunter-Gatherers: The Emergence of Cultural Complexity.* Orlando, Fla., 1985.

Pritchard, James B., ed. *The Ancient Near East: An Anthology of Texts and Pictures.* 6th ed. Princeton, N.J., 1975.

——. *Ancient Near Eastern Texts Relating to the Old Testament.* 2d ed., corrected and enlarged. Princeton, N.J., 1955.

Quirke, Stephen, and Jeffrey Spencer, eds. *The British Museum Book of Ancient Egypt.* London, 1992.

Redman, C. L. *The Rise of Civilization: From Early Farmers to Urban Society in the Ancient Near East.* San Francisco, 1978.

Reed, C. A. "A Review of the Archaeological Evidence on Animal Domestication in the Prehistoric Near East." In *Prehistoric Investigations in Iraqi Kurdistan,* ed. R. J. Braidwood and B. Howe. Studies in Ancient Oriental Civilization, no. 31. Chicago, 1960.

Renfrew, Colin. *Before Civilization: The Radiocarbon Revolution and Prehistoric Europe.* London: Cape, 1973.

Renfrew, Jane M. *Food and Cooking in Prehistoric Britain: History and Recipes.* [London], 1985.

——. *Palaeoethnobotany: The Prehistoric Food Plants of the Near East and Europe.* New York, 1973.

Riehm, Karl. "Prehistoric Salt-Boiling." *Antiquity* 35 (1961): 181–91.

Roux, Georges. *Ancient Iraq.* London, 1964.

Ruffer, Marc Armand. *Studies in the Paleopathology of Egypt.* Chicago, 1921.

———. *Food in Egypt*. Institût français d'archéologie orientale, Mémoire presenté à l'Institût Égyptien, no. 1. Cairo, 1919.

Saggs, H. W. F. *Everyday Life in Babylonia and Assyria*. New York, 1965.

———. *The Greatness That Was Babylon: A Survey of the Ancient Civilization of the Tigris-Euphrates Valley*. Rev. ed. London, 1988.

Salonen, A. "Die Ofen der alten Mesopotamer." *Baghdader Mitteilungen* 3 (1964): 100–124.

Samuel, Delwyn. "Ancient Egyptian Cereal Processing: Beyond the Artistic Record." *Cambridge Archaeological Journal* 3 (1993): 276–83.

———. "Their Staff of Life: Initial Investigations on Ancient Egyptian Bread Baking." In *Amarna Reports*, no. 5, ed. B. Kemp, 253–90. Egyptian Exploration Society. London, 1989.

Sauer, Carl O. *Agricultural Origins and Dispersals*. New York, 1952.

———. *Land and Life: A Selection from the Writings of Carl Orwin Sauer*, ed. John Leighley. Berkeley and Los Angeles, 1967.

Schorske, Carl E. "Freud's Egyptian Dig." *New York Review of Books*, 27 May 1993, 35–40.

Scott, Nora. "The Daily Life of the Ancient Egyptians." *Metropolitan Museum of Art Bulletin* (Spring 1973).

Sigrist, R. Marcel. "Offrandes dans le Temple de Nusku à Nippur." *Journal of Cuneiform Studies* 29 (1977): 169.

Sillen, Andrew. "Dietary Reconstruction and Near Eastern Archaeology." *Expedition* 28 (1986): 16–22.

Simmons, N. W., ed. *The Evolution of Crop Plants*. London, 1976.

Singer, Charles, et al., eds. *A History of Technology*, vol. 1: *From Early Times to Fall of Ancient Empires*. London: Oxford University Press, 1954.

Smith, E. Baldwin. *Egyptian Architecture as Cultural Expression*. New York, 1938.

Soler, Jean. "Sémiotique de la nourriture dans le bible." *Annales ESC* 28, no. 2 (1973): 943–55. Reprinted as "The Semiotics of Food in the Bible." In F. Foster and O. Ranum, eds., *Food and Drink in History: Selections from the Annales*, vol. 5, 126–38.

Spiegel, J. "Die Entwicklung der Opferszenen in den thebaischen Gräbern." *Mitteilungen des deutschen archäologischen Institutes für ägyptischen Altertumskunde in Kairo* 14 (1956): 190–200.

Starr, C. G. *Early Man: Prehistory and the Civilizations of the Near East*. New York, 1973.

Stein, Gil. "Herding Strategies at Neolithic Gritille: The Use of Animal Bone Remains to Reconstruct Ancient Economic Systems." *Expedition* 28 (1982): 8–15.

Stigler, Robert, et al. *The Old World: Early Man to the Development of Agriculture*, ed. R. Stigler. New York, 1974.

Stol, Marten. "Cress and Its Mustard." In *Jaarbericht van het vooraziatisch-egyptisch Genootschap* 28 (1985): 24–32.

Strouhal, Evzen. *Life of the Ancient Egyptians*. Norman, Okla., 1992.

Täckholm, Vivi, Gunnar Täckholm, and Mohammed Drar. *Flora of Egypt*. Vol. 1. Cairo, 1941.

Thompson, R. Campbell. *The Assyrian Herbal: A Monograph on the Assyrian Vegetable Drugs*. London, 1924.

———. *A Dictionary of Assyrian Botany*, London, 1949.

Trigger, Bruce G. *Beyond History: The Methods of Prehistory*. New York, 1968.

Trigger, B. G., B. J. Kemp, D. O'Connor, and A. B. Lloyd, eds. *Ancient Egypt: A Social History*. Cambridge, 1983.

Ucko, Peter J., and G. W. Dimbleby, eds. *The Domestication and Exploitation of Plants and Animals: Proceedings of a Meeting of the Research Seminar in Archaeology and Related Subjects held at the Institute of Archaeology, London University.* Chicago, 1969.

Ucko, Peter J., G. W. Dimbleby, and Ruth Tringham, eds. *Man, Settlement and Urbanism: Proceedings of a meeting of the Research Seminar in Archaeology and Related Subjects held at the Institute of Archaeology, London University.* London, 1972.

Van Zeist, W. "Pulses and Oil Crop Plants." *Bulletin on Sumerian Agriculture* 2 (1985): 33–37.

Viandier, J. *Manuel d'archéologie Égyptienne.* Vol. 4, *Bas-reliefs et peintures.* Paris, 1964.

———. *Manuel d'archéologie Égyptienne.* Vol. 5, *Scenes de la vie quotidienne.* Paris, 1969.

von Soden, Wolfram, ed. *Akkadisches Handwörterbuch.* 3 vols. Wiesbaden, 1967–81.

Währen, Max. *Brot und Gebäck im Leben und Glauben der alten Ägypter.* Bern, 1963.

———. *Brot und Gebäck im Leben und Glauben des alten Orient.* Basel, 1967.

Walker, Alan C. "Microwear of Mammalian Teeth as an Indicator of Diet." *Science* 201 (1978): 908–10.

Wells, Peter S. *Farms, Villages, and Cities: Commerce and Urban Origins in Late Prehistoric Europe.* Ithaca, N.Y., 1984.

Wendorf, Fred, R. Schild, and Angela E. Close. "An Ancient Harvest on the Nile." *Science* (1982): 68–73.

Wente, Edward F. "The Egyptian 'Make Merry' Songs." *Journal of Near Eastern Studies* 21 (1962): 118–28.

Whittle, A. W. R. *Neolithic Europe: A Survey.* Cambridge, 1985.

Wilson, Hilary. *Egyptian Food and Drink.* Aylesbury, England, 1988.

Wilson, J. V. Kinnier. *The Nimrud Wine Lists: A Study of Men and Administration at the Assyrian Capital in the Eighth Century B.C.* London, 1972.

Wing, Elizabeth, and Antoinette B. Brown. *Paleonutrition: Method and Theory in Prehistoric Foodways.* Studies in Archaeology series. New York, 1979.

Winlock, Herbert E. *Models of Daily Life in Ancient Egypt from the Tomb of Meket-Re at Thebes.* Metropolitan Museum Expeditions, no. 18. Cambridge, Mass., 1955.

Wiseman, D. J. "A New Stela of Assur-nasir-pal II: The Nimrud Tablets, 1951." *Iraq* 14 (1952): 24–39.

Wooley, Sir Leonard. *Ur Excavations.* Vol. 2, *The Royal Cemetery: A Report on the Predynastic and Sargonid Graves Excavated Between 1926 and 1931.* New York, 1934.

Wright, Gary A. *Obsidian Analyses and Prehistoric Near Eastern Trade: 7500 to 1500 B.C.* University of Michigan Anthrolopogy Papers, no. 37. Ann Arbor, 1969.

Young, T. Cuyler, Jr., Philip E. L. Smith, and Peder Mortensen, eds. *The Hilly Flanks and Beyond: Essays on the Prehistory of Southwestern Asia, Presented to Robert J. Braidwood, November 15, 1982.* Studies in Ancient Oriental Civilization, no. 36. Chicago, 1983.

Zaky, Ahmed and Z. Iskander. "Ancient Egyptian Cheese." *Annales du service des antiquités de l'Égypte* 41 (1942): 295–313.

Zeuner, Frederick E. "Cultivation of Plants." Chap. 14 in Singer et al., eds., *A History of Technology: From Early Times to Fall of Ancient Empires.* Vol. 1. London: Oxford University Press, 1954.

———. *A History of Domesticated Animals.* London, 1963.

Zihlman, Adrienne L. "Women in Evolution, Part II: Subsistence and Social Organization among Early Hominids." *Signs. Journal of Women in Culture and Society* 4 (1978): 4–20.

Zohary, Daniel and Maria Hopf. *Domestication of Plants in the Old World: The Origin and Spread of Cultivated Plants in West Asia, Europe, and the Nile Valley.* Oxford, 1988.

Greece and Rome

Abbe, Elfriede M. *The Plants of Virgil's Georgics.* Ithaca, N.Y., 1965.

Alföldi, Andreas. "Tonmodel und Reliefmedaillons aus dem Donau-ländern." In *Laureae Aquincenses memoriae Valentini Kuzsinszky dicatae.* 2 vols. Dissertationes Pannonicae ex Instituto numismatico et Universitatis de Petro Pazmany nominatae budapestinensis provenientes, 312–341. Ser. 2, no. 10. Budapest, 1938.

Alin, Per. "Mycenaean Decline: Some Problems and Thoughts." In *Greece and the Eastern Mediterranean in Ancient History and Prehistory,* ed. K.-H. Kinzl, 31–39. New York, 1977.

Amouretti, Marie-Claire. "Oleiculture et viticulture dans la Grèce antique." In *Agriculture in Ancient Greece,* ed. B. Wells, 77–86. Stockholm, 1992.

———. *Le pain et l'huile dans la Grèce antique.* Paris, 1986.

André, Jacques. *L'alimentation et la cuisine à Rome* [1961]. Paris, 1981.

———. *Lexique des termes de botanique en Latin.* Paris, 1956.

———. *Les noms d'oiseaux en Latin.* Paris, 1966.

Andrews, Alfred C. "Alimentary Use of Hoary Mustard in the Classical Period." *Isis* 34 (1942): 161–62.

———. "Alimentary Use of Lovage in the Classical Period." *Isis* 33 (1941): 514–18.

———. "The Carrot as a Food in the Classical Era." *Classical Philology* 44 (1949): 182–96.

———. "Celery and Parsley as Foods in the Greco-Roman Period." *Classical Philology* 44 (1949): 91–99.

———. "Marjoram as a Spice in the Classical Era." *Classical Philology* 56 (1961): 73–82.

———. "Melons and Watermelons in the Classical Era." *Osiris* 12 (1956): 368–75.

———. "The Parsnip as Food in the Classical Era." *Classical Philology* 53 (1958): 145–52.

———. "The Roman Craze for Surmullets." *Classical Weekly* 42 (1948–49): 186–88.

———. "The Silphium of the Ancients: a Lesson in Crop Control." *Isis* 33 (1941): 232–36.

Arndt, Alice. "Silphium." *Public Eating: Proceedings of the Oxford Symposium on Food and Cookery, 1991,* 28–35. London, 1992.

Ashley, A. "The *alimenta* of Nerva and His Successors." *English Historical Review* 36 (1921): 5–16.

Baldwin, Betty. "Trimalchio and Maecenas." *Latomus* 43 (1984): 402–43.

Balsdon, J. P. V. D. *Life and Leisure in Ancient Rome.* New York, 1969.

Becatti, Giovanni. *Case Ostiense del tardo impero.* Rome, 1948.

Bek, Lise. "Quaestiones conviviales: The Idea of the Triclinium and the Staging of Convivial Ceremonial from Rome to Byzantium." *Analecta Romana Institut Danici* 12 (1983): 81–107.

Bergquist, Birgitta. "Sympotic Space: A Functional Aspect of Greek Dining-Rooms." In *Sympotica,* ed. O. Murray, 37–65. New York, 1990.

Berthiaume, G. *Les rôles du mageiros: Étude sur la boucherie, la cuisine et le sacrifice dans la Grèce ancienne. Mnemosyne,* suppl. 70. Leiden, 1982.

Beyen, H.-G. *Über Stilleben aus Pompeji und Herculanum.* The Hague, 1928.

Bieber, Margarete. *Kuchenformen mit Tragödienszene.* Berlin, 1915.

Bilabel, Friedrich. "Kochenbücher." *RE,* vol. 11, no. 1 (1921): cols. 932–43.

———. "OPSARTYTIKA und Verwandtes." *Sitzungsberichte der Heidelberger Akademie der Wissenschaften.* Phil.-hist. Kl. 23 (1919): 1–93.

Billiard, R. *La vigne et le vin dans l'Antiquite.* Lyon, 1913.

Birley, Robin. *Vindolanda: A Roman Frontier Post on Hadrian's Wall.* London, 1977.

Bisconti, F. "A pranzo con i primi cristiani." *Archeo* 12 (1986): 36–39.

Blanck, Horst. "Ein spätantikes Gastmahl: das Mosaik von Duar-Ech-Chott." *Mitteilungen des deutschen archäologischen Instituts. Römische Abteilung,* 88 (1981): 329–44.

Boardman, John. *The Greeks Overseas: Their Early Colonies and Trade.* Rev. ed. New York, 1980.

———. "The Olive in the Mediterranean: Its Culture and Use." *Philosophical Transactions of the Royal Society* B 275 (1976): 187–96.

Bober, Phyllis Pray. "Identity with Mycenaean Ancestors in Cult Meals at Ancient Greek Sanctuaries." *Public Eating: Proceedings of the Oxford Symposium on Food and Cookery, 1991,* 50–53. London, 1992.

Boethius, Axel. "Nero's Golden House." *Eranos* 44 (1946): 442–59.

Bookidis, Nancy. "Ritual Dining in the Sanctuary of Demeter and Kore at Corinth: Some Questions." In *Sympotica,* ed. O. Murray, 86–94. New York, 1990.

Booth, Alan. "The Age for Reclining and its Attendant Perils." In *Dining in a Classical Context,* ed. W. J. Slater, 105–20. Ann Arbor, 1991.

Börker, Christoph. *Festbankett und griechische Architektur.* Xenia. Konstanz, Germany, 1983.

Borza, Eugene N. "The Symposium at Alexander's Court." *Archaia Makedonia: Ancient Macedonia,* 45–55. Proceedings of the 3d International Symposium, 1977. Thessalonika, 1983.

Boyancé, P. "Platon et le vin." *Bulletin de l'Association G. Budé* (1951): 3–19.

Bravo, Benedetto. "Le commerce des céréales chez les grecs de l'époque archaïque." In *Trade and Famine in Classical Antiquity,* ed. P. Garnsey and C. R. Whittaker, 17–29. Cambridge, 1983.

Brogan, Olwen. "Trade between the Roman Empire and the Free Germans." *JRS* (1936): 195–222.

Breeze, J., and Brian Dobson. *Hadrian's Wall* [1976]. London, 1978.

Brown, A. D. Fitton. "Black Wine." *The Classical Review,* n.s., 12 (1962): 192–95.

Bruhl, A. *Liber Pater: Origine et expansion du culte dionysiaque à Rome.* Bibliothèque des Écoles françaises, 175. N.p., 1953.

Brumfield, Allaire Chandor. *The Attic Festivals of Demeter and their Relation to the Agricultural Year.* New York, 1981.

Bruns, Gerda. *Küchenwesen und Mahlzeiten.* Archaeologia Homerica, vol. 2, pt. Q. Göttingen, 1970.

Bryson, R. A., H. H. Lamb, and D. A. Donley. "Drought and the Decline of Mycenae." *Antiquity* 48 (1974): 46–50.

Buecheler, F., ed. *Petronii Saturae et Liber Priapeorum et Varronis Menippearum Reliquiae.* Berlin, 1922.

Burkert, Walter. "Greek Tragedy and Sacrificial Ritual." *Greek, Roman and Byzantine Studies* 7 (1966): 87–121.

——. *Homo Necans: The Anthropology of Ancient Greek Sacrificial Ritual and Myth* [1972], trans. P. Bing. Berkeley and Los Angeles, 1983.

——. "Oriental Symposia: Contrasts and Parallels." In *Dining in a Classical Context*, ed. W. J. Slater, 7–24. Ann Arbor, 1991.

——. *Structure and History in Greek Mythology and Ritual*. Sather Classical Lecture, no. 47. Berkeley and Los Angeles, 1979.

Calza, Guido. "Le botteghe in Roma antica." *Capitolium* 14 (1939): 221–30.

Cambiano, Giuseppe and Luciana Repici. "Cibo e forme di sussistenza in Platone, Aristotele e Dicearco." In *Homo edens*, ed. O. Longo and P. Scarpi, 81–90. Verona, 1989.

Carcopino, J. *Daily Life in Ancient Rome*, trans. E. O. Lorimer and ed. H. T. Rowell. New Haven, 1940.

——. "Les fastes de la cuisine romaine." In *La Cuisine considerée comme un des Beaux-Arts*, 45–71. Paris, 1951.

Carroll-Spillecke, Maureen. "The Gardens of Greece from Homeric to Roman Times." *Journal of Garden History* 12 (1992): 84–101.

Casella, Domenico. "La frutta nelle pitture Pompeiane." *Pompeiana: Raccolta di studi per il secondo centenario degli scavi di Pompei*, 355–86. Naples, 1950.

Casson, Lionel. *Ancient Trade and Society*. Detroit, 1984.

Chadwick, John. "Mycenaean Wine and the Etymology of *glukús*." *Minos: Rivista di filologia Egea* 9 (1969): 192–97.

——. *The Mycenaean World*. Cambridge, 1976. [Chap. 7, on agriculture and aliment in Linear B, is an epitome of more extensive materials in his *Documents in Mycenaean Greek* (2d ed., 1973).]

Chiarini, Gioachino. "Metafore Plautine." In *Homo edens*, ed. O. Longo and P. Scarpi, 327–33. Verona, 1989.

Clark, Judith A., and Samuel A. Goldblith. "Processing of Foods in Ancient Rome." *Food Technology* 30 (1975): 30–32.

Clemente, Guido. "Le legge sul lusso e la società romana tra III e II secolo A.C." In *Modelli etici, Diritto e Trasformazioni Sociali*, ed. A. Giardina and A. Schiavone. Società Romana e Produzione Schiavistica, vol. 3. Bari: Istituto Gramsci, 1981.

Coleman-Norton, P. R., ed. *Studies in Roman Economic and Social History in Honor of Allan C. Johnson*. Princeton, N.J., 1951.

Compostella, Carla. "Banchetti pubblici e banchetti privati nell' iconografia funeraria romana del I secolo D.C." *Mélanges de l'École française de Rome Antiquité* 104, no. 2 (1992): 659–89.

Cooper, F., and S. Morris. "Dining in Round Buildings." In *Sympotica*, ed. O. Murray, 66–85. New York, 1990.

Coote, H. C. "Some Account of the Cuisine Bourgeoise of Ancient Rome." *Archaeologia* 41 (1886): 283–324.

Corbato, Carlo. "Symposium e teatro: dati e problemi." In *Spettacoli conviviali dall' antichità classica alle corti italiane del '400: Atti del VII Convegno di Studio, Viterbo, 27–30 Maggio 1982*, 65–76. Centro di studi sul teatro medioevale e rinascimentale. Viterbo, 1983.

Corcoran, T. "Roman Fish Sauces." *Classical Journal* 58 (1963): 204–10.

Croisille, J.-M. *Les natures mortes campaniennes: Répertoire descriptif des peintures de nature morte du*

Musée national de Naples, de Pompei, Herculanum et Stabies. Collection Latomus, vol. 76. Brussels, 1965.

Curtis Robert I. *Garum and Salsamenta: Production and Commerce.* Materia medica. Studies in Ancient Medicine, no. 3. New York, 1991.

———. "The Garum Shop of Pompeii Region I.xii.8." *Cronache Pompeiane* 5 (1979): 5–23.

Curtis Robert I., ed. *Studia Pompeiana et Classica in Honor of Wilhelmina F. Jashemski.* 2 vols. New Rochelle, N.Y., 1988.

d'Andrea, Jeanne. *Ancient Herbs in the J. Paul Getty Museum Garden.* Santa Monica, Calif., 1982.

D'Arms, John. *Commerce and Social Standing in Ancient Rome.* Cambridge, Mass., 1981.

———. "Control, Companionship, and *Clientela:* Some Social Functions of the Roman Communal Meal." *Échos du monde classique/Classical Views* 28 (1984): 327–48.

———. "The Roman *Convivium* and the Idea of Equality." In *Sympotika,* ed. O. Murray, 308–20. Oxford, 1990.

———. *Romans on the Bay of Naples: A Social and Cultural Study of the Villas and their Owners from 150 B.C. to A.D. 400.* Cambridge, Mass., 1970.

———. "Slaves at Roman Convivia." In *Dining in a Classical Context,* ed. W. J. Slater, 171–83. Ann Arbor, 1991.

D'Arms, John, and E. C. Kopff, eds. *Roman Seaborne Commerce: Studies in Archaeology and History. MAAR,* no. 36 (1980).

Dalby, Andrew. "The Banquet of Philoxenos," *Petits Propos Culinaires* 26 (1987): 28–36.

———. "Food and Sexuality in Classical Athens: The Written Sources." In *Food Culture and History,* vol. 1, ed. G. Mars and V. Mars, 165–90. London Food Seminar. London, 1993.

———. "In Search of the Staple Foods of Prehistoric and Classical Greece." *Proceedings of the Oxford Symposium on Food and Cookery, 1989,* 5–23. London, 1990.

———. "Silphium aand Asafoetida: Evidence from Greek and Roman writers." *Proceedings of the Oxford Symposium on Food and Cookery, 1992,* 67–72. London, 1993.

———. *Siren Feasts.* New York, 1997.

———. "On *Thria.*" *Petits Propos Culinaires* 31 (1989): 56–57.

———. "The Wedding Feast of Caranus the Macedonian by Hippolochus. *Petits Propos Culinaires* 26 (1988): 37–45.

Daniela Conta, Gioia. "Note sulle peschiere marittime nel mondo romano." In *Il livello antico del mare Tirreno,* by G. Schmiedt et al., 217–21. Florence, 1972.

Davies, R. W. "The Daily Life of the Roman Soldier." In *ANRW,* Principat, II, 1, pp. 299–338.

———. "The Roman Military Diet." *Britannia* 2 (1971): 122–42.

De Fidio, Pia. "Dieta e gestione delle risorse alimentari in età Micenea." In *Homo edens,* ed. O. Longo and P. Scarpi, 193–203. Verona, 1989.

Degani, Enzio. "On Greek Gastronomic Poetry." 2 parts. *Alma Mater Studiorum Bologna* (1990): 51–63; (1991); 164–75.

Delatte, Armand. *Essai sur la politique pythagoricienne.* 1922. Bibliothèque de la Faculté de philosophie et lettres de l'Université de Liége, no. 29. Geneva, 1979.

della Corte, Francesco. *Catone censore. La vita e la fortuna.* Florence, 1969.

Della Corte, Matteo. *Case ed abitanti di Pompei.* Naples, 1954.

De Lucca, M. S. "Recherches chimiques sur le pain et sur le blé découverts à Pompei." *Comptes-rendus Academie des sciences* 57 (1963): 475–79.

Dentzer, Jean-Marie. *Le motif du banquet couché dans le Proche-Orient et le monde grec.* Rome, 1982.

Deonna, Waldemar, and Marcel Renard. *Croyances et superstitions de la table dans la Rome antique.* Collection Latomus, vol. 46. Brussels, 1961.

de Ruyt, Clare. *Macellum: Marché alimentaire des romains.* Louvain, 1983.

de Sallengre, Albert-Henri. *Thesaurus antiquitatum Romanorum.* Dissertation 4, *De accumbendi et comedendi ratione.* The Hague, 1716.

Desjardins, E. *De tabulis alimentariis.* Paris, 1854.

Detienne, Marcel. "La cuisine de Pythagore." *Archives de sociologie des religions* 29 (1970): 141–61.

———. *Dionysos Slain,* trans. M. Mueller and L. Mueller. Baltimore, 1979.

Detienne, Marcel, and Jean-Pierre Vernant. *La cuisine du sacrifice en pays grec.* Centre de Recherches comparées sur les sociétés anciennes. [Paris], 1979. English ed., *The Cuisine of Sacrifice among the Greeks,* trans. Paula Wissing (Chicago, 1989).

———. *The Gardens of Adonis: Spices in Greek Mythology,* trans. J. Lloyd. Princeton, N.J., 1977.

DeWitt, Norman. "The Role of Vesta Unveiled." In *Studies in Honor of Ullman,* ed. Lillian B. Lawler, Dorothy M. Robathan, and William C. Korfmacher. [St. Louis], 1960.

Dickson, J. H., and C. A. Dickson. "Flour or Bread in a Roman Military Ditch at Bearsden, Scotland." *Antiquity* 53 (1979): 47–51.

Dillon, John. "Last Words: Great Eaters of Ancient Greece." *University Publishing* 8 (1979): 28. [Sample translation from Archestratos.]

Dion, Roger. *L'histoire de la vigne et du vin en France.* Paris, 1959.

Dohm, Hans. *Mageiros: Die Rolle des Kochs in der griechisch-römischen Komödie.* Munich, 1964.

Dombrowski, Daniel A. "Vegetarianism and the Argument from Marginal Cases in Porphyry." *Journal of the History of Ideas* (January–March 1984): 141–43.

Dosi, Antonietta. *I Romani in cucina.* Museo della Civilta Romana. Vita e costumi dei Romani antichi, no. 3. Rome, 1986.

Dosi, Antonietta, and François Schnell. *A tavola con i Romani antichi.* Rome, 1984.

Duncan-Jones, Richard P. *The Economy of the Roman Empire: Quantitative Studies.* Cambridge, 1974.

———. "The purpose and organization of the *alimenta.*" *PBSR* 32 (1964): 123–46.

———. "Scaurus at the House of Trimalchio." *Latomus* 32 (1973): 364–67.

Dupont, Florence. *Le plaisir et la loi: Du Banquet de Platon au "Satyricon."* Paris, 1977.

Durry, Marcel. "Les femmes et le vin." *Revue des études latines* 33 (1955): 108–13.

Edelstein, Ludwig von. "Antike Diätetik." *Die Antike* 7 (1931): 255–70.

Edmunds, Lowell. "Ancient Roman and Modern American Food: A Comparative Sketch of Two Semiological Systems." *Comparative Civilizations Review* 5 (1980): 52–69.

Edwards, Ruth B. *Kadmos the Phoenician: A Study in Greek Legends and the Mycenaean Age.* Amsterdam, 1979.

Étienne, Robert. *La vie quotidienne à Pompéi.* [Paris], 1966.

———. "Á propos du vin pompéien." In *Neue Forschungen in Pompeji,* ed. B. Andreae and H. Kyrieleis, 309–16. DAI. Recklinghausen, 1975.

Evans, J. A. S. "Candaules, whom the Greeks call Myrsilus." *Greek, Roman and Byzantine Studies* 26 (1985): 229–33.

Fayer, C. *Aspetti di vita quotidiana nella Roma arcaica.* Rome, 1982.

Finley, Moses I. *Economy and Society in Ancient Greece.* London, 1981.

Forbes, R. J. "Sugar and its Substitutes in Antiquity." Pp. 78–109 in vol. 5 of *Studies in Ancient Technology.* 9 vols. Leiden, 1955–64.

Fortsch, Reinhard. *Archäologischer Kommentar zu den Villen-briefen des jungeren Plinius.* Mainz, 1993.

Frank, Tenney. *Aspects of Social Behavior in Ancient Rome.* Martin Classical Lectures, no. 2. Cambridge, Mass., 1932.

———. *An Economic Survey of Ancient Rome.* 6 vols. Baltimore, 1938.

Frayn, Joan M. "Home Baking in Roman Italy." *Antiquity* 52 (1978): 28–33.

———. *Subsistence Farming in Roman Italy.* London, 1979.

———. "Wild and Cultivated Plants: A Note on the Peasant Economy of Roman Italy." *JRS* 45 (1975): 32–39.

Fregoni, Mario. *Origini delle vite e della viticoltura: Contributo dei popoli antichi.* N.p., 1991.

Friedlaender, Ludwig. *Roman Life and Manners under the Early Empire.* Translated by J. H. Freese and L. H. Magnus. London, ca. 1909. [A translation of the 7th, rev. ed. of Friedlaender's *Darstellung aus der Sittengeschichte Roms in der Zeit von August bis zum Ausgang der Antonine,* 3 vols.]

Frier, Bruce. *Landlords and Tenants in Imperial Rome.* Princeton, N.J., 1980.

Frost, Honor. Chapters 4 and 5 on Conservation and Diet, and chap. 11 on Pottery in *Notizia degli Scavi,* supplement to vol. 30, 1976 (Lilybaeum (Marsala) in Sicily), 1980.

Gabba, Emilio. "Mercati e fiere nell' Italia romana." *Studi classici e Orientali* 24 (1975): 141–63.

Gabba, Emilio, ed. *Tria corda: Scritti in onore di Arnaldo Momigliano.* Como, 1983.

Gallant, Thomas W. "The Agronomy, Production and Utilization of Sesame and Linseed in the Graeco-Roman World." *Bulletin on Sumerian Agriculture* 2 (1985): 153–58.

———. *Risk and Survival in Ancient Greece: Reconstructing the Rural Domestic Economy.* Stanford, Calif., 1991.

Gallo, Luigi. "Alimentazione urbana e alimentazione contadina nell'Atene classica." In *Homo edens,* ed. O. Longo and P. Scarpi, 213–30. Verona, 1989.

Garlan, Yvon. "Le commerce des amphores grecs." In *Trade and Famine in Classical Antiquity,* ed. P. Garnsey, and C. R. Whittaker, 37–44. Cambridge, 1983.

Garland, Robert. *The Greek Way of Life from Conception to Old Age.* London, 1990.

Garnsey, Peter. *Famine and Food Supply in the Graeco-Roman World: Responses to Risks and Crisis.* Cambridge, 1988.

Garnsey, P., T. W. Gallant, and D. Rathbone. "Thessaly and the Grain Trade of Rome during the Second Century B.C." *JRS* 74 (1984): 123–39.

Garnsey, Peter, and I. Morris. "Risk and the Polis: The Evolution of Institutionalised Responses to Food Supply Problems in the Early Greek State." In *Cultural Responses to Uncertainty,* ed. P. Halstead and J. O'Shea. Cambridge, 1988.

Gernet, Louis. *The Anthropology of Ancient Greece.* Baltimore, 1981.

Giannini, A. "La figura del cuoco nella commedia greca." *Acme* 13 (1960): 135–216.

Goethert, Klaus-Peter. "Il panettiere: Zur Geschichte einer Fehl-deutung." In *Festschrift für Nikolaus Himmelmann.* Bonner Jahrbücher Beihefte, no. 47. Mainz, 1989.

Goldstein, Michael Sanford. "The Setting of the Ritual Meal in Greek Sanctuaries, 600–300 B.C." Ph.D. diss., University of California, Berkeley, 1978.

Gourevitch, Danielle. "Le menu de l'homme libre: Recherches sur l'alimentation et la digestion dans les oeuvres en prose de Séneque le philosophe." *Mélanges-École française de Rome* 22 (1974): 311–44.

Gowers, Emily. *The Loaded Table: Representations of Food in Roman Literature.* Oxford, 1993.

Gozzini Giacosa, Ilaria. *A Taste of Ancient Rome,* trans. and ed. Anna Herklotz. Chicago, 1992. Originally published as *A cena da Lucullo* (Casale Monferrato, 1986).

Gras, Michel. "Vin et société à Rome et dans le Latium à l'époque archaïque." In *Modes et contacts et processus de transformation dans les sociétés anciennes; Actes su colloque de Cortone, 1981,* 1067–75. Collection de l'École française de Rome, no. 67. Rome, 1983.

Gray, Patience. *Honey from a Weed: Fasting and Feasting in Tuscany, Catalonia, the Cyclades and Apulia.* New York, 1987.

Greenewalt, Crawford H., Jr. *Ritual Dinners in Early Sardis.* Berkeley and Los Angeles, 1978.

Grimal, Pierre, and T. Monod. "Sur la véritable nature du garum." *Revue des études anciennes* 54 (1952): 27–38.

Grottanelli, C. "L'ideologia del banchetto e l'ospite ambiguo." *Dialoghi di archeologia* 33 (1981): 122–54.

Gruen, Erich S. *The Hellenistic World and the Coming of Rome.* 2 vols. Berkeley and Los Angeles, 1984.

Gunther, R. T. "The Oyster Culture of the Ancient Romans." *Journal of the Marine Biological Association* 4 (1897): 360–65.

Hagenow, Gerd. *Aus dem Weingarten der Antike: Der Wein in Dichtung, Brauchtum und Alltag.* Kulturgeschichte der antiken Welt, no. 12. Mainz am Rhein, 1982.

Hahn, Istvan. "Foreign Trade and Foreign Policy in Archaic Greece." In *Trade and Famine in Classical Antiquity,* ed. P. Garnsey and C. R. Whittaker, 30–36. Cambridge, 1983.

Halstead, Paul. "Towards a Model of Bronze Age Palatial Economy." In *Agriculture in Ancient Greece,* ed. B. Wells, 105–17. Stockholm, 1992.

Hansen, Julie H. "Agriculture in the Prehistoric Aegean: Data versus Speculation." *American Journal of Archaeology* 92 (1988): 39–52.

———. *The Palaeoethnobotany of Franchthi Cave.* Bloomington, 1991.

Hanson, Victor D. "Practical Aspects of Grape-growing and the Ideology of Greek Viticulture." In *Dionysus: a Social History of the Wine Vine,* by E. S. Hyams. London, 1965.

Harcum, Cornelia G. "Roman Cooks." Ph.D. diss., Johns Hopkins University, 1914.

Harmand, Jacques, *L'armée et le soldat à Rome de 107 à 50 avant notre ère.* Paris, 1967.

Hay, J. Stuart. *The Amazing Emperor Heliogabalus.* London, 1911.

Heichelheim, F. M. "Sitos." *RE,* suppl. 6 (1935): cols. 819–92.

Heichelheim, F. M. "Roman Syria." In *An Economic Survey of Ancient Rome,* by Tenney Frank. Vol. 4. Baltimore, 1938.

Helbaek, Hans. "Late Cypriote Vegetable Diet at Apliki." *Opuscula Atheniensis* 4 (1962): 171–86.

———. "Vegetables in the Funeral Meals of Pre-urban Rome." In *Early Rome.* Vol. 2, *The Tombs,* ed. E. Gjerstad, 287–94. Lund, 1956.

Hermansen, Gustav. *Ostia: Aspects of Roman City Life.* Alberta, 1982.

Hohendahl-Zoetelief, I. M. "Manners in the Homeric Epic." *Mnemosyne,* suppl. 63. Leiden, 1980.

Houghton, W. "Notices of Fungi in Greek and Latin Authors." *Annals and Magazine of Natural History,* Ser. 5, 15 (1885): 22–49.

Hudson, Nicola. "The Beast at the Feast, Food in Roman Verse Satire." In *Food Culture and History,* ed. V. Mars and E. Mars, 204–20. London, 1993.

Hug, A. "Symposion." *RE,* vol. 7, cols. 1266–70. [See also Mau on origins in vol. 4 (1931): col. 61ff.].

Humphreys, S. C. *Anthropology and the Greeks.* London, 1978.

Hutchinson, Valerie J. *Bacchus in Roman Britain: The Evidence for his Cult.* 2 vols. British Archaeological Reports, no. 151. Oxford, 1986.

Immerwahr, H. R. "An Athenian Wine-shop." *TAPA* 79 (1948): 184–90.

L'Instrumentum domesticum di Ercolano e Pompei nella prima età imperiale. Quaderni di cultura materiale, no. 1. Rome, 1977.

Irwin, J. R. "Galen on the Temperaments." *Journal of Psychology* 36 (1947): 45–64.

Isager, Signe, and Jens Erik Skydsgaard. *Ancient Greek Agriculture: An Introduction.* New York, 1992.

Isenberg, M. "The Sale of Sacrificial Meat." *Classical Philology* 70 (1975): 271–73.

Jameson, Michael H. "Agricultural Labor in Ancient Greece." In *Agriculture in Ancient Greece,* ed. B. Wells, 135–46. Stockholm, 1992.

———. "Sacrifice and Animal Husbandry in Classical Greece," In *Pastoral Economies in Classical Antiquity,* ed. C. R. Whittaker, 87–119. Cambridge, 1988.

Jardé, A. *Les céréales dans l'antiquité grecque.* Paris, 1925.

Jardin, Claude. "Garum et sauces de poisson de l'antiquité." *Rivista di studi Liguri* 27 (1961): 70–96.

Jashemski, Wilhelmina F. "The Contribution of Archaeology to the Study of Ancient Roman Gardens." In *Garden History: Issues, Approaches, Methods,* ed. J. D. Hunt, 5–30. Dumbarton Oaks, 1992.

———. "The Gardens of Pompeii: An Interim Report." *Cronache Pompeiane* 1 (1975): 48–81.

———. *The Gardens of Pompeii, Herculaneum and the Villas Destroyed by Vesuvius.* 2 vols. New Rochelle, N.Y., 1979, 1992.

———. "The Gardens of Pompeii, Herculaneum and the Villas Destroyed by Vesuvius." *Journal of Garden History* 12 (1992): 102–25.

———. "Recently Excavated Gardens and Cultivated Land of the Villa at Boscoreale and Oplontis." In *Ancient Roman Villa Gardens,* ed. E. B. MacDougal, 175–178. Dumbarton Oaks Colloquium on the History of Landscape Architecture, no. 10. Washington, D.C., 1987.

Jashemski, Wilhelmina F., and E. Salza Prina Ricotti. "Preliminary Excavations in the Gardens of Hadrian's Villa: The Canopus Area and the Piazza d'Oro." With appendix by John Foss. *AJA* 96 (1992): 579–97.

Jasny, Naum. *The Wheats of Classical Antiquity.* Baltimore, 1944.

Johnston, Patricia A. *Vergil's Agricultural Golden Age: A Study of the Georgics. Mnemosyne,* suppl. 60. Leiden, 1980.

Jones, Christopher P. "Dinner Theater." In *Dining in a Classical Context,* ed. W. J. Slater, 185–98. Ann Arbor, 1992.

Kinzl, K.-H., ed. *Greece and the Eastern Mediterranean in Ancient History and Prehistory.* Berlin, 1977.

Kirk, G. S. "Some Methodological Problems in the Study of Ancient Greek Sacrifice." In *Le sacrifice dans l'antiquité,* ed. O. Reverdin and B. Grange, 41–90. Entretiens sur l'antiquité classique, Fondation Hardt, no. 27. Geneva, 1981.

Kleberg, Toennes. *Hotels, restaurants et cabarets dans l'antiquité romaine.* Bibliotheca Ekmaniana-Universitatis Regiae Upsalaiensis, 61. [Uppsala], 1957.

Klotz. "Mago." *RE,* vol. 27, no. 15 (1928): col. 506f.

Knauer, Elfriede. "Ou gar en amis." *Greek Vases in the J. Paul Getty Museum* 2 (1985): 91–100.

Kolendo, Jerzy. "Parcs à huitres et viviers à Baiae sur un flaçon en verre de Musée national de Varsovie." *Puteoli* 1 (1977): 108–27.

Kristeller, Paul Oscar. *Greek Philosophers of the Hellenistic Age.* New York, 1991.

Labaste, A. *Les vins grecs.* Annales de Géographie, 49. Paris, 1939.

Lafon, X. "Á propos des villas de la zone de Sperlonga; les origines et le développement de la *villa maritima* sur le littoral tyrrhénien à l'époque républicaine." *Mélanges. École française de Rome* 93, no. 1 (1981): 297–353.

Landolfi, Luciano. *Banchetto e società romana, dalle origini al I secolo A.C.* Rome, 1990.

Lang, Mabel. *Cure and Cult in Ancient Corinth: A Guide to the Asklepieion.* Athens, 1977.

———. "The Palace of Nestor: Excavations of 1957," pt. 2. *AJA* 62 (1958): 181–91.

Lauffer, S., ed. *Diokletians Preisedikt.* Texte und Kommentare, no. 5. Berlin, 1971.

Lavin, Irving. "The House of the Lord: Aspects of the Role of Palace Triclinia in the Architecture of Late Antiquity and Early Middle Ages." *Art Bulletin* 44 (1962): 1–27.

Lehmann, Karl. "The Dome of Heaven." *Art Bulletin* 27 (1945): 1–54.

Leon, Ernestine F. "Cato's Cakes." *The Classical Journal* 38 (1942–43): 213–21.

Lepore, E. "Orientamente per la storia Sociale di Pompei." *Pompeiana,* 144–66. Naples, 1950.

Leuven, J. V. van. "Prehistoric Grain Explosions." *Antiquity* 53 (1979): 138–40.

Levi, Doro. *Antioch Mosaic Pavements.* Princeton, N.J., 1947.

Levick, Barbara. "Domitian and the Provinces." *Latomus* 41 (1982): 50–73.

Lincoln, Bruce. "Of Meat and Society, Sacrifice and Creation, Butchers and Philosophy." *L'uomo* 9 (1985): 9–19.

Lissarrague, François. *The Aesthetics of the Greek Banquet: Images of Wine and Ritual,* trans. Andrew Szegedy-Maszak. Princeton, N.J., 1990.

Lissarrague, François, and Schmitt-Pantel, P. "Partage et communauté dans les banquets grecs." In *La Table et le partage.* Rencontres de l'École du Louvre (January), 155–70. Paris, 1986.

Lloyd-Jones, Hugh, ed. *The Greeks.* Cleveland, 1962.

Loane, Helen J. *Industry and Commerce of the City of Rome: 50 B.C.–200 A.D.* 2 vols. Johns Hopkins Studies in Historical and Political Science, no. 56. Baltimore, 1938.

Lohmann, Hans. "Agriculture and Country Life-Classical Attica." In *Agriculture in Ancient Greece,* ed. B. Wells, 29–57. Stockholm, 1992.

Lombardo, Mario,"Pratiche di commensalità e forme di organizzazione sociale nel mondo greco: Symposion e Syssitia." In *Homo edens,* ed. O. Longo and P. Scarpi, 311–26. Verona, 1989.

Longo, Oddone, and Paolo Scarpi, eds. *Homo edens: Regimi, miti e pratiche dell'alimentazione nella civiltà del Mediterraneo.* Congresso della Fiera di Verona, April, 1987. Verona, 1989.

MacCormack, Sabine. *Art and Ceremony in Late Antiquity.* Berkeley and Los Angeles, 1981.

Mahaffy, J. P. *Social Life in Greece from Homer to Menander.* London, 1907.

Maiuri, A. *I Campi Flegrei.* Rome, 1934.

Makler, P. T. "New Information on Nutrition in Ancient Greece." *Klio* 62 (1980): 317–19.

Marsden, P. *Roman London.* London, 1980.

Martin, J. *Symposion: Die Geschichte einer literarischen Form.* Paderborn, 1931.

Mayeske, B. *Bakeries, Bakers and Bread at Pompeii: A Study in Social and Economic History.* Ann Arbor, 1972.

Mazzoli, Giancarlo, "Il cibo del potere: il mito dei Pelopidi e il *Tieste* di Seneca." In *Homo edens,* ed. O. Longo and P. Scarpi, 335–42. Verona, 1989.

McCracken, George. "The Villa and Tomb of Lucullus at Tusculum." *American Journal of Archaeology* 46 (1942): 325–40.

McDonald, W. A., and G. R. Rupp. *Minnesota Messenia Expedition: Reconstructing a Bronze Age Regional Environment.* Minneapolis, 1972.

McKay, Alexander G. "Pleasure Domes at Baiae." *Studia Pompeiana,* ed. R. I. Curtis, 2:155–72. New Rochelle, N.Y., 1988.

McPhee, Ian, and A. D. Trendall. *Greek Red-figured Fish-plates. Antike Kunst,* Beiheft 14. Basel, 1987.

Meiggs, R., and D. M. Lewis. *A Selection of Greek Historical Inscriptions to the End of the Fifth Century.* Oxford, 1969.

Meyer, Frederick G. "Food Plants Identified from Carbonized Remains at Pompeii and other Vesuvian Sites." In *Studia Pompeiana,* ed. R. I. Curtis, 1:183–229. New Rochelle, N.Y., 1988.

Michell, H. *The Economics of Ancient Greece.* Cambridge, 1957.

Miller, J. Innes. *The Spice Trade of the Roman Empire, 29 B.C. to A.D. 641.* Oxford, 1969.

Millett, P. C. "Hesiod and His World." *Proceedings of the Cambridge Philological Society,* 30 (1984): 84–115.

Minchin, Elizabeth. "Food Fiction and Food Fact in Homer's *Iliad.*" *Petits Propos Culinaires* 25 (1987): 42–49.

Mingazzini, P. "Gli antichi conoscevano i maccheroni?" *Archeologia classica* 6 (1954): 292–94.

———. "Tentativo ricostruzione grafica della 'coenatio rotunda' della Domus Aurea." *Quaderni,* 31–48 (1961), Festschrift Fasolo, 21–26.

Murray, Oswyn. "The Greek Symposion in History." In *Tria Corda: Scritti in onore de Arnaldo Momigliano,* ed. E. Gabba, 257–72. Como, 1983.

———. "The Symposion as Social Organization." In *The Greek Renaissance of the Eighth Century B.C.: Tradition and Innovation. Proceedings of the 2d International Symposium at the Swedish Institute in Athens, 1–5 June 1981,* ed. Robin Hägg. Stockholm, 1983.

———. "Symposium and Genre in the Poetry of Horace." *JRS* 75 (1985): 39–50.

Murray, Oswyn, ed. *Sympotica: A Symposium on the Symposion.* Oxford, 1990.

Murray, Oswyn, and Manuela Tecuşan, eds. *In Vino Veritas.* Conference proceedings, March 1991. British School at Rome in association with American Academy at Rome. London, 1995.

Murray, Philip. "Poetic translations from Martial." *Arion* 2 (1963): 75f.

Nenci, Giuseppe. "Pratiche alimentari e forme di definizione e distinzione sociale nella Greca arcaica." In *Homo edens*, ed. O. Longo and P. Scarpi, 25–30. Verona, 1989.

Noonan, T. S. "The Grain Trade of the northern Black Sea in Antiquity. *AJP* 94 (1973): 231–42.

Orth. "Kochkunst." *RE*, vol. 11, no. 1 (1921): cols. 964–82.

Osborne, Robin. "Classical Greek Gardens: Between Farm and Paradise." In *Garden History: Issues, Approaches, Methods*, ed. J. D. Hunt, 373–91. Dumbarton Oaks, 1992.

Packer, James E. *The Insulae of Imperial Ostia. MAAR*, no. 21 (1971).

Page, Denys L. *History and the Homeric Iliad*. Berkeley and Los Angeles, 1966.

Palmer, L. R. *Mycenaeans and Minoans: Aegean Prehistory in the Light of the Linear B Tablets*. New York, 1962.

Parke, Herbert W. *Festivals of the Athenians*. Ithaca, N.Y., 1977.

Pavlovskis, Zoe. *Man in an Artificial Landscape*. Leiden, 1973.

Perry, Charles. "Baklava not Proven Greek." *Petits Propos Culinaires* 27 (1987): 47–48.

———. "The Oldest Mediterranean Noodle: A Cautionary Tale." *Petit Propos Culinaires* 9 (1981): 42–45.

Plouvier, Liliane, "Ah! com'era bella la pasticceria!" In *La cucina e la tavola*, ed. J. Ferniot and J. Le Goff. Bari, 1987.

Pollitt, J. J. *Art and Experience in Classical Greece*. Cambridge, 1972.

Polombi, Arturo. "La fauna marina nei musaici e nei dipinti pompeiani." *Pompeiana*, 425–55. Naples, 1950

Pompei 1748–1980: i tempi della documentazione. Exhibition catalogue. Pompeii, 1981.

Ponsich, Michel, and Miguel Tarradell. *Garum et industries antiques de salsaison dans la Méditerranée occidentale*. Université de Bordeaux et Casa de Velasquez, Bibliothèque de l'École des hautes études hispaniques, no. 36. Bordeaux, 1965.

Pucci, Giuseppe. "Il fritto nel mondo greco." In *Homo edens*, ed. O. Longo and P. Scarpi, 45–48. Verona, 1989.

Purcell, N. "Wine and Wealth in Ancient Italy." *JRS* 75 (1985): 1–19.

Quentin, D. Henri. "*Clibanus. Pigella. Panis artopticus.*" *Rendiconti Pontificia Accademia Romana di archeologia* 4 (1925–26): 81–89.

Radcliffe, William. *Fishing from the Earliest Times* [1924]. Chicago, 1974.

Rankin, Edwin Moore. *The Role of the Mageiroi in the Life of the Ancient Greeks as depicted in Greek Literature and Inscriptions*. Chicago, 1907.

Renard, Marcel. "Pline l'Ancien et le motif de l'*asarotos oikos*." In *Hommages à Max Niedermann*, 307–14. Brussels, 1956.

Renfrew, C. *The Emergence of Civilization: the Cyclades and the Aegean in the Third Millenium B.C.* London, 1972.

Renfrew, Jane M. "Food for Athletes and Gods: A Classical Diet." In *The Archaeology of the Olympics*, ed. W. J. Rashke, 174–81. Wisconsin Studies in Classics. Madison, 1988.

Richardson, Lawrence, Jr. *Pompeii: An Architectural History*. Baltimore, 1988.

———. "Water Triclinia and Biclinia in Pompeii." *Studia Pompeiana*, ed. R. I. Curtis, 1:305–15. New Rochelle, N.Y., 1988.

Rickman, G. *Roman Granaries and Store Buildings*, Cambridge, 1971.

Robinson, David M., and Walter J. Graham. *Excavations at Olynthos.* Part 8, *The Hellenic House.* Baltimore, 1938.

Rose, Kenneth F. C. *The Date and Author of the Satyricon. Mnemosyne,* suppl. 16. Leiden, 1971.

Rose, Kenneth F. C., and J. P. Sullivan. "Trimalchio's Zodiac Dish." *Classical Quarterly,* n.s., 18 (1968): 180–84.

Rose, H. J. "The Cult of Volkanus at Rome." *JRS* 23 (1933): 46–63.

Rossi, L. "Il simposio greco arcaico e classico come spectacolo a se stesso." In *Spettacoli conviviali dall' antichità classica alle corti italiane del '400: Atti del VII Convegno di Studio, Viterbo, 27–30 Maggio 1982,* 41–50. Centro di studi sul teatro medioevale e rinascimentale. Viterbo, 1983.

Rossiter, Jeremy, and E. Haldenby. "A Wine-making plant in Pompeii. Insula II, 5." *Échos du monde classique/Classical Views* 18, n.s. 8, no. 2 (1989): 229–39.

Rostovtzeff, M. *A Large Estate in Egypt in the Third Century B.C.: A Study in Economic History.* Studia historica, no. 52. Rome, 1967. Reprint of Studies in the Social Sciences and History, no. 6 (University of Wisconsin, 1922).

———. *The Social and Economic History of the Hellenistic World.* 3 vols. Oxford, 1941.

Rotroff, Susan I., and J. H. Oakley. *Debris from a Public Dining Place in the Athenian Agora. Hesperia,* suppl. 25. Princeton, N.J., 1992.

Roux, Georges. "Salle de banquets à Delos." In *Études Déliennes. BCH,* suppl. 1 (1973): 525–54.

Runnels, C. N., and J. M. Hansen. "The Olive in the Prehistoric Aegean: The Evidence for Domestication in the Early Bronze Age." *Oxford Journal of Archaeology* 5 (1986): 299–308.

Salaman, Rena. "The Case of the Missing Fish, or *dolmathon* Prolegomena." *Proceedings of the Oxford Symposium on Food and Cookery, 1984,* 184–87. London, 1985.

———. "Wheat, Staple Food for the Dead." *Proceedings of the Oxford Symposium on Food and Cookery, 1989,* 213–15. London, 1990.

Sallares, Robert. *The Ecology of the Ancient Greek World.* London, 1991.

Salmonson, J. W. "Römische Tonformen mit Inschriften: Ein Beitrag zum Problem der sogennanten *Kuchenformen* aus Ostia." *Bulletin antieke Beschaving* 47 (1972): 88–113.

Salviat, F. "Le vin de Thasos: Amphores, vins et sources écrites." In *Recherches sur les amphores grecques,* ed. J.-Y. Empereur and Y. Garlan, 145–95. *BCH,* suppl. 13. Paris, 1986.

Salza Prina Ricotti, Eugenia. *L'arte del convito nella Roma antica.* Rome, 1983.

———. *Les cryptoportiques dans l'architecture romaine.* Rome, 1978.

———. "Cucina e quartieri servili in epoca romana." *Rendiconti Pontificia Accademia Romana di archeologia* 51–51 (1978–79/1979–80), 237–94.

———. "Il ferculum dello Zodiaco." *Rendiconti Pontificia Accademia Romana di archeologia* 55–56 (1983–84): 245–64.

———. "Forme speciali di triclini." *Cronache Pompeiane* 5 (1979), 102–49.

———. *Ricette della cucina romana a Pompei e come eseguirle.* Rome, 1993.

———. "Le tende conviviali e la tenda di Tolomeo Filadelfo." *Studia Pompeiana,* ed. R. I. Curtis, 199–239. Vol. 2. New Rochelle, N.Y., 1988.

———. "Villa Adriana nei suoi limiti e nella sua funzionalità." *Atti della Pontificia Accademia di Archeologia,* ser. 3, *Memorie,* 14 (1982): 25–55, Pls. 1–9.

Santini, Carlo. "Il lessico della spartizione nel sacrificio romano." *L'uomo* 9 (1985): 9–19 and 63–73.

Sarpaki, Anya. "The Palaeoethnobotanical Approach to the Mediterranean Triad, or is it a Quartet?" In *Agriculture in Ancient Greece*, ed. B. Wells, 61–76. Stockholm, 1992.

Sarton, George. *Galen of Pergamon*. Lawrence, Kansas, 1954.

Scarpi, Paolo. "La rivoluzione dei cereali e del vino: Demeter, Dionysos, Athena." In *Homo edens*, ed. O. Longo and P. Scarpi, 57–66. Verona, 1989.

Scheid, John. "Sacrifice et banquet à Rome: Quelques problemes." *Melanges École française de Rome, Antiquite* 97, no. 1 (1985): 193–206.

Schmeling, Garth. "Trimalchio's Menu and Wine List." *Classical Philology* 65 (1970): 248–51.

Schmiedt, G., ed. *Il livello antico del mar Tirreno: Testimonianze dei resti archeologici*. Florence, 1972.

Schmitt-Pantel, P. "Banquet et cité grecque: Quelques questions suscisitées par les recherches récentes" *Mélanges de l'École française de Rome* 97 (1985): 135–58.

———. *La Cité au Banquet: Histoire des repas publics dans les cités grecques*. Collection de l'École française de Rome, no. 157. Rome, 1992.

———. "Les repas au prytanée et à tholos dans l'Athènes classique. Sitesis, trophe, misthos: Reflexions sur le mode de nourriture democratique." *Annali dell'Istituto orientale de Napoli* 2 (1980): 55–68.

Schnur, Harry C. "Vinum Opimianum." *Classical Weekly* 50 (1957): 122–23.

Schraemli, Harry. "El banquète de Trimalcion." In H. Schraemli, *Historia de la gastronomia*, 254–59. Destinolibro series, no. 171. Barcelona, 1952.

Scranton, Robert L. *Aesthetic Aspects of Ancient Art*. Chicago, 1964.

Seltman, Charles. *Wine in the Ancient World*. London, 1957.

Shelmerdine, C. W. *The Perfume Industry of Mycenaean Pylos*. SIMA pocket book, no. 34. Göteborg, 1985.

Shero, L. R. "The *Cena* in Roman Satire." *Classical Philology* 18 (1923): 126–43.

Simon, Erika. *Festivals of Attika: An Archaeological Commentary*. Madison, 1983.

Skinner, F. G. *Ancient Weights and Measures*. London, 1967.

Skydsgaard, J. E. "Nuove ricerche sulla villa rustica romana fino all'epoca di Traiano." *Analecta Romana Instituti Danici* 5 (1969): 25ff.

Slater, William J., ed. *Dining in a Classical Context*. Ann Arbor, 1991.

Solomon, Jonathan, and Julia Solomon. *Ancient Roman Feasts and Recipes adapted for Modern Cooking*. Miami, 1977.

———. "*Tracta*: A Versatile Roman Pastry." *Hermes* 106 (1978): 539ff.

Soprano, Pietro. "I triclini all'aperto di Pompei." *Pompeiana*, 288–310. Naples, 1950.

Sparkes, B. A. "The Greek Kitchen." *JHS* 82 (1962): 121–37, pls. 4–8; 85 (1965): 162–63.

———. "Kottabos. An Athenian After-Dinner Game." *Archaeology* 13 (1960): 202–7.

Starr, Chester G. *The Economic and Social Growth of Early Greece 800–500 B.C.* New York, 1977.

Strong, Donald E. *Greek and Roman Gold and Silver Plate*. London, 1966.

Tanzer, Helen H. *The Common People of Pompeii, A Study of the Graffiti*. Johns Hopkins Studies in Archaeology, no. 29. Baltimore, 1939.

Taylor, Lily Ross. *Party Politics in the Age of Caesar*. Sather Classical Lectures, no. 22. Berkeley and Los Angeles, 1949.

Taylour, William Lord. *The Mycenaeans*. Ancient Peoples and Places series. New York, 1964.

Tchernia, André. *Le vin de l'Italie romaine*. Rome, 1986.

Tengstrom, E. *Bread for the People: The Corn-Supply of Rome during the Late Empire.* Stockholm, 1975.

Thédenat, Henri. *Pompei.* 3d ed., revised by André Piganiol. Paris, 1928.

Thoenges-Stringaris, R. "Das griechische Totenmahl." *Mitteilungen des deutschen archäologischen Instituts. Römische Abteilung* 80 (1965): 1–99.

Thompson, D'Arcy W. A. *A Glossary of Greek Fishes.* Oxford, 1947.

Thompson, Dorothy Burr, and R. E. Griswold. *Garden Lore of Ancient Athens.* American School of Classical Studies Picture Book, no. 8. Princeton, N.J., 1963.

Thompson, Homer A. *The Tholos of Athens and its Predecessors. Hesperia,* suppl. 4. Baltimore, Md., 1940.

Tilly, Bertha. *Varro the Farmer.* London, 1973.

Todd, O. J. "Frustum Porcinum." *Classical Philology* 47 (1952): 93–94.

Toller, O. "De spectaculis, cenis, distributionibus in municipiis Romanis imperatorum aetate." Diss. Leipzig, 1889.

Tomlinson, R. A. "Ancient Macedonian Symposia." In *Ancient Macedonia,* ed. B. Laourdas and C. Makaronas, 308–15. Proceedings of the 1st International Symposium, 1968. Thessalonika, 1970.

Torelli, Marco. "Gli spettacoli conviviali di età classica," in *Spettacoli conviviali dall' antichità classica alle corti italiane del '400: Atti del VII Convegno di Studio, Viterbo, 27–30 Maggio 1982,* 51–64. Centro di studi sul teatro medioevale e rinascimentale. Viterbo, 1983.

Trevor Hodge, A. "Vitruvius, Lead Pipes and Lead Poisoning." *AJA* 85 (1981): 486–91.

Turano, Gianfrancesco. "L'alimentazione nel linguaggio di Platone: il *Simposio.*" In *Homo edens,* ed. O. Longo and P. Scarpi, 97–102. Verona, 1989.

Uliano, Fulvio. *L'antica Roma a tavola: Il gusto dei cesari.* Ricette liberamente tradotte ed interpretate dal De re coquinaria di Celio Apicio. Naples, 1985.

Valerio, Nico. *La tavola degli antichi.* Milan, 1989.

Vallet, G. "L'introduction de l'olivier en Italie centrale d'après les données de la céramique." In *Latomus: Hommages à A. Grenier,* ed. Marcel Renard, 3:1554–63. Brussels, 1967.

van Ooteghem, J. *Lucius Licinius Lucullus.* Académie Royale de Belgique. Mémoires, lettres et sciences morales et politiques, no. 8. Facs. 4. Brussels, 1959.

Ventris, M., and J. Chadwick. *Documents in Mycenaean Greek.* 2d ed. Cambridge, 1973.

Vermeule, Emily. *Greece in the Bronze Age.* Chicago, 1964.

Vernant, Jean-Pierre. *Myth and Society in Ancient Greece* [1974], trans. J. Lloyd. London, 1980.

———. "Théorie générale du sacrifice et mise à mort dans la *thusia* grecque." In *Le sacrifice dans l'antiquité,* ed. O. Reverdin and B. Grange, 1–39. Entretiens sur l'antiquité classique, Fondation Hardt, no. 27. Geneva, 1981.

Veyne, Paul. *Bread and Circuses: Historical Sociology and Political Pluralism,* trans. Brian Pearce, with an introduction by Oswyn Murray. London, 1990.

Vickery Kenton F. *Food in Early Greece* [1936]. Chicago, 1980.

Warmington, E. H. *The Commerce between the Roman Empire and India.* Cambridge, 1928.

Wellmann, M., "Archestratus." *RE,* vol. 2 (1896): cols. 459–60.

Wells, Berit, ed. *Agriculture in Ancient Greece.* Proceedings, 7th International Symposium at the Swedish Institute of Athens, May 1990. Stockholm, 1992.

Westlake, H. D. "Athenian Food Supplies from Euboea." *Classical Review* 62 (1948): 2–5.

White, K. D. *Farm Equipment of the Roman World.* Cambridge, 1975.

———. "Roman Agricultural Writers, I: Varro and his predecessors." *ANRW* 1, no. 4 (1973): 439–97.

———. *Roman Farming.* Aspects of Greek and Roman Life, ed. H. H. Scullard. Ithaca, N.Y., 1970.

Whittaker, C. R., ed. *Pastoral Economies in Classical Antiquity.* Cambridge, 1988.

Wilkins, John. "Public (and Private) Dining in Ancient Greece 450–300 B.C." *Proceedings of the Oxford Symposium on Food and Cookery, 1992,* 306–10. London, 1993.

———. "Social Status and Fish in Greece and Rome." In *Food Culture and History,* ed. G. Mars and V. Mars, 191–203. London, 1993.

Wilkins, John, F. D. Harvey, and M. Dobson, eds. *Food in Antiquity.* Exeter, 1995.

Wilkins, John, and Shaun Hill. *Archestratus. The Life of Luxury: Europe's Oldest Cookery Book.* Totnes, Devon, England, 1994.

———. "The Flavours of Ancient Greece." *Proceedings of the Oxford Symposium on Food and Cookery, 1992,* 275–79. London, 1993.

Will, Ernst. "Banquets et salles de banquet dans les cultes de la Grèce et de l'Empire romain." In *Mélanges d'histoire ancienne et d'archéologie offerts à Paul Collart,* ed. Paul Ducrey et al., 353–62. Lausanne, 1976.

Wright, James C. "Empty Cups and Empty Jugs: The Social Role of Wine in Minoan and Mycenaean Societies." In *The Origins and Ancient History of Wine,* ed. P. E. McGovern, S. J. Fleming, and S. H. Katz. Philadelphia, 1995.

Zahn. "Garum." *RE,* vol. 7, no. 1 (1910): col. 841ff.

Early Medieval and Gothic Sources

Aebischer, Paul. "Un manuscrit valaisan du *Viandier* attribué à Taillevent." *Vallesia* 8 (1953): 73–100.

Alessio, G. "Storia linguistica di un antico cibo rituale: I maccheroni." *Atti della Accademia Pontiniana,* n.s., 8 (1958–59): 261–80.

Arminjon, Catherine. "Objets de table au Moyen Age: Le trésor de Coeffort." In *Les français et la table,* 164–78. Exhibit, Musée national des arts et traditions populaires, 20 Novembre 1985–21 Avril 1986. Paris, 1985.

Ashtor, Eliyahu. "The Volume of the Medieval Spice Trade." In *East-West Trade in the Medieval Mediterranean,* ed. B. Z. Kedar. London, 1986.

Austin, Thomas, ed. *Two Fifteenth-century Cookery Books.* Early English Text Society, no. 91. London, 1888.

Aymard, Marcel. "Pour l'histoire de l'alimentation: Quelques remarques de méthode." In *Annales ESC* 30 (1975): 431–44.

Aymard, Marcel, and H. Bresc. "Nourritures et consommation en Sicile entre 14e et 18e siècle." In *Annales ESC* 30 (1975): 592ff.

Baruzzi, Marina, and Massimo Montanari. "Porci e porcari nel Medioevo." *Bolognaincontri* 12, no. 6 (1981): 27–32.

Bautier, A. M. "Pain et patisserie dans les textes médiévaux latins antérieurs au 13e siècle." In *Manger et boire au Moyen Age*, ed. Denis Menjot, 1:33–65. Nice, 1984.

Beck, P. "L'Approvisionnement en Bourgogne ducale aux 14e et 15e siècles." In *Manger et boire au Moyen Age*, ed. Denis Menjot, 1:171–81. Nice, 1984.

Beichner, Paul E. "The Grain of Paradise." *Speculum* 36 (1961): 302–7.

Bell, Clair Hayden, ed. *Peasant Life in Old German Epics, Meier Helmbrecht and Die arme Heinrich, translated from Middle High German of the 13th Century.* New York, 1931.

Bennassar, Bartolomé, et al. "Contribution à l'histoire de la consommation alimentaire du 14e au 19e siècles." *Annales ESC* 30 (1975): 402–632.

Benoist, J. O. "Le gibier dans l'alimentation seigneuriale (11e–15e siècles). In *Manger et boire au Moyen Age*, ed. Denis Menjot, 1:75–87. Nice, 1984.

Berkhout, Barbara. "Taillevent, Cuisinier du Roi." *Gourmet* (February 1968): 16ff.

Black, Maggie. *Food and Cooking in Medieval Britain: History and Recipes.* English Heritage Pamphlet. N.p., 1985.

Bober, Harry. "*In Principio:* Creation before Time." In *Essays in Honor of Erwin Panofsky*, ed. M. Meiss, 13–28. Princeton, N.J., 1960. Reprint, New York University Press, 1961.

———. "The Zodiacal Miniature of the *Très Riches Heures* of the Duke of Berry: Its Sources and Meaning." *Journal of the Warburg and Courtauld Institutes* 11 (1948): 1–34.

Bolens, Lucie. "Les sorbets andalous (11e–12e siècles) ou conjurer la nostalgie par la douceur." In *Du manuscrit à la table*, ed. Carole Lambert, 257–72. Montreal, 1992.

Bourin, Jeanne, with Jeannine Thomassin. *Les recettes de Mathilde Brunel: Cuisine médiévale pour table d'aujourd'hui.* Paris, 1983.

Bowden, Muriel. *Commentary on the Prologue of Chaucer's Canterbury Tales.* New York, 1948.

Bresc-Bautier, G., H. Bresc, and P. Herbeth. "L'Équipement de la cuisine et de la table en Provence et en Sicile, 14e et 15e siècles: Étude comparée." In *Manger et boire au Moyen Age*, ed. Denis Menjot, 2:45–58. Nice, 1984.

Bryant, Joseph A. "The Diet of Chaucer's Franklin." *Modern Language Notes* (1948): 318–25.

Burcaw, George E. *The Saxon House: A Cultural Index in European Ethnology.* Moscow, Idaho, 1979.

Bynum, Caroline Walker. *Holy Feast and Holy Fast: The Religious Significance of Food to Medieval Women.* Berkeley and Los Angeles, 1987.

Carruthers, Mary J., and Elizabeth D. Kirk, eds. *Acts of Interpretation: The Text in its Contents, 700–1600: Essays in Medieval and Renaissance Literature in Honor of E. Talbot Donaldson.* Norman, Okla., 1982.

Cartellieri, Otto. *The Court of Burgundy: Studies in the History of Civilization* [1929]. London, 1972.

Carus-Wilson, E. M. *Medieval Merchant Venturers.* London, 1967.

Casanova, E. "Visita di un papa avignonese a suoi cardinali." *Archivio della Società Romana di Storia Patria* 22 (1899): 361–81.

Cawley, A. C. "The 'Grotesque Feast' in the *Prima Pastorum.*" *Speculum* 30 (1955): 213–17.

Chadwick, D. *Social Life in the Days of Piers Plowman.* New York, 1922.

Cherubini, G. "La *Civiltà* del castagno in Italia alla fine del Medioevo." *Archeologia medievale* 8 (1981): 247–80.

Clark, Peter. *The English Alehouse: A Social History, 1200–1830.* London, 1983.

Cogliati Arano. *The Medieval Health Handbook: Tacuinum Sanitatis.* New York, 1976.

Cosman, Madeleine P. *Fabulous Feasts: Medieval Cookery and Ceremony.* New York, 1976.

Cuttler, Charles. "Exotics in post-Medieval European Art." *Artibus et historiae* 12, no. 23 (1991): 163–79.

[Donzet, Bruno, and Christian Siret.] *Fastes du Gothique: Le siècle de Charles V, exhibite Grand Palais, octobre 1981–fevrier 1982.* Paris, 1981.

Dembińska, Maria. "Fasting and Working Monks: Regulations of the Fifth to Eleventh Centuries." In *Food in Change,* ed. A. Fenton and E. Kisbán, 152–60. Edinburgh, 1986.

Duby, Georges. *The Age of the Cathedrals: Art and Society, 980–1420.* Chicago, 1981.

Dyer, Christopher. "English Diet in the Later Middle Ages." In *Social Relations and Ideas: Essays in Honor of R. H. Hilton,* ed. T. H. Aston, P. R. Coss, C. Dyer, and J. Thirsk, 191–216. Oxford, 1983.

———. "Les régimes alimentaires en Angleterre, 13e–15e siècles." In *Manger et boire au Moyen Age,* ed. Denis Menjot, 2:263–74. Nice, 1984.

———. *Standards of Living in the Later Middle Ages: Social Change in England, c. 1200–1500.* Cambridge, 1989.

Eisenstein, Elizabeth L. *The Printing Revolution in Early Modern Europe.* Cambridge, 1983.

Elaut, E. "The Walcourt Manuscript: A Hygienis Vademecum for Monks." *Osiris* 13 (1958): 184–209.

Esposito, Mario. *"I Confetti" nella storia, nella letteratura e nel folklore.* Sulmona, 1990.

Faccioli, Emilio. "Le fonti letterarie della storia dell'alimentazione nel Basso Medioevo." *Archeologia medievale* 8 (1981): 71–82.

———. *Arte della cucina: Libri di ricette, Testi sopra lo scalco Il trinciante e i vini dal XIV al XIX secolo.* Milan, 1966.

Faraudo de Saint-Germain, Luis. *"Liber de totes maneres de confits:* Un tratado manual cuatrocentista de arte de dulceria." *Boletin de la Real Academia de Buenas Letras de Barcelona* 19 (1946): 97–134.

Fenton, A., and E. Kisbán, eds., *Food in Change: Eating Habits from the Middle Ages to the Present Day.* Edinburgh, 1986.

Flandrin, Jean-Louis. "Brouets, potages et bouillons." *Médiévales* 5 (1983): 5–14.

———. "Internationalisme, nationalisme et régionalisme dans la cuisine des 14e et 15e siècles: Le témoignage des livres de cuisine." In *Manger et boire au Moyen Age,* ed. Denis Menjot, 2:75–91. Nice, 1984.

———. "Le gout et la nécessité sur l'usage des graisses dans la cuisine d'Europe occidentale (14e et 15e siècles)." *Annales ESC* 38 (1983): 369–401.

———. "Médecine et habitudes alimentaires anciennes." In *Pratiques et discours alimentaires à la Renaissance,* ed. Jean-Claude Margolin and Robert Sauzat, 85–95. Paris, 1982.

———. "Structure des menus français et anglais aux 14e et 15e siècles." In *Du manuscrit à la table,* ed. Carole Lambert, 173–92. Montreal, 1992.

Flandrin, Jean-Louis, and Odile Redon. "Les livres de cuisine italiens des 14e et 15e siècles." *Archeologia medievale* 8 (1981): 393–408.

Freeman, Margaret. *Herbs for the Medieval Household for Cooking, Healing and Divers Uses.* New York, 1943.

Fudge, John D. "Supply and Distribution of Foodstuffs in Northern Europe, 1450–1500." *Medium Aevum Quotidianum* 13 (1988): 8–17.

Fussell, G. E. *The Classical Tradition in West European Farming.* Rutherford, N.J., 1972.

Girard, Alain. "Du manuscrit à l'imprimé: le livre de cuisine en Europe aux 15e et 16e siècles." In *Pratiques et discours alimentaires à la Renaissance,* ed. Jean-Claude Margolin and Robert Sauzat, 107–117. Paris, 1982.

Gislain, G. de. "Le rôle des étangs dans l'alimentation médiévale." In *Manger et boire au Moyen Age,* ed. Denis Menjot, 1:80–101. Nice, 1984.

Grewe, Rudolf, ed. *Libre de sent sovi (Receptari de cuina).* Els nostres clàssics: obres completes dels escriptors catalans medievals, coll. A. vol. 115. Barcelona, 1979.

———. "Catalan Cuisine, in an Historical Perspective." *National and Regional Styles of Cookery: Proceedings of the Oxford Symposium on Food and Cookery, 1981,* 170–78. London, 1982.

———. "An Early 13th Century Northern-European Cookbook." In *Current Research in Culinary History: Sources, Topics, and Methods.* Proceedings of a Conference at Radcliffe College, June, 1985. Culinary Historians of Boston. Cambridge, Mass., 1986.

Grieco, Allen J. "From the Cookbook to the Table: A Florentine Table and Italian Recipes of the Fourteenth and Fifteenth Centuries." In *Du manuscrit à la table,* ed. Carole Lambert, 29–38. Montreal, 1992.

———. "Savoir de poète ou savoir de botaniste? Les fruits dans la poésie italienne du XVe siècle." *Médiévales* 16–17 (1989): 131–46.

Guerreau-Jalabert, Anita. "Aliments symboliques et symbolique de la table dans les romans arthuriens (12e–13e siècles)." *Annales ESC* 45 (1992): 561–94.

Harington, Sir John, ed. and trans. *The School of Salernum: Regimen Sanitatis Salerni.* Salerno, 1957.

Haskins, Charles Homer. *Studies in the History of Medieval Science.* New York, 1960.

Hecht, Konrad. *Der St Gallen Klosterplan.* Sigmaringen, 1983.

Heers, Jacques. "Il commercio nel Mediterraneo alla fine del sec. 14 e nei primi anni del 15." *Archivio storico italiano* 113 (1955): 157–209.

———. *Fêtes, jeux et joutes dans les sociétés d'occident à la fin du moyen âge.* Conference Albert-le-Grand, 1971. Montreal, 1982.

Hémardinquer, J. J., ed. *Pour une histoire de l'alimentation: Recueil de travaux.* Paris, 1970.

Henisch, Bridget Ann. *Fast and Feast: Food in Medieval Society.* University Park, Pa., 1976.

———. "Unconsidered Trifles: The Search for Cookery Scenes in Medieval Sources." In *Current Research in Culinary History: Sources, Topics, and Methods,* 110–21. Cambridge, 1986.

Herbeth, Pascal. "Les utensiles de cuisine en Provence médiévale, 13e–15e siècles." *Médiévales* 5 (1983): 89–93.

Herlihy, David. *Medieval Households.* Cambridge, 1985.

Hieatt, Constance B. *An Ordinance of Pottage: An Edition of the Fifteenth-century Culinary Recipes in Yale University's MS Beinecke 163.* London, 1988.

———. "The 'Poignant' Flavour in Medieval Cooking." In *Taste: Proceedings of the Oxford Symposium on Food and Cooking, 1987,* 103–5. London, 1988.

———. "'Ore pur parler del array de une graunt mangerye': The Culture of the 'Newe Get,' circa 1285." In *Acts of Interpretation in Honor of E. Talbot Donaldson,* ed. M. J. Carruthers and Elizabeth D. Kirk, 219–33. Norman, Okla., 1982.

———. "The Roast or Boiled Beef of Old England." *Book Forum* 5 (1980): 294–99.

———. *Curye on Inglysch: English Culinary Manuscripts of the Fourteenth Century (Including the Forme of Cury)*. Early English Text Society, no. 58. London, 1985.

Hieatt, Constance B., and Sharon Butler. *Pleyn Delit: Medieval Cookery for Modern Cooks*. Rev. ed. Toronto, 1979.

Hilton, Rodney H. *English and French Towns in Feudal Society: A Comparative Study*. Cambridge, 1992.

Holmes, Urban Tignor, Jr. *Daily Living in the Twelfth Century: Based on the Observations of Alexander Neckam in London and Paris*. Madison, Wis., 1952.

Hoquet, J.-C. "Le pain, le vin et la juste mesure à la table des moines carolingiens." *Annales ESC* 40, no. 1 (1985): 661–86.

Horn, Walter, and Ernest Born. *The Plan of St Gall: A Study of the Architecture and Economy of . . . and Life in a Paradigmatic Carolingian Monastery. . . .* 3 vols. Berkeley and Los Angeles, 1979.

Huizinga, Johan. *The Waning of the Middle Ages*. New York, [1949] 1954.

Hyman, Mary. "Les 'menues choses qui ne sont de necessité': Les confitures et la table." In *Du manuscrit à la table*, ed. Carole Lambert, 273–83. Montreal, 1992.

Hyman, Philip, and Mary Hyman. "Les livres de cuisine et le commerce des recettes en France aux 15e et 16e siècles." In *Du manuscrit à la table*, ed. Carole Lambert, 59–68. Montreal, 1992.

Jones, George Fenwick. "The Function of Food in Medieval German Literature." *Speculum* 35 (1960): 78–86.

Jones, Peter Murray. *Medieval Medical Miniatures*. Austin, Tex., 1985.

Kernodle, George R. "Renaissance Artists in the Service of the People: Political Tableaux and Street Theaters in France, Flanders and England, 1380–1650." *Art Bulletin* 25 (1943): 59–64.

Kraus, Henry. *The Living Theatre of Medieval Art*. Philadelphia, 1967.

LaBahn, Patricia D. "Feasting in the Fourteenth and Fifteenth Centuries: A Comparison of Manuscript Illustrations to Contemporary Written Sources." Ph.D. diss., Saint Louis University, 1975.

Labarge, Margaret Wade. *A Baronial Household of the Thirteenth Century*. New York, 1965.

[Lacroix, Paul]. *Moeurs, visages et coutumes au Moyen Age et à l'époque de la Renaissance*. Paris, 1978.

Lafortune-Martel, Agathe. "De l'entremets culinaire aux pièces montées d'un menu de propagande." In *Du manuscrit à la table*, ed. Carole Lambert, 121–29. Montreal, 1992.

Lambert, Carole, ed. *Du manuscrit à la table: Essais sur la cuisine au Moyen Age et répertoire des manuscrits médiévaux contenant des recettes culinaires*. Études médiévales, University of Montreal. Montreal, 1992.

Langlois, Charles-Victor. *La vie en France . . . d'après des romans mondains du temps*. Vol. 1 of *La vie en France au Moyen Age*. Paris, 1924–28.

Laurioux, Bruno. "Les livres de cuisine en Occident à la fin du Moyen Age." In *Artes mechanicae en Europe médiévale*, ed. R. Jansen-Sieben, 113–26. Actes du colloque du 15 octobre 1987. Brussels, 1989.

———. "Modes culinaires et mutations du gout à la fin du Moyen Age." In *Artes mechanicae en Europe médiévale*, ed. R. Jansen-Sieben, 199–222. Brussels, 1989.

———. "Les premiers livres de cuisine." In *La cuisine et la table: 5000 ans de gastronomie*, ed. J. Ferniot and J. Le Goff, 51–55. Paris, 1962.

———. "Spices in the Medieval Diet: A New Approach." *Food and Foodways* 1 (1985): 43–76.

———. "Table et hiérarchie sociale à la fin du Moyen Age." In *Du manuscrit à la table*, ed. Carole Lambert, 87–108. Montreal, 1992.

———. "De l'usage des épices dans l'alimentation médiévale." *Médiévales* 5 (1983): 15–31.

Laurioux, Bruno, and Odile Redon. "La constitution d'une nouvelle catégorie culinaire? Les pâtes dans les livres de cuisine italiens de la fin du Moyen Age." *Médiévales* 16–17 (1989): 51–60.

Le Goff, Jacques. "Vestimentary and Alimentary Codes in *Erec et Enide*." In *The Medieval Imagination*, trans. Arthur Goldhammer, 132–50. Chicago, 1988.

Loomis, Laura Hibbard. "Secular Dramatics in the Royal Palace, Paris, 1378, 1389 and Chaucer's Tregetours." *Speculum* 33 (1958): 242–55.

Ludovisi, Stefano. "Forchette e compagni." *Appunti di gastronomia* 4 (1991): 57–60. Review of Marchese, *L'invenzione della forchetta* (1989).

Lysaght, Patricia. "Continuity and Change in Irish Diet." In *Food in Change: Eating Habits from the Middle Ages to the Present Day*, edited by Alexander Fenton and Eszter Kisbán, 80–89. Edinburgh, 1986.

MacDougall, Elisabeth B., ed. *Medieval Gardens*. Proceedings of the Ninth Dumbarton Oaks Colloquium on the History of Landscape Architecture, 1983. Washington, D.C., 1986.

Mane, P. "L'alimentation des paysans en France et en Italie aux 12e et 13e siècles à travers l'iconographie des calendriers." In *Manger et boire au Moyen Age*, ed. Denis Menjot, 1:319–33. Nice, 1984.

Manselli, Raoul. "La festa nel medioevo." In *Spettacoli conviviali dall' antichità classica alle corti italiane del '400: Atti del VII Convegno di Studio, Viterbo, 27–30 Maggio 1982*, 219–41. Centro di studi sul teatro medioevale e rinascimentale. 1982. Viterbo, 1983.

Marchese, Pasquale. *L'invenzione della forchetta . . . dai Greci ai nostri forchettoni*. Soveria Mannelli, 1989.

Martellotti, Anna and Elio Durante. *Libro di Buone Vivande: La cucina tedesca dell'eta cortese*. Fasano, 1991.

Mazzi, Curzio. "La mensa dei Priori di Firenze nel secolo 14." *Archivio storico italiano* 20 (1897): 336–68.

Mead, William Edward. *The English Medieval Feast* [1931]. New York, 1967.

Meiss, Millard. "Light as Form and Symbol in some Paintings of the Fifteenth Century." *Art Bulletin* 27 (1945): 43–68. Reprinted in his *The Painter's Choice: Problems in the Interpretation of Renaissance Art* (New York, 1976).

Menjot, Denis, ed. *Manger et boire au Moyen Age*. Actes du colloque de Nice, 15–17 octobre 1982. Centre d'études médiévales de Nice. Publication de la faculté des lettres et sciences humaines de Nice, no. 27. 2 vols. Nice, 1984.

Milliken, W. M. "A Table Fountain of the Fourteenth Century." *Bulletin of the Cleveland Museum of Art* 12 (1925): 36–39.

Monckton, H. A. *A History of English Ale and Beer*. London, 1966.

Montanari, Massimo. *Alimentazione e cultura nel Medioevo*. Bari, 1988.

———. "Note sur l'histoire des pâtes en Italie." In "Contre Marco Polo: Une histoire comparée des pâtes alimentaires." *Médiévales* 16–17 (1989): 61–64.

———. "Storia, alimentazione e storia dell'alimentazione: Le fonti scritte altomedievali. *Archeologia medievale* 8 (1981): 25–38.

———. "Valeurs, symboles, messages alimentaires durant le haut Moyen Age." *Médiévales* 5 (1983): 57–66.

Moore, Ellen W. *The Fairs of Medieval England: An Introductory Study.* Pontifical Institute of Medieval Studies. Montreal, 1987.

Moulin, Léo. "La bière, une invention médiévale." In *Manger et boire au Moyen Age,* ed. Denis Menjot, 1:13–31. Nice, 1984.

Mulon, Marianne. "Les premiers recettes médiévales." *Annales ESC* 19 (1964): 933–37. Reprinted in Hémardinquer, *Pour une histoire de l'alimentation* (1970).

———. "Deux traités inédits d'art culinaire." *Bulletin philologique et historique* 1:396–420. Paris, 1971.

Nuñez Rodriguez, Manuel. "El ritual de mesa en la miniatura *le bon repas* del duque de Berry." In *Manger et boire au Moyen Age,* ed. Denis Menjot, 2:33–43. Nice, 1984.

Oman, Charles. *Medieval Silver Nefs.* Victoria and Albert Museum Monograph, no. 15. London, 1963.

Panofsky, Erwin. *Abbot Suger on the Abbey Church of St. Denis.* Princeton, N.J., 1946.

Parsons, J. C. *The Court and Household of Eleanor of Castile in 1290.* Pontifical Institute of Medieval Studies. Montreal, 1977.

Peterson, T. "The Arab Influence on Western European Cooking." *Journal of Medieval History* 6 (1980): 117–41.

Pinto, G. "Le fonti documentarie bassomedievali." *Archeologia médiévale* 8 (1981): 39–58.

Platt, Colin. *Medieval England: A Social History and Archaeology from the Conquest to 1600 A.D.* New York, 1978.

Plouvier, Liliane. "Taillevent, la première star de la gastronomie." *L'histoire* 61 (1983): 93–94.

———. "La gastronomie dans le *Viandier* de Taillevent et le *Ménagier* de Paris." In *Manger et boire au Moyen Age,* ed. D. Menjot, 2:149–59. Niece, 1984.

———. "La 'letuaire,' une confiture du bas Moyen Age." In *Du manuscrit à la table,* ed. Carole Lambert, 243–56. Montreal, 1992.

Postan, M. M., ed. *The Cambridge Economic Life of Europe.* Vol. 1, *The Agrarian Life of the Middle Ages.* Cambridge, 1966.

———. *Medieval Trade and Finance.* Cambridge, 1973.

Pouchelle, Marie-Christine. "Les appétits mélancoliques." *Médiévales* 5 (1983): 81–88.

Power, Eileen. *Medieval English Nunneries.* Cambridge, 1922.

———. *Medieval People* [1924]. With a new introduction by Richard Smith. London, 1986.

Price, Leona. *The Plan of St. Gall in Brief: An Overview Based on the Work by Walter Horn and Ernest Born.* Berkeley and Los Angeles, 1982.

Puycousin, Perrin de, and Madeleine Blondel. *Moutarde à Dijon.* Catalogue. Ville de Dijon, Musée de la vie bourguignonne, 20 April–30 September 1984. Dijon, 1984.

Redon, Odile. "La reglementation des banquets par les lois somptuaires dans les villes d'Italie, 13e–15e siècles. In *Du manuscrit à la table,* ed. Carole Lambert, 109–19. Montreal, 1992.

Roach, Frederick A. *Cultivated Fruits of Britain: Their Origin and History.* Oxford, 1985.

Robertson, Eugenia Dufur. "Circa instans and the Salernitan materia medica." Ph.D. diss., Bryn Mawr, 1982.

Roden, Claudia. "Early Arab Cooking and Cookery Manuscripts." *Petits Propos Culinaires* 6 (1980): 16–27.

Rodinson, Maxime. "Recherches sur les documents arabes relatif à la cuisine." *Revue des études islamiques* (1949): 95–165.

Rogers, J. E. Thorold. *A History of Agricultural Prices in England, 1259–1793.* 7 vols. in 8. Oxford, 1886–1902.

Rose, Brenda S. "A Perfect Feast? Preventive Medicine and Diet in Medieval France." In *Proceedings of the Oxford Symposium on Food and Cooking, 1990,* 183–89. London, 1991.

———. "A Medieval Staple: Verjuice in France and England." In *Proceedings of the Oxford Symposium on Food and Cooking, 1989,* 205–12. London, 1990.

Ross, Anne. *Pagan Celtic Britain: Studies in Iconography and Tradition.* London, 1967.

Rouche, Michel. "La faim à l'époque carolingienne: Essai sur quelques types de rations alimentaires." *Revue historique* 250 (1973): 295–320.

———. "Les repas de fête à l'époque carolingienne." In *Manger et boire au Moyen Age,* ed. Denis Menjot, 1:265–96. Nice, 1984.

Sabban, F. "Le savoir-cuire, ou l'art des potages dans le *Ménagier* de Paris et le *Viandier* de Taillevent." In *Manger et boire au Moyen Age,* ed. D. Menjot, 2:161–72. Nice, 1984.

Sada, Luigi. "Spaghetti e compagni." *Appunti di gastronomia* 1 (February 1990): 16–35.

Salmen, Walter. "Tafelmusik im hohen und späten Mittelalter." In *Spettacoli conviviali dall' antichità classica alle corti italiane del '400: Atti del VII Convegno di Studio, Viterbo, 27–30 Maggio 1982,* 171–94. Centro di studi sul teatro medioevale e rinascimentale. Viterbo, 1983.

Santich, Barbara. "Les éléments distinctifs de la cuisine médiévale méditerranéenne." In *Du manuscrit à la table,* ed. Carole Lambert, 133–39. Montreal, 1992.

Santucci, M. "Nourritures et symboles dans le *Banquet du Faisan* et dans *Jehan de Saintré.*" In *Manger et boire au Moyen Age,* ed. Denis Menjot, 1:429–40. Nice, 1984.

Sass, Lorna J. "The Preference for Sweets, Spices and Almond Milk in Late Medieval English Cuisine." In *Food in Perspective,* ed. A. Fenton and T. M. Owen, 253ff. Cardiff, Wales, 1977.

———. "Religion, Medicine, Politics and Spices." *Appetite* 2 (1981): 7–13.

———. *To the King's Taste: Richard II's Book of Feasts and Recipes adapted for Modern Cooking.* New York, 1975.

Scully, Terence. "Medieval Cookery and Medicine." *Petits Propos Culinaires* 44 (1993): 11–20.

———. "The *Opusculum de saporibus* of Magninus Mediolanensis." *Medium Aevum* 54 (1985): 178–207.

———. "Les saisons alimentaires du *Ménagier de Paris.*" In *Du manuscrit à la table,* ed. Carole Lambert, 205–13. Montreal, 1992.

———. *The Viandier of Taillevent: An Edition of All Extant Manuscripts.* Ottawa, 1988.

Scully, Terence, ed. and trans. *Chiquart's "On Cookery": A Fifteenth-century Savoyard Culinary Treatise.* American University Studies series 9 (History), vol. 22. New York, 1986.

Sigerist, E. *The Earliest Printed Book on Wine.* New York, 1943.

Sinatti D'Amico, Franca. "Coltivazione e nutrizione nel medio evo mediterraneo." In *Homo edens,* ed. O. Longo and P. Scarpi, 67–72. Verona, 1989.

Skaarup, Bi. "Sources of Medieval Cuisine in Denmark." In *Du manuscrit à la table,* ed. Carole Lambert, 39–43. Montreal, 1992.

Sorrensen, W. "Gärten und Pflanzen im Klosterplan." In Johannes Duft, *Studien zum St Galler Klosterplan.* St. Gall, 1962.

Southern, R. W. *Medieval Humanism.* New York, 1970.

Spadaro di Pasanitello, Carmelo. "La fonte vaticana dei primi libri di cucina italiani." *Appunti di gastronomia* 5 (1991): 5–13.

Spencer, Judith, trans. *The Four Seasons of the House of Cerruti.* New York, 1983.

Stouff, Louis. *Ravitaillement et alimentation en Provence aux XIVe et XVe siècles.* Civilisations et sociétés, no. 20. Paris, 1970.

———. "Y avait–il à la fin du Moyen Age une alimentation et une cuisine provençales originales?" In *Manger et boire au Moyen Age,* ed. Denis Menjot, 2:93–99. Nice, 1984.

Sturtevant, E. Lewis. *Edible Plants of the World* [1919]. New York, 1972.

Taylor, Henry Osborne *The Medieval Mind.* 2 vols. 4th ed. [1925]. Cambridge, Mass., 1959.

Thomas, M. "La visite de l'empereur Charles IV en France d'après l'exemplaire des 'Grandes Chroniques' exécuté pour le roi Charles V." In *Congrès international des bibliophiles, Vienne 1969,* 85–89. Vienna, 1971.

Thorndike, Lynn. "A Medieval Sauce Book." *Speculum* 9 (1934): 183–90.

Toussaint-Samat, Maguelonne. "Une recette de 15e siècle." *Médiévales* 5 (1983): 94–95.

van Winter, Johanna Maria. "Obligatory Fasts and Voluntary Asceticism in the Middle Ages." In *Food in Change,* ed. A. Fenton and E. Kisbán, 161–66. Edinburgh, 1986.

———. "The Role of Preserved Food in a Number of Medieval Households in the Netherlands." In *Food Conservation,* ed. A. Riddervold and A. Ropeid, 56–72. London, 1988.

Vincent-Cassy, M. "Manger beau: L'exemple de Paris à la fin du Moyen Age." In *A tavola con il Principe: Alimentazione e cultura nella Ferrara degli Estensi,* ed. J. Bentini. Ferrara, 1988.

Warner, Richard, ed. *Antiquitates culinariae; or, Curious Tracts Relating to the Culinary affairs of the Olde English* [1791]. London, 1981.

Watson, Andrew M. *Agricultural Innovation in the Early Islamic World: The Diffusion of Crops and Farming Techniques, 700–1100.* Cambridge, 1983.

Way, A. S. *The Science of Dining (Mensa philosophica): A Medieval Treatise on the Hygiene of the Table and the Laws of Health.* London, 1936.

Weiss-Amer, Melitta. "The Role of Medieval Physicians in the Diffusion of Culinary Recipes and Cooking Practices." In *Du manuscrit à la table,* ed. Carole Lambert, 69–80. Montreal, 1992.

Wheaton, Barbara Ketchum. "How to Cook a Peacock." *Harvard Magazine* (November–December 1979): 63–65.

White, Lynn, Jr. *Medieval Technology and Social Change.* Oxford, 1962.

Whitmore, M. E. "Medieval English Domestic Life and Amusements in the Works of Chaucer." Ph.D. diss., Catholic University, 1937.

Wilson, C. Anne. "The Saracen Connection: Arab Cuisine and the Medieval West." 2 parts. *Petits Propos Culinaires* 7 (1981): 13–22; 8 (1981): 19–27.

Wiswe, Hans. "Ein mittelniederdeutsches Kochbuch des 15. Jahrhunderts." *Braunschweigisches Jahrbuch* 37 (1956): 19–55.

——. "Die mittelniederdeutsches Kochrezeptüberlieferung." *Braunschweigisches Jahrbuch* 37 (1956): 46–62.

Woolgar, C. M., ed. *Household Accounts from Medieval England*, Parts 1–2. Records of Economic History. The British Academy. Oxford, 1993.

Wright, Clifford A. *Lasagne*. Boston, 1995.

——. "Cucina Arabo-Sicula and Maccharruni." *Al-Masaq: Studies in Arabo-Islamica Mediterranea*, ed. Dionisius A. Agius, 9 (1996–97): 151–77.

Wright, Richard A., *A Volume of Vocabularies, Illustrating the Condition and Manners of our Fore-fathers . . . from the Tenth Century to the Fifteenth* [1857]. 2d ed. [London], 1882.

Wright, Thomas. *The Homes of Other Days: A History of Domestic Manners and Sentiments in England*. London, 1871.

Zambreno, Mary Frances. "The Moral Ambiguity of the Medieval Feast." *Medium Aevum Quotidianum* 13 (1988): 18–27.

Zambrini, Francesco. *Il libro della cucina del secolo 14*. Bologna, 1863. Reprint, 1968.

GENERAL BIBLIOGRAPHY
Bibliographic Aids

Attar, Dena. *A Bibliography of Household Books Published in Britain, 1800–1914*. London, 1987.

Axford, Lavonne B. *English Language Cookbooks, 1660–1973*. Detroit, 1976.

Berès, Pierre. *Nourritures*. Catalogue 82. Paris, 1991.

Bitting, K. G. *Gastronomic Bibliography* San Francisco, 1939. Reprints, Ann Arbor, 1971; London, 1981.

Cagle, William R. *A Matter of Taste: A Bibliographical Catalogue of the Gernon Collection of Books on Food and Drink*. Bloomington, Ind., 1990.

Driver, Elizabeth. *A Bibliography of Cookery Books Published in Britain, 1875–1914*. London, 1989.

Gabler, James M. *Wine into Words: A History and Bibliography of Wine Books in the English Language*. Baltimore, Md., 1984.

Feret, Barbara. *Gastronomical and Culinary Literature: A Survey and Analysis of Historically Oriented Collections in the U.S.A.* Metuchen, N.J., 1979. Reprint, London, 1981.

Longone, Jan, and D. T. Longone. *American Cookbooks and Wine Books, 1797–1950*. Library Exhibit, University of Michigan. Ann Arbor, 1984.

Lowenstein, Eleanor. *Bibliography of American Cookery Books, 1742–1860*, New York, 1972. [Based on Waldo Lincoln's earlier bibliography.]

Maggs Brothers, eds. *Food and Drink Throughout the Ages*. Auction Catalogue no. 645. London, 1937.

Maclean, Virginia. *A Short-Title Catalogue of Household and Cookery Books Published in the English Tongue, 1701–1800*. London, 1981.

Oxford, A. W. *English Cookery Books to the Year 1850*. London, 1913.

Pennell, Mrs. E. R. *My Cookery Books*. New York, 1903. Reprint, London, 1983.

Quayle, Eric. *Old Cook Books: An Illustrated History*. London, 1978.

Simon, André. *Bibliotheca Gastronomica: A Catalogue of Books and Documents before 1861, and in the Wine and Food Society* [1953]. London, 1978.

———. *Bibliotheca Vinaria: A Bibliography of Books and Pamphlets dealing with Viticulture, Wine-making, Distillation, the Management, Sale, Taxation, Use and Abuse of Wines and Spirits.* London, 1913. Reprinted, from author's annotated copy, as *Bibliotheca Bacchica* (London, 1979).

Sotheby's, eds. *Catalogue of a Collection of Books and Manuscripts of the 15th to the 20th Century on Food and Wines from the Well-Known Library of Harry Schraemli.* London, 1971.

———. *Marcus and Elizabeth Crahan Collection of Books on Food, Drink and Related Subjects.* Auction catalogue. New York, 1984.

Sutton, David C. *The History of Food: A Preliminary Bibliography of Printed Sources.* Coventry, England, 1982.

Vanossi, Lorenzo. *Bibliografia gastronomica italiana: Fino al 1950.* Pinerolo, Italy, 1964.

Vicaire, Georges. *Biblographie gastronomique.* Paris, 1890. Reprints, London, 1954, 1978; Geneva, 1983.

Westbury, Richard. *Handlist of Italian Cookery Books.* Florence, 1963.

Wheaton, Barbara, and Patricia Kelly. *Bibliography of Culinary History and Food Resources in Eastern Massachusetts.* Boston, [1988].

Periodicals

American Anthropologist.

Annales: Économies. Sociétés. Civilisations. [In addition to a volume of *Selections,* 5, edited by Forster and Ranum, see below. General history; Another volume of selections edited by J. J. Hémardinquer, *Pour une histoire de l'alimentation,* Paris, 1972.]

Appetite: Interdisciplinary Journal of Dietary Practice. 1980–.

Appunti di gastronomia. Edited by Claudio Benporat. 1990–.

Archaeology. Archaeological Institute of America.

The Art of Eating. Quarterly newsletter by Edward Behr, on individual ingredients, historically researched.

Ceres. Journal from UNESCO emphasizing alternate food sources and technologies.

Critical Reviews in Food Science and Nutrition.

Cuadernos de Gastronomia. Huesca.

The Digest: A Review for the Interdisciplinary Study of Food. American Folklore Society.

Expedition: The Magazine of Archaeology/Anthropology. University Museum, University of Pennsylvania.

Food and Foodways: Explorations in the History of Culture and Human Nourishment. Edited by M. Aymard, J.-L. Flandrin, and S. L. Kaplan. 1985–.

Food First. Institute for Food and Development Policy.

Food Technology. Society of Food Technologists.

Journal of Clinical Nutrition.

The Journal of Gastronomy. American Institute of Wine and Food. 1984–.

McIlvania: Journal of American Amateur Mycology. North American Mycological Association. 1973–.

Natural History. American Museum of Natural History (New York).

Newsletter. Culinary Historians of Boston. [In general, newletters are excluded from this list, but this bimonthly reproduces texts of the Society's lectures.]

Petites Propos Culinaires. Edited by Alan Davidson et al. Prospect Books (London).

Science.

Scientific American. [Particular issues, such as that of September 1975: "Food."]

Zhongguo Pengren. Beijing monthly on Chinese cookery. 1981–.

General Food History

An asterisk (*) denotes a work in dictionary form.

Alberini, M. *Storia del pranzo all'italiana.* Milan, 1966.

Anderson, Eugene N., Jr. *The Food of China.* Yale University Press, 1988.

Arnott, M. L. *Gastronomy: The Anthropology of Food and Food Habits.* The Hague, 1975.

Ashton, J. *The History of Bread.* London, 1904.

Barber, R. *Cooking and Recipes from Rome to the Renaissance.* London, 1973.

Baudrillart, Henri. *Histoire du luxe privé et public depuis l'antiquité jusqu'à nos jours.* 4 vols. Paris, 1879–81.

Bevilacqua, O., and G. Mantovano. *Laboratorio del gusto: Storia dell'evoluzione gastronomica.* Milan, 1992.

Blond, G., and G. Blond. *Histoire pittoresque de notre alimentation.* 2 vols. Paris, 1960. [To be used critically.]

* Castelot, A. *L'histoire à table.* Paris, 1972.

Chang, K. C., ed. *Food in Chinese Culture: Anthropological and Historical Perspectives.* New Haven, 1977.

Cutting, C. *Fish Saving: A History of Fish Processing from Ancient to Modern Times.* New York, 1968.

Drummond, J. C., and A. Wilbraham. *The Englishman's Food: A History of Five Centuries of English Diet.* London, 1939. Revised ed., 1964.

* Dumas, Alexandre [père]. *Le grand dictionnaire de cuisine* [1873]. Edited posthumously by D. J. Vuillemot. Reprints, London, 1958; Paris, 1978 (a complete reedition). Selections translated by A. Davidson and J. Davidson (Oxford, 1978).

Elkort, Martin. *The Secret Life of Food: A Feast of Food and Drink History, Folklore and Fact.* Los Angeles, 1991.

Ellwanger, G. H. *The Pleasures of the Table.* New York, 1902.

Ferniot, J., and J. Le Goff, eds. *La cucina e la tavola: Storia di 5000 anni di gastronomia.* Paris, 1986. Translation, N. Scaramuzzi (Bari, 1987).

* FitzGibbon, Theodora. *The Food of the Western World: An Encyclopedia of Food from North America and Europe.* New York, 1976.

Forster, F., and O. Ranum. *Food and Drink in History.* Vol. 5. Baltimore, 1979. [Selections from *Annales ESC*, 1961–.]

Francis, C. A. *A History of Food and its Preservation.* Princeton, N.J., 1937.

Franklin, Alfred. *La vie privée d'autrefois.* Vol. 3, *La cuisine,* and vol 6, *Le repas.* Paris, 1888. Reprint, Geneva, 1980.

Goody, Jack. *Cooking, Cuisine and Class: A Study in Comparative Sociology.* New York, 1982.

Gottschalk, A. *Histoire de l'alimentation et de la gastronomie depuis la préhistoire jusqu'à nos jours.* 2 vols. Paris, 1948.

Graubard, Mark Aaron. *Man's Food: Its Rhyme or Reason.* New York, 1943.

* Gutkind, Curt S. *Das Buch der Tafelfreuden aus allen Zeiten und breiten gesammelt.* Leipzig, 1929.

Hackwood, Frederick W. *Good Cheer: The Romance of Food and Feasting.* New York, 1911.

Harris, Marvin. *Cannibals and Kings.* New York, 1977.

Harrison, M. *The Kitchen in History.* New York, 1972.

Henderson, Alexander. *The History of Ancient and Modern Wines.* London, 1824. Reprint, Baltimore, n.d.

Horizon Cookbook and Illustrated History of Eating and Drinking Through the Ages, ed. W. H. Hale, and the editors of *Horizon,* with Mimi Sheraton. New York, 1968.

Incontri Lotteringhi della Stufa, Maria Luisa. *Desinare e cene dai tempi remoti alla cucina toscana del XV secolo.* Florence, 1965.

Ladurie, E. Le Roy. *Times of Feast, Times of Famine: A History of Climate since the Year 1000.* New York, 1971.

Leeming, Margaret. *A History of Food: From Manna to Microwave.* London, 1991.

Legrand d'Aussy, P. J.-B. *Histoire de la vie privée des français.* 3 vols. Paris, 1782; 1815.

Maurizio, A. *Histoire de l'alimentation végétale depuis la préhistoire jusqu'à nos jours.* Paris, 1932. [Original published in Polish.]

* McGee, Harold. *On Food and Cooking: The Science and Lore of the Kitchen.* New York, 1984.

———. *The Curious Cook: More Kitchen Science and Lore.* San Francisco, 1990.

* Montagné, Prosper. *Larousse gastronomique.* 1938. Revised, translated, and abridged, New York, 1961–.

Montanari, M. *La fame e l'abbondanza: Storia dell'alimentazione in Europa.* Rome, 1993.

———. *Convivio. Storia e cultura dei piaceri della tavola dall'Antichità al Medioevo.* Rome, 1989.

Multhauf, R. *Neptune's Gift: A History of Common Salt.* Johns Hopkins Studies in the History of Technology. Baltimore, 1978.

Norman [Makanowitzky], Barbara. *Tales of the Table: A History of Western Cuisine.* Englewood Cliffs, N.J., 1972.

Oberle, Gerard. *Les festes de Bacchus et de Comus, ou, Histoire de boire et du manger en Europe, de l'antiquité à nos jours, a travers les livres.* Paris, 1989.

Pullar, P. *Consuming Passions, Being an Historic Inquiry into Certain English Appetites.* Boston, 1970.

Revel, J.-F. *Culture and Cuisine: A Journey Through the History of Food.* Translated by H. R. Lane. New York, 1982. Originally published as *Un festin en paroles: histoire littéraire de la sensibilité gastronomique de l'Antiquité à nos jours* (Paris, 1979).

Ritchie, Carson I. A. *Food in Civilization: How History Has Been Affected by Human Tastes.* New York, 1981.

Seifert [Korschinski], Edeltraud, and Ute Sametschek. *Die Kochkunst in zwei Jahrtausenden: Das grosse Buch der Kochbücher und Meisterkoche, Mit Originalrezepten von der Antike bis 1900.* Munich, 1977.

* Simon, André. *A Concise Encyclopedia of Gastronomy.* New York, 1942.

Simoons, F. J. *Food in China: A Cultural and Historical Inquiry.* Boca Raton, Fla., 1991.

———. *Eat Not This Flesh: Food Avoidances in the Old World* [1961]. 2d ed. Westport, Conn., 1981.

* Soyer, Alexis. *The Pantropheon, or a History of Food and its Preparation in Ancient Times.* London, 1853. Reprint, London, 1977.

Spencer, Colin. *The Heretic's Feast: A History of Vegetarianism.* London, 1993.

Stewart, Katie. *The Joy of Eating: A Cook's Tour of History, Illustrated with a Cook's Selection of the Great Recipes of Every Era.* Owings Mills, Md., 1977. First published as *Cooking and Eating* (London, 1975). [To be used critically.]

Stokar, Walter. *Die Urgeschichte des Hausbrotes, ein Beitrag zur Entwicklungsgeschichte der Nahrung.* Lepzig, 1951.

Storck, J. and W. D. Teague. *Flour for Man's Bread: A History of Milling.* St. Paul, Minn., 1952.

Tannahill, Reay. *Food in History* [1973]. London, 1988.

———. *Flesh and Blood: A History of the Cannibal Complex.* London, 1975.

———. *The Fine Art of Food.* The Folio Society, 1968; New York, 1970.

* Toussaint-Samat, M. *A History of Food.* Translated by Anthea Bell. Oxford, 1992. Originally published as *Histoire naturelle et morale de la nourriture* (Paris, 1987).

Trager, J. *The Food Chronology: A Food Lover's Compendium of Events and Anecdotes, from Prehistory to the Present.* New York, 1995.

Walcher, D. N., N. Kretchmer, and H. L. Barnett, eds. *Food, Man and Society.* Third meeting, Organization for the Study of Human Development. Madrid, 1975.

* Ward, Artemus. *The Encyclopedia of Food.* 2 vols. ca. 1923. Reprint, New York, 1941.

Wilkins, John. *Food in European Literature.* Intellect: European Studies series, ed. K. Cameron. Exeter, 1996.

Wilson, C. Anne. *Food and Drink in Britain: From the Stone Age to Recent Times.* London, 1973.

Theoretical works

Aymard, M. "Pour l'histoire de l'alimentation: quelques rémarques de méthode." *Annales ESC* 30 (1975): 431–44.

Barker, L. M., ed. *Psychobiology of Human Food Selection.* Westport, Conn., 1981.

Barthes, Roland. *Mythologies.* Paris, 1978.

———. "Toward a Psychosociology of Contemporary Food Consumption." In *Annales ESC* 16 (1961). Reprinted in *Food and Drink in History,* ed. F. Forster and O. Ranum (Baltimore, 1979).

Braudel, F. *The Structures of Everyday Life.* Translated and revised by S. Reynolds. New York, 1981. [Sections on "daily bread," "food and drink," etc.]

Cappon, D. *Eating, Loving and Dying: A Psychology of Appetites.* Toronto, 1973.

Dembińska, Maria. "Symbolic Aspects of Food Production in the Light of a Thirteenth-century Polish Historical Source." In *Food in Perspective,* ed. A. Fenton and T. M. Owen, 69–76. Cardiff, Wales, 1977.

Douglas, Mary. "Deciphering a Meal." *Daedalus* 101 (Winter 1972): 61–81.

Elias, Norbert. *The Civilizing Process: The History of Manners,* vol. 1. Translated by E. Jephcoll. New York, 1978.

Fenton, A., and T. M. Owen, eds. *Food in Perspective: Proceedings of the 3rd International Conference on Ethnological Food Research.* Cardiff, Wales, 1977.

Harris, Marvin. *Cows, Pigs, Wars and Witches: The Riddle of Culture.* New York, 1974.

———. *Good to Eat: Riddles of Food and Culture.* New York, 1985.

Harris, Marvin, and Eric B. Ross, eds. *Food and Evolution: Toward a Theory of Human Food Habits.* Philadelphia, 1987.

Hörander, Edith. "The Recipe Book as a Cultural and Sociohistorical Document." In *Food in Perspective*, ed. A. Fenton and T. M. Owen, 118–44. Cardiff, Wales, 1977.

Lehrer, Adrienne. "Semantic Cuisine." *Journal of Linguistics* 5 (1969): 39–56.

Leininger, M. "Some Cross-Cultural, Universal and Non-Universal Functions, Beliefs and Practices of Food." In *Dimensions of Nutrition*, ed. J. Dupont, 153–79. Denver, 1970.

Lévi-Strauss, C. "Le triangle culinaire." *L'Arc* 26 (1965): 19ff.

———. *Mythologiques*, trans. by J. and D. Weightman. 4 vols. Chicago, 1969–78.

Moulin, Léo. *L'Europe à table: Introduction à une psycho-sociologie des pratiques alimentaires en Occident*. Paris, 1975.

Ritchie, Carson, I. A. *Food in Civilization: How History has been Affected by Human Tastes*. Economic Botany. New York, 1981.

Rozin, Elizabeth. "The Structure of Cuisine." In *Psychobiology of Human Food Selection*, ed. L. M. Barker. Westport, Conn., 1981.

Rozin, Paul. "Human Food Selection: The Interaction of Biology, Culture, and Individual Experience." In *Psychobiology of Human Food Selection*, ed. L. M. Barker. Westport, Conn., 1981.

———. "The Acquisition of Food Habits and Preferences." In *Behavioral Health: A Handbook of Health Enhancement and Disease Prevention*, ed. J. D. Matarazzo et al., 590–607. New York, 1981.

Schmauderer, E. *Studien zur Geschichte des Lebensmittelwissenschaft*. Vierteljahrsschaft für Sozial- und Wirtschaftsgeschichte, suppl. 62. Wiesbaden, 1975.

Sigerist, Henry E. *A History of Medicine*. Vol. 1: *Primitive and Archaic Medicine*. Oxford, 1967.

Singer, Charles J. ed. *A History of Technology*. Oxford, 1954–78.

Visser, M. *Much Depends on Dinner: The Extraordinary History and Mythology, Allure and Obsessions, Perils and Taboos of an Ordinary Meal*. New York, 1988.

———. *The Rituals of Dinner: The Origins, Evolution, Eccentricities, and Meaning of Table Manners*. New York, 1992.

Cookbooks

Black, Maggie. *The Medieval Cookbook*. London: British Museum, 1992.

Bottéro, Jean. *Textes culinaires Mésopotamiens: Mesopotamian culinary Texts*. In Mesopotamian Civilizations, ed. Jerold S. Cooper, vol. 6. Winona Lake, Ind., 1995.

Cosman, Madeleine Pelner. *Fabulous Feasts: Medieval Cookery and Ceremony*. New York, 1976.

Grieve, Mrs. M. *A Modern Herbal*. Edited by Mrs. C. F. Leyel. N.p., 1931

Jenkins, Nancy Harmon, *The Mediterranean Cookbook*. New York, 1994.

Kremezi, Aglaia, *The Foods of Greece*. New York, 1993.

Roden, Claudia. *A New Book of Mediterranean Food* [1968]. London, 1985.

Sass, Lorna. *To a King's Taste: Richard II's Book of Feasts and Recipes*. New York: Metropolitan Museum of Art, 1975.

Scully, Terence, and O. Eleanor Scully. *Early French Cookery: Sources, History, Original Recipes and Modern Adaptations*. Ann Arbor, 1995.

Wolfert, Paula. *The Cooking of the Eastern Mediterranean*. New York, 1994.

———. *Paula Wolfert's World of Food*. New York, 1988.

Index